A Companion to Latin
American Anthropology

# Blackwell Companions to Anthropology

The *Blackwell Companions to Anthropology* offers a series of comprehensive syntheses of the traditional subdisciplines, primary subjects, and geographic areas of inquiry for the field. Taken together, the series represents both a contemporary survey of anthropology and a cutting edge guide to the emerging research and intellectual trends in the field as a whole.

# A Companion
# to Latin
# American
# Anthropology

Edited by
Deborah Poole

**Blackwell**
Publishing

BLACKWELL PUBLISHING
350 Main Street, Malden, MA 02148-5020, USA
9600 Garsington Road, Oxford OX4 2DQ, UK

The right of Deborah Poole to be identified as the author of the editorial material in this work has been asserted in accordance with the UK Copyright, Designs, and Patents Act 1988.

Designations used by companies to distinguish their products are often claimed as trademarks. All brand names and product names used in this book are trade names, service marks, trademarks, or registered trademarks of their respective owners. The publisher is not associated with any product or vendor mentioned in this book.

This publication is designed to provide accurate and authoritative information in regard to the subject matter covered. It is sold on the understanding that the publisher is not engaged in rendering professional services. If professional advice or other expert assistance is required, the services of a competent professional should be sought.

First published 2008 by Blackwell Publishing Ltd

1  2008

*Library of Congress Cataloging-in-Publication Data*

A companion to Latin American anthropology / edited by Deborah Poole.
    p. cm.
Includes bibliographical references and index.
ISBN 978-0-631-23468-5 (hardcover: alk. paper) 1. Ethnology—Latin America. 2. Anthropology—Latin America. I. Poole, Deborah.

GN564.L29C64 2008
306.098—dc22

2007032294

A catalogue record for this title is available from the British Library.

Set in 10/12.5pt Galliard
by SPi Publisher Services Pondicherry, India
Printed and bound in Singapore
by Markono Print Media Pte Ltd

The publisher's policy is to use permanent paper from mills that operate a sustainable forestry policy, and which has been manufactured from pulp processed using acid-free and elementary chlorine-free practices. Furthermore, the publisher ensures that the text paper and cover board used have met acceptable environmental accreditation standards.

For further information on
Blackwell Publishing, visit our website at
www.blackwellpublishing.com

# Contents

# Notes on Contributors

**Ana M. Alonso** is Associate Professor of Anthropology at the University of Arizona. She has done ethnographic and historical research in Mexico and the US–Mexico borderlands on topics related to state formation, resistance and revolution, nationalism and ethnicity/race, legal narratives, social memory and material culture, space and place, gender and sexuality. She is the author of *Thread of Blood: Colonialism, Revolution, and Gender on Mexico's Northern Frontier* (1994). Recent publications include "Conforming Disconformity: 'Mestizaje,' Hybridity and the Aesthetics of Mexican Nationalism," *Cultural Anthropology* 19(4) (2004); "Sovereignty, the Spatial Politics of Security, and Gender: Looking North and South from the US–Mexico Border," in C. Krohn-Hansen and K. G. Nustad (eds), *State Formation: Anthropological Perspectives* (2005); and "Love, Sex and Gender in Mexican Legal Narratives," in H. Baitenmann, V. Chenaut, and A. Varley (eds), *Law and Gender in Contemporary Mexico* (2006).

**Jaime Arocha** is Professor of Anthropology and Director of the Afro-Colombian Studies Group at the National University of Colombia. His latest research has to do with peaceful mechanisms of conflict resolution by people of African descent, adaptations developed by victims of war belonging to the same ethnic affiliation to urban environments, and hyper-exaltation of their symbolical universes by the state, with the purpose of hiding territorial expropriation. His most recent books include *Ombligados de Ananse. Hilos tradicionales y modernos en el litoral Pacífico colombiano* (1999) and *Utopía para los Excluidos. El multiculturalismo en África y América Latina* (2005). He has edited two books published in 2007: *Nina de Friedemann, cronista de disidencias y resistencias* and *Las Africanías y Diáspora en Colombia*.

**Rossana Barragán** is Professor of History at the University of San Andrés (UMSA) at La Paz. She served for five years as director of the journal *T'inkazos* at the Program for Strategic Research (Programa de Investigaciones Estratégicas (PIEB)) in Bolivia. She is currently Director of the Historical Archive of the City of La Paz. Her research focuses on social processes, identity, and state formation in 19th and 20th century Bolivia. Her most recent publications include "El estado pactante: gouvernement et peuples. La configuration de l'état et ses frontières, Bolivie (1825–1880)" (Ph.D. thesis, EHESS, 2002), and "The 'Spirit' of Bolivian Law: Citizenship, Patriarchy, and Infamy," in Sueann Caulfield et al. (eds), *Honor, Status, and Law in Modern Latin America* (2005), and *Asambleas Constituyentes. Ciudadanía y elecciones, convenciones y debates (1825–1971)* (2006).

**Claudia Briones** is Professor of Anthropology at the University of Buenos Aires, and Researcher of the National Council for Scientific and Technological Research (CONI-CET), Argentina. Her primary research areas are indigenous movements, rights and policy; differentiated citizenships and national formations of alterity in Argentina; and kinship, knowledge and politics of the Mapuche People. Her most recent publications include *La Alteridad del Cuarto Mundo. Una deconstrucción antropológica de la diferencia* (1998), *Contemporary Perspectives on the Native Peoples of Pampa, Patagonia, and Tierra del Fuego: Living on the Edge* (coedited with J. Lanata, 2002), *Metacultura del estado-nación y estado de la metacultura* (2005), and *Cartografías Argentinas. Políticas indigenistas y formaciones provinciales de alteridad* (editor, 2005).

**Carlos Iván Degregori** is Professor of Anthropology at the Universidad Mayor de San Marcos in Lima, Peru, and Director of the Instituto de Estudios Peruanos (IEP). Between 2001 and 2003, Degregori served as Commissioner on the Peruvian Truth and Reconciliation Commission and chaired the editorial committee in charge of the Commission's final report. He has been director of the School of Anthropology at San Marcos (2000–02) and visiting professor at several universities: Princeton, Madison-Wisconsin, Columbia and Johns Hopkins (USA), Utrecht (The Netherlands), École des Hautes Études en Sciences Sociales (France) and Freie Universität, Berlin (Germany). His research and publications focus on ethnicity; political violence; and the teaching of anthropology in Peru. His edited books include *No hay país más diverso. Compendio de antropología peruana* (2000) and *The Peru Reader: History, Culture, Politics* (with Orin Starn and Robin Kirk, 1995).

**Guillermo Delgado** is Professor and Merrill College Fellow in the Latin American and Latino Studies Department, University of California, Santa Cruz. He is editor of the Bolivian Studies Electronic Journal/*RevistaE*, and coeditor with John M. Schechter of *Quechua Verbal Artistry: The Inscription of Andean Voices / Arte expresivo quechua. La inscripción de voces andinas* (2004).

**Brigittine M. French** is Assistant Professor of Anthropology at Grinnell College. Her research focuses on language politics, sameness/difference claims, and nationalism in Guatemala and Ireland. Her recent publications include "The Politics of Mayan Linguistics in Guatemala: Native Speakers, Expert Analysts, and the Nation," *Pragmatics* 13(4) (2003) and "Partial Truths and Gendered Histories: Ruth Bunzel in American Anthropology," *Journal of Anthropological Research* 61(4) (2005).

**Mark Goodale** is Assistant Professor of Conflict Analysis and Anthropology at George Mason University. He studies legal culture, the relationship between law and the practice of everyday life, the cultural construction of violence, and the impact of modern forms of subject-making in Bolivia. He is the author of *Dilemmas of Modernity: Bolivian*

*Encounters with Law and Liberalism* (2008) and *The Anthropology of Human Rights: Critical Explorations in Ethical Theory and Social Practice* (2008), and editor (with June Starr) of *Practicing Ethnography in Law* (2002) and (with Sally Engle Merry) of *The Practice of Human Rights* (2007). He currently serves as one of several editors of *The Bolivia Reader* (forthcoming).

**Gastón Gordillo** is Associate Professor of Anthropology at the University of British Columbia. His research has focused on the production of places, the spatiality of social memory, and the subjectivities associated with experiences of domination and resistance in the Gran Chaco region of northern Argentina. He is the author of *Landscapes of Devils: Tensions of Place and Memory in the Argentinean Chaco* (2004), *Nosotros vamos a estar acá para siempre: historias tobas* (2005), and *En el Gran Chaco. Antropologías e historias* (2006).

**Rosana Guber** is researcher at the National Council for Scientific and Technological Research (CONICET-Argentina). She chairs the Center of Social Anthropology of the Institute for Social and Economic Development (IDES) and is Coordinator of its Masters Program with the University of San Martín. Her primary research areas are social memory and nationalism concerning the Malvinas/Falklands War between Argentina and the United Kingdom (1982), and the ethnography of Argentine social anthropology. She has published *From Chicos to Veteranos* (2004), *Malvinas. De la causa justa a la guerra absurda* (2001), *Historia y estilos de trabajo de campo en la Argentina* (edited with Sergio Visacovsky, 2002), and two books on ethnographic fieldwork, *El salvaje metropolitano* (1991/2001) and *Etnografía. Método, campo y reflexividad* (2001).

**Charles R. Hale** is Professor of Anthropology at the University of Texas, Austin. He is author of *Resistance and Contradiction: Miskitu Indians and the Nicaraguan State, 1894–1987* (1994); coeditor (with Gustavo Palma and Clara Arenas) of *Racismo en Guatemala. Abriendo debate sobre un tema tabú* (1999); and coeditor (with Jeffrey Gould and Darío Euraque) of *Memorias del mestizaje. Cultura y política en Centroamérica, 1920 al presente* (2004) and *"Más que un indio": Racial Ambivalence and Neoliberal Multiculturalism in Guatemala* (2006). He is also author of numerous articles on identity politics, racism, ethnic conflict, and the status of indigenous peoples in Latin America. He was President of the Latin American Studies Association (May 2006–October 2007).

**Olivia Harris** is Professor of Social Anthropology at the London School of Economics. She pursues long-term anthropological and historical research in Bolivia, and comparative interests in Latin America more broadly. She is completing a book on understandings of historical time in Latin America, and among her recent publications are *To Make the Earth Bear Fruit* (2000) and *Qaraqara-Charka. Mallku, Inka y Rey en la provincia de Charcas, siglos XV–XVII* (with Tristan Platt and Thérèse Bouysse-Cassagne, 2006).

**Penelope Harvey** is Professor of Social Anthropology at the University of Manchester. She has done research in Peru, Spain and Manchester on the politics of knowledge and communicative practice with an ethnographic focus on language, science and technology, and the modern state in everyday life. She is joint editor (with Jeanette

Edwards and Peter Wade) of *Anthropology and Science: Epistemologies in Practice* (2007); and *Technologized Images, Technologized Bodies: Anthropological Approaches to a New Politics of Vision* (2007).

**Cori Hayden** is Associate Professor of Anthropology at the University of California, Berkeley. Her research interests include the anthropology of science, technology, and medicine; intellectual property and pharmaceutical politics; and kinship theory. She has conducted ethnographic research on plant-based drug discovery in Mexico and is currently researching the politics of generic medicines in Mexico and Argentina. Hayden is the author of *When Nature Goes Public: The Making and Unmaking of Bioprospecting in Mexico* (2003).

**Myriam Jimeno** is Titular Professor at the Departamento de Antropología and Centro de Estudios Sociales, Universidad Nacional de Colombia. Her research is on social conflict and violence; and the history of anthropology, ethnicity, state policy, and ethnic minorities. Her most recent publications include *Juan Gregoria Palechor. Historia de mi vida* (2006), *Crimen pasional. Contribución a una antropología de la emociones* (2004), and *Unos cuantos piquetitos. Violencia, mente y cultura* (2005).

**Carmen Martínez Novo** is Chair of the Anthropology Program at Facultad Latinoamericana de Ciencias Sociales in Ecuador. Her research focuses on indigenous identities and the relationship between indigenous peoples and non-indigenous actors in Mexico and Ecuador. She is the author of *Who Defines Indigenous?* (2006), and has also published, among other works, "We Are Against the Government Although We Are the Government," *Journal of Latin American Anthropology* 9(2) (2004); "The Making of Vulnerabilities," *Identities* 11(2) (2004); and "The Culture of Exclusion," *Bulletin of Latin American Research* 22(3) (2003).

**Adriana Maya** is Professor of History at the Universidad de Los Andes in Bogotá, Colombia. Her research focuses on racism, political conflict, Afro-Colombian identities and history, and postcolonial subjectivities. Her publications include *"Brujería" y reconstrucción de identidades entre los africanos y sus descendientes en la Nueva Granada, siglo XVII* (2004); *Balance y desafío de la historia de Colombia a finales del siglo XXI. Homenaje a Jaime Jaramillo Uribe* (with Diana Bonnett, 2003); and *Los Afrocolombianos*, vol. 6 of *Geografía humana de Colombia* (1998).

**Rodolfo L. Meyer** is a researcher at the Hemispheric Institute of the Americas (HIA), University of California, Davis. From 2002 to 2003 he served as associate editor for *Current Anthropology*. His research focuses on Western and indigenous epistemology, and on Aymara culture and its relation to popular urban culture in the Andes. He is working on the folklorization of ritual, a book based on his Ph.D. dissertation titled "Performance and Identity in Popular Culture's Re/presentations of Tinku Ritual by Andean People." His research on the ideology and rhetoric of the image, specifically in ethnographic film and issues of re/presentation in cinema can be seen in his recent essay-film *The Re/generation of Life* (2003–04).

**Salomón Nahmad Sittón** is a founding member and current Regional Director of Centro de Investigaciones y Estudios Superiores en Antropología Social (CIESAS)

Pacífico Sur in Oaxaca. He also served as director general of Mexico's Instituto Nacional Indigenista and the Indigenous Education section of Mexico's Public Education Secretaria. He has taught anthropology at the National Autonomous University of Mexico (UNAM), the National School of Anthropology and History (ENAH), the Universidad Iberoamericana and the Autonomous University "Benito Juarez" in Oaxaca (UABJO). His publications include *Fronteras étnicas análisis y diagnostico de dos sistemas de desarrollo: proyecto nacional vs. proyecto étnico. El caso de los ayuuk (mixes) de Oaxaca* (2003); *Fuentes etnológicas para el studio de los pueblos ayuuk (mixes) del Estado de Oaxaca* (1994); *Los Pueblos de la bruma y el sol* (1981); "Huichol Religion and the Mexican State: Reflections on Ethnocide and Cultural Survival," in Peter Furst and Stacey Schaefer (eds), *People of the Peyote: Huichol Indian History, Religion and Survival* (1996); and "El concepto de identidad en la frontera cultural, el poder político. El caso del pueblo mixe," in Joan Pujadas and Gunther Dietz (eds), *Etnicidad en Latinoamerica. Movimientos sociales, cuestión indígena y diásporas migratorias* (2005).

**Mariza Peirano** is Professor of Anthropology at the Universidade de Brasilia, Brazil. Her research focuses on politics and ritual, with special interest in the presence of the state in people's everyday life. The comparison between different conceptions and practices of anthropology has been a long-term concern. Her books include *Uma antropologia no plural. Três experiências contemporáneas* (1992), *A favor da etnografia* (1995), *O Dito e o Feito. Ensaios de antropologia dos rituais* (editor, 2001), *Rituais Ontem e Hoje* (2003), *A teoria vivida e outros ensaios de antropologia* (2006).

**Deborah Poole** is Professor of Anthropology and Director of the Program in Latin American Studies at Johns Hopkins University (Baltimore). Her research deals with issues of political culture, violence, race, visuality, and law in southern highland Peru and Oaxaca, Mexico. Her publications include *Unruly Order: Violence and Culture in The High Provinces of Southern Peru* (1989), *Peru: Time of Fear* (with Gerardo Rénique, 1992), *Vision, Race, and Modernity* (1998), and *Anthropology in the Margins of the State* (with Veena Das, 2004).

**Alcida Rita Ramos** is Professor of Anthropology at the University of Brasília and senior researcher of the National Council of Scientific and Technological Development (CNPq) in Brazil. Having done extensive fieldwork among the Yanomami in Brazil, she is currently working on indigenism and nation, comparing Brazil with other South American countries. She is the author of *Sanumá Memories: Yanomami Ethnography in Times of Crisis* (1995) and *Indigenism: Ethnic Politics in Brazil* (1998).

**Isaias Rojas Pérez** is a Ph.D. candidate in Anthropology at Johns Hopkins University. His ethnographic research focuses on law, violence, and human rights in post-conflict Peru. Currently, he is working on a critical examination of the experiences of truth and reconciliation commissions in Latin America. He has served for several years on the steering committee of the Instituto de Defensa Legal (IDL), in Lima, Peru, and the editorial board for IDL's magazine, *ideele*. During that time, he has written extensively on political violence and human rights in Peru. His recent publication is "Drug Control Policy, Human Rights, and Democracy in Peru," in C. A. Youngers and E. Rosin (eds), *Drugs and Democracy in Latin America: The Impact of US Policy* (2004).

**Pablo Sandoval** is Associate Researcher at the Instituto de Estudios Peruanos in Lima, Peru. He is currently completing his postgraduate studies in history at the Colegio de Mexico. His research focuses on political violence and the relationship between *indigenismo* and Andean anthropology. His recent publications include contributions to Carlos Iván Degregori (ed.), *No hay país más diverso. Compendio de antropología peruana* (2000), Carlos Iván Degregori (ed.), *Jamás tan cerca arremetió lo lejos. Memoria y violencia política en el Perú* (2003), and Elizabeth Jelin (ed.), *El pasado en el futuro. Los movimientos juveniles* (2006), and he is the editor (with Ramon Pajuelo) of *Globalización y diversidad cultural. Una mirada desde América Latina* (2004).

**Victoria Sanford** is Associate Professor of Anthropology at Lehman College/City University of New York. Her ethnographic research focuses on human rights, truth-telling, and political violence in Guatemala and Colombia. She is the author of *Buried Secrets: Truth and Human Rights in Guatemala* (2003), *Violencia y genocidio en Guatemala* (2003), *La Masacre de Panzós. Etnicidad, tierra y violencia en Guatemala* (2007), coeditor (with Asale Angel-Ajani) of *Engaged Observer: Anthropology, Advocacy and Activism* (2006) and coauthor of the Guatemalan Forensic Anthropology Foundation's Report to the Commission for Historical Clarification (2000).

**Linda J. Seligmann** is Professor of Anthropology at George Mason University. Her ethnographic research has focused on agrarian issues, political economy, and the dynamics of gender, class, and ethnicity in the informal economy in Andean Peru; and on transnational and transracial adoption in the United States. Her most recent books include *Between Reform and Revolution: Political Struggles in the Peruvian Andes* (1995) and *Peruvian Street Lives: Culture, Power and Economy among Market Women of Cuzco* (2004).

**Lynn Stephen** is Distinguished Professor of Anthropology at the University of Oregon. Her research explores political identities and their articulation with ethnicity, gender, class, immigration, and nationalism in the Americas. Her most recent books are *Transborder Lives: Indigenous Oaxacans in Mexico and the US* (2007), *Zapotec Women: Gender, Class, and Ethnicity in Globalized Oaxaca* (2005), and *Zapata Lives! Histories and Cultural Politics in Southern Mexico* (2002).

**Stefano Varese** is Professor of Native American Studies at the University of California, Davis. In addition to his anthropological and ethnohistorical research on the Asháninka peoples of Peru, he has been active in policy-making and legislative activity to protect indigenous territories and ethnic rights. During the last decades he has done ethnographic research in southeastern Mexico and on Latin America's indigenous diaspora in California. His publications include *Salt of the Mountain* (2002), *Indígenas y educación en México* (1983), *La ruta mixteca* (2004), and *Witness to Sovereignty* (2006).

**Peter Wade** is Professor of Social Anthropology at the University of Manchester. His publications include *Blackness and Race Mixture* (1993), *Race and Ethnicity in Latin America* (1997), *Music, Race and Nation: Música Tropical in Colombia* (2000), *Race, Nature and Culture: An Anthropological Perspective* (2002), and (as editor) *Race, Ethnicity and Nation: Perspectives from Kinship and Genetics* (2007). His current research focuses on issues of racial identity, embodiment, and new genetic and information technologies.

**Casey Walsh** is Assistant Professor of Anthropology at the University of California, Santa Barbara. From 2001 to 2007 he was a professor in the Graduate Program in Social Anthropology at the Universidad Iberoamericana, in Mexico City. His research centers on water, agriculture and society in the Mexico–US borderlands. He has published recently in *Latin American Perspectives*, the *Journal of Political Ecology*, and *Nueva Antropología*. His book *Building the Borderlands* (2008) shows how regional society in northern Mexico formed at the intersection of the transnational cotton industry, state-led irrigated development projects, and migrant labor.

# Acknowledgments

This book has been many years in the making. My first and greatest debt is owed to my contributing authors. Their great insight, humor and patience made it possible for the book to move forward, and I feel honored to have been able to work with such a distinguished group of international anthropologists. Many other friends also provided much needed advice and support. Of these, I would especially like to thank Valeria Procupez for her invaluable help in defining the scope and content of the book during the initial stages of this project, and Don Selby for his excellent editing of some very rough translations. Becky Daniels at the Johns Hopkins University Anthropology Department helped out with the formatting and bibliographic work. Veena Das and Naveeda Khan offered advice and encouragement during different phases of the project. Peggy Cornejo, Elizabeth Kilburn, and Lynn Bolton helped with translation on several chapters. Jane Huber and Emily Martin at Blackwell Publishing got the project up and running, and Rosalie Robertson and Deirdre Ilkson saw it to its completion. Finally, I would like to thank Gerardo and Lucas Renique for their patience and support.

# Introduction

*Deborah Poole*

In 1968, an article entitled "Anthropology and Imperialism" in the US journal *Monthly Review* challenged anthropologists to confront the worrying gap that seemed to separate their academic discipline from the political passions and complexities of a modernizing, capitalist, and militarized world. Arguing that "anthropology is a child of Western imperialism," the article's author, Kathleen Gough, charged that anthropologists had ignored this reality to act, either implicitly or explicitly, as defenders of their nations' colonial and imperial projects. Although some anthropologists had begun to study processes of urban migration, proletarianization, and social change, Gough argued that the hardening of imperial and revolutionary currents would now oblige them to expand their reach even further to include revolutionary movements, nationalist identities, and the political aspirations of the marginal or subject peoples with whom anthropologies had always worked.

In subsequent years, as anthropologists and their subjects have together moved through the antiwar and decolonization movements of the 1960s and 1970s, the postcolonial critique of the 1980s, and the rise in the 1990s of identity based, sectarian, and antisystemic politics, Gough's charge has lost its radical edge to assume instead the implicit force of a received truth. Anthropology today is invested in a wide range of ethical, political and humanitarian debates and most anthropologists readily accept the argument that their discipline should both be politically engaged and embrace distinctive, even discrepant political voices. As it has moved through crisis and recovery, the discipline has been significantly expanded. Anthropologists now study pretty much everything, from laboratory scientists and development workers, to financial markets, genomes and transnational political movements. Thus, if anthropology can still be somewhat broadly defined as "the study of other cultures and societies," the location of that "other" has been left up for grabs: The other is both out there in the world and inside the very methodologies, theoretical claims, and epistemologies that define the work of anthropology. However, although anthropology may well have lost its original claim to have a distinctive *subject matter* – the "non-Western" or "primitive" cultures of the world – its recovery has brought a new claim to disciplinary distinction grounded in methodologies of encounter and acknowledgment. Anthropology has thus grown, somewhat unevenly, into the social science discipline that is best positioned to acknowledge the philosophical and ethical priority of alterity as the necessary grounds for articulating responsible (and, in Gough's terms, nonimperialistic) claims to political and scientific knowledge. This move is, perhaps, best observed in anthropologists' growing commitment to redefine the political and ethical force of their discipline through a critical engagement with such traditional anthropological methodologies and concepts as ethnography, comparison, locality, culture, tradition, and indigeneity.

The Latin American anthropologies surveyed in this Companion offer a privileged perspective on the relevance, force and passion of anthropology as a discipline that studies and embraces both alterity and activism. Indeed, the very idea that anthropology could be anything *but* engaged is one that does not resonate easily with the experience of anthropologists working in Latin America. Since its emergence as a field of scientific study in the 19th century, the discipline took its cues from new liberal states whose national and cultural identities were formed in a complex dialogue with their Spanish and Portuguese colonizers. Throughout their history, Latin American anthropologists have also had to contend with the cultural and academic imperialism of their powerful neighbor to the north. Many have had to carry out their research in the shadow of repressive governments and dictatorships who were benefactors of US economic and military support. More recently still, Latin American anthropologists have been challenged by the demands of their own research "subjects" for the expanded participation of indigenous and other subaltern anthropologists.

The chapters collected in this Companion offer an entry into these experiences, histories and debates that comprise Latin American anthropology. They tell the story of anthropologies that developed in tandem with the liberal nation-state, and of anthropologists who often played critical roles in defining both the ideological contours of national cultures and the administrative and governmental policies through which culturally and ethnically diverse populations were governed and, at times, subdued. They also, however, tell stories of anthropologists who defended indigenous and economically marginalized populations from state abuses, who have struggled with the need to incorporate indigenous voices into their discipline and research, and who have crafted a regionally specific disciplinary agenda around issues of social justice and activism. Together these stories suggest that Latin American anthropologies were like European and US anthropologies to the extent that their theoretical priorities and applications were often shaped by the needs of conservative states and by the policies of internal colonialism through which states attempted to subjugate indigenous peoples. At the same time, they clearly point toward important regional differences in that – with very few exceptions – the "native" subjects of Latin American anthropologists did not live in far-off lands, but rather formed part of the same nation-state as the anthropologist. Although early US and European anthropologies were also founded, to differing degrees, on the study of internally colonized peoples, Latin American anthropologists often approached their "native" subjects with a desire to understand what it was that *they* shared, as national and cultural subjects, with their ethnographic subjects. As many of the authors in this volume argue, this understanding of anthropology as a discipline that is premised on concerns with intimacy and belonging gives the anthropology practiced by Latin American anthropologists a distinctive resilience, creativity, and salience in the modern world.

The culturally and linguistically diverse geographic region now known as Latin America has also played a distinctive role in the formation of the theoretical and comparative sensibilities of sociocultural anthropology. The Americans later known as "Indians" offered Europeans their first encounter with radical alterity, forcing the Catholic Church to rule on such matters as the distribution of souls, and Iberian intellectuals to come to grips with the existence of cities and states that were many times larger and richer than those of contemporary Europe. Somewhat later, the French philosopher Michel de Montaigne drew on his encounter with a Tupi-Guarani prince to launch a debate that would be foundational to the European Enlightenment. How, de Montaigne asked in his famous 1580 essay "Of Cannibals," can "we call these people barbarous in respect to the rules of reason; but not in respect to ourselves, who in all sorts of barbarity exceed them?" Similar curiosity about Inca governance, Tupi culture, and Aztec religion helped the 18th century philosophes to imagine more beneficent forms of governance and to conjure the utopian imaginaries that would fuel European political reform. The indigenous peoples of Latin America also figured prominently in the 19th century debates about racial origins, racial classification, language, and cultural evolution launched by anthropologists such as Alcides d'Orbigny, William Tylor, Daniel Brinton, and Lewis Henry Morgan. Although the positivist methodologies and racist premises of these debates were later rejected by post-Boasian and post-Durkheimian anthropologists, the discipline's claims to scientific status continued in many respects to rely on these early ethnological experiments in the comparative, predictive and classificatory study of Latin America's native civilizations.

If Latin America's indigenous peoples figured from the beginning as an inspiration for political theory, a source for museum collections, and a laboratory for ethnological and racial classification, its creole intellectuals and scientists also participated as important interlocutors for European and US anthropologists. Although most 19th century Latin American intellectuals actively embraced contemporary ideologies of progress, racial distinction, and societal evolution, many also contested the application of such theories to portray their nations as inferior and incapable of progress. Most notably, by the late 19th and early 20th century, some anthropologists and intellectuals in Latin America began to articulate theories concerning the "vigor" and resilience of their countries' mixed or *mestizo* races as a productive counterpoint to the charges of racial inferiority leveled against them by those who believed in the natural superiority of the European or "Anglo-Saxon" races. Although these proponents of mestizaje subscribed to the same doctrines of racial determination that drove European racial theories, they did so in the interests of defending the "civilizational" achievements of their nations and region. Thus, no matter how misguided these early racial anthropologies now appear, it is important to acknowledge that they shared with later, more critical perspectives on cultural difference an understanding that anthropology is necessarily configured through the intimate relationships that bind political polemic, social change, and nation-building to academic scholarship.

The social anthropologies that took shape in the universities, government offices, Catholic parishes, and indigenous and non-governmental organizations of 20th century Latin America assumed distinct political positions to those of their 19th century predecessors. These anthropologies were shaped by two intellectual traditions.

The first was the broad cultural, political, and intellectual movement known as *indigenismo*. Indigenistas defended the cultural traditions, histories and rights of their nations' "first peoples." Many also protested contemporary ideologies of indigenous racial inferiority by claiming indigenous racial and cultural attributes as part of their own personal identities. Others drew on philosophy to articulate intellectual and political agendas that privileged indigenous spiritual and cultural traditions as a counterpoint to the rapacious ideologies of economic development and "progress" that drove European science.

Although the indigenistas' willingness to speak *for* the Indians they claimed to represent has frequently been decried as a sign of their inauthenticity or even duplicity, the indigenista movement as a whole nevertheless set an important precedent for Latin American anthropology. Not only did they deploy their knowledge of indigenous culture and history to advocate for policies and laws which they believed would address problems of indigenous poverty and marginalization, but they also muddied the conceptual and perceptual divides through which US and European anthropologists framed their accounts of the "other" as an object of scientific inquiry. Even the most conservative of the indigenistas predicated their studies of Indians in terms of their actual or potential membership in a national community. For indigenistas, the "native" was both a subject of academic inquiry and an interiorized, often conflictive, dimension of the anthropologist's own identity and life.

A second crucial force shaping Latin American anthropology has been left-wing political movements and the struggle for social justice. The histories chronicled in these chapters describe the diverse affiliations, both critical and partisan, that linked Latin American anthropologists with their nations' left-wing political parties and organizations. Although many anthropologists viewed the traditional left's focus on class and the economy as a threat to a disciplinary subject matter focused on culture and race, others drew on Marxist theory to expand the reach of anthropological inquiry to include issues of economic dependency, internal colonialism, peasant economies, nationalism, and the state. In this way, Latin American anthropologists were able to locate their subjects – Indians, peasants, and the urban poor – within broader geographies of power, and to redefine the disciplinary staples of culture, kinship, and community to include considerations of inequality, class, and local political power. Even language – which was long considered as the key indicator of cultural continuity – was from the 1970s onward reconceptualized as a domain of cultural and political practice shaped by unequal access to political and economic power, as well as by historical strategies of resistance.

Armed with the new theoretical tools provided by their critical embrace of Marxist theory and by an increased awareness of how historical patterns of inequality played out in the lives of their "traditional" research subjects, anthropologists in Latin America formed crucial interlocutors for the indigenous and Afro-Latin American organizations that emerged in the final decades of the 20th century. These movements drew on international human rights law and the (limited) recognition of cultural rights offered by the neoliberal constitutional reforms of the 1980s to demand increased access to resources, territorial and political autonomy, and more participatory forms of democracy at a national level. Indigenous organizations have been at times critical of both anthropology, as a discipline that claimed expertise in indigenous lifeways, and indigenismo, as a politico-philosophical current that often spoke in the name of indigenous peoples. Over time, however, these conversations and quarrels between anthropology and indigenous organizations have been productive. They have produced what Rossana Barragán describes in her chapter on Bolivian anthropology as "bridges and chasms" that unite and separate anthropology and indigenous politics in a dynamic exchange of ideas. The end result has been an anthropology that has been strengthened by the inclusion of increasing numbers of professional anthropologists who study their own cultures and communities. Reciprocally, indigenous movements have also drawn critically on anthropologists' and historians' knowledge of their peoples' political practices, social forms, and histories to mobilize strategic definitions of cultural affiliation, ethnic territoriality, and political autonomy.

The activist and advocacy role of anthropologists in such popular political struggles for policy reform, legal recognition and political inclusion has reinforced the already strong historical links between anthropology and the nation-state in Latin America. As several chapters in this volume argue, the nationalist frameworks within which this engagement with indigenous politics has unfolded has proven troubling for many foreign anthropologists. Yet Latin America's indigenous and politically engaged anthropologies have contributed to discussions of ethical and political responsibility that extend well beyond the national and regional boundaries of Latin America. As Latin American anthropologists struggle to accommodate their understandings of what constitutes sound research practices and responsible claims to knowledge, they have helped to shift the discipline as a whole towards a greater capacity to acknowledge how local forms of life figure as alternative "civilizing projects" and how subaltern forms of knowledge can help us to rethink the ethical and political configuration of our academic disciplines.

The stories of research, theory building, government collaboration, and critical, even revolutionary, practice recounted in the different contributions to this Companion describe an arena of academic practice distinguished by considerable scientific and scholarly achievements. They tell the stories of Latin American anthropologists who have offered theoretical innovations to our understandings of ethnicity, kinship, inequality, social justice, violence, and resistance. Above all, they tell the story of anthropologists whose work and lives have much to teach to others who hope to reclaim the political, philosophical, and ethical relevance of anthropology in the current moment.

At the same time, the story of anthropology in Latin America has not always been a happy one. Each of the chapters in this book chronicles not only the achievements, but also the difficulties of "doing anthropology" in Latin America. Those professional anthropologists in Latin America who are lucky enough to get a job in a university often juggle two or more teaching positions. Others attempt to reconcile their political beliefs and scholarly standards to their professional reliance on state agencies and administrative work. Those who refuse to do so often face political repression and censorship. Others struggle to accommodate their research agendas to shifting fashions in the international development industry that contracts local anthropologists to carry out studies of indigenous and poor populations. Finally, with some exceptions, Latin American anthropologists must face misrecognition and marginalization within international anthropological circles dominated by English language journals, conferences and publications, and by anthropologists and theorists with more visible positions in the prestigious and relatively well-paid universities of "the North."

This book offers an entry to the history and experience of Latin American anthropologists. The chapters include contributions by anthropologists who work and live in the countries they study, as well as by anthropologists who study and teach on Latin America in British and US universities. Rather than providing comprehensive overviews or summaries, authors were asked to draw on their own work to engage thematic debates and histories within Latin American anthropology. By organizing – and in some cases, centering – their overviews of national anthropologies and theoretical debates around examples drawn from their own work, they provide the reader with a clear sense of how engaged ethnographic fieldwork has shaped the production of anthropological knowledge in the region. The eight chapters in part I, "Locations," provide an introduction to the anthropological traditions of Argentina, Bolivia, Brazil, Colombia, Ecuador, Guatemala, Mexico, and Peru. Together these chapters offer a sense of the intimate institutional, political and affective ties that bind anthropology to the nation-state in Latin America. The nine chapters grouped in part II, "Debates," provide an introduction to some of the key thematic and conceptual debates animating anthropological work in Latin America. Some chapters focus on what might be thought of as the historical "gate-keeping concepts" of race, place, language, kinship, and land reform that many anthropologists will easily associate with Latin American anthropology. Other chapters on law, borders, sovereignty, science, and statistics outline the important contributions which Latin American anthropologies have made to the ethnographic study of the state, globalization and the political economies of disciplinary knowledge. Together they offer a sense of the many innovative, critical and conceptual contributions through which anthropological work in Latin America has enlivened social, political and anthropological theory. The chapters gathered in part III, "Positions," all speak to Latin American anthropologists' enduring commitment to activism, collaboration and engagement. While some deal with polemics concerning identity, migration, voice and indigenous anthropologies, others chronicle anthropologists' efforts to bring disciplinary knowledges to bear on violence, suffering and the work of recovery in the aftermath of political conflict and state terror.

If a single quality could be said to characterize Latin America as a region, that quality might well be its unsettling diversity. Latin America is home to peoples who originally came from Africa, Europe, Asia and the Middle East. Its indigenous peoples today speak over 600 different languages, representing 56 language families. Over time, its political elites and states have governed through an amazing, and sometimes very creative array of political positions and ideologies. The social and political energies and abilities of the indigenous, subaltern, and marginal peoples whom anthropologists often study are astounding, lending strength to the region's resilient left-wing, critical and utopian traditions of social change. In similar spirit, the range of issues, questions, and methodologies deployed by the region's anthropologists are also far-ranging and diverse. This volume makes no claim to represent or much less speak for all of them. It was not possible, for example, to include chapters on all of the countries or even subregions of Latin America in part I. This Companion, for example, does not include chapters on the rich anthropological traditions of the Caribbean. Similarly, the overview of current debates in part II does not pretend to be inclusive of all of the contributions which Latin American anthropologies have made to broader disciplinary debates. Finally, the selection of "Positions" in part III is necessarily just that: a selection. Like the best traditions within Latin American anthropology, then, the chapters contained in this volume seek to be neither totalizing nor even particularly comprehensive in their claims to speak *for* a region, a people, or a place. Rather what this companion volume offers is a cross-section of voices speaking from within the varied spaces occupied by Latin American anthropologies. The space they describe is one in which political commitment and polemic have never been conceived of as outside the domain of anthropology, and in which anthropologists have played important roles in recrafting the conceptual, theoretical, and methodological boundaries of their discipline as a whole.

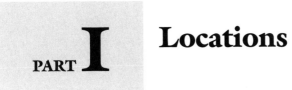

# PART I  Locations

# Argentina: Contagious Marginalities

CHAPTER **1**

## Claudia Briones and Rosana Guber

This chapter explores the development of anthropology in Argentina in relation to both ideas and practices of politics and the political, and official common-sense understandings of cultural diversity. As Ana María Alonso (1994) has warned us, anthropologists need to exercise caution when working with analytical categories such as *ethnicity*, *nation* and *state*, in that they also form part of our common knowledge as citizens. The Argentine experience suggests that such problems result less from the uncritical reproduction of commonly accepted categories, than from the exchange between scientific theories and wider social theories. The fact is that anthropologists, other academics, state agents, and the public all create meaning from direct and indirect practices permeated by state mechanisms. These practices inform the terms "ethnicity," "nation," "state," as well as "race" and "pueblo" (the people). We also, however, create meaning from notions and practices of what constitutes "politics," "realpolitik," and "the political," and from national formations of alterity. Together these constitute our civic subjectivity.

Although anthropological constructs were at times backed by the Argentine state in its most authoritarian and intrusive phases, we argue here that there are no automatic alignments between the constructs of diversity endorsed by ethnology, folklore and social anthropology and the "officially" sponsored ones.[1] The effects of a century-old journey, the alternately tense and complicit interaction between anthropology and the Argentine state, began in the mid 19th century with state centralization and the 1853 National Constitution. Territorial expansion into native populations by the military followed from 1870 to 1920, with the incorporation of survivors into the proletariat. The decades from 1880 to 1910 brought mass immigration from overseas, laws for compulsory and free education (1880), and the assimilation of second-generation immigrants and other native inhabitants into the military via the 1901 law of compulsory male conscription. Finally, in 1912 a new law mandated voting by secret ballot for all men, and the 1918 university reform granted autonomy to institutions of higher education. This foundational moment was followed by alternating phases of democracy, partial democracy, and dictatorship, until the infamous

Proceso de Reorganización Nacional (Process of National Reorganization, 1976–1983) and its 30,000 *desaparecidos* (disappeared persons). The democratic *apertura*, or opening, of 1983 paved the way to an unusually long period of constitutional institutionalization. This path of fitful twists and turns nonetheless contrasts with the extraordinary endurance of the matrix of "diversity" endorsed by the national state (Segato 2002). By relating sociological inequalities, read as cultural differences that are selectively rendered as ethnic or racial (Briones 1998), this state construct has operated in terms of marks and thresholds of uniformity and "alterity". The state-led ideal of Argentina as a country made up of "few Indians," "no Negroes," "mostly immigrants," and "criollos" (creoles) has shaped and stratified collective entities by "assigning them disparate qualities in terms of the consistency, porosity or even feebleness of their ethnic/racial boundaries and profiles" (Briones 2002).

The anthropological side of the story started with the first museums of "natural history" founded after 1870, and with the inclusion of anthropology courses into the teaching programs at the national universities. The first degrees in Ciencias Antropológicas (Anthropological Sciences) came out in 1957 and 1958. From then on, with varying degrees of success and duration, several undergraduate and graduate programs were established in Anthropology, Social Anthropology and Archaeology.[2]

As many others have noticed, the disciplinary process intertwines with political struggle in 20th century Argentina (Bartolomé 1980; Herrán 1985; Perazzi 2003; Ratier and Ringuelet 1997; Vessuri 1992). In its most obvious and dramatic sense this means that some colleagues paid – with their lives, in prison or in exile – the price of being seen as "dangerous dissidents" or "internal enemies." In a less obvious sense, it means that in some ways the political process shaped the professional and academic tasks of the discipline (setting objects of research, topics and formats of scientific debate and research teams). These in turn affected anthropological theory and methodology. Nonetheless the articulation between the two routes – one based on the nation-state and the other based on the discipline itself – is hardly a one-way relationship.

Here we show that anthropological constructs of otherness produced by ethnologists, folklorists and social anthropologists have differed from the hegemonic constructs of alterity sponsored by the state. Such differentiation depended upon the political and institutional positions held by each subdiscipline, as well as on the ways in which each one forged its objects of knowledge. Anthropological diversity, however, has itself often fueled divisiveness and animosity, while keeping its own secrets and maintaining its sense of marginality vis-à-vis "official alterity." The official construction of alterity promotes a white, eurocentric, "nonracist" nation, while it discriminates against indigenous people, Argentines of African descent, as much as against some immigrants and *criollos* by lumping them altogether as *cabecitas negras* ("little dark heads"), because of their "inadequacy" not only in terms of skin color, but also of class and political culture. Thus, despite shared denunciations of widespread and subtle racism, Argentine anthropologists have been unsuccessful not only in unmasking the hegemonic racialization of class and region and the "enclassement" of racial and territorial segments of society, but also in regarding objectively the political predicament of the identification of "internal enemies" by means of ubiquitous standards of "unbearable politicization."

"Anthropological styles" in Latin America have often been linked to national, social, political, and academic discourses (Cardoso de Oliveira and Ruben 1995;

L'Estoile et al. 2002; Ramos 1990; Visacovsky and Guber 2002). The point in noting these "styles" is not to uncover the complicity of anthropology and anthropologists with the colonial legacy or with neocolonialism and collaborationism, as occurred in the United States with the 1980s political critique of anthropology (Asad 1973). Rather the goal is to show that the same hegemonic force against which self-appointed opponents take their antagonistic stand ends up being part of this stand itself (Laclau 1993). In Argentina, anthropologists have often complained about the marginal status of their traditional "objects of study" (Indians, *Afro-argentines, cabecitas negras*) in an allegedly European country, whereas their own field becomes marginal to the social sciences and the humanities. Unlike in Mexico and Brazil, Argentine anthropology also ended up in the margins "of general interest and of the common good." Founded to study the relics or survivals of the past in the present, the origins of American man, mythic consciousness, or the persistence of rural workers in an apparently modern country, the discipline has not yet managed to find a conceptual and authorized place for itself vis-à-vis its local audience. This situation has reinforced the marginality and even public silence of anthropology as a discipline (see Gordillo, this volume).

## "Few Indians, No Blacks, Tons of Internal Enemies"

Since its modern formation, intellectuals and statesmen have characterized Argentina as a dual country, split into opposing segments that are difficult or impossible to reconcile. This characterization has had direct and indirect practical impact. First, the fate of the nation is conceived in terms of opposing factions, deeply rooted in the Argentine common sense (port–interior, centralists–federalists, civilization–barbarism, Peronists–anti-Peronists, authoritarianism–democracy) (Shumway 1991; see Neiburg 1998 for a critique). Second, Argentine dualism has set in motion a process through which political and social groupings have produced a myriad of internal enemies to be silenced, suppressed, or removed. As a result, the actors of modern history have taken part and taken sides, as allies or enemies, in the ensuing military coups and sudden *aperturas*. Between 1930 and 1983, there were 20 years of unconstitutional regimes, 13 years of partial democracies, and only 12 years of government by free and open elections. Hemispheric political trends and guidelines such as the US National Security Doctrine entered Argentina to enforce the ban of Peronism, and later on to eradicate the social and political militants of the early 1970s. The self-named "Proceso de Reorganización Nacional" – known today simply as either "el Proceso" (the Process) or "la dictadura" (the dictatorship) – was the climax of mounting accusations and repression, the traces of which can still be seen in the recent accusations against those who have voiced demands for indigenous rights (Muzzopappa 2000).

Encompassing ideas of "otherness" have tended to reproduce the traits that exclude both those groups identified as "unacceptable inappropriates" – who are defined in terms of their "differences" as internal others – and those sectors classified as "tolerable subordinates," that is, as the ones who are already seen as (actually or potentially) part of the national mainstream, despite their differences (Williams 1993). The moral elites of the 19th century adopted the trope of the "melting pot," less as a diagnostic than as a project of social engineering whose goal was to create a homogeneously white Europe at the southern tip of South America. Soon after the end of the wars of independence, the leaders of the 1810 Revolution abandoned the Enlightenment dream of abolishing all forms of difference and incorporating indigenous peoples into the new nation-state, while respecting the ideal of human equality before the law (Menni 1995). To the romantics of the generation of 1837, the *civilization* that belonged to an *external other* (Europe and/or the United States) became the guiding utopia for nation-building. While indigenous peoples were progressively externalized, the label of "barbarism" (*barbarie*) was also extended to those masterless rural residents – the *gauchos* and bandits – and to the Creole masses who formed the rural armies or *montoneras* who rebelled against the centralizing power of the Port of Buenos Aires. The collective term *criollo* gained a negative connotation of a lasting nature. Native romanticism represented by the organizers of the modern state – Juan B. Alberdi, D. F. Sarmiento, José Echeverría – was based on a social realism (Soler 1979) which turned the polarity of *civilización* or *barbarie* into a representation of society, a principle of legitimization of power, and the way in which moral elites planned to take it over (Svampa 1994). The symbolic geography of the nation thus coined two images of extraordinary interpretative and pedagogic strength: the "desert" as an empty space that the government should populate; and a country in need of filling its voids with people coming down "from the ships" – mostly Europeans whose human and cultural potential were seen as a "key to progress."

Decades later, the moral elites refined those two aesthetic tropes of territorialization to justify a military advance on "Indian territory." The resulting "Conquest of the Desert" spilled over the Pampa and Patagonia regions (1879–1885), whereas "the conquest of the green desert" (1884–1911) covered the Gran Chaco. Led by the ideals of "order and progress," the modernizing "generation of the '80s" did not establish a global indigenous policy to "civilize the barbarian Indians" (Briones and Delrio 2002). State intellectuals and large portions of the non-indigenous population believed that the civilizing crusade would solve the aboriginal question in due time and in its own way, by means of physical and cultural extinction, and by the encroachment of the white population (Lenton 1992). Even those who promoted more lenient policies toward these "barbarians" rejected the idea that the indigenous peoples had any cultural contribution to make to the Argentine nation.

This negative attitude toward the aborigines and the creoles was complemented with a positive attitude toward the European immigrants whose alterity, it was believed, would disappear through racial mixing and cultural assimilation, while improving and whitening the local inhabitants. Interestingly enough, this quality, which rendered the immigrants "assimilable" and which distanced them from the indigenous peoples, also removed them from the *criollo gaucho*. This other "native" element implied a social rift in economic, educational, cultural, and politico-ideological terms. The *gaucho* was out of control, since he dwelled on the margins of the Nation, as a liminal being (Archetti 1999).

The apparently unrestricted receptiveness toward European immigrants soon gave way to a call for more "authentic" national values. The *gaucho* – already tamed – was established as the national (social) symbol. This process paralleled the condemnation of those foreigners suspected of anarchism or left-wing activism. The 1902 Residency Law allowed for the deportation of "undesirable elements" from Argentine territory, although the hegemonic image of the Nation still maintained the civilizing and pedagogic potential of the European contingent, the absence of blacks and the scattered presence of *indios*.[3] These models for the "racialization" of both internal others and the nation in construction gave the Argentine melting pot a specific character in *mestiza* Latin America. Although Europeanness was a central and distinctive feature of the "Argentine mix," the overt exclusion of Indians and blacks (as well as "yellow" Asians), made it obvious that not just any kind of European immigrant could effect progress and civilization. In this classification game, those identified as "ethnically inconvenient elements" became markers that would devalue the chemistry of a racial, class, and politico-ideological pot.

The anti-immigration attitude and the conversion of "immigrants" into "foreigners" or "refugees" – labels which increased the threshold of "alterity" – paralleled the stock market crash of 1929 and its authoritarian effects in Europe and the Americas. The sectors that ran the state after 1930, the date of the first coup against a democratic government, until Juan D. Perón's decade (1946–55) shared a similar view concerning the "Argentine race." For example, Perón founded the Instituto Étnico Nacional (National Ethnic Institute, 1946–55) in order to regulate the entrance of foreigners. This was the first attempt at involving the national government in racial biopolitics in Argentina (Schneider 1994; Lazzari 2004). The subsequent emergence and consolidation of "Justicialismo" (or "Peronism") as a movement calling for the social and political inclusion of the urban and rural proletariat, however, was a turning point in the redefinition of the idea of the "Argentine people" (Martínez Sarasola 1992; Carrasco 1991). This notion referred first to the "pueblo trabajador" (the workers), a synonym for "pueblo peronista" which the elite or "antipatriotic oligarchy" (in Eva Perón's words) chastised as *cabecitas negras* (little black heads), *aluvión zoológico* (zoo-like alluvium), and *descamisados* (the shirtless ones) for trying to occupy the public sphere (Taylor 1979). Such labels resulted in a national core that included all those of humble economic status, no matter what their ethnic background. Therefore, the constitutional reform of 1949, which was in force until the 1955 anti-Peronist coup, acknowledged social and economic rights – mainly labor rights – for all citizens, while it revoked the only article that mentioned indigenous peoples.[4] To maintain such a distinction within the body of the Argentine people constituted, according to Perón, an act of flagrant and unforgivable discrimination. Paradoxically, if indigenous peoples were "integrated" for the first time into the "Argentine people" because they were unprivileged, they remained deprived of their character as original peoples, distinct, and predating the nation-state.

Anthropology established its professional credentials in the open wounds of the 1955 coup and the mounting repression of Peronists. Although the political change did not entail a radical transformation in the "official theories" of diversity, nor a uniform adoption of state proposals on the part of the subdisciplines within anthropology, the juncture reinforced the marginality of the "dark melting pot" vis-à-vis the nationality of the "white melting pot," and the anthropologists' marginality vis-à-vis the social sciences devoted now to promoting "social change." This racialization of the subaltern condition (Ratier 1971; Guber 2002; Margulis et al. 1998; Quijada et al. 2000) depicts a melting pot that parallels the Euro-Argentine one. The former is a symbolic space where the indigenous, the *Afro*, and the popular sectors of the provincial "interior" merge. Undesirable Europeans of Sicily and Calabria, of Andalusía and the Middle East were grouped with those thought of as "gauchos," "paisanos" or country-men, "montoneros," and poor "criollos." These nationals could not be made into foreigners, nor be symbolically removed from the nation, nor othered in any strong sense, because of the risk of losing critical mass and the possibility of an independent nation altogether. Just as the official and explicit *melting pot* "Europeanized" the Argentines by turning the European immigrants into Argentineans, the dark "melting pot" of the *cabecitas negras* "interiorized" a color line represented by the "interior" of the country (Ratier 1971). Here, the darkening of a generic condition of subalterneity epitomized as "tolerable subordinates" allowed for the reconstruction of a class system without questioning the assumption of whiteness as the attribute of the whole nation, nor the premises of progress and upward mobility which justified it, in order to establish its profile as a country of immigrants.

## ANTHROPOLOGICAL SCIENCES AS UNIVERSITY DISCIPLINE

The programs in Ciencias Antropológicas at La Plata (1957) and Buenos Aires (1958) started in what Argentine intellectuals have termed "the golden age of the university." Immediately after a decade of Peronist political interference with the administration of public universities,[5] a process of "normalization" took place: deans, rectors and faculty were replaced in order to put an end to academic "obscurantism," and to expel those involved with the regime of the so-called "fleeing tyrant" (*tirano prófugo*) (Sigal 1991; Neiburg 1998). In all, universities were heading for a successful process of modernization. In the early 1960s, Argentine universities were at the top of Latin American higher education. In 1957 the University of Buenos Aires launched programs in Sociology, Psychology and Educational Sciences, at the School of Philosophy and Literature. The three programs boasted a modern, professional and applied profile.

Ciencias Antropológicas – which opened in Buenos Aires in 1958 and began classes in 1959 – on the other hand, maintained a marked continuity with the previous period. The only changes were the forced retirement of Italian anthropologist José Imbelloni – former director of the Institute of Anthropology and of the Ethnographic Museum of the University of Buenos Aires and strongman of anthropology under Peronism (Garbulsky 1987) – and of the director of the Institute of Archaeology, Carlos Casanova. These resignations, however, did not jeopardize the hegemony of the Culture-Historical school in its Austrian version. In fact, although the faculty differed in their political sympathies – Fernando Márquez Miranda, the first chair of the Ciencias Antropológicas department, was a liberal, and Imbelloni a fascist – most of them operated with the same theoretical background. When in 1948 Oswald F. A. Menghin – a leading prehistorian who applied culture cycles to world prehistory, and who became rector of the University of Vienna in 1935–36 (Kohl and Pérez Gollán 2002) – and Marcelo Bórmida, an Italian with a bachelor's degree in Anthropology and a former *balilla* (from the Italian fascist youth organization Opera Nazionale Balilla), entered the Ethnographic Museum on Imbelloni's invitation, Anthropology was more attuned with the German Romantic trends that considered "culture" as the soul of peoples and nations, than with the blueprint of political and social organization.

Unlike the Department of Sociology – led by an antifascist Italian, Gino Germani, who instructed his students to look for the underlying sociocultural factors of Peronism – the three orientations in Ciencias Antropológicas (Archaeology, Ethnology and Folklore) continued to aim at the reconstruction of the origins of the American man and his heritage, and at salvaging material and symbolic mores under the threat of extinction. In their comparative studies ethnologists privileged indigenous peoples, as did ethnographers in their "description" of ways of life (Bórmida 1961; Lafón 1970). Folklore, a degree course in itself, led by literature professor Augusto R. Cortazar, entered Ciencias Antropológicas for the study of the "Folk." Unlike Robert Redfield's notion, in Argentina the "folk society" did not emphasize the indigenous pole, but rather the Spanish component of a Spanish–indigenous mix: the folklore of a people being seen to be made of cultural "survivals" of the colonial past, rather than as current expressions of social inequality (Cortazar 1949).

## Imbelloni's master plan

The division between Folklore and Ethnology was already contained within Imbelloni's blueprint, since each anthropological discipline had its own "object of study." Like other founding precursors and researchers, Imbelloni cultivated both fields as "full professor" at the University of Buenos Aires, in charge of the course on Anthropology and General Ethnology.[6] Imbelloni systematized the entire discipline along with its branches. Prehistory and Archaeology dealt with "lost civilizations"; Ethnography brought together "pottery, basketry, puzzles, dances, songs, prayers, cult rituals, funerary mores of the inhabitants of the territories where the natural civilization of the peoples described by nineteenth-century evolutionists as 'primitive' and 'savages' is still alive"; Folklore dealt with "the populations that belong to civilized nations" (Imbelloni 1959:17).

In Imbelloni's view, three notions justified the separation of Ethnography from Folklore: "survivals" (*supervivencias*), "stratum" (*estrato*) and "tradition." While the latter referred to the process through which a particular patrimony was preserved, "supervivencia" concerned that patrimony once preserved. The idea of "stratum" was twofold. On the one hand, it was related to the ways in which class, cultural and political elites within the "modern nations" acted as the cultural model for the "vulgo" (lower orders), that is, for the rural and urban masses who operated as "the substratum of the social hierarchy" (1959:34–35). On the other hand, it referred to the combination of modernization and the informal process of cultural transmission or "tradition" which resulted in the coexistence of modern and inherited forms, threatened by new cultural developments (1959:41–42). Such "inherited forms" were also defined as "substrata" from a temporal point of view, thus acknowledging the coexistence of different levels or layers from a remote to a recent past (1959:51). Imbelloni endowed Ethnography with populations and patrimonies that were not seen as underlying strata of the national culture, and Folklore with the "substrata" or popular heritages which had digested some fragments of the indigenous culture (1959:60), thus rooting his *Americanística* in the temporal–spatial margins of Argentineness.

This approach differed from the Boasian framework in the way it defined the objects for each subdiscipline, since demarcations hinged less on "cultural products" than on the human subjects to be dealt with. While for Boas and his students Folklore should study living systems of oral traditions, and Ethnography other remaining cultural products (Zumwalt 1988:29–30), in the Argentine case Folklore and Ethnography studied sectors with a different sociocultural distance from the national mainstream and the patterns of modernization.

Amid such a backdrop, the "professionalization" of Anthropology in the late 1950s resulted in a progressive separation of Ethnology and Folklore, two fields quite integrated in the past, as Imbelloni's own trajectory attested. The leading characters of this new arrangement were Marcelo Bórmida for Ethnology and Cortazar for Folklore. Their influence outreached their lives (1978 and 1974) even to the threshold of the democratic *apertura* in 1983, and shaped official anthropology, except during Perón's third government (1973–74).

## Ethnology's barbarians and Folklore's survivals

Bórmida learned physical anthropology and ethnology from Imbelloni, and the application of cultural cycles (*Kulturkreisse*) to preceramic Argentine archaeology from Menghin. After Imbelloni's expulsion, Bórmida pursued theoretical elaborations pointing at the autonomy of Anthropology from the Natural Sciences. Unlike Anthropology at the University of La Plata, *latu sensu* Anthropology was for him part of the Sciences of Spirit and of Universal History, rather than of the Sciences of Nature. He defined Anthropology as the study of the "barbarians," in its classic Greek sense of the "people we do not understand" (Bórmida 1956:7). Barbarianism could not, however, simply be dealt with from a civilizing project, as national statesmen had proclaimed since 1854, because – "irreducible" as it was – mythical consciousness expressed a feature of human subjectivity which epitomized a valued "temperament and manner of being in the world." Although myths were not exclusive to indigenous peoples, indigenous myths revealed the essence of an ahistorical, spontaneous logic, as opposed to Western rationality. Native mythologies were not only the privileged object of research, but also the guide to ethnographic work on the sociopolitical organization and the material lives (ergology) of their bearers.

Two conclusions ensue. First, myths resisted the causal-explanatory methods of modern science; and as a result, only a phenomenological ethnology based on Wilhelm Dilthey's interpretation of the sociological concept of *Verstehen* (understanding) was deemed suitable as a method for comprehending the true "cultural essence" these myths contained, without preconceptions (Bórmida 1969–70:27). Second, the *epojé* or epistemological disengagement required to approach the indigenous world with no trace of ethnocentrism and other reductionisms – economicism, sociologism – ended up fostering a more ontological than methodological relativism. In this framework, Bórmida's Ethnology called for the study of those immanent essences that formed the conceptual heiresses of the essences that had anchored the cultural cycles adopted by Imbelloni in his *Americanística* (Fígoli 1995). Now, if Imbelloni's anthropological studies of race, ethnicity, peoples and nations had the characterization of what was "Argentine" and "American" as a reference point, for Bórmida, Ethnology mainly offered incomparable access to the "inexorable" and immanent nature of the indigenous peoples. Historical contingencies such as their incomplete citizenship were beside the point. Moreover, by limiting its universalizing humanism with notions of objectivity and neutrality specific to positivism, Bórmida's Ethnology claimed a legitimacy denied to Folklore and to Social Anthropology, which had begun by the early 1960s to advocate scholarly "commitment" to the subjects of study as key actors in and for social transformation.

Extolling Ethnology and taking advantage of an increasing monopoly of directorial posts, Bórmida's approach shaped the academic field at the main Argentine university and, on account of its academic and geographical proximity, at the national agency for the promotion of scientific research, CONICET. Bórmida's presence throughout the institutional breaks of 1955, 1966, and 1974–6 moved his direct disciples – who grouped together in the Argentine Center of American Ethnology (Centro Argentino de Etnología Americana, CAEA) – to base their scientific practice not only on the acceptance of the radical alterity of indigenous peoples, but also on withdrawal both from indigenous needs and demands, and from applied anthropological knowledge (Califano et al. 1985).[7]

The professionalization of Folklore, by contrast, resumed an early path of union with the national state. Together with Peronism, increasing value was assigned to the "popular" and the "national." The National Institute of Tradition was founded in 1943, to be renamed according to political context as the National Institute of Philology and Folklore in 1955, the National Institute of Folkloric Research in 1960, the National Institute of Anthropology in 1964, and the National Institute of Anthropology and Latin American Thought in 1992. In the view of its first director, Juan Alfonso Carrizo, the Institute was meant to save "the spiritual patrimony inherited from our country," and to study "the recorded material in its historic and literary value, as well as in its relation with the other countries of America and Europe, especially with Spain and those of a Greco-Latin ancestry, to which the material belongs" (Carrizo 1953:26).

Folklore's "patrimonialist" perspective concentrated, as already stated, on sectors of the Argentine population termed "folk society." Scholars such as Cortazar and Imbelloni, but also Ismael Moya, Bruno Jacovella, Carlos Vega, and Armando Vivante, believed they could find values of the farming–stockbreeding oligarchy among the subaltern sectors arising from the early miscegenation of Spaniards and Indians (Blache 2002). Forever revealing its anonymous, common and oral character, folklore was precisely what could be found "like residual elements among subordinate sectors" (Cortazar 1949).

Cortazar's influence in Argentina and in most of Latin America resulted from his ability to seize concepts from the culture-historical theory of the cultural cycles, Malinowskian functionalism, North American culturalism, and folklore experts in North and South America. Although restricted by the theory of survivals, Cortazar confronted sociocultural totalities much in the way of community studies, a remarkable step forward in an environment that usually split cultures into particular features corresponding to this or that *kulturkreisse*. Nevertheless, the Cortazarian stance was established as a disciplinary dogma, not only on account of its theoretical and broadcasting merit, but also because of an academic promotion indebted to the political-academic process (Blache 2002). Cortazar's interpretation worked as a barrier against those readings of Argentine culture as "national and popular" which prevailed in the increasingly radicalized academic atmosphere surrounding Perón's return to Argentina in 1972 (Gurevich and Smolensky n.d.).

In any case, if the theory of the folk society was one of the very few hints of a quite absent theory of *mestizaje* (cross-breeding) in Argentina's hegemonic national ideology, the obvious predominance of the Spanish component within this framework showed once again the downplaying of the indigenous contribution to Argentine-ness, and also the exclusion of immigrants from the possibility of "producing 'authentic' folklore" (Blache 2002). In time, Folklore became more flexible. Rescuing folklore goods turned out to be less important than coping with the issues confronting "folk communities" (Lazzari 2002). From the 1960s onward, Folklore also made room for all things indigenous. But here "indigenous" meant less a feeble contribution to the early Argentine cultural patrimony than a powerful factor in the reproduction of marginal and marginalized communities, with their own cultural distinctiveness, and without full citizenship. Along with this gradual shift, Folklore also included people of European descent, first as objects of Argentinization and as recipients of Argentine folklore (taken to be emblematic of national culture), and later as subjects who were equally distinctive and valued in their contributions to Argentine-ness. Yet, seen as the product of a twofold shift – from an indigenous society to a European one, and from traditional to modern organization – the subject-objects of Folklore could not help being defined as marginal both in the past and in the present. Nonetheless, their marginality remained linked to an alterity seen as transitional rather than radical, like that of the subject-objects of ethnology.

In sum, the two main branches of Argentine Anthropology – Archaeology and Ethnology/Folklore – looked back to the past. This orientation stemmed in Ethnology and Folklore from their respective conceptualizations regarding the cultural products of groupings as emblematic either of prehispanic Argentina or of mestizaje. This division was also geopolitical; Ethnology and its junior partner Ethnography spread through Chaco and Pampa-Patagonia, that is, through the so-called "new provinces" of the Argentine territory that mushroomed in what were "Indian lands" until the late 19th century. Meanwhile, Folklore was located in central and north-west Argentina, in the "old provinces" arising from early Spanish colonization. While the dominant Ethnology was concerned with the native presence as radical and inexorable alterity, Folklore dealt with the rural "peasant" world as a transitional otherness.

Nevertheless, not all Anthropology would be concerned with times past. The marginalization of which ethnologists and folklore experts were so fond would change most dramatically among social anthropologists, for whom the formations of alterity resulted from the formative processes of inequality.

## Social Anthropology as a place of dissidence

The basis of "social anthropology" in Buenos Aires and La Plata, Rosario and other university centers revolved, for a long time, around the theoretical-ideological mix that prevailed in the 1960–1970s. For some anthropologists and sociologists, "social anthropology" referred to a combination of ethnography concerned with social change and intellectual commitment to the fate of social subjects. Such a mix surfaced in exchanges among Argentina's political and institutional processes and the modernizing enlightenment of the post-Peronist university (Terán 1991; Neiburg 1998), at times in line, at others in marked disagreement with British anthropology. In all, social anthropology, Argentine style, stemmed from three stances.

The modernizing Department of Sociology offered a course on social anthropology that was optional for sociologists and mandatory for anthropologists. Its first professor, as late as 1961, was US anthropologist Ralph Beals, who was succeeded by native and foreign experts. None of them belonged to the Ethnographic Museum. Apparently, the chair of Sociology considered anthropologists unable to teach a course in social anthropology that combined functionalism and structural functionalism, culture and personality, cultural ecology, neo-evolutionism, symbolic interactionism, ethnomethodology, and ethnographic fieldwork (Visacovsky et al. 1997). Interestingly enough, some faculty members at the Museum, such as Enrique Palavecino and Cortazar, taught British and American anthropology. But this was neither all, nor enough.

As for the second stance, Esther Hermitte – who graduated with a History teaching degree (*profesorado*) – encountered social anthropology in two visits to the Anthropology Department of the University of Chicago between 1947 and 1949. In 1957, before traveling to Chicago to pursue her doctorate in anthropology, Hermitte started to do research in the mining complex of El Aguilar, in the Argentine Puna. Here, she talked to Bolivian and *atacameño* miners and their families, and to the white-collar workers of the Aguilar company. But this time she was not concerned with cultural heritage or folk traditions, but rather with social relations at work, within the family and in the mining neighborhood as well. In 1958, Hermitte presented her conclusions as "applied anthropology," while her works were acknowledged by her two field assistants as social anthropology (Sanguinetti and Mariscotti 1958–59).[8] This line, however, was somehow interrupted when Hermitte departed to the US with a fellowship at CONICET, Argentina's National Science Foundation. The degree in Ciencias Antropológicas was created thereafter.

In contrast with Bormidian Ethnology and without labeling it "social" yet, the first students of the brand new degree in Anthropological Sciences at the University of Buenos Aires started to talk about a "committed" and "grass-roots" anthropology, aiming at "development" and "social change." Official anthropology at the Museum promptly identified social anthropology as a suspiciously modernizing, up-to-date, applied, Anglo-Saxon, mainly foreign kind of anthropology, as long as its main promoters were trained in the US (archaeologist Alberto Rex González at Columbia, Ph.D. 1959, and social anthropologist Hermitte at Chicago, Ph.D. 1964). Moreover, social anthropology was envisaged as a contaminated orientation tainted by its immediacy and its politicization (Bórmida 1961). For their part, committed young people accused the anthropological status quo of being "ahistorical" and also Nazi/fascist, in the troubled context of the Vietnam war, the Cuban revolution, Algerian independence, the events of May 1968 in France, and the growth of the first guerrilla groups in South America.

In any case, from the graduation in 1962 of the first bachelor in Anthropology at the University of Buenos Aires, Blas Alberti, to the first seminar on the modern Maya ethnography to be taught by Hermitte in 1966 (Hermitte 1971), students and young teaching assistants learned that anthropology could be undertaken among several groupings (rural inhabitants, people of African descent), in different areas (urban contexts), and from several theoretical approaches (structural functionalism, symbolic interactionism, and Marxism). Most of these approaches and topics were absent from the official anthropology. Far from merging with the projects of the Sociology Department, or even with open-minded career professors who were still teaching and even applying functionalism and structural-functionalism, the new degree holders attempted to forge a committed anthropology that would become the fourth orientation, along with Ethnology, Folklore and Prehistory.

The military coup of 1966 aborted those plans. After the violent police intervention at the university in July of that year, many teaching assistants resigned, along with a group of professors. Hermitte was among them, the only professor from the Anthropology Department to leave the university. Bórmida became the new chairman. Obviously enough, he did not encourage the consolidation of an orientation in Social Anthropology. In La Plata and Rosario there were fewer resignations, and Social Anthropology continued to be taught as a single course, albeit within an adverse context still dominated by the culture and history school. Meanwhile, those who had resigned from the University of Buenos Aires became advisors at public institutions, such as the Instituto de Tecnología Agropecuaria (Institute of Farming and Fishery Technology), Consejo Federal de Inversiones (Federal Investment Council), housing, education, and health departments. They were hired to deal with what federal and state administrations interpreted as the burdensome effects of anachronistic "peasant cultures," namely "resistance to change" and "traditionalism." In the "developmentalist" age influenced in Argentina and most of Latin America by the United Nations Economic Commission for Latin America and the Caribbean from the middle of 1950 and by marginalist theory, anthropologists contributed with their critical readings, based on Wright Mills, French and Italian versions of Marxism, and through ongoing debates on peasantries led by Eric Wolf, Sidney Mintz, June Nash, Rodolfo Stavenhagen, and Pablo González Casanova (see Seligmann, this volume).

These approaches made it possible to do research on *compadrazgo* (spiritual co-parenthood), *patronazgo* (patronage) and clientelism, which cleared the way for the study of politics. Together, Hermitte, the Argentine Ph.D. candidates who were coming back to do their fieldwork, and the young *licenciados* who had remained in the country started to explore the ties of the economic system with issues of social and political organization. With a strong empirical bias rooted in Malinowskian fieldwork – extended intensive stays with a holistic approach uncommon in Argentine Ciencias Antropológicas (Hermitte 2002; Vessuri 2002; Menéndez 1970) – social anthropology challenged the culturalist model prevailing among those trained in the Sociology Department. Social anthropologists such as Eduardo Archetti, Leopoldo Bartolomé, Santiago Bilbao, Esther Hermitte, Carlos Herrán, Eduardo Menéndez, Hugo Ratier, and Hebe Vessuri argued that Argentine underdevelopment resulted from unequal integration and dependence on the economic and political core. Argentina was not a dual entity split into a modern, industrial, fully capitalist, politically liberal and democratic half, on the one hand, and a traditional, rural, precapitalist and *caudillo*-led half, on the other. Argentina was an unequal whole, driven by "internal colonialism," and explained under the new paradigm of Fernando Cardoso's and Enzo Faletto's "dependency theory" (in Argentina, also of Miguel Murmis and José Nun).

Peronism was a case in point. While official sociology equated Peronism with the hindrances of tradition and backwardness, social anthropologists and *dependentista* sociologists thought of it rather as the expression of the underclass's material and political conditions, and of their attempts to gain control over their reproduction. Since such a debate was quite removed from the aims of official anthropology, social anthropologists decided to publish in social science journals (for example, *Desarrollo Económico* (IDES), *Revista Latinoamericana de Sociología, Coloquio, Índice*), rather than in strictly anthropological ones (*Runa, Cuadernos del INA*, and *Relaciones de la Sociedad Argentina de Antropología*). In fact, social anthropologists did not talk about "ethnographic" or folk groups. They referred to "cases" or units marked by their spatial location and by their place in the relations of production: *yerba mate* (Argentine tea), cotton and sugar growers and workers, small and big *poncho* weavers, and so forth. Research was defined by "problems and objectives situated 'here and now,' with a regional and/or national perspective and an ethno-historical dimension" (Menéndez 1968:49).[9] Thus, Social Anthropology in the 1960s and 1970s was located on the institutional, conceptual and editorial periphery of Ciencias Antropológicas, striving with some success to enter the social sciences debate, without surrendering, however, to the public discourse of other social sciences (Guber and Visacovsky 2000).

This disciplinary shift led to the opening of specific academic orientations in Antropología Social at the universities of Salta (L. Gatti), Mar del Plata (E. Menéndez) and Misiones (L. Bartolomé) between 1972 and 1974, and to the creation of a working group in the Latin American Council for Social Sciences (CLACSO), which brought together anthropologists from the Americas to define a thematic and theoretical agenda. The Social Anthropology degrees were led by graduates from the traditional Ciencias Antropológicas courses of Buenos Aires and La Plata, but their programs were totally innovative. Two of the three experiments were interrupted in 1974, when the Federal Administration took temporary control of the national universities. The CLACSO group coined the notion of "social articulation" to contest more traditional theses that labeled social and cultural relations as "acculturation," "transculturation," and "syncretism" (Hermitte and Bartolomé 1977). Launched from the Social Anthropology section at the Instituto Torcuato Di Tella, which Hermitte chaired from 1965 to 1974, this group brought together the main characters of the best of Latin American anthropology, such as Roberto Cardoso de Oliveira, Guillermo Bonfil Batalla and González Casanova, as well as social anthropologists from Argentina, Latin America and North America who were working in Argentina and Brazil. The group disbanded with the advent of the Argentine dictatorship in 1976, but set a vital precedent in shaping a way into otherness that stemmed from inequality.

## THE LOCATIONS OF ALTERITY, OR THE MARGINS FROM THE MARGINS

To sum up, we began our journey with the exploration of the effects of national formations of alterity and *politicity* (the ideas and practices of politics and the political) on the practices of Argentine anthropology and, conversely, with the analysis of how these practices coped with those very formations. First we looked at the composition of the Argentine nation-state, pointing to the formation of two parallel melting pots. We argued that, even when some cross-over was allowed, the civilizing, white and European-laden melting pot prevailed over the barbarizing, indigenous and criollo/

cabecita-laden one – the legitimacy and dominance of the former being rarely questioned. We then situated the emergence of professional anthropology in the context of a deepening political rift between Peronists and anti-Peronists. Even though the two polarities – the racial/ethnic and the political/partisan – do not overlap in any simple fashion, their coexistence and the use of such terms as *cabecita negra* as synonyms for *Peronista* show that this is a pivotal question for Argentine anthropology, as a discipline that must deal with otherness-diversity-inequality.

Ciencias Antropológicas, particularly those subdisciplines devoted to the present – ethnology, folklore and social anthropology – took a stance concerning the two melting pots as featuring sociocultural alterity, a stance that overreached the disciplinary field. Institutional continuities and breakdowns fostered or aborted the trajectories of some individuals and the theoretical standpoints and fields embodied by them. To talk about ethnology, social anthropology or folklore, therefore, means much more than simply referring to subdisciplines stemming from a common scientific field. It also entails political and academic positions that the opponents equate with a troubled past ravaged by bloodshed, persecution, military coups, university takeovers, generational breaks, legal and clandestine militancy, social utopias, images of science, personal decisions in light of political and academic shifts, models of the "committed intellectual," and the search for horizons other than the strictly academic. Social anthropologists, ethnologists and folklore experts made use of all this to establish their differences within and beyond anthropology and its subdisciplines. Boundaries among the subdisciplines were thus reproduced, dragging behind them political options and explanatory keys to the national formation of alterity, even if internal public debates usually called those ideas into question.

Once the program in Ciencias Antropológicas at the University of Buenos Aires was consolidated, "official" ethnology – always an official term – subscribed to a radical alterity as a means to understand humanity in its cultural diversity. Assuming that cultural difference had a greater chance of surviving and being imitated in the spiritual/representational field than in the daily practices of material reproduction, hegemonic ethnology concentrated on the study of native populations, far removed from the implicit national norm. Any less distance would imply a loss of authenticity, thus reducing the possibility of recording legitimate variants of humanity before they were wiped out by the (supposedly) homogenizing forces of modernity. The urge to collect paramodern, para-industrial, paracapitalist and paranational cultural responses discouraged further work with indigenous peoples visibly affected by processes rendering them both whiter and less visible, such as those who lived in urban shanty towns and/or were part of the industrial proletariat. Argentine *criollo* groups or those of foreign origin – whose cultural peculiarities could only be viewed from within and as emanating from their very modernity – were also side-stepped. Ethnology mimicked the territorialization of indigenous peoples, confined during their "pacification" to faraway enclaves and pushed toward the national borders. Its field was both geographically and socially distant, thus spatializing its fieldwork in the boundaries of the national territory, and even entering neighboring countries in search of the mores and goods that urbanization supposedly annihilated. Radical alterity, however, reflected only partially the hegemonic official rhetoric of the bureaucratic state circles and of the nation-building moral elites, since ethnology cast indigenous cultural differences in a positive light that had always been denied by those circles and those elites

(Vecchioli 2002; Visacovsky et al. 1997). But, paradoxically enough, this positive stance was presented and analyzed in ways that reinforced those very differences as a rarity on the margins of the lives of most Argentines. In this context, not even blackness could be considered a legitimate field of study. This was less because "blacks" were gone – as proclaimed by the founding myths of the nation – than because the black population had been "decultured" by the actions and effects of slavery. In this light, dominant ethnology remained as the established discipline of a mythical consciousness that would always survive outside or on the margins of modern Argentina.

Social Anthropology, on the other hand, set out to identify a structural otherness, produced and reproduced by exploitative social relations. In this view, any subordinate group – indigenous, *criollo*, immigrant, *Afro* – was a legitimate object of research mainly as a victim of domination, discrimination or oppression. But the explanatory focus was less on the reproduction of cultural practices than on the reproduction of class relations. At any rate, the "cultural" element was another factor to be taken into account, insofar as it might facilitate or resist the pattern of prevailing inequality. Social anthropologists, then, did not locate themselves within previously established ethnographic areas or folk regions, but rather according to a geopolitical and sociological division in terms of "center–periphery." This division demonstrated its effects both in rural and urban zones, even more so in a country spanned by "port–interior" inequality and dependence. In rural areas, the subordination was embodied by peasants, small producers, landholders, farm laborers, and tenant farmers; in towns and cities, it was embodied by industrial workers, slum dwellers, and *cabecitas negras* everywhere. To be black, aboriginal or foreign did not make anyone an object of study per se on account of their cultural traits, but rather because of their subaltern class reproduction. The marginal location of these subjects vis-à-vis those considered main actors of modernizing or revolutionary processes – whatever such processes could be – placed anthropological interests on a periphery of the Argentine social science mainstream. Meanwhile, social anthropology seriously challenged the hegemonic rhetoric of radical alterity, although it ended up recreating an official concept of citizenship by contract, which boasted of its color-blindness.

As for Folklore, it found its raison d'être in the premise of transitional otherness. Unlike ethnology and social anthropology, folklore was early implicated in a state biopolitics that advocated the cultural melting pot. Interest in the "Argentine people" and their traditions as a sphere of fusion, metamorphosis and cultural survival differed from ethnology's, since folklore experts appreciated indigenous culture precisely on account of the processes of cross-breeding, cultural change and whitening that ethnologists took as an obstacle to their work, or as evidence of their object's decline. In turn, that very interest came with a cultural emphasis that distanced folklore from social anthropology even when, in time, both disciplines would come to work on almost the same research subjects, rural and urban. Paradoxically, what caused the hegemonic folklore to be estranged from its sister subdisciplines became alluring to state racial biopolitics. In fact, folklore experts prevailed at the National Institute of Tradition (later on, renamed National Institute of Anthropology). This does not mean that folklore was the only discipline to provide organic intellectuals, who were instrumental to nation-building, either when folklorists focused on "folk society," conceived of as the fruit of a hispanic-indigenous womb located in the "old provinces" with colonial ancestry, or when they worked on immigrants' offspring. Along with those who endorsed the hegemonic formation of alterity, folklore also produced other more autonomous interpretations of a supposedly homogeneous "Argentine-ness," either by praising the recreation of cultural differences among those inhabitants enjoying access to full citizenship, or by positively valuing immigrant communities of Asian or Latin American origin, whose contributions official rhetoric tended to ignore. Interestingly enough, and largely for political/academic reasons, this subdiscipline ended up on the margins of Ciencias Antropológicas. As a repository for what neither ethnology nor social anthropology claimed for themselves, folklore became from 1984 onward a marginal orientation, squeezed by both the subdiscipline that had been hegemonic during the dictatorship, and the one that would take over with the arrival of democracy.

In 1983, still under military rule but with presidential elections in sight, the first Argentine Congress of Social Anthropology was held at the National University of Misiones. The tone of the encounter of colleagues and former students from different subdisciplines, places and trajectories foreshadowed the structures of feeling that would characterize the coming years. The joy of getting together in the open was not enough in itself to address openly the painful effects of internal and external exiles, the necessary revisions of what had taken place during the "leaden years," and the urgent need to discuss the role of anthropologists at this new juncture. In turn, theoretical and political/institutional disagreements became open disputes about the status of each subdiscipline and its involvement with a particular segment of the past, thus hindering the critical revision of each one's contribution to Argentine anthropology and to the knowledge of Argentine society and culture. By equating each subdiscipline *in toto* with a specific university and national administration – and all too frequently, with a theoretical orientation – such defensive claims, whether true or not, classified and ranked the anthropological branches with its ensuing hierarchy. While folklore's contribution was downplayed, responsibility and blame was attributed to ethnology or to social anthropology. These two subdisciplines, alternating academic power (ethnology in 1959–65, 1966–73, 1975–83, and social anthropology in 1966, 1973–74, and since 1984), became trapped in a duel between two supposedly homogeneous blocs, as mutually exclusive, noncomplementary endogamous halves.

In the early years of democratic transition, the symbolic reordering of an intellectual field ready to acknowledge and give hegemony to the previously banned social anthropology revived oppositions imprinted under the *Proceso* rule. Not only did social anthropologists *say* they did not study "ethnographic groups," they did not, in fact, study them; not only did they understand structural analysis to be of vital importance, they rejected the study of so-called "superstructural matters" such as arts, religion, and even kinship and material production. Myths, rituals and material objects – topics allied with ethnology during the *Proceso*, but also favorite areas of the best of anthropology globally – were taken as emblematic of reactionary and uncommitted anthropology. The baby was thrown out with the bath water: systems of anthropological ideas were banished with ethnology, still regarded as being concerned with irrelevant or marginal matters, even though ethnologists were now striving to analyze indigenous life within interethnic relations, and even though social anthropologists of the 1960s and 1970s had done work on indigenous peoples in Patagonia and Chaco (see Gordillo, this volume).

Nonetheless, it soon became anachronistic to summarize the newly opened political and academic process in these terms. First, in 1984 the University of Buenos Aires, as well as most other universities in the country, changed the programs of study for Ciencias Antropológicas. From then on, they offered only two orientations: archaeology and sociocultural anthropology. The year of 1984, however, was not 1973. The world was no longer "prerevolutionary," and the theoretical trends working on the relative autonomy of intellectual, political and belief systems were a far cry from classic Marxism. Secondly, the 1980s marked the appearance of political and ideological identities based on ethnicity, race, religion, nationality, gender, and memory. Such movements were based on demands for the recognition of legitimate differences, and the adoption of legal frameworks updated to institutionalize diversity in the language of rights.

Such processes, previously unknown to Argentines, have transformed anthropological debates in myriad ways as they experiment with novel approaches to new research areas and subjects. There is, consequently, a fresh questioning of the traditionally muted effects of hegemonic formations of alterity and politicity that have permeated the anthropological field. While the typical subjects of anthropology – indigenous and black groups – actively question their marginality and, along with newly organized groups such as retired senior citizens, *jubilados*, and the unemployed *piqueteros* take on an unprecedented visibility, we Argentine anthropologists have yet to come out of the margins. We still face the challenge of raising multiple, visible platforms to speak out, so that the public debates of Argentina's 21st century can address their anthropological dimensions from anthropological perspectives.

## NOTES

1 Although Prehistoric Archaeology, Physical or Biological Anthropology and Forensic Anthropology form an integral part of the Anthropological Sciences in Argentina, we are concerned here only with the fields of ethnology, folklore and social anthropology. For reasons of space, we also focus here on *porteño* or Buenos Aires anthropology, which is symbolically and materially tied to the Federal administration.

2 Undergraduate programs evolved in Buenos Aires, La Plata, Mar del Plata, Olavarría, Rosario, Posadas, Catamarca, Tucumán, Salta and Jujuy; Masters and Ph.D. programs are currently taught at Posadas, Buenos Aires, Córdoba and La Plata.

3 According to Reid-Andrews (1982) and Segato (1991), the "disappearance" of the blacks in Argentina was more ideological than demographic. Nevertheless the presence of blacks in the whole of Argentina is confirmed by names, census, birth registers and cultural activities (Bilbao 1962).

4 The constitution of 1853 stated that Congress should "provide for the security of the frontiers; conserve the peace accord with the 'indios' and promote their conversion to Catholicism" (article 67, inc. 15). The amendment of 1949 took out the article 67, inc. 15. It was put back in place again in 1955, and remained as such until the reform of 1994, when the recognition of indigenous rights as special rights was incorporated instead (Carrasco and Briones 1996).

5 From the reform of 1918 onward public universities have been led by an autonomous board of representatives of each "claustro" or segment: professors, pupils and graduates. Perón's intervention was direct and, among other measures, required card-carrying membership

in the Partido Justicialista in order to work in public administration, including the state universities.

6  Biased less toward the historic-cultural school than toward a strongly anti-evolutionist Italian historical Ethnology, Imbelloni promoted "la Americanística" or the study of the origins and patrimony of the American Man. This project included an editorial series (Humanior), a journal (*Runa*), and a degree course whose guidelines would be taken up again by Marcelo Bórmida to design the degree course of 1958 (Fígoli 1995).

7  See Gordillo (this volume) for more details on Bórmida's proposal and on official Ethnology at the University of Buenos Aires which, up to 1983, allowed little space for autonomous developments within the institution, such as those carried out by ethnologists and also UBA's professors Edgardo Cordeu and Alejandra Siffredi.

8  Almost at the same time, the third stance developed at the Rosario branch of the Universidad del Litoral. (Medical) Doctor Alberto Rex González – with a Ph.D. in archaeology from Columbia University – introduced a program of study in sociocultural anthropology in the Department of History. In 1959, part of this program involved the interdisciplinary study of cultural areas in the Valley of Santa María, Catamarca – of the type done by Julian Steward – and included social-anthropological fieldwork (Meister et al. 1964). In 1969, this sociocultural orientation was consolidated as a specialization within Anthropology in the Humanities School at the Universidad Nacional de Rosario, and as an undergraduate course in the Universidad Nacional de La Plata.

9  Some titles illustrate the aims of early Argentine Social Anthropology: "Social Structure of a Creole Provincial Town, Seen through Its Social Organization, Economic System and Local Power Forms" (Hermitte); "Sociocultural Study of a Migrant Community: San José del Boquerón (Prov. de Santiago del Estero)" (Bilbao); "Study of Agrarian *Fiestas* and Their Current Function in the Economic Context of the Southern *Sierra* of Perú (Kanas and Chumbivilcas, Depto. Cusco)" (Lischetti, Muñoz, and Gorbak); "Assimilation of European Ethnic Groups to a Community of the Center of Entre Ríos Province" (Menéndez); "Archaeological and Socio-Anthropological Study with Special Emphasis on Cultural Ecological Problems, East of the Quebrada de Humahuaca" (Madrazo) (*Actualidad Antropológica* 1968).

## REFERENCES

*Actualidad Antropológica* (1968) Journal of Museo Dámaso Arce, Olavarría, Provincia de Buenos Aires.

Alonso, A. M. (1994) The Politics of Space, Time and Substance: State Formation, Nationalism, and Ethnicity. *Annual Review of Anthropology* 23:379–405.

Archetti, E. P. (1999) *Masculinities: Football, Polo and the Tango in Argentina*. Oxford: Berg.

Asad, T. (1973) *Anthropology and the Colonial Encounter*. Atlantic Highlands, NJ: Humanities Press.

Bartolomé, L. (1980) La antropología en Argentina. Problemas y perspectivas. *América Indígena* 40(2):207–215.

Bilbao, S. (1962) Las comparsas del Carnaval porteño. *Cuadernos del Instituto Nacional de Investigaciones Folklóricas* 5:155–187.

Blache, M. (2002) Folklore y nacionalismo en la Argentina. Su vinculación de origen y su desvinculación actual. In S. Visacovsky and R. Guber (eds), *Historias y estilos de trabajo de campo en Argentina* (pp. 127–152). Buenos Aires: Editorial Antropofagia.

Bórmida, M. (1956) Cultura y ciclos culturales. Ensayo de etnología teorética. *Runa* (Universidad de Buenos Aires, Facultad de Filosofía y Letras) 7(1):5–28.

Bórmida, M. (1961) Ciencias antropológicas y humanismo. *Revista de la Universidad de Buenos Aires* 6(3):470–490.

Bórmida, M. (1969–70) Mito y cultura. Bases para una ciencia de la conciencia mítica y una etnología tautegórica. *Runa* (Universidad de Buenos Aires, Facultad de Filosofía y Letras) 12.

Briones, C. (1998) *La alteridad del "Cuarto Mundo." Una deconstrucción antropológica de la diferencia.* Buenos Aires: Ediciones del Sol.

Briones, C. (2002) Mestizaje y blanqueamiento como coordenadas de aboriginalidad y nación en Argentina. *Runa* (Universidad de Buenos Aires) 23:61–88.

Briones, C. and Delrio, W. (2002) Patria sí, colonias también. Estrategias diferenciales de radicación de indígenas en Pampa y Patagonia (1885–1900). In A. Teruel, M. Lacarrieu, and O. Jerez (eds), *Fronteras, ciudades y estados...*, vol. 1 (pp. 45–78). Córdoba: Alción Editora.

Califano, M., Pérez Diez, A., and Balzano, S. M. (1985) Etnología. Centro Argentino de Etnología Americana. In *Evolución de las ciencias en la República Argentina, 1872–1972. Antropología.* Special issue of *Sociedad Científica Argentina* 10:9–71.

Cardoso de Oliveira, R. and Ruben, G. R. (1995) *Estilos de antropología.* Campinas: Editora da Unicamp.

Carrasco, M. (1991) Hegemonía y políticas indigenistas argentinas en el Chaco centro occidental. *América Indígena* (Mexico City) 51(1):63–122.

Carrasco, M. and Briones, C. (1996) *La tierra que nos quitaron. Reclamos indígenas en Argentina.* Serie Documentos en Español, no. 18. Copenhagen: IWGIA.

Carrizo, J. (1953) *Historia del folklore argentino.* Buenos Aires: Ediciones Dictio.

Cortazar, A. R. (1949) *El Carnaval en el folklore Calchaquí.* Buenos Aires: Editorial Sudamericana.

Fígoli, L. (1995) A antropología na Argentina e a construçao da naçao. In R. Cardoso de Oliveira and G. Ruben (eds), *Estilos de antropología* (pp. 31–63). Campinas: UNICAMP.

Garbulsky, E. (1987) José Imbelloni. Positivismo, organicismo y racismo. *Cuadernos de la Escuela de Antropología* (Universidad Nacional de Rosario) 3:3–23.

Guber, R. (2002) "Antropología Social": An Argentine Diaspora between Revolution and Nostalgia. *Anthropology Today* (Royal Anthropological Institute, London) 18(4):8–13.

Guber, R. and Visacovsky, S. E. (2000) La antropología social en la Argentina de los '60 y '70. *Desarrollo Económico* 40(158):289–316.

Gurevich, E. and Smolensky, E. (n.d.) La antropología en la UBA. 1973–1983. MS, Buenos Aires.

Hermitte, E. A. de (1971) *Poder sobrenatural y control social.* Mexico City: Instituto Indigenista Interamericano, no. 57. Reprint 2004, Buenos Aires: Editorial Antropofagia.

Hermitte, E. A. de (2002) La observación por medio de la participación. In S. Visacovsky and R. Guber (eds), *Historias y estilos de trabajo de campo en Argentina* (pp. 263–288). Buenos Aires: Editorial Antropofagia.

Hermitte, E. A. and Bartolomé, L. (eds) (1977) *Procesos de articulación social.* Buenos Aires: Editorial Amorrortu.

Herrán, C. A. (1985). Antropología social en la Argentina. Apuntes y perspectivas. Paper presented at the Simposio sobre Teoría e Investigación de la Antropología Social Mexicana. El Colegio de México, May 11–14.

Imbelloni, J. (1959) Introito. Concepto y praxis del folklore. In J. Imbelloni et al., *Folklore Argentino* (pp. 7–83). Buenos Aires: Editorial Humanior.

Kohl, P. and Pérez Gollán, J. (2002) Religion, Politics, and Prehistory: Reassessing the Lingering Legacy of Oswald Menghin. *Current Anthropology* 43(4):561–586.

Laclau, E. (1993) *Nuevas reflexiones sobre la revolución de nuestro tiempo.* Buenos Aires: Ediciones Nueva Visión.

Lafón, C. R. (1970) *Nociones de introducción a la antropología.* Buenos Aires: Editorial Glauco.

Lazzari, A. (2002) El indio argentino y el discurso de cultura. Del Instituto Nacional de la Tradición al Instituto Nacional de Antropología. In S. Visacovsky and R. Guber (eds), *Historias y estilos de trabajo de campo en Argentina* (pp. 153–202). Buenos Aires: Editorial Antropofagia.

Lazzari, A. (2004) Antropología en el estado. El Instituto Etnico Nacional (1946–1955). In
  F. Neiburg and M. Plotkin (eds), *Intelectuales y expertos. La constitución del conocimiento
  social en la Argentina* (pp. 203–230). Buenos Aires: Editorial Paidós.
Lenton, D. (1992) Relaciones interétnicas. Derechos humanos y autocrítica en la generación
  del '80. In J. Radovich and A. Balazote (eds), *La problemática indígena. Estudios antropológ-
  icos sobre pueblos indígenas de la Argentina* (pp. 27–65). Buenos Aires: CEDAL.
L'Estoile, B. de, Neiburg, R., and Sigaud, L. (eds) (2002) *Antropología, impérios e estados
  nacionais*. Rio de Janeiro: Relumé Dumará.
Margulis, M., et al. (1998) *La segregación negada. Cultura y discriminación social*. Buenos
  Aires: Editorial Biblos.
Martínez Sarasola, C. (1992) *Nuestros paisanos los indios. Vida, historia y destino de las comuni-
  dades indígenas en Argentina*. Buenos Aires: Sudamericana.
Meister, A., Petruzzi, S., and Sonzogni, E. (1964) *Tradicionalismo y cambio social. Estudio de
  área en el Valle de Santa María*. Rosario, Argentina: Universidad Nacional del Litoral.
Menéndez, E. L. (1968) Correo antropológico. *Actualidad Antropológica* (Olavarría, Provin-
  cia de Buenos Aires, Museo Dámaso Arce) 3:48–51.
Menéndez, E. L. (1970) Ideología, ciencia y práctica profesional. In *Ciencias sociales. Ideología
  y realidad nacional* (pp. 101–124). Buenos Aires: Tiempo Contemporáneo.
Menni, A. (1995) *Relaciones interétnicas en Argentina y Chile del siglo XIX*. Serie Tierra Indígena
  Americana, no. 6. Neuquén: IREPS–APDH.
Muzzopappa, E. (2000) Metáforas estratégicas. El concepto de cultura en y sobre el ámbito de
  la seguridad. Undergraduate dissertation in Anthropological Sciences, University of Buenos
  Aires.
Neiburg, F. G. (1998) *Los intelectuales y la invención del peronismo*. Buenos Aires: Editorial
  Alianza.
Perazzi, P. (2003) *Hermenéutica de la barbarie. Una historia de la antropología en Buenos Aires,
  1935–1966*. Buenos Aires: Sociedad Argentina de Antropología.
Quijada, M., Bernard, C., and Schneider, A. (2000) *Homogeneidad y nación con un estudio de
  caso. Argentina, siglos XIX y XX*. Colección Tierra Nueva e Cielo Nuevo, no. 42. Madrid:
  Consejo Superior de Investigaciones Científicas.
Ramos, A. R. (1990) Ethnology Brazilian Style. *Cultural Anthropology* 5(4):452–457.
Ratier, H. (1971) *El cabecita negra*. Buenos Aires: CEDAL.
Ratier, H. and Ringuelet, R. (1997) La antropología social en la Argentina. Un producto de la
  democracia. *Horizontes Antropológicos* (Porto Alegre, Universidade Federal do Río Grande
  do Sul) 3(7):10–23.
Reid-Andrews, G. (1982) *Los afroargentinos del Río de la Plata*. Buenos Aires: Ediciones de la Flor.
Sanguinetti, A. C. and Mariscotti, A.M. (1958–59) Notas para el estudio de la cultura de la
  Puna. *Runa* (Universidad de Buenos Aires, Departamento de Ciencias Antropológicas) 9:1–2.
Schneider, A. (1994) The Two Faces of Modernity: Concepts of Melting Pot in Argentina.
  *Critique of Anthropology* 15(2):173–198.
Segato, R. (1991) Uma vocação de minoria. A expansão dos cultos Afro-Brasileiros na Argentina
  como processo de reetnicização. *Dados, Revista de Ciências Sociais* (Rio de Janeiro)
  34(2):249–278.
Segato, R. (2002) Identidades políticas y alteridades históricas. Una crítica a las certezas del
  pluralismo global. *Nueva Sociedad* (Venezuela) 178:104–125.
Shumway, N. (1991) *The Invention of Argentina*. Berkeley: University of California Press.
Sigal, S. (1991) *Intelectuales y poder en la década del sesenta*. Buenos Aires: Puntosur.
Soler, R. (1979) *El positivismo argentino. Pensamiento filosófico y sociológico*. Mexico City:
  Universidad Nacional Autónoma de México.
Svampa, M. (1994) *El dilema Argentino. Civilización o barbarie. De sarmiento al revisionismo
  peronista*. Buenos Aires: Ediciones El Cielo por Asalto.
Taylor, J. (1979) *Eva Perón: The Myths of a Woman*. Chicago: University of Chicago Press.
Terán, O. (1991) *Nuestros años sesenta*. Buenos Aires: Puntosur.

Vecchioli, V. (2002) A través de la etnografía. Representaciones sobre la nación en la producción etnográfica sobre los tobas. In S. Visacovsky and R. Guber (eds) *Historias y estilos de trabajo de campo en Argentina* (pp. 203–228). Buenos Aires: Editorial Antropofagia.

Vessuri, H. M. C. (1992) Las ciencias sociales en la Argentina. Diagnóstico y perspectivas. In Enrique Oteiza (ed.), *La política de investigación científica y tecnológica argentina. Historia y perspectivas* (pp. 87–126). Buenos Aires: Centro Editor de América Latina.

Vessuri, H. M. C. (2002) La observación participante en Tucumán (1971). In S. Visacovsky and R. Guber (eds), *Historias y estilos de trabajo de campo en Argentina* (pp. 289–316). Buenos Aires: Editorial Antropofagia.

Visacovsky, S. E. and Guber, R. (eds) (2002) *Historias y estilos de trabajo de campo en Argentina*. Buenos Aires: Editorial Antropofagia.

Visacovsky, S. E., Guber, R., and Gurevich, E. (1997) Modernidad y tradición en el origen de la carrera de Ciencias Antropológicas de la Universidad de Buenos Aires. *Redes* (Universidad Nacional de Quilmes) 10:213–257.

Williams, B. (1993) The Impact of the Precepts of Nationalism on the Concept of Culture: Making Grasshoppers of Naked Apes. *Cultural Critique* 24:143–191.

Zumwalt, R. (1988) *American Folklore Scholarship: A Dialogue of Dissent*. Bloomington: Indiana University Press.

# CHAPTER 2

# Bolivia: Bridges and Chasms

## *Rossana Barragán*

One of the proposals put forward by indigenous social organizations for representation in the 2006 Constituent Assembly – itself a symbol of a new foundation for Bolivia – is for the election of 16 men and 16 women from the predominantly indigenous regions of the Andean highlands. This gender complementarity (*Chacha Warmi* or man/woman) is conceived in accordance with customs and practices employed in the ethnic districts of Jacha Carangas, Jatun Quillacas Asanaques Aransaya, Jatun Quillacas Asanaques Urinsaya, Uros, Chichas, Lípez, Charcas, Karakara Aransaya, Karakara Urinsaya, Soras Aransaya, Soras Urinsaya, Pacajes Aransaya, and Pacajes Urinsaya (Coordinadora de la Mujer 2004). This list of modern-day ethnic regions corresponds almost exactly to those that appear on a 16th century map published some 20 years earlier by the French historical anthropologist Thérèse Bouysse-Cassagne (1980). A comparison with this map also reveals a striking continuity between the ethnic territories on this 16th century map and the present-day territories of the Federation of Southern Oruro (or FASOR), the Federation of Ayllus and Communities of the Province of Ingavi (or FACOPI), and the Federation of Originary Ayllus of Northern Potosi (FAONP).

Can this really be the case? The longest standing organization, FASOR, is after all less than 20 years old (1986). Yet what this correspondence would seem to suggest is that, far from being mere survivals, these organizations of ayllu associations,[1] communities and districts are in fact modern recompositions that draw on both the existing segmentary structure of the communities found in these regions, *and* the content of anthropological, historical and ethnohistorical work that has been carried out in these regions in the last 20 years.

This chapter reflects on this dynamic interaction between anthropology and indigenous politics (see also Rivera 1993). Rather than attempt a comprehensive historical analysis of Bolivian anthropology, its theoretical influences, contributions to the discipline, and relations to power, I instead focus on the close relationship and connection between research and academic thinking on the one hand, and political action and social movements on the other. In addition, this chapter offers a very concrete example of the invention of traditions and the construction of "imagined communities" (Anderson 1983), with the peculiarity that, rather than analyzing nationalism and the construction of the nation from the viewpoint of the state and the power it implies, I demonstrate this process from the angle of civil society, analyzing the interrelation between institutions, leaders, intellectuals, and political or social movements. This relation between research and civil society functions on two levels: on the one hand, social movements influence the topics and questions addressed by academics; and on the other, social movements reappropriate the results of this research. To capture this dynamic, I use here the image of bridges to describe the relations that have been and continue to be built between anthropology and indigenous movements in Bolivia (see Rivera 1993).

Given that the present necessarily influences the questions posed by researchers, it could be argued that this relation is neither peculiar nor special to Bolivia. I argue, however, that in the case of Bolivia this relation is much more direct than in many other countries due to the relatively late academic institutionalization of history and sociology (around 1970) and anthropology and archaeology (around 1980). Another factor is the virtual absence until recently of research opportunities both within and outside the national universities. As a consequence, in Bolivia it has not been possible to construct sustainable, autonomous and self-referential spaces for reflection. In effect, both professionals and academics are nomads moving between simultaneous and sequentially held posts as university professors, consultants, political militants, and state employees. This situation, which has become even more acute in the last few decades, is one crucial point of differentiation between Bolivian anthropology and the institutionally and financially more stable academic worlds of the northern hemisphere (see also Martínez Novo, this volume).

My first argument, then, is that the results of research in anthropology, history and ethnohistory can be traced in the content and arguments that indigenous organizations have developed concerning such issues as territoriality. Conversely, the topics that originated within the indigenous movements can be identified in academic works. Specifically, I expand on this general exchange of information and perspectives by tracing the links between (1) academia and the indigenous movement, (2) professionals and indigenous leaders, (3) the topics broached by researchers and those that form part of the movements' demands, (4) research results and their appropriation and reappropriation, (5) a prehispanic territory rendered meaningful through ethnohistorical and anthropological research, and (6) the demands for territorial rights and political autonomy put forward by social and political movements in recent years.

My second argument is that these sorts of linkages have been made possible by two related factors: The first is the theoretical and conceptual shift that took place in the 1980s and 1990s from models based on class, to ones based on ethnicity, people (pueblo) and nation (Aymara, Quechua, Guaraní, etc.). The second is the fact that Bolivian sociologists, historians and anthropologists have, for the most part, held, and continue to hold, views that fall to the left of the political spectrum. Although these include a number of indigenous intellectuals, I argue here that it would be wrong to attribute this entire process to indigenous actors. Lastly, the relation between social movements, indigenous demands and public policies has been possible due to the participation of certain intellectuals, of both indigenous and nonindigenous origin (Simón Yampara, Mauricio Mamani, Victor Hugo Cárdenas, Iván Arias, Alvaro García Linera, Juan Ramón Quintana, among others) in state positions at various levels.

My third argument is that anthropological and historical research has provided, and continues to provide, the academic arguments and historical legitimacy on which indigenous organizations base their demands for greater political and economic participation, and for the recognition of territories, autonomies, and nations. This political and academic process, however, has also given rise to greater polarization and radicalization, as well as to distances and even chasms. The enduring and traditional dualisms that oppose "whites" (known in Aymara as *q'aras*) to indigenous peoples fail to account for the complex connections and social interrelations, the identifications or lack of identifications, of many social groups, working class or otherwise, as well as those existing in different regions of the country. This has gradually led to another major rupture in the guise of regional conflicts that make use of their own reinventions, and which act as a cover for regional economic interests. These sorts of conceptual oppositions based on either ethnicity (indigenous versus nonindigenous), or the geographic and demographic distinctions between the populations of Bolivia's eastern (*camba*) and western (*colla*) provinces, conceal conflicting economic and political projects in racial terminology and language.

In what follows, I develop these arguments in four parts. First, I discuss the shift that took place, roughly, between 1970 and 1990, from class based analyses to frameworks that privilege culture and ethnicity. In the second part, I examine the move in Bolivian anthropology from a perspective which emphasized the "vision of the vanquished" to the subsequent refusal of the image of defeat and the denunciation of oppression. I next analyze how subaltern subjects were rendered as national subjects, "making history and anthropology a material reality," when the ancient territories took the tangible form of ayllu federations. The territorial demands proved to be particularly important in the context of the contentious "celebration" of 1992 which culminated in the alliance of the Revolutionary Nationalist Movement (MNR) and the Tupac Katari Revolutionary Liberation Movement (MRTKL), the appointment of an Aymara leader as vice-president of Bolivia, and even more radical approaches that grew out of popular resistance to political and neoliberal economic reforms. Opposition to these reforms – and in particular to government attempts to privatize gas and other natural resources – led to broad based political mobilizations in the city of El Alto (La Paz) and other regions of the country, and to the 2005 election of Evo Morales, Bolivia's first indigenous president. In the fourth section, I connect the plan for a "different Bolivia" based on the recognition of "nationalities" with the social demand for a Constituent Assembly that arose in the context of the severe political crisis of 2000 onward. A long postponed demand, the 2006 Constituent Assembly is regarded as a national refounding, and as a new pact for popular sovereignty. The current political context since 2000 is without doubt a time of acute polarizations in which each of the extremes created and constructed its own "imagined nation."

## CENTERS AND MARGINS

> One people that oppresses another cannot be free…We peasants…feel economically exploited and culturally and politically oppressed. In Bolivia, rather than an integration of cultures, one culture has been superimposed onto another and has dominated it.
>
> Manifesto of Tiwanaku, 1973

In the late 1960s and early 1970s, the upsurge in popular movements in Latin America resulted in military dictatorships. In Bolivia, following the guerrilla war led by Che Guevara in 1967 and the Popular Assembly or "Parallel Power" sustained by miners and factory workers in 1970, a military coup brought Hugo Bánzer to power in 1971. In spite of Bánzer's repressive measures, Marxist currents continued to dominate within both the political movements and the nascent social sciences. Key concepts at that time were means of production, social formation, class antagonism and contradiction. As a conceptual category focused on production and wage labor, "class" framed "peasants" as relatively passive actors within the economically driven processes of depeasantization, urbanization, internal migration and proletarianization. As a result, the political demands of intellectuals in Bolivia, as elsewhere in Latin America, were concerned with defending the proletariat, miners, peasants or the "people" (*el pueblo*), and not with culture-bearing "Indians" (see Seligmann, this volume).

The fact that the Bolivian state had seized control of progressive arenas such as universities, and that many intellectuals of the period had been driven into exile by the Bánzer dictatorship, meant that there was a relocation of activities in new institutions, often linked to religious organizations. One such institution was the Institute of Cultural Research for Popular Education (INDICEP), founded in 1969 and supported by Brother Santiago Gelinas. INDICEP's approach to popular education, which drew on the work of Paulo Freire, was rooted in the mining communities and contributed to the creation in 1966 of the "Bolivia" radio station. In the context of the period, popular education in the style of Paulo Freire was the model to be followed. Since this was a Canadian institution, it was sensitive to cultural differences and raised issues of cultural domination and the ineffectiveness of political projects that failed to take sociocultural forces into account. It was in this context that, in one of its posters, INDICEP revived the image of the indigenous couple who had led the great uprising of the late 18th century: Julián Apaza, known as Túpac Katari, and his companion Bartolina Sisa (Hurtado 1986:254, 255).

The Tiwanaku Manifesto of 1973, which today is considered to have laid the foundations for the Indianista political movements, was connected to INDICEP. It is alleged to have been drawn up by Raimundo Tambo, Rosendo Condori and J. Velarde with the collaboration of Gregorio Iriarte, a priest and member of INDICEP. Tambo was one of the pioneers of the autonomous peasant union movement and a founder of MRTKL (Hurtado1986:58). The Manifesto was also signed by Genaro Flores and other prominent peasant union leaders (Dunkerley 1987–2003:264).

The Center for Research and Promotion of the Peasantry (CIPCA), founded in January 1971 by the Catalan (now Bolivian) priest, linguist and anthropologist Xavier Albó, was another crucial religious organization that sought to strengthen the peasant organizations and then later fought against the Bánzer dictatorship. Among its more important activities was the production of a radio narrative about the life of Túpac Katari (Hurtado 1986:256). As we will see, in years to come CIPCA would play a crucial role in both Bolivian anthropology and the indigenous movement.

The problems of indigenous cultural and social particularity were not, however, central to the intellectual or the political agendas of the 1970s. This fact makes the Tiwanaku Manifesto all the more exceptional. Some of the most prestigious intellectuals of the time – such as the Trotskyst labor chronicler Guillermo Lora (1967), the French theorist of revolutionary struggles Régis Debray, and even the Bolivian theorist of "national-popular" consciousness René Zavaleta Mercado (1983, 1986) – believed that Indian communities were backward organizations with limited class consciousness. Some authors even characterized them as "infrapolitical" (Hurtado 1986:245). Toward the end of the 1970s, the indigenous question began to assume greater importance. The Túpac Katari Indigenous Movement (MITKA) was established in 1978, and among its founders was the priest Julio Tumiri, who was also involved in its precursor organization MINK'A (a Quechua term that refers to a system of collective work). In its newspaper, *Collasuyo*, MITKA activists and intellectuals addressed the question of recuperating "Bolivian identity based on a policy of community life with a socialist outlook, without identifying ourselves with the political struggle of traditional organizations of left and right" (cited in Dunkerley 1987–2003:262–263). The most influential figure here was Ramiro Reinaga, son of Fausto Reinaga, one of the first Indianista intellectuals. For Reinaga and other MITKA activists, the defense of "Indianismo" – or the quality of being "indigenous" – implied as well a struggle to refine the epistemological and conceptual relationship between historical and cultural knowledge, on the one hand, and political or ideological alignment on the other. In this view, the knowledge gained through learning is what gives a political position both substance and legitimacy:

> MITKA holds *indianismo* to be its ideological basis ... It is an ideology constituted from the input of hundreds of scientists of all nationalities, who, through their research in different branches of learning, have contributed to the clarification of reality ... In effect, archaeology, anthropology, social psychology, [and] linguistics ... have unearthed mysteries, interpreted events. In this way, a millenarian historical consciousness and way of thinking have emerged. (Cited in Hurtado 1986:264; see also, for indigenismo, Pacheco 1992)

## FROM CLASS EXPLOITATION TO ETHNOHISTORY

The decade of the 1970s was a particularly agitated time as far as academia was concerned. A number of young academics, mainly from the United Kingdom and France, established ties with the country through their doctoral work. Another group of Bolivians emerged from the new history and sociology courses taught at the national university. Politically active against Bánzer's dictatorship and imbued with utopian ideas of a more egalitarian and socialist society, this new generation approached popular themes, and their proletarian and peasant subjects, from diverse perspectives and with varying degrees of commitment.

At the same time, the few existing nongovernmental organizations (NGOs), which were mainly religious organizations, began to recruit the professionals who had either been left unemployed after the military government closed the universities in 1972, or been excluded from them after their reopening later in the 1970s. They also played a fundamental role in the diffusion of academic works. By 1978, CIPCA had 14 publications in its Research Notes series and 19 in its Popular Series Notes. These included important works on kinship and ayllu structure (Albó 1972; Albó and Harris 1976; Platt 1976), language politics (Albó 1976); social organization and ethnic identity (Albó 1975, and see 1979); and Aymara history (Barnadas 1976a, 1976b).

Another important institution was the Center for Studies on Economic and Social Reality (CERES), headed by anthropologist Jorge Dandler. CERES brought together researchers with mainly sociological backgrounds, such as Fernando Calderón, Juan Torrico and José Blanes. Its output was considerable and among its publications figured such important works as Brooke Larson's (1992) colonial history of Cochabamba and Gonzalo Flores's study of early 20th century peasant movements.

A number of the professionals and intellectuals from these institutions collaborated in 1978 on two issues of a new magazine, *Avances*. The publication, which proved to be epoch-making, featured pieces by Silvia Rivera, René Arze, Roberto Choque, Gustavo Rodríguez, Enrique Tandeter, Tristan Platt, Olivia Harris, John V. Murra, Ramiro Condarco Morales, Thierry Saignes, Brooke Larson, and Xavier Albó. Although a diverse group, these authors shared a sense of the need to question Bolivian reality by reclaiming the country's "indigenous roots," not only by speaking out against the widespread myths of "Indian passivity" and Western "progress," but also by identifying alternative bases from which to construct an "economically and culturally thriving Bolivian massif" (*Avances* 1978a:2). The only two issues published clearly reflect the main influences of the period: ethnohistory in the first, Marxism in the second.

In *Avances* 1, three topics were given precedence. The first dealt with the forms of vertical ecological control through which indigenous ayllus and communities had diversified their production strategies in the Andean landscape. In *Avances*, the work of Bolivian Ramiro Condarco Morales was set alongside that of John V. Murra, the more famous and widely read theorist of Andean vertical ecologies (Murra 1978). Condarco Morales, however, had earlier postulated the same view as Murra under the name of "interzonal symbiosis," as well as being the first to highlight, in 1965, the role of the late 19th century indigenous leader Pablo Zárate Willka. The second thematic focus, explored in articles by Rivera, Choque and Arze, concerned *caciques*, the traditional colonial indigenous leaders whose histories suggested the need to "unravel the complexity of the Andean and Iberian connection" (*Avances* 1978a:5). Following the lead of French anthropologist Nathan Wachtel (1971) and the historian Nicolás Sánchez Albórnoz (1978), yet a third set of articles by Tristan Platt and Enrique Tandeter sought to analyze the characteristic features of Bolivian colonial reality.

In its second and final issue, *Avances* tackled a new set of issues revolving around large rural estates and oligarchy. In what would become classic studies, Rivera and Rodríguez located the expansion of large agrarian estates in the 19th century republican period rather than, as was previously assumed, in the colonial period. Their analyses called for rethinking the links between capitalism and the "feudal" relations characteristic of Bolivian haciendas. The testimony of a former estate worker, and historical articles by Albó, Rojas and Larson, provided tools for rethinking the relations of production on the Bolivian haciendas. Finally, *Avances* introduced comparative perspectives with articles on other Andean countries by Andrés Guerrero (Ecuador) and Alberto Flores Galindo (Peru).

By the late 1970s, new researchers, topics, regions, and publications had emerged. The anthropological viewpoint was reflected in Albó's linguistic and ethnographic studies of social organization in the Andean commuity of Jesús de Machaqa (Albó 1972); William Carter and Mauricio Mamani's now classic ethnographies of Irpa Chico and coca use (1982); and Tristan Platt's (1976, 1982) and Olivia Harris's focus on ayllus, segmented societies, ecological integrations, symbolic dualism, and ethnic economies (Harris 1978; Harris and Larson 1987). From a sociological standpoint, on the other hand, CERES and its directors Fernando Calderón and Jorge Dandler (1986; see also Dandler 1983) worked on the peasantry, its power within the popular movement, rural proletarianization and the antipeasant state (Urioste 1984). Finally, French anthropologist Nathan Wachtel and his students Thérèse Bouysse-Cassagne and Thierry Saignes drew on historical and anthropological methodologies to study the history of Bolivia's indigenous peoples. In Bolivia itself, a new history program was set up at the Universidad Mayor de San Andrés in La Paz. René Arze's thesis on popular participation in the wars of Independence unearthed new material on indigenous social movements. Finally, Roberto Choque undertook two research projects: the first demystifying the "revolutionaries" of the creole independence movement, and the second exploring indigenous *caciques* of the 16th century.

Although ethnohistory and anthropology reached their apogee from 1977 to 1980, they represented only small groups of researchers. Indeed, for many Bolivian students, discussing "vertical control" in sociology courses and referring to Murra was sufficient to be branded a reactionary and accused of employing language that obscured relations of production, exploitation and class. Indeed, the sorts of analyses put forward in *Avances* concerning late 19th century liberalism and community resistance to the nation-state occupied a minority position in Bolivian academic circles and politics. Instead, intellectuals continued to debate passionately the problems of urbanization, depeasantization and the class differences that existed within indigenous and peasant communities.

In marked contrast to the Bolivian publications, Wachtel and Murra put together a special issue of the French journal *Annales*, dedicated to Andean societies (Annales 1978; Murra, Revel and Wachtel 1986). Unlike the magazine *Avances*, which featured both Bolivian and non-Bolivian authors, only one out of 18 authors published in *Annales* was Bolivian. What the issue did do well, however, was to bring together the complementary disciplinary perspectives and insights of anthropology and history. From the outset, it put forward the notion that we were at an impasse: between the visions of the "macrocosm" of the Inka state and the microcosm of the modern-day community, without the historical dynamic of a relation between the two (*Annales* 1978:890). The perspective presented by Murra was fundamental in this sense. It made it possible to link the native ethnic groups with the organization of the Inka state, and, through this connection, to establish a bridge toward the present-day communities. Indeed, the compilation included one part entitled "From Ethnic Groups to Communities," dealing with changes in the prehispanic structures and the fragmentation of indigenous communities. Despite Wachtel's and Saignes's emphasis on colonial readjustments and changes, in the second part of the issue other authors continued to emphasize structural continuities and the enduring logic of ancient Andean cultural systems. These authors analyzed underlying concepts of Andean social organization, including Inka kinship, the modern classificatory system used by Andean llama herders, and the "language" of textiles. Structural analysis was a particular feature of the works by R. T. Zuidema on irrigation networks in the Inka empire; by T. Bouysse-Cassagne on the spatial organization of the 16th century Aymaras; and by Platt (1986) and Harris (1978) on the Macha and Laymi communities.

These publications as a whole marked a change in the orientation of anthropological work, similar in tone to Wachtel's influential 1971 publication *La Vision des vaincus* (translated as *The Vision of the Vanquished* in 1977). Through structural and historical analysis of social organization, dances, and myth, Wachtel proposed to bring the ideas of structural and cultural continuity then prevalent in Andeanist anthropology into conversation with a more historical approach that recognized the unique perspective and experience of the indigenous polities' "defeat" and colonization. Ten years later, a book by Wachtel's student Thérèse Bouysse-Cassagne (1980) gained surprising popularity, in large part due to the inclusion of maps showing Bolivia's 16th century ethnic domains or "nations." As we have seen, these maps showing the physical and historical reality of Aymara unity would later find their way into the territorial and political imaginations of some of Bolivia's most important indigenous organizations. Bouysse-Cassagne's study, Murra's work on the Lupaqas (Murra 1964, 1978), and Saignes' synthesis of Aymara ethnohistory (1986) together marked the beginning of a series of research projects aimed at reconstructing the major political units of the late 16th century. Other scholars undertook ethnic and regionally focused histories of the Urus (Wachtel 1990), Carangas (Rivière 1982), the Charcas and Qaraqaras (Platt 1982; Saignes 1986; Bouysse-Cassagne 1980; Albó and Harris 1976; Arze and Medinaceli 1991), the Quillacas federation (Espinoza Soriano 1969; Molina Rivero 2006; and see Abercrombie 1998; Barragán 1982), and finally, the southern valleys (Presta and del Río 1995; Barragán 1994). This collection of studies was fundamental in consolidating the linguistic term "Aymara" (see specially the studies compiled by Albó in 1988) as a replacement for the ethnic and spatial category of "Collas," which had been commonly used up to that point. It also provided historical backing for the territorial distribution of languages analyzed by Albó.

Over the course of the 1980s, several fundamental changes came about in the Bolivian political context and academic sphere. On the one hand, these changes created a certain distance between foreign and Bolivian researchers. On the other hand, however, they also led to an increasing recognition of the distinctive research tendencies, theoretical affinities and political emphases that existed within the fields of Bolivian anthropology and ethnohistory. The conditions within Bolivian academia as well as social and political demands themselves led to two very different pathways: stability for the Bolivianistas, and dispersion and a nomadic existence for the Bolivians. The former continued their intellectual careers in academic posts in their countries of origin. At the same time, other anthropologists and historians appeared, particularly from the US, to do their theses on Bolivia. However, the fact that they tended to relate more to the rural communities where they worked than to urban academics, and also their shorter periods of stay, meant that they would become increasingly distanced from their Bolivian counterparts (see Hale, this volume).

The 1980s were also marked by the increasing dispersion of Bolivian academics, and the political and ideological division between the Movimiento de Izquierda Revolucionario (MIR), on the one hand, and Katarista and Indianista tendencies, on the other. At the same time, independent trade unionism grew in strength, as did the Katarista movement, which was founded in 1978 in La Paz. The Katarista movement had strong links from its very beginnings to rural migrants (Hurtado, 1986:32–33). During the mid 1980s, it would become one of the dominant political forces in the country.

The ideological split between MIR and Katarismo strengthened the emerging links between indigenous movements and intellectuals. One of the clearest expressions of this was Silvia Rivera's *Oprimidos pero no vencidos. Luchas del campesinado aymara quechwa de Bolivia, 1900–1980* (Oppressed but Not Defeated: Struggles of the Aymara and Qhechwa Peasantry, 1900–1980) (Rivera 1984). The phrase "oppressed but not vanquished" – which is said to have been coined by Josep Barnadas (cf. Hurtado 1986:92) and which can also be found in the Thesis of the Peasantry of 1978 and 1979 – was intended as a direct rebuttal to Wachtel's emphasis on the Indians' "defeat" in *The Vision of the Vanquished*. The intellectual influence on the peasant movement is clear, but so too is the influence this movement had on the researchers. Silvia Rivera (1984), for example, gave equal weight to the Indians' exploitation as economic producers (class antagonism) and their colonial oppression as a society and culture (see also Rivera 1993). This view had already been put forward by Victor Hugo Cárdenas in 1978:

> In Bolivia, the problem of the great Aymara, Quechua, and Guaraní nationalities for those on the left, is a problem that does not exist. They cannnot see: that is one of their biggest mistakes. For example, there are many of us who…claim to be part of the *katarista* tendency. Immediately we are described as being racist. It is also obvious to us that workers are beginning to understand it this way. This could be a new phenomenon.

Rivera's study concludes by citing a political document in which the United Trade Union Confederation of Bolivian Peasant Workers (CSUTCB) proposed to reject social and political analyses based only on class ("Political Thesis," Second National Congress of the CSUTCB, La Paz, 1983; see also Ticona 1996:9, 22). The vocabulary used, as in Rivera's own text, alludes simultaneously to class and ethnicity, but the terms "oppression, exploitation, racism, discrimination" are already present. Finally the document proposes a society without exploitation or oppression and, perhaps for the first time, "a multinational state" (in Rivera 1984:185–187). It was also in this same year of 1983 that Silvia Rivera founded the Oral Andean History Workshop (THOA). Rivera's role was principally concerned with the training and formation of Aymara intellectuals. (On the role and impact of THOA, see Stephenson 2000).

## FROM PROLETARIANS AND PEASANTS TO NATIONS, AYLLU FEDERATIONS, AND COMMUNITY LANDS OF ORIGIN

The years from 1985 to the 1992 "Quincentennial" were critical in the shift from studies in which proletarian workers and miners figured as the lead characters, to those focusing specifically on indigenous individuals, communities and pueblos (peoples). At an international level, Gorbachev's reforms and the political changes taking place in Eastern Europe culminated symbolically in the fall of the Berlin Wall in 1989. At the domestic level, the Popular Democratic Unity (UDP) government – an alliance of left-wing parties which came to power in 1982 amid great expectations and support – collapsed in 1985. The economic crisis and unprecedented inflation levels, the opposition of right-wing parties, and the social demands for both wage increases and more radical government, all culminated in 1985 when more than 12,000 miners took over the streets of La Paz demanding new elections and the resignation of the

president. The winner of the subsequent elections was the former dictator Hugo
Bánzer, although the national congress subsequently elected Víctor Paz Estensoro,
the candidate who had come second in the voting.

The first measure introduced by the new government was a neoliberal economic
policy that stabilized the economy at an extremely high social cost, with more than
20,000 mining workers losing their jobs. The defeat of the UDP and the collapse of
the international reference points that, up to this point, had been vital to the political
parties on the left, led to a crisis and the eventual fragmentation of the parties. At the
same time, miners and proletariat lost the central leadership role they had previously
held in the once strong Bolivian Workers Union (COB). In this context, various Indianista tendencies took hold, as did new parties that appealed to "popular" themes of
solidarity and patriotism (CONDEPA or Consciousness of the Fatherland (*patria*),
and the UCS or the Civic Solidarity Union in 1988). The emphasis on ethnicity and
cultural diversity began to gain ground discursively, but more importantly, it also
began to take the material or concrete form of political actions and projects.

It was in this context that the Association of Anthropologists of the Andean South
(ASUR) – and more specifically the work of anthropologist Ramiro Molina Rivero in
the Quillacas region – inspired the formation of the First Federation of Ayllus of
Southern Oruro (FASOR) in 1987.[2] One of the objectives of FASOR was to
reconstitute ancient political alliances of its member ayllus going back to the 16th
century. Although FASOR was perhaps the first indigenous organization to privilege
the search for ancient ayllu alliances, others would follow suit in the aftermath of the
debate sparked by the 1992 Quincentennial of the "discovery" of America. (See table 2.1
for the principal indigenous organizations.) From 1993, THOA, for example, assumed
the "reconstitution of the ayllu" as a central part of its activities, citing the need for a
return to "native roots" and "decolonization" (Choque 2001:205, 211, 217). In this
same process, Ricardo Calla contributed to the territorial reorganization of ayllus and
rural communities in the department of Potosí. This resulted in the 1995 Potosi
ayllus map (Calla and Arismendi 1995) and, later, to popular support for the constitutional recognition of Community Lands of Origin.

A different yet related line – privileging the notion of ethnodevelopment – was
promoted by Gabriel Martínez and Verónica Cereceda in ASUR Chuquisaca. The
practical experiences of these two anthropologists were extraordinary, and have yet to
be equaled 20 years later. They sought to promote textiles as works of art, as part of
a complex process of recuperating indigenous memory and technology, creative tradition and innovation. To do so, they embarked on an economic experiment designed
to reinforce identities. In this process, it was often the indigenous actors themselves
who best articulated the debate concerning identity:

> Who are we ultimately? We still do not have the answer … We need our own ideology,
> based on culture and the current reality of exploitation … When we talk of the 500 years
> since the Spanish Conquest, we must think about … finding our own identity; decide if we
> are really Indians, indigenous people, peasants, ethnic groups, second class citizens or
> whether we are Bolivians. I do not believe we are any of these denominations. What is our
> own cultural and national identity? (Juan de la Cruz Villca, in UNITAS 1991:117–118)

This testimony retraces history through a terminological sequence: The *indios* of the
colonial period are first transformed into *indígenas* in the 19th century, then into

**Table 2.1**  Principal indigenous organizations

| Acronyms of the organizations | Names of the organizations | Date of foundation | Related NGOs and anthropologists |
|---|---|---|---|
| FASOR | Federación de Ayllus del Sur de Oruro (Federation of Ayllus of Southern Oruro) | 1987 Quillacas | ASUR Ramiro Molina Rivero |
| FAONP | Federación de Ayllus Originarios del Norte de Potosí (Federation of Aboriginal Ayllus of Northern Potosi) | August 29, 1993 in the ayllu Karacha | |
| FACOPI | Federación de Ayllus y Comunidades Originarias de la Provincia Ingavi (Federation of Aboriginal Ayllus and Communities of the Ingavi Province) | January 1, 1993 in Tiwanaku (12 ayllus of Jesús de Machaqa) | THOA Silvia Rivera Carlos Mamani M. E. Choque  CIPCA Xavier Albó |
| FAMQAPM | Federación de Ayllus y Marcas Qhichua-Aymara de la Provincia Muñecas (Federation of Qhichua-Aymara Ayllus and Marcas of Muñecas Province) | 1995 | THOA |
| CACOU | Federación de Comunidades Originarias y Ayllus de la Marka de Achacachi, Prov. Omasuyos (Federation of Native Communities and Ayllus of the Achacachi Marka, Omasuyos Province) | | THOA |

*Sources*: Date of foundation of FASOR provided by Molina Rivero; information on FASOR, FAONP and FACOPI taken from Ticona 1996; information on FAMQAPM and CACOU in the final column is the author's.

peasants (*campesinos*) after the 1952 nationalist revolution, into ethnic groups (*grupos étnicos*) in the 1970s and 1980s, and finally on a different but related register, into citizens and Bolivians (*ciudadanos bolivianos*). All of these groups carried the burden of history and of exclusions, but it is as though they were all mutually exclusive. Equally, it would appear that the act of naming made it possible to create subjects with demands and lines of action to pursue. Thus, what this extract demonstrates, above all else, is an almost desperate quest for definition and certainty. This was the purpose of the sometimes defiant appeals to those who were presumed to know: professionals and NGOs.

The above extract was taken from a 1991 publication, *La revuelta de las nacionalidades* (The Revolt of the Nationalities), which focuses on the actions of NGOs and the close relations between indigenous leaders, syndicalists and intellectuals (UNITAS 1991). The words "revolt" and "nationalities" chosen for the title demonstrate the connection between a Marxist tendency and the Katarista-Indianista one. The Spanish term *revuelta*, which includes the meanings of turn around, revolution and change, evokes what in Quechua is called *pachakuti* (from *pacha* meaning earth and time; and *kuti*, meaning "to return" or "revolve"). In fact, the book was the product of a seminar organized by UNITAS (National Union of Institutions for Social Action), the coordinating body for over 40 NGOs addressing development and multiculturalism. By linking development and multiculturalism, UNITAS and its member NGOs not only sought to highlight the presence of diverse "nationalities" and peoples within the country. They also raised the urgent issue of how these nationalities were to be represented within the existing structure of the Bolivian nation (UNITAS 1991:15). In addition, the book – and the seminar on which it was based – also represented an attempt to bring together the differing perspectives of indigenous peoples in Bolivia's western highlands and eastern lowlands. Coming on the heels of earlier regional seminars, the UNITAS event also came at a favorable moment politically, since the historic "March for Territory and Dignity" from the lowlands to the capital of La Paz had been held only recently, in 1990. The conclusions of the western regional seminar stressed the theme of territory (Albó in UNITAS 1991). What these demands made clear is that there had been a shift in emphasis away from the problem of land and the ownership of land, toward a broader sense of territory and the collective rights of territorially defined "pueblos" (Calla and Molina 2003:63).

This shift from land to territory had only come about, however, as a result of earlier historical research, undertaken on behalf of political and social organizations, into the territorial fragmentation and destructuring of the highlands following Spanish colonization in the 16th century. But it was also linked to organizations and congresses of lowland indigenous peoples, including the Guaraní, Guarayo, Ava-Guaraní, Chiquitano and Ayoréode. These groups, from 1982 on and particularly following the fourth congress of the CIDOB (Confederation of Indigenous Peoples of Bolivia) in 1985, had established important relationships with the International Labor Organization (ILO) (Soliz 2002:68–92).

In addition to its emphasis on territory, the UNITAS publication also gave considerable importance to the problems of identity, and the acculturation and alienation brought about by both internal migration and expanding colonization of the lowland frontier areas (UNITAS 1991:43). The introduction to the volume advised Bolivia's historically privileged mestizo sectors "to recognize their minority status and ... [the fact that] there is a majority power that must be included in the institutions of decision-making and power" (1991:48). Two of the main proposals put forward in the volume were for self-determination for the "diverse nations" in the "practice of a true democracy," and the creation of an Assembly of Unity of the Native Nations that would bring together the two most important regional organizations: the CIDOB, representing indigenous peoples in the eastern lowlands, and the CSUTCB, a national peasant trade union confederation that has assumed a strong ethnic discourse among the highland or western indigenous peoples. Commissions were also set up for elaborating political proposals, and for drafting a new constitution recognizing alternative forms of representation other than the national parliament, and changes in the executive and judicial systems (UNITAS 1991:51).

Speaking from the "peasant perspective," then, this "popular historical project" as articulated by Albó in the UNITAS volume argued for the existence of *peoples* and *nations* and with *territorial* rights. Two different types of rights were identified: the substate right of native people to inhabit a territory and hold principal rights to that territory's resources; and the rights of the multinational state which included all the substate territories, both multinational and nonnational (large cities, for example). The proposal for state organization and the coexistence of the different nationalities signified the end of the "unitary and restrictive" state, the challenge being to construct a new multicultural, multinational state (UNITAS 1991:64, 131). The recorded debate included the following testimony:

> We must plan so that in October 1992 we can constitute the great Confederation of the Ayllus, which has to be a plurinational state, a Tawantinsuyo, a New Republic. We regard the republican stage as one small step – maybe even as a slip up, nothing more.... If we want to understand the nationalities, we must take off the straitjacket of syndicalism, and if we want to understand Tawantinsuyo, we must take off that of Bolivianness. (1991:135–137)

Tawantinsuyo, the ancient Inka state, thus came to stand as at once a symbol of the past and a project for the future. As a model for a state in which various ethnic groups could coexist, the image of Tawantinsuyu invoked here is reminiscent of the ideas of John V. Murra, while the denunciations of republicanism's homogenizing Bolivianness and trade unionism similarly evoke Rivera's earlier criticisms of Bolivia's liberal republican state (Rivera 1984). But what we also see in this paragraph is that certain perspectives begin to be regarded as opposites, mutually exclusive of one another: nationalities become the antithesis of syndicalism (although Katarism itself emerged from the peasant union movement), while Tawantinsuyo comes to stand as the anthithesis of a homogeneous, mestizo "Bolivianness."

## CONSTITUTIONAL REFORMS AND ACADEMIC DISPERSION (1990s)

Despite the government's harsh neoliberal economic policies, the 1989 elections once again handed victory to neoliberals from the nationalist revolutionary party, MNR, Bánzer's Nacionalist Democratic Action (ADN) and in the formerly left-wing Movement of the Revolutionary Left (MIR). However, following the defeat of the UDP government in 1985 and the ensuing (temporary) slowdown of the country's social movements, new and more radical expressions of discontent began to appear as a response to the political and economic reforms ushered in by the neoliberals. A first manifestation of popular discontent was the emergence in 1991 of the Túpac Katari Guerrilla Army (EGTK) led by Felipe Quispe. Quispe – who would later become known as "el Mallku" – the title of the highest community authority – would later assume leadership of the United Trade Union Confederation of Bolivian Peasant Workers (CSUTCB). A second expression of discontent was the 1990 March for Territory and Dignity, which led to state recognition of Mojeños, Chimanes, and other eastern ethnic territories.

By 1993, the situation had changed so much that Gonzalo Sánchez de Lozada ("Goni"), from the MNR party, a representative of neoliberalism, invited Víctor Hugo Cárdenas to be his vice-president. The son of a rural Aymara teacher, Cárdenas had studied philosophy and education before becoming the leader of the MRTKL

(Túpac Katari Revolutionary Liberation Movement), the dominant tendency within the Peasant Confederation up to that point. Cárdenas's speech on the day he assumed office included paragraphs in Aymara, Quechua and Guaraní announcing that a new era was beginning, that is to say a *pachakuti*. Goni's campaign – which he summed up in the slogan "A Plan for All" – involved four main reforms: at the economic level, the "capitalization" of the principal state-owned companies (practically a privatization), including the hydrocarbon sector; and at a sociopolitical level, "Popular Participation" comprising educational reform, judicial reform, and land reform. Cárdenas also contributed to the 1994 reformulation of the Bolivian constitution, which for the first time referred to the country's multiethnic and multicultural character. The new constitution backed bilingual education, legal recognition of indigenous communities, and a new law of Popular Participation gave formal meaning and constitutional validity for the first time to the terms "indigenous," "native peoples," and "territory." Although opinion is divided regarding Cárdenas's time in government – ranging from those who think it was a betrayal, to others who see it as a merely symbolic gesture on part of the neoliberal system – there is no doubt that it was a milestone.

Two changes were crucial to the political and social dynamic of the 1990s. The first was the shift that occurred from the recognition of "the indígena" as a culturally marked individual to the recognition of "pueblos indígenas" or indigenous peoples. The second was the related shift from "land" to "territory." The term employed by the law of Popular Participation – "indigenous people" – implied collective recognition. Indeed, the term had generated debate within the United Nations itself, where it was associated with the right to self-determination (Velasco 2001:24). In much the same way, the change from land to territory became a reality in the form of what are known as Community Lands of Origin (Tierras Comunitarios de Origen, or TCO):

> The designation of community lands of origin incorporates the concept of indigenous territory, in accordance with the definition laid down in part II of Agreement 169 of the International Labor Organization, ratified [in Bolivia] by Act/Law 1257 of 11 July 1991. The deeds to community lands of origin grant the indigenous and native peoples and communities collective ownership of their lands, recognizing their right to put to sustainable use the renewable natural resources present there. (Article 3, III, Law 1715 of the Nacional Agrarian Reform Service, October 18, 1996)

Although the very notion of a TCO implies recognition by a separate governmental authority or central state, decisions concerning the distribution of land were removed from the jurisdiction of the central state and returned to the communities:

> The distribution and redistribution [of land] for individual and family use within the collectively owned community lands of origin will be governed by the rules of the community, according to its norms and customs. (Article 3, III, Law 1715, October 18, 1996)

How was it possible for such demands as the multicultural recognition of indigenous peoples and the right to bilingual and intercultural education to become state policies? A first explanation lies in the longevity of the demands that were articulated by organizations such as the CSUTCB or by NGOs, but which circulated as constant claims on the state. In addition, this process was linked to international agreements such as ILO Convention 169, which was signed by Bolivia in 1991. This treaty calls for the recognition of territory and for the respect and protection of the social, economic and cultural rights of indigenous peoples. It is legally binding and prevails over national laws. Secondly, this situation came about as a result of the alliance between the government of Sánchez de Lozada (MNR) and the Katarista movement (MRTKL). A number of anthropologists, historians and sociologists who had worked in different capacities with the social movements participated directly and indirectly in the day-to-day running, advisory functions, policies and diagnoses of the Sánchez de Lozada government. These included Xavier Albó, who was for a long time either an advisor on educational reform or closely involved in the process; Iván Arias, who served as an advisor to Vice-President Cárdenas; Ramiro Molina Rivero, who served as First Under-secretary of Ethnic, Gender and Generational Affairs; Gonzalo Rojas Ortuste, who had previously worked in CIPCA (see Ticona, Rojas and Albó 1995) and was Director of Popular Participation; and Miguel Urioste, who worked on the agrarian reform. Many intellectuals and activists, however, condemned the MRTKL's participation in the government, arguing that the social reforms were either instrumental to the neoliberal economic measures, or a "perversion" of their radical political potential.

While all of this was taking place, foreign Bolivianistas such as Platt, Harris, Rivière, Larson and Wachtel continued their relations with Bolivia, albeit more sporadically. Wachtel, who in 1990 published his book on the Uru Chipayas (Wachtel 1990), was one of the few academics who sought, until at least the mid-1990s, to establish some form of ongoing dialogue with the country's intellectuals by each year inviting several Bolivian academics to the École des Hautes Études en Sciences Sociales in Paris. By that time, of course, there was a new generation of Bolivianistas. During the ten year period from 1990 to 1999 at least ten doctoral theses on Bolivia were published each year in English, mainly within anthropology (Kruse 2001:171). However, most of them, just like the publications they have led to, are unknown in Bolivia. (It would seem that we have not advanced much since Albó wrote his article entitled "Bolivia: Do You Speak English?") The fact is that, unlike their predecessors, the new young Bolivianistas do not spend such extended periods in the country; they do not return so frequently; nor do they establish the same type of relationships. Thus, paradoxically, the same period (1990s) that was marked in international arenas by fiery criticism of the colonial roots of anthropological writing and ethnographic authority was marked in Bolivia by scant communication between researchers in the country and those abroad. It may well be that the dispersion and nomadic existence of Bolivian researchers, brought about by the absence of centers of reflection and research, did not help the process of international communication. This relationship, in cases where it does exist, tends to be highly individualized and, above all, unequal, with "local" intellectuals serving primarily as "key informants" or disliked mestizos. But, what has happened in recent years?

## FROM THE TWO REPUBLICS TO TWO BOLIVIAS TO A CONSTITUENT ASSEMBLY

The social reforms undertaken during Sánchez de Lozada's first administration (1993–96) were overshadowed by the neoliberal policies, illegality and corruption that also characterized the government. Large-scale protests and social movements sprang up in response to the deepening economic crisis, the government's corrupt practices, the so-called "capitalization" – or de facto privatization – of state-owned companies, and, finally, the loss of credibility of those political parties taking turns in wielding state power. The Cochabamba Water War of 2000 marked the beginning of a new cycle. The Water War was a mass urban movement that, in alliance with peasant mobilizations, opposed the increases in utility prices accompanying the privatization of the city's water supply. The movements forced the government to break its contract with the multinational Aguas de Tunari water company, which was also forced to leave the country (Assies 2001).

Within this context, an intellectual group, La Comuna, whose members included Alvaro García Linera, Raúl Prada and Luis Tapia, began to articulate more sweeping anti-establishment positions. The Comuna – whose name was an allusion to both the Paris Commune and the Andean communites or ayllus – succeeded in uniting a cultural, ethnonational vision – predominant among historians and anthropologists – with a Marxist analysis of emergent political and social movements. Its members would also play an important role in the academic delegitimization of political parties, and the legitimization of the new forms of organization and protest which they proposed might serve as the foundations of the country's future political life. Luis Tapia, for example, published a series of articles in which he argued that Bolivia was a "multisocietal" country. Building on René Zavaleta Mercado's idea of "lo abigarrado" – an ensemble of overlapping yet unequal social components – Tapia described Bolivia as made up of a "wide range of societies existing in a situation of more or less colonial domination." He further denounced liberal multiculturalism as a covert form of racism, affirming that there could only be intercultural equality once political forms of self-government were recognized on equal terms (Tapia 2001:226–229; see also Tapia 2002). García Linera, for his part, argued against the common assumption that the 1985 mine closings had led to the demise of the workers' movement. Although it may well have signified the death of the union in the form of the COB (Bolivian Workers Union), García Linera argued that it did not necessarily imply the end of the workers' movement as a whole. He also identified the emergence of new forms of groupings such as the "multitude" defined by a flexible unification of territory. These were further characterized by claims to control over resources and resource management (including and especially water, access to land, and basic services) rather than as wage related demands (García Linera 2001:52–54). However, more importantly for our study of Bolivian anthropology, García Linera took up the community as a form of organization, defining it as:

> Bearer of the most developed political and discursive understanding of contemporary indigenous identity, bearer of a long trajectory of struggle for the autonomy and independence of indigenous nationalities with respect to the patronage and cooption of the state... (2001:67)

As an example, he cited the Aymara uprising of September and October 2001 in which a supraregional communal political power came to serve as an effective substitute for central state power. The system of state authorities was dissolved, and police, judges and other authorities were expelled from communities, to be replaced by a complex system of communal and union authorities (2001:68–69).

A central figure in these revolts, which were closely followed and analyzed by the Comunagroup, was Felipe Quispe ("el Mallku"). As secretary of the United Trade Union Confederation of Bolivian Peasant Workers (and as a history student), Quispe had previously been a member of MITKA and, after 1988, of the Red Offensive of Katarista Ayllus, the armed wing of which was the EGTK or Túpaj Katari Guerrilla Army from 1991 to 1992 (Albó 2002:80). Quispe touched a public nerve when he contended that there were in fact two Bolivias. The metaphor was certainly a powerful one. It already had a direct and indirect precedent in the social "schism" that Rivera had spoken of when she referred to the concept of "internal colonialism," first developed by Mexican anthropologist Pablo Gonzalez Casanova (1965; see also Nahmad Sitton this volume), and to the reproduction of the "two republics" inherited from the Spanish colony (Rivera 1984:16).

The demand for a new Constituent Assembly was itself a product of the important relationship that had developed over time between the country's social movements and its intellectuals. Indeed, the 1991 CIPCA publication *Por una Bolivia diferente* (For a Different Bolivia) can be seen as a forerunner of the Constituent Assembly, in the sense that it imagined an opportunity to refound the nation. *Por una Bolivia diferente* presented itself as a "provocation" intended to stir up debate on the "colonialist and antipeasant" state (p. 9). More specifically, it proposed a project for a new state and society grounded in "a peasant perspective on both levels, as a class and as a nation" (p. 11). This state was to be an egalitarian, democratic and self-governing society with no exploitation of classes. It was, moreover, to be based on community organizations and the coexistence of nations, thereby creating a "multinational state" rather than a "nation-state" (pp. 19–22, 64). The book also proposed the political recognition of peoples on three different levels: that of communal and microregional governments; that of the local governments of each nation, understood as a "cultural, historical and geographical unit" (p. 28); and that of regional governments (p. 28). These concrete suggestions included a proposal for a "new Constitution of the Multinational State" (p. 35) recognizing the relative autonomy of each region and substate nation. Congress was to be made up of representatives from the substate nations (and no longer from towns and cities, p. 24) and from the regions, which would be represented proportionally according to their demographic density (pp. 164, 165). In addition, at the level of executive power, there was to be representation by class based organizations like the COB, the CSUTCB, the unions, and producer organizations (pp. 35–36).

*Por una Bolivia diferente* included contributions from over 32 intellectuals from diverse professions and regions, representing such academic institutions and universities as the Bolivian Center for Multidisciplinary Studies (CEBEM), the Latin American Institute for Social Research (ILDIS), the Latin American Social Science Faculty (FLACSO), the Center for Research and Documentation of the Beni (CIDDEBENI), and CIPCA. Other chapters represented the viewpoints of militants from progressive political parties, including the Revolutionary Left Movement (MIR), the United Left (IU), and the MRTKL, and the media (in this case, CEDOIN, the Center for Documentation and Information).[3] The concept of "going back to native roots" contained in the book referred to historical and anthropological concepts of an Andean worldview oriented toward reciprocity and "complementarity" (between men and women, beween the mountainous western highlands and the humid eastern lowlands).

This idea of a unity that does not destroy its component units evokes the historical example of Tawantinsuyu, as well as the regular rotation of political posts that characterizes Andean communal democracy, and the territorial combat that intensifies difference and unity while avoiding overt violence (CIPCA 1991:84). Filimón Escóbar, a well-known left politician and a former mining leader, pointed out, for example, that the new generation of leaders are "young lovers of Andean culture" who are thinking about "returning" to rural areas, "to the ayllu system of production, to the vertical control of the various ecological layers of the country by a community" (cited by Yapura 2003:46).

In Bolivia, a long process has led from the denial of all things ethnic to their current prestige and political centrality. The 2002 election brought the first mass vote for indigenous parties and candidates, including Evo Morales's Movement toward Socialism (MAS) and Felipe Quispe's Pachakuti Indigenous Movement (MIP). In those elections, indigenous representation in government grew to include 42 members of parliament (33 congressional deputies and 8 senators). Following the October 2003 crisis and "Gas War" and the resulting forced resignation of President Sánchez de Lozada, popular movements further consolidated around the demand for a Constituent Assembly. Envisioned as the opportunity for establishing a new constitutional pact, the promise inherent in a Constituent Assembly – a promise which was perhaps first articulated in 1991 in CIPCA's "academic" publication *Por una Bolivia diferente*, and even more explicitly in the Comuna group's 2001 analysis (Comuna 2001) – had come, by the time of the 2005 national elections, to occupy the central place in Bolivia's national agenda. On August 6, 2006 – the day on which Bolivian independence is celebrated – the Morales government inaugurated the Asamblea Constituyente.

## BRIDGES AND CHASMS

This chapter has sought to analyze the processes of interrelation – the *bridges* – that have been built between such ostensibly heterogeneous groups as NGOs, anthropologists, sociologists, indigenous elites and organizations, and popular social movements. These are the associations that have helped bring about legal changes such as the declaration of multiculturalism in the Bolivian constitution, the concept of indigenous and native peoples, legislation on Community Lands of Origin or TCOs, and intercultural educational reforms. These legal changes have contributed to even greater transformations. Central topics in ethnohistorical and anthropological research have not only laid the foundations for social and political changes, but they have also provided the concepts and terminology that today circulate widely in Bolivian political and social debate. Among these topics are the notions of "territory" and "indigenous" people, the concept of *ayllu* as an economic, political, social and governmental authority (with an emphasis on ethnic group), the recognition of language as a fundamental grounding of worldview, the history of the pillaging of community lands, and the economic and political domination of the country's many indigenous peoples.

However, during the lengthy process described throughout the chapter, certain chasms have also opened up. These have taken the form, in the first place, of economic tensions. Leaders of communities and social movements have seen first-hand how many NGOs and their largely middle-class directors and technicians make a living "in their name." There have also been considerable intellectual tensions. Indigenous leaders and intellecturals have remarked that the NGOs "work on behalf of the Indians and for the Indians, but without the Indians." According to some, they are the Trojan horses of the Indian movement, and every NGO seeks "its own Indian" to give it legitimacy (Agreda 2004). Indigenous representatives have also questioned the power that the authorized and glorified words of nonindigenous officials have when they speak in the name of the indigenous peoples. When the press asked Felipe Quispe, "the Mallku," whether he was advised by nonindigenous intellectuals such as García Linera or Albó, he replied that he should be advising them. It may well be that the need for self-affirmation can explain his merciless criticisms of anthropologists Silvia Rivera and Xavier Albó, and his one-time comrade García Linera. This need for self-affirmation and independence also forms part of political debate. The Council of Ayllus and Markas of Qullasuyo (CONAMAQ, founded in 1997 in Azanaques, Killacas territory, where FASOR first emerged) was not only the culmination of the process of reconstituting the ayllus, but also a response to the union organization led in Northern Potosí by a traditional left-wing group, the Free Bolivia Movement (MBL). In their dispute with the CSUTCB (the top national peasant organization led by Quispe), the ayllu representatives of CONAMAQ, who present themselves as the "Government of the Qullasuyu" (see www.aymara.org), cite continuity of norms, cultures and practices from the prehispanic era to claim greater "authenticity" when compared, for example, with union organizations and leaders (Andolina 2001:13–14). The unions themselves have become "Indianized" and in rural areas traditional posts today receive indigenous names, even if it is just a matter of a simple translation. This political stance of self-affirmation often implies a Manichean view of good, associated with all things indigenous and native, and evil, associated with things Western and nonindigenous. It is a view that implicitly and explicitly denies the associations and relations between them, while allowing for a certain essentialization of Andean culture. The fact is that the social and political radicalism and polarization that has gradually emerged also pervades academia. In the Mallku's radical nationalism, affirmation and essentialization are part of a political strategy with its roots in the lengthy historical and political process outlined above:

> We indigenous [peoples] have our own territories. This territory does not belong to Westerners and colonizers…We have our own history, our own philosophy, our laws, religion, language habits and customs. From this perspective, we Aymara consider ourselves to be a nation, hence the idea of self-determination. We do not follow the tricolor Bolivian flag carried by our oppressors. We have the *wiphala*…

The Indianista objective, Quispe continues in a 2002 interview, is to

> de-ideologize our brothers, take the foreign ideology out of the Indian mind. Then comes the task of re-indianization…We have our own authorities and we are the owners of the territory: of the soil, the subsoil, the products that grow on the soil and the airspace above the soil. There, soon, we will have autonomy, although we know that this will not happen easily, that this process is going to cost us blood. But there it is: We have to shed a lot of blood, but we are certain that we are going to have our own form of organization, our own indigenous nation.[4]

Perhaps the greatest challenge, however, has come from the proposals for regional autonomy that emerged after the political crisis of the Gas War and the resignation of "Goni" Sánchez de Lozada. These proposals seem almost as though they were in response to voices such as that of "el Mallku." The regionalist movements from the eastern lowlands intensified as a result of the decisions taken about gas, and the economic, political and social polarization associated with them. The eastern regions, and more specifically Santa Cruz, became identified with companies successfully exporting agricultural produce, with gas and oil, with a vigorous economy, with mestizaje, with modernity and work. The very mention of "East," "South," and "West" constitute objectifications and essentializations. Most importantly, and even paradoxically, the same terms employed by the indigenous movements of the altiplano (high altitude plateau) – "multiculturalism," "territory," "identification as distinct peoples," and "self-determination" – are now promoted by elites from the eastern regions and their representatives. In their name during the political crisis of October 2003, the Civic Committee of Santa Cruz demanded the "refounding of the country" and the establishment of a new republic with regional self-determination.[5]

The idea of refounding the nation is also a product of a process in which the construction of identities has been fundamental. This invention has been forged in recent years around the Camba and "Cruceño" identity, in reference to the tropical eastern region of Santa Cruz. The extreme right-wing group Camba Nation – whose representative the press calls "the Mallku of the East" – relies on the same concepts used to analyze the indigenous situation in the west of the country. This means that internal colonialism is identified with the centralism of the state, which is in turn accused of exploiting lowland (eastern) regions as "colonies."

The polarization in "racial" terms that is being created between the regions constitutes yet another important social chasm. Both Santa Cruz and Tarija, where the majority of the population is not indigenous, claim they do not feel represented by the debates, decisions and choices taking place in La Paz, all of which are strongly influenced by the dynamic of the indigenous movements. Meanwhile the radical indigenous leaders denounce as their enemies the nonindigenous politicians and intellectuals with whom they have established and continue to establish relations on a daily basis. At the other extreme, the social elites are imbued with profoundly discriminatory and racist ideas. Thus a number of chasms have gradually opened up and broad sectors of the urban population – which today is over 60 percent – appear to be subject to a choice between polarities.

By 2005 there was no doubt that the Bolivian state had lost its legitimacy and been "stripped bare" by, on the one hand, its own neoliberal economic policies and, on the other, a profound questioning of its raison d'être (Petras 2002). The process gave rise to fragmentation and tensions that worsened following the gas crisis in 2003. This explains the preoccupation with social divisions, often expressed in apocalyptic terms:

> The country's division is fourfold, it has an ethnic slant (Q'aras versus Indians), a regional one (Collas versus Cambas), another that is economic (rich versus poor) and lastly a new political tone (government versus opposition). The division has already appeared and no one should be celebrating. Add to the pot a fair number of guns and age-old hatreds and "there you have it": Will the last one to leave, please turn off the lights? (Archondo 2003:88)

Other authors have been less pessimistic. Some are of the opinion that, inflammatory rhetoric notwithstanding, a more democratic society is being constructed. After a period of acute political crisis from 2003 to 2005, the elections of 2005 gave 54 percent of the popular vote to Evo Morales, leader of the coca producers (cocaleros), founder of the Movement to Socialism (MAS), and, since January 2006, Bolivia's first indigenous president. The idea of a refounding of the country emerged six months later in the inauguration of the national constituent assembly, with its impressive indigenous presence.

Regardless of the outcome in the short or medium term, there is no doubt that history and anthropology in Bolivia have taken a very particular course: The paradigm shift from proletariat to indigenous people has taken place as part of a dialogue between political leaders, social movements and NGOs supported by international organizations (see also Andolina 2001). The indigenous movement has drawn on historical and anthropological research to argue for the legitimacy of its demands. Linguistic studies have supplied the foundations for unity. Countless historical, anthropological and sociological studies have contributed to a new historical consciousness, and a rethinking of the foundation on which communities were historically established, reconstituted and reinvented. Anthropologists and other academics have been constantly inspired by the challenges presented to them by the social movements, and, when they have participated as advisors or officials, their relationships and connections with the indigenous population have given them visibility, legitimacy and political power. The indigenous intellectuals have also played a fundamental role as activists and advisors throughout this entire process (see for example, Stephenson 2000). Thus they have all contributed to the Aymara emergence, even though some academics would have thought it neither possible nor desirable. But in the process of building bridges, the chasms have also widened. The fact is that the current political context consists of conflicting nationalist projects, some more radical than others. The existing forms of nationalism include extremism, and nationalist demands often depend on a rejection of "otherness" altogether. Let us not forget that, in Latin America as elsewhere in the world, many social and also national identities have been constructed by devaluing, denying, diminishing, annulling and discriminating against a perceived adversary. The denial of others, but also of the self, only perpetuates, or re-expresses, colonial relations.

Lastly, in this whole process the distances between academic anthropology in Bolivia and the rest of the world have been increasing. The differences in work conditions and research opportunities appear to be ever more pronounced. In Bolivia there is not even minimal access to journals from neighboring countries. Teachers are largely paid by the hour and usually receive no benefits. Hence they are like nomads, juggling responsibilities between one university and another, one program and another, or one job and another. Research, when it is possible, is above all a personal and individual initiative and it is difficult to believe that it is still carried out at all. Bolivia is nevertheless a place where major cultural and historical processes are taking place. For many they provide fascinating research experiments, while for others they are a matter of day-to-day experience.

## NOTES

1  Ayllus are flexible kindred based social units that can extend from small family residential groups to communities and broader territorial affiliations. In common use the name is often used as a synonym for "community" as an affective and territorial or geographic grouping.
2  Personal communication, Ramiro Molina Rivero. ASUR members included Ramiro Molina Rivero, Ricardo Calla, Silvia Arce, Ramiro Molina Barrios, Ximena Medinaceli, and the author.

3   It is worth noting, however, that the book included only one female author, Zulema Lehm.
4   In www.narconews.com/felipe1eng.html, accessed Oct. 11, 2007.
5   "For a New Republic," Oct. 17, 2003, on the website of the ProSanta Cruz Committee at www.comiteprosantacruz.org/comite/pronunciamientos/nuevarepublica.htm, accessed Oct. 12, 2007.

## REFERENCES

Abercrombie, T. A. (1998) *Pathways of Memory and Power: Ethnography and History among an Andean People*. Madison: University of Wisconsin Press.

Agreda, Mario (2004) Las ONGs son el caballo de Troya del movimiento indio. ¿Son las Ongs la industria de la solidaridad? *Ekintza Zuzena*, no. 31. At www.nodo50.org/ekintza/articlephp3?id_article=106, accessed Oct. 11, 2007.

Albó, X. (1972) Dinámica en la estructura intercomunitaria de Jesús de Machaca. *América Indígena* 32–33.

Albó, X. (1975) *La paradoja Aymara. Solidaridad y faccionalismo*. Cuadernos de Investigación, no. 8. La Paz: CIPCA.

Albó, X. (1976) *Lengua y sociedad en Bolivia*. La Paz: Instituto Nacional de Estadísticas.

Albó, X. (1979) ¿Khitipxtansa? ¿Quiénes somos? Identidad localista, étnica y clasista en los aymaras de hoy. *América Indígena* 39(3):477–527.

Albó, X. (ed.) (1988) *Raíces de América. El mundo Aymara*. Madrid: Alianza América.

Albó, X. (2002) *Pueblos indios en la política*. CIPCA, Cuadernos de Investigación, no. 55. La Paz: Plural.

Albó, X. and Harris, O. (1976) *Monteras y guaratojos, campesinos y mineros en el norte de Potosí*. La Paz: CIPCA.

Anderson, B. (1983) *Imagined Communities: Reflections on the Origin and Spread of Nationalism*. London: Verso.

Andolina. R. (2001) Between Local Authenticity and Global Accountability: The Ayllu Movement in Contemporary Bolivia. Paper for conference on Beyond the Lost Decade: Indigenous Movements and the Transformation of Democracy and Development in Latin America, Princeton, Mar. 2–3.

*Annales* (1978) *Anthropologie historique des sociétés andines*. Special issue of *Annales: Économies, Sociétés, Civilisations* (Paris), nos 5–6. For English trans., see Murra, Revel and Wachtel 1986.

Archondo, R. (2003) ¿Y si organizamos la incertidumbre? In R. Archondo et al., *Cercados pero despiertos. Bolivia después del 30 de Junio del 2002*. La Paz: Eureka–La Epoca.

Arze, S. and Medinaceli, X. (1991) *Imágenes y presagios: El escudo de los Ayaviri*. La Paz: Edit. HISBOL.

Assies, W. (2001) David vs. Goliat en Cochabamba. Los derechos del agua, el neoliberalismo y la renovación de la propuesta social en Bolivia. *T'inkazos* (Pieb. La Paz.) 8.

*Avances* (1978a) *Avances: Revista Boliviana de Estudios Históricos y Sociales* (La Paz), no. 1.

*Avances* (1978b) *Avances: Revista Boliviana de Estudios Históricos y Sociales* (La Paz), no. 2.

Barnadas, Joseph (1976a) *Los aymaras dentro de la sociedad boliviana*. Cuadernos de Investigación, no. 12. La Paz: CIPCA.

Barnadas, Joseph (1976b) *Apuntes para una historia aymara*. La Paz: CIPCA.

Barragán, Rossana (1982) *Etnicidad y verticalidad ecológica de Sicasica, Ayú-Ayo y Calamarca, siglos XVI–XVII. El acceso vertical y el nacimiento de la hacienda en Palca (1596–1644)*. La Paz: Museo Nacional de Etnografía y Folklore.

Barragán, Rossana (1994) *¿Indios de arco y flecha? Entre la historia y la arqueología de las poblaciones del norte de Chuquisaca*. Sucre: Antropólogos del Surandino, Interamerican Foundation.

Bouysse-Cassagne, T. (1980) *La identidad aymara. Aproximación histórica. Siglo XV, siglo XVI*. La Paz: HISBOL.

Calderón, F. and Dandler, J. (eds) (1986) *Bolivia. La fuerza histórica del campesinado*. Geneva: CERES–UNRISD.

Calla, R. and Arismendi, W. (1995) *Mapa preliminar de ayllus y comunidades rurales en el departamento de Potosí. Fines del siglo XX*. Proyecto de Desarrollo Forestal Comunal La Paz–FAO Holanda.

Calla, R. and Molina B., R. (2003) Los pueblos indígenas y la construcción de una sociedad plural (1993–1996). In R. Calla, *Indígenas, políticas y reformas en Bolivia*. Guatemala: Ediciones ICAPI.

Carter, W. and Mamani, M. (1982) *Irpa Chico*. La Paz: Juventud.

Choque, M. E. (2001) Reconstitución del ayllu y derechos de los pueblos indígenas: el movimiento indio en los Andes de Bolivia. *Journal of Latin American Anthropology* 6(1):202–224.

CIPCA (1991) *Por una Bolivia diferente. Aportes para un proyecto histórico-popular*. La Paz: CIPCA.

Comuna (2001) *Tiempos de rebelión*. Grupo Comuna. La Paz: Editorial Muela del Diablo.

Coordinadora de la Mujer, Viceministerio de la Mujer, Foro Político de Mujeres, Red Ada, Plataforma de la mujer y AMUPEI (2004) *Asamblea Constituyente: fundamentación sobre la representación y paridad de género. Documento de trabajo elaborado por el Equipo de Apoyo a la Asamblea Constituyente*.

Dandler, J. (1983) *El sindicalismo campesino en Bolivia. Los cambios estructurales en Ucureña*. La Paz: CERES.

Dunkerley, J. (1987–2003) *Rebelión en las venas. La lucha política en Bolivia. 1952–1982*. La Paz: Plural.

Espinoza Soriano, W. (1969) *El memorial de Charcas. Crónica inédita de 1582*. Lima: Universidad Nacional de Educación.

García Linera, A. (2001) Sindicato, multitud y comunidad. Movimientos sociales y formas de autonomía política en Bolivia. In A. García Linera, R. Gutiérrez, R. Prada, and L. Tapia, *Tiempos de rebelión*. La Paz: Muela del Diablo Editores.

Gonzalez Casanova, Pablo (1965) Internal Colonialism and National Development. *Studies in Comparative International Development* 1(4):27–37.

Harris, O. (1978) De l'assymétrie au triangle. Transformations symboliques au nord de Potosí. *Annales* 33/5–6:1108–1125. In English as: From Asymmetry to Triangle: Symbolic Transformations in Northern Potosi. In J. V. Murra, J. Revel and N. Wachtel (eds), *Anthropological History of Andean Polities* (pp. 260–280). Cambridge: Cambridge University Press.

Harris, O. and Larson, B. (eds) (1987) *Participación indígena en los mercados surandinos*. La Paz: CERES. English trans. as *Ethnicity, Markets and Migration in the Andes*. Durham, NC: Duke University Press, 1995.

Hurtado, J. (1986) *El Katarismo*. La Paz: HISBOL.

Kruse, T. (2001) Lo que dicen de nosotros. Tesis universitarias del mundo anglohablante, 1990–1999. Primera Parte y Segunda Parte. *T'inkazos* (Pieb. La Paz) 9 and 10.

Larson, B. (1984) *Explotación agraria y resistencia campesina en Cochabamba*. Cochabamba: CERES.

Larson B. (1992) *Colonialismo y transformación agraria en Bolivia. Cochabamba, 1500–1900*. La Paz: CERES–HISBOL.

Lora, G. (1967) *Historia del movimiento obrero boliviano*. 4 vols. La Paz: Editorial Los amigos del Libro. In English as G. Lora, L. Whitehead, and C. Whitehead, *A History of the Bolivian Labour Movemenet 1848–1971*. Cambridge: Cambridge University Press, 1977.

Molina Rivero, Ramiro (2006) *De memorias e identidades. Los Aymaras y Urus del Sur de Oruro*. La Paz: IEB-ASDI-DIALOGO.

Murra, J. V. (1964) Una apreciación etnológica de la Visita. In J. V. Murra, W. Espinoza, and W. Espinoza Soriano (eds), *Visita Hecha a la Provincia de Chucuito por García Diez de San Miguel en el año 1567*. Lima: Casa de la Cultura.

Murra, J. V. (1978) *Formaciones económicas y políticas del mundo andino*. La Paz: IEP.

Murra, J. V., Revel, J., and Wachtel, N. (1986) *Anthropological History of Andean Polities*. Cambridge: Cambridge University Press. English translation of *Annales* 1978.

Pacheco, D. (1992) *El indianismo y los indios contemporáneos en Bolivia*. La Paz: HISBOL–MUSEF.

Petras, J. (2002) El rostro comunitario del nacionalismo.

Platt, T. (1976) *Espejos y maíz. Temas de la estructura simbólica andina*. La Paz: CIPCA, no. 1.

Platt, T. (1982) *Estado boliviano y ayllu andino. Tierra y tributo en el norte de Potosí*. Lima: Instituto de Estudios Peruanos.

Platt, T. (1986) Mirrors and Maize: The Concept of Yanantin among the Macha of Bolivia. In J. V. Murra, J. Revel and N. Wachtel (eds), *Anthropological History of Andean Polities* (pp. 228–259) (English translation of *Annales* 1978). Cambridge: Cambridge University Press.

Presta, A. M. and del Rio, M. (1995) Un estudio etnohistórico en los corregimientos de Tomina y Yamparaez. Casos de multietnicidad. In A. M. Presta (ed.), *Espacio, etnias, frontera. Atenuaciones políticas en el Sur del Tawantinsuyu. Siglos XV–XVIII* (pp. 189–218). Sucre, Bolivia: ASUR, 4.

Rivera Cusicanqui, S. (1984) *Oprimidos pero no vencidos. Luchas del campesinado aymara quechwa de Bolivia, 1900–1980*. La Paz: HISBOL–CSUTCB. In English as S. Rivera Cusicanqui, *Oppressed but Not Defeated: Peasant Struggles among the Quechua and Aymara in Bolivia, 1900–1980*. Geneva: United Nations Research Institute for Social Development, 1987.

Rivera Cusicanqui, S. (1993) La raíz. Colonizadores y colonizados. In *Violencias encubiertas en Bolivia. Cultura y política*, vol. 1. La Paz: CIPCA-Aruwiyiri.

Rivière, Gilles, *Sabaya: structures socio-economiques et representations symboliques dans le Carangas-Bolivie*. Tesis de Doctorado, Ecole de Hautes Etudes en Sciences Sociales, Paris, Francia, 1982.

Saignes, Thierry (1986) *En Busa del doblamiento étnico de los Andes bolivianos (Siglos XV y XVI)*. La Paz: Museo Nacional de Etnografía y Folklore.

Sánchez Albórnoz, N. (1978) *Indios y tributos en el Alto Perú*. Lima: IEP.

Soliz, Carmen (2002) El territorio de los pueblos indígenas del Oriente. Discurso sobre el territorio indígena en los pueblos indígenas de las tierras bajas desde la perspectiva de la Confederación de los Pueblos Indígenas de Bolivia (CIDOB): 1982–2000. Tesis de Licenciatura, Carrera de Ciencias Políticas, Universidad Nuestra Señora de La Paz.

Stephenson, M. (2000) The Impact of an Indigenous Counterpublic Sphere on the Practice of Democracy: The Taller de Historia Oral Andina in Bolivia. Working Paper 279, Kellogg Institute, Notre Dame; at www.nd.edu/kellog/wps/279.pdf, accessed Oct. 12, 2007.

Tapia, L. (2001) El movimiento de la parte maldita. In Comuna, *Tiempos de rebelión*. La Paz: Muela del Diablo.

Tapia, L. (2002) *La condición multisocietal. Multiculturalidad, pluralismo, modernidad*. La Paz: Muela del Diablo–CIDES–UMSA.

Ticona, Esteban (1996) *CSTUCB. Trayectoria y desafíos*. La Paz: CEDOIN.

Ticona, E., Rojas, G., and Albó, X. (1995) *Votos y wiphalas. Campesinos y pueblos originarios en democracia*. Cuadernos de Investigación, no. 43. La Paz: CIPCA.

UNITAS (1991) *La revuelta de las nacionalidades*, ed. D. Cuadro. La Paz: UNITAS.

Urioste, M. (1984) *El estado anticampesino*. La Paz: CINCO.

Velasco L. (2001) Areas de desarrollo indígena y distritos municipales indígenas. El desarrollo indígena desde las políticas de Chile y Bolivia. *Revista MAD (Magíster en Antropología y Desarrollo)* (Departamento de Antropología, Universidad de Chile), no. 4 (May). At http://rehue.csociales.uchile.cl/publicaciones/mad/04/paper05.htm, accessed Oct. 12, 2007.

Wachtel, N. (1971) *La Vision des vaincus*. Paris: Gallimard.

Wachtel, N. (1990) *Le Retour des ancêtres. Les Indiens Urus de Bolivie XXe–XVIe siècle. Essai d'histoire régressive*. Bibliothèque des Sciences Humaines. Paris: Gallimard.

Yapura, G. (2003) Mallku, Evo y Goni. Volvemos al campo. In R. Archondo et al., *Cercados pero despiertos. Bolivia después del 30 de Junio del 2002*. La Paz: Eureka–La Epoca.

Zavaleta Mercado, René (1983) *Las masas en noviembre*. La Paz: Juventud.

Zavaleta Mercado, René (1986) *Lo nacional-popular en Bolivia*. Mexico: Siglo XXI.

# Brazil: Otherness in Context

CHAPTER **3**

*Mariza Peirano*

For a long time anthropology was defined by the exoticism of its object of study and by the distance, conceived as cultural and geographical, that separated the researcher from his or her group. This situation has changed. Even (and perhaps mostly) in the socially legitimate centers of anthropological production, the ideal of an encounter with some sort of radical alterity is no longer considered an essential dimension of the anthropological perspective. Anthropology is not about an object, it is about difference.

Of course, this viewpoint has been present in the international scene since the 1960s, but it would not surface easily in the minds of anthropologists. Despite the fact that anthropology's interest had shifted from far away (the Trobrianders, the Azande, Kwakiutl, Bororo) to less exotic places (the Mediterranean countries, for example), and then to settings and groups close by, when it really did reach "home" in the 1980s, in some quarters it turned itself to an array of *studies* – cultural studies, science studies, feminist studies and so on (cf. Peirano 1998).

In Brazilian anthropology, as in Latin American more generally, difference came to refer to a plurality of notions which can be either historical or simultaneous. In Brazil, though exoticism has never been an issue in itself, some dimension of alterity has been and continues to be a basic trait of anthropology. Briefly, a notion of otherness involving indigenous peoples and their contact with the regional population dominated the scene up until the 1960s; in the following decades, these studies coexisted with "softer" alterities in which anthropologists turned their attention to the peasantry and then to urban contexts, until, more recently, during the 1980s, their concerns began to include social scientists' intellectual careers and production. Otherness has thus shifted from a concept of distant to minimal alterities, many anthropologists having developed interests in several kinds over the course of their academic career. The result has been a steady incorporation of new topics and an enlargement of the discipline's research universe. Today, all these modes of conceiving alterity (indigenous peoples, urban population, peasantry, social scientists themselves) live together in a pluralistic way.

The Brazilian example reveals that, though exoticism is the sociogenetic foundation of anthropology, *for anthropologists themselves* difference can assume many meanings. While in canonical terms it was radical to the point of (ideally) being foreign, when acculturated in other latitudes alterity has often translated into relative rather than exotic difference. Whether near or far, these differences can be cultural, social, economic, political, religious, territorial. In other words, the process that in the metropolitan centers took a century to develop – that is, bringing the discipline home from abroad – in Brazil took no more than three decades. Even though there are of course intellectual and/or empirical priorities as well as trends (theoretical or regarding objects/subjects), there are no real restrictions in relation to this multiplicity of alterities.

This relative freedom is related to many factors, and I shall raise a few of them. First, Brazil (or South America, for that matter) has never experienced any historical resentment for having been the object of anthropological curiosity by the metropolitan centers (as was the case in the first half of the century with Melanesia, South and Southeast Asia, and Africa). Second, sociologists have been the main interlocutors for anthropologists – and not archaeologists, physical anthropologists or linguists. If neighboring disciplines (as models or rivals) must always be considered in order to focus a specific field of knowledge, then permanent dialogue with sociology and political science has prevailed. In Brazil, anthropology is one of the social sciences. Third, indigenous peoples – the presumed prototype of a radical alterity – were researched within the boundaries of the national territory. This situation reveals less a problem of financial resources – although this needs to be considered – than the choice of an object of study which includes, or is mixed with, a concern over differences. A last point to mention is the dominant influence of a French/Durkheimian perspective (over a German one, for instance), in which different ways of conceiving society stand side by side, thus playing down any strict interests in peculiarities or singularities. (The exhilaration which Lévi-Strauss produced in Brazil in the 1960s may be explained by this situation.)

Given this general context, this chapter centers on (but is not restricted to) the last three to four decades, when anthropology gained legitimacy and became a prestigious field of social inquiry in Brazil. Because it emerged as a kind of rib to sociology – a feminine agency, for that matter – it also inherited sociology's basic tension, that of combining theoretical excellence with social commitment. All this has to do with the institutionalization of the social sciences back in the 1930s, an Enlightenment project to help forge a political elite to govern the country and create a "national" ideal. Since then, this external dialogue with sociology has been internalized in the discipline as a dichotomy between indigenous ethnology "made in Brazil" and anthropological research *about Brazil*. Today we may say that an anthropology made in/about Brazil is a general goal.

## EXOTICISM AND IDEAL TYPES: THE CASE OF BRAZIL

From the perspective of the classic concern about taboos, exoticism is a distant and remote alterity which also includes a sort of fascination. In other words, rather than delineating a forbidden territory, it calls for scrutiny. But alterity as *difference* or as *exoticism* diverge: while exoticism always implies some sort of difference, not every difference is exotic. This is basic Durkheim. In the first case, political dimensions are intrinsic to its very existence. In the latter, politics are beyond, far away or in any case separate. One more aspect is that the emphasis on difference is inherently compara-tive, whereas the emphasis on exoticism does not require contrasts.

Since exoticism was the sociogenetic trait of anthropology, I will take it as the relevant element in relation to which examples can be measured. The aim is to focus on how it was acculturated in Brazil by means of a shift in emphasis toward difference. I identify four ideal types, in the Weberian sense: (1) radical alterity, (2) contact with alterity, (3) nearby alterity, and (4) minimum alterity. These types are not mutually exclusive and, as mentioned, throughout their academic careers anthropologists move back and forth among and within them. In chronological terms, a certain sequence can be noted: the research project of radical alterity pre-ceded the study of contact of regional with indigenous populations. In turn, this interest was followed by research carried out at home, especially in urban contexts. Today sociological production itself has become an anthropological problem. In the past decade, the trend to transpose national boundaries (but in a different mode from orthodox anthropologists) has been not only accepted but praised. I will look closer at these cases but, for editorial reasons, I will transform long and productive academic careers into a single reference, and sometimes not even that. I apologize to my colleagues in advance. (For a more inclusive listing, see Peirano 1999.)

## Radical alterity

The search for a rigorous sort of alterity can be illustrated in Brazil by two forms of geographical and ideological distancing. First, in the classic study of indigenous popu-lations; second, in the more recent project of going beyond the country's own territo-rial limits. In neither case, however, compared to a central or "international anthropology" (as per Gerholm and Hannerz 1982), is alterity extreme (though it may be argued that indigenous peoples represented the "available exoticism," and that studying abroad is what anthropologists should do).

Let me begin by looking at the study of indigenous peoples. Today apprentices in the field can detect some dichotomies: Tupi or Jê; social organization or cosmology; Amazonia and Central Brazil or Xingu; history or ethnography; political economy or descriptive cosmology (Viveiros de Castro 1995). As with any dichotomy, the empiri-cal options are far greater. But in this context, research on the Tupi, having practically disappeared from ethnology in Brazil during the 1960s (see Laraia 1964, 1986), has made a return in the past two decades (Viveiros de Castro 1992, 1998; Fausto 2001; among others). At the same time, research on indigenous peoples has provoked a sys-tematic interest in kinship systems: though a classic area of anthropology, in Brazil's local scene it was considered a novelty (Viveiros de Castro 1995; Villaça 1992; Gonçalves 1993; Teixeira Pinto 1997).

Before the 1980s, the Jê was the most studied group in Brazil. Following the classic works of Nimuendaju (for example, 1946), the Jê caught the attention of Lévi-Strauss (for instance, 1952) and, shortly thereafter, of the Harvard-Central Brazil Project (Maybury-Lewis 1967, 1979). In a short time, the results of this ambitious research project became the main support for structuralist Ph.D. dissertations. This field experience was central for a whole generation of Brazilian anthropologists (for example, DaMatta 1976; Melatti 1970). In the following decades, research on the Jê continued, although the question of hegemony over the Tupi research was no longer an issue: see, for example, Vidal (1977), Carneiro de Cunha (1978), Seeger (1981), Lopes da Silva (1986), among others. (For the ethnology of Xingu musicology see Seeger 1987, followed by Menezes Bastos 1999.)

This brief overview indicates that research has been consistently carried out in Brazilian territory. The specialists, however, do not consider they are studying "Brazilian Indians"; for them the relevant fact is that these indigenous groups are *situated* in Brazil as a matter of chance. There are, however, political and ideological implications deriving from this location – anthropologists are often called to participate in the demarcation of Indian lands, for instance. But even if the main motivation for research is not exoticism but rather the (social, cultural, cosmological) difference between social groups, this line of research best corresponds to the traditional concerns of anthropology. It follows that it is within this area of study that debates with the "international" community are most frequent (see the debate between Brazilian and French ethnologists in Viveiros de Castro 1993 and Copet-Rougier and Héritier-Augé 1993; see Viveiros de Castro 2003). The question thus remains: is *our* difference *others'* exoticism?

One more word in retrospect. Since it is considered the classic field of anthropology, specialists have access to a large body of literature on South American ethnology. It traces back to the German expeditions of the 19th century seeking answers in Brazil to European questions about the nature of primitive groups, and continues onward to recent generations, such as the works of Nimuendaju about the social organization of the Jê, or research in the 1930s about the Tupi (for example, the monographs by Herbert Baldus, Charles Wagley and Eduardo Galvão, as well as the works by Darcy and Berta Ribeiro about the Urubu-Kaapor, by Florestan Fernandes concerning Tupinambá social organization and Tupinambá war, and Egon Schaden on the Guarani (see references in Melatti 1984; Peirano 1999).

Then there is a second case of radical alterity. In this situation, otherness is basically geographical but not historically distant. In fact, though Brazilian anthropologists are increasingly breaking with the common practice of conducting fieldwork within the country's borders, an ideological bond to Brazil remains the rule. This happens in two ways: first, following Brazilians abroad, and second, looking at populations who were once colonial subjects of Portugal.

Let us see both. The first tendency leads us straight to the United States, which has acquired a social value of paradigmatic alterity for comparative purposes (see G. Velho 1995 for references of studies published from the 1950s to the 1990s; see also Wade, this volume). This practice builds upon the classic study about racial prejudice by Oracy Nogueira (1986), but also includes analyses of hierarchy and individualism by DaMatta (1973, 1980). Later developments are, for example, L. Cardoso de Oliveira (2002) and Kant de Lima (1995a, 1995b). A second direction leads us to Portugal's former colonies and to the ethnographic interest they inspire. Fry (e.g. 1991, 1999, 2005) compares colonial experiences in the matter of color and race in Brazil, the United States, Mozambique and Zimbabwe. Trajano Filho (1993, 1998) examines the national projects for a Creole society, with reference to Guiné-Bissau, and in a similar mode, but this time in the Cape Verde Islands, are Dias (2004) and Rego (2001). Thomaz (2002) examines the Portuguese "third empire," thus confirming the deep-rooted link to Portugal. Dialogues between Portuguese and Brazilian scholars can be found in Bastos, Almeida and Bianco (2002), G. Velho (1999), and *Etnográfica* (2000). Of course, there are exceptions to the rule concerning direct links to Brazil, and some authors have developed studies on other settings such as Argentina (G. Ribeiro 1991; Neiburg 1997), France (Fonseca 1986; Eckert 2003), and Syria (Pinto 2002).

A new trend may be detected in recent concerns about international and supranational affairs. Among these studies, Góes Filho (2003) looks at meetings of the General Assembly in the United Nations as rituals; Silva (2004) examines the role of the United Nations in East Timor state-building processes; Leite Lopes (2004) focuses on the proliferation of nuclear plants in small towns in Brazil and the issue of environmentalism.

## Contact with alterity

If radical alterity consisted of studies *about* indigenous groups, studies looking at relations *with* indigenous groups are of a different kind, which I call contact with alterity. Today, a considerable body of literature is beholden to indigenist concerns, long discussed separately from mainstream ethnological monographs in the 1940s. Contact itself became a legitimate academic topic during the following decades: after D. Ribeiro (1957, 1962) focused in on the issue of Indian integration, R. Cardoso de Oliveira (1978) adopted a perspective *from within* and crafted the notion of "interethnic friction."

Interethnic friction is considered a theoretical innovation by many. It appeared as part of a bricolage of indigenist concerns and sociological theory, revealing "a situation in which two groups are dialectically put together through their opposing interests" (R. Cardoso de Oliveira 1963:43). Interethnic friction was proposed in a context where the theories of contact, both British (Malinowski) and American (Redfield, Linton and Herskovitz), had proven inadequate. The combination of an anthropological subject and a sociological inspiration (Fernandes and the French sociologist Georges Balandier) resulted in a proposal which became fundamental in the consolidation of several M.A. and Ph.D. programs.

In the 1960s, when the notion of interethnic friction was proposed, a structuralist oriented project was also being developed in the same institutional space (Museu Nacional), curiously involving many of the same researchers (Laraia and DaMatta 1967; DaMatta 1976; Melatti 1967). The literature produced from these two projects focused, respectively, on interethnic contact from a sociological orientation, and on indigenous social systems in a structuralist mode.

In the late 1970s research about "contact" received a new impulse. Oliveira Filho (see 1998, 1999) expanded interethnic concerns by reshaping them to include historical dimensions. A group of researchers followed suit and unfolded this thematic approach by discussing relations between indigenists and government policies, the demarcation of Indian lands, the role of the military and frontiers, the notion of *territorialization* and the two-way process that derives from it, the examination of "mixed Indians" in the Brazilian northeast and Indian rights. Souza Lima (1995) refocuses some of these concerns by looking at research programs on "indigenism," described as a set of ideas related to the insertion of indigenous peoples into nation-state societies, and Souza Lima and Barroso-Hoffoman (2002) look at several dimensions inherent in the association between anthropology and the state regarding indigenous policies. They discuss the regulation of Indian rights in Brazil, confronting the paradox that social policies often create and maintain social inequalities despite their discourse to the contrary. One sensitive nerve touched by the probing of these issues is the national myth about an integrated society derived from the "mixture of three races" and the role of the state as mediator.

Parallel to this front, Baines (1991) looks at relations between indigenous groups and the National Indian Foundation. For further studies of indigenous legislation and the conditions of South American Indians, see Carneiro da Cunha (1993) and Santos (1989). After a canonical trajectory in ethnology, Alcida Ramos developed an increasing concern with indigenism, evaluating Yanomami ethnography in a context of crisis and examining the idea that indigenism is for Brazil what orientalism is for the "West" (Ramos 1995, 1998).

Here, I pause just to mention, without further elaboration, the anthropological study of peasants – a highly relevant field which deserves a study of its own (see Seligmann, this volume). I only indicate that during the 1970s the concern with contact incorporated the theme of expanding frontiers. This in turn made topics such as internal colonialism, peasants and the development of capitalism legitimate anthropological concerns (O. Velho 1972, 1976). At the same time, studies about peasants gained an independent thematic status, involving both anthropologists and sociologists (for the former see Palmeira 1977, Sigaud 1980, Moura 1988, Seyferth 1999, and the works of Klaas Woortmann (1990) and Ellen Woortmann (1995), among others). To the degree that alterity shifted its locus from Indian groups to contact with Indians, and then to peasants, the path was somehow completed with the inclusion of the peripheries of big cities (for instance, Leite Lopes 1976).

## Nearby alterity

Since the 1970s, anthropologists in Brazil have carried on research in large cities. Given that the teaching of anthropology is part of the social sciences curriculum, it is common for anthropology to become a counterpoint to sociology. Under the political authoritarianism of the 1960s, anthropology was seen by many as an alternative to (Marxist) challenges coming from sociology, in a more or less silent dialogue that has persisted ever since. The attraction to anthropology rested both on its qualitative approach and on the promise of answers to understand both the country's diversity and its unity.

In the case of nearby otherness, the object of study has generally been chosen in close association with specific theoretical options. In Brazil, theory is not just an approach, but a political statement. Thus, G. Velho pulled together, by way of a bricolage, the symbolic interactionism from the Chicago school of sociology, and 1960s British social anthropology (Clyde Mitchell, Raymond Firth, E. Bott) to open up the possibility for research on sensitive urban topics. Those included middle class lifestyles, cultural behaviors of what is called in Brazil "psychism" (psychoanalysis etc.), drug consumption, violence, and politics. See for example G. Velho (1981, 1994). In this context, Velho's pioneering fieldwork in urban anthropology in the early 1970s focused on a specific overpopulated building in the Rio de Janeiro neighborhood of Copacabana (G. Velho 1973).

Later, this line of research expanded into other areas, including poverty, the elderly, gender issues, prostitution, kinship and family, music and politics. A central goal of this comprehensive project as a whole has been to reveal some urban values of Brazilian society. In this sense, this research project not only situated phenomena in the city, but also sought to analyze, in the path opened by Simmel, conditions of sociability in metropolitan areas. The production of this thematic line is voluminous and broad-ranging. (See Peirano 1999 for references.) For violence in the city, the extensive work by Zaluar is essential (see Zaluar 1999 for a review article on violence and crime).

DaMatta (1973, 1980) found in structuralism a legitimate theoretical approach with which to begin his research about Carnival. The horizontality this perspective conferred to different societies allowed him to leap from his 1960s study on indigenous peoples to national society as a whole. Later on, he added Gilberto Freyre (a former student of Franz Boas) as a predecessor for the examination of a possible national ethos. DaMatta (1973) may be considered the transition point, with a canonical structuralist analysis placing side by side an Apinajé myth, a short story by Edgar Allan Poe and Carnival as *communitas*. This line of research was later expanded in order to examine "what makes brazil, Brazil" (DaMatta 1984).

In this expansion toward urban topics, the relevance of researching at home was never seriously questioned. There was a brief discussion about the nature of fieldwork in general in the 1970s, but the whole issue was solved by the 1980s.

In the period that begins in the 1960s, other topics have emerged, some related to the social integration of oppressed sectors of the society and, later on, to minorities' rights. Despite occasional rivalries between anthropology and sociology regarding the study in urban settings, both disciplines have had a long association, which can be attested in a large bibliography related to immigration, race relations, feminism and gender studies, messianism, Afro-Brazilian cults, crime, citizenship. To mention only a few examples, the review article on religion and Afro-Brazilian cults by Montero (1999) offers a basic bibliography (but see also Maggie 1975, 1992; Carvalho 1992; O. Velho 1995). Popular festivities are the subject of Magnani (1984), Chaves (2003), and Cavalcanti (1994), among others. The investigation of Brazil as a nation-state is exemplified in DaMatta (1980) and Oliven (1992). The subject of gender is exemplified in Grossi (2003) and Fonseca (2000); crime and citizenship in Caldeira (2000). For studies focused directly on politics from a native's perspective, see the more than 30 volumes of the Coleção Antropologia da Política (published by Relume Dumará, Rio de Janeiro), which puts together studies on several topics including, for instance, the National March of Landless Workers (Chaves 2000), honor among Congressmen (Teixeira 1998), the presence of the state in the everyday life of a shantytown (Borges 2004), political networks, favors and personal dependency in governmental spheres (Bezerra 1999), kinship, family and rural labor unions (Comerford 2003), and elections and political representation (Palmeira and Goldman 1996). Palmeira and Barreira (2005) puts together contributions by the project's principal researchers.

## Minimum alterity

As if to confirm that the social sciences in Brazil have a debt to Durkheim – for whom other forms of civilization should be looked at in order to explain what is near to us – since the 1980s anthropologists have launched a series of studies about themselves and their craft. For the most part, these studies aim at understanding science as a manifestation of modernity. Topics vary from the study of historical contexts for science and biographies of social scientists (mostly in Brazil) to inquiries about classical sociological authors. Some examples are studies examining the development of anthropology in museums and universities (Castro Faria 1993); the historiography of the discipline in the country (Corrêa 2003); intellectual biographies (such as one of Lévy-Bruhl, see Goldman 1994) and memories (Peixoto, Pontes and Schwarcz 2004); comparative projects concerning the social sciences in Brazil (Miceli 1999); the social sciences in São Paulo (Pontes 1998); comparisons between intellectual careers (such as Gilberto Freyre and Roger Bastide in Peixoto 2000; Gilberto Freyre and Sérgio Buarque de Holanda in Castro Santos 2003; Mario de Andrade in Brazil and Béla Bartok in Hungary in Travassos 1997); investigations on scientists and the race question in Brazil (Schwarcz 1996, 1999; Maio 1996); a bibliographical guide to the study of Brazilianists (Peixoto and Schwarcz 2002). The interest that Brazilian scholars generally manifest in educational issues is discussed in Bomeny (2001), and a comprehensive bibliography of anthropology in Brazil until the 1980s appears in Melatti (1984).

A broad-based research project dealing with different national styles of anthropology was inaugurated in R. Cardoso de Oliveira and Ruben (1995). Conceived as an inquiry into "peripheral" anthropologies, it is inspired by the work of philosopher G. Gaston Granger. Before that, in the late 1970s, I started a research project with the intention of analyzing the discipline from an anthropological perspective. Challenged by Dumont's proposal, in which he submits that anthropology is defined by a hierarchy of values in which universalism encompasses holism, I examined anthropology in Brazil, with France and Germany as control cases (Peirano 1981). This study was followed by a comparison between Brazil, India, and the United States, resulting in the proposal for an "anthropology in the plural" (Peirano 1992). The analysis of the relationship between social science and the national ideology was refined by Vilhena (1997), who examines the role of regional intellectuals in the 1950s and 1960s, and the struggle by folklorists to survive in an environment in which sociology was becoming hegemonic. A new project on the relationship between anthropological perspectives and state-building processes is presented in L'Estoile, Neiburg and Sigaud (2002). Psychoanalysis has also proved to be a fertile field of study for anthropology in Brazil. A dialogue within this field has developed into a solid research program; see Duarte (1986, 1996, 2000).

In sum: the studies in which alterity is found among social scientists generally focus on the Brazilian case, often with a comparative perspective in mind, but also on topics related to broad Western intellectual traditions. Since most of the publications are in Portuguese, the audience is limited. This scenario is enlarging with publications in English, but overall these are still a tiny minority. An important question thus arises concerning the audience for these studies. To what extent does it make sense to undertake comprehensive and exhaustive investigations if they have no immediate overseas audience? Or, put in another way, why enter into a dialogue with the sources of scholarship if the desired debates do not occur due to the very language of enunciation? It seems that the link with the wider intellectual world – by means of inquiries about the works of recognized scholars – is sought for its illocutionary effect at home, as it is considered essentially "theoretical." Accustomed to the exotic gaze of investigators from abroad, the idea of "minimum alterity" thus hides a proposal of "maximum (theoretical) alterity" that remains incomplete at heart, since no feedback is generally available.

## MULTIPLE INTERLOCUTORS

If the Brazilian example reinforces the idea that categories of alterity are contextual for anthropologists themselves, it is necessary to turn, by way of comparison, to the consecrated traditions in order to remember that they never were totally radical: Africa was relatively *home* for the British when they transferred the notion of totality to the Tallensi, the Azande and the Ndembu, thus renouncing sociology in favor of a flourishing anthropology. Up until the mid-1950s the discipline was limited to the metropolis, but social recognition of structuralism during the 1960s produced an unexpected by-product. If it is true that human practices are horizontal, it was possible to imagine both the emergence of "indigenous anthropologies" along with the endorsement that today, in the words of Clifford Geertz, "we are all natives."

The center's acceptance seems to have legitimated the many conferences held since then by, and/or for, "non-Western" specialists, but the matter remained controversial. One example is Kuper (1994), who criticizes "nativist" manifestations of anthropology using the case of Greece. Denying that only natives can have a proper understanding of their own society, and that natives are the best judges (even censors) of ethnography, this sensible viewpoint is followed by a not so thoughtful proposal for a "cosmopolitan anthropology" which would exclude not only curious foreigners, armchair voyeurs, but also the native community of specialists (social scientists, planners, intellectuals in general). Anthropology is a social science allied to sociology and history, and should not be linked to political programs – that is the conclusion.

In Brazil, the alliance between anthropology, sociology and history has been common practice, but the same does not hold for the exclusion of political viewpoints. Actually, in different guises, political agendas have always been part of scientific projects – in Brazil as elsewhere. In Brazil, efforts to achieve theoretical excellence rest on classical sociological authors, on critical dialogues with contemporary specialists (foreigners and local), and on the impact of new empirical evidence. In other words, in Brazil theoretical bricolage is the foundation for new intellectual lineages, with social responsibility being pervasive.

One specific feature, however, is relevant here: foreign interlocutors *from the metropolis* have been social scientists' fashionable preference. They have been chosen from several blends of Marxism since the 1960s, then Lévi-Strauss's structuralism, interpretativism in Clifford Geertz's style, and more recently, Foucault and Derrida's postmodernism. For those who take it for granted that the center is where theory is (and vice versa), parochialism is simply avoided by means of the immediacy of the empirical data. This may partially explain why there is not much ongoing exchange with peers from other Latin America countries (Mexico and Argentina are exceptions).

Since the basic triangular dialogues in Brazil are with local social scientists in general, with native subjects (generally conceived as socially oppressed), and with Western traditions of scholarship in the discipline (where legitimate theory is supposed to develop best), it would be necessary to make a new effort to include other Latin American traditions into this configuration.

## MULTIPLE ALTERITIES

The institutionalization of the social sciences as part of nation-building processes is a well-known phenomenon (see Peirano 1981), as is the paradox of the existence of a critical social science surviving the interests of the elite that created it. In these moments, the new social science is not specialized because the project of nation-building and state formation encompasses several academic disciplines. Alterity is rarely neutral and the interested aspects, in a Weberian sense, are in many cases explicit. Anthropology and sociology only break apart in a process which is at once political, institutional and conceptual. Specializations are often needed when the process of nation-state building demands separated areas of investigation, for instance on the conditions for development (sociology) and cultural diversity (anthropology).

During the 1930s in Brazil, the social sciences were adopted in order to provide a scientific approach to the project of a new nation. It was believed that social sciences would substitute for the socioliterary essay which (more than philosophy or human sciences) had performed the task of reflecting on social issues. Thus, from the 1930s to the 1950s, sociology was understood as encompassing all social sciences. But an emerging *"made-in-Brazil* sociology," which combined theoretical demands with political concerns, was to become hegemonic during the following decades (Fernandes 1958, 1963). Meanwhile, ethnological studies of indigenous groups represented the canonical model for anthropology, even though soon afterwards it adopted topics considered to be related to sociology. There was a fundamental disparity between sociology and anthropology, though: while problem-solving projects dominated sociology, the examination of social and/or cultural *difference* was the concern of anthropology. Difference, however, was to be found inside Brazil's own borders. Nowadays, even when anthropologists do venture out of the country, the quest for some sort of "Brazilianness" is unavoidable (as attested by the studies of former Portuguese colonies or Brazilian immigrants).

Social sciences from Brazil were never part of the circuits dominated by the centers of intellectual production. Curiously, though, we still consider ourselves as legitimate interlocutors of recognized authors of the Western tradition. It seems that the isolation of the Portuguese language has an affinity with the (local) political role reserved for the social scientist. This affinity, first of all, justifies alterity's ideal types and strategies, while on the other hand it spotlights a paradox: when we look for difference, we often find a supposed singularity (which is "Brazilian"). Apart from this puzzling aspect, however, the complex process of intellectual and political debates has over time contributed positively to the consolidation of an effective academic community. On that note, I conclude this essay by pointing to three aspects:

*In terms of exoticism*    For Brazilian anthropologists it has been difference, whether social or cultural, and not exoticism, that has provided the focus of attention when they look for alterity. This characteristic perhaps explains why, as opposed to the places where exoticism is threatening to destroy the discipline, or at least displace it, Brazilian anthropologists tend to share an optimistic perspective.

*In political terms*    Though the political dimension has always been present wherever social sciences develop, in Brazil it has been directed toward a specific type of ideal nation-state, in which differences should be respected and a (national) singularity sought out and revealed.

*In theoretical terms*    Conceived as part of the Western world but not speaking an international language, Brazil finds itself in a *sui generis* position, in which theoretical dimensions assume a critical role as the noble path to modernity. In Brazil, the political implications of social theory lead to a bricolage of specific objects of study and theoretical options. In recent years, the more successful attempts in the social sciences have come from the above-mentioned summation of previous and still valuable theoretical approaches and the empirical situations at hand. In this context, there is room for a variety of approaches. Room first of all for pure mimetism, produced from a belief that we are all part of a homogeneous world that does not exist. This situation leads to the acritical absorption of current foreign authors as a shortcut to the modern world. Second (as a variation on the first approach), there is room for a trivial practice whereby the data are ours but the theory is imported – the interlocution between empirical data and theory is abandoned, and data become the mere illustration of theory. There is a third, perhaps more rewarding option. It rests on the idea that anthropology (and the social sciences in general) develops better when expanding, redirecting and broadening previous questions, thus posing renewed problems and questions. In this case, anthropology defines itself as eternally surpassing itself – and in this sense partaking of the Weberian eternal youth ideal of the social sciences. This project does not deny political differences among intellectual communities, but rests on a sociological understanding of them. If it is correct to think that "a world culture of the times" develops by constant exchanges – out of the "centers" to the ideological peripheries *and vice versa* – then the implicit promise is for theoretical and empirical dialogues surpassing boundaries toward "plural universalisms" to take root. In this context, where one lives – in Brazil or elsewhere – is an important but not the only factor at play. Anthropology is one and many: while anthropology is practiced in Brazil, there is not of necessity a "Brazilian anthropology."

## REFERENCES

Baines, Stephen (1991) *É a funai que sabe*. Belém: Museu Emílio Goeldi.
Bastos, Cristiana, with Almeida, Miguel V., and Bianco, Bela (eds) (2002) *Trânsitos coloniais. Diálogos críticos luso-brasileiros*. Lisbon: Ed. Imprensa de Ciências Sociais.
Bezerra, Marcos Otávio (1999) *Em nome das bases. Política, favor e dependência pessoal*. Coleção Antropologia da Política. Rio de Janeiro: Relume Dumará.
Bomeny, Helena (2001) *Os intelectuais da educação*. Rio de Janeiro: J. Zahar.
Borges, Antonádia (2004) *Tempo de Brasília. Etnografando lugares-eventos da política*. Coleção Antropologia da Política. Rio de Janeiro: Relume Dumará.

Caldeira, Teresa (2000) *City of Walls: Crime, Segregation and Citizenship in São Paulo*. Berkeley: University of California Press.

Cardoso de Oliveira, Luís R. (2002) *Direito legal e insulto moral. Dilemas da cidadania no Brasil, Quebec e Estados Unidos*. Coleção Antropologia da Política. Rio de Janeiro: Relume Dumará.

Cardoso de Oliveira, Roberto (1963) Aculturação e "fricção" interétnica. *América Latina* 6:33–45.

Cardoso de Oliveira, Roberto (1978) *A sociologia do Brasil indígena*. Rio de Janeiro: Tempo Brasileiro.

Cardoso de Oliveira, R. and Ruben, Guillermo (eds) (1995) *Estilos de antropologia*. Campinas: Unicamp.

Carneiro da Cunha, Manuela (1978) *Os mortos e os outros*. São Paulo: Hucitec.

Carneiro da Cunha, Manuela (1993) *O futuro da questão indígena*. São Paulo: EdUSP.

Carvalho, José Jorge (1992) *Shango Cult in Recife, Brazil*. Caracas: Fundef.

Castro Faria, Luiz (1993) *Antropologia. Espetáculo e excelência*. Rio de Janeiro: UFRJ/Tempo Brasileiro.

Castro Santos, Luiz A. (2003) *O pensamento social no Brasil*. Campinas: Edicamp.

Cavalcanti, Maria Laura (1994) *Carnaval carioca. Dos bastidores ao desfile*. Rio de Janeiro: Editora da UFRJ/MinC/Funarte.

Chaves, Christine A. (2000) *A marcha nacional dos sem-terra*. Coleção Antropologia da Política. Rio de Janeiro: Relume Dumará.

Chaves, Christine A. (2003) *Festas de política. Uma etnografia da modernidade no Sertão (Buritis, MG)*. Coleção Antropologia da Política. Rio de Janeiro: Relume Dumará.

Comerford, John (2003) *Como uma família. Sociabilidade, territórios de parentesco e sindicalismo rural*. Coleção Antropologia da Política. Rio de Janeiro: Relume Dumará.

Copet-Rougier, E. and Héritier-Augé, F. (1993) Commentaires sur commentaire. Réponse à E. Viveiros de Castro. *L'Homme* 33:139–148.

Corrêa, Mariza (2003) *Antropólogas e antropologia*. Belo Horizonte: Editoral UFMG.

DaMatta, Roberto (1973) *Ensaios de antropologia estrutural*. Petrópolis: Vozes.

DaMatta, Roberto (1976) *Um mundo dividido. A estrutura social dos Índios Apinayé*. Petrópolis: Vozes.

DaMatta, Roberto (1980) *Carnavais, malandros e heróis*. Rio de Janeiro: Zahar.

DaMatta, Roberto (1984) *¿O que faz o Brasil, Brasil?* Rio de Janeiro: Guanabara.

Dias, Juliana B. (2004) Mornas e coladeiras de cabo verde. Versões musicais de uma nação. Doctoral dissertation, Universidade de Brasília.

Duarte, Luiz F. Dias (1986) *Da vida nervosa (nas classes trabalhadoras urbanas)*. Rio de Janeiro: J. Zahar/CNPq.

Duarte, Luiz F. Dias (1996) Distanciamento, reflexividade e interiorização da Pessoa no ocidente. *Mana* 2(2):163–176.

Duarte, Luiz F. Dias (2000) Dois regimes históricos das relações da antropologia com a psicanálise no Brasil. In Paulo Amarante (ed.), *Ensaios. Subjetividade, saúde mental, sociedade* (pp. 107–139). Rio de Janeiro: Editora Fiocruz.

Eckert, Cornelia (2003) *O tempo e a cidade*. Porto Alegre: IFCH/UFRGS.

*Etnográfica* (2000) *Antropologias brasileiras na viragem do milénio*. Theme issue of *Etnográfica* 4(2).

Fausto, Carlos (2001) *Inimigos fiéis. História, guerra e xamanismo na Amazónia*. São Paulo: EdUSP.

Fernandes, Florestan (1958) *O padrão de trabalho científico dos sociólogos brasileiros*. Estudos Sociais e Políticos, 3. Belo Horizonte: UFMG.

Fernandes, Florestan (1963) *A organização social dos Tupinambá*. São Paulo: Difusão Européia do Livro.

Fonseca, Claudia (1986) Clochards et dames de charité. Une étude de cas parisien. *Ethnologie Française* 16:391–400.

Fonseca, Claudia (2000) *Família, fofoca e honra. Etnografia de relações de gênero e violência em grupos populares*. Porto Alegre: Editora da Universidade.

Fry, Peter (1991) Politicamente correto em um lugar, incorreto em outro. *Estudos Afro-Asiáticos* 21:167–177.

Fry, Peter (1999) Color and the Rule of Law in Brazil. In J. E. Mendez, G. O'Donnel, and P. S. Pinheiro (eds), *The (Un)Rule of Law and the Underprivileged in Latin America* (pp. 186–210). Notre Dame: University of Notre Dame Press.

Fry, Peter (2005) *Racismo persistente. Brasil e África Austral*. Rio de Janeiro: Civilização Brasileira.

Gerholm, T. and Hannerz, U. (1982) Introduction. In *The Shaping of National Anthropologies*. Theme issue of *Ethnos* 42:5–35.

Góes Filho, Paulo (2003) *O clube das nações. A missão do Brasil na ONU e o mundo da diplomacia parlamentar*. Coleção Antropologia da Política. Rio de Janeiro: Relume Dumará.

Goldman, Marcio (1994) *Razão e diferença. Afetividade, racionalidade e relativismo no pensamento de Lévy-Bruhl*. Rio de Janeiro: Grypho.

Gonçalves, Marco Antonio (1993) *O significado do nome. Cosmologia e nominação entre os Piraha*. Rio de Janeiro: Sette Letras.

Grossi, Miriam (2003) Gênero e parentesco. Famílias gays e lésbicas no Brasil. *Cadernos Pagu* 21:261–280.

Kant de Lima, Roberto (1995a) Bureaucratic Rationality in Brazil and in the United States: Criminal Justice System in Comparative Perspective. In R. DaMatta and David Hess (eds), *The Brazilian Puzzle* (pp. 241–269). New York: Columbia University Press.

Kant de Lima, Roberto (1995b) Da inquirição ao júri, do *trial by jury* à *plea bargaining*. Full Professorship thesis. Universidade Federal Fluminense, Rio de Janeiro.

Kuper, Adam (1994) Culture, Identity and the Project of a Cosmopolitan Anthropology. *Man* (NS) 29:537–554.

Laraia, Roque de Barros (1964) Review of *A organização social dos Tupinambá*. *América Latina* 7(3):124–125.

Laraia, Roque de Barros (1986) *Tupi. Índios do Brasil Atual*. São Paulo: FFLCH/Universidade de São Paulo.

Laraia, Roque and DaMatta, R. (1967) *Índios e Castanheiros*. São Paulo: Difusão Européia do Livro.

Leite Lopes, José Sérgio (1976) *O vapor do diabo*. Rio de Janeiro: Paz e Terra.

Leite Lopes, José Sérgio (2004) *A ambientalização dos conflitos*. Coleção Antropologia da Política. Rio de Janeiro: Relume Dumará.

L'Estoile, Benoit, with Neiburg, Federico, and Sigaud, Lygia (2002) *Antropologia, impérios e estados nacionais*. Rio de Janeiro: Relume Dumará.

Lévi-Strauss, Claude (1952) Les Structures sociales dans le Brésil central et oriental. In Sol Tax (ed.), *Indian Tribes of Aboriginal America* (pp. 302–310). Chicago: University of Chicago Press.

Lopes da Silva, Aracy (1986) *Nomes e amigos. Da prática xavante a uma reflexão sobre os Jê*. São Paulo: FFLCH/Universidade de São Paulo.

Maggie, Yvonne (1975) *Guerra de Orixá. Um estudo de ritual e conflito*. Rio de Janeiro: Zahar.

Maggie, Yvonne (1992) *Medo do feitiço. Relações entre magia e poder no Brasil*. Rio de Janeiro: Arquivo Nacional.

Magnani, J. G. (1984) *Festa no pedaço. Cultura popular e lazer na cidade*. São Paulo: Brasiliense.

Maio, Marcos Chor (ed.) (1996) *Raça, ciência e sociedade*. Rio de Janeiro: Editora Fiocruz.

Maybury-Lewis, David (1967) *Akwë-Shavante Society*. Oxford: Oxford University Press.

Maybury-Lewis, David (1979) *Dialectical Societies: The Gê and Bororo of Central Brazil*. Cambridge, MA: Harvard University Press.

Melatti, Julio Cezar (1967) *Índios e criadores. Situação dos Krahó na área pastoril do Tocantins*. Rio de Janeiro: Instituto de Ciências Sociais.

Melatti, Julio Cezar (1970) O sistema social Krahó. Doctoral dissertation, Universidade de São Paulo.

Melatti, Julio Cezar (1984) A antropologia no Brasil. Um roteiro. *Boletim Informativo e Bibliográfico de Ciências Sociais – BIB* 17:3–52.

Menezes Bastos, Rafael (1999) *A musicológica Kamayurá. Para uma antropologia da comunicação no Alto-Xigu.* Florianópolis: Editora da UFSC.

Miceli, Sergio (ed.) (1999) *O que ler na ciência social brasileira (1970–1995).* 3 vols. São Paulo: Editora Sumaré.

Montero, Paula (1999) Religiões e dilemas da sociedade brasileira. In Sergio Miceli (ed.), *O que ler na ciência social brasileira (1970–1995),* vol. 1: *Antropologia* (pp. 327–367). São Paulo: Editora Sumaré.

Moura, Margarida M. (1988) *Os deserdados da terra. A lógica costumeira e judicial dos processos de expusão e invasão da terra camponesa (MG).* Rio de Janeiro: Bertrand Brasil.

Neiburg, Federico (1997) *Os intelectuais e a invenção do Peronismo.* São Paulo: EdUSP.

Nimuendaju, Curt (1946) *The Eastern Timbira.* Berkeley: University of California Press.

Nogueira, Oracy (1986) *Tanto preto quanto branco. Ensaios de relações raciais.* São Paulo: T. A. Queiroz.

Oliveira Filho, João Pacheco (1998) Uma etnologia dos "índios misturados"? Situação colonial, territorialização e fluxos culturais. *Mana* 4(1):47–78.

Oliveira Filho, João Pacheco (1999) *Ensaios em antropologia histórica.* Rio de Janeiro: Editora da UFRJ.

Oliven, Ruben (1992) *A parte e o todo. A diversidade cultural no Brasil-nação.* Petrópolis: Vozes.

Palmeira, Moacir (1977) Emprego e mudança sócio-econômica no nordeste. *Anuário Antropológico* 76:201–238.

Palmeira, Moacir and Barreira, César (eds) (2005) *Política no Brasil. Visões de antropólogos.* Coleção Antropologia da Política. Rio de Janeiro: Relume Dumará.

Palmeira, Moacir and Goldman, M. (eds) (1996) *Antropologia, voto e representação.* Rio de Janeiro: Contracapa.

Peirano, Mariza (1981) The Anthropology of Anthropology: The Brazilian Case. Ph.D. dissertation, Harvard University.

Peirano, Mariza (1992) *Uma antropologia no plural. Três experiências contemporâneas.* Brasília: Editora da UnB.

Peirano, Mariza (1998) When Anthropology Is at Home: The Different Contexts of a Single Discipline. *Annual Review of Anthropology* 27:105–128.

Peirano, Mariza (1999) Antropologia no Brasil (alteridade contextualizada). In Sergio Miceli (ed.), *O que ler na ciência social brasileira (1970–1995),* vol. 1: *Antropologia* (pp. 225–266). São Paulo: Editora Sumaré.

Peixoto, Fernanda (2000) *Freyre e bastide. Os dois lados da luneta.* São Paulo: Fundação Memorial da América Latina.

Peixoto, Fernanda and Schwarcz, Lilia (eds) (2002) *Guia bibliográfico dos Brasilianistas.* São Paulo: Sumaré.

Peixoto, Fernanda, with Pontes, Heloisa, and Schwarcz, Lilia (eds) (2004) *Antropologias, histórias, experiências.* Belo Horizonte: Editora UFMG.

Pinto, Paulo Hilu (2002) Mystical Bodies: Ritual, Experience and the Embodiment of Suffism in Syria. Ph.D. dissertation, Boston University.

Pontes, Heloísa (1998) *Destinos mistos. Os críticos do grupo clima em São Paulo, 1940–1968.* São Paulo: Companhia das Letras.

Ramos, Alcida (1995) *Sanumá Memories: Yanomami Ethnography in Times of Crisis.* Madison: University of Wisconsin Press.

Ramos, Alcida (1998) *Indigenism: Ethnic Politics in Brazil.* Madison: University of Wisconsin Press.

Rego, Maria S. (2001) Re-inventing Cape Verde. Ph.D. dissertation, University of California, San Diego.

Ribeiro, Darcy (1957) Culturas e línguas indígenas do Brasil. *Educação e Ciências Sociais* 2:5–100.

Ribeiro, Darcy (1962) *A política indigenista brasileira.* Rio de Janeiro: Ministério da Agricultura.

Ribeiro, Gustavo (1991) *Empresas transnacionais. Um grande projeto por dentro.* São Paulo: Marco Zero/Anpocs.

Santos, Silvio C. (1989) *Os povos indígenas e a constituinte.* Florianópolis: Editora da UFSC.

Schwarcz, Lilia (1996) *O espetáculo das raças. Cientistas, instituições e questão racial no Brasil.* São Paulo: Companhia das Letras.

Schwarcz, Lilia (1999) Questão racial e etnicidade. In Sergio Miceli (ed.), *O que ler na ciência social brasileira (1970–1995)*, vol. 1: *Antropologia* (pp. 267–327). São Paulo: Editora Sumaré.

Seeger, Anthony (1981) *Nature and Society in Central Brazil.* Cambridge, MA: Harvard University Press.

Seeger, Anthony (1987) *Why Suyá Sing: A Musical Anthropology of an Amazonian People.* Cambridge: Cambridge University Press.

Seyferth, Giralda (1999) Etnografia de um sistema lógico. A lavoura camponesa dos Sitiantes de Sergipe. *Anuário Antropológico 97.*

Sigaud, Lygia (1980) A nação dos homens. *Anuário Antropológico* 78:13–114.

Silva, Kelly Cristiane (2004) Paradoxos da autodeterminação. A ONU e o processo de state-formation em Timor Leste. Doctoral dissertation, Universidade de Brasília.

Souza Lima, Antonio Carlos (1995) *Um grande cerco de paz.* Petrópolis: Vozes.

Souza Lima, A. C. and Barroso-Hoffoman, Maria (eds) (2002) *Além da tutela. Bases para uma nova política indigenista.* 3 vols. Rio de Janeiro: Contracapa.

Teixeira, Carla Costa (1998) *A honra da política. Decoro parlamentar e cassação de mandato no Congresso Nacional 1949–1994.* Coleção Antropologia da Política. Rio de Janeiro: Relume Dumará.

Teixeira Pinto, Marnio (1997) *Ieipari. Sacrifício e vida social entre os Índios Arara (Caribe).* São Paulo: Hucitec.

Thomaz, Omar R. (2002) *Ecos do Atlântico Sul. Representações sobre o terceiro império português.* Rio de Janeiro: Editora da URFJ.

Trajano Filho, Wilson (1993) A tensão entre a escrita e a oralidade na Guiné-Bissau. *Soronda* 16.

Trajano Filho, Wilson (1998) Polymorphic Creoledom: The "Creole Society" of Guinea-Bissau. Ph.D. dissertation, University of Pennsylvania.

Travassos, Elizabeth (1997) *Os mandarins milagrosos. Arte e etnografia em Mário de Andrade e Béla Bartók.* Rio de Janeiro: J. Zahar.

Velho, Gilberto (1973) *A utopia urbana. Um estudo de antropologia social.* Rio de Janeiro: J. Zahar.

Velho, Gilberto (1981) *Individualismo e cultura.* Rio de Janeiro: Zahar.

Velho, Gilberto (1994) *Projeto e metamorfose. Antropologia das sociedades complexas.* Rio de Janeiro: J. Zahar.

Velho, G. (ed.) (1995) *Quatro viagens. Antropólogos brasileiros no exterior.* Comunicações do PPGAS, 6. Rio de Janeiro: Museu Nacional/UFRJ.

Velho, G. (1999) *Antropologia urbana. Cultura e sociedade no Brasil e em Portugal.* Rio de Janeiro: J. Zahar.

Velho, Otávio (1972) *Frentes de expansão e estrutura agrária.* Rio de Janeiro: Zahar.

Velho, Otávio (1976) *Capitalismo autoritário e campesinato.* São Paulo: Difel.

Velho, Otávio (1995) *Besta-Fera. Recriação do mundo.* Rio de Janeiro: Relume Dumará.

Vidal, Lux (1977) *Morte e vida de uma sociedade indígena brasileira. Os Kayapo-Xikrin do Rio Catete.* São Paulo: Hucitec.

Vilhena, Luís Rodolfo (1997) *Projeto e missão. O movimento folclórico brasileiro (1947–1964)*. Rio de Janeiro: Funarte/Fundação Getúlio Vargas.

Villaça, A. (1992) *Comendo como gente. Formas do canibalismo Wari*. Rio de Janeiro: Editora da UFRJ.

Viveiros de Castro, Eduardo (1992) *From the Enemy's Point of View: Humanity and Divinity in an Amazonian Society*. Chicago: University of Chicago Press.

Viveiros de Castro, Eduardo (1993) Structures, régimes, stratégies. *L'Homme* 133:117–137.

Viveiros de Castro, Eduardo (ed.) (1995) *Antropologia do parentesco. Estudos Ameríndios*. Rio de Janeiro: Editora da UFRJ.

Viveiros de Castro, Eduardo (1998) Dravidian and Related Kinship Systems. In T. Trautmann, with M. Godelier and F. Tjon Sie Fat (eds), *Transformations of Kinship* (pp. 332–385). Washington, DC: Smithsonian Institution.

Viveiros de Castro, Eduardo (2003) *And*. Manchester Papers in Social Anthropology, 7. University of Manchester, Manchester.

Woortmann, Ellen (1995) *Herdeiros, parentes e compadres*. São Paulo: Hucitec.

Woortmann, Klaas (1990) Com parente não se neguceia. O campesinato como ordem moral. *Anuário Antropológico* 87:11–76.

Zaluar, Alba (1999) Violência e crime. In Sergio Miceli (ed.), *O que ler na ciência social brasileira (1970–1995)*, vol. 1: *Antropologia* (pp. 13–107). São Paulo: Editora Sumaré.

CHAPTER 4

# Colombia: Citizens and Anthropologists

## Myriam Jimeno

In this paper I propose to outline some of the debates and positions that have shaped anthropology in Colombia since it was established as a disciplinary and professional field in the mid-1940s. Although archaeology, linguistics or biological anthropology might also be interesting perspectives from which to approach this subject, my intention here is to focus on sociocultural anthropology. I will argue that the evolution of anthropology can be understood in terms of the tension between the global orientations of the discipline (concerning dominant narratives and practices, theories, fieldwork, relations between subjects of study) and the way they are put into practice within the Colombian context. In the anthropological practice of countries like Colombia there is a constant uneasiness about either adopting the dominant anthropological concepts and orientations, or else modifying, adjusting or rejecting them and proposing alternatives. This need to adapt the practice stems from the specific social condition of anthropologists in these countries, that is, our dual position as both researchers and fellow citizens of our subjects of study, as a result of which we are continually torn between our duty as scientists and our role as citizens.

From this perspective, there is a danger of falling into a nationalistic interpretation of the history of anthropology in Colombia. As Claudio Lomnitz (1999) ironically comments, such is the case of Mexican anthropology, which has gradually represented itself as a family tree rooted in its own precolumbian and precolonial tradition. I am, however, more concerned with the practice of anthropologists in Colombia, since, as in other countries in similar situations, this practice has been continuously upset by discussions on the place of cultural differences within the hierarchy of power in our society; on the relationships of subjection and exclusion that afflict certain sectors; on the basis of their ethnicity, class or gender; or on the dilemmas posed by so-called "development." The questions raised have frequently come from outside of the discipline itself, from social organizations or movements, or as a result of situations of violence and internal conflict. This has meant that the certainties of a practice oriented toward academic knowledge have been shaken by questions about the social repercussions of our interpretations and images on the populations being studied. Moreover, we are plagued by an interminable controversy regarding the social and political significance of intellectuals in our society. This controversy expressed itself as a rift between the generation commonly referred to as "pioneers" and the one that suddenly emerged in the university system at the beginning of the 1970s (Arocha and Friedemann 1984; Jimeno 1984, 1999; Barragán 2001, 2005; Caviedes 2004). But, rather like a weed that is impossible to eradicate, the controversy has sprung up again today, phrased in a new language that expresses the confrontation between new subjects and new preoccupations. In other words, from its very beginnings, Colombian anthropology has had to face a long and persistent social preoccupation, which has not been without its share of ambiguities or contradictions, and which is part of the aforementioned dual position of anthropologists. This instantiates a dialogue (sometimes a shouting match without communication) between the anthropologist and the struggles of different social sectors around projects of national construction. It reflects certain anthropological emphases that vary over time, and even conflict, but share an anchoring in a questioning, now and then, about the requirements of democracy for national reconstruction, about the place of those we study – since they tend to be the most underprivileged in society – and about their relationship with what we call the state.

It is possible to point out some dominant trends and a number of breaks that appear to me to have been significant during the six decades of anthropology in Colombia. These can be grouped together into three broad tendencies which are not consecutive, but rather have coexisted and overlapped since the establishment of anthropology as an academic discipline. They also act as cut-off points, since each has characterized a particular period. The first tendency has to do with the predominance of a descriptive approach, especially with the intention of carrying out a detailed inventory of Amerindian societies from the settlement and development of prehispanic societies, to aspects of physical anthropology, linguistics and the social organization of existing indigenous societies within the limits of the national territory.

The second is particularly concerned with the place of social inequality and cultural difference within the nation-state, with the representations that nourish them, and with the relations of subjection in the local and national context. This tendency, as we shall see, adopted two opposing positions. One supported integration into national society and was particularly prevalent from the 1950s to the 1970s, though it is still present in "development" positions that during those years employed concepts such as assimilation and cultural integration. The other position also arose in the 1970s, in opposition to the first, since it confronted the suppositions of national integration in terms of its cultural homogeneity and racial supremacy. This particular stance was encouraged by the emergence of social movements seeking recognition of the rights of ethnic and peasant populations and by the ideological influence of Marxism, which was particularly strong during that period (Jimeno and Triana 1985; Jimeno 1996). The emphasis was a militant anthropology and largely apocryphal, as Mauricio Caviedes (2004) calls it, for its habit of debating, participating a lot and writing very little. At its height between the 1970s and 1980s, this approach sought to transform the symbolic markers of national identity and refute the orientation grounded in the ideology of one language, one religion and one nation. Its aim was to accompany the new ethnic movements in the creation of a "counternarrative," an alternative version of events, with which to challenge the cultural hegemony that ostracized the indigenous communities and other social sectors, regarding them as sources of the country's backwardness.

The third tendency is a marked growth in anthropology that coincides with the consolidation of anthropology in universities, postgraduate studies and research centers such as the Colombian Institute of Anthropology and History. Although there are no exact figures on the number of anthropology degrees and students nationwide, the National University alone has produced over 1,000 anthropology graduates and Colombia today is home to around 3,000 professional anthropologists. This has brought about divisions in an academic community with very diverse interests and approaches, ranging from global processes and ecology to the most varied social subjects. At the same time, there is a large number of professionals, many more than there are academics, whose job it is to apply their knowledge in a vast array of public and private institutions. Nonetheless, there is a good deal of interchange between the application of knowledge and academic life, since the division between the two is relative and very often temporary. Many anthropologists, as well as sociologists – Orlando Fals Borda being a prime example – retain an interest in the practical and political implications of their studies, to the extent that they usually participate in debates and involve themselves in proposals on public policies. A recent example is their participation, in 1991, in the process of constitutional reform and development, with regard to the recognition of cultural and ethnic rights.

## Anthropologists and Citizenship

Veena Das (1998) suggests that anthropological knowledge is constructed on the basis of maps of otherness made up of theories of the Other rather than theories of the self. It is for this very reason that the sociopolitical proximity between anthropologists and their subjects of study in Latin America has resulted in a very particular anthropological output (Ramos 1999–2000, 2004). The construction of anthropological knowledge, as well as the entire anthropological practice, is carried out in conditions in which the Other is an essential and problematic part of the self. This shapes the anthropologist's relationship to his or her own work, since a good proportion of anthropologists do not regard their subjects of study as being exotic worlds that are isolated, distant and cold, but instead consider them to be coparticipants, with a voice of their own, in the construction of the nation and its democracy.

Thus, the overall tone of anthropological practice in Colombia is precisely that of the indistinct boundary between the practice of anthropology as a discipline and social action taken as citizens. This is why it is not a question of establishing or initiating critical thinking in relation to what could be seen as mere self-indulgence. Rather, it is important to remember that in countries such as ours, social thinking has been repeatedly shaken by intellectual polemics. These are contradictory ways of understanding the concepts of State and democracy, which are given concrete form in institutions, legislation and opportunities in life for certain sectors of society. Contact with the Other has made it possible to criticize anthropological approaches such as "inflexible holism," as Veena Das (1998) calls it, which has been left behind by experimentation on ethnographical representations and by the reconceptualization of certain categories commonly used in anthropology. Das demonstrates that in India it was precisely the emergence of new communities, as political communities, which led to the discussion and creation of new anthropological categories, given the confrontation between the diverse sectors that make up this abstract concept of community. In short, by trying to understand new social actors that come into play on the same social stage as itself, and by reclaiming their particular narratives, the anthropology carried out in these countries reconsiders overgeneralizing rhetoric, reformulates analytical categories, and recuperates variations of gender, class, history and place. It does not settle for being the object of thought; instead it declares itself to be an instrument of thought (Das 1998:30–34).

I have named myself the citizen researcher (Jimeno 2000) in order to highlight the close relationship that exists between exercising one's profession as a researcher and exercising one's rights as a citizen. Krotz (1997) has underlined the fact that, for what he terms "southern anthropologies," the Other, the Others, are at the same time both fellow citizens and research subjects. The fact that we are fellow citizens of the subjects of our research pervades the practice of anthropology in countries like ours, making it more like the practice of politics, as a kind of *natiocentrism*. Every characterization has repercussions on the everyday lives of the people and on the practical significance of exercising citizenship. Hence the statement by Alcida Ramos that "in Brazil, like in other countries of Latin America, practicing anthropology is a political act" (Ramos 1999–2000:172). Roberto Cardoso de Oliveira (1995, 1998) also had this in mind when he put forward the concept of *style* to characterize Latin American anthropology (for a discussion on this topic see Jimeno 1999, 2000; Krotz 1996; Uribe 1997). Esteban Krotz (1997) criticizes the diffusionist anthropological model based on images of "extension" or "adaptation" for its failure to recognize that the production of scientific knowledge is a process of cultural creation, just like any other, and cannot be analyzed merely as symbolic systems that are separate from other aspects of a more comprehensive social reality.

Thus, the structure of the nation-state pervades the emergence and development of anthropology and provides the backdrop for the dialogue taking place between anthropologists and the Others. This is why I believe that, of all the social concepts proposed by Norbert Elias (1989), the idea of *natiocentrism* is a particularly useful one. I would like to expand this concept in order to emphasize the diversity of meanings and interests that are brought into play when anthropologists ask themselves about the relationship between their work and their responses to questions about who participates, how and in what circumstances, in what nation, in what state. There is still much to be said regarding the answers to these questions, and they continue to pervade the theoretical output and indeed the entire work of intellectuals. With the idea of *natiocentrism* Norbert Elias seeks to underline the relationship between concepts and the social conditions in which they are created and employed, with specific reference to the intellectual orientation centered on the concept of "nation." Elias demonstrates how this *natiocentrism* is found throughout much of the output of the social sciences. To illustrate this point, he offers the example of the concepts of civilization and culture, which *natiocentrism* first gives rise to and then transforms, as the societies and social strata in which they originate are themselves gradually transformed (Elias 1989). The concepts therefore go through a dual process of "nationalization," being adopted by the both nation and the state. Other concepts that allude to social units, such as that of society, also take on this nationalized quality, in the sense that they are adapted to the project of national construction through ideas of equilibrium, unity, and homogeneity, and with the intention of presenting them to the world as stabilized and divided into clearly defined units (Elias 1989; Neiburg 1998; Fletcher 1997).

As numerous authors have already pointed out (Fletcher 1997), Elias's observations are fundamentally critical of *natiocentrism* as an intellectual current that is connected to the rise of the European nation-state. However, his theories can be applied to our own historical situation, if we emphasize the fact that here there is no conceptual homogeneity regarding the constitution of the nation, nationality and the nation-state. On the contrary, some analysts have suggested that the violent confrontation that has been affecting Colombia for the past two decades, as well as the one it lived through in the middle of the last century, can be understood as a struggle between opposing demands on the state, in which the competition between opposing sides plays a role in the spread of violence (Roldán 2003). In the view of Daniel Pécaut (1987), for the past half a century the intensification of partisan rivalry for state control has contributed to the increasingly widespread use of violence, which has never entirely been a state monopoly. The recent confrontation in Colombia, which escalated from the mid-1980s on, has again involved a confrontation between very heterogeneous forces, in dispute over the precise nature of the formation of the state. But leaving aside the fact that the opponents in this struggle are armed, their conflicting viewpoints and perspectives are formed within an arena of debate in which Colombian intellectuals also participate.

Now let us look at the three main tendencies spanning the practice of anthropology in Colombia.

## THE EARLY DEBATES

An early tendency in Colombian anthropology was marked by an inclination that is common in Boasian anthropology, namely that of practicing a generalizing ethnography on the existing native groups of the country and considering them as being in danger of extinction or cultural decline. However, there was already a tendency among the pioneers of this current to blend universal theories and models, or to apply them in a fairly unorthodox fashion, which is a tendency that persists to this day. Anthropology was established as a professional discipline in Colombia at the beginning of the 1940s, thanks to the efforts of Gregorio Hernández de Alba and the French ethnologist Paul Rivet. The latter found refuge from the war in Europe in Colombia, and in 1941 set up the National Institute of Ethnology. The first generation of professional anthropologists was made up of a handful of young graduates, some of whom had come from other disciplines. Among them they combined an exclusive interest in ethnography with Rivet's interest in the origin of American settlement and the diffusion of cultural traits, all of which meant research in archaeology, ethnohistory and physical anthropology, in search of enduring sociocultural sequences. This early generation played a fundamental role in the organization of anthropology courses at Colombian universities from the 1960s onwards. The same can be said of the Colombian Institute of Anthropology of 1952, a state research center which absorbed the former ethnological one and began to dedicate itself to research in the four fields of anthropology, and to the preservation of archaeological heritage (Barragán 2001, 2005). Thus, this first handful of anthropologists (there would be fewer than 50 in the following two decades) practiced their profession in the context of public research institutions. The social sciences, particularly sociology and history, were only just starting up in a limited number of university centers.

What were the preoccupations of this early generation of anthropologists? The first issue of the *Revista Colombiana de Antropología* (Colombian Anthropology Review), an institute publication, came out 50 years ago in certain rural areas. At the time, Colombia was immersed in a violent confrontation in a number of rural areas, which took the form of a partisan struggle. It was the height of cold war suspicions and the fear of communism was rife. It is said that during this period, the partisan affiliations of those who worked at the Institute determined whether or not their work received support, and even whether they were to continue to be employed there. In this first issue of the Review articles appeared on the following subjects: "contacts and cultural exchange in the Sierra Nevada of Santa Marta" by Gerardo Reichel Dolmatoff, "La Guajira, a region, a culture of Colombia" by Milcíades Chaves, "the social and economic aspects of coffee growing in Antioquia" by Ernesto Guhl, and "food distribution in a transitional society" by Alicia Dussán. There were also contributions by Segundo Bernal on mythology and folk tales from a Paez community, Federico Medem on the taxonomy of the alligator, and Nils Holmer and Jean Caudmont on the linguistics of two indigenous groups. Not a word then was said about the violent confrontation taking place in a large area of rural Colombia. But on the other hand, the government was already experimenting with a type of applied anthropology in what were called programs of rural social security, which sought to resolve the problem of the rural violence.

Others might note, as Marco Martínez (2004) has done, the conspicuous absence of any theoretical discussion, or explicit reference to a question or to a methodology employed in the work. Their writings appear to assume that reality is in front of our very eyes, ready to be revealed by the expert. In archaeology, the focus was on establishing cultural areas across the Colombian territory and elaborating chronological sequences. We might say, then, that the focus of these works was on "local worlds" and the "objective" description of closed cultures. However, this emphasis was qualified by the preoccupation that is apparent in almost all of the texts, and is particularly explicit in those of Alicia Dussán and Gerardo Reichel, with "contact" and "cultural exchange" and with the effects of "acculturation," particularly where they perceived a "cultural loss." It was also qualified by the appearance of applied anthropology projects in certain communities, or on matters such as urban housing. Which is to say that the anthropologists were not unaware of the fact that these local worlds existed in relation to a history and a regional context that were imposed on them and that in general placed them at the bottom of the social hierarchy, or that they were facing pressing new social conditions and necessities. What they did was limit themselves to context of the Colombian national territory.

In this first issue of the Review it is also apparent that the anthropologists drew conclusions from their studies with the aim of modifying the deeply rooted prejudices that provided the ideological justification for the subordination of indigenous societies. For example, Milcíades Chaves begins the piece on the Guajira, a peninsula in the north of Colombia, with the subtitle "Colombia, a tropical country," and after examining the influence of the climate on man, he takes the opportunity to say that, behind many theories on geographical influence, there are hidden racist theories that ignore man's adaptation to his environment. He emphasizes the fact that the region should be considered "as a culture of Colombia," when in ordinary language this term was only applied to esthetic and refined representations, and the indigenous peoples were commonly referred to as "savage tribes" and "barbarians." Chaves finishes by arguing that the "guajiros [are an example of] astonishing adaptation."

Nowadays we might argue that the anthropological representation of the ecological Indian, to which the native peoples stake their claim, is largely an anthropological "invention" (Orrantia 2002). Nonetheless, although this praise for cultural adaptation might now seem naive to us, there is no doubt about how strange Chaves's words must have sounded in a society where racism toward Indians and Afro-Colombians was prevalent. This was not just intellectual pie in the sky; as is often the case with ethnographic representations (Ramos 2004), there were implications for the way in which Amerindian societies were perceived in Colombia. There is no denying that the results of a change in the public image of the indigenous peoples would take several more decades to become apparent, and would require prolonged and repeated work on the value of cultural diversity. It would also be necessary for the ethnic reaffirmation movements and ethnographic representation to come together. Nonetheless, it was the first step toward seeking an improved position for these societies.

In this first issue of the *Revista Colombiana de Antropología* in 1953, it is also apparent that the anthropological emphasis on indigenous societies soon went beyond a mere interest in these societies as exotic objects. But equally obvious are the tensions between the various approaches to the subject of these indigenous societies. The Review was announced as the "modern and more scientific" replacement for the *Revista del Instituto Etnológico Nacional* (National Ethnographical Institute Review) and the *Boletín de Arqueología* (Archaeological Bulletin), publications belonging to the former National Ethnological Institute. Under legal guidance, the management of the Institute announced the establishment of the following sections: Archaeology, Physical Anthropology, Ethnography, Social Anthropology, Linguistics, and Folk Studies, emphasizing that in the near future there would be

> a very particular section devoted to the Protection of the Indian, which will study the specific problems of each community, in order to suggest to the government measures that might rescue the indigenous peoples from their precarious condition, thereby incorporating them into the national identity, since with 10 percent of pure Indians, 40 percent of mestizos of Caucasian descent and 30 percent of mestizos of Afro-Colombian descent, Colombia urgently needs the solutions that anthropology can offer it in this respect. (Andrade 1953:13)

Before announcing the opening of a three-year course for training anthropologists, the Institute's director, Andrade, declared that anthropology could not escape from the problems facing the nation, or avoid offering an answer to the question of what it meant to be American. Andrade himself, however, was responsible for failing to start up the aforementioned section, for fear that its research would "become politicized." Thus, the idea that anthropologists might act as mediators between the state and the indigenous peoples turned out to be problematic in itself, since it raised the question of whether it was possible to sustain the dichotomy between objectivity and commitment to the populations being studied.

Many of these anthropologists included in their bibliographies the likes of Melville Herzkovits, Ralph Linton, Abraham Kardiner, Margaret Mead, and also Malinowski. But they didn't neglect to study in detail the chroniclers of the Indies, as well as regional histories and monographs. A certain posture of innocent discoverers was challenged by a dual requirement: on the one hand, to put new names on the Columbian map; and on the other, to respond to the place that these populations would occupy in the nation as a whole, defining itself as a nation still in formation. Thus, they clearly demonstrated their desire to participate in the very formation of Colombian nationality, in a role similar to that of the cartographies, museums and censuses described by Benedict Anderson (1983).

There was no unanimity among this early generation regarding how they should resolve the problematic relationship between knowledge and political position, nor was there agreement as to how far their concrete proposals on social questions should go. In the fourth issue of the Review, Virginia Gutiérrez de Pineda (1955) relates how during an "expedition" to la Guajira she was struck by the high infant mortality rate among the indigenous community then known as "guajiros." She then goes on to look at the high infant mortality in Colombia and immediately suggests that if cultural models of child rearing and nutrition were reconsidered, Colombia could reduce this high rate. Virginia was only just beginning her career, but the question of how to translate anthropological knowledge into public policies on health and the family, in accordance with the cultural particularities of each Colombian region, was one she would spend her life addressing. An important part of her work as an anthropology professor was giving classes in the faculty of medicine of the National University.

Other colleagues adopted more radical positions, inspired by the ideas of the Peruvian José Carlos Mariátegui, among others. According to this viewpoint, the problem of the indigenous peoples, the agrarian problem and the national problem were all one (Mariátegui and Sánchez 1987). Roberto Pineda Giraldo, another of the pioneers, recently recounted (Caviedes 2004; Barragán 2005) how two contrasting tendencies soon appeared among the first generation of anthropologists. One favored "objective" knowledge of "in vitro" societies in danger of extinction, while the other, which was termed *indigenista*, backed the political claims of the Indians. Despite the fact that the two tendencies coexisted within the Ethnological Institute from 1940 to 1952, they separated their production; while the purely ethnographical texts were published in the National Ethnological Institute Review, the articles on the social situation of the indigenous peoples came out in the Archaeological Bulletin.

By the 1960s and 1970s, this difference had taken another form. Although some remained distrustful of official policy and continued to denounce the situation of indigenous communities, others jumped on the bandwagon of the "development" current within the Colombian state apparatus. They even laid the foundations for an official policy designed to assimilate the indigenous communities into the stream of Colombian national identity, largely influenced by Mexican indigenismo. During this period, the development argument permeated the Colombian state and made use of a new crop of scientists and technicians, who set out to "plan" social intervention in their capacity as participants in the public administration (Jimeno 1984). It was at this time that the two principal mechanisms employed by the development camp were consolidated: professionalization and institutionalization (Escobar 1996).

As far as professionalization was concerned, this was the time when the first three university programs in anthropology were opened up (undergraduate to begin with), replacing the training given by the Colombian Institute of Anthropology. As was the case in other areas, like sociology, the organization of the programs largely followed North American university models and their creators were distinguished members of the first generation of anthropologists, namely Gerardo and Alicia Reichel-Dolmatof, Luis Duque Gómez and Graciliano Arcila. The aim was to train both scientists and professionals in the four fields of anthropology. By the mid-1970s the number of graduates was increasing throughout the country and they were rapidly being incorporated into various official agencies. There was also, however, rapid expansion of a student movement within the universities, particularly the public ones, encouraged by the Cuban Revolution of 1959, by anticolonial and "third world" social protest movements, and by the student movements that had emerged in the late 1960s throughout the first world. It was thought at that time that Latin America could be home to a utopia of social equality. The anthropology students of the late 1960s joined the movement with enthusiasm and included in their questioning of the social order the interrogation of anthropology as a colonial product, and of their professors as docile followers of such orientations (Caviedes 2004; Jimeno 1999). This questioning soon led to intergenerational conflict, resulting in the early dismissal of several of the first anthropologists from university classrooms, where they were replaced by young radicals heavily influenced by Marxism and critical dependency theory, who tried to reorient training along these lines.

The second mechanism employed by development ideology was institutionalization. We have already mentioned that some of the pioneers of anthropology actively supported new state "development" institutions, including those concerned with land reform and indigenismo. Some of them maintained that the role of anthropologists would be to plan cultural changes, in order for development and technological improvements in agriculture to make room for the integration of peasant and indigenous populations into the social structure of the nation (Jimeno and Triana 1985). Here they were implicitly following the Andean regional model, which consisted of civilizing the periphery. The anthropologist Gregorio Hernández de Alba was the inspiration for the new official agency, the Division of Indigenous Affairs, the aim of which, according to his own definition, was "social improvement and the effective incorporation into active life and national progress of territories and inhabitants that could be classified as marginal" (quoted in Jimeno and Triana 1985:82). From as early as 1940, the concept of *national integration* had been at the very core of indigenismo, which was spread throughout Latin America by Manuel Gamio. This indigenismo affected the formulation of Colombian policies toward the indigenous societies in the early 1960s (Jimeno and Triana 1985). The anthropologists of the time saw themselves as bureaucratic agents assigned to assimilate the indigenous peoples, who were considered to be marginalized individuals who needed to be put on the path to progress. Hernández de Alba believed that a more modern and efficient kind of action on behalf of the state might reduce the enormous influence the Catholic Church had maintained over the indigenous populations since the 19th century, on the explicit orders of the Colombian state itself (Jimeno and Triana 1985).

The first article of the decree proclaiming the creation of the new agency stated that its function would be "to study stable indigenous societies, as a basis for the facilitation of any cultural, social and economic changes that might be advisable, with a view to encouraging the progress of these societies" (quoted in Jimeno and Triana 1985:82). This directive included highly concrete forms of action with respect to indigenous populations, and in particular their lands. As is still the case today, the indigenous societies were scattered throughout the peripheral regions of Colombia, in groups of low population density with pronounced cultural differences. Some retained legal protection of their lands, dating back to Spanish colonial legislation, which they had secured through legal and political battles against various expropriation attempts since the declaration of the Republic in the 19th century. The policy of development considered collective territorial rights to be a transitional stage on the way to individual ownership, much as the liberal ideology had done in the 19th century. Thus, in 1962, the Land Reform Institute was given the task of breaking up communal lands. It also, however, opened up the possibility of allocating lands beyond the economic border. This small crack introduced the movement for defense and expansion of indigenous lands, which would achieve a great deal in the following decade.

In the early 1970s social unrest spread among peasants seeking land inhabited by indigenous communities. The latter not only refused to divide up their common lands, but also reclaimed lands invaded in the past by landowners, or demanded rights guarantees in border regions. To the surprise of the peasant movement's paternal wing, indigenous peoples formulated their own claims through newly established ethnic organizations in which dozens of young anthropologists and other intellectuals actively participated (Jimeno 1996; Caviedes 2004).

## A Militant Anthropology

Caviedes argues that in the 1970s there was a break in the practice adopted by anthropology, its most drastic element being the way anthropologists became activists in peasant and indigenous social movements (Caviedes 2002; Arocha and Friedemann 1984; Barragán 2001). In Caviedes' opinion, this break did not occur simply because of a movement within anthropology influenced by Marxism and the proximity to the indigenous movement (particularly the Indigenous Regional Council of the Cauca, CRIC), as some of us have suggested (Jimeno 1999). Instead, he argues, it came about as a result of attempts during that decade to rethink the power relationship both between Colombian society and the indigenous peoples, and also at the heart of Colombian society as a whole. This would mean that the rethinking of anthropology was a result of the struggles to transform this power relationship. Caviedes is probably more right than those of us who were too closely involved in the process during those years. In fact, I myself belong to the generation that questioned the orientation of the anthropology curriculum at one of the universities between 1968 and 1970, precisely on account of its lack of "commitment" to social movements. Shortly after, I was able to participate in the debate on the orientation of land policies, in support of the new ethnic organizations. Many of those I have mentioned as contributing to the first issue of the Review were affected by our criticisms, in some cases quite profoundly. During that period, the answer to the question "What is the purpose of knowledge?" was emphatic – to transform social injustice in our society. The practical response, which was more enthusiastic than reflective and rather more naive than prepared, consisted of accompaniment and even fusion with the social movements of the time.

During the 1960s and 1970s, the land distribution problem was at the center of national debate. On one side, there was pressure from peasants and left-wing organizations; and on the other, from the principal rural landowners, who mobilized support from the most conservative sections of the party political system and from a third sector within the government, which proposed agricultural modernization within a moderate framework of technological innovation and improvements in productivity. The result was an ineffectual land reform project that proved to be incapable of modifying the concentration of land ownership in a country that was already largely urban. The rural organizations, however, consolidated themselves, particularly the indigenous organization bringing together the three main indigenous groups from the southwest in the CRIC (Jimeno 1996). Their demands could be summed up in two words: *land* and *culture*. Many of us who at the time had recently become professors at the public universities (National, el Cauca and Antioquia) embraced the indigenous cause with enthusiasm. In it we saw the possibility of achieving the "commitment" between science and politics that we had so desired.

One way of contributing to the cause was by producing short texts written in the fervent language of the activist, denouncing abuses, especially by landowners, the Catholic Church and local police forces, and attacking official policies toward the indigenous communities as "ethnocide." We also promoted countless meetings so that indigenous leaders could put forward their point of view in the cities, we attended meetings and conventions organized by the indigenous communities themselves, or we took advantage of work-related trips throughout the country to act as liaisons between the indigenous groups that were cut off from each other. We were *collaborators* (*colaboradores*). One of the numerous examples of this militant literature was the newspaper *Yaví*, produced by a small group of anthropologists, lawyers and sociologists, which was circulated among intellectuals and indigenous organizations from 1978 to 1983. The assassination of indigenous leaders during that period, as well as the imprisonment of others, was one of the driving forces behind the publication, which also examined local confrontations and praised the variety and wealth of indigenous beliefs and practices. As for the researchers from the Colombian Institute of Anthropology, they set up work stations, known as "anthropological stations," in indigenous communities with the purpose of bringing together research and work in the community, on ethno-education, health and organization.

We collaborators concentrated on circulating ethnic demands: the right to "territory" and "self-determination," the right to live according to their cultural practices and to condemn relations of submission and exploitation in the local environment. We were active image creators, advocating the intrinsic value of the Amerindian cultures as a political means of rethinking both the relationship between these societies and official policies, and the place of the native American in society and in the national consciousness. In a sense, we continued the work that had already been started by the pioneers. The limits of this activity and its ambiguities would only become apparent some time later. The indigenous communities appropriated ethnographical images and transformed them into a new ethnical topography.

Militant activity, however, was not limited to students and university professors. The expansion of official institutions involved a large number of professionals, anthropologists and other intellectuals who sympathized with the indigenous cause. They saw themselves, not as agents of the official order, but as its subversives, working discreetly, even secretly, and at times more openly and defiantly. This work had two main purposes. One was to influence official policy to rethink the role of ethnic and cultural diversity. The other was to promote the creation of new local indigenous organizations designed to demand recognition of the rights of indigenous communities. It also had the intention of putting different groups in contact with each other, by promoting the idea of a national indigenous movement with common demands and courses of action. We also worked on promoting a rethinking of official land policy, and established the ideological and practical bases for what would be a long struggle to obtain official recognition of indigenous lands in different parts of the country. "Ideological" in that they rejected the idea of dividing up communal lands and advocated the opposite: the advantage of maintaining the existing ones and applying the same scheme of community lands to the peripheral regions of the forest. "Practical" because they led to intense promotional activity with local and regional organizations throughout the country.

The action taken by anthropologists, though, was fairly diverse. We can demonstrate this by examining their casework in relation to the construction of the Urrá hydroelectric dam in an indigenous territory in the north of Colombia, the same dam studied by Caviedes (2004). Between 1960 and 1970, a local environmental development agency began a feasibility study on the construction of a dam in the region of the Embera Katío, near to the Caribbean plains. The plan had the financial backing of multinational corporations, and attracted interest from landowners and politicians in the region. Over the next three decades, there was a succession of technical assessments by social and environmental scientists. The Embera also made their voice heard and, in a fairly haphazard manner, with a number of internal disagreements still unresolved, presented legal claims and organized public protests. The Embera were opposed to the reservoir and dam because it meant having to abandon their territory, in exchange for much less productive land. They also argued that the dam would adversely affect their lives through its impact on plants, animals and the regional water system. The landowners, for their part, saw the reservoir as an opportunity to expand their haciendas through increased control of seasonal water flow and by moving the Indians off their lands. During the course of the debate on Urrá, anthropologists were to be found working on various sides. On several occasions they acted as consultant technicians on the social impact of the dam. The first participants, anthropologists Piedad Gómez and Roberto Pineda Camacho, maintained their negative view of the relationship between environmental destruction of the forest and rivers and the survival of the Embera, despite veiled pressure from contractors and powerful local interests. Others, though, understated indigenous demands (Caviedes 2004).

Parallel to the conflicting technical studies, Antonio Cardona, another young anthropologist, recently graduated from the public university, traveled the region in the early 1980s as a public employee of an agency on indigenous affairs (Caviedes 2004). His job consisted of seeking out a site for the creation of a protected, communal territory, but very soon he was forced to take a position on the construction of the dam. He then worked to group the local communities together into new organizations that took the form of "cabildos" – organizations of Spanish colonial origin that were adopted as a model by the national indigenous movement. Supported by other anthropologists who had recently graduated from other universities and also sympathized with the indigenous struggle, Cardona used his knowledge of mobilizations that he had acquired as a student in contact with the peasant organization and the CRIC, and succeeded in putting the Embera in contact with each other and with other indigenous organizations. This marked the start of a slow but continuous process of participation by the Embera in meetings, and they even ventured into the unknown – to the capital, Bogotá. Supported by anthropologists who worked with them, they traveled on to the south of Colombia to attend the first national indigenous meeting in 1981, which led to the formation of the National Indigenous Organization (ONIC). Numerous events, such as the assassination of indigenous leaders, harassment by the Colombian army and armed groups, both "paramilitary" and guerrilla, have marked the protest movement against the dam. In spite of everything, the first phase of the construction began in 1989. Antonio Cardona opted, as he remembers it, for open "commitment" in opposition to the dam – and lost his job (Caviedes 2004).

The central concept guiding the action of the militant anthropologists was that of *commitment*, which they understood as a moral duty to confront what they believed was damaging communities. Many practiced it to the full, as in the case of the Urrá dam, and some still continue with this approach, but others chose to become more conciliatory and modify their positions. In time, the combative young anthropologists of the 1980s gave way to others who put their expert knowledge to use in a new way: now as consultants to the Constitutional Court, studying the damage caused by the dam that had already been built. In 1998, based on anthropological opinion, the Court ruled that the dam had caused sweeping changes that threatened the survival of the Embera and awarded compensation to their communities. At this stage, new challenges appeared. Firstly, there was the matter of reaching agreement on how to manage these fairly considerable sums of money. Secondly, there was the question of the Embera's very survival in the midst of a war between guerrilla factions who had accused them of siding with the "enemy," on the one side, and paramilitaries who besieged them and kept close watch on their movements, on the other. We know all this thanks to anthropologists such as Caviedes, who works for the public administration on the defense of human rights in a small town in the region. But that is another story, of history in the making.

## BETWEEN POLITICAL CONSTITUTION AND CONFLICT

From the second half of the 1980s onward, two distinct situations began to come together. On the one hand, anthropology was reaping the rewards of its consolidation as an academic discipline, with a considerable number of professionals practicing applied anthropology in a wide range of areas. On the other hand, there was a substitution of the concept of *commitment* as political activism in the community by a greater interest in the actual production of knowledge and by a greater sectorization of anthropology according to the social, regional and institutional affiliation of the researcher. The subject of indigenous societies now became the domain of a limited number of specialists, at the same time as the indigenous organizations and their spokespeople were becoming increasingly visible politically, and could speak for themselves. For some researchers, including Caviedes, this meant that the bulk of anthropology had distanced itself from social movements. But it can also be seen as an overall reorientation of the discipline, which in Colombia covers a wide variety of topics and approaches. The influence of debates within the social sciences in the US, and to a lesser extent in France, has replaced the former contact with Latin American critical theory. Moreover, there has been a shift in the function of *commitment*, which is no longer understood as being a political and moral bond with local communities. Instead, it is now seen as fostering political debate at the national level. The best of example of this is perhaps the process that led to the constitutional reform of 1991, as well as the determination of many anthropologists to defend and build on some of their social achievements.

The constitutional reform came about in 1991 partly as a result of the peace agreements with the M-19 guerrillas. The country was still reeling from a wave of assassinations and bombings carried out by the drugs cartels, who were attempting to put pressure on the authorities to abandon the official measures taken against them. Many sectors of society saw the constitutional reform as a ray of hope in the midst of the conflict; as the possibility of a new social pact and the chance to make progress on social rights and economic guarantees. For certain intellectuals, including some anthropologists, it was an opportunity to leave behind the political constitution of 1886, which proclaimed one official religion and culture and left the Amerindian and Afro-Colombian populations in a state of social exclusion and disadvantage. It was also an opportunity to support the ethnic organizations in their demands. Thanks to their active participation in the formulation of the new constitution, the indigenous communities improved their public image and received recognition for a host of safeguards and rights for which they had fought long and hard, such as the recognition of their cultural diversity, their territorial rights, their native language and education. The same cannot be said for the Afro-Colombian populations, who lacked such experienced forms of representation and organization. Even so, thanks to the activities of a group of anthropologists, the constitution included a norm that led to moderate advances in the recognition of the exclusion of these populations and in territorial guarantees for some of them. It was no coincidence that the headquarters for work on legal aspects of the constitution was the Colombian Institute of Anthropology.

Here we encounter a difference between the perspective of foreign intellectuals and that of Colombian ones. Most foreign observers look on the progress achieved through negotiation with considerable skepticism, and see each accomplishment as merely confirmation of the existing order, since the changes have been minor ones. They see a tendency to endorse the state and accept its overall authority (Gros 2001). Jaime Arocha (2004) demonstrates precisely this difference in perspective. While foreign anthropologists are skeptical about the sociopolitical events affecting the Afro-Colombian population, for example, through the law establishing their ethnoterritorial and political rights, the dominant position taken by Colombian anthropologists is one of attachment and commitment to the political achievements concerning the recognition of these peoples.

Indeed, the majority of Colombian anthropologists make a more positive political assessment of every advance made against discrimination and historical forms of domination, or in the unequivocal process of the empowerment of the indigenous peoples. For some, it is a question of attaining a new social order. For us, it is about working in a field of day-to-day struggles to expand democracy, in the midst of a long and violent confrontation. Again, the difference in perspective has to do with our historical position as researchers and citizens, which is continually challenged by controversial ideas on the state, the nation and the democracy we are seeking to build.

The proliferation of subjects and approaches, and the shift in interest toward the national public arena, have occurred within the context of increasing internal conflict in Colombia. It is well documented that the characteristic feature of this conflict is the complex criss-crossing of local situations and struggles for control of the state between state forces and insurgents from across the political spectrum. The money and interests generated by the traffic in illegal drugs permeates this conflict, further complicating the panorama of alliances, negotiations and confrontations. This adds a particular kind of tension, not only for those who have to live with the immediate effects of the violence, but also for the rest of Colombian society, which is afraid of becoming inadvertently caught up in it. Since 1985, much of the escalating confrontation has taken place in rural areas, which are paying the highest price for the violence. Thus, there is a relative degree of protection to be found in urban life. To some extent, however, the atmosphere of worry and fear is inescapable.

In this sense, anthropologists who work in Colombia do so "under fire," to use the expression from the book by Nordström and Robben (1995). How has practicing anthropology in the context of this conflict affected the work of research, the relationship between the researcher and the research subjects, and the field itself or its theory? The events of the conflict are like accumulating layers that shake our consciousness and personal sensibilities, to the point where none of us can ignore the fact that our environment is becoming increasingly unsafe. How does this translate into the work of the anthropologist? Those anthropologists who work in a strictly professional capacity, in the countless social institutions in the areas of conflict, have to make an ongoing effort to ensure that their institutional cover is the general frame of reference for their actions. Like many other civilians, they go about their business with the utmost caution, which, among other things, involves showing neutrality toward all parties and constantly negotiating what we might call civil neutrality. This attitude must be demonstrated in daily conversation and in their choice of relations. It also means not inquiring about people, places or critical actions. But the struggle to achieve the neutrality that protects them and the people they work with can easily be destabilized, forcing the anthropologist to abandon the area in order to ensure his or her survival.

From the point of view of elemental research, there has undoubtedly been a decrease in the amount of work being carried out in high risk zones, particularly in some rural areas. But there is a great deal of interest in studying political and other forms of violence, even though there tend to be more political scientists than anthropologists in this field. One effect of the conflict on anthropological practice has been to reinforce the general tendency toward opening up new topics of investigation, as we have previously seen. This has entailed redefining what exactly is meant by the "field" and "fieldwork" of anthropology. The avoidance or prevention of violence has led anthropologists to abandon their former interest in localized communities in favor of general or multi-sited processes. It has also brought about methodological innovations, including varied strategies for approaching research subjects, from the use of visual texts, to the internet, or changes in traditional writing formats.

The relationship of anthropologists with their subjects of investigation has also undergone a process of reevaluation. The naive position of committed activism has been left behind, although it still exists among some young anthropologists with pronounced loyalties toward the most disadvantaged sectors of society. This change can be seen as the emergence of a new understanding of political action, "apolitical politics," as Barragán (2005) calls it, which is now oriented toward environmental impact, gender identity, emotional youth communities (musical, literary), or globalization processes. The concept of *complicity* put forward by George Marcus (1999), and used by Sara Shneiderman to show the adaptation in the relationship between social scientists and their informants in Nepal (Shneiderman, Pettigrew and Harper 2004), might prove useful to those working in conflict zones or on violence-related topics. According to this concept, neither the anthropologist nor the subject of investigation can limit his or her project to the local; they must work together to place themselves in a wider context, agreeing on their purposes and commitment to an external "third party." In Shneiderman's work this entailed new forms of *complicity* with local colleagues, insofar as their common goal was to guarantee the safety of those involved and to understand the changing situation. Indeed, those working in Colombia emphasize both the need to guarantee the safety of all concerned, and the way in which this creates special bonds between them and their research subjects. Together they begin to participate in a whole range of small, vital strategies, such as avoiding certain places, people and times, maintaining a degree of mobility within the area and paying close attention to rumors. In our case, however, this concept is limited by the fact that the internal conflict makes it difficult for social scientists to regard the opposing parties with indifference, and in general they adopt a definite position of either sympathizing with them or not, as the case may be. Thus, it is impossible for them to form a bond of *complicity* with some of their research subjects, for example, in the case of paramilitary or guerrilla groups. Nevertheless, they must walk a fine line between relying on the approval of armed groups in order to move about freely and claiming civil neutrality.

Another factor affecting an anthropologist's relationship of *complicity* is that it is so difficult to avoid arousing suspicion, however cautious they may be. Female researchers are said to be safer in such situations, as the fact that they are women protects them from the automatic assumption that they are combatants. By way of contrast, we can cite the case of our colleague Hernán Henao, which provides a dramatic example with which to end this analysis. A university professor whose research subject for a number of years was the relationship between region, territoriality and culture, in 1999 Henao finished a study on territorial conflicts in a region of western Colombia known for its preponderance of paramilitary groups. In May of that year he was murdered by a commando in his own office at the University of Antioquia. As occurs with most violent deaths, conflicting versions of the reasons for the attack immediately began to circulate. According to some of the versions, what made him an enemy of these groups was the fact that an NGO had used his work abroad to support a claim of territorial usurpation. This particularly painful example demonstrates the difficulty of operating in a changing terrain dominated by the use of force.

## Conclusion

The practice of anthropology in Colombia has been pervaded by the tension between the global orientations of the discipline and the way they are put into practice in the Colombian context. This is due to the fact that the practice must be adapted to the social condition of anthropologists as fellow citizens of their subjects of study. In this sense, the practice of anthropology has been *naciocentric*, since our cultural production is permeated by disparate and polemical ideas regarding the makeup of the state and what it means to construct a nation, democracy and citizenship.

This is why anthropological practice in Colombia has been far from just an acritical repetition of imported models. We anthropologists have been forced to account for the tangle of perspectives and social interests in which we find ourselves immersed, and to exercise the function of citizen-researcher. The three main tendencies that sum up the six decades of anthropology in Colombia point to certain dominant trends and a few breaks, which have not been consecutive, but rather have coexisted and over-lapped since it became an academic discipline in the 1940s. At one extreme we find an ethnography with a generalizing "blanket" mentality, and at the other, a militant anthropology. Between the two we can identify a range of positions and discussions, the distinguishing feature of which has been the ill-defined boundary between prac-ticing anthropology as a discipline and acting as citizens. In one sense this limits our anthropological practice, but in another sense it also opens it up.

## REFERENCES

Anderson, B. (1983) *Imagined Communities*. London: Verso.

Andrade, A. (1953) Presentación. *Revista Colombiana de Antropología* 1.

Arocha, J. (2004) Metrópolis y puritanismo en Afrocolombia. *Revista de Ciencias Sociales* (Universidad de los Andes).

Arocha, J. and Friedemann, N. (1984) *Un siglo de investigación social*. Bogotá: Etnos.

Barragán, C. A. (2001) Antropología en Colombia. Del Instituto Etnológico a los programas universitarios. Tesis de grado, Departamento de Antropología, Universidad de Los Andes.

Barragán, C. A. (2005) *Antropología en Colombia: 1890–1980*. Bogotá: Instituto Colombiano de Antropología e Historia.

Cardoso de Oliveira, R. (1995) Notas sobre uma estilística da antropologia. In R. Cardoso de Oliveira and G. Raul Ruben (eds), *Estilos de antropologia* (pp. 177–196). Campinas: Editora da UNICAMP.

Cardoso de Oliveira, R. (1998) *O trabalho do antropólogo*. Brasilia: Paralelo 15/Editora da UNESP.

Caviedes, M. (2002) Solidarios frente a colaboradores. Antropología y movimiento indígena en el Cauca en las décadas de 1970 y 1980. *Revista Colombiana de Antropología* 38:237–260.

Caviedes, M. (2004) Antropología apócrifa y movimiento indígena. Desde los cuarenta hasta el apoyo a los Embera Katío. Tesis de maestría en Antropología, Universidad Nacional de Colombia, Bogotá.

Das, V. (1998) *Critical Events: An Anthropological Perspective on Contemporary India*. Delhi: Oxford University Press.

Elias, N. (1989) *El proceso de la civilización*. Mexico City: Siglo XXI Editores.

Escobar, A. (1996) *La invención del tercer mundo*. Bogotá: Norma.

Fletcher, J. (1997) *Violence and Civilization: An Introduction to the Work of Norbert Elias*. Cambridge: Polity Press.

Gros, C. (2001) *Políticas de la etnicidad. Identidad, estado y modernidad*. Bogotá: ICANH/CES.

Gutiérrez de Pineda, V. (1955) Causas culturales de la mortalidad infantil. *Revista Colombiana de Antropología* 4:11–86.

Jimeno, M. (1984) Consolidación del estado y antropología en Colombia. In J. Arocha and N. Friedemann (eds), *Un siglo de investigación social* (pp. 200–230). Bogotá: Etnos.

Jimeno, M. (1996) Juan Gregorio Palechor. Tierra, identidad y recreación étnica. *Journal of Latin American Anthropology* 1(2):46–76.

Jimeno, M. (1999) Desde el punto de vista de la periferia. Desarrollo profesional y conciencia social. *Anuário Antropológico* 97:59–72.

Jimeno, M. (2000) La emergencia del investigador ciudadano. Estilos de antropología y crisis de modelos en la antropología colombiana. In J. Tocancipá (ed.), *La formación del estado nación y las disciplinas sociales en Colombia* (pp. 157–190). Popayán: Taller Editorial, Universidad del Cauca.

Jimeno, M. and Triana, A. (1985) *Estado y minorías étnicas en Colombia*. Bogotá: FUNCOL.

Krotz, E. (1996) La generación de teoría antropológica en América Latina. Silenciamientos, tensiones intrínsecas y puntos de partida. *Maguaré* 11–12:25–39.

Krotz, E. (1997) Anthropologies of the South: Their Rise, Their Silencing, Their Characteristics. *Critique of Anthropology* 13(3):237–251.

Lomnitz, C. (1999) Descubrimiento y desilusión en la antropología mexicana. In *Modernidad indiana. Nueve ensayos sobre nación y mediación en México* (pp. 79–97). Mexico City: Editorial.

Marcus, G. (1999) The Uses of Complicity in the Changing Mise-en-Scène of Anthropological Fieldwork. In S. Ortner (ed.), *The Fate of Culture: Geertz and Beyond* (pp. 86–109). Berkeley: University of California Press.

Mariátegui, J. C. and Sánchez, L. A. (1987[1927 and 1928]) *La polémica del indigenismo. Textos recopilados por Manuel Aquézolo*. Lima: Mosca Azul Editores.

Martínez, M. (2004) *Panorama general Revista Colombia de Antropología*. Bogotá: Inédito.

Neiburg, F. (1998) O natiocentrismo das Ciências Sociais e as Formas de Conceituar a Violência Política e os Processos de Politizacao da Vida Social. In L. Waizborg (ed.), *Dóssier Norbert Elias* (pp. 37–62). São Paulo: Editora da Universidade de São Paulo EDUSP.

Nordström, C. and Robben, A. (1995) *Fieldwork under Fire: Contemporary Studies of Violence and Survival*. Berkeley: University of California Press.

Orrantia, J. C. (2002) Matices Kogui. Representaciones y negociación en la marginalidad. *Revista Colombia de Antropología* 38:45–75.

Pécaut, D.(1987) *Orden y violencia en Colombia. 1930–1954*. Bogotá: Siglo XXI Editores.

Ramos, A. (1999–2000) Anthropologist as Political Actor. *Journal of Latin American Anthropology* 4(2) and 5(1):172–189.

Ramos, A. (2004) Los Yanomami. En el corazón de las tinieblas blancas. *Relaciones* 98(25):19–47.

Roldán, M. (2003) *A sangre y fuego. La violencia en Antioquia, Colombia, 1946–1953*. Bogotá: Instituto Colombiano de Antropología e Historia.

Shneiderman, S., Pettigrew, J., and Harper, I. (2004) Relationships, Complicity and Representation: Conducting Research in Nepal during the Maoist Insurgency. *Anthropology Today* 20(1):20–25.

Uribe, C. A. (1997) A Certain Feeling of Homelessness: Remarks on Esteban Krotz's Anthropologies of the South. *Critique of Anthropology* 13(3):253–261.

# CHAPTER 5

# Ecuador: Militants, Priests, Technocrats, and Scholars

## Carmen Martínez Novo

In *Ethnography in Unstable Places*, US anthropologist Carol Greenhouse (2002) makes the claim that research under conditions of dramatic change allows us to question reifications of state and society because structures cease to be a given.[1] Large-scale systems are revealed to be fragile amalgams of improvisatory arenas and expanded agency, and social projects and understandings that would otherwise be latent in society are able to surface. Thus, instability allows for more productive theorization, and expands opportunities for thinking reflexively about both ethics and ethnographic methods as ethnographers become implicated in the situations about which they write.

Greenhouse, however, looks at Third World instability from the standpoint of the relative stability of the researcher in the academia of the North – reducing the principle of "instability," in addition to the opportunities described above, to the risk and danger that anthropologists experience under the conditions of ethnographic fieldwork. The fieldwork trip, however, implies a condition of relative impermanence: no matter how long she is in "the field," the ethnographer is there as an outsider who will, eventually, leave and whose livelihood and permanent security does not depend on conditions in the field. Thus, what the book does not consider is how the related questions of "conjuncture" and "instability" shape research and writing done by academics located in the academies of "unstable places." Ecuadorian social scientists, for example, often complain that "the conjuncture can eat you up." Things change so rapidly that a study or interpretation may be obsolete in a couple of days. This vertiginous course of events may present problems as well as opportunities for academic reflection. Sometimes there is not enough time to reflect academically on the events. In addition, many scholars feel pressure to change topics of study according to the conjuncture, sacrificing long-term academic reflection. On the other hand, however, periods of intense change and the insertion of the scholar within the social fabric under analysis may allow for research agendas that are more socially and politically relevant. As Arturo Escobar has noted:

> US based Latin Americanist academic fields have treated Latin America largely as an object of study, even if many of its practitioners have done so from a political perspective

and have built a practice of solidarity along the way. In contrast, critical perspectives arising from Latin America have been as a whole more prone to foreground radical political questions and positions. (2006:12)

This chapter takes this question of conjuncture – and timing – to reflect on the institutional, political-economic, and epistemic conditions that have shaped Ecuadorian anthropology since the early 1970s, when the first anthropology department was created in Quito at the Pontificia Universidad Católica del Ecuador (Catholic University of Ecuador), until the present. This period coincides with the two issues that have most occupied Ecuadorian anthropologists: the agrarian reform and the rise of one of Latin America's most powerful indigenous movements.

I define Ecuadorian anthropology as scholarship written from within Ecuadorian institutions by either Ecuadorian nationals or foreigners who reside and work in the Ecuadorian academy. For a number of reasons, silence often surrounds this production. Reviews of the literature on Ecuador written in the United States often do not take into account the work of Ecuadorian authors, leading many Ecuadorian scholars to complain that they are treated as mere native informants or field assistants by academics from the North who adopt their ideas, but who most of the time do not quote their works or add their name to publications. Similarly, in many respects, Ecuadorian anthropology tends to be more open toward the outside, to new things coming from abroad, than it is to the idea of recovering a national tradition. This tendency may be explained by a combination of factors, including the intellectual dependency that results from the colonial legacy, fear of conflict and its consequences for one's academic career, and the "politicization" of the universities in the 1970s and 1980s. During these decades, academics were not conceived of as intellectuals but as party members who were understood as either allies who should not be questioned, or opponents who needed to be ignored (Francisco Rhon, interview, August 14, 2006).[2]

Its emphasis on politically engaged and applied work adds interest to a revision of Ecuadorian anthropology because anthropological ideas have had important social consequences. Reviewing anthropology-making institutions and anthropologists in Ecuador, I found that the same two actors that interacted with indigenous peasants and contributed to their political organization were also the ones producing anthropological knowledge: namely, the Catholic Church and the political left. In addition, I found that the boundaries between these two institutional fields were often blurred by actors who worked together in the field and shared academic spaces. Thus, a review of anthropological literature in Ecuador provides important clues about debates on the Ecuadorian left, as well as the impact of religious ideas and practices at all levels of Ecuadorian society.

Ecuadorian anthropology has had many influences from abroad, and the resulting cosmopolitan character is an interesting value in itself. Some Ecuadorian anthropologists studied in North America or have been influenced by anthropologists who work in the US and Canada. Other anthropologists working in the Ecuadorian academia have studied in Europe, particularly France and Germany, and more recently in Spain. Similarly, French, German, Spanish, and other European anthropologists have done research in Ecuador and influenced Ecuadorian researchers. Latin American scholars and currents have been even more influential. There is an old and strong relationship between Mexican and Ecuadorian anthropology, for example. Moisés Sáenz, one of the fathers of Mexican indigenismo, came to Ecuador in the early 1930s to carry out a study of the situation of Andean Indians. Later, Mexican indigenismo influenced the work of Misión Andina (1950s–1970s), a development program sponsored by the United Nations and carried out by the International Labor Organization in collaboration with Ecuador and other Andean states (Bretón 2001). These influences and relationships have led a number of Ecuadorian anthropologists to study in Mexico. Other scholars, particularly those working for Centro Andino de Acción Popular (CAAP, see below) were influenced by Peruvian and Bolivian anthropology. Finally, in the late 1970s and early 1980s, there was an important presence of political exiles escaping military dictatorships in Argentina and Chile.

Rather than tracing these intellectual genealogies in terms of national – or international – traditions, in this chapter I instead frame the history of Ecuadorian anthropology in terms of the important "moments" or "conjunctures" that have shaped debates within the discipline. I begin by considering the institutional landscapes through which the political and philosophical agendas of the state, the Catholic Church, and more recently nongovernmental organizations have shaped anthropological production. I then consider the important influence of the Ecuadorian left on anthropological discussions of peasant economies, indigenous culture, and gender. I conclude by looking at anthropological responses to the rise of the indigenous movement, the restructuring of the Ecuadorian state, and the diffusion of neoliberal academic agendas in the 1990s.

## INSTITUTIONAL MARKS

Ecuadorian anthropology has been shaped in important ways by the country's regional fragmentation and political and economic centralism. Most Ecuadorian anthropologists have focused on the indigenous peasantries of the Andean highlands. This fact is not unrelated to the centralism of Ecuadorian academia and the heavy concentration of universities and NGOs in the highland capital city of Quito, as well as to the political agendas of the left. The educational institutions of coastal Guayaquil, on the other hand, have been more inclined to promote "practical" specializations such as economics, business management, engineering, and agriculture, although there has also been an important archaeological tradition in the Ecuadorian coast centered around the Center for Archaeological and Anthropological Studies of the Escuela Superior Politécnica del Litoral (Polytechnic School of the Coast) and the Central Bank of Ecuador (for a classic study see Estrada 1979; for a recent critical perspective see Benavides 2006). Despite this general tendency to focus on indigenous peasants of the highlands, there is a less developed tradition of work on the coast and populations of African descent. North American anthropologist Norman Whitten (1965, 1974), Afro-European anthropologist Jean Muteba Rahier (1998), and Spanish anthropologist Paloma Fernández Rasines (2001) have developed work on populations of African descent, as have Ecuadorian scholars such as Diego Quiroga (2003), Carlos de la Torre (2002), and Maria Eugenia Chaves (1998). A few anthropologists have worked with indigenous populations of the coast like the tsáchilas (Ventura i Oller 1999), and there is also some anthropological work on coastal cities by anthropologists Marcelo Naranjo (1980) and Xavier Andrade (2004). Finally, there is a tradition of work on coastal plantations by Ecuadorian and foreign scholars such as Manuel Chiriboga (1980), Andrés Guerrero (1980), and more recently Steve Striffler (2002).

There has been historically less work by Ecuadorian anthropologists on the Amazonian region than on the highlands. Foreigners dominated Amazonian anthropology for a long time (Moreno 1992). Some of these foreign researchers were perhaps seeking culturally diverse, relatively isolated communities, whereas Ecuadorian social scientists preferred to focus on the inherently political dynamics of the agrarian reform. However, some foreign anthropologists such as Blanca Muratorio (1991) have been influential in placing Amazonian peoples in larger contexts and in modernity. Nevertheless, interest in the Amazonian region grew slowly within Ecuadorian academia in the 1970s. One trigger was the historical and cultural research stimulated by evangelization, especially, as we will see, by Salesian fathers working with the Shuar in southeastern Ecuador. On the other hand, the Ecuadorian state became increasingly invested in the Amazonian region or Oriente in the 1970s due to the colonization that accompanied agrarian reform and the first exploitation of oil resources. Today there are a number of Ecuadorian researchers focusing on the Amazon. Many of them, as well as foreign scholars, study conflicts between indigenous populations and oil companies in a context in which oil companies are among the most important sponsors of scholarship (Fontaine 2003; Sawyer 2004).

Following the creation in 1972 of the Catholic University's Anthropology Department, Quito has remained the institutional center for Ecuadorian sociocultural anthropology. According to Andrés Guerrero (interview, January 20, 2006) the impetus behind the new anthropology department originated in a meeting of progressive Jesuits whose concern for the plight of Ecuador's highland peasants was at least partly inspired by the Vatican II Catholic Church Council (in 1962–65) and the Conference of Latin American Bishops in Medellin (in 1968). Francisco Rhon (interview, August 14, 2006) adds that progressive groups supported the creation of an anthropology department because they felt the need to promote critical, empirically grounded scholarship that would transcend the rigid, theoretically oriented explanations of orthodox Marxism. Originally, the department had two research lines. One, inspired by leftist politics and the agrarian reform, focused on peasant issues and sociopolitical change and was represented by anthropologists like Diego Iturralde and Fernando García. Another, led by Jesuit father Marco Vinicio Rueda, who studied for his doctorate in France, responded to the religious character of the institution and studied popular manifestations of Catholicism.

By this time (1972), the debate on the agrarian reform process (which had begun in 1964) was at its peak. In this context the applied and politically engaged aspects of Ecuadorian anthropology were reinforced. Researchers in anthropology and other social sciences asked themselves what would happen to peasants after the reform. Would they become successful subsistence peasants and improve their standard of living? Would they become proletarians or semiproletarians, or small capitalists? What role could state-led development play in bettering the lives of Ecuador's peasant population? These questions were framed within a Latin American wide debate, the *campesinista–descampesinista* debate, which discussed how peasants were articulated to capitalist modes of production (Chiriboga 1988; see also Seligmann, this volume). The answers to these questions had consequences for the revolutionary strategies of leftist parties; what was discussed was whether the left should focus their political strategies on urban proletarians or on the countryside and peasants. The research lines of the newly formed anthropology department of the Catholic University were connected to these debates (García 1980). Influenced by the work of Russian agrarian economist Chayanov (who had been translated into Spanish by the Argentine exile and then Ecuadorian resident Eduardo Archetti), anthropologists at the Catholic University studied how reciprocity, kinship, and communal labor had allowed for peasant survival during the colonial and hacienda periods and encouraged peasant resistance to capitalism. Others worried to what extent capitalism was in fact eroding these traditional cultural strategies.

Others at the Catholic University focused on popular religion through collective fieldwork on religious rituals, particularly in the highlands (Rueda 1982). Much of this work was inspired by liberation theology and the Catholic Church's unprecedented acceptance – following Vatican II – of popular religion as a legitimate religious form. Another important influence was the Barbados Conference of 1971, which emphasized the importance of non-Western cultural elements for evangelization (see Varese, Delgado and Meyer, this volume).

The Salesian Order also played an important role in the development of Ecuadorian anthropology. Starting in the late 19th century, the Ecuadorian government has granted the Salesian Order the authority to "civilize and Christianize the Shuar" in Ecuador's southeastern lowlands and, in the process, to ensure Ecuadorian presence along the highly contested border with Peru (Botasso 1986; Rubenstein 2005; Audiovisuales Don Bosco, *Misiones en el Oriente*, n.d.). The original goal of the Salesians was to transform Shuar culture into a European or "Western" and Christian model. A first step was to compile information on Shuar language, myths and customs (Pelizzaro 1990). However, by the mid 20th century, the Salesians had begun to reflect on the importance of preserving an indigenous culture that was increasingly threatened by the colonization of Amazonian regions following the 1964 Agrarian Reform and Colonization Law. The Salesians led a process of organization that resulted in the formation in 1964 of one of the first indigenous organizations in Latin America: The Federación Interprovincial de Centros Shuar, or FISCH (Interprovincial Federation of Shuar Centers). According to the missionaries' own account, they were pioneers in promoting the Catholic Church's awareness of cultural and ethnic diversity in the first (1971) Barbados conference (Juan Botasso, at the 2005 FLACSO conference; J. Manangón, personal communication 2002).

In 1975, the Salesians started to publish their own research, along with work by Ecuadorian and indigenous intellectuals and translations of foreign works, in the collection Mundo Shuar (Shuar World). In 1980, stimulated by the growth of the indigenous movement and the implementation of bilingual-bicultural education, the order expanded the collection to a series entitled Mundo Andino (Andean World). In 1983, they unified both collections in a publishing house named Abya Yala, which has been the most important publisher of anthropological research in Ecuador until today. From its foundation, the main goal of Abya Yala was to promote respect for indigenous peoples and cultural diversity among non-Indians in Ecuador, while providing materials to indigenous communities for a better self-understanding and self-reflection on their own identity (Cucurella 2005; Audiovisuales Don Bosco, *Abya Yala*, n.d.).

In 1987 the Salesians, led again by Juan Botasso, founded the school of applied anthropology. Applied anthropology was used in the 19th and 20th centuries to improve the administration of colonized groups, particularly by the British (Kuper 1973). However, in the 1960s, critical anthropologists, among them liberation theology priests, proposed using anthropology to advocate on behalf of indigenous organizations and to help them in their development plans. Specifically, the School of Applied Anthropology was founded to encourage mission personnel to take cultural factors into account in their evangelization and human development work (Bartoli 2002). The Salesians have also been pioneers in allowing access to higher education to indigenous, Afro-Ecuadorian, and other disadvantaged students at the Universidad Politécnica Salesiana (Salesian Polytechnic University) founded in 1994.

The Facultad Latinoamericana de Ciencias Sociales (FLACSO, Latin American Faculty of Social Sciences) in Ecuador has also provided Ecuadorians and foreigners with graduate degrees in Andean History, Amazonian Studies, and Anthropology. It has been a meeting place for scholars coming from Latin America, Europe, and North America. FLACSO is an international system of research and graduate teaching in the social sciences created in 1957 with the aim of elaborating Latin American development theories and proposals for the region. As with the other institutions mentioned above, the idea of applied and politically engaged social science was present from its foundation. Although the international system of FLACSO was first created in Chile, that center had to close after the brutal 1973 coup d'état of General Augusto Pinochet. The centers in Mexico and Ecuador were founded in 1975 to give asylum to Chilean and later Argentinean academics escaping dictatorships. The anthropology department, which was opened in the early 1990s, had few permanent professors and was mainly based on the teaching of invited professors from North America, Europe, and other Latin American countries. Among them were Europeans like Penelope Harvey, Olivia Harris, Joan Pujadas, Philippe Descola, and Anne Christine Taylor, academics working in North America like Deborah Poole, Ruth Behar, Joanne Rappaport, William Roseberry, Blanca Muratorio, and James Fernández, and Latin Americans like Guillermo de la Peña. This was a list of cutting edge scholars most of whom were examples of critical thought and many of whom were women. According to the director of the program at the time, Xavier Izko (personal communication), receiving classes and conferences from women scholars was unusual at the time in Ecuador, and was only made possible by the fact that FLACSO's director, Amparo Menendez Carrión, was a woman. A few Ecuadorian scholars like Andrés Guerrero and Diego Quiroga were also hired to teach classes at FLACSO.

The history of FLACSO and the list of invited scholars attest to a characteristic of Ecuadorian academia that it still retains: its cosmopolitanism and its tendency to look abroad for inspiration, a tendency that could also be read as intellectual dependency. Preference for foreign over national scholarship was not only intellectually and politically questionable; it also brought institutional costs. Faced with a mounting financial crisis, FLACSO was forced to emphasize the sorts of applied research that could attract external funding. An interesting initiative in the anthropology department in the last years has been a graduate program in ethnic studies that has been attended by a number of indigenous leaders.

The role of the state has been weaker than the role of religious orders in the promotion of anthropological scholarship. However, in the 1970s, thanks to funds originating in the oil boom and in the context of nationalist military dictatorships, there was considerable funding for cultural matters. According to Andrés Guerrero (interview, January 20, 2006), the Central Bank of Ecuador was a very important sponsor of archaeology and FODERUMA (Fondo de Desarrollo Rural Marginal, Development Fund for Rural and Marginal Areas) employed many anthropologists in development programs. In addition, the Central Bank created the Instituto Otavaleño de Antropología (IOA, Otavalo Institute of Anthropology), an institution that sponsored archaeological and anthropological research linked to museums. However, according to Francisco Rhon (interview, August 14, 2006), most anthropologists who worked for the state through FODERUMA carried out narrowly focused consulting jobs that did not have an important intellectual impact besides that of providing a living for researchers.

Nongovernmental organizations have been another important site for the production of anthropological knowledge. The older NGOs such as the Centro Andino de Acción Popular (CAAP, Andean Center for Popular Action) and the Centro de Planificación y Estudios Sociales (CEPLAES, Center for Planning and Social Studies), for example, started to function in the 1970s in the context of radical political struggles that required independent research. Many others appeared in the following decades, particularly in the 1990s, when neoliberal reforms to reduce the size of the state led to an NGO boom in Ecuador and in Latin America more generally. The lack of long-term positions for social scientists within state agencies and universities, together with the scarcity of research and development funding, has led scholars to create these nongovernmental centers to provide jobs for themselves. The pressure to seek private funds for research, however, has often resulted in the imposition of external theoretical agendas and the proliferation of short-term, narrowly focused, quickly written case studies.

However, some of the older centers like CAAP have resisted these trends, sponsoring independent academic research. CAAP has produced anthropological knowledge and development work for more than 30 years and publishes one of the most established journals in the social sciences in Ecuador: *Ecuador Debate*. This institution started in 1975 under the direction of Francisco Rhon. CAAP carried out organizational activities among peasants, development programs, and research simultaneously, providing an ideal environment for the kind of engaged, applied anthropology that developed in that period. CAAP promoted important *campesinista* (and some *descampesinista*) scholarship and brought to Ecuador debates on the Andean community and *lo Andino* (Andean identity) inspired in Peruvian and Bolivian scholarship.

## ECUADORIAN ANTHROPOLOGY AND DEBATES WITHIN THE LEFT

Many agrarian scholars believed that the agrarian reforms of 1964 and 1973 would result in a transition toward capitalism and the formation of new peasant sectors. Marxist and other scholars had understood large properties in the highlands as feudal since they relied on servile labor until 1964. Similarly, relatively independent peasant communities were assumed to possess a different logic from capitalism, one that the agrarian reforms and the process of modernization were starting to break (Chiriboga 1988). Some researchers thought that contact with capitalism would cause the disintegration and proletarianization of the peasant community (L. Martínez 1984), whereas others noticed complex processes of semiproletarianization and recampesinization taking place in the Ecuadorian countryside (Farga and Almeida 1981). Rural–urban migration was seen as the main mechanism of contact with capitalism and the main source of destruction of these rural/indigenous cultures of resistance (Sánchez Parga 2002). Thus, there is a tradition of stigmatization of migration in Ecuadorian social science that still permeates perceptions of international migration.

A connected debate was that of the transition of large agrarian properties to modernization and capitalism. The large properties of the coast had been perceived as linked to capitalism since the late 19th century because they exported cocoa and later bananas and other products to the world market (Chiriboga 1980; Guerrero 1980; Striffler 2002), whereas highland haciendas produced for the national market using nonwage labor arrangements. Despite the fact that the highland hacienda has been described as feudal, Andrés Guerrero (1983) showed that landowners thought and acted as capitalists when they sold hacienda products on the national market and imported agrarian technologies from the world market. However, labor relationships within haciendas were not based on salaries, but on historically grounded customary rights and duties that subordinated workers to landowners while simultaneously preserving some prehispanic indigenous customs (Guerrero 1991).

While European and North American structuralists and cultural ecologists had described the Amazonian peoples as relatively isolated, Ecuadorian anthropologists scrutinized these same societies for evidence of historical colonization, state domination, and the penetration of oil and timber companies. Ernesto Salazar's (1986) *Pioneros de la selva. Los colonos del proyecto Upano-Palora* (Pioneers of the Rain Forest: The Settlers of the Upano-Palora Project), for example, examines rain forest colonization, state policies, and the environment in order to argue for new colonization policies. In this same vein, Teodoro Bustamante's (1988) *La larga lucha del kakaram contra el sucre* (The Long Struggle of Kakaram [shuar concept of strength or power] against the Sucre [earlier Ecuadorian currency]), analyzes Shuar violence not as an intrinsic feature of their "culture," but rather as a historical reaction to colonialism. Interpreting the creation of the Salesian backed Shuar Federation in 1964 as a reaction to the wave of colonization provoked by the agrarian reform, Bustamante frames the process of ethnogenesis underlying Shuar political organization as a process of modernization, rather than as a form of "preserving tradition."

## THE DEBATE ON CULTURE, DISCRIMINATION, AND RESISTANCE

It has become common sense to argue that the 1970s Latin American left was characterized by a class based approach with little sensitivity for the political potential of culture and ethnicity. However, Ecuadorian debates on culture, and its role in the political organization of peasants, challenge these widely held assumptions. Some authors such as Hugo Burgos (1970) – a progressive indigenist who was not part of the militant left – Diego Iturralde (1980) and Gladys Villavicencio (1973), all of whom studied in Mexico, began to focus on ethnic differences as a legacy of colonialism, internal colonialism, elite and state domination. Burgos carries out an analysis of central aspects of what is understood as indigenous culture and demonstrates how they constitute mechanisms of social subordination: One example is the minga (communal work), which was used by the Inkas, the Spaniards, hacendados and the state to extract free labor from peasants for public works. Syncretic religious festivities were also an important factor of exploitation, according to Burgos, when local elites and the traditional Church extracted economic profits from peasants through the rental of public spaces, customs, religious objects and other necessities, and the sale of food and alcohol. Peasants were so indebted after these celebrations that they were forced to mortgage or sell their land to local *chicheros* (sellers of *chicha*, a native beer) who were also moneylenders. This argument contrasts with the point of view of Rueda (1982), who understood peasant religious festivals as a factor of resistance to colonization and as peasant creativity.

Similarly, Iturralde (1980) argued that the 1937 communal law (passed as a means of controlling a unionized and increasingly radical peasantry), and its revamping with the 1964 agrarian reform, had resulted in increased state control over the community. Like Burgos, Iturralde believed that the ethnic label "indigenous," and the sense of belonging to a community that accompanied it, actually facilitated peasant co-optation. Likewise, Gladys Villavicencio (1973) observed during her fieldwork in Otavalo that local mestizos encouraged Otavalos to keep their traditional indigenous dress and hairstyle, as well as to remain monolingual in Quichua, to produce a clearly distinguishable group that they could exploit and discriminate against. Those Otavaleños who were able to speak Spanish or who adopted mestizo appearance were perceived as uppity and unmanageable (*alzados*) and were not hired in mestizo businesses. However, Villavicencio also noticed that one group of upwardly mobile indigenous textile manufacturers were reinforcing their ethnic pride, and contributing to the formation of an indigenous nationality as a strategy to fight discrimination. More established indigenists like Gonzalo Rubio Orbe (1973), however, rejected this conclusion.

Although some earlier indigenista authors (e.g. Buitrón 1971) had indirectly addressed the topic, Burgos's and Villavicencio's vivid descriptions of discrimination in the markets, public spaces, and public and private institutions of mestizo cities were among the first detailed analyses of racism in Ecuador, a topic that has only begun to be taken up again recently (J. Almeida 1996; de la Torre 1996, 2002; Cervone and Rivera 1999; Rahier 1998).

Researchers at CAAP, meanwhile, set out to rescue cultural differences for leftist politics by emphasizing the historical traditions and strategies for resistance that characterized the Andean community. CAAP's focus on the community had several sources of inspiration, including cultural anthropologists' models of Andean reciprocity and solidarity, John Murra's model of environmental micro-verticality, José Carlos Mariátegui's and Chayanov's notion of "the peasant commune … as the cell form of a future communist society" (Roseberry 1989:176), and the Catholic idea of religious base communities (Andrés Guerrero, interview, January 20, 2006).

The foundational book in this tradition was *Comunidad andina. Alternativas políticas de desarrollo* (The Andean Community: Political Alternatives for Development) (CAAP 1981). Although published only a year after Iturralde's sweeping critique of the community, the authors of *Comunidad andina* do not engage either Iturralde's argument or the Ecuadorian tradition of thought on the political importance of the indigenous community (e.g. Jaramillo 1922). On the contrary, the authors in

*Comunidad andina* and its continuation, *Estrategias de supervivencia en la comunidad andina* (Survival Strategies in the Andean Community) (CAAP 1984), draw on an eclectic mix of Russian, Mexican and Peruvian scholarship to argue that kinship and the Andean ayllu form the bases of peasant survival. Many of the authors in the volume were heavily influenced by both functionalist understandings of kinship and social cohesion, and by the seemingly contradictory tenets of Marxism. This harmonic view of the community was not only an interpretation of reality, but also an integral part of CAAP's political project and development work. For example, CAAP encouraged peasants to put into practice the very strategies of solidarity that had supposedly characterized them in the past.

Ethnolinguists were another left group whose ethnic and cultural agenda influenced the social movement. Linguists, for example, designed and helped to implement bilingual education, an institution that is key to understanding the political culture and organizational efficiency of the indigenous movement (Martínez Novo 2004). Ethnolinguists were based at the department of linguistics of the Catholic University, a program founded as a counterweight to the influence of the Protestant Summer Institute of Linguistics (Francisco Rhon, interview, August 14, 2006). Another ethnolinguist, José Yánez (interview, May 5, 2006), argues that while the indigenous movement and some academics close to it like himself still sponsored class based politics, ethnolinguists like Consuelo Yánez and Ruth Moya promoted an ethnicity centered agenda. The recent Secretary of Education in the government of Alfredo Palacio (2005 to 2006), Consuelo Yánez Cossío, for example, designed the intercultural bilingual program and elaborated Kichwa grammars, textbooks, and other materials. Ruth Moya and her sister Alba also worked on written materials for bilingual education and implemented the first degree in Andean linguistics for indigenous students at the University of Cuenca. By providing indigenous intellectuals with access to higher education, they helped to form those cadres who would later implement intercultural bilingual education in different regions of the country. Ruth Moya, who graduated at the University of Ottawa in Canada, mixed Marxism and structuralism in her work *Simbolismo y ritual en el Ecuador andino* (Symbolism and Ritual in Andean Ecuador) (1981). Similarly to *campesinista* authors, Moya interprets the survival of Andean symbols, customs, and practices as cultural resistance to colonization, modernization, and capitalism. Another important ethnolinguist, Ileana Almeida (1996), who studied linguistics in the Soviet Union, imported the Stalinist concept of oppressed nationalities, a concept that under her influence and that of other ethnolinguists was adopted by the Confederation of Indigenous Nationalities of Ecuador (CONAIE).

Somewhat different is the focus of José Yánez's *Yo declaro con franqueza. Cashnami causashcanchic* (I Sincerely Declare: We Have Lived in This Way) (1988). His book focuses on the oral history of a hacienda in Pesillo, Cayambe. Yánez emphasizes the political significance of collaborative research for raising peasant consciousness and promoting organization, as well as for learning about peasant historical rebellions, unionization processes, and political resistance to the hacienda system. After many years of working closely with the indigenous movement and in bilingual intercultural education, today Yanez's project focuses more on building interculturalism among mestizos in Ecuador through his classes in Kichwa language and anthropology. The idea is to make mestizos aware of their indigenous self so that they stop being secretly ashamed of themselves, become more indigenous, proud, and politically conscious.

Yánez's political project would thus seem to resonate with the work of early 20th century Andean intellectuals, such as the Peruvian indigenista José Uriel Garcia (1930) who rejected the idea of a "pure" Andean culture, and argued instead for a dynamic and flexible understanding of identity based on cultural mestizaje (see also Poole 1997).

## GENDER AND ETHNICITY

Gender studies in Ecuador started to develop in the 1980s (Cuvi 2006) and became incipiently institutionalized in academia in the 1990s (Herrera 2001). This scholarship was triggered in Ecuador by two concerns: the need for recognition of gender inequality and gender rights by a mostly urban, middle class feminist movement, and the agendas of international development organizations that in the 1980s start to require a gender component. Thus, the majority of work has been applied, and has been carried out from outside academia. Herrera (2001) argues that, for these reasons, a reflection on the articulations between gender and ethnicity has been scarce. Most work has centered on the oppression of women and the formation of their identity in private urban, middle class spaces, the inequality of women in public domains like the economy and politics, and the agendas of international organizations in topics such as gender and development. Paradoxically, according to Herrera, most foreign scholars working on gender in Ecuador have been anthropologists, and as such, they have privileged the study of indigenous and rural women (see, for example, Stolen 1987; Weismantel 1988; Crain 1991, 1996).

Studies of gender in indigenous contexts in Ecuador focused first on the role of female labor in peasant economies. These studies emphasize the flexibility of labor roles in indigenous peasant contexts, as well as the dignity of women's status within indigenous communities (Poeschel 1986; A. Martínez 1998). However, the seminal work of Stolen (1987) triggered reflection within Ecuador on the oppression and violence suffered by peasant women in the highlands, a violence that was characterized by Sanchez Parga (1990) as a way to restore Andean harmony, and as an Andean tradition of ritual fight linked to the Pan-Andean *tinkuy* (the violent union of opposites). Since then, the debate on gender and ethnicity has continued to focus on whether indigenous societies are egalitarian from a gender point of view, or unequal and characterized by discrimination and violence toward women. This debate is not, of course, restricted to Ecuador, but rather reaches across the Andean countries (see Harris, this volume). The discourse of gender complementarity, which is part of the official self-description of indigenous organizations, would seem to justify indigenous women's privileging of ethnic discrimination over gender oppression, as well as their lack of common agendas with the white-mestizo and urban-centered feminist movement (Prieto 1998; Prieto et al. 2005). On the other hand, it has been argued that indigenous societies are hierarchical from a gender point of view and that indigenous women would benefit from joining a feminist agenda and adding to it, while feminists would benefit from making their movement more inclusive (Prieto 1998; Prieto et al. 2005).

The differences between the highlands and the Amazonian region have also been pointed out (Cervone 1998). Whereas indigenous women in the highlands, despite sometimes acknowledged inequalities, have benefited from the flexibility of gender roles and from expanded spaces for political action, gender in the Amazon has been characterized by separate spaces for men and women, and women seem to have lost power and independence with processes of modernization that have encroached on their traditional spaces (Cervone 1998). Often, the violence and oppression against Amazonian, and Andean, women is interpreted as a Western and capitalist influence that has disrupted traditional gender relations described as harmonious. This assumption is challenged by Blanca Muratorio (2001), who uses archival and oral sources to show that gender violence among the Napo-Kichwas of the Ecuadorian Amazon has roots both internal to the culture and colonial.

## Anthropology and the Indigenous Movement

Starting in the early 1980s, Ecuadorian Indians had begun to take the first steps toward the formation of a united indigenous movement that would transform national politics in Ecuador. Although many regional, or second tier, indigenous organizations and communal associations had been active for many years, it was not until 1986 that the largest organization of highland Indians, ECUARUNARI, joined with the lowland CONFENIAE (Confederación de Nacionalidades Indígenas de la Amazonía Ecuatoriana, Confederation of Indigenous Nationalities of the Ecuadorian Amazon) to form the united Confederation of Indigenous Nationalities of Ecuador, or CONAIE. Four years later, CONAIE organized its first nationwide indigenous uprising. The uprising paralyzed the country, creating awareness among mestizo Ecuadorians of the organizational strength that indigenous peasants had acquired. Since then, periodical national uprisings have succeeded in halting or slowing the implementation of neoliberal reforms in Ecuador. Indigenous revolts have focused on the resolution of land claims, opposition to the 1994 law that sought to put an end to the process of agrarian reform, the declaration of Ecuador as a pluricultural state, opposition to the elimination of subsidies for basic products including natural gas and gasoline, intercultural education, and the demarcation of indigenous territories. In 1995, the indigenous social movement was enriched with its own political party, Pachakutik. In 1998, the Ecuadorian constitution was reformed to include the multicultural character of the nation as well as an array of indigenous rights.

The indigenous movement has definitely changed a country that until the 1980s was still very much based on a past of haciendas, servitude, and lack of citizenship rights. However, as critics have pointed out (Bretón 2001; Santana 2004), despite the formation of an indigenous middle class, most indigenous communities still live in poverty. Moreover, although constitutional indigenous rights were achieved, the secondary laws necessary for their implementation have not been developed. In addition, the indigenous movement participated in a military coup d'état in the year 2000 and reached governmental power in 2002 with Colonel Lucio Gutierrez. Once in power, Pachakutik for a number of reasons, including growing differences with the military president, did little to transform the country. In the 2006 presidential elections, we find a fragmented and weakened movement that was only able to get little above 2 percent of the vote in support of Luis Macas, its presidential candidate, while retaining some of its strength in Congress and at the local level.

How has this process been interpreted by anthropologists in Ecuador? Beginning in the mid-1980s, Ecuadorian anthropologists – influenced by their own activism with indigenous people and by an international academic turn toward the study of resistance – had begun to study the history and forms of indigenous protest (Prieto 1980; Moreno 1985; Ramón 1987; Yánez 1988; Bustamante 1988). The fact that many authors failed to fully comprehend the importance of the powerful organizational machinery that was in the making can be attributed, on the one hand, to the indigenous peasants' politically strategic (and historically justified) silence about their political activities, and on the other, to the role of the Catholic Church in the early indigenous organizations (Martínez Novo 2004; Rubenstein 2005). Many leftist scholars were anticlerical and dismissed the activities of the Church as reinforcing the status quo. For instance, Father Juan Botasso (1986) was well aware that strong political organizations based on indigenous identity are being built with the help of the missionary Catholic Church.

After the first indigenous uprising of 1990, and following the recurring mobilizations of the indigenous movement, a number of books and articles were published. These studies reflected an important characteristic of social sciences in Ecuador: many were studies of the conjuncture. One of the first books written by anthropologists after the 1990 indigenous uprising challenged traditional indigenista policies, while also criticizing the left for not having given importance to ethnic differences in the past (Moreno and Figueroa 1992). Two influential collective works written immediately after the indigenous uprising of 1990 are *Indios. Una reflexión sobre el levantamiento indígena de 1990* (Indians: A Reflection on the 1990 Indigenous Uprising) (Cornejo 1991) and *Sismo étnico en el Ecuador* (Ethnic Earthquake in Ecuador) (Almeida et al. 1993). *Indios* brought together scholars who worked on indigenous issues and social actors such as indigenous activists, landowners and the military, while *Sismo étnico* also featured academic analyses by both white/mestizo and indigenous intellectuals. A more recent book by Fernando Guerrero and Pablo Ospina (2003) focuses on the connections between indigenous mobilization and neoliberal structural adjustment. The authors, however, also note the collaboration of the indigenous movement with what they characterize as neoliberal governments since the movement's entrance into the political sphere in 1995. Other authors have focused on particular aspects of indigenous struggles, such as the search for legal pluralism (García 2002). While documenting a wide array of indigenous legal uses, some of these works also reflect a romantic view of the community and fail to be critical when indigenous legal practices collide with human rights.

Such complexities attest to the ambiguities and contradictions of the indigenous movement, and present a challenge to anthropologists in their attempts to describe and understand indigenous "resistance." Here it is important to note that much of the work done since 1990 on the indigenous movement has been done by anthropologists working as consultants for (or otherwise funded by) international agencies. The majority of this work has supported the movement even in moments of crisis or when it has made important mistakes (for example, during the 2000 coup d'état or the alliance with Lucio Gutierrez). In fact, some of these scholars are themselves advisors to the movement or collaborate closely with it in consulting or development work. This close collaboration makes it difficult for authors to defend a critical position with respect to the indigenous movement, especially because scholars now often require the approval of indigenous organizations to get funds from international agencies.

Substantial critiques of the indigenous movement have been made by Roberto Santana and Víctor Bretón. Santana (2004), who teaches in France, draws on his long-term work on Ecuadorian indigenous politics to describe how the movement's organizational "fetishism" prevents it from developing a coherent political project. Bretón (2001, 2005) shows that development projects and particularly the World Bank's Development Program for Indigenous and Black Peoples (PRODEPINE, Programa de Desarrollo de los Pueblos Indígenas y Negros) – which has been widely embraced by the indigenous movement – have failed to improve indigenous peoples' lives, and led to the political demobilization of a once radical movement. Bretón's work contributed to the indigenous movement's recent rejection of the second phase of PRODEPINE. Some critiques have also been presented by the Catholic Church. Father Miguel Angel Cabodevilla (2004) of the Aguarico Vicariate, has written a moving and passionate book about the genocide of what he calls the "hidden peoples," indigenous groups neighboring the more numerous Huaorani, and still living with little contact with Ecuadorian society. Cabodevilla argues that oil and timber companies are encouraging the Huaorani Indians who lead the Organización de la Nacionalidad Huaorani del Ecuador (a branch of CONFENIAE and CONAIE) to exterminate these other peoples. Father Cabodevilla is ethically involved in protecting the human rights of these peoples – who, paradoxically, are legally represented in relation to the Ecuadorian state by the very organization that is annihilating them.

## INDIGENOUS SCHOLARS AND ANTHROPOLOGY

Although every Ecuadorian has enjoyed a constitutional right to elementary education since the 19th century (Ramón 1991), in practice most indigenous peoples were functionally illiterate and excluded from public education until the 1970s. The educational efforts of the Communist Party, which opened clandestine schools for indigenous peasants in the 1940s, the work of the progressive Catholic Church, and the struggles of the indigenous organizations themselves have allowed for the formation of a group of indigenous intellectuals. These intellectuals started to acquire literacy, high school diplomas, higher education, and more recently access to graduate education and international grants. Despite these achievements, their insertion in academia is not yet complete. Unlike what happened 20 years ago, indigenous peoples now participate in academic conferences as students, speakers and audience. However, most indigenous intellectuals find jobs in politics or intercultural bureaucracies, and remain underrepresented in academic institutions. As a result, indigenous intellectuals have, to date, not published as much as their nonindigenous counterparts, a problem that is often noted at meetings of the indigenous movement (Kar Atamaint, personal communication). With this history of difficulties and exclusion in mind, I will briefly comment on a few published works by indigenous authors.

In the 1970s, the Salesians started to publish the work of Shuar intellectuals in the collection Mundo Shuar. José Vicente Jintiach, a historic leader of the Shuar Federation and one of the first to get access to higher education, at the Catholic University, published his reflections on the difficult adjustments facing the Shuar youth who entered Salesian boarding schools. Jintiach's book (1976) portrays the Shuar as a people fully integrated into, and fond of, modernity, who enjoyed the few movies to which they had access in Sucúa and the music of the Beatles. As is typical of the egalitarian Shuar culture, Jintiach is very critical of the Salesians' authority. According to Jintiach, Shuar adolescents find the lack of personal liberty and the sexual repression they encounter in the boarding schools particularly painful. However, Jintiach unambiguously recognizes the importance of the opportunity provided by the Salesian schools for education in the dominant culture. A much more recent work that also questions essentialism and presents indigenous peoples as fully integrated into modernity is Gina Maldonado's *Comerciantes y viajeros. De la imagen etnoarqueológica de lo indígena al imaginario del Kichwa Otavalo universal* (Merchants and Travelers: From the Ethnoarchaeological Image of Indigenous People to the Universal Quichua Otavalo Imaginary) (2004). Maldonado, who obtained her M.A. in anthropology at FLACSO-Ecuador, draws on interviews with young Otavaleños who are business people and who often travel to Europe, the United States, and other Latin American countries to question the anthropological image of Otavaleños as a people who are "frozen in the past." Instead, she argues that Otavaleños are themselves struggling to define what it means to be indigenous within modernity and globalization.

By contrast with Jintiach and Maldonado, another recent book by another anthropology M.A. from FLACSO, Raul Ilaquiche (2004), represents indigenous culture as fixed since prehispanic times, arguing that such a representation is necessary in order to legitimize the claims of the indigenous movement to legal pluralism (a right that was recognized for the first time in the 1998 constitution). Ilaquiche is also uncritical of the tensions between indigenous justice and human rights, which is one of the most important bottlenecks for the implementation of indigenous legal systems, as well as of the legacy of hacienda practices in indigenous customary legal practices. Thus, the work of indigenous scholars – although not abundant given their difficult access to the sorts of academic jobs where writing is encouraged and possible – do enrich Ecuadorian anthropology with a variety of different perspectives.

## CONCLUSION: ACADEMICS OR CONSULTANTS?

How, then, does living in an economically and politically unstable environment affect the intellectual work of anthropologists residing in Ecuador? Instability does good and bad things to our ability to produce knowledge and to the kind of knowledge produced for those who not only study, but also live in unstable places (Greenhouse 2002). It is important to note that in Ecuador academic jobs are limited, institutions tend to be fragile, and the state does not now – and perhaps never did – provide anthropologists with a reliable framework within which to work. Since the mid-1980s, academics in Ecuador have relied more and more on consulting work for international agencies like the World Bank, the Inter-American Development Bank, and the United Nations. Others have been forced, or have chosen, to work for private companies – including oil companies, which now finance some Amazonian anthropology. Others have had to work with the validation of the social actors they study. Of course, this has had important ethical implications for those whose desirable role might be to provide a perspective of critical distance. Even those who are lucky enough to work for more or less stable academic institutions, such as the universities, are required to bring in private funds that can sustain these institutions financially. While this process is certainly linked to the neoliberalization of academia that is also taking place in the North, the stakes are much higher in an "unstable" and poorer country with virtually no safety net for those intellectuals who do not succeed in the entrepreneurial world of consultancies (Escobar 2006). On the other hand, rejecting external private funds and depending on state money makes institutions vulnerable to political influences and to uncontrollable factors like oil prices in an oil-fueled state.

In addition to the lack of diversity discussed earlier, another problem in Ecuadorian academia relates to the position of women. Although, as has been pointed out throughout the chapter, some of the most important contributions to Ecuadorian anthropology have been made by women, whose works often do not receive the attention they merit, they tend to be in academic positions that are more fragile than those of men; they are not invited to the conferences and debates that deal with public issues; and their contributions to research tend to remain unrecognized.

Another difficulty facing Ecuadorian anthropologists is that solid academic work is often restricted to theses and dissertations. Many academic contributions to Ecuadorian anthropology by authors such as Galo Ramón (1987), Mercedes Prieto (2004), Susana Andrade (2004), and Eduardo Kingman (2006) have been published theses. For instance, Prieto's *Liberalismo y temor. Imaginando los sujetos indígenas en el Ecuador postcolonial* (Liberalism and Fear: Imagining Indigenous Subjects in Postcolonial Ecuador) (2004) draws on a rigorously researched review of congressional and other political debates, as well as academic texts, to trace liberal debates about indigenous peoples in the first half of the 20th century. Prieto characterized these debates as being marked by a tension between fear of popular groups, ethnic subordination, and the longing for a certain degree of equality. Susana Andrade's *Protestantismo indígena* (2004) is based on long-term fieldwork and reflection among indigenous Protestants in Chimborazo. She looks at indigenous Protestantism in the context of processes of economic, social, and political change, and shows how a religious current of North American origin becomes inserted within, and transformed by, local and Kichwa logics. Kingman (2006) discusses how concepts of the urban and the modern which circulated in early 20th century Quito, rendered invisible the city's indigenous migrants and lower classes.

However, as Greenhouse (2002) and the authors of *Ethnography in Unstable Places* note, instability and fragility can often lead to insights and creative solutions. As I have discussed at length, Ecuadorian anthropologists in the last decades have overcome institutional obstacles to play major roles in public debates on important social and political transformations, and they have tended to avoid trivial discussions in an environment where the contribution of academia to the understanding and improvement of a fragile reality is deemed fundamental.

## NOTES

1    I would like to thank Deborah Poole for her comments and thorough editorial work. Víctor Bretón, Francisco Rhon, José Yánez, Andrés Guerrero, Carlos de la Torre, and the colleagues at FLACSO-Ecuador provided valuable insights as well.

2    Some of the same reasons have been used to explain the "conspiracy of silence" that surrounds Ecuadorian literary works from this time period (Arcos Cabrera 2005).

## REFERENCES

Almeida, Ileana (1996) *Temas y cultura quichua en el Ecuador*. Quito: Abya Yala.

Almeida, José (1996). Fundamentos del racismo ecuatoriano. *Ecuador Debate* 38:55–71.

Almeida, José et al. (1993) *Sismo étnico en Ecuador*. Quito: CEDIME/Abya Yala.

Andrade, Susana (2004) *Protestantismo indígena. Procesos de conversión religiosa en la provincia de Chimborazo, Ecuador*. Quito: FLACSO.

Andrade, Xavier (2004) Burocracia. Museos, políticas culturales y flexibilización laboral en Guayaquil. *Iconos* 20:64–72.

Arcos Cabrera, Carlos (2005) Los avatares de la literatura ecuatoriana. El caso Chiriboga. *Letras* (Chile), Sept.

Audiovisuales Don Bosco (n.d.) *Abya Yala*. DVD. Quito.

Audiovisuales Don Bosco (n.d.) *Misiones en el Oriente*. DVD. Quito.

Bartoli, Laura (2002) *Antropología aplicada. Historia y perspectivas desde América Latina*. Quito: Abya Yala.

Benavides, Hugo (2006) La representación del pasado sexual de Guayaquil. Historizando a los enchaquirados. *Iconos* 24:145–160.

Botasso, Juan (1986) Las nacionalidades indígenas, el estado y las misiones en el Ecuador. *Ecuador Debate* 12:151–159.

Bretón, Víctor (2001) *Cooperación al desarrollo y demandas étnicas en los Andes ecuatorianos*. Quito: FLACSO.

Bretón, Víctor (2005) *Capital social y etnodesarrollo en los Andes*. Quito: CAAP.

Burgos, Hugo (1970) *Relaciones interétnicas en Riobamba*. Mexico City: Instituto Indigenista Interamericano. Republished Quito: Corporación Editora Nacional, 1997.

Buitrón, Aníbal (1971[1949]) *El valle del amanecer*. Otavalo: Instituto Otavaleño de Antropología.

Bustamante, Teodoro (1988) *La larga lucha del kakaram contra el sucre*. Quito: Abya Yala.

CAAP (Centro Andino de Acción Popular) (1981) *Comunidad andina. Alternativas políticas de desarrollo*. Quito: CAAP.

CAAP (Centro Andino de Acción Popular) (1984). *Estrategias de supervivencia en la comunidad andina*. Quito: CAAP.

Cabodevilla, Miguel Angel (2004) *El exterminio de los pueblos ocultos*. Quito: CICAME.

Cervone, Emma (1998) *Mujeres contracorriente. Voces de líderes indígenas*. Quito: CEPLAES.

Cervone, Emma and Rivera, Freddy (1999) *Ecuador racista. Imágenes e identidades*. Quito: FLACSO.

Chaves, María Eugenia (1998) *María Chiquinquirá Días. Una esclava del siglo XVIII. Acerca de las identidades de amo y esclavo en el Puerto colonial de Guayaquil*. Guayaquil: Archivo Histórico del Guayas-Banco Central de Ecuador.

Chiriboga, Manuel (1980) *Jornaleros y gran propietarios en 135 años de explotación cacaotera*. Quito: CIESE.

Chiriboga, Manuel (1988) *El problema agrario en el Ecuador*. Quito: ILDIS.

Cornejo, Diego (ed.) (1991) *Indios. Una reflexión sobre el levantamiento indígena de 1990*. Quito: ILDIS/Duende/Abya Yala.

Crain, Mary (1991) Poetics and Politics in the Ecuadorian Andes: Women's Narratives of Death and Devil Possession. *American Ethnologist* 18(1).

Crain, Mary (1996) The Gendering of Ethnicity in the Ecuadorian Andes. In A. Stolen and M. Melhus (eds), *Machos, Mistresses and Madonnas*. New York: Verso.

Cucurella, Leonella (2005) *Abya Yala. Tierra en plena madurez*. Quito: Abya Yala.

Cuvi, María (2006) *Pensamiento feminista y escritos de mujeres en el Ecuador. 1980–1990*. Quito: UNIFEM–UNICEF.

de la Torre, Carlos (1996) *El racismo en el Ecuador. Experiencias de los indios de clase media*. Quito: CAAP (2nd edn 2002 with Abya Yala).

de la Torre, Carlos (2002) *Afroquiteños. Ciudadanía y racismo*. Quito: CAAP.

Escobar, Arturo (2006) Revisioning Latin American and Caribbean Studies: A Geopolitics of Knowledge Approach. *Latin American Studies Association Forum* 37(2):11–14.

Estrada, Víctor Emilio (1979) *Ultimas civilizaciones prehistóricas de la cuenca del río Guayas.* Guayaquil: Publicaciones del Archivo Histórico del Guayas.

Farga, Cristina and Almeida, José (1981) *Campesinos y haciendas de la sierra norte.* Otavalo-Ecuador: Instituto Otavaleño de Antropología.

Fernández Rasines, Paloma (2001) *Afrodescendencia en el Ecuador. Raza y género desde los tiempos de la colonia.* Quito: Abya Yala.

Fontaine, Guillaume (2003) *El precio del petróleo. Conflictos socio-ambientales y gobernabilidad en la región amazónica.* Quito: FLACSO.

García, Fernando (1980) Introducción. *Revista de la Universidad Católica* 8(26):7–14.

García, Fernando (2002) *Formas indígenas de administrar justicia.* Quito: FLACSO.

Garcia, José Uriel (1930) *El nuevo indio.* Lima: Colección de autores peruanos.

Greenhouse, Carol (2002) Introduction. In C. Greenhouse, E. Mertz, and K. Warren (eds), *Ethnography in Unstable Places: Everyday Lives in Contexts of Dramatic Political Change* (pp. 1–34). Durham, NC: Duke University Press.

Guerrero, Andrés (1980) *Los oligarcas del cacao.* Quito: El Conejo.

Guerrero, Andrés (1983) *Haciendas, capital y lucha de clases andina.* Quito: El Conejo.

Guerrero, Andrés (1991) *La semántica de la dominación. El concertaje de indios.* Quito: Libri Mundi.

Guerrero, Fernando and Ospina, Pablo (2003) *El poder de la comunidad. Ajuste estructural y movimiento indígena en los Andes Ecuatorianos.* Quito: CLACSO.

Herrera, Gioconda (2001) Los estudios de género en el Ecuador. Entre el conocimiento y el reconocimiento. In G. Herrera (ed.), *Antología de estudios de género.* Quito: FLACSO.

Ilaquiche, Raul (2004) *Pluralismo jurídico y administración de justicia indígena en Ecuador.* Quito: Hans Seidel.

Iturralde, Diego (1980) *Guamote. Campesinos y comunas.* Otavalo-Ecuador: Instituto Otavaleño de Antropología.

Jaramillo, Pío (1922) *El indio ecuatoriano.* Quito: Corporación Editora Nacional.

Jintiach, José Vicente (1976). *La integración del estudiante Shuar en su grupo social.* Quito: Mundo Shuar.

Kingman, Eduardo (2006) *La ciudad y los otros. Quito 1860–1940.* Quito: FLACSO.

Kuper, Adam (1973) *Antropología y antropólogos. La escuela británica.* Mexico City: Fondo de Cultura Económica.

Maldonado, Gina (2004) *Comerciantes y viajeros. De la imagen etnoarqueológica de lo indígena al imaginario del Kichwa otavalo universal.* Quito: FLACSO/Abya Yala.

Martínez, Alexandra (1998) La producción de esteras en Yahuarcocha y la construcción del significado de ser mujer y ser hombre. In C. Landázuri (ed.), *Memorias del primer congreso ecuatoriano de antropología.* Quito: PUCE-Marka.

Martínez, Luciano (1984) *De campesinos a proletarios.* Quito: el Conejo.

Martínez Novo, Carmen (2004) Los misioneros salesianos y el movimiento indígena de Cotopaxi 1970–2004. *Ecuador Debate* 63:235–268.

Moreno Yánez, Segundo (1985) *Sublevaciones indígenas en la Audiencia de Quito desde comienzos del S. XVIII hasta finales de la colonia.* Quito: PUCE.

Moreno Yánez, Segundo (1992) *Antropología ecuatoriana. Pasado y presente.* Quito: Ediguias.

Moreno Yánez, Segundo and Figueroa, José (1992) *El levantamiento indígena del Inti Raymi.* Quito: Abya Yala.

Moya, Ruth (1981) *Simbolismo y ritual en el Ecuador Andino.* Otavalo-Ecuador: Instituto Otavaleño de Antropología.

Muratorio, Blanca (1991) *The Life and Times of Grandfather Alonso: Culture and History in the Upper Amazon.* New Brunswick: Rutgers University Press.

Muratorio, Blanca (2001) History and Cultural Memory of Violence against Indigenous Women in the Ecuadorian Upper Amazon. MS.

Naranjo, Marcelo (1980) *Etnicidad, estructura social y poder en Manta*. Otavalo: Pendoneros.

Pelizzaro, Siro (1990) *Arutam. Mitología Shuar*. Quito: Abya Yala.

Poeschel, Ursula (1986) *La mujer salasaca*. Quito: Abya Yala.

Poole, Deborah (1997) *Vision, Race and Modernity: A Visual Economy of the Andean Image World*. Princeton: Princeton University Press.

Prieto, Mercedes (1980) Haciendas estatales. Un caso de ofensiva campesina. In O. Barsky et al. (eds), *Ecuador: cambios en el agro serrano*. Quito: FLACSO/CEPLAES.

Prieto, Mercedes (1998) El liderazgo en las mujeres indígenas. Tendiendo puentes entre género y étnia. In E. Cervone (ed.), *Mujeres contracorriente*. Quito: CEPLAES.

Prieto, Mercedes (2004) *Liberalismo y temor. Imaginando los sujetos indígenas en el Ecuador postcolonial*. Quito: FLACSO.

Prieto, Mercedes, Cuminao, Clorinda, Flores, Alejandra, Maldonado, Gina, and Pequeño, Andrea (2005) Las mujeres indígenas y la búsqueda del respeto. In *Mujeres ecuatorianas. Entre la crisis y las oportunidades*. Quito: FLACSO.

Quiroga, Diego (2003) The Devil and Development in Esmeraldas: Cosmology as a System of Critical Thought. In N. Whitten (ed.), *Millennial Ecuador* (pp. 154–183). Iowa City: University of Iowa Press.

Rahier, Jean Muteba (1998) Blackness, the Racial Spatial Order, Migrations and Miss Ecuador 1995–1996. *American Anthropologist* 100(2):421–430.

Ramón, Galo (1987) *La resistencia andina. Cayambe 1500–1800*. Quito: CAAP.

Ramón, Galo (1991) Ese secreto poder de la escritura. In D. Cornejo (ed.), *Indios*. Quito: ILDIS/Duende/Abya Yala.

Roseberry, William (1989) *Anthropologies and Histories*. New Brunswick: Rutgers University Press.

Rubenstein, Steven (2005) La conversión de los Shuar. *Iconos* 22, special issue on politics and religion: 27–48.

Rubio Orbe, Gonzalo (1973) Prólogo. In G. Villavicencio, *Relaciones interétnicas en Otavalo*. Mexico City: Instituto Indigenista Interamericano.

Rueda, Marco Vinicio (1982) *La fiesta religiosa campesina*. Quito: Ediciones de la Universidad Católica.

Salazar, Ernesto (1986) *Pioneros de la selva*. Quito: Abya Yala.

Sánchez Parga, José (1990) *¿Por qué golpearla? Etica, estética y ritual en los Andes*. Quito: CAAP.

Sánchez Parga, José (2002) *Crisis en torno al Quilotoa. Mujer, cultura y comunidad*. Quito: CAAP.

Santana, Roberto (2004) Cuando las élites indígenas giran en redondo. El caso de los lideraz- gos indígenas en Ecuador. *Ecuador Debate* 61:235–258.

Sawyer, Suzana (2004) *Crude Chronicles: Indigenous Politics, Multinational Oil, and Neoliber- alism in Ecuador*. Durham, NC: Duke University Press.

Stolen, Kristi Anne (1987) *A media voz. Relaciones de género en la sierra ecuatoriana*. Quito: CEPLAES.

Striffler, Steve (2002) *In the Shadows of State and Capital: The United Fruit Company, Popular Struggle and Agrarian Restructuring in Ecuador*. Durham, NC: Duke University Press.

Ventura i Oller, Montserrat (1999) Ser Tsáchila en el Ecuador contemporáneo. *Ecuador Debate* 48:95–118.

Villavicencio, Gladys (1973) *Relaciones interétnicas en Otavalo. ¿Una nacionalidad india en formación?* Mexico City: Instituto Indigenista Interamericano.

Weismantel, Mary (1988) *Food, Gender, and Poverty in the Ecuadorian Andes*. Philadelphia: University of Pennsylvania Press.

Whitten, Norman (1965) *Class, Kinship, and Power in an Ecuadorian Town: The Negroes of San Lorenzo*. Stanford: Stanford University Press.

Whitten, Norman (1974) *Black Frontiersmen: Afro-Hispanic Culture of Ecuador and Colom- bia*. Prospect Heights, IL: Waveland Press.

Yánez, José (1988) *Yo declaro con franqueza. Cashnami causashcanchic*. Quito: Abya Yala.

# CHAPTER 6 Guatemala: Essentialisms and Cultural Politics

*Brigittine M. French*

Consider the following reflection on Maya culture in Guatemala: "Los indígenas no pueden tener cultura, ya que son cerrados, analfabetos, atrasados y haraganes y encima de todo ladrones" [The Indians can't have culture, they are closed, illiterate, backward, lazy, and, on top of it all, thieves] (quoted in Casaús Arzú 1992:274). Now juxtapose it with this antithetical perspective: "Xtik'atzin ta k'a chi ke ri taq ixtani' taq alab'o' re eral jal, e ral ixim ruma pa kiq'a rije' k'oj wi ri k'ak'a rusaqarisab'al ri Maya Amaq" [To the boys and girls of the corn who are the future of the Maya people, because the new radiant dawn of Maya culture and the continuation of Mayan languages is in their hands] (Garcia Matzar and Rodriguez Guaján 1997:4).[1] The former is a commonplace conception of "Indian" identity articulated by a 59-year-old elite ladina (non-Indian, mestizo); the latter is a visionary book dedication written by two Maya-Kaqchikel linguists. Taken together as emblematic, they underscore the importance of Maya culture in Guatemalan national discourse and highlight its contested meanings and locations. Their juxtaposition also indicates that objectified constructions of culture are implicated in essentialized notions of social difference, in this case indigenous identity. The issue of essentialist constructs of social difference, Maya Indian and ladino ones specifically, has fundamentally structured scholarly inquiries in the anthropology of Guatemala.

In the pages that follow, I take up a consideration of the anthropology of Guatemala around the history, politics, and theoretical polemics of essentialism. I begin by historicizing essentialist constructions of Maya identity relative to nation-building in Guatemala and go on to connect constructions of "Indians" as "Others" within the nation to the late 20th century genocide against Maya populations. I then move to consider strategic essentialism as it is self-consciously deployed by the Maya movement to reconfigure the Guatemalan nation as a multilingual and multicultural imagined community. I show how this tension between competing essentialisms with radically different political agendas situates the particularities of Guatemalan anthropology squarely in theoretical debates about essentialism in the discipline. I argue that the anthropology of Guatemala in the post-conflict era does not try to resolve the paradox of strategic essentialism; rather anthropological scholarship embraces its irresolution. In accepting the irresolution of the paradox of strategic essentialism for a potentially libratory politics, anthropological scholarship about contemporary Guatemalan social life moves beyond the theoretical question to "celebrate" or "criticize" essentialist constructions of collective Selves when authored by historically disenfranchised Others. More specifically, current research on collective identity construction among Guatemala's multiethnic communities reframes questions of essentialism and politics in a variety of innovative ways that productively focus on the multiplicity of agents involved in the creation of essentialist identities, the regimes of knowledge that are efficacious and contested in essentialist cultural politics, the erasure of alternate forms of collective identification, and the transnational economic forces that shape the politics of essentialism in Guatemala.

## ESSENTIALISM, VIOLENCE, AND THE STATE

One place to enter into a discussion of collective identity construction, cultural politics, and inequality in Guatemala is the modernist moment of nation-building and its concomitant gestures of exclusion. Indeed, since the beginning of the nation-building period during the early 19th century, the nation has been erected upon the stark opposition between two groups: "Indians" and ladinos (Smith 1990a). Constituting meaningful categories of social boundedness, ladino refers to the minority of Guatemala's citizens who are of European, usually Spanish and indigenous ancestry, while "Indian" refers to members of any of the 21 ethnolinguistic groups belonging to the family of Mayan languages, defined by shifting but persistent notions of marked cultural difference, who constitute the majority of Guatemala's rural and impoverished population.[2]

Seizing upon the social opposition between these two categories, the Guatemalan state has actively circulated a conception of "Indians" as an undifferentiated and inherently inferior group that has stood stubbornly in the way of the nation's progress toward unity and development, modeled after Western paradigms of nation-building (Gellner 1983). In other words, the Guatemalan nation has been imagined not, as Benedict Anderson (1991) would have it, by means of an opposition to other nations – an external "they" – but by means of an internal opposition, a division within. From this perspective, to be Guatemalan has meant to be ladino, and to be ladino means to be non-Indian. Within this commonplace and hegemonic logic, the persistence of the "Indian problem" has been the bane of the nation's project of crafting a homogeneous national community. As Carol Smith has shown, "each attempt by the modern Guatemalan state to eradicate cultural divisions in order to create a unified nation has been either brutal or half-hearted, such that the attempt has merely recreated the division between Indians and non-Indians in stronger form" (1990b:6).

These enduring essential constructs of "Indians" as inherently "backward, uncivilized, and ignorant" (Casaús Arzú 1992) in 20th century Guatemalan national discourse have had material and violent consequences for the majority Maya population. Robert Hayden (2002) highlights the productive link between exclusive constructions of national identity in multiethnic contexts and the possibility of state-sponsored violence against Others within the nation's borders. Hayden argues that such essentialist discourse in the context of nation-building can be "a matter of making heterogeneous communities unimaginable. In formal terms, the point has been to implement an essentialist definition of the nation... the brutal negation of social reality in order to reconstruct it. It is this reconstruction that turns the imagination of a community into a process that produces real victims" (2002:232). In the Guatemalan context, such essentialist constructions of Indian identity as antithetical to definitions of Guatemalan national identity have been a productive part of the conditions of possibility for state-sponsored violence against Maya populations. Ultimately, the essentialist construction of "Indians" was a condition of possibility that, along with the confluence of several other economic, social, and political factors, led to genocide (Menchú Túm 1983; Montejo 1987; Carmack 1988; Grandin 2004). From the late 1970s to the mid-1980s, the military, under the leadership of presidents/generals Lucas García and Ríos Montt, unleashed a genocidal campaign against Maya populations. During "La Violencia," the army and its agents annihilated 626 villages, leaving over 200,000 people dead and another million people displaced, the overwhelming majority of whom were Maya (CEH 1999).

## STRATEGIC ESSENTIALISM AND THE MAYA MOVEMENT

Rising out of this unprecedented period of repression, some Maya people have become committed to a vibrant ethnonationalist movement that seeks to promote Maya cultural difference within the nation-state and to craft a collective Pan-Maya identity in the face of a national policy of assimilation and violence (COMG 1991; Cojtí Cuxil 1991, 1994, 1995; Fischer and Brown 1996; Warren 1998). It is a movement launched both against the nation-state and in favor of the nation as reconstituted and redefined by the politics of cultural difference. The Maya movement's cultural revitalization project based centrally (although not exclusively) around the Mayan languages is linked to the dual political objectives of promoting cultural autonomy for Maya peoples and reconfiguring the Guatemalan nation into a multilingual and multicultural democracy.

    Central to the pursuit of the Maya movement's goals of cultural self-determination and progressive political reform within the Guatemalan state is the strategically essential linking of Mayan languages with the ideal of a unified Maya *pueblo* (people/ nation) (French 1999). In other words, Mayan languages hold a unique place among several aspects of culture that are objectified as the fundamental essences of Maya identity, as the foundation upon which a collective identity, based upon difference within the nation, is erected. This nationalist language ideology linking Mayan languages with the ideal of collective Maya identity has acted as an effective means for structuring notions of difference and legitimizing calls for cultural autonomy. Indeed, the few but important victories Maya leaders have won involve the state's recognition of difference based upon the uniqueness of Mayan languages and their provisional inclusion in the Guatemalan national community. These include the development of the Unified Alphabet for Mayan languages in 1987, the creation of the autonomous Mayan Languages Academy in 1990, and the recent reconfiguration of DIGEBI (General Directorate of Bilingual and Intercultural Education), an explicitly intercultural bilingual education program in 1995. Such accomplishments are particularly significant because they demonstrate how Maya activists and scholars have managed to challenge the modernist project of nation-building and its foundational ideals of cultural continuity and ethnic homogeneity (Handler 1988). They also reveal the extent to which Mayan activism has obliged the Guatemalan state to shift its position on the relation of difference within the nation from the antithetical to the problematic.

## Essentialisms and Anthropological Scholarship

Within this historical context, we can once again consider the tension that introduced this essay, namely, the competing constructions of an essentialized indigenous identity, one promoted by the state in service of the hegemonic and violent project to create a homogeneous Guatemala, and one endorsed by the Maya movement in a self-conscious attempt to reconfigure the Guatemalan nation into a multicultural democracy. It is this tension between competing essentialisms with radically different political agendas that situates the particularities of Guatemala anthropology at the center of broader disciplinary debates about the theoretical and ethical implications of essentialism.

At the beginning of the 21st century, many anthropologists and postcolonial scholars are theoretically well versed in the construction of "Otherness" and widely critical of its concomitant essentialized notions of collective identity that work in service of systems of domination (Said 1979). From this perspective, constructions of essential Others function productively both to justify and further hegemony. Such an understanding of the relationships between essentialism, identity construction, and power necessarily implicates scholarly discourse, including anthropological research, in hegemonic representations (Abu-Lughod 1991; Trouillot 1991; Domínguez 1994). Engaging this broad concern with the production of essentialist identities, in the specific ethnographic scholarship about Guatemala, begins to reveal an intellectual history of essentialist constructs of "Indian" identity by anthropologists (Tax 1937; Wagley 1949; Redfield 1962) and recent critiques of those constructions (Casaús Arzú 1992; Smith 1999; Montejo 2002; French 2005b).

While they are generally critical of essentialist constructs of collective identity that work in service of domination, there is little consensus among anthropologists on how to deal productively with essentialism when it is authored by disenfranchised Others. In other words, there is much debate about how to engage essential identity construction when the authors of these constructions are precisely those social groups who have been marginalized by colonial, national, and/or anthropological endeavors – as is the case with scholars and activists involved in Maya ethnonationalism in Guatemala. Daniel Segal articulates these pressing disciplinary questions in the following way: "How should we, as ethnographers, relate to the identity politics of variously marginalized ethnographic subjects? Should some identities, even if they involve essentializing, be celebrated by ethnographers as acts of resistance by the oppressed? Or should ethnographic analysis position itself as resisting any and all essentialized identities?" (1996:431). The problematics of dealing with strategically essential identity constructs "cut across the boundaries of various area literatures" in anthropology (1996:431), particularly as former anthropological subjects in a variety of ethnographic contexts author their own analyses in the service of cultural rights (Cojtí 1990; Briggs 1996; Trask 1999).

Serious engagement with these theoretical debates in anthropology, coupled with the specific horrors of state-sponsored violence (Falla 1992; REHMI 1998; Sanford 2003) and the hopes of ethnonationalist politics in Guatemala (OKMA 1993; Cojtí 1994, 1995; Montejo 1997), has necessarily pushed the intellectual trajectory in the anthropology of Guatemala in new directions. More specifically, the anthropology of Guatemala in the post-conflict era does not try to resolve the paradox of strategic essentialism for potentially libratory politics; rather it begins with it. Recognizing the irresolution of the paradox as a point of entry into anthropological research allows us to move beyond the theoretical question Segal raised, namely, to "celebrate" or "criticize" essentialist constructions of collective Selves when authored by historically disenfranchised Others. Instead, recent scholarship about collective identity construction in Guatemala reframes questions of essentialism and politics in a variety of ways that engender new theoretical perspectives and ethnographic inquiries. Specifically, such work raises the questions: Who are the agents of essentialism? What regimes of knowledge enable the conditions of its possibility for essentialist constructions of identity and in what ways are these epistemologies contested? What erasures are entailed in discourses of essentialism? How is essentialism implicated in transnational economic forces? Taken together, these questions concern not only the politics of representation, but also their concrete manifestations in political inclusions and exclusions.

I now turn to take up some ethnographically rich and theoretically informed answers to these questions.

## AGENTS OF STRATEGIC ESSENTIALISM

As we have seen, the state and Maya intellectuals/activists have productively authored essentialist constructions of Maya identity for radically different political ends. Recent scholarly inquiry into the Maya movement illustrates how to move beyond the paradox of strategic essentialism so as to examine critically its current agents and their assumptions, strategies, and fields of involvement in the post-violence era. Demetrio Cojtí Cuxil's book *Ri Maya' Moloj pa Iximulew* (The Maya Movement in Guatemala) (1997) comprehensively maps several factors involved in the development of the Maya movement, its objectives, its strategies, and its involvement with national and international organizations. Originally prepared for the internal use of those involved in the Maya movement (1997:11), Cojtí crafts his analysis from the unique and self-conscious perspective provided by his positioning within the movement itself (1997:13). Specifically, Cojtí frames his analysis of the movement as a particular response to the condition of internal colonialism. He devotes analytic attention to the definition of internal colonialism, working analogically through a cross-cultural comparison with the anticolonial African independence movements of the 1970s, to argue that the economic, political, and social position of the Maya population within the Guatemalan nation confirms that the "country evolved from a colonial dictatorship to a colonial democracy" (1997:23). As such, he defines the Maya movement as fundamentally anticolonial (1997:43) and is quick to point out, rather than negate, the contradictions inherent in essentialist identity politics. Indeed, Cojtí recognizes contradictions as a point of entry into further analysis and action. He situates the paradoxical position of Maya cultural activism in the following way:

> The first internal contradiction among the members of the Maya nation is the two antagonistic options to resolve the colonial situation that they have suffered... In effect, confronted with the situation of internal colonialism, there are two basic and contradictory solutions: the assimilation of the dominated nation advised by the dominant nation or the recognizing of their autonomy revindicated principally by the dominated nation. (1997:37–38)

In effect, Cojtí emphasizes that the struggle for cultural difference within the nation must be conceived as a struggle that is always, already defined in relationship to the ongoing process of homogeneity and domination.

Although Cojtí is the most visible and senior leader of Maya ethnonationalism, he is quick to stress the heterogeneity of actors within the movement. He underscores that the Maya movement

> is a movement effected by an infinite number of actors – individuals, groups, institutions, and collectives that take action without having only one executive leadership, nor are they all in the same stage or level of advancement in thought and action... The Maya movement cannot be understood as an organization with a stable structure, but rather as a trend concretized in a thousand and one ways by different actors. (1997:11)

From this perspective, we come to understand the diversity of agents and actors actively involved in the production of strategically essential Maya identity for political ends.

The emphasis on the diversity of agents within the movement is a locus of inquiry advanced in the work of Victor Montejo (2002), Kay Warren (2002), and Diane Nelson (1999). Critical of Cojtí's political orientation, Montejo's recent work focuses particularly upon ideological diversity within the Maya leadership and argues for a shift from an extreme nationalist orientation to a regenerationist one as the best way to carry out the movement's struggles to reconfigure the Guatemalan nation (2002:143). He places the thrust of his analytic attention toward recognizing a diversity of Maya voices and inserting their multiple orientations more centrally into national legislative politics. Montejo explains: "The multiple voices of the contemporary Maya should be heard, because they are no longer silent or sunken in centuries-old amnesia... We have to listen to the multiplicity of Mayan voices, because in the past the international solidarity community, mostly leftist, has created pictures that purported to represent Mayan or Indian America as a homogenous whole" (2002:124). Here Montejo argues for the necessity of a Maya political party (not exclusive of ladinos) that will represent several different sectors of Maya communities, including intellectuals, advocates, peasants, and traditional religious leaders (2002:143). Montejo suggests that this incorporation of a multiplicity of Maya voices will be key to the development of a highly politicized front that can eventually collaborate with ladinos to create a multicultural democracy in Guatemala.

Like other contemporary scholars of culture and politics in Guatemala, Montejo takes on as a given, rather than attempts to resolve, the paradox of Maya strategic essentialism. "The agenda of Mayan scholars and activists is not to embellish ourselves with a romantic past or to wrap ourselves in ancient Mayan garb but to revitalize our Mayan identity and weave back in the sections worn away by centuries of neglect... It is not, then, a bad thing to have the essential parts of our culture, such as language and respect for our land and the elders, as the foundation of this dynamic process of self-representation we are promoting for ourselves" (2002:129). A similar focus on the necessarily dialectic relationship between constructivist and essentialist understanding of Maya identity in the Guatemalan context is foregrounded in the work of Kay Warren.

In *Indigenous Movements and Their Critics: Pan-Maya Activism in Guatemala* (1998), Kay Warren self-consciously and critically articulates the tension between Pan-Maya intellectuals, who craft essentialist understandings of Maya identity in their scholarship, and North American anthropologists, who assume a constructivist approach to collective identity formation. Subjecting her own work to interrogation, Warren discusses how she theorized collective identity in a public venue in Guatemala to her Maya interlocutors as:

> A collage of conflicting meanings, simultaneously advanced by different actors in social systems. In this process-oriented formulation, ethnicity becomes the practice, representation, negotiation, resistance, and appropriation of identity for all parties. Due to powerful economic, cultural, and political constraints on individual and collective action, identity formation is not a free market of personal options for self-definition. Rather, a whole host of groups are in the identity production business... From this viewpoint, there is no Maya or ladino except as identities are constructed, contested, negotiated, imposed, imputed, resisted, and redefined in action. (1998:72–73)

Warren narrates that Maya responses provided "complex counterpoint" that resituated anthropology as a potentially colonial endeavor. In other words, Maya scholars quickly marshaled a "political critique of foreigners as neocolonial academics" (1998:74) and publicly questioned North Americans' motives for research among Maya communities, laying bare the disparate political stakes involved in representations of Maya collective identity, depending upon the social position of the author.

Returning to the question of diversity within the movement, Warren, who has spent over 30 years professionally engaged with Maya leaders, examines the multiplicity of agents and agendas involved with the project of an essentially framed cultural revitalization and political rights movement. Here Warren masterfully furthers anthropological understandings of diversity within the Maya movement through an examination of three generations of activism within one Kaqchikel family and the concomitant conflicts that activism produced among them. Warren's earlier ethnography (1978) showed how indigenous activism was locally based and religiously focused in the Kaqchikel community of San Andrés Semetabaj. She describes how, over the course of three decades, younger generations of the same family became increasingly active in indigenous cultural politics through their involvement in rural development projects, education for Maya communities, shamanism, and linguistic science at regional, national, and international levels. Consequently, inter- and intragenerational definitions of Maya identity and ways of framing cultural continuity are discrete and often at odds. Warren argues that "the ideological diversity of the Maya Movement is not solely a product of regional language difference, decentralized community loyalties, or emerging class cleavages. Additionally, Maya cultural constructions of the person, structures of kinship relations, and the political experiences of different historical generations contribute to diverse definitions of antiracism activism and critiques of Pan-Mayanism" (1998:31).

While Warren and Montejo take up the myriad of individual agents involved in the production of Maya identities, Nelson's ethnography (1999) focuses on institutional agents, particularly the Guatemalan state. With self-consciously postmodern sensibilities, Nelson challenges the notion of the state as a unified "bounded thing that homogenizes and hegemonizes," and instead offers an understanding of the state as a fragmented, multisited entity made up of several different facets such as members of governmental ministries, the Congress, judges, the executive branch, interest groups, laws, enforcers, and rituals that attempt to "articulate, or fix identifications in the short term" (1999:33). Nelson's work underscores the duplicitous nature of the Guatemalan state – at once the site of demand and the stake of struggle – in national cultural politics. She captures the contradictory nature of state power in her theorization of the "piñata effect, the contradictory but simultaneous moves of hitting the state and expecting sweets" (1999:77).

## REGIMES OF KNOWLEDGE

As the work of Cojtí (1990, 1997), Montejo (2002), and Warren (1998) indicates, the production of scholarly knowledge about collective identities in Guatemala is necessarily situated in a larger political field that structures systems of hierarchy and exclusion. Anthropological representations of national, ethnic, and local identifications and experiences may provide the opportunity to "speak truth to power," as Sanford (2003) claims, in service of revealing oppression. Such representations also may function to reinscribe it. While social actors and institutions mobilize several disciplinary epistemologies to define Guatemalan communities, the particular epistemology of linguistic science has been especially visible and efficacious (Cojtí 1990; England 1995, 1998; Maxwell 1996) in late 20th century cultural politics.

In their counterhegemonic efforts to reconfigure the Guatemalan nation, Maya scholar-activists appropriate and, indeed, privilege linguistic science as a valuable tool for challenging national social inequality. As I have recently argued, such an appropriation of scientific epistemology emerged in a recent history of the transformation of linguistics as an authoritative regime of knowledge linked to various political projects (French 2003). The history of contemporary linguistic analysis of Mayan languages in Guatemala during the early 20th century may very well begin with the work of W. Cameron Townsend, the founder of the Summer Institute of Linguistics (SIL), also known as the Wycliffe Bible Translators, in the early 1920s. Townsend began his career and international missionary project in 1919 as an ambulatory Bible vendor turned proselytizer among Kaqchikel speakers in the Guatemalan highland communities of Patzun, San Antonio Aguas Calientes, and Comalapa (Stoll 1982). As Townsend became more involved in and committed to spreading Christianity in these Kaqchikel areas, he became troubled that new congregations in Maya communities "were springing up around poorly apprehended Spanish Bibles" (1982:36). Convinced of the need to spread more clearly and efficiently the world of God in the local language, Townsend took a keen interest in the structure of Kaqchikel. Soon after, he completed its first 20th century grammar, in 1926. The Guatemalan government courted SIL linguistic work on Mayan languages, under the auspices of the National Indigenous Institute and National Bilingual Education Program, until the mid-1970s, for the explicit purpose of linguistic assimilation.

From the mid-1970s to the mid-1980s, with the support of and training from secular North American linguists, professional Mayas systematically challenged the Summer Institute of Linguistics regimentation of Mayan languages through their own use of linguistic science. A pivotal moment in this process was the transfer of leadership in the Proyecto Lingüístico Francisco Marroquín to an all-Maya directorship and staff that explicitly dedicated themselves to "becoming a center of technical resources in linguistics made up of native speakers of different Mayan languages properly chosen and trained" in linguistic science (López Raquec 1989:53). Mirroring the SIL's stated commitment to the scientific analysis of Mayan languages, the PLFM centered its mission on the development of scientific linguistic research. But it also underscored – as it does still today – a linguistic science both *by Mayas* and *for Mayas*, a goal that challenged directly the inherited model of expert knowledge by undermining the division between expert analysts and native speakers (French 2003). This comprised a strikingly different epistemology from that construed by SIL, which had defined the subject of expert linguistic knowledge tautologically, as the scientific linguist/analyst. Within a new epistemological reconfiguration that depended upon rather than denied the linguistic and cultural identity of the would-be analyst, a distinct manner of linking linguistics and politics emerged. It situated scientific linguistic analysis as a tool for challenging the national hegemony that excluded Mayas and their languages. Thus, scientific epistemology, what Bauman and Briggs identify as "the wellspring of modernity" (2003:4), was used strategically to challenge the explicitly homogenizing and exclusionary goals of what Benedict Anderson (1991) calls the "most universally legitimate political form" of modern times.

While Maya scholars have used linguistic science for the counterhegemonic purposes of challenging their exclusion from the Guatemalan nation, their efforts also confirm Bauman and Briggs's suggestion that "contemporary critical projects themselves bolster key foundations of the modernity that they claim to challenge" (2003:309). Indeed, as the Maya movement creates new experts to regiment language through linguistic science, it simultaneously contributes to the creation of what Bauman and Briggs call the "power/knowledge syndrome" in which the intellectual, as "legislator," is authorized on the basis of claims to superior knowledge to make authoritative statements about the "maintenance and perfection of the social order" (2003:309). In this case, the social order that these legislators seek to perfect is the essential connection between Mayan languages and a collective Maya identity supported by their scientific analyses (French 2005a).

Following the theoretical trajectory Bauman and Briggs (2003) enumerate in such a process, the construction of "tradition" and its ideological mapping onto language acts as a necessary condition to further instantiate hegemony and social inequality. However, this perspective is open to at least one challenge, as I have recently shown. Specifically, I argue that the invocation of tradition – both assumptions about it and claims to it–can provide a site for challenging nascent hegemonies and burgeoning expert legislators (French 2005a). In the Guatemalan case, Maya linguists' project of linguistic unification and concomitant Pan-Maya identification are challenged by locally held and experienced ideologies of linguistic tradition. In other words, local constructions of language and tradition challenge the tacit gestures of exclusion that the critical Pan-Maya project may unwittingly reinscribe. The example of the K'iche'– Achi language debate shows how local experiences of linguistic tradition, relative to history, problematize Pan-Maya homogenization. The case of Maya women from the urban area of Chimaltenango who self-identify as Spanish monolingual show that gendered experiences of linguistic tradition actively frustrate Pan-Maya goals to reproduce an exclusive form of Mayan-ness among future generations (French 2005a).

## ERASURES

Current anthropological scholarship about contemporary Guatemala highlights the multiplicity of agents and interrogates the epistemologies involved in the production of essentialist collective Maya, ladino, and Guatemalan identities. Accepting the irresolvable paradox of essentialism in the construction of collective Maya identity also provides the impetus for scholars of Guatemala to question what identities have been silenced, overlooked, and unrecognized in the dualistic model of Guatemalan people-hood. While ladino has been and continues to be named category of social sameness, it has tended to be an unmarked collective identity that constitutes Guatemalan national belonging defined only in relation to the negative Maya. How "ladino" came to be naturalized and universalized in this manner is an inquiry taken up by Greg Grandin (2000). Grandin uses a historical approach to interrogate the consolidation of ladino identity and state efforts to engender ladino collective identifications as iso-morphic with Guatemalan national ones. He underscores the concomitant macro forces that led to the production of ladino identities, cogently arguing that "colonial-ism, capitalism, and state formation have produced a variety of outcomes, including ladino identity" (2000:15). Grandin elucidates this thesis through an analysis of the cholera epidemic of 1837, showing how "elite responses to the epidemic emerged from the racial and political logic of colonialism" (2000:85) and ultimately reconfig-ured a "disease of the poor" into a "disease of the indigenous poor." In so doing, Grandin shows how "the collapsing of class into ethnicity and equating the result with the disease provided fragmented and politically weak ladinos with an opportunity to culturally consolidate their identity and legitimacy" (2000:85). Yet the active con-struction and consolidation of ladino identity is only one of myriad collective identifi-cations that have been overlooked in the nationalist binary of Maya/Guatemalan peoplehood. In my own work (French 2005a), I suggest that it may be productive to reframe this aspect of the identity question semiotically – to consider what kinds of collective identifications are *erased* in the various discourses of cultural politics. Irvine and Gal (2000) provide a clear understanding of the mechanism of erasure. In their semiotic and ethnographic inquiry into the construction of social difference, they argue that there are three universal semiotic processes at work to produce and repro-duce socially meaningful categories of difference. For our consideration of strategic essentialism and identity construction in contemporary Guatemala, erasure – the process by which an ideology, in simplifying a social field, renders some forms of dif-ference invisible (Irvine and Gal 2000:38) – is particularly salient. Reconfigured as part of this orientation, the work of Marta Elena Casaús Arzú, Todd Little-Siebold, and Christa Little-Siebold can be seen to historically and ethnographically interrogate the erasures entailed in the discourses of essential Maya and ladino identities.

Marisol de la Cadena rightly draws attention to the general erasure of "whiteness" and "blackness" in discourses of identity that have been structured by nationalist agendas in Latin America. She claims: "A feature that Guatemala shares with other

Latin American countries (including Peru, Mexico, Ecuador, and Bolivia) is that raciali-zed nation-building projects (concerned with the assimilation of 'indigenous popula-tions') officially silenced both blackness and whiteness" (2001:261). The innovative work of Casaús Arzú (1992, 1998) uncovers the importance of whiteness in elite con-ceptions of race and identity among the Guatemalan ruling class. In *Guatemala. Linaje y racismo* (1992), Casaús Arzú meticulously documents the kinship structure and mar-riage alliances of the Guatemalan oligarchy from the colonial era (1524) through the late 20th century. Her historical analysis is complemented by the dual project of socio-logically and ethnographically investigating how elite families conceive of collective identity and race. Casaús Arzú cogently argues that the oligarchy is ultimately a mes-tizo (mixed) group with an ethnocentric, ladino (non-Indian) worldview that is both elitist and endogamous in its family structure. Despite the empirical evidence of racial/ethnic "mixing," members of the oligarchy overwhelming consider themselves white, that is to say without any mixing of indigenous blood (1992:21).

While effectively erased from essentialist discourses of identity in the national context, the significance of whiteness to collective identification among the elite is paramount. Casaús Arzú interrogates the prevailing conception of whiteness among elite families to show how it is based upon an ideology of racial purity – *la pureza de sangre* (blood purity). She underscores how the high degree to which elites are invested in the notion of blood purity leads some families to produce "evidence" of their "pure" white lineage by proving absence of *mestizaje* in their familial lines through certificates of blood purity from the colonial era and by documenting the persistence of O negative blood type – a biologically inherited trait from their European Basque ancestors (1992:213). Here, social difference among Guatemala's elite oligarchy is perceived to be inherent in blood; conceptions of blood serve to naturalize the inherent superiority of the elite and the essential inferiority of indigenous Mayas based upon the biology of race. One of Casaús Arzú's informants explained: "The genetic transmission of the Indians is of an inferior race. The genes of the white race are superior and this superior race produces great inventions and artists, the other hasn't created anything" (1992:220). Casaús Arzú argues that such racist ideology among self-identified white elites is a fundamental prin-ciple of socialization among the group regardless of one's age, gender, or profession (1992:23). Her more recent work (1998) provocatively suggests that such a conception of blood purity and color hierarchy pervades all segments of Guatemalan society, thus demonstrating a clear need for further empirical investigation in this area.

Todd Little-Siebold (2001) broadens the historical inquiry into the erasure of collective identities through an analysis of named categories of social boundedness during the first 50 years of Guatemalan independence. This era is particularly signifi-cant in that it marks the transition in 1821 from Spanish colonial rule to an era of liberal nation-building and the formation of an urban elite class. Such a substantial change in power structures, from "Spanish" elites to "Guatemalan" ones, as well as in concomitant political entities, from colony to nation, necessitated the immense task of redefining forms of collective identity. In this context, Little-Siebold demonstrates that the post-independence struggle was ultimately "between and within regions and locales." He argues that this local and regional struggle vis-à-vis the nascent elite of the capital resulted in the emergence of a "Guatemala that was a state of pueblos, a nation of municipalities, where localist politics (including those of identity) remained the most important arena of socio-cultural interaction for all but a tiny urban minority" (2001:113).

Through an examination of parish registers and census documents, Todd Little-Siebold demonstrates the tremendous diversity in systems of identification and their variability from community to community. For example, *Españoles, Indios, Mestizos, Ladinos, Mulatos, Pardos, Negros, Sambos, Castizos, Caciques, Laborios* were all named identities that were locally meaningful and unevenly distributed in various communities from 1750 to 1820. Little-Siebold highlights the importance of these classifications according to *calidades* – broad terms used in the Spanish colonial world to denote a person's social position (2001:115). Here, we see the legacy of Spanish colonialism for collective identification in a rich, varied, and ultimately local manner in the era immediately following independence. Such diversity points to "the contradictions between the politics of identity implied by the official assimilations aspirations of the nation's urban elite and the radical diversity of Guatemalan's lived identities on the local level (2001:107).

Christa Little-Siebold's (2001) ethnographic inquiry into local forms of collective identification complements the historical analysis of identities that are erased in essentialist conceptualizations of collective identity. Little-Siebold uncovers the contextually situated and persistently shifting collective identifications deployed in the eastern highland communities of Quetzaltepeque. She shows how particular understandings of such social classifications as *natural, indio, misteado, moreno,* and *sambo* circulate in everyday discourse. In other words, she argues that the pervasive "language of ethnic identity politics that proliferated elsewhere in Guatemala, namely ladinos and Indians, was almost non-existent in the area" (2001:178).

A closer examination of Christa Little-Siebold's data shows not a simple negation of the collective identity categories of indigenous and nonindigenous, but rather a complication of them: both their signifiers and their flexibility remain imbued with traces of essentialist understandings. For example, Little-Siebold explains a fellow Guatemalan's response to her professional interest as an anthropologist in identity:

> "Lo que pasa es que a Christa le interesa ir a estudiar a los doctores" (What's going on is that Christa is interested in studying the doctors). The term *doctores*, that usually refers to medical doctors, is used by some ladinos of the *Oriente* as an inverse image to make fun of the men who wear the traditional white cotton pants and shirts that identify them as Indians. The irony here, of course, is to counterpose the most prestigious professional title in the country with the ignorance often associated with the Indian. (2001:186)

I want to underscore that, while the derogatory term *indio* is not invoked, its indirect indexical connections (Hill 2001) to the essentialist construct of Indianness are. Working in response to the paradox of essentialist identity politics, Little-Siebold's work returns to its resilient persistence, even as she complicates its categories.

## GLOBAL FORCES AND LOCAL ARTICULATIONS

As I have argued, the anthropology of post-conflict Guatemala, through its engagement with the paradoxes of strategic essentialism, redirects disciplinary preoccupations with resolving the paradox of essentialist identity constructs for political ends toward new inquiries. In effect, such new inquiries focus on the social agents of essentialist constructions, the particular epistemologies involved in the production of efficacious and problematic cultural politics, and the erasures of other forms of collective identification entailed in them. Another innovative area of inquiry emerging in the anthropology of Guatemala focuses on transnational political and economic forces and their articulations with local communities. Charles Hale's recent work (2002, 2005) on the theoretical relationship between neoliberalism and multiculturalism and Walter Little's (2004) ethnographic treatment of Maya-Kaqchikel tourist vendors illustrate the breadth of inquiry in this emergent scholarly direction.

Hale (2002) raises the provocative question, "Does multiculturalism menace?" in direct response to the implications of the Maya movement's cultural rights work and the Guatemalan state's responses to it. To speak of cultural rights that are bestowed upon a collective group by the nation requires an essential understanding of collective identity whose boundedness is conceptualized as the objectified "culture" which unifies a collective people (Handler 1998; Domínguez 1989; Légáre 1995). In other words, one must necessarily presuppose the construction of a strategically essential Maya identity to entertain the question of cultural rights in Guatemala. From there, Hale boldly posits that the seemingly libratory promise of cultural rights activism may actually work in favor of neoliberal political and economic policies. He begins by illustrating the co-occurrence of indigenous mobilization throughout Latin America and the ascendancy of neoliberal economic and political reforms in the region during the 1990s. Moving beyond current scholarly wisdom that "indigenous struggles and neoliberal ideologies stand fundamentally opposed to one another," Hale argues that "proponents of the neoliberal doctrine pro-actively endorse a substantive, if limited, version of indigenous cultural rights, as a means to resolve their own problems and advance their own political agendas" (2002:487).

Hale's thesis centers on the concept of "neoliberal multiculturalism," whereby the state, private sector capitalists, and transnational institutions like the World Bank and the US Agency for International Development (USAID) recognize Maya culture and endorse multicultural ideals even as these are "precautionary and pre-emptive reforms, actions taken to cede carefully chosen ground in order to more effectively fend off more far-reaching demands, and even more important, to pro-actively shape the terrain on which future negotiations of cultural rights take place" (2002:488). Hale marshals theoretical sophistication and ethnographic evidence such as interviews with high governmental officials, World Bank economists, and provincial ladino elites to demonstrate the limits and possibilities of social change organized around the recognition of difference in carefully circumscribed ways.

Hale's theoretical account of the powerful institutions that embrace neoliberal political and economic doctrine, and their concomitant influences on the "politics of recognition" (2002:521) for Maya cultural difference in Guatemala, provides a powerful framework for interrogating the dialectic between strategic uses of difference to promote social equality and the neoliberal project that further instantiates structural inequality. The ground-breaking analysis of Velásquez Nimatuj (2005) provides a striking empirical example of this complex, contradictory dilemma. Specifically, she discusses how three particular Maya-Mam communities actively seek out ways to take advantage of World Bank policies to advance their demands to obtain arable land, with some measure of success. Velasquez Nimatuj illustrates that such a remarkable victory in the history of peasant/indigenous land struggles in Guatemala necessarily comes at a very high price: "Becoming the '*el indio permitido*' (the permissible Indian) within the neoliberal project" reveals "the most important challenge is not only to obtain land, but how to make it produce ... Allowing some groups to obtain multimillion dollar loans that cannot be repaid only fortifies the perpetuation of the racial exclusion of those groups" (2005:6, 8).

Walter Little considers one particular facet of transnational capitalism – tourism – and its relationships to local, national, and global conceptions of Maya identity. The roughly 500,000 tourists who come to Guatemala annually (Little 2004:7) are, no doubt, drawn by the essentialized portrayals of the "exotic" and "colorful" Maya culture they find in guidebooks, postcards, and travel literature. Such objectified representations serve to sustain tourism as Guatemala's second largest industry. Little's ethnography centers on one particular group of *tipica* vendors from the Kaqchikel community of San Antonio Aguas Calientes who market their goods to these national and international tourists. In particular, he connects the global and local not through a usual anthropological consideration of displacement and diaspora (Appadurai 1996), but rather through analytic attention to how the "global and local converge in places where Maya vendors live and work" (Little 2004:10). In order to do so, Little focuses on quotidian practices like vending, eating meals, everyday conversation, and child care to "find evidence of how global processes are part of household organization and local identity concepts" (2004:11). Reynolds's (2002) critical ethnography of *Antoñero* childhood demonstrates how local children and youth negotiate the transnational flows of images, commodities, and identities through their imaginative play.

Of particular interest for our consideration of innovative responses to the paradox of strategic essentialism are the self-conscious performances of Maya identity that Little analyzes. He elucidates the ways that Maya identity among Antoneco vendors shifts according to the social context in which they unfold. Here the shifting character of Maya identity is not expressed relative to ladino identity, but rather relative to the salient social networks that translocal Maya vendors maintain. He captures the vendors' dismissal of Maya strategic essentialism for the political goals of the Pan-Maya movement and their concomitant creation of essentialized identity for other aims: "Maya handicraft vendors reject the calculated use of identity for cultural goals using it instead for economically oriented purposes" (Little 2004:18). In other words, this group of Maya vendors does not support essentialist constructions of Maya identity as part of a self-conscious cultural politics; at the same time, they craft their own essentialist constructions of Maya identity for economic gain – through tourism. Little reveals how *Antoñero* families self-consciously perform quintessential Maya culture for North American and European tourists. He carefully analyzes one moment I take to be emblematic of these performances. Little describes how members of the Lopez family, who speak Spanish fluently and live in a "modern" house built of concrete, with electricity, stoves, and refrigerators, can quickly transform their house into a "theater-in-the-round that involves partitioning off private areas of the house and removing electrical appliances and other signs of non-Maya material culture" (2004:213). The family then borrows selectively from essentialized versions of Maya culture during their staged performances for tourists of the "typical Indian life" in highland Guatemala. For example, Little discusses how the guests are directed through the old section of the house with cane walls and dirt floors. They then are greeted by the Lopez women in full traditional dress, surrounded by *tipica* weavings, and hear

Kaqchikel spoken among the members of the family (2004:214–216). Such local enactments of Maya cultural practices reinscribe essential constructs of Maya identity for alternate audiences and new ends – transnational tourists and the economic advancement of local households.

## CONCLUSION

Taken together, recent work in the anthropology of Guatemala has made the important conceptual step of accepting, rather than challenging the irresolvable paradox of strategic essentialism – a paradox that has been both theoretically and ethically "unsettling for anthropologists working in a wide range of ethnographic contexts" (Segal 1996:431). Consequently, its inquiries and interventions productively redirect anthropological scholarship about essentialism and cultural politics to new terrains. Recent ethnographic inquiries in post-conflict Guatemala consider the multiplicity of agents, epistemologies, erasures, and transnational forces implicated in the construction of collective identities. Their particular analyses of Guatemala challenge our general anthropological understanding of collective identity construction in multiethnic and politically charged contexts.

## NOTES

1  All translations are the author's.
2  There are 21 Mayan languages spoken in Guatemala recognized by the ALMG (Mayan Languages Academy of Guatemala). They are: K'iche', Achi, Mam, Kaqchikel, Q'eqchi', Q'anjob'al, Tz'utujiil, Ixil, Ch'orti', Poqomchi', Popti', Poqomam, Chuj, Sakapulteko, Akateko, Awakateko, Mopan, Sipakapense, Uspanteko, Teko, Itzaj.

## REFERENCES

Abu-Lughod, Lila (1991) Writing against Culture. In Richard G. Fox (ed.), *Recapturing Anthropology: Working in the Present*. Santa Fe: School of American Research Press.

Anderson, Benedict (1991[1983]) *Imagined Communities: Reflections on the Origin and Spread of Nationalism*. London: Verso.

Appadurai, Arjun (1996) *Modernity at Large: Cultural Dimensions of Globalization*. Minneapolis: University of Minnesota Press.

Bauman, Richard and Briggs, Charles (2003 ) *Voices of Modernity: Language Ideologies and the Politics of Exclusion*. Cambridge: Cambridge University Press.

Briggs, Charles (1996) The Politics of Discursive Authority in Research on the "Invention of Tradition." *Cultural Anthropology* 11(4):435–469.

Carmack, Robert (ed.) (1988) *Harvest of Violence: The Maya Indians and the Guatemalan Crisis*. Norman: University of Oklahoma Press.

Casaús Arzú, Marta (1992) *Guatemala. Linaje y racismo*. Costa Rica: FLACSO.

Casaús Arzú, Marta (1998) *La metamorfosis del racismo en Guatemala*. Guatemala: Editorial Cholsamaj.

CEH (Comisión para el Esclarecimiento Histórico) (1999) *Guatemala. Memoria del silencio*. Guatemala City: United Nations.

Cojtí Cuxil, Demetrio (1990) Lingüística e idiomas Mayas en Guatemala. In Nora England and Stephen Elliot (eds), *Lecturas sobre la Lingüística Maya* (pp. 1–26). South Woodstock, VT: Plumsock Mesoamerican Studies.

Cojtí Cuxil, Demetrio (1991) *La configuracíon del pensamiento politico del pueblo Maya.* Quetzaltenango, Guatemala: Talleres de El Estúdiante.

Cojtí Cuxil, Demetrio (1994) *Políticas para la reivindicación de los Mayas de hoy.* Guatemala: Editorial Cholsamaj.

Cojtí Cuxil, Demetrio (1995) *Políticas para la reivindicación de los Mayas de hoy* (2nd part). Guatemala: Editorial Cholsamaj.

Cojtí Cuxil, Demetrio (1997) *Ri Maya' Moloj pa Iximulew. El Movimiento Maya en Guatemala.* Guatemala: Editorial Cholsamaj.

COMG (Consejo de Organizaciones Mayas de Guatemala) (1991) *Rujunamil Ri Mayab' Amaq'. Derechos específicos del Pueblo Maya.* Guatemala: Editorial Cholsamaj.

de la Cadena, Marisol (2001) Comments: Ambiguity and Contradiction in the Analysis of Race and the State. *Journal of Latin American Anthropology* 6(2):252–266.

Domínguez, Virginia (1989) *People as Subject, People as Object: Selfhood and Peoplehood in Contemporary Israel.* Madison: University of Wisconsin Press.

Domínguez, Virginia (1994) A Taste for the Other: Intellectual Complicity and Racializing Practices. *Current Anthropology* 35(4):333–348.

England, Nora C. (1995) Linguistics and Indigenous American Languages: Mayan Examples. *Journal of Latin American Anthropology* 1(1):122–149.

England, Nora C. (1998) Mayan Efforts toward Language Preservation. In Leonore A. Grenoble and Lindsay J. Whaley (eds), *Endangered Languages: Current Issues and Future Prospects* (pp. 99–116). Cambridge: Cambridge University Press.

Falla, Ricardo (1992) *Masacres de la Selva. Ixcán, Guatemala, 1975–1982.* Guatemala: Editorial Universitaria.

Fischer, Edward and Brown, R. McKenna (eds) (1996) *Maya Cultural Activism in Guatemala.* Austin: University of Texas Press.

French, Brigittine M. (1999) Imagining the Nation: Language Ideology and Collective Identity in Contemporary Guatemala. *Language and Communication* 19:277–287.

French, Brigittine M. (2003) The Politics of Mayan Linguistics in Guatemala: Native Speakers, Expert Analysts, and the Nation. *Pragmatics* 13(3–4):483–498.

French, Brigittine M. (2005a) Language Ideologies and the Politics of Inclusion: Maya Linguistics and Modernity. Paper presented at the University of Chicago, Department of Anthropology seminar, Nov. 21.

French, Brigittine M. (2005b) Partial Truths and Gendered Histories: Ruth Bunzel in American Anthropology. *Journal of Anthropological Research* 61:513–532.

García Matzar, Pedro (Lolmay) and Rodríguez Guaján, José Obispo (Pakal B'alam) (1997) *Rukemik ri Kaqchikel Chi'. Gramática Kaqchikel.* Guatemala: Editorial Cholsamaj.

Gellner, Ernest (1983) *On Nations and Nationalism.* Ithaca: Cornell University Press.

Grandin, Greg (2000) *The Blood of Guatemala: A History of Race and Nation.* Durham: Duke University Press.

Grandin, Greg (2004) *The Last Colonial Massacre: Latin America in the Cold War.* Chicago: University of Chicago Press.

Hale, Charles R. (2002) Does Multiculturalism Menace? Governance, Cultural Rights and the Politics of Identity in Guatemala. *Journal of Latin American Studies* 34:485–524.

Hale, Charles R. (2005) Neoliberal Multiculturalism. *PoLAR: Political and Legal Anthropology Review* 28(1):10–19.

Handler, Richard (1988) *Nationalism and the Politics of Culture in Quebec.* Madison: University of Wisconsin Press.

Hayden, Robert M. (2002) Imagined Communities and Real Victims: Self-Determination and Ethnic Cleansing in Yugoslavia. In Alexander Laban Hinton (ed.), *Genocide: An Anthropological Reader* (pp. 254–285). Oxford: Blackwell.

Hill, Jane (2001) Language, Race, and White Public Space. In Alessandro Duranti (ed.), *Linguistic Anthropology: A Reader* (pp. 450–464). Oxford: Blackwell.

Irvine, Judith and Gal, Susan (2000) Language Ideology and Linguistic Differentiation. In Paul V. Kroskrity (ed.), *Regimes of Language: Ideologies, Polities, and Identities* (pp. 35–84). Santa Fe: School of American Research Press.

Légaré, Evelyn (1995) Canadian Multiculturalism and Aboriginal People: Negotiating a Place in the Nation. *Identities: Global Studies in Culture and Power* 1(4):347–366.

Little, Walter E. (2004) *Mayas in the Marketplace: Tourism, Globalization, and Cultural Identity.* Austin: University of Texas Press.

Little-Siebold, Christa (2001) Beyond the Indian-Ladino Dichotomy: Contested Identities in an Eastern Guatemalan Town. *Journal of Latin American Anthropology* 6(2):176–197.

Little-Siebold, Todd (2001) Where Have All the Spaniards Gone? Independent Identities: Ethnicities, Class, and the Emergent National State. *Journal of Latin American Anthropology* 6(2):106–133.

López Raquec, Margarita (1989) *Acerca de los idiomas Mayas de Guatemala.* Guatemala: Ministerio de Cultura y Desportes.

Maxwell, Judith (1996) Prescriptive Grammar and Kaqchikel Revitalization. In Edward F. Fischer and R. McKenna Brown (eds), *Maya Cultural Activism in Guatemala* (pp. 195–207). Austin: University of Texas Press.

Menchú Túm, Rigoberta (1983) *I Rigoberta Menchú: An Indian Woman in Guatemala.* London: Verso.

Montejo, Victor R. (1987) *Testimony: Death of a Guatemalan Village.* Willimantic, CT: Curbstone Press.

Montejo, Victor R. (1997) Pan-Mayanismo. La pluriformidad de la cultura maya y el proceso de autorrepresentación. *Mesoamérica* 18(33):93–123.

Montejo, Victor R. (2002) The Multiplicity of Mayan Voices: Mayan Leadership and the Politics of Self-Representation. In Kay B. Warren and Jean E. Jackson (eds), *Indigenous Movements, Self-Representation, and the State in Latin America* (pp.123–148). Austin: University of Texas Press.

Nelson, Diane (1999) *A Finger in the Wound: Body Politics in Quincentennial Guatemala.* Berkeley: University of California Press.

OKMA (Oxlajuuj Keej Maya' Ajtz'iib') (1993) *Maya' chii. Los idiomas Mayas de Guatemala.* Guatemala: Editorial Cholsamaj.

Redfield, Robert (1962) *La cultura y la educación en el altiplano medio occidental de Guatemala, cultural indígena de Guatemala, ensayos de antropología social.* Guatemala: SISG.

Reynolds, Jennifer F. (2002) Maya Children's Practices of the Imagination: (Dis)playing Childhood and Politics in Guatemala. Ph.D. dissertation, Department of Anthropology, University of California at Los Angeles.

REHMI (Proyecto Interdiocesano de Recuperación de la Memoria Histórica) (1998) *Guatemala. Nunca más.* Guatemala City: Oficina de Derechos Humanos del Arzobispado de Guatemala.

Said, Edward (1979) *Orientalism.* New York: Vintage Books.

Sanford, Victoria (2003) *Buried Secrets: Truth and Human Rights in Guatemala.* New York: Palgrave Macmillan.

Segal, Daniel (1996) Resisting Identities. *Cultural Anthropology* 11(4):431–434.

Smith, Carol A. (1990a) Introduction: Social Relations in Guatemala over Time and Space. In Carol A. Smith (ed.), *Guatemalan Indians and the State: 1540 to 1988* (pp. 1–30). Austin: University of Texas Press.

Smith, Carol A. (1990b) Origins of the National Question in Guatemala: A Hypothesis. In Carol A. Smith (ed.), *Guatemalan Indians and the State: 1540 to 1988* (pp. 72–95). Austin: University of Texas Press.

Smith, Carol A. (1999) Racismo en el analisis socio-historico sobre Guatemala. Una critica geneologica. In Clara Arenas, Charles Hale, and Gustavo Palma (eds), *¿Racismo en Guatemala? Abriendo el debate sobre un tema tabu* (pp. 93–126). Guatemala: FLACSO.

Stoll, David (1982) *Fishers of Men or Founders of Empire: The Wycliffe Bible Translators in Latin America.* London: Zed Press.

Tax, Sol (1937) The Municipios of the Midwestern Highlands of Guatemala. *American Anthropologist* 39:423–444.

Trask, Huanani Kay (1999) *From a Native Daughter: Colonialism and Sovereignty in Hawai'i.* Hawai'i: University of Hawai'i Press.

Trouillot, Michel-Rolf (1991) Anthropology and the Savage Slot: The Poetics and Politics of Otherness. In Richard G. Fox (ed.), *Recapturing Anthropology: Working in the Present* (pp. 17–44). Santa Fe: School of American Research Press.

Valásquez Nimatuj, Irma Alicia (2005) Indigenous Peoples, the State and Struggles for Land in Guatemala: Strategies for Survival and Negotiation in the Face of Globalized Inequality. Ph.D. dissertation, Department of Anthropology, University of Texas at Austin.

Wagley, Charles (1949) *The Social and Religious Life of a Guatemalan Village.* Memoirs of the American Anthropological Association, 71. Menasha, WI: American Anthropological Association

Warren, Kay B. (1978) *Symbolism of Subordination: Indian Identity in a Guatemalan Town.* Austin: University of Texas Press.

Warren, Kay B. (1998) *Indigenous Movements and Their Critics: Pan-Maya Activism in Guatemala.* Princeton: Princeton University Press.

Warren, Kay B. (2002) Voting against Indigenous Rights in Guatemala: Lessons from the 1999 Referendum. In Kay B. Warren and Jean E. Jackson (eds), *Indigenous Movements, Self-Representation, and the State in Latin America* (pp. 149–180). Austin: University of Texas Press.

## SUGGESTIONS FOR FURTHER READING

Adams, Abigail E. (2001) The Transformation of the Tzuultaq'a: Jorge Ubico, Protestants and Other Verapaz Maya at the Crossroads of Community, State, and Transnational Interests. *Journal of Latin American Anthropology* 6(2):198–233.

Adams, Richard (1970) *Crucifixion by Power.* Austin: University of Texas Press.

Annis, Sheldon (1987) *God and Production in a Guatemalan Town.* Austin: University of Texas Press.

Arias, Arturo (ed.) (2001) *The Rigoberta Menchú Controversy.* Minneapolis: University of Minnesota Press.

Asturias, Miguel (1923) *Sociologia guatemalteca. El problema social del indio.* Guatemala: Universidad Nacional de Guatemala.

Bastos, Santiago (1993) *Quebrando el silencio. Organizaciones del Pueblo Maya y sus demandas.* Guatemala: FLACSO.

Bastos, Santiago (1995) *Abriendo caminos. Las organizaciones Mayas desde el Nobel hasta el Acuerdo de Derechos Indígenas.* Guatemala: FLACSO.

Brintnall, D. E. (1979) *Revolt against the Dead: The Modernization of a Mayan Community in the Highlands of Guatemala.* New York: Gordon and Breach.

Bunzel, Ruth (1959[1952]) *Chichicastenango: A Guatemalan Village.* Seattle: University of Washington Press.

Ehlers, Tracy (1990) *Silent Looms: Women and Production in a Guatemalan Town.* Boulder, CO: Westview Press.

Goldín, Liliana R. (2001) Maquila Age Maya: Changing Households and Communities of the Central Highlands of Guatemala. *Journal of Latin American Anthropology* 6(1):30–57.

Green, Linda (1999) *Fear as a Way of Life: Mayan Widows in Rural Guatemala.* New York: Columbia University Press.

Guzmán, Bockler (1970) *Guatemala: Una interpretación histórico social.* Mexico City: Siglo XXI.

Manz, Beatriz (1988) *Refugees of a Hidden War: Aftermath of Counterinsurgency in Guatemala.* Albany: SUNY Press.

Martínez Peláez, Severo (1970) *La patria del criollo.* 13th edn. Mexico City: Universidad Autónoma de Puebla.

Oakes, Maud (1951) *The Two Crosses of Todos Santos: Survivals of Mayan Religious Ritual.* New York: Pantheon.

Otzoy, Irma (1992) Identidad y trajes mayas. *Mesoamerica* 23:95–112.

Pitarch, Pedro and López García, Julián (eds) (2001) *Los derechos humanos en tierras Mayas. Política, representaciones y moralidad.* Madrid: Sociedad Española de Estudios Mayas.

Sam Colop, Luis Enrique (1991) *Jub'aqtun Omay Kuchum K'aslemal. Cinco sigos de encubrimiento.* Seminario Permanente de Estudios Mayas, Cuaderno no. 1. Guatemala: Editorial Cholsamaj.

Schirmer, Jennifer (1998) *A Violence Called Democracy: The Guatemalan Military Project.* Philadelphia: University of Pennsylvania Press.

Sieder, Rachel (2002a) *Who Governs? Guatemala Five Years after the Peace Accords.* Cambridge, MA: Hemisphere Initiatives.

Sieder, Rachel (2002b) *Multiculturalism in Latin America: Indigenous Rights, Diversity, and Democracy.* New York: Palgrave Macmillan.

Skinner-Klée, Jorge (1995) *Legislación indigenista de Guatemala, segunda edicion.* Mexico City: Instituto Indigenista Interamericano.

Stoll, David (1993) *Between Two Armies.* New York: Columbia University Press.

Taracena Arriola, Arturo (1997) *Invención criolla, sueño ladino, pesadilla indígena. Los Altos de Guatemala, de region a estado.* La Antigua, Guatemala: CIRMA.

Tedlock, Barbara (1992[1982]) *Time and the Highland Maya.* Albuquerque: University of New Mexico Press.

Watanabe, John M. (1992) *Maya Saints and Souls in a Changing World.* Austin: University of Texas Press.

Wilson, Richard (1995) *Maya Resurgence in Guatemala: Q'eqchi Experiences.* Norman: University of Oklahoma Press.

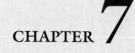

CHAPTER 7

# Mexico: Anthropology and the Nation-State

## Salomón Nahmad Sittón

For a long time Mexicans believed that the pursuit of knowledge would bring its own rewards. In recent years, however, the legitimacy of the notion of a pure, self-contained, impartial science has become increasingly questionable. In no scientific field has this proved to be so true as in the social sciences. Anthropologists, in particular, have been quick to point out the ways in which historical misrepresentations, racial doctrines and nationalistic dogmas have distorted the social needs of ethnic "minorities," producing as a result more detrimental effects than human well-being. As the Australian anthropologist Nadel rightly points out: "A science that could be thus abused must no longer hope to recover its spurious detachment. It will find redemption only in closeness to the problems of our existence as society and civilization" (Nadel 1942:vi). More recent critiques have led to what some see as a permanent identity crisis within sociocultural anthropology, even among those who have attempted to replace such models with more revolutionary approaches (e.g. García Mora and Medina 1983, 1986).

Events and observations made from within the Latin American social sciences, however, would seem to suggest that this "crisis" has been less devastating and more productive than some would claim. This is particularly true of one of the most important developments in Latin American anthropology: the emergence of an anthropology that is practiced and applied within the ethnic group or social unit itself: an anthropology, in short, that is practiced by its own indigenous research subjects. This phenomenon of intellectuals and social thinkers reclaiming local and national histories is widespread throughout the Third World, particularly in Africa (Mazrui 1986; Owusu 1989) and South America, where we might think of such figures as Domingo Antun (1979) of the Ecuadorian Shuar Federation, the Peruvian anthropologist Stefano Varese (1995), or the renowned Brazilian intellectual Darcy Ribeiro (Ribeiro and Gomes 1995). These authors have emphasized the importance of involving indigenous organizations in anthropology, thereby transforming – and in some cases eliminating – the subject/object ("the other") of anthropological study and of ethnology in particular (see also chapters by Hale, Ramos, and Varese, Delgado and Meyer, this volume). This is especially true for linguistic anthropology, a disciplinary subfield that will no doubt someday belong to the academies and institutes of each existing indigenous language (see French, this volume). This transformation of the subject of sociocultural anthropology may ultimately bring about the most important change of all: the disappearance of indigenismo itself as the only option for sociocultural anthropology, and along with it the idea that anthropology is a discipline reserved for intellectuals of the dominant society.

All of these trends can be noted with special force in the case of Mexican anthropology. In Mexico, for example, the professional training of ethnolinguists began in the late 1970s and early 1980s. These ethnolinguists have questioned national policies that discriminate against original Mexican languages. Most recently, in 2003, they were instrumental in drafting a new law recognizing language rights (The Law of Linguistic Rights of Indigenous Peoples). Another important development is the role now played by indigenous intellectuals within their own communities, municipalities, regions and states. Some have become prominent figures in national politics; others have mobilized their people locally to fight for recognition of cultural and political rights.

Anthropology has never had the necessary force or prestige to attempt the sort of decolonization of knowledge that might allow for more fundamental changes in the asymmetrical and colonial relations that have shaped the experience of indigenous peoples with the modern nation-state. An anthropology that is directed toward the study and observation of the researcher's own culture and civilization, however, can only strengthen the forms of ethnographic observation – "the anthropological way of seeing things" – that have distinguished it as a science. Native or indigenous anthropologies, in other words, will help anthropology as a whole to grasp the complexity of the epistemological, methodological, theoretical and substantive problems that constitute ethnographic fieldwork. In this respect, an anthropology that is practiced directly by members of the ethnic group itself will prove to be of considerable importance for any profound debate on anthropology's so-called "identity crisis." Finally, on a national level, the emergence of indigenous anthropology will contribute to the revival and construction of a national society that includes and recognizes the cultural and ethnic diversity of Mexico.

## INDIGENISTA ANTHROPOLOGY AND THE REVOLUTIONARY STATE

Modern Mexican anthropology can be said to begin with Manuel Gamio's ambitious collaborative study of the mestizo populations who lived in the Teotihuacan region of central Mexico (Gamio 1916, 1972, 1979; see also Walsh, this volume). Insofar as most of Gamio's study population in Teotihuacan did not speak an indigenous language or self-identify as "Indians," his study in 1915 set a model for studying non-indigenous populations, for the use of interdisciplinary methods, and for defining a study population in terms of regional configurations. It also laid the foundations for an anthropology that would define itself as political, nationalist, and "action oriented." Given the revolutionary commitments of its practitioners, this was an anthropology that would not only work closely with the state, but also share the goal of assimilating Indians and mestizos into Mexico's modern, Spanish speaking nation.

Assimilation was a common theme in many state-led projects during the early postrevolutionary period. The rural schools of the 1920s (Ramírez 1928, 1976) and the 1930s agrarian reform incorporated both mestizos and the many indigenous communities who fell within the ejido system into the notion of "Mexican-ness" (*mexicanidad*).[1] Anthropologists such as Gamio (1916), Sáenz (1970) and Ramírez (1928) initially supported these attempts to impose Spanish as a common, unifying language. By the early 1940s, however, with the consolidation of the revolutionary nation-state and the reduced threat of US intervention, they reversed their position to press for the preservation and teaching of indigenous languages as a means to build and preserve "national" culture.

Greater political acknowledgment of the cultural and social presence of the Indian is also suggested by the expanding institutional framework for the administration and study of indigenous populations. In 1936, for example, the Mexican state, led by President Lázaro Cárdenas, created the Autonomous Department for Indigenous Affairs as one component of a program for analyzing indigenous demands. Cárdenas's intention in creating the department was not to single out indigenous peoples as separate ethnic groups. On the contrary, the administration hoped to assimilate them into the nation (see for example, the Declaration of the Principles of the Autonomous Department for Indigenous Affairs cited in Comas 1964). In his opening speech for the Indigenous Regional Congress in September 1936, President Cárdenas spoke of the government's intention to solve the problems of irrigation, education and unsanitary living conditions affecting the country's indigenous groups. This was the first of several annual regional congresses organized by the state in locations with indigenous populations so that the people themselves could communicate their needs and suggest possible solutions. That same year (1936), the National Polytechnic Institute was founded, with the active participation of Miguel Othón de Mendizábal, an anthropologist who organized teaching and research in anthropology at the Institute's School of Biological Sciences. The creation of the Anthropology Department was an attempt to bring together anthropologists, who up to that point had carried out their activities independently and in isolation, and to encourage joint anthropological research. Teaching programs for the new anthropology course were prepared and approved by the Ministry of Public Education. From that moment on anthropological activities had a plan, a structured program and also a budget provided by the National School of Biological Sciences.

Academic anthropology was accompanied from its foundation by state-led policy initiatives. The first Inter-American Indigenista Congress, which was held in Pátzcuaro, Michoacán in 1940, drew up an integrating policy proclaiming respect for the dignity and cultures of indigenous peoples, paying special attention to the languages that constituted their means of expression and creativity. Eight years later, with the creation of the National Indigenista Institute (INI), Mexican anthropologists and other social scientists were given the opportunity to put into practice the indigenista policies formulated at the Pátzcuaro Congress. The INI was initially headed by anthropologist Alfonso Caso, who a decade earlier had promoted the creation of the National Institute of Anthropology and History (INAH). As part of the state apparatus, the INAH was responsible for training ethnologists, archaeologists, linguists, and physical anthropologists. Social anthropologists received their training at the National Polytechnic Institute and, somewhat later, the National School of Anthropology and History (ENAH), which was founded in 1942.

Anthropologists' ongoing relationship with the state – and their commitment to "action anthropology" – gave particular salience to the theoretical paradigms embraced and promoted by Mexican anthropologists. From the beginning these paradigms were dominated by indigenismo, a set of theoretical and administrative practices that combined theories of cultural relativism with paternalistic policies for the defense, improvement and assimilation of Mexico's indigenous populations. Viewed within the framework of contemporary theories of race and culture, "indigenismo" appears as a broadly eclectic set of theories ranging from ideas of indigenous racial inferiority to relativist accounts of indigenous culture and appeals to indigenous civilization as the basis of Mexican national culture. More than a theoretical corpus, indigenismo constituted a conceptual and political position from which "the Indian" was constituted as a voiceless, passive subject for intellectual contemplation and administrative reform. It is this, somewhat contradictory, stance toward the Indian as research subject that characterizes the Mexican anthropology of the 1930s and 1940s.[2]

By the 1950s, anthropologists were beginning to rethink somewhat their commitment to indigenismo to address the relationship between indigenous peoples and the nation-state. Of particular importance here were theories of acculturation and a spatial model of cultural integration that was perhaps best summed up in Gonzálo Aguirre Beltrán's (1979) conceptualization of the "region of refuge" as a space that is itself defined by regional power relations that subordinate indigenous communities to nonindigenous or "dominant" social sectors and to the state. Given their structural position with these regional power structures, Aguirre Beltran argued that the only way to improve the Indians' condition was through their acculturation and assimilation into the dominant society. In developing his theory of acculturation, Aguirre Beltrán drew on the work of the US anthropologist Melville Herskovitz (1938), with whom he had studied briefly at Northwestern University (Aguirre Beltrán 1957). Acculturation also formed the cornerstone of the INI Regional Coordinating Centers established by Caso and Aguirre Beltran in Chiapas and other regions. The idea behind these coordinating centers, which were staffed by professional anthropologists, was to promote regional economic and cultural integration, thereby eliminating the sources of ethnic exploitation – as well as the forms of cultural identification – that characterized the "region of refuge."

Others responded critically to this model of integration or acculturation. Among the most influential of these critics was Pablo González Casanova (1965a), who proposed the concept of "internal colonialism" as a means to explain the unique forms of cultural, ethnic, political and economic marginalization that characterized minority and indigenous populations in Mexico and other Latin American nations. "Internal colonialism," wrote González Casanova, "corresponds to a structure of social relations based on domination and exploitation among culturally heterogeneous, distinct groups. If it has a specific difference with respect to other relations based on subordination, it inheres in the cultural heterogeneity that is historically produced by the conquest of some peoples by others" (1965b:33). The notion of internal colonialism placed Mexican anthropology in conversation with international debates concerning decolonization and the characteristics of "new nations" in Africa and other postcolonial regions. It also generated heated debate among national anthropologists, in that it directly attacked the doctrines of assimilation that lay at the heart of Mexican indigenismo. The most prominent opponent of the concept was Aguirre Beltrán (1970), who argued that internal colonialism was a mere "entelechy" for which González Casanova had provided "no proof whatsoever." At stake in this debate was whether the marginalization and poverty of Mexico's indigenous groups could be best explained as an expression of class relations (as in Aguirre Beltran's model), or as a *colonial* relation that combined class, race and ethnic domination.

Yet other critics of acculturation theory such as Guillermo Bonfil Batalla, Rodolfo Stavenhagen, Salomón Nahmad, and Leonel Durán combined ethnology with the theory of internal colonialism to posit a distinction between the "Imaginary Mexico" of the national Europeanizing elites, and a "Profound Mexico" (Bonfil Batalla 1987) in which indigenous cultural influences continue to play an important constructive and civilizing role in shaping Mexico's national history and culture. Their position – which was characterized as "ethnicista" – was supported by the new model of anthropological collaboration proposed at the Barbados meetings of 1971, 1977 and 1993 by Latin American anthropologists such as Darcy Ribeiro, Guillermo Bonfil, Stefano Varese, Miguel Bartolomé, George Grünberg, Alicia Barabas, Nelly Arvelo-Jiménez, Esteban Emilio Mosonyi, Silvio Coelho dos Santos, Joao Pacheco de Oliveira, Víctor Daniel Bonilla, and Alberto Chirif (see Varese, Delgado and Meyer, this volume). This model, which assigned a constructive and civilizing role to indigenous peoples, was opposed to the goals of integration and acculturation that had been defended at each of the nine Inter-American Indigenista Congresses. In its place, they envisioned the possibility of a new political strategy for reclaiming the cultural achievements of Latin America's indigenous peoples. These new ideas were heavily criticized by Aguirre Beltrán in his book on vernacular languages (1983), which considered this entire anthropological current to be anarchistic and nonconformist. In 1988, faced by criticism from the new anthropological currents, Aguirre Beltrán declared that he was

> immersed in countless controversies, arguments and disputes, in defense of the doctrine (of acculturation and integration) that I myself conceived and presented in books, articles, papers and interventions of all kinds. We are all familiar with the philosophy and the practice advocated by [the concept of] integration and I am not going to repeat it; I would just like to point out that it functioned honestly and efficiently for 22 years under Alfonso Caso's management, and for six years under my own, with complete congruence between thought and deed. (Aguirre Beltrán 1988)

The anthropological critique formulated by Robert Jaulin (1973) on ethnic cleansing offered yet another mortal blow to the old integrationist formula, and further distanced the new Mexican anthropology that took shape in the 1980s from such "old school" ideologues as Aguirre Beltrán, Alfonso Villa Rojas and Agustín Romano.

The concept of integration, however, continued to linger among certain Marxist anthropologists who saw class as a form of identification that was necessarily opposed to "ethnicity" or "culture," and who assigned a role in social change to the state. The sharpest critique of this model came from Marxist anthropologists themselves and specifically from a failed project, led by Mexican anthropologists, in the Misquita area of Nicaragua. Faced with Misquito resistance, the Mexican architects of the project (Díaz Polanco 1993) eventually had to modify their original project of forced collectivization and to adopt, in its place, a Soviet-style collective farm in the indigenous Misquita communites of Nicaragua. This experiment led to a war between the Misquito communities and the Sandinista government, which finally resulted in the official recognition of multiculturalism and multilinguism and the right to autonomy for the indigenous peoples of Nicaragua. What soon became apparent to all, however, was that the experiment had failed because of Marxist anthropology's reluctance to account for the indigeneity and cultural specificity of the indigenous peoples. This experience also constituted a break, in the mid-1980s, from the theory of social classes put forward by Mexican anthropologists such as Ricardo Pozas, Isabel Horcasitas, Gonzalo Aguirre Beltrán, Roger Bartra, Andrés Medina and Daniel Casés, all of whom had argued for a Marxist-style integrationism in which the state would serve as an institution for planning and organizing society and culture in a hegemonic and progressive linear direction. (See tables 7.1, 7.2 and 7.3 for the theoretical and institutional context of Mexican anthropology.)

Despite increasing criticism from both "ethnicists" and Marxists, indigenismo continued as the dominant current in Mexican anthropology, in part because anthropology's institutional dependence on the state had led as well to close links with the ruling PRI party.[3] The effects on anthropology of this close relationship with Mexico's de facto one-party state were complex. On the one hand, it led to institutional complacency. On the other, it produced a willingness to confine anthropology's domain of influence to questions of indigenous – or, rather, "indigenista" – policy and debate. As handmaiden of the revolutionary state, however, Mexican anthropology was able to avoid, in the words of anthropologist Esteban Krotz:

> the sorts of mass repression of intellectual activity, particularly within the field of academia, that occurred in the cases of Chile or Argentina. Although many may, naively, have exaggerated the freedom brought by such a situation, it is certain that it permitted the generation, reception and circulation of ideas and approaches, as well as the carrying out of research, free from the restrictions to which our colleagues from other parts of the continent have so often been subjected. (1993:362)

## ANTHROPOLOGY AS CRITIC OF THE STATE

Anthropology's romance with the state began to falter after 1968, when student protests against the state disrupted the ideological equilibrium and questioned the discourse of revolutionary nationalism in which anthropological work was framed. Anthropologists who were militants within left-wing political parties clashed with other anthropologists whose perspectives were left-wing but who did not actively participate in a political party. Until this time, a majority of the country's archaeologists, physical anthropologists, ethnologists and linguists had openly sympathized with the governing PRI party (Partido Revolucionario Institucional) through their affiliation with government institutions such as the INAH, INI and ENAH. With the crisis unleashed by the student protests and the massacre of Tlatelolco in 1968, these groups were increasingly isolated from Mexico's largest public university, the UNAM (Autonomous National University of Mexico), leading to the creation of the Instituto de Investigaciones Antropológicas as a separate institute within the UNAM. Other social anthropology programs were set up at the University of Veracruz and the Iberoamerican University in Mexico City. These programs signaled a process of separation from the federal government, and the formation of a more or less autonomous academic system, similar to that in more "developed" countries.

**Table 7.1**   Theoretical and applied anthropology in development projects in Mexico

| PERIOD | Theoretical and conceptual frameworks | Mexican anthropologists | Foreign anthropologists working in Mexico | Research projects |
|---|---|---|---|---|
| 1920–1940 | Incorporation and assimilation | Manuel Gamio Othón de Mendizábal | Robert Redfield John Collier Parsons | Indigenous Student House (Casa del Estudiante Indígena) |
|  | Revolutionary nationalism | Moisés Sáenz Alfonso Villa Rojas Alfonso Fabila Juan Comas Carlos Basauri | W. Thousand | Proyecto Tarasco de Educación de los 11 Pueblos Department of Indigenous Affairs, Instituto Nacional de Antropología e Historia (INAH) |
| 1940–1950 | Social and cultural change | Julio de la Fuente Arturo Monzón Fernando Cámara Ricardo Pozas Evangelina Arana | B. Malinowski R. Beals R. Weitlaner M. Swadesh | "Pacification" of Maya in Quintana Roo Yaqui and Otomí Project (Sonora) Instituto Nacional Indigenista (INI) |
|  | Urban–folk continuum |  |  |  |
| 1950–1970 | Acculturation and integration | G. Aguirre Beltrán F. Plancarte Agustín Romano M. Muñoz C. Incháustegui G. González | E. Vogt N. McQuown J. Murra E. Wolf R. Adams A. Ichon R. Bastide | Centros Coordinadores Indigenistas (INI) Papaloapan Commission Chicago and Harvard projects Ejidal and Agrarian banks Mexican Coffee Institute (INMECAFE) |
|  | Linear evolution |  |  |  |
| 1970–1990 | Marxism and class analysis | P. González Casanova M. Olivera R. Bartra R. Stavenhaghen | M. Godelier M. Diskin H. Favre M. Cernea | PIDER program General Coordination of the National Plan for Depressed Zones and Marginal Groups (COPLAMAR) |
|  | Internal colonialism |  |  |  |

| Period | Approach | Authors | Authors | Programs/Initiatives |
|---|---|---|---|---|
| | Dependency theory | L. Pare<br>H. Díaz Polanco<br>A. Medina<br>G. López y Rivas<br>I. Horcasitas de P.<br>C. García Mora | | Agrarian Bank (Banco Agropecuario) |
| 1980–2000 | Peasant economy | M. Nolasco<br>A. Warman<br>C. Hewit<br>L. Arizpe<br>J. Lameiras | D. Barkin<br>S. Robinson<br>B. Thomsen<br>T. Downing | SOLIDARIDAD (federal antipoverty program)<br>Businesses in SOLIDARIDAD<br>Ejido Union<br>Program for Certification of Ejidal Rights and Titling (PROCEDE) |
| 1970–2000 | Ethnicity and culture | A. Palerm<br>G. Bonfil | G. Collier<br>T. Weaver | Bilingual and bicultural education |
| | Multilineal evolution | R. Stavenhaghen<br>L. Duran<br>S. Nahmad<br>L. Reyes<br>M. Bartolomé<br>A. Barabas<br>F. Báez | A. Colombres<br>N. Rodríguez<br>S. Varese<br>N. Modiano<br>N. Canclini<br>R. Cardoso<br>D. Riveiro<br>J. Nash | Popular culture initiatives<br>Training of indigenous ethnolinguists |
| 1990–2000 | Neoliberalism | A. Warman<br>J. del Val<br>C. Bueno<br>M. Perez Lisaur<br>E. Saldívar | S. Davis<br>A. Molnar | Federal poverty elimination programs (PROGRESA and OPORTUNIDADES) |
| | Economic globalization, environmental conservation, and cultural diversity | | | Intercultural education<br>Land privatization programs |

**Table 7.2**  Anthropology schools and research centers

| Location | University, school or research center |
| --- | --- |
| Mexico City | Escuela Nacional de Antropología e Historia (ENAH) |
|  | Universidad Iberoamericana |
|  | Universidad Nacional Autónoma de México (UNAM),* |
|  |     Instituto de Investigaciones Antropológicas |
|  | Universidad Autónoma Metropolitana Ixtapalapa (UAM-I) |
|  | Centro de Investigaciones y Estudios Superiores en |
|  |     Antropología Social (CIESAS)* |
| Xalapa, Veracruz | Universidad Veracruzana (UV), Facultad de Antropología |
| Cholula, Puebla | Universidad de las Américas |
| Puebla, Puebla | Universidad Autónoma de Puebla |
| Mérida, Yucatán | Universidad Autónoma de Yucatán (UADY), Facultad |
|  |     de Antropología |
| Toluca, Estado de México | Universidad Autónoma del Estado de México (UAEM), |
|  |     Facultad de Antropología |
| San Cristóbal de las Casas, | Universidad Autónoma de Chiapas, Escuela de |
|     Chiapas |     Antropología |
| Chihuahua, Chihuahua | Escuela de Antropología de Chihuahua |
| Zamora, Michoacán | Colegio de Michoacán* |
| Guadalajara, Jalisco | CIESAS – Occidente* |

* Grants masters and doctoral degrees.

Along with a critique of the authoritarian state and anthropology's relation to it came an equally radical criticism of the universalizing and nationalist theoretical postures of Mexican anthropology, orthodox Marxism and indigenismo.[4] Some hoped to create a Marxist anthropology that would address problems of internal colonialism at home and situate Mexican social problems within the oppressive social reality of the peoples of the world who had been colonized by European powers. The Mexican Communist Party, which maintained strong ties with some branches of Mexican anthropology, was influential in promoting a sense of crisis and ideological struggle in the schools and research centers that cultivated anthropological knowledge. Students at the ENAH sharply criticized the foundations upon which homegrown Mexican anthropology rested and demanded that

> (a) anthropology abandon the study of indigenous communities considered to be in a degree of isolation that does not exist in reality, (b) that the anthropological disciplines detach themselves from the politics of the state, and (c) that anthropology open itself to theoretical currents, particularly Marxism, which might examine and explain social realities more clearly and efficiently. (Guerrero 1996:123)

Other pressures for reform came from outside of Mexico. The cold war assigned to the social sciences a relevant role in the construction of a human society ruled by multilateral organizations such as the UN, the International Labor Organization, UNESCO, the Organization of American States, and the Economic Commission for Latin America and the Caribbean. In the case of anthropology, this involved multilateral organizations such as the Interamerican Indigenista Institute, the Regional Center of Basic Education for Latin America, and the Panamerican Union of Geography and

History. These institutions promoted public policies aimed at eliminating slavery and the exploitation of indigenous workers, recognizing communal lands, and seeking equality of opportunity in education, health, living conditions and general well-being. The single most important factor pushing Mexican anthropologists toward a redefinition of their disciplines, however, was the shifting political fortunes of Mexico's one-party state. Although similar critiques of anthropology sprang up in Europe and the United States, the fact that anthropology in those countries maintained a certain distance from the state meant that critique of anthropology in those countries was focused more on questions of ideological and theoretical "complicity" with imperialism, capitalism and racism, and less directly aimed at the *institutional* foundations of the discipline as a whole. In Mexico, by comparison, the fact that anthropology had always been so closely dependent on the state meant that critiques of state and discipline could not easily be separated.

Given this situation, it is perhaps not surprising that party politics played an important role in defining the new Mexican anthropology that would emerge after 1968. From the early 1970s until the end of the century, the discipline experienced a struggle among anthropologists who were activists from left-wing parties, anthropologists who were active members of the PRI, and anthropologists who had left-wing social views but were not political activists. Many of those who defended the new anthropology began a process of legitimizing state and local governments and electoral campaigns affiliated with opposition parties such as the center-left PRD (Revolutionary Democratic Party) headed by Cuauhtémoc Cárdenas (the son of Lázaro Cardenas, the president who had been, as we have seen, a driving force behind the formation of indigenista anthropology in the 1930s). Following the fragmentation of the PRI, the resulting alliance of left-wing forces was consolidated as a political anthropology which sought "to construct an authentic national anthropology in the service of the working classes, which is part of the social processes and the lines of thinking of our time" (García Mora and Medina 1983, 1986).

Marxism was a dominant tendency among these anthropologists seeking to reform Mexican anthropology. As elsewhere in Latin America, orthodox Marxist models of class struggle and structural change were challenged by the fall of the Berlin Wall and the breakup of the Soviet Union. Another challenge to orthodox Marxist politics came in the 1994 revolt by the Zapatista National Liberation Army (Ejercito Zapatista de Liberación Nacional, EZLN) in Chiapas. The Zapatista movement altered popular perceptions – including those held by many indigenista anthropologists – of indigenous peoples as passive social actors, suggesting instead that Indians were intellectual and political actors with the power to transform the unequal and asymmetrical relations that characterized Mexican society as a whole. Today indigenous organizations throughout Mexico play a forceful political role as critics, not only of the system of government that emerged from the Mexican Revolution, but also of the political party system that dominates politics in early 21st century Mexico.

Despite these changes, in practice social anthropology was not able to break its ties with the government until the beginning of this new century. Indeed in the immediate aftermath of the 1960s guerrilla and student movement, the state created additional jobs for anthropologists and initiated new indigenista programs directed toward Mexico's impoverished indigenous majorities (García Mora and Medina 1983, 1986). The INAH was also strengthened through the creation of new state delegations.

**Table 7.3** International meetings and their impact on applied anthropology in Mexico

| Date and place | Events | Recommendations | Impact in Mexico |
| --- | --- | --- | --- |
| 1940 Pátzcuaro, Michoacán, Mexico | Interamerican Indigenist Congresses promoted throughout Latin America | Respect and protect indigenous peoples in development and create national institutions specialized in indigenous affairs | The second Interamerican Indigenist Institute (III) is held with the agreement of the member nations. The National Indigenista Institute (INI) is created by the Mexican government in 1948 |
| 1949 UNESCO, Paris, France | Creation of the Regional Center for Fundamental Education in Latin America (CREFAL) in Pátzcuaro, Michoacán (1951) | Train specialized personnel in indigenous education | Has stimulated and positively influenced educational projects in indigenous communities throughout Mexico and Latin America |
| 1959–1968 Organization of American States (OAS), Washington DC, USA | OAS establishes Program in Applied Social Sciences in Mexico (OAS Projects 104 and 208) | Train professional applied anthropologists in Latin America, and Mexico in particular | Anthropologists working through INI and other federal organizations promote indigenous education initiatives, and support and help to organize indigenous communities |
| 1957, 1989 International Labor Organization (ILO) | ILO promotes two Conventions, 107 (1957) and 169 (1989) on indigenous and tribal peoples | The concepts from these Conventions define cultural, religious and economic rights of indigenous peoples in international law | Mexican government ratifies ILO Convention 169, which thereby gains force in Mexican national law as basis for recognizing indigenous rights and indigenous demands for legal recognition |
| 1971, 1977, 1993 Barbados meetings | Anthropologists and indigenous representatives from across Latin America meet to discuss internal colonialism and dependency affecting indigenous peoples | The Barbados Declarations call for indigenous liberation, struggle for human rights and an end to ethnocide | Encourages the formation of grassroots, national and state-led indigenous organizations throughout Latin America |

| | | | |
|---|---|---|---|
| 1969 Second Vatican Council, Rome, Italy | Vatican II promotes liberation theology among indigenous peoples through base communities and evangelizing missions | Seeks to guarantee that the work of priests, missionaries, and catechists furthers the cause of indigenous rights | Catholic Church organizes and supports indigenous organizations and community-led projects in Chiapas and other Mexican states |
| 1994 United Nations (UN), New York, USA | UN declaration on the rights of indigenous peoples | The UN Human Rights Commissioner (OHCHR) recognizes the urgent need to respect the basic human rights, land, territories, resources and cultures of indigenous peoples across the world | Has important impact on legislative proposals at both national and state levels. Indigenous organizations demand that the federal government recognize the universal rights of indigenous peoples |
| 1992 Inter-American Development Bank (IDB), Madrid, Spain | IDB agrees to administer the Indigenous Peoples Endowment Fund, to assure the permanent flow of resources for development initiatives benefiting native peoples of the region | To define mechanisms to support sustainable development of indigenous peoples, communities and organizations | As signatory of the Convention, the Mexican state agrees to provide economic and human resources for the development of indigenous peoples |
| 1991 World Bank, Washington DC, USA | World Bank approves Operational Directive 4.20 on indigenous populations | OD 4.20 stipulates that all governmental loans must include provisions guaranteeing that projects will not adversely affect indigenous peoples and their development | Mexican rural development projects linked to World Bank funds have included indigenous participation in such areas as community forestry and education |

The INI too was briefly expanded through new coordinating centers for indigenous affairs before being dismantled in 2003.[5] Anthropology also expanded into new teaching fields at Mexico City's Autonomous Metropolitan University, and academic research in social anthropology was encouraged through the creation in 1973 of CISINAH (Centro de Investigaciones Superiores del INAH), the predecessor of today's influential CIESAS (Centro de Investigacion y Estudios Superiores en Anthropología Social) which maintains programs of research and teaching in Mexico City, Oaxaca, Guadalajara San Cristóbal de Las Casas, Merida, Xalapa and Monterrey. Anthropology programs also opened at state universities in Yucatán, México, Querétaro, Chihuahua, Chiapas, and the Postgraduate College of the University of Chapingo. Finally, masters and doctoral programs were created at UNAM and later at CIESAS and at the College of Michoacán. (See tables 7.1 and 7.2 above.)

Thus, although many feared that the crisis within anthropology would eliminate research and teacher training opportunities, in fact it had the opposite effect, creating new lines of research and action in the fields of health, education, linguistics, urbanism, ruralism, the peasantry, agrarian studies, and geography. In spite of the controversy that took place during the last 30 years of the 20th century, the depth of analysis undertaken in the various subject areas helped to establish common directions for anthropology, and also to dilute criticism by separating the discipline somewhat from its historically dependent relationship with the state and government. At the same time, this crisis converted anthropology into an interlocutor that helped to change accepted paradigms of postrevolutionary state legitimization, by formulating proposals for a democratizing, multiparty anthropology.

## ANTHROPOLOGY IN THE SERVICE OF POLITICAL CURRENTS

For most anthropologists in Mexico, as elsewhere in the Third World, anthropological research carries with it a disciplinary obligation to pursue social transformation on behalf of the marginal and subaltern populations they study. Transformation can range from promoting concrete changes in the social structures of exploitation and domination, to encouraging the acceptance and preservation of cultural diversity. On the one hand, as we have seen, social anthropology in Mexico – in large part thanks to its ties to the nation-state – has always been not only a theoretical, but also an applied social science. Anthropologists have managed to formulate pragmatic recommendations to better the lives of their research subjects, direct or even reorient government proposals for such things as land reform, and to set up social programs that were first aimed at ethnic groups, then at peasants in general, and somewhat later at poor urban populations. Although some anthropologists (e.g. Warman 2003) have recently spoken out in support of neoliberal measures such as the counter land reform of 1992[6] and in defense of existing power and party structures, most Mexican anthropologists have remained committed from the outset to promoting progressive social change. Indeed, as Ignacio Rodríguez has argued, professional anthropologists working both within and outside the state apparatus became increasingly involved in policy formation during the last 30 years of the 20th century. This political orientation of Mexican anthropology, however, has at times been seen to undermine the scientific criteria for research design and implementation. Thus, as Rodríguez goes on to note:

because the origins and aims of anthropological projects are often politically motivated, they are often not based on scientific considerations; meaning that the academic goals will necessarily be less important than the political ones. Even when the specific purpose of each project has been based on an academic rationale defended by the specialists in charge, such a choice was supported by opportunistic personal motives and not by an academic consensus originating from a general research program. (1996:102)

Such research projects, moreover, have been subject to the shifting political priorities of federal and state governments that change every six years, regardless of the momentum the research investigations may have acquired. As Rodríguez goes on to ask:

Is there no other alternative? Or rather we should ask, do we want another alternative? Are we prepared to join together to confront a state accustomed to imposing its ideological visions on academic needs? How long could we exist without the regular budget donations we now receive? Would we be able, as a civil society, to produce a nonpolitical/ideological use for archaeological remains? Would it be in the interest of civil society and specialists to reduce the role of the state in archaeology, and then have to face the very unacademic visions that would surely be generated by its imminent privatization? We do not know. All we do know is that a dignified reply to these and other questions is only to be found through rigorous academic debate and the organization of a collective effort. (1996:103)

After 1968, as we have seen, ethnological analysis split in two directions, Marxist and "ethnicist." Although these two currents agreed on many theoretical elements, they diverged with respect to their understandings of how theory should be applied to public policies. The Marxists accused those who worked with the state of putting anthropology at the service of capitalism, and called on anthropologists to abandon the study of indigenous communities considered in isolation. This criticism was a huge distortion of a regional research tradition which – since its foundation in Gamio's Teotihuacan project – had focused on the important relationship between communities and their regional, state and national environments. The "ethnicist" group echoed the Marxists' calls for greater autonomy vis-à-vis state politics. They called for the creation of new spaces for the development of anthropology, as in the case of the Metropolitan University or the CIESAS.

Nevertheless, by the 1990s orthodox Marxist anthropologists working through left-wing parties began to introduce themselves into the government apparatus, just as the "official" anthropologists had who had worked for earlier PRI governments. In the year 2000, when the extreme right-wing National Action Party (PAN) won the presidential elections, orthodox Marxist anthropologists established the same relationships with it as they had done with the campaigns and elected governments of the PRD. Thus, although their party allegiances may have shifted, Marxist anthropologists have yet to achieve the distancing or independence they claimed to desire with respect to the Mexican state.

During the 1980s and 1990s, many other anthropologists became intermediaries for indigenous communities, peasants, and the urban poor as researchers or employees for nongovernmental organizations, or NGOs (known as Asociaciones Civiles in Mexico). The NGO movement, which was financed by international and transnational foundations located in the industrialized nations, successfully convinced Marxist and dissident intellectuals to work within the framework of neoliberal, globalizing world politics by giving them resources to carry out research projects and to organize local communities. In this way, anthropology became a tool for bolstering the neoliberal system, due to the fact that in the last 20 years (up to 2004) governments cut financing for the social services in which anthropologists had previously played a central role. Thus, NGOs run by anthropologists found themselves representing and speaking in the name of indigenous and peasant communities. Similarly, funds were collected from both national governments and international agencies, without the participation or intervention of indigenous communities and organizations.

When the Mexican welfare state was dismantled between 1970 and 2004, neoliberal anthropologists supported judicial and constitutional measures to privatize common property and ejido lands Some, such as Arturo Warman, had gone from orthodox Marxism, to ethnicism, only to end up embracing an ideology in which their ethnology would serve as a means to justify the 1992 counter land reform (Warman 2003). Warman and others also questioned the San Andrés Larráinzar Accords that purportedly brought an end to the conflict between the EZLN and the Mexican state, and the accompanying resolution by the Comisión de Concordia y Pacificación de la Cámara de Diputados Nacional (COCOPA). Warman, for example, considered the EZLN's position on autonomy and cultural rights to be "worn out and in decline." The subject, he ventured (incorrectly), "has lost interest and priority; it has eroded with time." In a similar vein, Viqueira and Sonnleitner (2000), who write from within the same neoliberal tendency of electoral anthropology as does Warman, suggested that indigenous municipalities should be incorporated into the party system of Mexico's electoral democracy. Such a suggestion reflects the neoliberal imperative of dividing indigenous peoples through rural education projects and corporatist models of governance. It also runs counter to the demands of indigenous organizations and communities across Mexico for increased autonomy from Mexico's political party system.

## Pluralism and Autonomy

Although some anthropologists have supported the counter reform measures and authoritarian politics of Mexico's neoliberal state, a majority have assumed critical positions with respect to both neoliberalism and the particular forms of multiculturalism it has ushered in. Along with state reforms intended to decentralize state administration, encourage regional and local fiscal "responsibility," and facilitate the penetration of national markets by foreign capital, the neoliberal model in Mexico – as elsewhere in Latin America – has also brought with it constitutional recognition of ethnic pluralism. In Mexico, the federal constitution was amended in 1992 to recognize the pluricultural nature of the Mexican nation. Even before the federal reform, however, some states within Mexico's federal system had moved to recognize the multi-ethnic and multicultural characteristics of regional populations. In the southeastern state of Oaxaca, for example, the constitution was amended in 1989 to include explicit recognition of the rights of indigenous peoples. Anthropology and sociology have played important supportive roles in these juridical reforms, which many anthropologists saw as one means to address the historical exclusion of indigenous peoples from a national project that began, with Mexico's national independence, in the early 19th century. Today, as a result of these efforts to legislate, recognize and include ethnic pluralism within the structure of state-led reform projects, we are becoming increasingly immersed in a labyrinth of terminological contradictions. It is fascinating to reflect, however, how concepts we discussed as doctoral students in the late 1960s at UNAM in our classes with Aguirre Beltrán and Angel Palerm today occupy center stage in national debates concerning the nature and reach of indigenous autonomy and national sovereignty. How should we define (and legislate) "the Indian"? What should we understand as a "nation," an "ethnicity," or a "people"? How should we think about national and ethnic frontiers? These are the anthropological questions that all Mexicans must now confront as they debate the character of Mexico's "pluri-ethnic" national society.

Since 1970, when I began teaching the Sociology of Minorities and the Sociology of Indigenous Cultures at UNAM, I have discussed with students the place of indigenous peoples in terms of the profound political and structural conflicts caused by their exclusion from Mexico's national project. In these classes we analyzed how indigenism had effectively silenced any discussion of a national project that might include indigenous peoples. When Pablo González Casanova introduced the concept of internal colonialism in his 1965 book on democracy in Mexico (González Casanova 1965a), he struck at the very foundations of Mexican nationalism. When Guillermo Bonfil, Rodolfo Stavenhagen, Leonel Durán, and others of us resurrected the concept of ethnicity as a central and foundational element in the construction of a nation, we invoked a geopolitical reordering of Mexican diversity. The Marxists denounced our position as "ethnicist." As inheritors of indigenismo, they proposed instead that it would be through acculturation and education that Mexico's indigenous ethnicities could be integrated, through their affiliation with the proletariat, into Mexico's class structure. The First National Congress of Indigenous Peoples in 1975 set off the final unraveling of liberal Mexican nationalism with its call for a new inclusive and multi-ethnic national project that would recognize indigenous rights, rights that had remained unacknowledged in Mexico since the first constitution of 1824.

In short, anthropology has provided invaluable contributions to this struggle through its theoretical work on concepts such as autonomy, ethnicity, self-determination, community, and self-government – all terms that now circulate outside the academic confines of institutional anthropology. In Oaxaca, for example, anthropologists have played a particularly important role in reshaping public consciousness and debate concerning such things as limited and partial autonomy, and indigenous and cultural rights. In 1987, when the International Congress of Applied Anthropology was held in Oaxaca City, the national director of CIESAS announced the creation of a new branch of the institution dedicated to the study of cultural, social and political processes in Oaxaca. In the 16 years since its founding, CIESAS-Oaxaca has used its limited resources to carry out research on Oaxacan languages and cultures, ethnohistory and contemporary history, interethnic relations and the political articulation of indigenous communities with regional, state and national government. More recently, CIESAS-Oaxaca has added areas of research specialization in gender, environment, and indigenous technologies. With the support of Oaxacan indigenous linguists, CIESAS has also mounted an important program in ethnolinguistics and bilingual and intercultural education. In all these research areas, CIESAS-Oaxaca has sought to shape an anthropology that can contribute to public policy formation in areas such as health, justice, and indigenous communities. Most notably, anthropologists from

Oaxaca – including the author of this chapter – helped to conceive and draft the Law of Indigenous Peoples' Rights passed in 1998 (Ley de los Derechos de los Pueblos Indígenas). With this law, Oaxaca became the first state in Mexico to recognize diversity as a political and juridical principal, and to acknowledge the distinctive cultures and histories of its majority indigenous population (Nahmad 2001).

One way of accounting for the dramatic changes to Oaxaca's juridical structure over the past ten years is as a process of internal decolonization in which anthropology plays an important role in attenuating – or even someday hopefully eliminating – the economic inequality and political exclusion that have characterized Oaxacan society for the past two hundred years. In the drafting, conceptualization and defense of the new laws, for example, Oaxacan anthropologists had to hold dialogue and consult continuously with indigenous communities, as well as with non-indigenous sectors of Oaxaca's vibrant civil society. This kind of dialogue extended into the working of anthropology itself, as Zapotec and Mixtec anthropologists such as Gerardo Garfias, Víctor de la Cruz, and Juan Julián Caballero, sociologists such as Jaime Bailón and Víctor Raúl Martínez, and other intellectuals who have made Oaxaca their home, including Gustavo Esteva, Miguel Bartolomé, Stefano Varese, and myself, worked together to convince the Oaxacan state political apparatus to approve the reforms. By amending the state constitution and by passing new laws, such as the Ley de los Derechos de los Pueblos y Comunidades Indígenas, these anthropologists have contributed to an eventual dismantling of internal colonialism by helping to create a greater awareness of cultural diversity in Oaxaca and by supporting indigenous communities' claims to partial administrative, territorial and juridical autonomy. Of course, there are still many – including those in the current state government – who argue for the importance of maintaining a system of internal colonialism based on the exclusion of indigenous peoples. There are even some who argue that ethnic diversity should be eradicated in the interests of building a more "modern" civilization. Such arguments, for example, were widely aired in the state congress in the discussion of the 1998 reforms, and they continue to circulate widely in Oaxacan society and government offices today as a response to proliferating demands for justice, autonomy, and the recognition of existing social and political rights on the part of Oaxaca's indigenous communities and urban poor.

## AN ANTHROPOLOGY "FROM WITHIN"

As we have seen, Mexican anthropology has had close historical ties to "Western" (or European) models of social research and nation-building. Today, however, Mexican anthropology seeks to relocate itself within a broader, and always changing, global political context, and also to address the serious conflicts of interest that have been generated within anthropology itself through its historical allegiances to state policies and internal colonialism. Within this context, the anthropological task of translation or representation of other cultures becomes a political act, and not simply an academic pastime for relatively well-off university intellectuals.

These changes have been bolstered by the important transformations that have taken place since 1968 in how the subjects of anthropology view the ethnographers for whom they serve as informants, interpreters and hosts. Since the late 1970s a growing number of indigenous intellectuals, educated within "Western" academic traditions, have chosen to use their academic training to conduct fieldwork, investigation and historical research in their own communities and regions. These are anthropologists who work from a political commitment, and whose work addresses the development and protection of ethnic rights through objective ethnographic description of their own cultures and social institutions. They are also intellectuals who have been historically marginalized in (or excluded from) the Mexican educational system, or relegated to oral tradition. Their project begins from the premise that the history of an ethnic group as written by outsiders is apt to be not only incorrect in its facts and conclusions, but also lacking access to the many different interpretations of tradition that can exist within one group, relying instead on the information that can be obtained from a single individual or "informant" (see also Ramos, this volume). This trend toward an anthropology that is practiced by "insiders" or community members has been felt as a threat by some members of the anthropological profession. Yet, as Miguel Bartolomé points out in his reflections on the future of Mexican anthropology, "anthropology cannot not be a dialogue, given that we are no longer alone, although it may still be difficult for us to accept it. Stronger professional relations with our indigenous colleagues offer one route to recognition and dialogue, and dialogue is constitutive of the egalitarian intercultural relationships that our times demand" (2003:34). It is likely that the threat posed to mainstream sociocultural anthropology by the emergence of an indigenous anthropology will continue to be felt to the extent that ethnographic research, and theoretical interpretations that come from anthropology, fail to address questions of power, domination and poverty. The compromise of indigenous scholars – to accept the challenge to study and speak for their own cultures – is felt as a pressing duty (*un deber impostergable*). These are politically committed scholars who work for the protection and extension of ethnic rights, while also defending an intellectual commitment to providing objective descriptions and analyses of their people's culture, society and institutions.

Social applied anthropology in Mexico thus holds in reserve (*tiene reservada*) the important task of helping help ethnic minorities, the "first peoples" of Mexico, attain a more active participation in the national policies and programs most directly affecting their own populations. The anthropologist's responsibility is that of all academics across the world: to orient her consciousness, her ethics and her knowledge to the well-being of the community she studies; to contribute to the humanism of a universal society; and finally, to achieve peace and harmony among peoples, cultures and nations. As an example of this trend, we have seen how anthropologists in Oaxaca have worked to create a new juridical framework for the defense of indigenous cultural and linguistic rights. In Oaxaca, anthropologists have responded to the challenge of indigenous anthropology with both political and scientific commitment, although at times they have perhaps not always been sufficiently aware of the divergences between indigenous and non-indigenous interests.

While many anthropologists in Latin America embrace the new move toward an indigenous anthropology, the task of building an anthropology that is committed to furthering the work and participation of indigenous intellectuals brings with it potential risks. As Christian Gros notes:

> The surge in identity based, ethnic, religious, linguistic and cultural demands occurs across the modern world, and yet unfolds in different national contexts. In the more

industrialized European countries, familiar and persistent regional demands are duplicated by the problems provoked by the difficult integration of a new wave of immigrants from culturally distant countries. In the former communist block, ethnonationalism has emerged to fill the gap left by the decline of authoritarian regimes that had contained populations separated by long history of conflict. In other recently decolonized regions, what some call "tribalism" feeds off the subordinate place occupied by minority populations that once benefited from the self-interested protection of colonial powers. And in Latin America, where political independence occurred long ago, ethnically based demands threaten countries that made mestizaje the cornerstone of their national projects – countries that once believed they had effectively resolved the dilemmas generated by a unique history of "encounter" between different worlds. (2001:1)

To address these dramatic changes in our national and global worlds, anthropology counts on a rich reserve of theories and analytical instruments from the days when the discipline searched for cultural and human universals. In fact, it is possible to argue that anthropology was the first global social science and that, as such, it occupies a privileged position in studying the cultural and social phenomenon of globalization, and the migrations that accompany it. Indeed, for some time now, anthropology has ceased to study indigenous and peasant societies as "closed" or self-contained worlds, and has instead emphasized the multiple dynamic relationships that link these groups with national societies. Today anthropology studies transnational movements, migration, communication and patterns of consumption in a global frame. This framework lends renewed force to ethnographic perspectives on the transformation of cultural, ethnic and national identities.

The new relationship of the Mexican state to its indigenous peoples, however, will require even greater social and political commitment from anthropologists. Social and applied anthropology must play a central role in designing new strategies to eliminate and invalidate the paternalist and indigenista perspectives that have prevailed since the Mexican Revolution, replacing them with a more inclusive, participatory and dynamic relationship between indigenous peoples and the nation-state, a relationship in which indigenous peoples can exercise direct control over their natural and cultural resources and territories. Indigenous anthropologists, linguists, and archaeologists will certainly play a central role in forging political projects in which indigenous peoples will be strengthened in their political, social, cultural and economic rights. To achieve this, Mexican anthropology as a whole needs to cultivate a relationship to the political that is not subject to the circumstantial, and changing, interests and criteria of governments, parties and interest groups. This political program should promote (1) the opening of inclusive spaces and practices through which indigenous peoples can participate in political decision-making processes; (2) the promotion of a culture of pluralism and tolerance among different sectors of national society, and greater acceptance of different forms of life, worldviews and concepts of development; and (3) the sponsorship of actions that help to raise levels of production and employment, and increase access to justice, health care, education and cultural and social well-being. In each of these, anthropology shares responsibility with the peoples it once "studied" and with whom it now works as equal partners in anthropology inquiry.

## NOTES

1  The ejido is one form of collective property found within Mexican indigenous communities. The ejido system was reinforced and expanded through land redistributions carried out as part of a state-led land reform in the 1930s and 1940s.
2  For discussions about English indigenismo and its relation to national and racial ideologies in Mexico, see Dawson 1998 and Knight 1990.
3  PRI (Partido Revolucionario Institucional) controlled the Mexican government for nearly 70 years. Although there were other political parties, such as the Popular Socialist Party (Partido Popular Socialista), the National Action Party (Partido Acción Nacional, PAN), the Authentic Party of the Mexican Revolution (Partido Auténtico de la Revolución Mexicana), to name but a few, absolute control lay in the hands of the President of the Republic and an electoral system controlled by the government itself. The PRI lost control over the federal government in 2000 when PAN candidate Vicente Fox was elected President of Mexico.
4  For an overview of the controversy within anthropology, and its partial rupture with the Mexican state, see García Mora and Medina 1983, 1986.
5  The INI was effectively dismantled in 2003 when it was transformed into the Comisión Nacional Para el Desarrollo de los Pueblos Indígenas (CDI). See Saldívar 2002.
6  In 1992, President Salinas de Gortari amended the Mexican constitution to allow for the privatization of collective ejido lands that had been distributed in the land reforms of the 1930s and 1940s.

## REFERENCES

Aguirre Beltrán, Gonzalo (1957) *El proceso de aculturación*. Colección Problemas Científicos, no. 3. Mexico City: UNAM.

Aguirre Beltrán, Gonzalo (1970) Guatemala. Una interpretación histórico social por Carlos Guzmán y Jean Loup. *Anuario Indigenista* (Instituto Indigenista Interamericano, Mexico City) 30:307–322.

Aguirre Beltrán, Gonzalo (1979) *Regions of Refuge*. Washington, DC: Society for Applied Anthropology.

Aguirre Beltrán, Gonzalo (1983) *Lenguas vernáculas, su uso y desuso en la enseñanza. La experiencia de México*. Mexico City: CIESAS.

Aguirre Beltrán, Gonzalo (1988) Sobre teoría e investigación en la antropología social mexicana. In *Teoría e investigación en la antropología social mexicana* (pp. 7–14). Cuadernos de la Casa Chata, no. 160. Mexico City: CIESAS and Universidad Autónoma Metropolitana Unidad Iztapalapa.

Antun, Domingo (1979) ¿Qué es la federación Shuar? In *Indianidad y descolonización en América Latina. Documentos de la 2ª reunión de Barbados* (pp. 79–83). Mexico City: Nueva Imagen.

Bartolomé, Miguel (2003) Las palabras de los otros. La antropología escrita por indígenas en Oaxaca. *Cuadernos del Sur* 9(18):23–50.

Bonfil Batalla, Guillermo (1987) *México profundo. Una civilización negada*. Mexico City: Secretaría de Educación Pública, CIESAS, INAH and IISUABJO.

Comas, Juan (1964) *La antropología aplicada en México. Trayectoria y antología*. Serie Antropología Social, no. 1. Mexico City: Instituto Indigenista Interamericano.

Dawson, Alex (1998) From Models for the Nation to Model Citizens: Indigenismo and the Revindication of the Mexican Indian, 1920–1940. *Journal of Latin American Studies* 30:278–308.

Díaz Polanco, Héctor (1993) Las regiones autonomas en Nicaragua. In Lourdes Arizpe and Carlos Serrano (eds), *Balance de la antropología en América Latina y el Caribe* (pp. 543–554). Mexico: CRIM–UNAM.

Gamio, Manuel (1916) *Forjando patria*. Mexico City: Porrúa.

Gamio, Manuel (1972) *Arqueología e indigenismo*. Mexico City: SepSetentas.

Gamio, Manuel (1979) *La población del Valle de Teotihuacan*. Mexico City: Edición Facsimilar del Instituto Nacional Indigenista.

García Mora, Carlos (ed.) (1987) *La antropología en México. Panorama histórico 2. Los hechos y los dichos (1880–1986)*. Mexico City: INAH.

García Mora, Carlos and Medina, Andrés (eds) (1983) *La quiebra política de la antropología social en México. I. La impugnación*. Instituto de Investigaciones Antropológicas, Serie Antropológica, Antropología Social, no. 69. Mexico City: UNAM.

García Mora, Carlos and Medina, Andrés (eds) (1986) *La quiebra política de la antropología social en México. II. La polarización*. Instituto de Investigaciones Antropológicas, Serie Antropológica, Antropología Social, no. 69. Mexico City: UNAM.

González Casanova, Pablo (1965a) *La democracia en México*. Mexico City: Editorial Era.

González Casanova, Pablo (1965b) Internal Colonialism and National Development. *Studies in Comparative International Development* 1(4):27–37.

Gros, Christian (2001) Etnicidad, estado y violencia. La paradoja latinoamericana. Conferencia dictada en CIESAS. Instituto de Investigaciones Sociológicas de la UABJO.

Guerrero, Javier (1996) El desencuentro del Marxismo y la antropología en México 1970–1990. In M. Rutsch (ed.), *La historia de la antropología en México* (pp. 117–129). Mexico City: Universidad Iberoamericana, INI/Plaza y Valdés.

Herskovits, Melville (1938) *Acculturation: The Study of Culture Contact*. New York: J. J. Augustin.

Jaulin, Robert (1973) *La paz blanca. Introducción al etnocidio*. Buenos Aires: Tiempo Contemporáneo and Instituto Indigenista Interamericano.

Knight, Alan (1990) Racism, Revolution and Indigenismo: Mexico, 1910–1940. In R. Graham (ed.), *The Idea of Race in Latin America* (pp. 71–113). Austin: University of Texas Press.

Krotz, Esteban (1993) Antropología y antropólogos en México. Elementos de balance para construir perspectivas. In Lourdes Arizpe and Carlos Serrano (eds), *Balance de la antropología en América Latina y el Caribe* (pp. 361–380). Mexico City: CRIM–UNAM.

Mazrui, Ali A. (1986) *The Africans: A Triple Heritage*. Boston: Little, Brown.

Nadel, S. F. (1942) *A Black Byzantium*. Oxford: Oxford University Press.

Nadel, S. F. (1955) *Fundamentos de antropología social*. Mexico City: Fondo de Cultura Económica.

Nahmad Sitton, Salomón (1990) Oaxaca y el CIESAS. Una experiencia hacia una nueva antropología. *América Indígena* 50(2–3):11–32.

Nahmad Sitton, Salomón (2001) Autonomía indígena y la soberanía nacional. El caso de la ley indígena de Oaxaca. In Lourdes de León (ed.), *Costumbres, leyes y movimientos indios en Oaxaca y Chiapas* (pp. 19–48). Mexico City: CIESAS/Miguel Ángel Porrua.

Owusu, Maxwell (1989) La etnología de los etnógrafos y la etnografía. Teoría y práctica de la antropología sociocultural, una reconstrucción. In *Anuario de Etnología y Antropología Social*, vol. 2. Mexico City: Colegio de Etnólogos y Antropólogos Sociales.

Ramírez, Rafael (1928) *Como dar a todo México un idioma*. Mexico City: Talleres Graficos de la Nación.

Ramírez, Rafael (1976) *La escuela rural mexicana*. Mexico City: SepSetentas.

Ribeiro, Darcy and Gomes, Mercio (1995) Etnicidad y civilización. In *Articulación de la diversidad. Tercera reunión de Barbados*. Ecuador: Abya Yala.

Rodriguez, Ignacio (1996) Recursos ideológicos del estado mexicano. El caso de la arqueología. In M. Rutsch (ed.), *La historia de la antropología en México. Fuentes y transmisión* (pp. 83–103). Mexico City: Universidad Iberoamericana/INI/Plaza y Valdés.

Sáenz, Moisés (1970) *Carapan. Bosquejo de una experiencia.* Antología, prologo y selección de Gonzalo Aguirre Beltrán. Mexico City: Oasis.

Saldívar Tanaka, Emiko (2002) Everyday Practices of Indigenismo: An Ethnography of Mexico's Instituto Nacional Indigenista. Doctoral thesis, Political and Social Sciences Faculty, New School University, New York.

Varese, Stefano (1995) Pueblos indígenas y globalización en el umbral del tercer milenio. In *Articulación de la diversidad. Tercera reunión de Barbados.* Ecuador: Abya Yala.

Viqueira, Juan Pedro and Sonnleitner, Willibald (eds) (2000) *Democracia en tierras indígenas. Las elecciones en los altos de Chiapas.* Mexico City: CIESAS, Colegio de México, IFE.

Warman, Arturo (2003) *Los indios mexicanos en el umbral del milenio.* Mexico City: Fondo de Cultura Económica.

# CHAPTER 8

# Peru: From Otherness to a Shared Diversity

*Carlos Iván Degregori and Pablo Sandoval*

For a long time, anthropology privileged the study of "distant and different societies" (Augé 1995:12). As a result, classical anthropology came to be seen as the science or study of the Other, the radically different, the non-Western. Why this interest in studying "the other"? Curiosity and a spirit of adventure drove the chroniclers, travelers and explorers of antiquity who we now consider as precursors in the anthropological pantheon. Later, when anthropology emerged and developed as an academic discipline, such curiosity was rendered as "scientific," but it was never completely innocent. At least two underlying objectives lurked behind this interest in knowing the Other. First, there are those who studied "others" in order to dominate them better. The clearest example of this trend was British anthropology during the period of European imperial expansion (Asad 1991; Said 1989). On the other extreme, there were those who sought to know "the other" better so as to idealize him as the "noble savage." Between these two extremes, the best of classical anthropology contributed to broadening the concept of humanity itself, encouraging tolerance and positively recognizing cultural diversity at a time when "scientific" or biological racism was still a dominant mode of thought. As Stocking (2004:367) asserts, it is in this context that we should situate the cultural relativism of Franz Boas, who is widely considered the father of culturalism as well as being an important influence on the Latin American anthropologies that began to take shape at the beginning of the 20th century (see chapters by Walsh and Nahmad Sitton in this volume).

No one, however, can totally escape from the times in which they live. Even relativism shared in classical anthropology's tendency to dehistoricize the Other by rendering it as exotic or essential, either as a "noble savage" whose purity has to be protected, or as a "primitive" who is destined to disappear (Said 1990; and for the Andean context, Starn 1992). The anthropologist, who was almost always a white male citizen from an imperial state, could only rarely avoid looking at or depicting the Other with an "imperial eye" (Poole 1998; Pratt 1993).

What happens, however, when the Other is not on a faraway island, an impenetrable jungle or a scorching desert, but a resident of the same country as the anthropologist – perhaps someone who resides just around the corner, or even inside the anthropologist herself? In other words, what happens when the Others who constituted classical anthropology's subject of study themselves become the social scientists? If European anthropology was a product of North Atlantic expansion toward the rest of the world, in Asia, Africa and Latin America it was a product of the countervailing processes of national liberation and nation-state formation that arose in response to European and US imperial ambition (Cardoso de Oliveira 2001:77; Stocking 2001a, 2001b:287).

Just as in any other place, anthropology in Latin America offers dangers and possibilities. As several authors in this volume point out, "Southern" anthropologists always have and still do tend to study their own countries. This affords Latin American anthropologists the comparative advantage of "localized knowledge" and a capacity for "dense description" which is very difficult for foreign professionals to match. On the other hand, being too close to the tree can blur the view of the woods. By studying only his or her own country, the anthropologist may lose the special perspective afforded by distance which has traditionally stood as a prerequisite for successful ethnographic observation in the cultural and social anthropologies of the US and Europe. Finally, anthropologists may study their own country, but they do not necessarily study their own [sub]culture. When anthropology paints its Others as essential, it sees them as homogeneous and monolithic, although in reality, of course, they are not. We, the anthropologists of the *periphery*, are no exception to this rule. Indeed, Latin American anthropologists form part of an intelligentsia that is often differentiated from the rest of the population by education, social class, ethnicity and even "race."

In Peru, for example, the academic community tends to reproduce the same ethnic and class divides that traverse – and characterize – the country as a whole. This gap divides private from public universities, the capital city of Lima from the predominantly rural Andean and Amazonian regions, and the indigenous Andes from the "creole" or mestizo coast (Degregori and Sandoval 2006). Nevertheless, Latin American anthropology was also moved by a nostalgic or narcissist desire to (re)construct a homogeneous "us." Three currents where we can track this desire are (1) the theoretical gesture of indigenismo that dominated early 20th century anthropology in Peru, (2) the ideological paradigm of "national integration" that grew up during the mid to late 20th century as a product of anthropology's relationship to populist politics and the state, and (3) the ideology of revolution that tended to dominate much of the anthropology of the 1960s, 1970s and 1980s. Despite their differences, each of these three currents shared a view of culture as that which is both common and uniform, and a vanguardist concept of social change.[1]

These different views influenced Latin American anthropology to differing degrees, and at different points in time. But even when it was marked by dreams that would reveal themselves, once power was gained, to be impossible, anthropology was not only and in many cases not even mainly, an instrument of power. If we locate it in its historical context, we will find that anthropology has also been characterized both by the production of critical knowledge about social reality and by lines of flight that point toward other social and political horizons.

## CROSSED GLANCES: THE ORIGINS OF ANTHROPOLOGY IN PERU

In the case of Peru, the best of anthropology contributed to broadening the "family photo" and thereby to transforming "the imagined community" called Peru.[2]

A country originally conceived by its elites as western and creole gave way to another one that was more contradictory but also more plural. The central input of anthropology in its first decades (1940–60) was to contribute to national articulation,[3] by exploring undiscovered territories in both the literal and geographical sense, and also by metaphorically entering into unknown sociocultural and temporal environs.

In those times (and perhaps even today), when they left to do fieldwork in distant communities, Peruvian anthropologists felt themselves, and in fact acted as explorers in a country where foreigners had mainly been in charge of exploration, while the children of creole elites tended to act as foreigners in a strange country. As travelers and transcultural translators, collectors and folklorists of the 1930s and 1950s incorporated manifestations of what we now speak of as "subaltern groups" into their concept of a national culture. As time travelers, archaeologists and ethnohistorians further contributed to this expansion of national history by adding to it the thousands of years that preceded the Spanish Conquest in 1532.[4] But let us start from the beginning and proceed in order, specifying, expanding and also questioning these initial, perhaps too celebratory, statements.

## CHRONICLERS, EXPLORERS, AND TRAVELERS

If anthropology arises from an encounter with the Other, then the most ancient precursors of Peruvian anthropology are located in the times of the Spanish Conquest. Spanish historians or chroniclers attempted to make intelligible the radical Otherness of the Inka Empire, or Tawantinsuyo. Priests from different religious orders elaborated the first dictionaries in Quechua and Aymara. Bureaucrats charged with censustaking accumulated ethnographic data by interviewing ethnic lords and registering their subjects as tribute-paying "Indians" (Brading 1991:chs 2–4, and 7). Writing about Mexican anthropology, Claudio Lomnitz (1999:83) emphasizes that "this tension between the world of what is known and the seduction of exotic experiences that cannot be narrated, forms the original context of our anthropologies" (see also Lomnitz 2001).

But this immersion, or "intercultural translation," also brings dangers. The evangelists, for example, worried about a dangerous corruption of both signs and morality. To what extent were they adequately translating Christian categories? To what extent did translation imply a reaffirmation of the native culture and a consequent perversion of Christian doctrine? They worried, in short, that "the process of learning necessarily implies submission, albeit provisionally, to a foreign logic" (Lomnitz 1999:81–82). This same mixture of fascination and horror is found in Peru in figures such as the Cusco mestizo Jesuit, Francisco de Ávila (1573–1647). De Ávila's collection of myths, which he gathered while working as an extirpator of idolatries, has been described as "a sort of Popol Vuh of Peruvian Antiquity, a small regional Bible…" (Arguedas 1966:9; on de Ávila's life and work, see also Duviols 1966).

But soon other voices appeared, other crossed glances that offer us contradictory stories, absent in Lomnitz's tale of Mexican anthropology where "corruption" seems to be a one-way street. In the Peruvian case, Inca Garcilaso de la Vega (1539–1616) uses the same word to refer to the Spaniards who "corrupt… almost all the terms that they take from the language of the Indians of this land," starting with the name itself of

Peru. Through such corruptions, he argued, they misinterpreted the "real" history of the Inkas. But regarding the moral and religious sense of the word corruption, Garcilaso hesitates. He corrects the Spanish chronicler Pedro Cieza de León, who referred to Pachacamac, the great Pan-Andean divinity, as a "demon." Citing his own native ancestry, Garcilaso argues that Cieza, "was a Spaniard who did not therefore know the language as well as I do, since I am an Inca" (Garcilaso de la Vega 1960:58). Furthermore, he adds:

> On the other hand, they are right because the demon talked in those rich times acting as God under this man, keeping it for himself. But if I am asked ... now: what is God called in your language?, I would say "Pachacamac" because in that general language of Peru there is no other name to make reference to God but this one, and all the others ... either they do not come from the general language or they are corrupt. (1960:134–135)

Divinity or demon? In his vacillation lies outlined one of the recurrent dilemmas of anthropology and a significant part of today's Peruvian culture. These are the dilemmas of a mixture or cultural mestizaje that is far from being harmonic and without contradictions, and which is instead plagued by tearings, sutures and tensions at the edge of two worlds.[5]

So what happens when the Other is inside ourselves? The question is not only valid for Garcilaso but also for indigenous chroniclers such as Santa Cruz Pachacuti Yamqui, or Felipe Guamán Poma de Ayala, whose monumental letter to the King of Spain mixes Spanish and Quechua writing and iconography. His lavishly illustrated and passionate 1,200 page "letter" – which was lost until its discovery in Copenhagen in 1908 – never reached the King of Spain. It was first published in 1936 by the French anthropologist and linguist Paul Rivet. In the letter, Guamán Poma offers us "an ethnographic insight that is unique among the chroniclers" (Murra 1980:xvii). His critiques of Spanish colonial administration are harsh; and yet he leaves an opening toward the Catholic religion and the often violent campaigns it waged against Andean "idolatries." As Murra goes on to note, Guamán Poma's "ambivalence is notable. He defends the use of Andean dances and songs that others try to forbid. But like his contemporary, Francisco de Ávila, Waman Puma denounces the 'ydúlatras' (idolaters) among the Andean lords" (1980:vii). Indeed, Murra concludes, "his work, like that of Ávila, paves the way for the great campaigns to extirpate Andean religions."

Far from providing a thorough review of this first precursory moment for Peruvian anthropology, our interest here is instead to suggest how, from a very early date, the oppositions of domination and resistance, Andean and Western, and tradition and modernity were rendered as both complex and intertwined, and how this process has eroded the boundaries between Us and Others. Indeed, taken together, Garcilaso's and Guamán Poma's work suggests that, within only a few decades after the Conquest, a dominant discursive frame already defined the main topics around which, and in terms of which, contestation and struggle could occur (Joseph and Nugent 1994:20). Mestizo identity claims and indigenous protests alike appealed to symbols and institutions that had emerged from the same historical processes that had formed them as subordinate, colonial subjects.

After the great surge of exploration associated with the Conquest and the search for El Dorado, the fire burned out. As the shock of the new gave way to the routines of colonial life in Peru's Andean highlands and Pacific coast, the attractions of a proto-anthropology shifted to missionaries engaged in the "discovery" and spiritual conquest of Peru's eastern Amazonian lowlands. This period too would wane, however, when the 1740s Ashaninka rebellion led by Juan Santos de Atahuallpa forced the Franciscans from this last Amazonian frontier. Only a few decades later, the Spanish Crown followed suit by expelling the entire Jesuit Order from its New World colonies. With the removal of the Jesuits, curiosity about the Other was replaced by what Lomnitz has described as a compulsion to "ignore the other, so as to control her, so as not to be absorbed by her, so as to maintain Christianity in its purest form" (1999:83). By the 1780s, the great rebellions led by Túpac Amaru and Túpac Katari forced the Spaniards and creoles to retreat still further behind the walls of their "lettered cities." This was not so much a physical withdrawal, since both the early 19th century wars for independence and the civil wars that marked Peru's early Republican period developed in the countryside. Rather it was a shift in attitudes toward the indigenous Other. This shift was symbolized perhaps most evocatively in the country's very rapid retreat from its early liberal proclamations of equality and its quick return to colonial forms of ethnic taxation, discrimination and unpaid labor (Méndez 2005).

With the retreat of Peru's lettered, liberal elite, explorers and travelers, mostly foreigners, assumed the mantle of anthropological precursors (Degregori 2000). Neither the advance of liberalism, nor the abolition of indigenous taxation in the 1860s brought a significant change of attitude on the part of the oligarchical elites who – as Peruvian anthropologist José María Arguedas first pointed out – had always celebrated historical Indians while ignoring their contemporary descendants (Méndez 1996). Liberalism in Peru brought not tolerance and understanding, but rather a violent expansion of large landed estates or haciendas in what one historian has called the second conquest of the Andes (Larson 2004). But, despite its archaic wrapping, the context in which the 19th century land grab occurred was radically different, and had distinct consequences. Perhaps the most notable of these was indigenismo, an intellectual defense of indigenous culture and rights that emerged in response to both capitalist market expansion and the national trauma brought on by Peru's defeat by Chile in the War of the Pacific (1879–83).

## INDIGENISMO AND THE BIRTH OF ANTHROPOLOGY

Indigenismo questioned the exclusionary viewpoints that either kept the indigenous majorities out of the imagined national community, or incorporated them as a servile or "degenerate" substrate. During the late 19th and early 20th centuries, indigenismo carved a space for the recognition of the Indian in Peru's national conscience, culture and politics. The wide and varied literature on indigenismo reveals a heterogeneous and complex movement that covers several fields – philanthropic, social, political and artistic – and traverses different historical junctures (see, among others, Cornejo Polar 1980, 1994; Franco 1990; Lauer 1997; Martínez and Samaniego 1977; Poole 1997). For many scholars (e.g. Kristal 1991), indigenismo was animated by an "urban vision of the Andes" that was simultaneously paternalistic, exoticizing and often homogenizing with respect to its conceptualization of the role played by mestizos or Indians in Peruvian nation-building. Peruvian anthropology, which emerged as a university discipline in 1946, is the offspring of indigenismo and, as such, it is necessary to locate the origins of our discipline against this background.

Lauer (1997) makes an interesting distinction between an indigenismo that is mostly sociopolitical and another that is cultural (literary, plastic, architectonic or musical). The first strand, which lasted from the end of the 19th century until the 1920s, was mobilizing, modernizing and combative (*revindicativo*). As such, it assumed an important place in Peruvian national debates. By 1927, the polemic launched by indigenismo involved such prominent intellectual and political personalities as José Carlos Mariátegui (founder of Peru's Socialist Party), Luis Alberto Sánchez (a founding member of the APRA party, the Alianza Popular Revolucionario Americana) and José Ángel Escalante (a prominent Cusco indigenista) (see Aquézolo 1976 for examples). In its most radical form, indigenismo assumed utopian and even apocalyptic features, as in the writings of Luis E. Valcárcel,[6] or simply radical ones, as in *El Nuevo Indio* by another Cusqueño, Uriel García. In a subordinate way, many of the ideas were incorporated in the competing political programs that Victor Raúl Haya de la Torre and José Carlos Mariátegui drew up for Peru's two most influential opposition parties, the APRA and the Socialist Party, respectively.

By contrast, cultural indigenismo was "more than a subversive proposal or negation of [Peru's] creole identity," it was "a nationalist ideal whose moment seemed to have come, an effort to expand from its margins what counted as creole" (Lauer 1997: 46–47). As such, cultural indigenismo formed yet another instance of a long chain of attempts, dating back to colonial times, by Peru's creole elite to assimilate the autochthonous by "outlining a clear course of incorporation of what is not creole to what is creole" (Lauer 1997:16). In this guise, after suffering various mutations and with its more rebellious implications silenced, indigenismo was recovered and deployed as a sort of backdrop in official speeches until the 1980s. The historian Jorge Basadre traces the passage of "indigenismo 1" to "indigenismo 2" to the 1930s: "The decade from 1920 to 1930," Basadre suggests, "represented a significant increase in the image of the Indian within the conscience of the Peruvian intelligentsia." Yet this awareness gave way, in "the period corresponding to 1931–1942, to a period of Hispanic reaffirmation" (Basadre n.d: 33). The Hispanic counteroffensive occurred in a global climate of conservative, if not fascist offensive. The climate in which the so-called "indigenous problem" creates space on the national agenda yields to another in which it is possible for the philosopher Alejandro O. Deustua to affirm that: "Peru owes its disgrace to this indigenous race that, in its psychic dissolution, obtained the biological rigidity of beings who have definitively closed their cycle of evolution and who have been unable to transmit through miscegenation the very racial virtues of the period of its progress" (Deustua in 1937 quoted in Degregori et al. 1979:234). It was during this decade, described by another Peruvian historian as "the worst years of Peru's 19th century Republican history" (Macera 1968:92), that anthropology was born as a university discipline.

From that time onward, indigenismo assumed the form of a defensive idea that retreats to the past and toward the margins of national life. Valcárcel turned his attention to the ethnohistory of ancient Peru, and indigenismo as a movement found refuge in fields and institutions that did not explicitly challenge power, such as schools of fine arts or the Museum of Peruvian Culture. There, anthropology matured. Even on the defensive, the "indigenista group" waged its battles until finally, in 1946, in a favorable national and international context, anthropology was institutionalized as a university discipline. The Second World War had just ended and the cold war had not yet begun. In Peru, under the administration of José Luis Bustamante and Rivero (1945 to 1948), there was a short-lived democratic spring. Luis E. Valcárcel (whose indigenismo had already lost its utopian edge) was appointed Minister of Education in 1945, and under his office in 1946 the Institute of Ethnology and Archaeology was created in San Marcos University. At the same time, the Faculty of Anthropology was created in Cusco's University of San Antonio Abad.[7] By this time, Valcárcel and other indigenistas hoped to legitimate anthropology as an applied science, "moving it away from generalizations, utopias and panaceas" (Valcárcel 1964:12). In the first ten years, for example, more than 40 research papers on indigenous communities and three projects of technical assistance and cultural promotion were created at the Institute. Under Valcárcel's direction, this institution also cooperated with the Ministry of Education on its plans for primary and adult education.

One can describe the period between the 1920s and 1960s as a long and difficult passage from the exclusionary modernizing paradigm of the oligarchy to another, more inclusive, populist or "national popular" project. Part of this passage is the development of state-led indigenismo. Since the administration of Augusto B. Leguía (1919 to 1930), and lasting until the 1940s, indigenismo enjoyed intermittent and peripheral support from the Peruvian state. Under Leguía the state enacted laws to protect and regulate indigenous culture and life. In 1921 the Ministry of Public Works (Ministerio de Fomento) created the Section of Indigenous Affairs, as well as the Pro-Indigenous Rights Committee "Tahuantinsuyo." A year later, the same ministry created the Council of the Indigenous Race (Patronato de la Raza Indígena) and, following the First Inter-American Indigenista Congress held in 1949 in Pátzcuaro, Mexico, the Peruvian Indigenista Institute was established by executive decree as a dependent body within the Ministry of Justice and Labor. Peruvian anthropology grew up in a compromise between this pale version of an "official indigenismo," and the militant mobilizations led during these same decades by Peru's "real Indians," many of whom had begun to organize to protest against their exploitation by both wool merchants and local landowners.

Throughout these years, Mexico appears as a constant point of reference and contrast for Peruvian anthropologists. In Mexico, anthropology lived its Golden Age in what Bonfil (1970) has characterized as a long and comfortable marriage with the populist, postrevolutionary and integrationist state. This relationship started to sour with the 1968 massacre in Tlatelolco (see Nahmad Sitton, this volume). In Peru, by comparison, anthropology's relationship with the state can best be described as diplomatic, nearly a compact. If the Golden Age of Mexican anthropology was tightly linked to the revolutionary state, in Peru it was mostly related to financing by US philanthropic foundations and to European academic institutions such as the French Institute of Andean Studies (IFEA), founded in 1948. Universities and NGOs have worked with them for many years. By strange coincidence, it was during the reformist government of General Velasco (1968 to 1975) that anthropology (and sociology) began its brief romance with the state. Two of the first graduates of the new anthropology faculty occupied important positions in the military regime: Carlos Delgado, one of the architects of Velasco's 1969 Agrarian Reform Act, and Mario Vásquez, a disciple of Alan Holmberg who helped to create the 1972 Peasant Community Act.

Anthropology's romance with the military state was interrupted, however, by the conservative transition that took place in the mid-1970s. But by that point, Peruvian anthropology had already been a university discipline for two decades and it had also lived through its own "golden age."

The tenuous relationship between anthropology and the state during these first decades was at the same time its strength and its weakness. On the one hand, anthropology had to strive to make some social space, to get resources, and to make itself appear legitimate in the eyes of the state. On the other hand, anthropology was not overly constrained by its dependence on state projects, and it was in fact relatively free to move back and forth between the transcultural experience of fieldwork, a search for state legitimacy, and a hegemonic national culture dominated by the homogenizing implications of "acculturation," as it came to be formulated within modernization theory (Aguirre Beltrán 1967).

Somewhere between discovery and integration – or perhaps more appropriately, between the old dichotomy of "knowledge" versus "destruction" – anthropologists appeared as liminal or borderline figures who were neither fully incorporated within the state, nor wholeheartedly in favor of a full-scale sociocultural integration of the Indian. This phase unfolded as a flurry of bureaucratic reports for the Ministry of Labor and Indigenous Affairs and the immersion by the discipline's first graduating class into the little-known world of professional anthropology. Perhaps trying to come closer to the experience of the anthropological classics in distant islands or isolated "tribes," these young professionals chose to write their theses about distant communities where they hoped to find relics of prehispanic culture (e.g. Matos Mar 1949, Matos Mar et al. 1959, Avalos de Matos 1952). There is a time arch that goes from these first theses to the research projects led by anthropologists from San Marcos University in the Lurin and Chancay valleys (Matos Mar et al. 1959; Matos Mar and Ravines 1971; see also the list of theses in Rodríguez Pastor 1985). That same spirit was alive, simultaneously, in Cusco under the guidance of Óscar Núñez del Prado; and in Ayacucho too, where Efraín Morote Best held research seminars that shaped subsequent generations of anthropologists. In each of these sites, anthropology tended to be dominated by holistic studies of communities, folkloric studies and applied anthropology projects.

A certain tension between the contradictory mandates to exoticize and to acculturate "the other" also characterized applied anthropology projects, which were in turn influenced by theories of modernization, developmentalism and functionalism. These programs were criticized for their link to or coincidence with the interests of imperial power and their limited "demonstration effect." Allan Holmberg, director of the Vicos Project (1952 to 1962), the most important program of applied anthropology developed in Peru, stated that "it seems to us that the current process of Westernization of the peoples appears to us to consist of the introduction of modern "fundamental postulates" within cultures that lack them" (1966:59).[8] Such assertions reflect a contemporary intellectual context in which notions of tradition and modernity were perceived as mutually exclusive or opposing poles. But what attracts the most attention in Holmberg's Vicos project is not within the community of Vicos itself, but rather what occurs outside of it – that is, the massive peasant and left-wing political protests in which organized Andean peasants recovered, between 1958 and 1964, hundreds of thousands of hectares of land. The anthropologists' indigenous countrymen, without the intervention of supportive "development projects," effectively destroyed the ancient latifundio system – and they did so in a remarkably nonviolent manner, given both the magnitude of the protests and the continuing political sensitivities surrounding issues of land redistribution (Guzmán and Vargas 1981; Remy 1990; see also Seligmann, this volume).

## POINTS OF ESCAPE AND NEW HORIZONS

This tension between the seduction of the exotic and the need to assimilate is related to the form in which the discipline posits the relationships between anthropology's "others" and what Lomnitz calls a "normative citizen" – in this case the urban creole or mestizo:

> We could say that the Indian in Mexico was the "other" of the normative citizen, in comparison to the way in which African Americans, Indians or Mexicans were the "others" of the normative citizen in the United States at the beginning and mid-century… Thanks to the Mexican revolution, however, there is an important difference… although both the African American and the Mexican Indian were the other of the normative citizen in their corresponding countries, the Indian in Mexico was placed as the very subject of nationality, a subject that would be transformed by education and racial mixture. Thus, Mexican anthropology was "indigenist" while it was a modernizing anthropology that worked in a particular nationalist formula. (Lomnitz 1999:87–88)

Without the support of a social revolution (as in Mexico) and with the partial exception of the years when General Velasco's government celebrated peasant political consciousness (1968 to 1975), the Peruvian Indian takes longer to situate himself or herself in "the very root of nationality" (or perhaps never actually succeeds in doing so). For indigenismo, however, as for early Peruvian anthropology, it was obvious that the indigenous person was located there at the origins of the Peruvian nation. Perhaps because of that, even when the country experienced an accelerated process of modernization, urbanization and articulation, anthropologists reproduced, in another context and with less drama, the old dilemmas of Cieza de León, Garcilaso and Guamán Poma. Although they never managed fully to escape the dominant, homogenizing paradigm of "modernization," they did find opportunities to certify and produce knowledge about "the other," and to express sympathy for cultural diversity.

Throughout the 1960s, Peruvian anthropology began to spill over the boundaries that had been set for it by the early indigenista anthropologists with their focus on rural Andean communities, folklore, cultural relativism, and the sacred rites of ethnographic fieldwork. This overflow occurred gradually as new fieldsites, topics and influences were incorporated into anthropology. Among the new topics introduced during this period were urban studies about shantytowns and provincial clubs (Sandoval 2000), ethnohistorical studies that transformed not only our knowledge of the 16th century, but also our understanding of the contemporary Andean world (Murra 1975; Thurner 1998), and studies of Amazonian societies that were both geographically and academically little known (Varese 1968). Boundaries of "the field" were also stretched in a geographical sense. Going beyond earlier studies of isolated communities, anthropologists began to study broader social units, or what Matos Mar (1969) called microregions. Theoretical influences also expanded and changed. R. T. Zuidema (1962) introduced structuralist theories of social organization and religion, and John Murra (1975) reinforced the influence of cultural ecology and introduced ideas of substantivism derived from the work of Karl Polanyi. But the great rupture was produced by dependency theory – the first theoretical current to emerge from Latin America and to have an international impact on the social sciences. Dependency theory shaped, for example, the Project to Study the Changes of Peruvian Peoples that was jointly organized by San Marcos University, Cornell University and the Institute of Peruvian Studies in the Chancay Valley between 1964 and 1969 (see for example, Matos Mar et al. 1969; Fuenzalida et al. 1970; Degregori and Golte 1973; and the theses of Bonilla 1965, Fonseca 1966, and Celestino 1970).

Dependency theory introduced topics until then neglected by the discipline, such as conflict, domination and power. It influenced Peruvian anthropology and sociology at a time when these disciplines were transiting from description to interpretations of national scope. In that sense, the 1960s were an exceptional moment in which social sciences sought for the first time to "occupy central spaces in culture and politics." Enrique Mayer (1970) and Fernando Fuenzalida (1970) launched discussions of interethnic relations; sociologist Julio Cotler (1968) questioned the nature of traditional local power as a "baseless triangle"; and in 1964 sociologist Aníbal Quijano theorized *cholificación* (the process of cultural adoption or mimicry) as the expression of a diversity that was no longer confined to distant places, but rather a crucial, even defining, feature of the country as a whole (Quijano 1980).

Whether through their emphasis on conflict, structural transformation or cultural diversity, indigenista and culturalist anthropologies reached a strategic limit in which they were gradually overwhelmed by the experiences and hopes of new generations of predominantly provincial anthropologists. Above all, anthropology became attentive to the need to find a different paradigm that could finally overcome both the mutually exclusive opposition of tradition/modernity and the tension between knowledge and destruction that had haunted anthropology since its origins. But the great leap toward a new paradigm was frustrated.

José María Arguedas is the emblematic figure for how one possible transition was frustrated. In both his anthropological and his literary work, Arguedas perceived the possibility of a "diverse us" beyond colonial splittings and homogenizing miscegenations (see for example, Arguedas 1957, 1964, 1968a). Building on his own vital experience and drawing from both culturalism and liberation theology, Arguedas achieved insights that define him as a precursor of an interculturality that had theoretical support and became popular only 10 or 15 years after his death. Thus, upon receiving the Inca Garcilaso de la Vega Award in 1968, Arguedas defined himself as a "modern Quechua individual" – a concept which amounted, in contemporary modernization thinking, to squaring a circle. "I am not acculturated," he writes. "I am a Peruvian man who is proud, like a happy demon, to speak Christian and Indian, Spanish and Quechua." Further, he proclaims his desire "to live happily [as the expression of ] all [Peru's] fatherlands" ("vivir feliz todas las patrias"). If Peruvian anthropology has opened any horizon in a half century of existence, perhaps it could be synthesized in these phrases of Arguedas:

> There is no other country more diverse, more multiple in earthly and human variety; all the degrees of heat and color, of love and hate, of intrigues and subtleties, of used and

inspired symbols. It was not just for fun, as the so-called common people would say, that all this was created here: Pachacámac and Pachacútec, Huamán Poma, Cieza and Inca Garcilaso, Túpac Amaru and Vallejo, Mariátegui and Eguren, the feast of Qoyllur Riti and the Lord of the Miracles; the hot tropical valleys of the coast and the Andes; the agriculture at 4,000 meters; ducks that talk in the lakes of high altitude where all the insects of Europe would drown; hummingbirds that reach up to the sun to drink its fire and flame over the flowers of the world. To imitate someone from here is considered to be somewhat scandalous. (1968a:8)

In November 1969, Arguedas took his own life. We could say that just like a character in search of an author, his intuitions (and distress) did not find a social, organized subject with whom to talk and become nourished. They were the result of what we might describe as an *indigenismo without indigenous people*. The ethnic movements that would later emerge in Bolivia, Ecuador, and Guatemala had not yet appeared. The contingent of young people who could have led a similar movement in Peru, while they sympathized with Arguedas, were eventually seduced by another proposal to overcome the dilemmas of anthropology and Peruvian culture through structural transformations by way of revolution, fighting not only to occupy central places in the cultural and political life of the country but also to obtain state power. This proposal was the extremely dogmatic and economistic version of Marxism (and especially Maoism) that was disseminated in Peruvian universities during the 1970s.[9] As a form of Marxism that left no room for culture, it failed to realize its academic promise and instead became a victim of ideology. It was a "textbook Marxism" (Degregori 1990) that left empirical research aside, replacing it with a reverential reading not even of the classics of Marxism, but of Marxist handbooks that supposedly contained all truth and thus rendered superfluous the very concept of empirical research.

Nor were competing anthropological trends free from the oppressive dominance of structural analysis. Many of those who did not opt for a Marxist framework instead became Lévi-Straussian structuralists with little facility for integrating history – or indeed the nearly 500 years of European presence in Peru – into their analyses of Andean culture and society (e.g. Ortiz 1973; Ossio 1973). Then, in the midst of the political violence launched after 1980 by the Communist Party of Peru-Sendero Luminoso (Shining Path) (PCP-SL), culturalist anthropology, indigenismo and textbook Marxism confronted their own demise. This demise had the emblematic name of Uchuraccay.

## BANKRUPTCY OF ESSENTIALISM AND ECONOMISM

On January 23, 1983, the Peruvian press described the killing of an undetermined number of PCP-SL members in Huaychao, a peasant community in the highlands of Huanta (Ayacucho). The news seemed to confirm existing rumors that the communities known as Iquichanas were confronting PCP-SL on their own – without the assistance of the Peruvian armed forces. A group of eight journalists interested in finding out what happened traveled from Lima to the investigate what had happened. Shortly after leaving Huanta, they were brutally murdered in Uchuraccay, a neighboring community of Huaychao.

Because of the national impact of the massacre, the government appointed an investigative commission chaired by the novelist Mario Vargas Llosa. The commission included well-known anthropologists as consultants, thus putting a profession that specialized in the study of indigenous communities in the public spotlight. As Fernando Fuenzalida later explained, the anthropologists agreed to participate out of a moral and professional commitment that was animated not by the journalists' deaths per se, but rather because the killings had taken place in an Andean community (Ossio and Fuenzalida 1983:6). Their participation, however, had the effect of giving "scientific" support to the commission's otherwise highly dubious conclusions. As a description of fact, the report presented only a very rough sketch of what had happened: it said merely that peasants had murdered the journalists. Yet as a theoretical statement, the Vargas Llosa commission drew on anthropology to explain the tragedy as a "natural" product of the Iquichana community's secular isolation, poverty, "primitivism," and "archaism" – all traits that supposedly distanced Uchuraccay from the the nation's modern or "Western" culture (Vargas Llosa, Guzmán and Castro 1983:23ff). The anthropological reports of Ossio and Fuenzalida (1983) that formed part of the commission's scope revealed the inability of a certain sort of culturalist gaze to go beyond a general bewilderment at the killings. Instead, the anthropologists organized their report as a description of the "indigenous condition" and "community tradition," all within an essentially indigenista worldview that pitted "official Peru" against "the real Peru" (*el Perú profundo*). What is perhaps most surprising is that, as we have seen, other anthropologists had worked to undo this same dichotomy since at least the mid-1960s.

Twenty years later, the commission's general findings – that the journalists were killed by peasants – were corroborated by documentary evidence, as well as by the oral testimonies of peasants presented to the Peruvian Truth and Reconciliation Commission (Comisión de la Verdad y Reconciliación, CVR, 2001–3). The truth commission, however, carried out research on the case with new ethnographical and file materials from the ethnographic research of Ponciano del Pino (2003; CVR 2003:vol. 5). Del Pino's work revealed that, at the time of the killings, Uchuraccay had four stores and a school with one teacher, that peasants from the community migrated regularly to find wage labor, and that many of them were bilingual. In short, it showed that Uchuraccay was a far cry from the image of distance and isolation attributed to it by the anthropologists who wrote for the Vargas Llosa report.

The Uchuraccay case made patent the political and theoretical implications of the sorts of essentialized understandings of indigenous communities and peoples that had been promoted by an earlier, indigenista anthropology (for anthropological critiques of the report see, among others, Degregori and Urrutia 1983; Lumbreras 1983; Montoya 1983, 1984; Mayer 1992). It also, however, offered a challenge to dogmatic Marxism in that the Iquichana communities had risen up against the very party (PCP-SL) that had taken the logic of the "Marxist manuals" to its most demented extremes. This same party had also criticized the "querulous-magical nationalism" of José María Arguedas (*El Diario*, June 9, 1988, p. 12, quoted in Degregori 1990:213). During the 1980s, PCP-SL performed several punitive incursions against Uchuraccay and, during the final years of war, it multiplied its attacks against Andean and Amazonian communities, arguing that these had refused to side with the "laws of History" which the PCP-SL claimed to fulfill. This blindness to culture in general, and Andean indigenous culture more specifically, contributed to a significant degree to both the defeat of PCP-SL and the subsequent bankruptcy of "textbook Marxism" (Degregori 1990).

## THE RETURN OF CULTURE

In the midst of the violence and political crisis that characterized the 1980s in Peru, anthropology managed to set a new course for itself through a somewhat belated engagement with the debates that were transforming the discipline in the rest of the world. A double return, then, took place: "the return of the actor" (c.f. Touraine 1987) and the return of culture. To prioritize the study of social actors also means the return of history. Both had been expelled from the "simple and elegant" models of Lévi-Straussian structuralism and also from the more dogmatic forms of Marxism that perceived actors as solely determined by their position within an economic or productive structure. Authors such as E. P. Thompson (1979) drew attention to the fact that actors make history and that, in doing so, they sometimes betray the narrow class-bound scripts that Marxism had historically assigned them. This is what José Nun (1989) has called "the rebellion of the chorus." The effects in Peru can be observed perhaps most clearly in the multidisciplinary project developed in the 1980s at the Institute of Peruvian Studies (IEP) on Popular Classes and Urbanization (Golte and Adams 1987; Degregori et al. 1986). Curiously, although the resistance of rural communities to the Shining Path's armed struggle seemed to constitute a prototypical example of the "rebellion of the chorus," studies of political violence in Peru's rural and native communities were carried out, for the most part, by foreign anthropologists.[10] On other fronts, there was also a boom in studies of "new social movements" as a phenomenon (allegedly) distinct from the class-based claims of the unions and peasant organizations.

Of these "new social movements," those which proved to have the greatest political and theoretical impact were based on ethnicity and gender. In Peru studies on ethnicity, racism and ethnic movements appeared relatively late, compared with other Latin American countries. While movements such as Katarismo in Bolivia, the Confederation of Indigenous Nationalities (CONAIE) in Ecuador, the Mayan movement in Guatemala, or Zapatismo in Mexico challenged anthropologists to rethink their theoretical priorities, Peruvian ethnic movements were restricted to the Amazon region and they did not generally find a base among the Quechua and the Aymara majorities of the Peruvian Andes (Degregori 1998; Pajuelo 2003; and from the point of view of sociology, Cotler 2005; Quijano 2006). Studies of gender, on the other hand, experienced a sort of boom, as a result of both women's movements and the increasing currency of feminist theory (Anderson 1993, 1997; Fuller 2003; Oliart 1995). In the 1990s gender studies gained an institutional base with the creation of a Diploma in Gender Studies at Lima's Catholic University; and a Masters degree in Gender Studies at San Marcos University.

The return of culture allowed anthropologists to address some of the same concerns that had characterized earlier folkloric studies through the new theoretical lens of "popular culture."[11] More recently, other approaches linked to interpretative, symbolic and reflective aspects of anthropology, and also to subaltern studies, have overcome the dichotomy between domination and resistance. Of particular importance here have been studies on music, dance, folklore and ritual performances in the Andes by Romero (1993, 2001), Mendoza (2000, 2006) and Cánepa (2001). Such developments have gone along with a relaunching in the 1980s of folklore congresses, which had not been held since the late 1950s. As events that attract mainly provincial intellectuals, it is worth asking to what extent they reflect a hardening of the historical gap separating state and private universities, and Lima and the provinces. The folklore congresses, and conferences on Man and Andean Culture (Hombre y la Cultura Andina), once again represent as they did in the 1930s – although this time in an even more defensive mode – "the line of resistance drawn by provincial elites against the historical concentration of prestige and the cultural power in Lima" (Macera 1968).

On the other hand, during those years, anthropologists began their tardy journey from the country to the city, following rural subjects who had been the protagonists of massive migrations since the 1950s. Although anthropologists have studied migration since the early 1960s (Altamirano 1980), urban anthropology only really took off in the 1980s. While its early expressions were best characterized as an "anthropology in the city," whose subjects were immigrants, networks, associations, and micro-entrepreneurs, urban anthropology has since expanded to include studies of transnational migrations (e.g. Altamirano 1984; Berg and Paerregaard 2005; Golte and Adams 1987; Adams and Valdivia 1991; Degregori et al. 1986; Huber 1997). Today anthropologists in Peru study their urban subjects through the lens of new identities and mentalities, urban popular culture, religiosity, violence, organizations and youth identities, consumption, and differentiation (see Sandoval 2000). Thus, while one of the classical dichotomies of the anthropological agenda was based on the urban–rural duality, today that division is becoming increasingly blurred and more complex (Diez 1999; Urrutia 2002).[12]

Finally, other topics link themselves more directly with professional activity. Anthropology has moved in this respect from the old applied anthropology of the mid 20th century, through the social engineering carried out by the military state in the 1970s, to encompass now the sorts of promotional work sponsored by the NGOs that have become the most important site for professional anthropology. With the NGO boom, topics such as ecology and sustainable development take center stage for anthropology (Mayer 1994, 2004). Another challenge to anthropology comes from a state which has distanced itself from the homogenizing paradigm of earlier forms of liberal nation-building, to embrace a neoliberal rhetoric of cultural diversity. Taking up the notion of "socialization" – which had played only a very small role in earlier anthropologies – anthropologists have introduced theories of interculturality and bilingual education into debates on public education (Ames 2000; Ansión 2003). Older topics such as customary law and traditional medicine are repackaged as alternative forms of justice and health services (Polia 1994). Finally, the professional dimension of gender studies has meant increased attentiveness to questions of gender equity in many areas of public policy formation.

## From Homogeneity to the Construction of a "Diverse We" (*un nosotros diverso*)

While increasing opportunities for anthropological work, the expansion of anthropological expertise has also exposed dangerous flanks, in that expansion has occurred at a time when the gap is widening between Lima and the provinces, state and private universities, and research and development work. In other words, there is a widening gap between the academic and the professional wings of anthropology. Such gaps reflect similar forms of inclusion/exclusion to those that also characterize the current process of globalization. This dynamic produces, at one extreme, a "global" minority capable of entering transnational academic communities, and at the other, a "localized" majority seeing regional specialization as a refuge and emphasizing professionalization. Critical academic discussions are thus sacrificed in the interests of a pragmatism that paradoxically does not come from an accommodated sector, but rather from sectors with a great need of making a place for themselves in a restricted job market that most of the time will incorporate them in only the most subordinate positions (Degregori and Sandoval 2006).

If there is a single issue in Peruvian anthropology in which these sorts of risks and potentialities are most clearly framed, it is the issue of cultural diversity and its attendant concepts of multiculturalism and interculturality. Multiculturalism, as a claim to the right of difference, has been essential in strengthening the self-esteem of discriminated groups, in gaining rights and developing affirmative action programs. But insofar as multiculturalism begins with the idea that each "culture" or group exists as such prior to starting a relationship with the others, as if they were prebuilt discrete blocks, it has also tended to conceive of communities as homogeneous. It emphasizes ideals of equity among groups and *tolerance* toward Others, more than the enrichment and mutual transformation that take place as a result of the interaction of differences. For some, multiculturalism and the politics of recognition end up as reflections or functions of multinational capitalism (e.g. Favre 1998; García Canclini 2004; Žižek 1998).

Within this perspective, toward the end of the 1970s, a different concept emerged from Latin America and Canada: interculturality. The term started to be used in the field of bilingual education, where it was contrasted to the notion of biculturality that emerged in the United States (Lopez 2000). With the concept of interculturalism, a long history of the contacts, exchanges and bridges that exist among different cultures despite inequalities of wealth and power gives way to imagining another possibility: the elimination of inequality but not of the exchanges themselves. The goal, in other words, is to eliminate domination without aspiring to a clear separation among cultures. With time, the concept of interculturality has moved beyond debates on education to address problems of cultural diversity more generally. Its advantages reflect its origins in pedagogy. These include an emphasis on relational processes, locating the self in history and sorting out essentialisms, progressing from simple tolerance to the possibility of mutual enrichment among subjects who are increasingly connected through globalization (Hopenheyn 2004; for discussions of interculturalism in Peru see, among others, Aikman 2003; Callirgos 1993; Fuller 2003; Heise, Tubino and Ardito 1994; Godenzzi 1996; Poole 2003; Romero 1999).

Recent reflections on interculturality echo the Arguedian utopia of "joining opposing streams," not as the archaism that Vargas Llosa imagines it to be (1997), but rather as the possibility of bringing Peru's many different cultures into conversation. Arguedas's proposals seem incipient because they were made early and they were made in a Peru before agrarian reform, still marked by the contrast between lords and servants. Arguedas feels the distress of being unable to escape from the dialectic of master and slave, the shame of belonging to a universe of dominant people and despair for their insensitivity before the cultural wealth of the dominated Other. Arguedas's insights remind us that interculturality can only be obtained among citizens with equal rights and under conditions of at least a minimum of economic equity. Similar concerns have shaped ethnographic studies, especially since the 1990s when Peruvian anthropology was again strongly influenced by both subaltern studies and the more symbolic and reflexive wings of US anthropology, where scholars called for rethinking the relationships between culture and power through both history and ethnography (de la Cadena 2000; del Pino 2003; Poole 1997; Starn 1999; Jiménez 2005; Sendón 2003; Wilson 2001). This new thematic view, with its own theoretical genealogies, methodological approaches and ethnographic strategies, provides the backdrop for the transition from indigenismo to an intercultural paradigm (de la Cadena 2006).

This new approach to the study of culture and power, however, has also been characterized by an absence or, at best, scarcity of studies about the internal armed conflict that shook the country between 1980 and 1990, and its consequences, especially in the rural field and among the indigenous peoples who were always the privileged topics of anthropology.[13] This scarcity is felt even more because the final report of the Truth and Reconciliation Commission that worked in Peru between 2001 and 2003 clearly pointed to exclusion, ethnic and cultural discrimination, and racism as among the most important causes of the conflict, and as determining factors of the violence that proliferated during its course (CVR 2003:vol. 8, chs 1 and 2.2, and vol. 5). With some exceptions, such as the book written by the anthropologist and artist from Ayacucho, Edilberto Jiménez (2005), works about the internal armed conflict and its consequences have been carried out by Peruvian cultural critics, social psychologists or anthropologists who study or work abroad (see Rojas Pérez, this volume).

In this context, what is the role of anthropology in a post-conflict society whose elites once again reveal their "desire to ignore," a desire that is expressed not only in the neoliberal model but in their belligerent refusal to acknowledge, discuss or debate the findings of the Truth and Reconciliation Commission. Instead, the country's governing elites opt aggressively to demonstrate a racism that we thought had been removed from public space since the 1970s. This is a question to which the younger generation of anthropologists must now speak.

## NOTES

1    We refer to them as vanguards in the sense that they each conceived of themselves as privileged leaders who would design projects of modernization, national construction or revolution. These three very different projects also shared the common premise that diversity had to be rendered homogeneous. For modernization theorists, homogeneity would be produced mainly around the dissemination of an "American lifestyle." Indigenistas by comparison worked to forge a sole collective actor, the mestizo – which the Mexican intellectual José Vasconcelos called the "cosmic race." For the revolutionary left, the collective actor was the proletariat, which would be anchored in the productive structure, and thus transcend national frontiers as well as biological or cultural determinations.

2    In this section we draw on previous studies of Peruvian anthropology by Salomón (1982, 1985), Montoya (1975), Murra (1984), Osterling and Martínez (1985), Urrutia (1992), Poole (1992), Rivera Cusicanqui (1993), Marzal (1993), Ansión (1994), Guerrero and Platt (2000), Burga (2005) and Bonilla (2005).

3    We differentiate integration from articulation. Although integration is synonymous with homogenization and uniformization, articulation alludes to a unity in which differences are maintained.

4    Until 1969, archaeology, ethnohistory and ethnology formed part of the same faculty in the Institute of Ethnology and Archaeology at Lima's University of San Marcos, the country's most important and largest public university.

5   Regarding Inca Garcilaso's difficulties assuming his mestizo identity, see Hernández 1993. Regarding his critique of the concept of miscegenation, Cornejo Polar 1994.

6   See for example, Valcárcel's influential 1927 publication Tempestad en Los Andes: "One day the Sun of Blood, Yawar Inti, will bring light and the waters will turn red. The defeated party feeds its hate in silence, and coldly calculates the compound interest of five centuries of cruel insults. Would a million white victims be enough?" He further adds, "Who knows from which group of silent farm workers, of baleful shepherds, will the Andean Spartan arise? Who knows if he is already alive, still lost, in the high Plateau of Puno, in the rocky terrain of Cuzco. The dictatorship of the indigenous proletariat is in search of its Lenin" (Valcárcel 1970:24, 126).

7   According to Valcárcel (1947:16) "ethnologic activities in Peru started" in the 1930s, with the arrival in Cusco of US based ethnologist Harry Tschopik (1930). Another landmark was the publication of the Handbook of South American Indians (Steward 1946).

8   For a detailed bibliography regarding this project, see Dobyns and Vázquez (1966) and a critical evaluation in Stein (2000). An interesting evaluation prepared by the inhabitants themselves of the community has been recently published, Memorias de la comunidad de Vicos (Vicos 2005).

9   There are some who remained as solitary figures such as Rodrigo Montoya, who tries to establish an almost impossible dialogue between the concept of culture and ideology (1980), César Fonseca, who more successfully attempts a dialogue between substantivism and Marxism in economic anthropology (1972), and also several of Murra's disciples who appear among the authors of Reciprocidad e intercambio en los Andes Peruanos (Reciprocity and Exchange in the Peruvian Andes) (Alberti and Mayer 1974). For a wider analysis of this point, see Degregori (1995).

10  For a critique of the explanatory models of the political violence developed by some political scientists, see Poole and Rénique (1991).

11  The classic studies of folklore favored such expressive dimensions of culture as music, craftsmanship, narrative, rituals and theater. They posited a singular and genuine rural culture, and tended to disregard the wider sociopolitical contexts of the rural communities and their cultural experiences (Joseph and Nugent 1994:17). If such wider dynamics are taken into account, then the uneven distribution of cultural power is evident. When this occurs, the object of folkloric studies enters a process of redefinition (see especially Lloréns 1983).

12  The most complete view of the changes in Peruvian rural society may be found in the publications of the Permanent Seminar on Agrarian Research (SEPIA) which have been issued since 1985; see www.sepia.org.pe/web/frames.html.

13  The findings of the Truth and Reconciliation Commission revealed that 75% of executed victims during the internal armed conflict spoke Quechua as a mother tongue in comparison to only 17% of Peruvian people who claimed to speak it in the 1992 national census – a census that corresponded to the most difficult time of the conflict. Likewise, the commission's final report states that 65% of victims came from rural areas (CVR 2003).

# REFERENCES

Adams, Norma and Valdivia, Néstor (1991) Los otros empresarios. Ética de migrantes y formación de empresas en Lima. Lima: Instituto de Estudios Peruanos.

Aguirre Beltrán, Gonzalo (1967) Regiones de refugio. El desarrollo de la comunidad y el proceso dominical en mestizo América. México: Instituto Indigenista Interamericano.

Aikman, Sheila (2003) La educación indígena en Sudamérica. Interculturalidad y bilingüismo en Madre de Dios. Lima: Instituto de Estudios Peruanos.

Alberti, Giorgio and Mayer, Enrique (eds) (1974) Reciprocidad e intercambio en los Andes peruanos. Lima: Instituto de Estudios Peruanos.

Altamirano, Teofilo (1980) *El campesinado y la antropología urbana*. Lima: Pontificia Universidad Católica del Perú.

Altamirano, Teofilo (1984) *Presencia Andina en Lima Metropolitana. Estudio sobre migrantes y clubes provincianos*. Lima: Pontificia Universidad Católica del Perú.

Ames, Patricia (2000) ¿Escuela es progreso? Antropología y educación en el Perú. In Carlos Iván Degregori (ed.), *No hay país más diverso. Compendio de antropología peruana*. Lima: Red para el Desarrollo de las Ciencias Sociales en el Perú.

Anderson, Jeanine (1993) La feminización de la pobreza en el Perú. *Revista Peruana de Ciencias Sociales* (Fomciencias, Lima) 3(13).

Anderson, Jeanine (1997) *Sistemas de género, redes de actores y una propuesta de formación*. Montevideo: CEAAL-REPEM.

Ansión, Juan (1994) Transformaciones culturales en la sociedad rural: El paradigma indigenista en cuestión. In Carlos Iván Degregori, Javier Escobal, and Benjamín Marticorena (eds), *SEPIA V*. Lima: SEPIA.

Ansión, Juan (2003) La antropología al servicio de una educación intercultural. In Norma Fuller (ed.), *Interculturalidad y política: desafíos y posibilidades*. Lima: Red para el Desarrollo de las Ciencias Sociales en el Perú.

Aquézolo, Manuel (ed.) (1976) *La polémica del indigenismo*. Lima: Mosca Azul.

Arguedas, José María (1957) Evolución de las comunidades indígenas. El valle del Mataro y la ciudad de Huancayo: un caso de fusión de culturas no comprometida por la acción de las instituciones de origen colonial. *Revista del Museo Nacional* (Lima) 26.

Arguedas, José María (1964) Puquio una cultura en proceso de cambio. In José María Arguedas (comp.), *Estudios sobre la cultura actual del Perú*. Lima: UNMSM.

Arguedas, José María (1966) Introducción a Dioses y Hombres de Huarichirí. In *Dioses y Hombres de Huarichirí. Narración quechua recogida por Francisco de Ávila*. Bilingual edn trans. José María Arguedas. Lima: IEP.

Arguedas, José María (1968a) Ceremony of the Inca Garcilaso de la Vega award, Lima.

Arguedas, José María (1968b) *Las comunidades de España y del Perú*. Lima: UNMSM.

Arguedas, José María (1985[1965]) *¿He vivido en vano? Mesa redonda sobre "Todas las sangres."* Lima: IEP.

Asad, Talal (1991) Afterword: From the History of Colonial Anthropology to the Anthropology of Western Hegemony. In George W. Stocking (ed.), *Colonial Situations: Essays on the Contextualization of Ethnographic Knowledge*. Madison: University of Wisconsin Press.

Augé, Marc (1995) *Hacia una antropología de los mundos contemporáneos*. Barcelona: Gedisa.

Avalos de Matos, Rosalía (1952) El ciclo vital de la comunidad de Tupe. *Revista del Museo Nacional* (Lima) 21.

Basadre, Jorge (n.d.) *Historia de la República*, Book 16. Lima: Universo.

Berg, Ulla and Paerregaard, Karsten (eds) (2005) *El quinto suyo. Transnacionalidad y formaciones diaspóricas en la migración peruana*. Lima: Instituto de Estudios Peruanos.

Bonfil, Guillermo (1970) Del indigenismo de la revolución a la antropología crítica. In Arturo Warman et al. (eds), *De eso que llaman antropología mexicana*. Mexico City: Nuestro Tiempo.

Bonilla, Heraclio (1965) *Las comunidades campesinas tradicionales del valle de Chancay*. Anthropological Series, no. 1. Lima: Museo Nacional de la Cultura Peruana.

Bonilla, Heraclio (2005) Situación y tendencias de la investigación antropológica en los países andinos. In Heraclio Bonilla, *El futuro del pasado. Las coordenadas de la configuración de los Andes*, Book 1. Lima: Fondo editorial del Pedagógico San Marcos, Instituto de Ciencias y Humanidades.

Brading, David (1991) *Orbe indiano. De la monarquía católica a la República criolla, 1492–1867*. Mexico City: Fondo de Cultura Económica.

Burga, Manuel (2005) Historia y antropología en el Perú (1980–1998). Tradición, modernidad, diversidad y nación. In Manuel Burga, *La historia y los historiadores en el Perú*. Lima: Fondo editorial de la Universidad Nacional Mayor de San Marcos.

Callirgos, Juan Carlos (1993) *El racismo. La cuestión del otro y de uno.* Lima: Centro de Estudios y Promoción del Desarrollo.

Cánepa Koch, Gisela (ed.) (2001) *Identidades representadas. Performance, experiencia y memoria en los Andes.* Lima: Pontificia Universidad Católica del Perú.

Cardoso de Oliveira, Roberto (2001) Vicisitudes del "concepto" en América Latina. In Miguel León Portilla (ed.), *Motivos de la antropología americanista. Indagaciones en la diferencia.* Mexico City: Fondo de Cultura Económica.

Celestino, Olinda (1970) Conflicto social y redistribución de poder. La comunidad de Lampian. Thesis for Bachelor's degree, Universidad Nacional Mayor de San Marcos, Department of Arts and Human Sciences, Lima.

Cornejo Polar, Antonio (1980) *La novela indigenista. Literatura y sociedad en el Perú.* Lima: Lasontay.

Cornejo Polar, Antonio (1994) *Escribir en el aire. Ensayo sobre la heterogeneidad socio-cultural en las literaturas andinas.* Lima: Horizonte.

Cotler, Julio (1968) La mecánica de la dominación interna y el cambio social en el Perú. In José Matos et al., *Perú Problema no. 1.* Lima: Instituto de Estudios Peruanos.

Cotler, Julio (2005) Bolivia, Ecuador and Peru, 2003–04: A Storm in the Andes? Working Paper 51. Real Instituto Elcano de Estudios Internacionales y Estratégicos, Madrid.

CVR (Comisión de la Verdad y Reconciliación) (Truth and Reconciliation Commission of Peru) (2003) *Final Report.* Lima: CVR.

Degregori, Carlos Iván (1990) La revolución de los manuales. La expansión del marxismo-leninismo en las ciencias sociales y el surgimiento de Sendero Luminoso. *Revista Peruana de Ciencias Sociales* (Lima), no. 3.

Degregori, Carlos Iván (1995) El estudio del otro: cambios en el análisis sobre etnicidad en el Perú. In Julio Cotler (ed.), *Perú, 1964–1994. Economía, sociedad y política.* Lima: IEP.

Degregori, Carlos Iván (1998) Movimientos étnicos, democracia y nación en Perú y Bolivia. In Claudia Dray (ed.), *La construcción de la nación y la representación ciudadana en México, Guatemala, Perú, Ecuador y Bolivia.* Guatemala: FLACSO.

Degregori, Carlos Iván (2000) Panorama de la antropología en el Perú. Del estudio del Otro a la construcción de un nosotros plural. In Carlos Iván Degregori (ed.), *No hay país más diverso. Compendio de Antropología peruana.* Lima: IEP.

Degregori, Carlos Iván and Golte, Jürgen (1973) *Dependencia y desestructuración social en la comunidad de Pacaraos.* Lima: Instituto de Estudios Peruanos.

Degregori, Carlos Iván and Sandoval, Pablo (2006) Modernización neoliberal y comunidad académica de ciencias sociales. Antropología y antropólogos en el Perú. Research report presented to the Latin American Council for Social Sciences (CLACSO), Buenos Aires.

Degregori, Carlos Iván and Urrutia, Jaime (1983) Reflexiones sobre ocho muertes peruanas. *El Diario* (Lima), Feb. 14, p. ii.

Degregori, Carlos Iván et al. (1979) *Indigenismo, clases sociales y problema nacional.* Lima: CELATS.

Degregori, Carlos Iván, Blondet, Cecilia, and Lynch, Nicolás (1986) *Conquistadores de un nuevo mundo. De invasores a ciudadanos en San Martín de Porres.* Lima: Instituto de Estudios Peruanos.

de la Cadena, Marisol (2000) *Indigenous Mestizos: The Politics of Race and Culture in Cuzco, Peru, 1919–1991.* Durham, NC: Duke University Press.

de la Cadena, Marisol (2006) The Production of Other Knowledges and Its Tensions: From Andeanist Anthropology to Interculturalidad? In Gustavo Lins Ribeiro and Arturo Escobar (eds), *World Anthropologies: Disciplinary Transformations within Systems of Power.* Oxford: Berg.

del Pino, Ponciano (2003) Uchuraccay. Memoria y representación de la violencia política en los Andes. In Ponciano del Pino and Elizabeth Jelin (eds), *Luchas locales, comunidades e identidades.* Madrid: Siglo XXI.

Diez, Alejandro (1999) Diversidades, alternativas y ambiguedades. Instituciones, comportamientos y mentalidades en la sociedad rural. In Víctor Agreda, Alejandro Diez, and Manuel Glave (eds), *Perú: El problema agrario en debate. SEPIA VII.* Lima: ITDG, SOS-FAIM.

Dobyns, Henry and Vázquez, Mario (1966) El proyecto Perú-Cornell. Personal y bibliografía. In Allan Holmberg (ed.), *Vicos. Método y práctica de la antropología aplicada.* Lima: Editorial Estudios Andinos.

Duviols, Pierre (1966) Estudio bibliográfico de Francisco de Avila. In *Dioses y hombres de Huarochirí. Narración quechua recogida por Francisco de Avila.* Bilingual edn trans. José María Arguedas. Lima: IEP.

Favre, Henri (1998) *El indigenismo.* Mexico City: Fondo de Cultura Económica.

Fonseca, César (1966) Sindicatos agrarios del valle del Chancay. Thesis for Bachelor's degree in Anthropology, Universidad Nacional Mayor de San Marcos, Department of Arts and Human Sciences, Lima.

Fonseca, César (1972) Sistemas económicos en las comunidades campesinas del Perú. Doctoral thesis in Anthropology, Universidad Nacional Mayor de San Marcos, Department of Arts and Human Sciences, Lima.

Franco, Carlos (1990) Impresiones del indigenismo. *Hueso Húmero* (Lima), no. 26:44–68.

Fuenzalida, Fernando (1970) Poder, raza y etnia en el Perú contemporáneo. In Fernando Fuenzalida et al., *El indio y el poder en el Perú.* Lima: Instituto de Estudios Peruanos.

Fuenzalida, Fernando et al. (1970) *El indio y el poder en el Perú.* Lima: Instituto de Estudios Peruanos.

Fuller, Norma (2001) *Masculinidades. Cambios y permanencias.* Lima: Fondo Editorial PUCP.

Fuller, Norma (ed.) (2003) *Interculturalidad y política. Desafíos y posibilidades.* Lima: Red para el Desarrollo de las Ciencias Sociales en el Perú.

García Canclini, Néstor (2004) *Diferentes, desiguales y desconectados: mapas de la interculturalidad.* Barcelona: Gedisa.

Garcilaso de la Vega, Inca (1960) *Comentarios reales de los Incas (estudio preliminar de José Durand).* Lima: UNMSM.

Godenzzi, Juan Carlos (ed.) (1996) *Interculturalidad y educación en los Andes y la Amazonía.* Cusco: Centro Bartolomé de las Casas.

Golte, Jürgen and Adams, Norma (1987) *Los caballos de Troya de los invasores. Estrategias campesinas en la conquista de la gran Lima.* Lima: Instituto de Estudios Peruanos.

Guerrero, Andrés and Platt, Tristan (2000) Proyecto antiguo, nuevas preguntas. La antropología histórica de las comunidades andinas de cara al nuevo siglo. In Hans Joachim König, Tristan Platt and Colin Lewis (eds), *Estado-nación, comunidad indígena, industria. Tres debates al final del milenio.* Notebooks no. 8, Asociación de Historiadores Latinoamericanistas Europeos.

Guzmán, Virginia and Vargas, Virginia (1981) *El campesinado en la historia. Cronología de los movimientos campesinos 1956–1984.* Lima: IDEAS.

Heise, María, Tubino, Fidel, and Ardito, Wilfredo (1994) *Interculturalidad. Un desafío.* Lima: Centro Amazóncio de Antropología y Aplicación Práctica.

Hernández, Max (1993) *Memoria del bien perdido. Conflicto, identidad y nostalgia en el Inca Garcilaso de la Vega.* Biblioteca Peruana de Psicoanálisis. Lima: IEP.

Holmberg, Allan (ed.) (1966) *Vicos, método y práctica de la antropología aplicada.* Lima: Estudios Andinos.

Hopenhayn, Martín (2004) La aldea global. Entre la utopía transcultural y el ratio mercantil: paradojas de la globalización cultural. In Ramón Pajuelo and Pablo Sandoval (eds), *Globalización y diversidad cultural. Una mirada desde América Latina.* Lima: IEP.

Huber, Ludwig (1997) Etnicidad y economía en el Perú. Working Paper 83, Anthropology Series, no. 11. Instituto de Estudios Peruanos, Lima.

Jiménez, Edilberto (2005) *Chungui. Violencia y trazos de memoria.* Lima: Comisedh.

Joseph, Gilbert and Nugent, Daniel (eds) (1994) *Everyday Forms of State Formation: Revolution and the Negotiation of Rule in Modern Mexico.* Durham, NC: Duke University Press.

Kristal, Efraín (1991) *Una visión urbana de los Andes. Génesis y desarrollo del indigenismo en el Perú: 1848–1930.* Lima: Instituto de Apoyo Agrario.

Larson, Brooke (2004) *Trials of Nation Making: Liberalism, Race, and Ethnicity in the Andes, 1810–1910.* Cambridge: Cambridge University Press.

Lauer, Mirko (1997) *Andes imaginarios. Discursos del indigenismo 2*. Cusco: SUR, Centro Bartolomé de las Casas.

Lloréns Amico, José (1983) *Música popular en Lima. Criollos y andinos*. Lima: Instituto de Estudios Peruanos, Instituto Indigenista Interamericano.

Lomnitz, Claudio (1999) Descubrimiento y desilusión en la antropología mexicana. In C. Lomnitz, *Modernidad indiana. Nueve ensayos sobre nación y mediación en México*. Mexico City: Planeta.

Lomnitz, Claudio (2001) Bordering on Anthropology: Dialectics of a National Tradition. In *Deep Mexico, Silent Mexico: An Anthropology of Nationalism*. Minneapolis: University of Minnesota Press.

López, Luis Enrique (2000) Interculturalidad, educación y gestión del desarrollo. MS.

Lumbreras, Luis Guillermo (1983) Dr Luis Guillermo Lumbreras Declares: Incomplete and Descriptive Report of Uchuraccay. *El Observador* (Lima), Mar. 18 and 19.

Macera, Pablo (1968) La historia en el Perú. Ciencia e ideología. *Amaru* (Lima), no. 6 (Apr.–June).

Martínez, Héctor and Samaniego, Carlos (1977) *Política indigenista en el Perú. 1946–1969*. Notebooks no. 4. Lima: CEPES.

Marzal, Manuel (1993) *Historia de la antropología. 1. La antropología indigenista. México y Perú*. Mexico City: UAM-Iztapalapa.

Matos Mar, José (1949) Tupe: una comunidad del área cultural del Kauke en el Perú. Geografía y economía. Thesis for Bachelor's degree, Universidad Nacional Mayor de San Marcos, Lima.

Matos Mar, José (ed.) (1957) *La propiedad en la isla de Taquile, Lago Titicaca*. Lima: Universidad Nacional Mayor de San Marcos, Instituto de Etnología y Arqueología.

Matos Mar, José (1958) La estructura económica de una comunidad andina. Taquile, una isla del Lago Titicaca. Doctoral thesis, Universidad Nacional Mayor de San Marcos, Lima.

Matos Mar, José (1969) Microregión y pluralismo. In José Matos Mar et al., *Dominación y cambios en el Perú rural*. Lima: IEP.

Matos Mar, José and Ravines, Roger (1971) *Bibliografía peruana de ciencias sociales (1957–1969)*. Lima: Instituto de Estudios Peruanos, Campodónico Ediciones.

Matos Mar, José et al. (1959) *Las actuales comunidades de indígenas. Huarochirí en 1955*. Lima: Instituto de Etnología y Arqueología, Universidad Nacional Mayor de San Marcos.

Matos Mar, José et al. (1969) *Dominación y cambios en el Perú rural*. Lima: Instituto de Estudios Peruanos.

Mayer, Enrique (1970) Mestizo e indio. El contexto social de las relaciones inter-etnicas. In Fernando Fuenzalida et al., *El indio y el poder en el Perú*. Lima: Instituto de Estudios Peruanos.

Mayer, Enrique (1992) Peru in Deep Trouble: Mario Vargas Llosa's Inquest in the Andes' Reexamined. In George E. Marcus (ed.), *Rereading Cultural Anthropology*. Durham, NC: Duke University Press.

Mayer, Enrique (1994) Recursos naturales, medio ambiente, tecnología y desarrollo. In Óscar Dancourt, Enrique Mayer, and Carlos Monge (eds), *Perú. El problema agrario en debate. SEPIA V*. Lima: SEPIA.

Mayer, Enrique (2004) *Casa, chacra y dinero. Economías domésticas y ecología en los Andes*. Lima: Instituto de Estudios Peruanos.

Méndez, Cecilia (1996) Incas sí, Indios no. Apuntes para el estudio del nacionalismo criollo en el Perú. Working Paper 56. IEP, Lima.

Méndez, Cecilia (2005) *The Plebeian Republic: The Huanta Rebellion and the Making of the Peruvian State: 1820–1850*. Durham, NC: Duke University Press.

Mendoza, Zoila (2000) *Shaping Society through Dance: Mestizo Ritual Performance in the Peruvian Andes*. Chicago: University of Chicago Press.

Mendoza, Zoila (2006) *Crear y sentir lo nuestro. Folclor, identidad regional y nacional en el Cuzco, siglo XX*. Lima: Pontificia Universidad Católica del Perú.

Montoya, Rodrigo (1975) Colonialismo y antropología en Perú. *Nueva Antropología: Revista de Ciencias Sociales* (Mexico City), no. 2.

Montoya, Rodrigo (1980) *Capitalismo y no capitalismo en el Perú. Un estudio histórico de su articulación en un eje regional.* Lima: Mosca Azul.

Montoya, Rodrigo (1983) Interview with Dr Rodrigo Montoya: Uchuraccay ¿crimen sin castigo? *La República* (Lima), Mar. 19.

Montoya, Rodrigo (1984) Otra pista para entender lo ocurrido en Uchuraccay. *La República* (Lima), special supplement, Jan. 26.

Murra, John (1975) *Formaciones económicas y políticas en el mundo andino.* Lima: Instituto de Estudios Peruanos.

Murra, John (1980) Waman Puma, etnógrafo del mundo andino. In John Murra and Rolena Adorno, *El primer Nueva Crónica y Buen Gobierno (Felipe Guamán Poma de Ayala). Siglo XXI.* Mexico City: IEP.

Murra, John (1984) Andean Societies. *Annual Review of Anthropology* 13:119–141.

Nun, José (1989) *La rebelión del coro.* Buenos Aires: Nueva Visión.

Oliart, Patricia (ed.) (1995) *¿Todos igualitos? Educación y género.* Topics on Sociology series. Lima: Fondo Editorial PUCP.

Ortiz, Alejandro (1973) *De Adaneva a Inkarri (Una visión indígena del Perú).* Lima: Retablo de Papel.

Ossio, Juan (1973) *Ideología mesiánica del mundo andino.* Lima: Ignacio Prado Pastor.

Ossio, Juan and Fuenzalida, Fernando (1983) *Informe presentado a la comisión investigadora de los sucesos de Uchuraccay.* Lima: Editora Perú.

Osterling Jorge and Martínez, Héctor (1985) Apuntes para una historia de la antropología social peruana, décadas de 1940–1980. In Humberto Rodríguez Pastor (ed.), *La antropología en el Perú.* Lima: Concytec.

Pajuelo, Ramón (2003) Fronteras, representaciones y movimientos étnicos en los países centroandinos en tiempos de globalización. In Daniel Mato (ed.), *Políticas de identidades y diferencias sociales en tiempos de globalización.* Caracas: FACES–UCV.

Polia, Mario (1994) *Cuando dios lo permite: encantos y arte curanderil. Las estructuras culturales de la medicina tradicional andina.* Lima: Prometeo.

Poole, Deborah (1992) Antropología e historia andinas en los EE.UU.: buscando un reencuentro. *Revista Andina* (Centro Bartolomé de las Casas, Cusco), no. 19.

Poole, Deborah (1997) *Vision, Race, and Modernity: A Visual Economy of the Andean Image World.* Princeton: Princeton University Press.

Poole, Deborah (1998) Landscape and the Imperial Subject: US Images of the Andes, 1859–1930. In Gilbert Joseph, Catherine LeGrand, and Ricardo Salvatore (eds), *Close Encounters of Empire: Writing the Cultural History of US–Latin American Relations.* Durham, NC: Duke University Press.

Poole, Deborah (2003) Democracia y cultura en la educación intercultural peruana. At www.andes.missouri.edu/ANDES/Comentario/DP_Cultura.html, accessed Sept. 8, 2006.

Poole, Deborah and Rénique, Gerardo (1991) The New Chroniclers of Peru: US Scholars End Their "Shining Path" or Peasant Rebellion. *Bulletin of American Research* (New York) 10(1).

Pratt, Mary Louise (1993) *Imperial Eyes: Travel Writing and Transculturation.* London: Routledge.

Quijano, Aníbal (1980[1964]) Lo cholo y el conflicto cultural en el Perú. In Aníbal Quijano, *Dominación y cultura.* Lima: Mosca Azul.

Quijano, Aníbal (2006) El "Movimiento Indígena" y las cuestiones pendientes en América Latina. *Revista San Marcos* (UNMSM, Lima), no. 24, First Semester.

Remy, María Isabel (1990) ¿Modernos o tradicionales? Las ciencias sociales frente a los movimientos campesinos en los últimos 25 años. In Héctor Bejar et al., *La presencia del cambio. Campesinado y desarrollo rural.* Lima: Desco.

Rivera Cusicanqui, Silvia (1993) Anthropology and Society in the Andes. *Critique of Anthropology* 13.

Rodríguez Pastor, Humberto (ed.) (1985) *La antropología en el Perú*. Lima: Concytec.

Romero, Raúl (ed.) (1993) *Música, danzas y máscaras en los Andes*. Lima: Pontificia Universidad Católica del Perú.

Romero, Raúl (1999) De-esencializando al mestizo andino. In Carlos Iván Degregori and Gonzalo Portocarrero (eds), *Cultura y globalización*. Lima: Red para el Desarrollo de las Ciencias Sociales en el Perú.

Romero, Raúl (2001) *Debating the Past: Music, Memory, and Identity in the Andes*. Oxford: Oxford University Press.

Said, Edward (1989) Representing the Colonized: Anthropology's Interlocutors. *Critical Inquiry* 15:205–225.

Said, Edward (1990) *Orientalismo*. Madrid: Libertarias/Prodhufi.

Salomón, Frank (1982) Andean Ethnology in the 1970s: A Retrospective. *Latin American Research Review* 17.

Salomón, Frank (1985) The Historical Development of Andean Ethnology. *Mountain Research and Development* 5(1).

Sandoval, Pablo (2000) Cultura urbana y antropología en el Perú. In Carlos Iván Degregori (ed.), *No hay país más diverso. Compendio de antropología peruana*. Lima: Red para el Desarrollo de las Ciencias Sociales en el Perú.

Sendón, Pablo (2003) Cambio y continuidad en las formas de organización social de las poblaciones rurales del sur peruano. *Debate Agrario* (CEPES, Lima), no. 36.

Starn, Orin (1992) Antropología andina, "Andinismo" y Sendero Luminoso. *Allpanchis* (IPA, Cusco) 23(39):15–72.

Starn, Orin (1999) *Nightwatch: The Politics of Protest in the Andes*. Durham, NC: Duke University Press.

Stein, William (2000) *Vicisitudes del discurso del desarrollo en el Perú: Una etnografía sobre la modernidad del Proyecto Vicos*. Lima: SUR, Casa de Estudios del Socialismo.

Steward, Julian H. (ed.) (1946) *Handbook of South American Indians*. Bureau of American Ethnology, Bull. 143. Washington, DC: Smithsonian Institution.

Stocking, George W., Jr (2001a) Delimiting Anthropology: Historical Reflections on the Boundaries of a Boundless Discipline. In George W. Stocking, Jr, *Delimiting Anthropology: Occasional Essays and Reflections*. Madison: University of Wisconsin Press.

Stocking, George W., Jr (2001b) The Shaping of National Anthropologies: A View from the Center. In George W. Stocking, Jr, *Delimiting Anthropology: Occasional Essays and Reflections*. Madison: University of Wisconsin Press.

Stocking, George W., Jr (2004) *A formação da antropologia americana, 1883–1911. Antologia/ Franz Boas*. Rio de Janeiro: Universidade Federal do Rio de Janeiro/Contraponto.

Thompson, E. P. (1979) *Tradición, revuelta y conciencia de clase. Estudios sobre la crisis de la sociedad preindustrial*. Barcelona: Editorial Crítica.

Thurner, Mark (1998) Después de la etnohistoria: encuentros y desencuentros entre discursos antropológicos e históricos. In Franklin Pease (ed.), *Actas del IV Congreso Internacional de Etnohistoria (Lima)*, Book 2. Lima: Pontificia Universidad Católica del Perú.

Touraine, Alain (1987) *El regreso del actor*. Buenos Aires: Editorial Universitaria de Buenos Aires.

Tschopik, Harry (1946) *Highland Communities of Central Peru: Regional Survey*. Publication no. 5. Washington, DC: Smithsonian Institute of Social Anthropology.

Urrutia, Jaime (1992) Comunidades campesinas y antropología. Historia de un amor (casi) eterno. *Debate Agrario* (CEPES, Lima), no. 14.

Urrutia, Jaime (2002) Espacio, poder y mercado. Preguntas actuales para una vieja agenda. In Manuel Pulgar-Vidal, Eduardo Zegarra, and Jaime Urrutia (eds), *Perú. El problema agrario en debate. SEPIA IX*. Lima: SEPIA, Consorcio de Investigación Económica y Social.

Valcárcel, Luis E. (1947) Arqueólogos y etnólogos norteamericanos en el Perú. *Revista del Museo Nacional* (Lima), Book 16.

Valcárcel, Luis E. (1964) Indigenismo en el Perú. In Luis E. Valcárcel, *Estudios sobre la cultura actual del Perú* (pp. 10–12). Lima: UNMSM.

Valcárcel, Luis E. (1970[1927]) *Tempestad en los Andes.* Lima: Populibros Peruanos.

Varese, Stefano (1968) Las minorías étnicas de la montaña peruana. Esquema para una antropología de urgencia. *Letras* (Department of Arts and Human Sciences, San Marcos University, Lima), nos 7–8.

Vargas Llosa, Mario (1997) *La utopía arcaica. José María Arguedas y las ficciones del indigenismo.* Mexico City: Fondo de Cultura Económica.

Vargas Llosa, Mario, Guzmán, Abraham, and Castro, Mario (1983) *Informe de la Comisión Investigadora de los sucesos de Uchuraccay.* Lima: Editora Perú.

Vicos (2005) *Memorias de la comunidad de Vicos. Así nos recordamos con alegría. Comunidad campesina de Vicos.* Huaraz: Vicos Rural Community, Mountain Institute, Asociación Urpichallay.

Wilson, Fiona (2001) In the Name of the State? Schools and Teachers in an Andean Province. In Thomas Blom Hansen and Finn Stepputat (eds), *States of Imagination: Ethnographic Explorations of the Postcolonial State.* Durham,NC: Duke University Press.

Žižek, Slavoj (1998) Multiculturalismo o la lógica cultural del capitalismo multinacional. In Fredric Jameson and Slavoj Žižek, *Estudios culturales. Reflexiones sobre el multiculturalismo.* Buenos Aires: Páidos.

Zuidema, Tom (1962) *The Ceque System of Cuzco: The Social Organization of the Capital of the Inca.* Leiden: J. Brill.

**PART II** **Debates**

# CHAPTER 9

# Race in Latin America

*Peter Wade*

Since the Second World War, most biologists have agreed that race is not an analytic category to understand human biological diversity. Humans vary to some extent in their DNA and their outward physical appearance or phenotype, but this diversity cannot be organized into "racial groups" or "races," even if some genetic and phenotypical variation seems to correlate very broadly with continental geography. Humans are too similar genetically and intracontinental genetic variation is too great to be able to categorize humans into races. So race is a set of *ideas* about human similarity and difference. But what kind of ideas?

Scholars hold different views (Wade 2002b:ch. 1). This is partly because, as Goldberg says, "Race is not a static concept with a single sedimented meaning"; in fact as a signifier it is "almost, but not quite empty" (1993:80–81). While the word "race" began to appear in European languages from about the 14th century, its meaning has changed greatly since then. Banton (1987) traces how the concept first referred to genealogical linkages between a related set of people (or animals). This was "race as lineage": all the descendants of a single ancestor or group of ancestors were connected genealogically and thus of the same lineage or race; physical appearance was not a key feature. Before the 19th century, European representations of Andean people did not show them as physically different from Europeans (D. Poole 1997: ch. 2). From the late 18th century, there was a shift to the idea of race as "type," in which humans were categorized into a few racial types (African, European, Mongol, etc.), seen as primordial and relatively fixed; physical appearance was key to identifying racial type. This was the era of so-called scientific racism, when scientists developed "race" as a key biological category for understanding human physical variation and behavior; they legitimated racial hierarchies in which Europeans were at the top. During the 20th century, scientific racism was slowly dismantled, being mainly replaced, among scholars, by the concept of race as a "social construction," a set of ideas about humans which can have very powerful social consequences such as racial discrimination and racial violence. At the same time, so-called cultural racism has been identified, in which categories of people familiar from the older conceptions of race – such as "whites," "blacks," "Indians" and "Asians" – continue to be identified and to discriminate or be discriminated against, but now on the basis of their "culture" rather than their biology (Stolcke 1995).

The question remains: What kind of ideas are racial ideas? First, many social scientists say that racial ideas refer to human physical variation: bodily appearance, biology, genealogy, heredity, "blood" or genes. This is true but needs specifying further: These aspects of human biology are too general. People are fat and thin, tall and short, male and female. Any of these traits could be talked about in terms that included reference to such aspects.

Second, then, racial thinking also refers to human physical variation in relation to *particular kinds* of perceived human difference, which began to be perceived when Europeans started to colonize the globe and encounter different continents. Racial thinking is, typically, a way of thinking about historical categories such as "black," "white," "Indian," "African," "Asian," and so on. The qualifier, "and so on," is important because racial thinking can proliferate beyond such key categories – John Beddoe's *The Races of Britain* (published in 1885) divided up the population of Britain into racial subtypes. Also, it is important that the key categories are not stable: the definition, meaning and perception of them has changed over time and place.

Third, racial thinking is not just about dividing people into physical categories, but also about explaining their behavior. Race is about nature, but also about culture. Culture is explained through naturalization, that is by rooting observed behavior in something taken to be "natural" – although what is taken to be natural has varied over time and can include the realms of environment and cosmology as well as biology. Human nature can be thought to be shaped by the environment, the supernatural (including God) and biology (MacCormack and Strathern 1980; Wade 2002b). This third point is important in understanding "cultural racism." Although explicit reference to biology and indeed to race itself may be absent or muted in this discourse, there may still be a sense in which culture is naturalized, seen as part of a person's or a group's "nature" or perhaps seen as heritable in a quasi-biological way.

In sum, racial ideas are about human physical difference of various kinds, refer typically but not exclusively to key historical categories of colonial origin, and produce naturalizing explanations of culture. This is a fairly broad view of race. Some scholars prefer to limit the concept of race to a "worldview" that was typified by Europe and the US during the era of scientific racial typologies and when systematic, institutional racial discrimination was practiced in many colonial regimes and in the US (Smedley 1993). One can then trace the rise and fall of this worldview – and the way it influenced other areas of the globe – to construct a history of race. I think that this approach is not the best when looking at Latin America: It tends to measure the region against a US or European benchmark which establishes a norm for understanding race.

## HISTORICAL BACKGROUND

Spanish and Portuguese colonists exploited local indigenous peoples and African slaves to fulfill labor demands. African slaves were widespread in the Iberian Americas, but tended to concentrate where indigenous peoples suffered the worst decimation and/or were difficult to exploit as labor: the Caribbean islands, Brazil, the circum-Caribbean mainland and some areas of the Pacific littoral of South America (see Arocha and Maya, this volume). African slaves attained freedom in many areas and a free black population developed. Sexual relations between Europeans, Africans and indigenous people led to "mixed" people, *mestizos*, who were recognized as socially distinct from their parents and were enumerated using specific categories by colonial censuses. This mixed population became numerically dominant in some areas by the late 18th century. A broad contrast existed here with the US where, although such mixtures occurred, they were less recognized socially – especially during the 19th century – and the mixed children were placed socially, and often in censuses, into the racial category of the subordinate parent.

In Iberian colonies, a socially stratified pyramid emerged, with Europeans at the apex, black slaves and *indios* (indigenous people) at the bottom and an ambiguous and contestable set of intermediate categories in the middle in which ancestry, appearance (including dress), occupation and wealth all influenced social standing. In the Spanish colonies, this was sometimes known as a *sociedad de castas*, a society of "castes" (or breeds, or stocks). In New Spain (Mexico), this was illustrated by the 18th century *casta* paintings which depicted parents of different racial categories and their mixed offspring – a caption might read "Spaniard and Mestiza produce a Castiza" (Katzew 2004). The exact role "race" played in this system is the subject of debate. "Racial" status – for example, whether a person was classified in a census as castizo or mestizo – was not fixed, could change between censuses and could be influenced by occupation (Cope 1994). But there was a strong interest in genealogy and inherited blood as markers of status in a hierarchy which was structured in part by whiteness, African blackness and indigeneity. Legal disputes could ensue if a person who considered himself white was called a mestizo by another person. Some legislation in the late 1700s tried to control marriages between whites, indigenous people and blacks, while "sumptuary" legislation attempted to prevent black and mulatto people from using high-status clothes and accoutrements (Mörner 1967; Wade 1997:29–30).

Spanish notions of *limpieza de sangre* (cleanliness of blood) also worked in the colonies. In Spain, these ideas had been used from the mid 15th century to discriminate against "New Christians" – Jews and Muslims who had converted to Christianity. New legislation required people to prove the "purity" of their Old Christian genealogy to gain admittance to certain administrative positions. Although this was mainly a religious measure, there was an intense concern with genealogy and the perceived inherited "contamination" that came from Jewish or Muslim "blood" (S. Poole 1999). Limpieza de sangre was a manifestation of what Banton calls race as lineage (see above). In the colonies, limpieza de sangre was recast to discriminate also against African and indigenous heritage (Manrique 1993; Martínez 2004). This recasting was fueled by the numerous rebellions organized by indigenous people and slaves and by the perceived religious heterodoxy of indigenous, slave and free black people, many of whom retained aspects of indigenous and African religious systems alongside their avowed Catholicism (Harding 2000; Stern 1987). Colonial persecution of those seen as rebellious, heretical or religiously suspect was linked to perceptions of racial status.

In the postcolonial period, there were radical changes. The category *indio*, which had been a key colonial administrative status, defined by residence in a community and the payment of tribute, began to be dismantled in the context of influential

European ideologies of liberalism which envisaged new republics comprising equal citizens. Slavery was mainly abolished by the mid-1800s, although later in Brazil (1888), Cuba (1886) and Puerto Rico (1873). During the colonial period, indigenous people had always filtered out of the status of *indio* and into the mestizo population, while African slaves and their offspring had continuously entered the ranks of the free and the mixed. Now the very categories of *indio* and slave which had helped define the colonial racial hierarchy were being undermined or abolished. At the same time, countries such as Cuba, Peru, Brazil and Mexico received large numbers of migrants from China, Japan and the Middle East who complicated the situation (Bonfil Batalla 1993; Wilson 2004).

However, ideologies of race took on more important and, to the observer of today, more familiar patterns. Intellectual and political elites in the newly independent countries were very concerned with issues of race and the building of nations. In Europe and the US, scientists, medics and intellectuals were developing theories about race which gave it huge significance. The British physician Robert Knox (1850) affirmed: "Race is everything: literature, science, art – in a word, civilization depends on it." In the late 19th century, eugenics became fashionable with its progressive agenda of creating fitter and more morally upstanding populations through controlling sexual reproduction and improving the family environment. In these raciological theories, black and indigenous people were ranked as racially inferior and race mixture was seen as degenerative.

Latin American elites had an ambivalent relationship to these theories (Appelbaum, Macpherson and Rosemblatt 2003; Graham 1990). On the one hand, they saw their black and indigenous populations as inferior and their large mestizo populations as a burden. It was up to the whiter populations to lead nations into modernity. Many countries began to enact immigration legislation that sought to restrict the entry of black people, while European immigration was encouraged. While Asian immigration was significant in many countries, Chinese migrants in northern Mexico, and elsewhere, were seen as racially inferior (Rénique 2003). Deborah Poole (1997:chs 5, 6) shows how images of Andean people, created by Europeans and by Peruvians, began to focus on the physical appearance of the body as a key to classification. Throughout Latin America, typological theories which saw each body as analytically reducible to a racial "type" went hand in hand with new technologies of visual imaging which allowed the serial reproduction and circulation of multiple photographic images as instances of racial types: photographic portraits of black and indigenous peoples circulated widely in Latin America and Europe.

On the other hand, elites could not escape the mixedness of their populations – although this varied markedly from one country to another, being more prominent in Mexico than Argentina or Chile. Mixture could however be defined as a process of whitening. The perceived superiority of whites would tip the nation's biological and cultural balance in their favor, helped by European immigration (Stepan 1991). In the early decades of the 20th century, some nations began to take a more positive attitude to mixture: *mestizaje* or *mestiçagem* (racial and cultural mixture) was the basis for national identity. The mixture of African, indigenous and European peoples was the founding origin myth of the nation. Mestizaje was something to be celebrated as a distinctive feature; indigenous and African people had, it was said, made useful contributions to the cultures of, for example, Mexico or Brazil. There was, in short, some resistance to European ideologies that simply condemned Latin American nations as mixed and inferior. In postrevolutionary Mexico, in 1925, writer and education minister José Vasconcelos celebrated the "cosmic race" as a superior mixed race which was in the process of evolving, particularly on Latin American soil, and which would undermine US ideologies about the superiority of "pure" segregated races (Vasconcelos 1997). Ironically, in Mexico, this ideology was consolidated by anti-Chinese racism, which pitted a national mestizo identity against an Asian presence seen as alien (Rénique 2003). In 1930s Brazil, intellectual Gilberto Freyre was very influential in promoting the idea of a distinctive mixed nation, with indigenous and African contributions, which avoided the notorious problems of racism and segregation seen to affect the US. The image of the mestizo nation was also influential in Colombia, Central America and, to a lesser extent, Peru (de la Cadena 2000; Gould 1998; Hale 1996; Wade 1993).

However, mestizaje was still seen by many Latin Americans as a progressive process in which black and indigenous people would be integrated into a mestizo nation that was moving toward whiteness. Ideologies of *indigenismo* (indigenism) were prominent in countries such as Peru and Mexico, which had large indigenous populations (see chapters by Nahmad Sitton and Seligmann, this volume). But while indigenismo celebrated the nation's indigenous populations, it tended to extol indigenous history, rather than contemporary indigenous populations (de la Cadena 2000; Knight 1990). In Mexico, prominent indigenista Manuel Gamio studied indigenous populations, but focused on archaeology and overall took an integrationist perspective, envisaging the assimilation of indigenous populations into the mestizo nation (see Walsh, this volume). With the partial exception of Brazil and Cuba, black populations were much less subject to glorification as national ancestors.

## RACE AND CULTURE IN LATIN AMERICA

De la Cadena (2000) argues that from about the 1920s in Peru, intellectuals began to abandon notions of race and to talk of indigenous peoples in terms of "spirit" or soul rather than biology. This can be seen to mark a shift toward the cultural explanations of human difference that became more commonplace in the later 20th century. The indigenous spirit was seen as largely a product of the environment, but was also seen as deeply ingrained and in some sense innate, even if the language of racial biology was eschewed. "Culture" was thus understood in quite a determinist – one could say naturalized – way. Nevertheless, it could be argued that this shift sets the scene for a specifically Latin American approach to race, which is distinct from that in North America and Europe. This is a key point because scholarly and popular views of race in Latin America have frequently made explicit or implicit use of a comparison with the US.

This comparison has a long history and entered into the way intellectuals such as Freyre in Brazil or Vasconcelos in Mexico defined their countries as relatively free from racial prejudice in comparison with the US (Graham 1990; Wade 2004). Tannenbaum (1948) initiated a historical debate by arguing that slavery had been more benign and colonial society more open to the assimilation of slaves in Iberian colonies than Anglo-Saxon ones. He was wrong about the benevolence of Latin American slavery, but there was no doubt that slaves found it easier to become free in this region than in North America, that mixture between racial categories was more frequent, and that the offspring of such unions were, in the long term, recognized more fully as a mestizo social category, intermediate between black, white and indigenous.

The nature of Latin American societies as mestizo – with the variations that run from Argentina, where the image of mixture is downplayed in favor of whiteness, to Brazil or Mexico, where mixture is foregrounded in discourse on the nation – has powerfully shaped ideas about race in the region. One view is that race is not important: there is little racism and little sense of racial identity for most people. Indigenous people may have their particular ethnic identities, based on local cultures, and people in general may recognize phenotypical differences that are linked to skin color and other typically "racial" features, but none of this creates a society in which racial identities are the basis for significant social divisions and exclusions – the subtext here is usually, "in comparison with the USA" (Wade 1997:51–57). This view is most explicit in the claim that Latin America enjoys "a racial democracy." The opposing view holds that, while Latin American racism is different from that in the US, it still operates to create significant disadvantage for indigenous and black people as collective categories.

Debates on this theme have focused mainly on comparisons of Brazil and the US (Sant'Anna and Souza 1997). In the 1950s, in the wake of Nazism, UNESCO began a series of studies of Brazil designed to explore a racial democracy. In fact, few scholars unequivocally supported the idea of a racial democracy, but many saw race as much less significant than in the US and becoming more insignificant. It was widely argued that class was the key division in Brazil, while race was secondary (Winant 1992). A key factor was mixture itself. First, according to censuses, over a third of Brazilians identify themselves as *pardo* (brown), indicating some kind of mixedness. Second, the prevalence of mixture has created vagueness about who is who in racial terms (Sansone 2003:ch. 1; Telles 2002). Much was made then, and still is now, of the fact that, rather than using a small number of terms such as black, white and indigenous, Brazilians use dozens of descriptive terms, which often try to describe actual shade of skin color. A photograph of a person will elicit different terms depending on how the person is dressed and who is doing the classifying. Racial categorization is shifting and contextual, influenced by appearance, dress, behavior, and, especially, class status: blackness is strongly associated with lower class position. Terms that indicate some degree of mixedness are very common: *moreno* (brown) is common in Brazil and elsewhere, but can include a light-skinned person with dark hair and a person with quite dark skin and of clear African ancestry. If there is little agreement on who is black (or white or indigenous), how can discrimination take place in any systematic way? In contrast, in the US, there is generally a much clearer definition of racial identity, based on a few key categories: black, white, Native American (and Asian and Pacific Islander). This clarity was fundamental both to the institutionalized "Jim Crow" racial segregation that operated for decades until after the Second World War and to the informal discrimination and segregation that still persist. There needs to be general agreement about who is black and white for such systems to operate.

Contrasting views argue that, despite the apparent plethora of racial terms, a few key terms and categories are salient, focused on black, white, indigenous and two or three basic mixed categories. Most importantly, shifting and contextual terminologies lead to shifting and contextual discriminations, rather than the simple absence of them. Sansone shows that racial terminology in Salvador, Brazil, shifts according to context – "a son can be *preto* [black] to his mother and *moreno* [brown] to his father" – and is characterized by a "pragmatic relativism" (2003:46, 50). He also traces recent shifts in terminological usage, with younger, dark-skinned people more prepared to identify as *negro* (black), a term that was previously rather pejorative, but now signifies a more self-conscious, and globalized, political identity based on race. Yet in his view all this does not indicate an absence of racism.

A person can still discriminate against someone she or he *perceives* as "black" or "brown" or "indigenous" and if there is some kind of overlap in perceptions among people who racially discriminate and also control access to valued resources, then this will result in ongoing racial inequalities. Statistical evidence for Brazil shows that racial inequalities do exist which are not just the legacy of slavery or an effect of the fact that many dark-skinned people are in the lower classes and tend to remain there through "normal" processes of class stratification (Hasenbalg and Silva 1999). Lovell (1994) shows that average income difference between white and black men is partly due to the impact of educational background on ability to compete in the job market (which may itself be due to patterns of racial discrimination outside that market), but that 24 percent of the difference is due to processes of discrimination within the job market. The figure is 51 percent when comparing white men with black women. Data on Afro-Colombians reinforce this overall picture (Barbary and Urrea 2004; Wade 1993). Data on indigenous people in Latin America show generalized poverty for indigenous people. Up to 50 percent of income differentials between indigenous and non-indigenous workers may be due to discrimination in the Guatemalan, Peruvian and Mexican labor markets (Psacharopoulos and Patrinos 1994:xxi).

The key to race in Latin America, then, is that racism and mixture coexist and inter-weave (Wade 1993). There is great demographic and social variety across the region, yet some broad generalizations can be made. The coexistence of racism and mixture creates societies in which categories such as "black" and "indigenous" exist and occupy important places in the national imaginary. There are also often subregions associated with blackness or indigenousness – for blackness, the northeast of Brazil, the Pacific coastal region of Colombia and of Ecuador and Peru, and much of the Caribbean coastline of Central America (see Arocha and Maya, this volume); for indigenousness, the Amazon basin, the Andes, and the highlands of Central America (see Varese, Delgado and Meyer, this volume). These categories and subregions are generally low down in national hierarchies of value, although they may enjoy high symbolic status in particular stereotyped domains (e.g. black people may be seen as superior musicians, dancers and sportspeople; indigenous people as ecologically minded and powerful healers). People identified as black or indigenous do suffer racial discrimination to some degree. Modernity, development and high status are often associated with whiteness or at least mixedness. Race and gender often intersect in ways that give lighter-skinned men access to both lighter- and darker-skinned women, with their unions with the latter often being informal. Darker-skinned men are more constrained by class and color, while women are constrained by moral codes of honor. Darker women may have informal unions, but run the risk of being labeled as loose (Caulfield 2003; Smith 1996).

However, "black" and "indigenous" are often vaguely defined and there is an inde-cisive, subjective distinction between them and "mixed" people and between the latter and "whites" (hence the problems of enumerating these populations). There is often not a clear socio-racial hierarchy. In Brazil and Colombia, although many black people are poor, the lower classes are mixed and include many whites; people with evident African ancestry are also found in the middle classes. In Peru and Central America, although the elite is fairly white, people with indigenous physical features are not confined to the lower classes. Racial discrimination does occur but it is often unsystematic, individualistic, silent and masked. Racial identities are often not very important to people: for Brazil, Sansone (2003) calls this blackness without ethnicity (i.e. without a collective, self-conscious sense of identity). Racial identities are rarely key factors in electoral politics (although some Andean countries provide recent partial counterexamples here).

Few would contest nowadays that racism as a practice and race as an idea are significant in Latin America, but there is disagreement about how to analyze them. Twine (1998), Hanchard (1994) and Winant (1994) tend to see mixture as a problem for Brazil. The absence of clear racial identities, the existence of hegemonic ideologies which purvey the myth of racial democracy, together with the devaluation of blackness and the actual practice of racism, create a system in which black political consciousness is hampered and people are encouraged to "whiten" (to identify with whiteness and to actually marry whiter partners). For Winant (1994:156), "The public articulation and exploration of *racial dualism* [a clear black–white distinction] would itself be a major advance" in Brazil. Scholars such as Ferreira da Silva (1998), Sansone (2003) and Fry (2000) see such analyses as ethnocentric, using the US history of black political organization as a benchmark to evaluate the black Brazilian experience and judge it lacking (for a similar approach to Cuba, see also de la Fuente 2001:6–9). For them, Brazil has to be judged on its own terms: black consciousness, for example, might look more class oriented than in the US; antiracism might not depend on clear racial identities, but be based on a more inclusive, universalist project. Hanchard (1999:11) responds by emphasizing that the US and Brazil are variants on a common theme and are linked by transnational connections which undo a binary comparison between them. It is not a question of benchmarking one against the other.

In analyses of race in the Andes and Central America, something similar emerges. In this context, race has been seen by scholars as less relevant than ethnicity. Key distinctions between indigenous and mestizo people were analyzed as ethnic because they seemed to involve "cultural" distinctions of language, dress and behavior rather than "racial" distinctions of physical appearance and ancestry. I argue that this conceptual split is inadequate because (1) it denies the clearly racial discourse that surrounded ideas about indigenous peoples, alongside black people, during the colonial period and especially in the 19th and early 20th centuries (D. Poole 1997; Stepan 1991); (2) it assumes that culture (changeable, malleable) and race (permanent, fixed) are necessarily separate, when we know that identification of blackness also depends – and not only in Latin America – on cultural factors such as clothing, speech and class status; and (3) it ignores the discrimination that indigenous-looking people can suffer, for example in urban contexts (Wade 1997:37–39).

More recently, scholars both inside and outside Latin America have been willing to apply the concept of race to the Andes and Meso-America (Callirgos 1993; de la Torre 1996). The ethnocidal wars in Guatemala and Peru, which targeted these countries' indigenous populations, made public difficult issues of racism (Arenas

Bianchi, Hale and Palma Murga 1999; Casaús Arzú 1992; Nelson 1999). Famously, in 2005, indigenous activist Rigoberta Menchú brought several politicians to court in the country's first racism case; and in Peru the Truth and Reconciliation Commission pointed to racism in their analysis of counterinsurgency violence in the 1980s war (Comisión de la Verdad 2004). In Mexico, the war in Chiapas and the explicit denunciation of racism by the EZLN (Zapatista National Liberation Army) have also forced issues of race onto the agenda, while Mexico's black population is getting increasing recognition (Castellanos Guerrero 2003; Nash 2001; Vaughn 2005). For Peru, de la Cadena argues that biological notions of race began to disappear from discourse about the Peruvian Andes, but "racialized notions of cultural heritage" were retained (2000:155). De la Cadena contends that the notions of mestizo and mestizaje are themselves hybrid concepts, mixing pre-Enlightenment, colonial notions of limpieza de sangre, genealogy and purity of lineage with Enlightenment notions of scientific racial typologies: "the new scientific taxonomies continued to evoke language, faith and morality" (2005:268). More than a hybridization between 19th century concepts of biology and culture – which was not unique to Latin America – this was an epistemological mixing of "two regimes of knowledge, faith and science" which enabled "a conceptual politics where the pull to define race tilted towards culture" (2005:268–269).

Weismantel also deploys a culturalized notion of race, arguing that Andean people talk about race as a physical reality but also changeable: a person's race can alter over time. In the Andes, race can be part of the body and yet be changeable because race accumulates in the body over time; it is the embodied product of history:

> in the interactions between bodies and the substances they ingest, the possessions they accumulate, and the tools they use to act on the world, we can really see race being made, and making the society around it. This kind of race is neither genetic nor symbolic, but organic: a constant, physical process of interaction between living things. (Weismantel 2001:266)

Indigenous and white people's bodies accumulate things – both in the body (hard skin, soft skin; gnarled feet, smooth feet), in/on the body (smells) and on the body (clothes) – that mark them as racially distinct. Gose objects that Weismantel "simply assumes that 'race matters' in the Andes" and that she, speaking from an "omnipotent American standpoint," "accentuates the racism in Andean social life and presents it as absolute and unqualified" (Gose 2003:194). As with the debate on Brazil, we find scholars divided over whether North American understandings of race are being imposed onto a Latin American reality. In this case, however, Weismantel (and de la Cadena) are putting forward very Latin American notions of race as naturalized but still malleable culture and it is hard to accuse either of using US notions of race as a benchmark. As in the debate about Brazil, accusations of ethnocentrism, while potentially valid, can gloss over the way Euro-American notions of race both influenced and were fed by Latin American realities (D. Poole 1997).

In my view, Latin America concepts of race are sui generis, but not therefore the polar opposites of things North American or European. The culturalized versions of race that are particularly prominent in Latin America are not unique to the region: race always involves an interweaving between notions of nature and culture (Wade 2002b) and even in the heyday of scientific, biological theories of race, there were very powerful discourses of morality and what we would now call culture (Stoler 1995). The emergence of "cultural racism" is another case in point (see above). But in Latin America, the coexistence of mestizaje and racism gives a particular twist to the natural-cultural construct of race, making Latin American notions of race particularly culturalized and open to be thought and experienced through, say, class, region and gendered sexuality. Streicker (1995), for example, explored ideas of race among working class black people in Cartagena, Colombia. For them, race was not an everyday way of talking about and identifying people. Most people in the neighborhood he studied were varying shades of black and brown; there was a strong notion that everyone was equal and that racism did not loom large. Ideas about race, however, formed a discourse of the moral evaluation of behavior and status. Perceptions of class status, racial identity and sex/gender behavior all evoked each other. Being *negro* meant being of low class status and also being a father/husband or mother/wife who was sexually promiscuous and did not fulfill family obligations. This worked in reverse too, so that to impute sexual looseness to a woman evoked images of blackness and low class status. Race was not prominent, but it worked through other culturalizing-naturalizing perceptions.

## Mestizaje, Difference, Multiculturalism, and Globalization

If the coexistence of mestizaje and racism is the key to Latin American concepts of race, then it is also true that mestizaje has many different dynamics within it. It can be the very manifestation of racism when it takes the form of a nation-building ideology that devalues blackness and indigenousness, consigns them to the past and straitjackets them into stereotyped molds. But it can also be a space – always ambiguous and often ambivalent – in which to reaffirm blackness and indigenousness in practical everyday ways. Postcolonial theorists have recently made much of the potentially subversive nature of hybridity, a process of mixture which can be seen as linked to mestizaje and which can create a "third space" that unsettles colonial binaries of power and racial categorization (Bhabha 1994). Some Latin Americanist scholars have been cautious, well aware of the history of mestizaje and its potential to be the regional face of racism (Hale 1999; Wade 2004). Analyzing Guatemala, Hale (2002:524) recognizes the problems of romanticizing mestizaje, but still holds out the possibility that "some notion of 'mestizaje from below' could emerge as an articulating principle" decentering dominant ideas of mestizo society and the "acceptable" face of indigenous identity. In a related way, de la Cadena (2000) argues for a concept of "de-Indianization" which results in the formation of "indigenous mestizos." These are Andean people who self-identify as mestizos, but also claim indigenous heritage and culture as their own. They are indigenous and mestizo at the same time; being mestizo means having gained respect through hard work and economic success, rather than having sloughed off indigenous culture. But these indigenous mestizos also hand out racist insults to those they classify as simply *indio*. French (2004) also sees mestizaje as a "supple analytical tool" which allows us to conceptualize how people who are part of northeast Brazilian peasant culture and who look as African-descended as neighbors identifying as descendants of black slaves can nevertheless make land claims as indigenous people. These people are mestizos and indigenous at the same time, but through a process of "re-Indianization" (see also Warren 2001). I have also analyzed everyday notions of mestizaje in Colombia as involving the living out of cultural-racial elements through the physical body, with blackness felt to express itself through music, dance and heat, or through affective ties with family members, or through possession by racialized spirits in religious contexts. Being mestizo allows an inclusive space for difference as well as exclusive definitions of sameness (Wade 2005).

This is important when we come to consider recent moves toward official multiculturalism in Latin America, with the emergence of legal and constitutional measures which, in regionally uneven ways, recognize black and indigenous minorities in more explicit fashion and in some cases give them land and other cultural rights (see Arocha and Maya, this volume). In Brazil, there have been heated debates about affirmative action programs for Afro-Brazilians, with quotas for places in some universities and government entities (Htun 2004). This is not the place for an analysis of these changes and the black and indigenous movements involved in them (see Arocha and Maya, and Varese, Delgado and Meyer, this volume; see also Hale 2002; Sieder 2002; Van Cott 2000; Wade 1997). The question is how they have shaped Latin American concepts of race. One view is that such changes represent a radical departure from previous Latin American nationalisms based on mestizaje understood as homogenization. My view is that, when mestizaje is understood to encompass difference, these official multiculturalisms are not quite such a seismic shift. Still, blackness and indigenousness are beginning to occupy places on a different-looking terrain.

This terrain, at once new and familiar, is defined by struggles between local social movements and national states, but also by transnational and globalizing dynamics. First, nation-states are responding to new global notions of democracy as multicultural and neoliberal governance as creating and operating through self-reliant, self-organizing communities (including ethnically defined ones). Second, black and indigenous social movements are linked into transnational concepts of, and movements for, human and indigenous rights, and into globalizing images of blackness, Africa and indigenousness which also circulate in a world commodity market and a global NGO network. Third, the migration of black and indigenous people to North America and Europe (but also to Africa) has created stronger interactions between differing, but not opposing, conceptions of race and identity.

Latin American states were pushed into legal and constitutional reform by black and indigenous protest, but in some cases, they also took up the torch with a certain alacrity. Some have argued that it suited particular state interests to recognize black and indigenous minorities and thus control them more effectively while also promoting new forms of neoliberal governance (Hale 2002; Laurie, Andolina and Radcliffe 2003). In Colombia, for example, it has been argued that the state was interested in combining defense (and commercial exploitation) of biodiverse forest zones with the creation of Afro-Colombian and indigenous community land rights in those areas: the communities would be cast as stewards of the environment, thus tapping into images of a "natural" predisposition toward ecological sensitivity among indigenous and, to a lesser extent, black people (Escobar 1997; Gros 1997; Wade 2002a). By linking these populations to "nature" – in a way not necessarily challenged and even endorsed by ethnic social movements – there may be subtle processes of the renaturalization and essentialization of racial identities (see Hayden, this volume).

Black and indigenous social movements have from an early date been linked into transnational networks. This is not necessarily new: for example, Afro-Brazilian leaders have since the late 19th century been involved in interactions and dialogues about racism, religion and Africa with both North Americans and Africans, in a Latin American version of Gilroy's "Black Atlantic" (Gilroy 1993; Matory 1999; Sansone 2003:ch. 2). Sansone shows how objects of black culture (e.g. dance and religious forms) have been commodified for some time, but that recent globalization and the growth of the black movement has led new objects (notably the black body itself and its fashion accessories) to become more conspicuous and commodified (2003:76–79). This links with an increasing willingness among some black people to identify explicitly with the political and self-consciously ethnic category *negro*. In Colombia, too, black icons such as Martin Luther King, Nelson Mandela and Bob Marley have served as inspiration for black activists alongside homegrown heroes of slave resistance (Wade 1999).

Indigenous and black organizations frequently have close links to the Church and other international entities that provide them with support and advice. Radcliffe, Laurie and Andolina (2000) found that transnational institutions and actors have influential effects on how indigenous people represent their identity, starting with the fact that defining oneself as indigenous in the first place enhances access to resources and leads people to emphasize indigenous social capital in ways that reify "tradition." However, these transnational networks open up spaces for contestation, in which, for example, indigenous women can challenge dominant ideas of "gender and development." Interestingly, indigenous people have generally had greater success than black people in establishing themselves as distinct cultures, deserving of special rights. Black people in Latin America tend to be seen as culturally closer to the mainstream and it has been harder to carve out a distinctive legal space, based on cultural difference. One strategy for Afro-Latins – which some states have encouraged – has been to make themselves look more like indigenous groups (Hooker 2005; Wade 1997, 2002a).

Indigenous and black people are also involved in important transnational migrations. Kearney (2000) shows how Mixtecs from Oaxaca (southern Mexico) migrate to California and create a cultural space called "Oaxacalifornia" in which Mixtec identity becomes more self-conscious and explicit, creating the basis for organizations which defend Mixtec rights in the US and in Mexico. Various studies trace how migrants who do not see themselves as "black" are redefined as such in the US context. Duany (1998) shows how Dominican migrants resist this classification and try to retain the concept of an intermediate mixed identity, based on being Latino or Hispanic. Ramos-Zayas (2003:ch. 6) also shows how Puerto Rican nationalists in Chicago sometimes use images of Puerto Rican blackness in a critique of US racism and segregation This blackness is presented, however, in a specifically Latin American discourse, as inclusive and based on mestizaje, rather than exclusive and divisively segregated.

In sum, the effect of globalizing ethnic movements on Latin American concepts of race is uncertain. On the one hand, ideas of race may be taking on more North American dimensions (with globalized imagery): definitions of blackness and indigenousness become clearer and perhaps more polarized; and they include the use of commodified images of indigenous Greenness and spiritual healing alongside a collage of transnational black imagery (reggae, rap, "African" motifs, US black hero figures); in some countries, affirmative action programs are implemented which target black and indigenous people. On the other hand, there is something resilient about Latin

American notions of mestizaje and its irreducibility to a set of US-style racial classifications. The resistance of some US based Latinos to black–white racial binaries is a case in point. Also, it is not yet clear that affirmative action programs for Afro-Colombians and Afro-Brazilians – which so far seem to be progressing in the absence of a clear social consensus on who is black – will necessarily lead to US-style racial categories. In Colombia, university places reserved for Afro-Colombians have been allocated in flexible ways that retain typically Latin American contextual definitions of blackness.

It is perhaps the resilience of mestizaje that leads some commentators to see it as a critique of US notions of race, a way to shatter their sharp boundaries and exclusive definitions of identity (Saldaña-Portillo 2001; Wade 2004). I think great caution is needed with this idea – after all, racism and mestizaje coexist in Latin America. But it may be that Latin American notions of race are colonizing North America as much as the other way round. The sheer number of Latinos in the US has been complicating the traditional racial categories of the US for some time now: the category "Hispanic" is not meant to be a racial category for the census (Hispanics can belong to any census racial category), but it tends to act as one when it is routinely deployed alongside other racial categories in reporting data. One of the keys to understanding race in Latin America is to grasp that it has always been defined in opposition to the US – this was the concern of intellectuals such as Freyre and Vasconcelos in the 1920s. In fact, both regions are variants on a theme and have been in a constant process of mutual racial formation. If globalizing US concepts of race and identity are clarifying racial categories for some Latin Americans, it may be that Latin American concepts of race are blurring the clarity of racial definitions for some North Americans – without this implying that racism is therefore ameliorated.

## REFERENCES

Appelbaum, Nancy P., Macpherson, Anne S., and Rosemblatt, Karin A. (eds) (2003) *Race and Nation in Modern Latin America*. Chapel Hill: University of North Carolina Press.

Arenas Bianchi, Clara, Hale, Charles R., and Palma Murga, Gustavo (eds) (1999) *¿Racismo en Guatemala? Abriendo debate sobre un tema tabú*. Guatemala: Asociación para el Avance de las Ciencias Sociales en Guatemala.

Banton, Michael (1987) *Racial Theories*. Cambridge: Cambridge University Press.

Barbary, Olivier, and Urrea, Fernando (eds) (2004) *Gente negra en Colombia. Dinámicas sociopolíticas en Cali y el Pacífico*. Paris, Cali: IRD, Colciencias, Univalle.

Bhabha, Homi (1994) *The Location of Culture*. London: Routledge.

Bonfil Batalla, Guillermo (ed.) (1993) *Simbiosis de culturas. Los inmigrantes y su cultura en México*. Mexico City: Fondo de Cultura Económica.

Callirgos, Juan Carlos (1993) *El racismo. La cuestión del otro (y de uno)*. Lima: DESCO.

Casaús Arzú, Marta (1992) *Guatemala. Linaje y racismo*. San José, Costa Rica: FLACSO.

Castellanos Guerrero, Alicia (ed.) (2003) *Imágenes del racismo en México*. Mexico City: Universidad Autónoma Metropolitana, Plaza y Valdés.

Caulfield, Sueann (2003) Interracial Courtship in the Rio de Janeiro Courts, 1918–1940. In N. P. Appelbaum, A. S. Macpherson, and K. A. Rosemblatt (eds), *Race and Nation in Modern Latin America* (pp. 163–186). Chapel Hill: University of North Carolina Press.

Comisión de la Verdad y Reconciliación (2004) *Informe final. Peru: 1980–2000*. Lima: Univ. Nacl Mayor de San Marcos y Pont. Univ. Católica del Perú.

Cope, R. Douglas (1994) *The Limits of Racial Domination: Plebeian Society in Colonial Mexico City, 1660–1720*. Madison: University of Wisconsin Press.

de la Cadena, Marisol (2000) Indigenous Mestizos: The Politics of Race and Culture in Cuzco, 1919–1991. Durham, NC: Duke University Press.

de la Cadena, Marisol (2005) Are *Mestizo* Hybrids? The Conceptual Politics of Andean Identities. *Journal of Latin American Studies* 37:259–284.

de la Fuente, Alejandro (2001) *A Nation for All: Race, Inequality, and Politics in Twentieth Century Cuba.* Chapel Hill: University of North Carolina Press.

de la Torre Espinosa, Carlos (1996) *El racismo en Ecuador.* Quito: Centro de Acción Popular-CAAP.

Duany, Jorge (1998) Reconstructing Racial Identity: Ethnicity, Color and Class among Dominicans in the United States and Puerto Rico. *Latin American Perspectives* 25(3):147–172.

Escobar, Arturo (1997) Cultural Politics and Biological Diversity: State, Capital and Social Movements in the Pacific Coast of Colombia. In R. G. Fox and O. Starn (eds), *Between Resistance and Revolution: Cultural Politics and Social Protest* (pp. 40–64). New Brunswick, NJ: Rutgers University Press.

Ferreira da Silva, Denise (1998) Facts of Blackness: Brazil Is Not (Quite) the United States ... and Racial Politics in Brazil? *Social Identities* 4(2):201–234.

French, Jan Hoffman (2004) *Mestizaje* and Law-Making in Indigenous Identity Formation in Northeastern Brazil: "After the Conflict Came History." *American Anthropologist* 106(4): 663–674.

Fry, Peter (2000) Politics, Nationality, and the Meanings of "Race" in Brazil. *Daedalus* 129(2):83–118.

Gilroy, Paul (1993) *The Black Atlantic: Modernity and Double Consciousness.* London: Verso.

Goldberg, David (1993) *Racist Culture: Philosophy and the Politics of Meaning.* Oxford: Blackwell.

Gose, Peter (2003) Review of Cholas and Pishtacos: Stories of Race and Sex in the Andes by Mary Weismantel. *Journal of the Royal Anthropological Institute* 9(1):193–194.

Gould, Jeffrey L. (1998) *To Die in This Way: Nicaraguan Indians and the Myth of the Mestizaje, 1880–1960.* Durham, NC: Duke University Press.

Graham, Richard (ed.) (1990) *The Idea of Race in Latin America, 1870–1940.* Austin: University of Texas Press.

Gros, Christian (1997) Indigenismo y Etnicidad: el Desafío Neoliberal. In M. V. Uribe and E. Restrepo (eds), *Antropología en la modernidad. Identidades, etnicidades y movimientos sociales en Colombia* (pp. 15–60). Bogotá: Instituto Colombiano de Antropología.

Hale, Charles R. (1996) *Mestizaje*, Hybridity and the Cultural Politics of Difference in Post-Revolutionary Central America. *Journal of Latin American Anthropology* 2(1):34–61.

Hale, Charles R. (1999) Travel Warning: Elite Appropriations of Hybridity, Mestizaje, Antiracism, Equality, and Other Progressive-Sounding Discourses in Highland Guatemala. *Journal of American Folklore* 112(445):297–315.

Hale, Charles R. (2002) Does Multiculturalism Menace? Governance, Cultural Rights and the Politics of Identity in Guatemala. *Journal of Latin American Studies* 34:485–524.

Hanchard, Michael (1994) *Orpheus and Power: The Movimento Negro of Rio de Janeiro and São Paulo, Brazil, 1945–1988.* Princeton: Princeton University Press.

Hanchard, Michael (1999) Introduction. In M. Hanchard (ed.), *Racial Politics in Contemporary Brazil* (pp. 1–29). Durham, NC: Duke University Press.

Harding, Rachel E. (2000) *A Refuge in Thunder: Candomblé and Alternative Spaces of Blackness.* Bloomington: Indiana University Press.

Hasenbalg, Carlos and Silva, Nelson do Valle (1999) Notes on Racial and Political Inequality in Brazil. In M. Hanchard (ed.), *Racial Politics in Contemporary Brazil* (pp. 154–178). Durham, NC: Duke University Press.

Hooker, Juliet (2005) Indigenous Inclusion/Black Exclusion: Race, Ethnicity and Multicultural Citizenship in Contemporary Latin America. *Journal of Latin American Studies* 37(2):285–310.

Htun, Mala (2004) From "Racial Democracy" to Affirmative Action: Changing State Policy on Race in Brazil. Latin American Research Review 39(1):60–89.

Katzew, Ilona (2004) *Casta Painting: Images of Race in Eighteenth-Century Mexico*. New Haven: Yale University Press.

Kearney, Michael (2000) Transnational Oaxacan Indigenous Identity: The Case of Mixtecs and Zapotecs. *Identities: Global Studies in Culture and Power* 7(2):173–195.

Knight, Alan (1990) Racism, Revolution and Indigenismo in Mexico, 1910–1940. In R. Graham (ed.), *The Idea of Race in Latin America* (pp. 71–113). Austin: University of Texas Press.

Knox, Robert (1850) *The Races of Men: A Fragment*. London: Henry Renshaw.

Laurie, Nina, Andolina, Robert, and Radcliffe, Sarah (2003) Indigenous Professionalization: Transnational Social Reproduction in the Andes. *Antipode* 35(3):463–491.

Lovell, Peggy (1994) Race, Gender and Development in Brazil. *Latin American Research Review* 29(3):7–35.

MacCormack, Carol and Strathern, Marilyn (eds) (1980) *Nature, Culture and Gender*. Cambridge: Cambridge University Press.

Manrique, Nelson (1993) *Vinieron los Sarracenos. El universo mental de la conquista de América*. Lima: DESCO.

Martínez, María Elena (2004) The Black Blood of New Spain: Limpieza-de-Sangre, Racial Violence, and Gendered Power in Early Colonial Mexico. *William and Mary Quarterly* 61(3):479–520.

Matory, J. Lorand (1999) The English Professors of Brazil: On the Diasporic Roots of the Yorùbá Nation. *Comparative Studies in Society and History* 41(1):72–103.

Mörner, Magnus (1967) *Race Mixture in the History of Latin America*. Boston: Little, Brown.

Nash, June C. (2001) *Mayan Visions: The Quest for Autonomy in an Age of Globalization*. London: Routledge.

Nelson, Diane M. (1999) *A Finger in the Wound: Body Politics in Quincentennial Guatemala*. Berkeley: California University Press.

Poole, Deborah (1997) *Vision, Race and Modernity: A Visual Economy of the Andean Image World*. Princeton: Princeton University Press.

Poole, Stafford (1999) The Politics of Limpieza de Sangre: Juan de Ovando and His Circle in the Reign of Philip II. *Americas* 55(3):359–389.

Psacharopoulos, George, and Patrinos, Harry A. (1994) Executive Summary. In G. Psacharopoulos and H. A. Patrinos (eds), *Indigenous People and Poverty in Latin America: An Empirical Analysis* (pp. xvii–xxiii). Washington, DC: World Bank.

Radcliffe, Sarah, Laurie, Nina, and Andolina, Robert (2000) Transnationalism, Indigenous People and Development in Ecuador and Bolivia. Research Briefing 6. ESRC Transnational Communities Programme, Oxford. At www.transcomm.ox.ac.uk/briefings.htm.

Ramos-Zayas, Ana Y. (2003) *National Performances: The Politics of Class, Race and Space in Puerto Rican Chicago*. Chicago: University of Chicago Press.

Rénique, Gerardo (2003) Race, Region and Nation: Sonora's Anti-Chinese Racism and Mexico's Postrevolutionary Nationalism, 1920s–1930s. In N. Appelbaum, A. S. Macpherson, and K. A. Rosemblatt (eds), *Race and Nation in Modern Latin America* (pp. 211–236). Chapel Hill: University of North Carolina Press.

Saldaña-Portillo, Josefina (2001) Who's the Indian in Aztlán? Re-writing Mestizaje, Indianism and Chicanismo from the Lacandón. In I. Rodríguez (ed.), *The Latin American Subaltern Studies Reader* (pp. 402–423). Durham, NC: Duke University Press.

Sansone, Livio (2003) *Blackness without Ethnicity: Constructing Race in Brazil*. Houndmills: Palgrave Macmillan.

Sant'Anna, Alayde, and Souza, Jessé (eds) (1997) *Multiculturalismo e racismo. Una comparação Brasil–Estados Unidos*. Brasilia: Paralelo 15.

Sieder, Rachel (ed.) (2002) *Multiculturalism in Latin America: Indigenous Rights, Diversity and Democracy*. Houndmills: Palgrave Macmillan.

Smedley, Audrey (1993) *Race in North America: Origin and Evolution of a Worldview*. Boulder: Westview Press.

Smith, Carol A. (1996) Race/Class/Gender Ideology in Guatemala: Modern and Anti-Modern Forms. In B. Williams (ed.), *Women Out of Place: The Gender of Agency and the Race of Nationality* (pp. 50–78). New York: Routledge.

Stepan, Nancy Leys (1991) *"The Hour of Eugenics": Race, Gender and Nation in Latin America.* Ithaca: Cornell University Press.

Stern, Steve J. (ed.) (1987) *Resistance, Rebellion and Consciousness in the Andean Peasant World, 18th to 20th Centuries.* Madison: University of Wisconsin Press.

Stolcke, Verena (1995) Talking Culture: New Boundaries, New Rhetorics of Exclusion in Europe. *Current Anthropology* 36(1):1–23.

Stoler, Ann Laura (1995) *Race and the Education of Desire: Foucault's "History of Sexuality" and the Colonial Order of Things.* Durham, NC: Duke University Press.

Streicker, Joel (1995) Policing Boundaries: Race, Class, and Gender in Cartagena, Colombia. *American Ethnologist* 22(1):54–74.

Tannenbaum, Frank (1948) *Slave and Citizen: The Negro in the Americas.* New York: Vintage.

Telles, Edward E. (2002) Racial Ambiguity among the Brazilian Population. *Ethnic and Racial Studies* 25(3):415–441.

Twine, France W. (1998) *Racism in a Racial Democracy: The Maintenance of White Supremacy in Brazil.* New Brunswick: Rutgers University Press.

Van Cott, Donna Lee (2000) *The Friendly Liquidation of the Past: The Politics of Diversity in Latin America.* Pittsburgh: University of Pittsburgh Press.

Vasconcelos, José (1997[1925]) *The Cosmic Race.* Bilingual edn, trans. D. T. Jaén. Baltimore: Johns Hopkins University Press.

Vaughn, Bobby (2005) Afro-Mexico: Blacks, Indians, Politics, and the Greater Diaspora. In A. Dzidzienyo and S. Oboler (eds), *Neither Enemies nor Friends: Latinos, Blacks, Afro-Latinos* (pp. 117–136). New York: Palgrave Macmillan.

Wade, Peter (1993) *Blackness and Race Mixture: The Dynamics of Racial Identity in Colombia.* Baltimore: Johns Hopkins University Press.

Wade, Peter (1997) *Race and Ethnicity in Latin America.* London: Pluto Press.

Wade, Peter (1999) Working Culture: Making Cultural Identities in Cali, Colombia. *Current Anthropology* 40(4):449–471.

Wade, Peter (2002a) The Colombian Pacific in Perspective. *Journal of Latin American Anthropology* 7(2):2–33.

Wade, Peter (2002b) *Race, Nature and Culture: An Anthropological Perspective.* London: Pluto Press.

Wade, Peter (2004) Images of Latin American Mestizaje and the Politics of Comparison. *Bulletin of Latin American Research* 23(1):355–366.

Wade, Peter (2005) Rethinking Mestizaje: Ideology and Lived Experience. *Journal of Latin American Studies* 37:1–19.

Warren, Jonathan W. (2001) *Racial Revolutions: Antiracism and Indian Resurgence in Brazil.* Durham, NC: Duke University Press.

Weismantel, Mary (2001) *Cholas and Pishtacos: Stories of Race and Sex in the Andes.* Chicago: University of Chicago Press.

Wilson, Tamar Diana (2004) East Asian Migrations to Latin America: Introduction. *Latin American Perspectives* 31(3):3–17.

Winant, Howard (1992) Rethinking Race in Brazil. *Journal of Latin American Studies* 24: 173–192.

Winant, Howard (1994) *Racial Conditions: Politics, Theory, Comparisons.* Minneapolis: University of Minnesota Press.

# Language States

CHAPTER **10**

*Penelope Harvey*

From the moment the Europeans first arrived in the Americas they engaged in reflexive conversation about language, drawing their new interlocutors into discussions about which forms to adopt and which to avoid, about when to speak and when to remain silent, about what to permit and what to refuse. Over the centuries language has taken center stage in iconic accounts of first contact, registering incomprehension and cultural distance, enunciating the gulf between the parties to these first encounters, articulating the violent ambition carried by European assumptions about the power of the Word. The very first modern Spanish grammar had only recently appeared (in 1492), and in the preface to that work Nebrija offers language to the Spanish monarchs in the service of their new imperial project, famously declaring that "language was always the companion of empire" (Nebrija 1909). Language subsequently becomes the object of policy decisions and the subject of alternatives to power in confrontations that have repeated themselves across the centuries and across the vast territories of Latin America.

This deeply political framing of language use has marked the contribution to the studies of language and politics from Latin American ethnographers of language. It also resonates as the unspoken background to the highly influential and path-breaking studies on ethno-poetics, performance and communicative practice that were developed through the study of those indigenous groups who for centuries remained apart from arenas of state power in the rain forests of Amazonia and Central America. In the contemporary world where pan-American indigenous politics directly engages the corporations dedicated to the extraction of natural resources, and where young people are increasingly drawn to travel to the growing urban centers, even if they do not necessarily choose to stay there, we find a new ethnographic focus on cultural encounters. However, such encounters are now knowing, deliberate and often fascinatingly disruptive of the policies and plans laid down by bureaucrats, politicians and capitalists. This chapter opens with a brief review of the anthropologically informed discussion of language politics at the heart of both colonial and republican states. Specifically, I explore the projections, accommodations and challenges that language articulated as Europeans embarked on the colonization process in the 15th century, and as Latin

Americans later sought to build independent nation-states in the 19th century. The second section of the chapter looks in more detail at the communicative practices of Amazonian and Central American peoples who held no store by a theory of language that links communicative possibilities to a common language, but who are more attentive to the ambiguities and intrinsic deceptiveness of form and who seek meanings beyond that which is most immediately visible. In the final section I show how contemporary anthropologists have begun to draw these two fields of interest together in work on hybridization, transformation and provocation.

Language was a key ideological tool in the three great empires that the Spaniards encountered when they reached the Americas. The Inka, Aztec and Maya ruling elites controlled massive territories in which thousands of different languages were spoken, and in which powerful common languages were developed for trading and bureaucratic functions in both horizontal and hierarchical relationships of exchange and/or control. Dynamic and mobile, the peoples encountered by the first Europeans were no strangers to outsiders. Indeed, for many, their social worlds were quite clearly constituted through a continual process of incorporation and exclusion as kin based polities integrated through complex circuits of exchange. Yet the arrival of the Europeans was strangeness of a different order and marked, at least briefly, by moments of total incomprehension – or rather of total projection as each party to the encounters used what they already knew of the world to make sense of the Other and to consider what communicative strategy to adopt in seeking to establish some kind of relationship.

## FOUNDATIONAL DRAMAS OF INCOMPREHENSION

One of the more bizarre practices revealed by early records of encounter was the reading of the *Requerimiento*. The *Requerimiento* was a formal statement, read out in Spanish, claiming territories for the Spanish monarchs and warning native people that while obedience would be rewarded, resistance would be punished. These "readings" were patently absurd even to some eye-witnesses at the time. They constituted a cynical and perverse ritual that proceeded as if there were no serious language barrier between the Native Americans and the Europeans. As such they were clearly part of the ideological apparatus of Conquest that attempted to preserve the moral integrity of the aggressors. Nevertheless they highlight a powerful communicative intent (and its failure) at the moment of encounter, which suggests the possibility of a belief in something akin to a common language that would at least make this communicative gesture plausible. Indeed, Todorov has argued that Columbus believed all European languages to be intrinsically comprehensible (Todorov 1984:29–33). The possibility of comprehension might explain the lengths to which the Spaniards would go to prevent native peoples from actually hearing the reading:

> It was read to trees and empty huts... Captains muttered its theological phrases into their beards on the edge of sleeping Indian settlements, or even a league away before starting the formal attack... Ship captains would sometimes have the document read from the deck as they approached an island, and at night would send out enslaving expeditions whose leaders would shout the traditional Castilian war cry "Santiago" rather than read the *Requirimiento* before they attacked. (Hanke 1949:33–34, cited in Seed 1991:13)

Another notorious example of mutual incomprehension was the dramatic confrontation between the Inka ruler Atahuallpa and the Dominican priest Fray Vicente Valverde, who accompanied the Spanish conquistador Francisco Pizarro (Lara 1989; Ortiz Rescaniere 1973; Wachtel 1977). The encounter focused on Atahuallpa's inability to comprehend the communicative force of the Bible, his understanding that this object did "speak" in some way, his attempt to hear what it said by holding it to his ear, and his subsequent dismissal of the object as it fell, or was thrown to the floor. In the European tradition, this mythic scene conjured the impossibility of mutual comprehension, the gulf between literate and illiterate peoples. But even in this version the narrative holds within it the possibility that the Inka did somehow comprehend, and that the enormity of his misjudgment – his dropping the book – was replete with the possibility of a knowing rejection of the Holy Word. As evidence of his dangerous pride and perfidy, his "failure to marvel" (Seed 1991) provided justification for the immediate violent reprisal. Taken prisoner by Pizarro, Atahuallpa was held to ransom and subsequently executed. In this way, a small group of Spaniards took strategic advantage of a deep rift within the Inka ruling elites to bring about this historic defeat.

Hundreds of years later, when Claude Lévi-Strauss encounters the Nambiquara in the Brazilian Amazon there is a similar exchange of gifts and mutually incomprehensible speeches. As in earlier encounters between literate and nonliterate peoples, the dynamic again revolves around the book. In this case the Nambiquara chief is reported to be enthralled by writing. Like Atahuallpa he appears to understand its power but not how that power is actualized. Mistaking form for substance, he attempts to appropriate that power through a mimetic performance of writing, and soon finds himself abandoned by a people who rejected his aspirations to this technology of political control (Lévi-Strauss 1973). The description of this encounter is central to Derrida's work *On Grammatology* in which he makes a detailed critique of Lévi-Strauss's analysis, rejecting his conclusions as to the oppressive and exploitative function of writing and opening up a far wider ranging philosophical discussion of the relationship between speech and writing in European intellectual traditions (Derrida 1976).

These mythic accounts of first encounter are important for the ways in which they enshrine the notion of absolute discontinuity and produce stark and compelling imaginaries that focus on the gaps and spaces between cultural worlds. That these cultural worlds are also cast both as linguistic worlds and as worlds which are separated by the technology of writing is also highly significant for the ways in which Latin American states went on to develop language policies in relation to these gaps. However, the history of communicative practice in the Americas also clearly shows that from the very moment the first Europeans arrived there were other stories to tell, stories of translation, interpretation and mutual adaptation that filled the gaps and complicated the problem of stark cultural difference.

## Translators and "Go-Betweens"

Perhaps most famous of the go-betweens is Malintzin, or La Malinche as she became known. Born to an elite Nahautl speaking Aztec family she entered the circuits of interethnic exchange and enslavement (Stern 1995:342) that characterized prehispanic indigenous politics. Malintzin was subsequently given as a gift to the conquistador

Hernán Cortés and became his consort. The sexual betrayal of subsequent generations of Mexican men (Paz 1959) was accompanied by a more devastating linguistic betrayal, as Malintzin, fluent in the languages of the diverse polities through which she had passed in her life as exchange object, became a crucial interpreter between the indigenous and the Spanish worlds. The mythic figure of La Malinche concentrated in her person the deep ambivalence of value that communication between these worlds implied (see Harris, this volume). For linguistic capacity signalled intimacy, the intimacy of collaboration, coupled with the potential for turning the betrayal back on the Spaniards themselves (Greenblatt 1991:145; Todorov 1984; Appel and Muysken 1987).

The position occupied by La Malinche was reproduced throughout the colonial world. In the early years of settlement, the Spaniards would kidnap local people to teach them Spanish. They understood the importance of building affective ties and tried to offer caring relationships that might be conducive to loyalty rather than incite betrayal (Greenblatt 1991). But such support could never be counted on. Suspicion of betrayal – and of misunderstanding – continued to characterize these relationships.

The anxiety and ambiguity that attached to these cultural go-betweens was reproduced across the colonial and postcolonial states, and came to characterize the more subtle but no less devastating colonial politics of evangelization, and the modern politics of education and development.

The "queasy oscillation" characteristic of the sentiments of the early conquistadores (Greenblatt 1991) was repeated in the policies of Church and state during the colonial period, the linguistic policies of the republics, and even in contemporary indigenous politics. This issue has been explored with direct reference to language policy by anthropologists. Mannheim (1984) shows how in the Andean region a balance was never finally struck between the advantages and disadvantages (for both rulers and ruled) of assimilation and integration as opposed to sustained difference and autonomy. In the 20th century, Mexican revolutionary politics provided the basis for more radical and far-reaching educational policies promoting simultaneous castellanization and ethnic assimilation. Nevertheless, the impact of these policies varied considerably according to specific regional histories (de la Cruz 1993; Poole 2004; Vaughan 1997).

## THE CREATION OF CHRISTIAN SUBJECTS

Questions surrounding the possibility of translation and its effects were of central importance in the evangelization process, for reasons clearly articulated by Hanks in his useful formulation of the extralinguistic understandings that are inherent to communicative practice:

> Translation is based on a series of contingent judgements about the meaning of an original statement, the appropriate rendering of that meaning in the translation, and how to handle portions of the original deemed to be "untranslatable," whether by reason of unintelligibility, subtlety of meaning, or moral-ethical reprehensiveness. In the highly charged contexts of religious conversion, legal dispute, and conflict, these judgements become focal. (Hanks 1996:279)

The need to respond effectively to such judgments in order to ensure even a modicum of communication often set the official positions emanating from the Vatican and the

Spanish Court at odds with the everyday practices of priests and catechists who were charged with implementing such policies. The possibilities for misunderstanding inherent in "translations" of religious texts were an early source of concern to ecclesiastical authorities, who officially persisted in the view that the Christian message could not be adequately expressed in native languages, and should, ideally be communicated through the use of Spanish. Castilian Spanish was deemed to be the perfect instrument of empire not least because of its supposedly inherent capacity to express the values and significance of Christianity (Heath 1972).

However, from the perspective of those responsible for religious instruction Castilian Spanish had of necessity to engage with the thousands of local languages that persisted in the early colonial period, and with the inevitability of miscommunication, however adept the translators and interpreters (Hanks 1996; Mannheim 1991). Added to the impossibility of coherent interpretation was the fact that it was not always in the interest of ecclesiastical elites to extend the language of power to their Indian subjects. As a result the 16th century saw relatively liberal linguistic policies. The Council of Trent (1545 to 1563) recognized the importance of using vernacular languages to explain the sacraments to people, which in turn allowed priests to ignore the more general ruling to promote the use of Castilian Spanish. Local linguistic diversity was huge. Priests were often trying to teach in areas where as many as 700 languages were spoken (Heath and LaPrade 1982).

The response to this situation was ultimately the founding of a middle ground for cultural translation which both preserved the integrity of written, standard forms while elaborating a possibility for meaningful engagement with indigenous languages. This middle ground consisted in the elaboration and spread of the great common languages of the colonial period – Quechua in the Andes, Tupi-Guaraní in the regions of modern day Brazil and Paraguay, and Nahuatl in central Mexico. These languages were extended far beyond their precolonial repertoires, and most significantly harnessed for the business of the colonial state through the elaboration of standard, written forms. This practice of elaborating vernacular standards in the Americas was continuing a process initiated in Spain on the eve of Conquest where the process of systematizing vernacular forms as national languages had begun with Nebrija's grammar. These vernaculars that emerged in early modern Europe replaced previous ideas and practices that stressed translocalism. The abstraction of spoken language into stable rule-governed forms began to lend language a timeless form and facilitate the emergent association of language with singular, person-specific identities or ethnicity (Pollock 2000).

Nevertheless the process of imposing particular linguistic forms was neither straightforward nor one-sided. Heath and LaPrade (1982) discuss the case of Quechua and Aymara in some detail to show how official policy to impose Castilian Spanish not only failed to materialize, but created quite distinct linguistic histories for Quechua and Aymara, with implications for future language use. In the case of Quechua, the Spanish adopted what Heath and LaPrade call an additive policy (1982:136). This entailed the selective education of a small Indian elite in both Quechua and Spanish literacy. The training of such individuals allowed Quechua to develop as a language of state. By severely restricting access to such education the ruling elites could in effect school their own translators, granting them privileged status. The assumption was that the creation of a literate Quechua elite would render the Spaniards less vulnerable to the double standards of the less "schooled" translators. Furthermore, the partial abstraction of the Quechua language from the lived linguistic realities of the majority of Quechua speakers further disassociated this official Quechua from linguistic values of unschooled subjects. Through literacy the language was rendered appropriate to the task of translation. A chair in Quechua was established in the San Marcos University in Lima as early as 1580 (Heath and LaPrade 1982:129; see also Mannheim 1991).

This treatment of Quechua contrasted with the status of Aymara, previously an important lingua franca of the southern Andean region. Throughout the colonial period Aymara continued to serve as a strong identifier of a relatively homogeneous indigenous grouping, which in turn ensured its survival in the contemporary political domain as a viable national language (in Bolivia) and as the basis for the organization of the new indigenous politics. Despite its colonial status as an elite language, Quechua has not made this transition in the context of contemporary Peru, in large part because of the difficulty of shaking off the associations of ethnic and racial domination, or even inferiority, that today cling to all but the most literate of Quechua speakers.

In the 20th century we find very similar processes operating in lowland South America in regions that were largely ignored by the state until the frontier explorations of the late 19th and early 20th centuries began the search for natural resources and governments began to create and patrol frontiers in order to safeguard their national rights to these resources. In linguistic terms these explorations extended the domains of state anxiety, anxieties that were conveniently met by US evangelical institutions, particularly the Wycliffe Bible Translators, who, through the Summer Institute of Linguistics (SIL), were allowed from the 1940s onward to operate in the Catholic states of South America (see chapters by Seligmann, French, and Varese, Delgado and Meyer, this volume). The SIL convinced governments across Latin America of the importance of thorough documentation and description of minority indigenous languages and a blind eye was turned to what was in effect a new application of the theory of language that had motivated the early Catholic missionaries – that adequate translation would ensure the spread of the Word of God, and the related values of Christian civilization (Stoll 1982). That such values were largely forged in the crucible of capitalist modernity provided a link to the interests of the nominally Catholic states and the competition between Catholicism and evangelical Protestantism was seen as ultimately less threatening than that between Christianity and unknown indigenous alternatives. For our purposes the key point to make in relation to the translation process is that translation continued to relate fundamentally to conversion rather than the possibility of a two-way conversation. The SIL continued this trend with a commitment to learn the language from chosen native people who would be "returned" to their communities as indigenous catechists helping to instil a common ethos.

The other obvious reason why the Catholic states were not particularly worried by the presence of the SIL was that by the time they were working in Amazonia and Central America, the creation of Christian subjects had become of secondary importance to the creation of national subjects. In this transition, however, language remained at the center of this uneasy relationship between centralized power and the diverse populations nominally represented by, or directly subject to these powers.

## The Creation of National Subjects

By the 19th century, nationalist movements had begun to influence policy decisions in relation to language. The issue of "translation" was particularly acute in those nation-states that sought to articulate the "nation" to a linguistic group that had effectively been marginalized to a space of ignorance and absence of civility. It was in this context that the cultural revivalism of the various indigenista movements sought to recover value for certain indigenous languages from their abandonment by the cultured classes (Becker 1995; de la Cadena 2000; Hill and Hill 1986; Knight 1990; Lomnitz-Adler 1992; Mannheim 1991; Poole 1997; Torero 1974; Urban 1991b). In drawing these distinctions between an elite vernacular "heritage" and the degenerate linguistic forms of uneducated people, the indigenistas were repeating the "additive" policies of the ecclesiastic authorities of the colonial period, and further entrenching the notion of one language one culture on which nationalist politics so often rely (Mannheim 1984). However, the experiences of nation-building across Latin America were quite heterogeneous with respect to the notion of one language and one culture (see French, this volume). Thus, while countries such as Mexico or Peru appealed to ancient vernacular identity as the rhetorical grounding of national identities, in Argentina, Chile and Uruguay there was, by comparison, virtually no political will to recognize the indigeneity of surviving native populations (see Gordillo, this volume).

Within anthropology, Urban's (1991b) analysis of the semiotics of state–Indian linguistic relationships marked an important attempt to disarticulate language and identity in nationalist projects by comparing how grammars (languages) work as indexical signs in Paraguay, Brazil and Peru. His work challenged the notion that the linguistic code functions as a marker or index of a social group (ethnic group, nationality), and argues instead that the meanings elicited by the use of particular languages are contextually embedded in a relational field in which several languages are simultaneously in use.

For example, in the Andean countries the relationship between Spanish and Quechua was forged in relation to the linguistic practices of the Inka state. Quechua was imposed as a language of state (the Inka royal lineage having their own language which was not spoken by the rest of the Andean populations) and worked as a lingua franca in this very specific imperial context. By contrast, Tupinamba, the lingua franca encountered by both the Spanish and the Portuguese along the Atlantic coast, was a trade language that did not index relationships of social inequality, but pointed rather to communicative needs of a more horizontal kind. For many Andean peoples the arrival of the Spanish held out the possibility of liberation from Inka rule, and there was a resurgence of local languages (Edmonson 1983:96). Quechua has thus had a complex imperial history, encouraged by both the Inka and the Spaniards for reasons of state. It also stood as the language of the dominated, and by the 18th century came to hold the value of native tongue when most of the other Andean languages had disappeared. Quechua thus acquired the symbolic possibility of standing in opposition to Spanish and became available as a powerful symbol of resistance (although somewhat less powerful than neighbouring Aymara, for the reasons discussed above).

By contrast, in the Paraguayan and Brazilian contexts language was indexical of a widespread distinction between insiders and outsiders, where outsiders could equally be enemies, trading partners and potential affines. The Guarani allied themselves to the Spanish in the 16th century within this wider system of warfare and alliance. Again many languages disappeared during the colonial period, but through alliance rather than domination Guarani became a language of equal status with Spanish within the new state of Paraguay. In Brazil, on the other hand, a combination of the expulsion of the Jesuit priests, who had promoted the use of a Tupian lingua franca, and the arrival of the exiled Portuguese monarch created a space for the use of Portuguese as a new symbol of nationhood but in a context where the idea of the indigenous lingua franca maintained its horizontal and alliance-building significance.

Urban recognizes that the relational indexicality of languages changes over time, and relates also to the particular circumstances of use: "Language as symbol is more than a reflection of social relations. It is one of the devices used in constituting and modifying those relations" (1991b:325). The broad contrast between "alliance" and "domination" in the linguistic histories of Latin America is, however, an important characterization to which specific national linguistic histories can usefully be related.

## Twentieth-Century Language Politics

Notwithstanding the varying contexts of linguistic pluralism, pointed to by Urban, the new nation-states of Latin America were all involved in creating new social objects, the official languages through which these nations represented their own diversity, or homogeneity, to themselves. Furthermore, it was not until the second half of the 20th century that the vote was extended beyond the literate populations. Quechua was made an official language in Peru in 1975, and the first attempts at bilingual education programs and legal representation in Quechua were initiated. Despite the codification of six varieties of Quechua in grammars and dictionaries there was insufficient political will in the medium term to sustain the resources needed to carry these initiatives through in any meaningful way (Mannheim 1984).

In recent years contemporary indigenous movements have found space within the political economies of neoliberal regimes to demand the right to education, and particularly for meaningful access to languages of power. Interestingly these claims now embrace English as much as Spanish and/or Portuguese. These claims on power also came to be made in terms of a right to state-sponsored education in the vernacular, that is the right to learn in one's own language. Here the politics becomes more complex and directly challenges the model of diglossia (differentiated language use by function and/or social context) which the liberal state has fostered in recent decades. Claims to education in Spanish (or English) in some ways reinforce the functional distinctions between indigenous languages and European languages, with the former most often relegated to domains of intimacy and affect, while the European languages dominate in political debate, and in legal and scientific matters. In those nation-states with long histories of linguistic oppression, official languages, surrounded with the paraphernalia of literacy, could be used to silence and exclude, while laying claim to values of civilization, knowledge and justice (Harvey 1994, 2003). In these settings, indigenous demands for education in European languages are a pragmatic response to social inequality, enabling people to sidestep confrontational contexts in which an inability to use Spanish fluently was hugely disadvantageous in engagements with state power.

However, a politicized reading of diglossia in contexts such as those of the Andean countries saw indigenous languages as "oppressed" rather than functionally specific. As a result, people began to make demands on the state not simply for education in European languages, but for the full rehabilitation of indigenous languages, particularly through education programs which placed indigenous languages, and their cultures, at the heart of the curriculum. In these contexts the demand is for the right to learn in one's own language, not through the cultural lens of the language of power. Thus we find today that the basic parameters of language struggles in schools revolve around the tension between the liberal (descriptive) notion of diglossia and the more radical analysis of oppressed languages (Albó 1973, 1974; Arnold and Yapita 2000; Canessa 2004; Hornberger 1987, 1996; Howard-Malverde and Canessa 1995; King 2001; Mannheim 1991; Pozzi-Escott, Zuniga and Lopez 1991).

I have elaborated in some detail on the Andean case, but the theories of language implicated by these debates resonate across Latin America. Claims for education and citizenship inevitably revolve around modern (Western) understandings of personhood in which language indexes identity rather than relation (see Varese, Delgado and Meyer, this volume). These claims thus also reflect European understandings of language itself as a transparent instrument of social connection, a unifying cultural form through which diverse individuals can meet in the democratic process, which in turn relies on open discussion and negotiated settlements of competing interests. Modern political systems provoke anxiety about language loss, and the paradoxical concern that loss of diversity in expressive form is the price paid for diversity of opinion and interest in the political domain. Hence the politics of standardization that lies behind even the more radical proponents of linguistic representation, as they seek to formalize the diversity of spoken forms to the more static registers of official vernaculars. The arguments seem to offer the (non)choice between exclusion (held back by the "wrong" language that isolates people from benefits of modern life) and loss (as the yearning for dominant languages puts the more fragile vernaculars at risk). It is in this context that people have begun to think in a more focused way about attempts to develop alternative modernities – a topic to which I return in the final section of this chapter.

There are obvious problems inherent in the politics of standardization, not least in relation to who gets to "own" the new language object, who gets to develop the new standards, and how these are effectively imposed (Luykx 2003). Radical moves to establish new vernaculars, or to change the status of existing vernaculars, inevitably reproduce practices of exclusion in relation to nonwritten (noncodified) linguistic forms. Modern political movements of necessity work through modern political categories, of which language is one. Only through an exclusionary agreement to adopt one specific linguistic route at the expense of others can claims to language rights be made. Luykx (2003) gives examples from Bolivia where Spanish borrowing is referred to as "the enemy" in programs that seek to salvage archaic forms and impart the importance of learning "correct" language. Needless to say, those imposing these standards are usually highly educated bilinguals who use mostly Spanish in their daily lives. Such linguistic cleansing also tends to be enforced at the lexical level while ignored at the possibly more significant grammatical level. Jamieson (1999) discusses in a similar vein how the (Nicaraguan) Pearl Lagoon basin variety of Miskitu is considered a degraded form of language due to the presence of English nouns and verbs, despite the fact that these forms are often grammaticalized in ways that fully integrate them into Miskitu. Discussion of "belonging" in terms of the relationship between words and languages inevitably reproduces the notion of originary linguistic states of purity, authentic origins and subsequent "corruption." Jamieson argues that from an anthropological perspective it is more interesting to look at which lexical items are thought of as "loans," which as "originary," and which hold ambiguous repertoires.

Those language policies that fail to recognize the normative assumptions that hold equally to the notion of originary language as to "correct" language inevitably reinforce and institutionalize diglossic distinctions. For many the enforcement of standards is acceptable and a price worth paying for facilitating engagement with modernity. Such standards form the basis on which claims to rights in the modern state are built. The downside is that such claims feed the power of cultural reasoning (Briggs 2001), the notion of a categorical world of discrete and purified difference.

Through this brief discussion of the anthropology of language and education in contemporary Latin America we return, indirectly, to the go-betweens of the colonial encounter. For the politics of standardization produces people who move between and who, as a result, continue to be stigmatized as untrustworthy. Structurally ambivalent, these in-between spaces nevertheless offer opportunities for some to develop a strategic response to modern life from within them. The work of Hill and Hill (1986) on Mexicano offers an exemplary study of the ways in which these ambiguous spaces were taken up by the speakers of Mexicano in the Malinche towns of the Puebla region of Mexico. Mexicano could be described as a mix of Spanish and Nahuatl, but is not thought of in these terms by the Malinche, who claim to abhor mixture. They, by contrast, stress the importance of distinguishing a language of power (in which Spanish influences on Nahuatl are positively valued) from a linguistic purism that engages fundamental values of a community of insiders, particularly those associated with the complex system of honorifics through which respect is expressed and assumed. The value of these alternatives lies in the possibilities for the coexistence and creative manipulation of ways of speaking, and of techniques that allow people to blend languages as a means to signal both continuity and discontinuity between persons. The Malinche stress the importance of "speaking two." They attend to the degrees of mixing and forms of mixing that are appropriate and relevant to diverse contexts of engagement. Mixings are complex and may refer to the "borrowing" of lexical items, or phonological and syntactic convergence between Spanish and Nahuatl. One of the ground-breaking aspects of Hill and Hill's study was the ethnographic focus on "translinguistics" (the ways in which people juxtapose the possible "voices" that inhere in language), revealing how the ideological ambiguity of particular linguistic forms are fundamental to the communicative process. The study moved beyond normative understandings of language use (that characterized earlier studies of diglossia and bilingualism) to reveal a creative engagement with the rich indexical potential of language.

My work on the language of drunks in Andean Peru (Harvey 1991) also looks at how speakers disrupt the diglossic model of functional difference by deliberately using inappropriate language, particularly in the supposedly innocent use of bilingual punning. Drunks enjoy deliberately misinterpreting the propositional force of another's words by drawing out plausible but unintended meaning, playing with language in ways that demonstrate how Spanish and Quechua are always intrinsically meaningful in relation to each other and can never escape the translinguistic effect that each exercises on the other. The laughter that such practice provokes in those who observe drunken linguistic performances points to a general recognition of dual frames of reference, and of the pleasure gained by revealing the instability of categories. Hill (2001) emphasizes however that the "disorderly order" of disruptive practice is not equally available to all. The impact of drunken speech is diminished by the convention of discounting what drunks say. There is even a specific tense marker in Quechua to link what is said by drunks to states devoid of intention of responsibility such as dreaming or distant childhood. Nevertheless, the general point holds, that the objectification of sharp differences between languages is itself a linguistic assertion, not a background condition. Here the anthropological interest lies in understanding how the potential to foreground or background such distinctions is intrinsic to all communicational contexts. The specificity of the Latin American case lies in the particular ways in which significant distinctions have been produced and reproduced over time.

Thus, the violent and confrontational politics of Latin America has provided the impetus for generations of scholars to discuss how language ideologies hold the histories of state, Church and modern political struggle together in these specific cultural objects we call languages. Language is saturated with values that curtail social possibilities, often drastically restricting what can be said, but also providing resources for resistance. The Spanish colonial regime enshrined a dichotomized understanding of the nation in law, a dichotomy which has been repeated and re-presented in various ways and with varying moral connotations throughout the history of the Latin American nation-states. However, these categorical distinctions by no means dictate how distinctions are understood, nor the extent to which they are held to be important.

In the following section of this chapter I turn to those areas of Latin America where the notion of transformation and flux are seen as fundamental dimensions of being, and inform the experience and the resources required for living between categories. Here, in contrast to the paradigms of modern states, anthropologists work with people who celebrate the foundational importance of difference for the generation of productive sociality.

## COMMUNICATIVE PRACTICES ON THE MARGINS OF THE STATE

Anthropologists working in Amazonia and the tropical forests of Central America have been extremely influential in the development of new forms of discourse analysis that have focused on the ethnography of communication, ethno-poetics and verbal performance. Moving beyond the descriptive approach of formal linguistics, these anthropologists looked instead at discursive practice, providing descriptions that integrated the analysis of verbal forms with attention to the embodied practice of performance, and the contextual dynamics of social interaction (Hanks 1996). Their analysis of speech styles and discourse patterns, speech genres, participation frameworks, and the poetics of verbal performance generated new forms of ethnographic writing that worked around precise transcriptions of both language and prosody, attending to the ways in which meanings are generated intersubjectively through the skilled manipulation of grammatical forms (such as evidential systems and position markers), discursive patterns (such as parallelism, echo speech and dialogism), and the semantic possibilities afforded by multilingual speech communities. Furthermore, they began to identify common discursive genres – such as ceremonial greeting, ritual wailing, myths, songs, oratory and verbal duelling – across a huge diversity of linguistic groups.

One of the distinctive features of these ethnographers was the attention paid to language as evidence of ways of being that differed substantially from Euro-American habitual practice. In his work on Yucatan Mayan speakers, Hanks (1996) was particularly interested in the analysis of deixis (expressions which point to features of the surrounding context), as a way of understanding how people categorize the experiential and interpersonal contexts of speaking. His radical conclusions challenged established linguistic approaches to the relationship between language and context by claiming that language becomes meaningful through indexicality (the emergent and open-ended relationship between utterance and context) rather than semantics (where meanings derive from an altogether more static linguistic structure). More specifically, Hanks studies not language per se, but rather the communicative practices – or "language system" – emerging from the embodied practice of communication and the ideological values that come to inhere in speech over time. This approach allows for a new perspective on the relationship between verbal meaning and social context in that it reveals how language *is* context, and how context is in itself fundamentally constitutive of how "meaning" happens through speech, silence, bodies, and thought.

This formulation is far more dynamic than traditional ways of thinking about "language loss" in Latin America and about linguistic forms as somehow predisposing people to hold particular worldviews. Concern over the threat to indigenous languages and the urgency of "salvage anthropology" to capture these ways of speaking before they disappear certainly motivated many of the studies referred to above. However, there is a contradiction inherent in such approaches which is reminiscent of the dilemmas produced by the education debates discussed earlier. Beier, Michael and Sherzer (2002:121), for example, proposed a theory of linguistic diffusion across lowland South America to account for the commonalities of discursive practices across what are otherwise seen as "distinct genetic linguistic affiliations." Despite theoretical understandings of the primacy of discursive practices (such as genres of speech making, poetry and narrative), with the grammatical markers moving "behind" the more general "ways of speaking," these scholars are attentive to the dilemmas of "language loss," and seek to document "endangered languages" as "unique forms of human expression" (2002:138). What is unclear in these formulations is how the sociopolitical threats to the autonomy of indigenous peoples relate to the particular expressive forms they deploy. Or to put it another way, what exactly is it that disappears as linguistic forms change? The cultural practices themselves appear to be deeply embedded beyond the particularities of linguistic form through which they are expressed.

For example, in a recent paper Viveiros de Castro analyses a conversation in which a Spanish speaking schoolteacher and a Piro woman (in western Amazonia) demonstrate that "common language" offers no stable ground for effective communication (Viveiros de Castro n.d., drawing on a report by Gow). The teacher is giving advice to the Piro woman about how to look after her children, urging her to boil water to avoid intestinal infection. The woman replies that while she appreciates that water can give rise to illness in people from Lima, the Piro have different bodies, and it is in fact the boiled water that gives them parasites. The two women share their understandings of the surface meanings of the exchange, but there is no shared indexical ground for their conversation. Viveiros de Castro interprets the exchange as an example of ontological difference, referring to his understanding of the dominant perspectival ontology of Amazonian peoples. Fundamental to this indigenous philosophy is the notion that human being is culturally homogeneous (all beings are intrinsically human and have souls). What differs in the unicultural, multinatural world are the bodies through which beings live in the world. Thus, while the schoolteacher might think the Piro woman less cultured, and ignorant of the workings of the (singular) biological human body, the Piro woman posits that in fact it is their bodies that are different. Such difference is not biological, of course (for to posit that argument would return us to a singular nature), but indexical of different relationships. In this respect the body of her child which was the original subject of their exchange is effectively removed from the domain of the teacher's expertise, which is subtly refused in this short interchange.

The understandings drawn on for this exchange to be possible go far beyond the specific forms of particular languages and are found across the huge diversity of Amazonian languages, and they are not necessarily abandoned when Amazonian people communicate in Spanish. For what appears paradoxical within the terms of modern Western thought is quite basic to many Amerindian notions of linguistic diversity, namely that diversity itself can provide the common ground without the need for the kind of metalevel unity mobilized by state-sponsored education policies. The famously multilingual peoples of the Vaupés River in southeast Colombia (or western Brazil?) (C. Hugh-Jones 1979; S. Hugh-Jones 1979; Jackson 1974, 1983, 1995; Sorensen 1967, 1985) provide a paradigmatic example of such an understanding, practicing linguistic exogamy and articulating their cultural homogeneity with reference to linguistic difference.

Another wonderful example comes from bilingual speakers of Miskitu and English in the Nicaraguan Pearl Lagoon basin (Jamieson 1998). As noted above, these particular Miskitu speakers are seen as speaking a dialect tainted by continual contact with English speakers over the centuries. However, his ethnographic study of marriage preferences and kinship terms produced a fascinating twist to what might otherwise be dismissed as a case of imminent language loss. Jamieson found that the traditional distinction between cross-cousins and parallel-cousins (still important to the kinship and marriage practices of other Miskitu speaking groups) had been displaced in the Pearl Lagoon basin by a more powerful and pervasive differentiation between English and Miskitu speakers. On further investigation he found that the ideal partnership between an English-speaking man and a Miskitu-speaking woman was the more traditional, and had been posited as ideal during an earlier period of intense trade with English speakers. The contemporary form of cross-cousin marriage was seen as a poor but necessary substitute, adopted when English speakers proved less available as partners than had been hoped. The consequences for language use in this area are interesting.

> Ironically, the preference for village exogamy, and the consequent tendency of cross-sex adolescents of the same village to see one another as being somewhat unmarriageable, seem to have contributed to actually preserving the Miskitu language in villages such as Kakabila. Kakabila children, many of whom spend their early years speaking mostly

English, tend to switch into Miskitu as they reach adolescence, since they have no wish to present themselves to fellow villagers as the potential affines implied by the use of English. (Jamieson 1998:727)

Thus, alongside the concerns about language loss (the fear that the drive to a common language could erase the rich linguistic diversity of the region), there is an acknowledgment that language change is a continual process and that contact between discrete linguistic groups will always give rise to "borrowing." Writing of indigenous lowland South America, Beier, Michael and Sherzer assert:

> From the period of our earliest knowledge up to the present day, there is much travel, bilingualism, intermarriage and trade. In this view, linguistically distinct cultural groups in a given area come into contact and begin to interact intensely, borrowing discourse forms and processes from one another, such as myths, songs, and even entire ceremonies. Subsequently, phonological, morphological, syntactic, and/or semantic features embedded in these borrowed discourse forms begin to surface in the grammar of the group that has borrowed the discourse forms. In this picture, the sharing of discourse forms, which can be motivated on political and cultural grounds, mediates the borrowing of grammatical forms. (2002:137)

While anthropological linguists working in this tradition have recognized the significant history of group interaction within lowland South America, a somewhat artificial barrier is often set up between what are effectively understood as indigenous peoples living on the margins of states (those with a perspectival ontology and common repertoire of discourse forms) and those more clearly engaged with modern political institutions, and the philosophical tenets of "modern" European thought. However, as general theoretical paradigms render hybridizing processes more visible to analysts, and perhaps more interestingly in terms of future research directions, as indigenous Latin American peoples themselves find new ways to articulate claims on states, it is clear that the "borrowings" and influences between indigenous and European languages offer sites for the analysis of linguistic complexity and vitality as important as the borrowings and influences between Amerindian languages.

Hybridization, as Hanks's (1996) analysis of historical Yucatec Mayan materials reminds us, is always a two-way process. The Maya incorporated values and practices of their Spanish oppressors during the early colonial period when subjected to Spanish rule. They sought to become effective communicators with their new rulers, and in the process came to incorporate not just a new language, but many of the practices and sentiments that habitual speech forms engender. Asymmetries of power were deeply significant and in many ways the linguistic changes did express a deep and subtle cultural subordination. However, it is crucial to remember that just as the Maya were marked by their submergence in Spanish expressive forms, so too Spanish was open to Mayan influences. Thus today, even in areas that were clearly centers of Spanish colonial influence, such as the Peruvian Andes, contemporary Spanish is very strongly marked by the centuries of coexistence with Quechua. The inevitability of hybridization as intrinsic to all communicative process leads me to the final section of this chapter, in which I discuss recent work that focuses on the dynamics of interaction and engagement, and particularly on the place of language in people's creative engagement with power. This work challenges the notion that indigenous peoples of Latin America are in danger of death by translation.

## ALTERNATIVE MODERNITIES

Campaigners to save endangered languages focus primarily on the possibility of a reconfigured habitus implied by the shift to dominant national or international languages, and a desire to support and maintain alternative philosophies and anthropologies that challenge the hegemony of modernist thinking. And while they are not wrong to point out the deep structural inequalities which many indigenous peoples are forced to negotiate on a daily basis in order to be heard at all, it is also the case that Native American peoples have found ways to participate in the modern world without abandoning alternative values and priorities to those that underwrite the habitual practices of the majority of language planners. Positioning oneself in relation to power is not necessarily a point of capitulation, and although not without serious dangers, there are many contexts in which people assume the position of go-between, in a creative appropriation of hegemonic cultural forms:

> In the wake of colonization, cultural hybridization may be the only means whereby an effective indigenous discourse of resistance can evolve: the "authentically indigenous" is an inescapable anachronism in such a setting, while the alternative to hybridization is the engulfment of the indigenous by the hegemonic cultural forms and values of the colonising society. From this point of view, hybridization generates a space for the formulation of new meanings, by combining re-use and transformation of the indigenous, with appropriation and adaptation of symbols originating with the dominant culture. (Howard-Malverde 1997:15)

Hybridization allows a strategy of simultaneous accommodation and resistance, whereby the efficacy of certain modes of power are acknowledged, but precisely in order to articulate a point of difference (and autonomy) from such power. These attitudes of mimetic approximation, that nevertheless crucially maintain lines of distinction between orders of being, are characteristic of one of the most distinctive fields of practice in the canon of Latin Americanist anthropology, that is the field of shamanic knowledge and communicative practice. Platt (1997), for example, describes how Macha shamans, in highland Bolivia, incorporate metaphors of alphabetic literacy and legalism as they seek to conjoin the powers of mountain gods, government officials and the state itself. Shamanic healers exemplify the kinds of intercultural engagement that run counter to the procedures of standardization and singularity that characterize state-led language policy. Viveiros de Castro refers to Amazonian shamans as "nodes of translation." These are men who have to find ways to communicate with the spirit world. Moving beyond the habitual practices of human communication they enter a dangerous realm in which they seek to approximate the lifeworld of dangerous, cannibalistic beings in order to see and to know in ways that can help cure other humans or direct them in their everyday lives. Shamans have their own languages, and their visions come through the ingestion of hallucinogenic drugs and through the songs of the spirits.

Occupying the space of the go-between, they attempt to acquire the power of the nonhuman world through mimetic techniques, just as the first interpreters did in the early years of colonial encounter. Now as then, shamans are susceptible to accusations of betrayal from both the spirit and the human worlds. In some areas of Amazonia, the dynamics of incomprehension and projection that characterized the violent encounters with colonial and postcolonial powers fill the visions and provide the affective charge which renders magical practices effective. Taussig's (1987) work on the Colombian Putumayo is an analysis of how contemporary shamans from this region draw from the legacy of fear and the violent fantasies of the rubber barons, negotiating the "space of death" where savage cruelty and murderous desire were projected onto native peoples, and then enacted on their bodies in retribution for the imagined provocation. The highland shamans work with the images that animate such confrontations, the energies that inhere in envy and fear. Seeking always to establish a degree of control through ritual chanting, they approach the murky source of power to learn something of the truth beyond language, to penetrate realities that language too easily conceals.

Shamanic knowledge across lowland South America works with deeply held assumptions about vision and illusion, about communication and deception. Tobacco and more powerful hallucinogenic drugs allow shamans to receive "words" and "visions" in dreams and songs which hold valid and authoritative knowledge not merely in their content but in their forms. Shamanic performances thus often require careful attention to voice quality, performance style and the grammatical markers that invoke authority, indicate quotation or distance speakers from responsibility. In shamanic practice we find implicit theories of language that do not propose standards of codification or belief in the value of transparent interaction, but which are more likely to operate an economy of competitive insight. Aesthetically, they signal a pleasure in the verbal arts of deception, joking and innuendo that engage participants in tantalizing exchanges which reveal and conceal in a flirtation with "truth."

The performance of mythic narratives also reveals a similar approach to language. Writers like Urban (1991a) showed, through their attention to mythic performance, that the significance of discourse was not simply referential, but rather lay in the ways that mythic performances created social solidarity and continuity in contexts where formal political leadership was not recognizable in Euro-American terms. Anthropologists have long recognized that mythic forms express indigenous philosophies and values, not least as pertains to the illusory nature of being and the instability of bodily forms (Allen 1988; C. Hugh-Jones 1979; S. Hugh-Jones 1979; Kaplan 1975). Basso (1987) writes of how Kalapalo storytelling compresses information, interpretation, speculation and imaginative play. She notes the importance of dialogic modes of performance in which speakers create images for listeners, who in turn draw the images forth from speakers by asking appropriate questions. She argues that in ritual dialogues the Kalapalo create illusory intimacy through the co-conjuring of images. The performances bridge the gaps between categories of being, not through establishing a mood of sympathy (and identification), but rather through trickier techniques, using music and song to entrance and thereby control. Tricksters are key figures in the mythic narratives, archetypal go-betweens who acknowledge asymmetrical power relations, but who nevertheless also believe in the possibility of reversals and transformations brought about through the power of insight and imitation. As speakers and listeners draw together in their coproduced experience of assertion and doubt, differences are not collapsed but acknowledged and activated.

The drive for engagement rather than purity and the drawing together of incompatible forms to knowingly create alternatives are a form of strategic accommodation that has implications for how we might approach the linked issue of national integration and even of language loss. In many ways, anthropologists working in this field are taking the lead from the considered practice of Amerindian people, who certainly debate these issues among themselves (Graham 2002; Howe 1986). In the Vaupés, for example, changes are taking place in the context of the implementation of a new constitution in which Colombia declares itself an ethnically and culturally plural society. In this context native people seek first to protect their territory and find that the creation of a viable native identity is fundamental to their land claims. To this end the multilingual Vaupés Indians have begun to objectify themselves as "ethnic groups" in ways that convincingly evoke an enduring heritage of linguistic difference. In the process, they obscure the huge fluidity between groups that has long characterized linguistic practices in this area. In some respects the national constitution has pushed these people to create difference in a particular way, a way that fits the commodifying logics of contemporary capital and the understandings of the multiculturalism of neo-liberal states. It remains to be seen whether the official naming of groups leads to a subsequent bounding of groups that radically changes social organization and cultural understandings in this region.

There is no reason to suppose that cultural homogenization is the only plausible outcome. Certainly dominant languages such as English and Spanish have produced huge variation as they spread around the world, influencing but influenced in turn by those they encounter. Graham (2002) writes of how the Shavante, once a classic hunting society as described by Maybury-Lewis, now live in settled communities as dry rice cultivators. Shavante leaders continue to use dreams to articulate futures through dialogue with the ancestors. Her ethnography shows how contemporary leaders try to preserve the specificity of their way of life while participating in wider national arenas. They respond to change with their established cultural possibilities, that include new experiences as well as old, and often embrace new technologies to assist in the preservation of traditional knowledge. In the process differences within communities as well as between them are frequently negotiated or highlighted.

A final example illustrates this point, and returns us to the arrival of Columbus with a tale of translation, prompted by the transcription and translation of a chant, performed by the Panamanian Kuna chief Olopinikwa to the linguistic anthropologist Joel Sherzer. Having recorded the chant, which told of the arrival of the Spaniards and the way in which they treated the Kuna, Sherzer employed a young bilingual man, Alberto Campos, to transcribe and translate the chief's performance. However, the work was far more interpretative than Sherzer had wanted, as Campos transformed the oral performance into a written form, and in the process subtly changed the communicative effect of the piece. Sherzer expressed the problem in the following terms:

> Campos belongs to a new generation of bilingual and bicultural Kunas; he is now a schoolteacher in Sasartii-Mulatuppu, married to the daughter of a chief, the granddaughter of Chief Olopinikwa. His mediating voice straddles two worlds, two literacies, and at least two sets of poetic/rhetorical conventions. The struggle between the older prestige of oral tradition and the newer prestige of the written word is characteristic of Latin America today. (1994:922)

The example is interesting as it reveals how Chief Olopinikwa and Alberto Campos were both fully engaged in the politics of language as they articulated and reproduced the chant. They were not simply giving or documenting an account. The chief was "enacting his authority and role as representative of tradition, ethnic identity, and historical struggle" (Sherzer 1994:922). The younger man was articulating his own relationship both to the chief and to the chant itself, as he sought to reveal his own connections to a literate world of scholarship, while engaging with the specificity of his own Kuna "tradition." Sherzer saw his own role as "getting it all down and getting it right" (1994:923). In the process he finds himself overruling Campos and producing an alternative translation that reproduces the poetic structure which Campos had ignored.

This example captures in many ways the contemporary field of Latin American anthropological linguistics, and the challenges for the future – the concern to document distinctive forms and competing models of difference, the need to understand social change often from the perspective of people who deploy understandings of temporality quite at odds with a Western historical tradition, the desire to support the articulation of alternatives in a world where the charged dynamics of inequality favour standardization and normative solutions, and the interest in tracking instability and syncretic forms in contexts where purity is asserted from all points of the political spectrum. Contemporary understandings of the indexical quality of language have shown how even the most routine encounters involve complex referential circumstances that connect linguistic forms to embodied practice and historically situated ideas. Ethnographic studies of language use thus offer a privileged point of entry for studies of how historical process informs contemporary cultural practice, of how value inheres in material forms, and for the realization that it is not ultimately the linguistic forms that carry meaning, but the relationships through which the forms are rendered significant.

## REFERENCES

Albó, X. (1973) *El futuro de los idiomas oprimidos en los Andes.* La Paz: Centro de Investigación y Promoción del Campesinado.

Albó, X. (1974) *Los mil rostros del Quechua.* Lima: Instituto de Estudios Peruanos.

Allen, Catherine (1988) *The Hold Life Has: Coca and Cultural Identity in an Andean Community.* Washington, DC: Smithsonian Institution Press.

Appel, R. and Muysken, P. (1987) *Language Contact and Bilingualism.* London: Edward Arnold.

Arnold, D. and Yapita, J. (2000) *El rincón de las cabezas. Luchas textuales, educación y tierras en los Andes.* La Paz: UMSA/ILCA.

Basso, E. (1987) *In Favor of Deceit: A Study of Tricksters in an Amazonian Society.* Tuscon: University of Arizona Press.

Becker, Marjorie (1995) *Setting the Virgin on Fire: Lázaro Cardenas, Michoacán Peasants, and the Redemption of the Mexican Revolution.* Berkeley: University of California Press.

Beier, C., Michael, L., and Sherzer, J. (2002) Discourse Forms and Processes in Indigenous Lowland South America: An Areal-Typological Perspective. *Annual Review of Anthropology* 31:121–145.

Briggs, C. L. (2001) Modernity, Cultural Reasoning, and the Institutionalization of Social Inequality: Racializing Death in a Venezuelan Cholera Epidemic. *Society for Comparative Study of Society and History* 43(4):665–700.

Canessa, Andrew (2004) Reproducing Racism: Schooling and Race in Highland Bolivia. *Race, Ethnicity and Education 7.*

de la Cadena, Marisol (2000) *Indigenous Mestizos: The Politics of Race and Culture in Cuzco, Peru, 1919–1991.* Durham, NC: Duke University Press.

de la Cruz, Víctor (1993) Brothers or Citizens: Two Languages Two Political Projects in the Isthmus. In H. Campbell (ed.), *Zapotec Struggles: Histories, Politics and Representations from Juchitán, Oaxaca* (pp. 241–248). Washington, DC: Smithsonian Institution Press.

Derrida, J. (1976[1967]) *Of Grammatology*, trans. Gayatri Chakravorty Spivak. Baltimore: Johns Hopkins University Press.

Edmonson, B. (1983) The Pre- and Post-Conquest Use of Quechua as a Lingua Franca. *Human Mosaic* 17:88–115.

Graham, L. R. (2002) How Should an Indian Speak? Brazilian Indians and the Symbolic Politics of Language Choice in the International Public Sphere. In J. Jackson and K. Warren (eds), *Indigenous Movements, Self-Representation, and the State in Latin America*. Austin: University of Texas Press.

Greenblatt, S. (1991) *Marvelous Possessions: The Wonder of the New World*. Oxford: Clarendon Press.

Hanke, L. (1949) *The Spanish Struggle for Justice*. Philadelphia: University of Pennsylvania Press.

Hanks, W. (1996) *Language and Communicative Practices*. Boulder: Westview.

Harvey, P. (1991) Drunken Speech and the Construction of Meaning: Bilingual Competence in the Southern Peruvian Andes. *Language in Society* 20:1–36.

Harvey, P. (1994) The Presence and Absence of Speech in the Communication of Gender. In P. Burton, K. Dyson, and S. Ardener (eds), *Bilingual Women*. Oxford: Berg.

Harvey, P. (2003) Elites on the Margins: Mestizo Traders in the Southern Peruvian Andes. In C. Shore (ed.), *Elite Cultures*. London: Routledge.

Heath, S. B. (ed.) (1972) *Telling Tongues: Language Policy in Mexico: Colony to Nation*. New York: Teachers College Press.

Heath, S. B. and LaPrade, R. (1982) Castilian Colonization and Indigenous Languages: The Cases of Quechua and Aymara. In R. L. Cooper (ed.), *Language Spread*. Bloomington: Indiana University Press.

Hill, J. (2001) Language, Race, and White Public Space. In A. Duranti (ed.), *Linguistic Anthropology: A Reader*. Oxford: Blackwell.

Hill, J. and Hill, C. (1986) *Speaking Mexicano: Dynamics of Syncretic Language in Central Mexico*. Tuscon: University of Arizona Press.

Hornberger, N. H. (1987) Bilingual Education Success, but Policy Failure. *Language in Society* 16(2):205–226.

Hornberger, N. H. (ed.) (1996) *Indigenous Literacies in the Americas: Language Planning from the Bottom Up*. The Hague: Mouton.

Howard-Malverde, R. (1997) Introduction: Between Text and Context in the Evocation of Culture. In R. Howard-Malverde (ed.), *Creating Context in Andean Cultures*. Oxford: Oxford University Press.

Howard-Malverde, R. and Canessa, A. (1995) The School in the Quechua and Aymara Communities of Highland Bolivia. *International Journal of Educational Development* 15:231–243.

Howe, J. (1986) *The Kuna Gathering: Contemporary Village Politics in Panama*. Austin: University of Texas Press.

Hugh-Jones, Christine (1979) *From the Milk River: Spatial and Temporal Processes in Northwest Amazonia*. Cambridge: Cambridge University Press.

Hugh-Jones, Stephen (1979) *The Palm and the Pleiades: Initiation and Cosmology in Northwest Amazonia*. Cambridge: Cambridge University Press.

Jackson, J. (1974) Language Identity of the Colombian Vaupes Indians. In D. Bauman and J. Sherzer (eds), *Explorations in the Ethnography of Speaking*. Cambridge: Cambridge University Press.

Jackson, J. (1983) *The Fish People: Linguistic Exogamy and Tukanoan Identity in Northwest Amazonia*. Cambridge: Cambridge University Press.

Jackson, J. (1995) Culture, Genuine and Spurious: The Politics of Indianness in the Vaupes, Colombia. *American Anthropologist* 22:3–27.

Jamieson, M. (1998) Linguistic Innovation and Relationship Terminology in the Pearl Lagoon Basin of Nicaragua. *Journal of the Royal Anthropological Institute* 4:713–730.

Jamieson, M. (1999) En inglés y la variedad de miskito en la cuenca de Laguna de Perlas. *Wani* 24:24–32.

Kaplan, Joanna Overing (1975) *The Piaroa: A People of the Orinoco Basin.* Oxford: Clarendon Press.

King, K. (ed.) (2001) *Language Revitalization, Processes and Prospects: Quichua in the Ecuadorian Andes.* Clevedon: Multilingual Matters.

Knight, Alan (1990) Racism, Revolution and Indigenismo: Mexico 1910–1940. In Richard Graham (ed.), *The Idea of Race in Latin America, 1870–1940.* Austin: University of Texas Press.

Lara, J. (1989[1957]) *Tragedia del fin de Atawallpa. Atau Wallpaj p'uchukakuyninpa wankan.* Cochabamba: Los Amigos del Libro.

Lévi-Strauss, C. (1973) *Tristes Tropiques.* London: Jonathan Cape.

Lomnitz-Adler, Claudio (1992) *Exits from the Labyrinth: Culture and Ideology in the Mexican National Space.* Berkeley: University of California Press.

Luykx, A. (2003) Whose Language Is It Anyway? *Current Issues in Comparative Education* 5:1–10.

Mannheim, B. (1984) Una nación acorralada: Southern Peruvian Quechua Language Planning and Politics in Historical Perspective. *Language in Society* 13(3):291–309.

Mannheim, B. (1991) *The Language of the Inkas since the European Invasion.* Austin: University of Texas Press.

Nebrija, A. de (1909[1492]) *Gramática castellana.* Halle: Niemeyer.

Ortiz Rescaniere, A. (1973) *De Adaneva a Inkarrí.* Lima: Retablo de Papel.

Paz, O. (1959) *El laberinto de la soledad.* Mexico City: Fondo de Cultura Económica.

Platt, T. (1997) The Sound of Light: Emergent Communication through Quechua Shamanic Dialogue. In R. Howard-Malverde (ed.), *Creating Context in Andean Cultures.* Oxford: Oxford University Press.

Pollock, S. (2000) Cosmopolitan and Vernacular in History. *Public Culture* 12:591–625.

Poole, D. (1997) *Vision, Race, and Modernity: A Political Economy of Andean Photography.* Princeton: Princeton University Press.

Poole, D. (2004) An Image of Our Indian: Type Photographs and Racial Sentiments in Oaxaca, 1920–1940. *Hispanic American Historical Review* 84(1):37–82.

Pozzi-Escott, I., Zuniga, M., and Lopez, L. E. (1991) *Educación bilingue intercultural. Reflexiones y desafíos.* Lima: Fomenciencias.

Seed, P. (1991) "Failing to Marvel": Atahualpa's Encounter with the Word. *Latin American Research Review* 26:7–32.

Sherzer, J. (1994) The Kuna and Columbus. *American Anthropologist* 96:902–924.

Sorensen, A. (1967) Multilingualism in the Northwest Amazon. *American Anthropologist* 69:670–684.

Sorensen, A. (1985) An Emerging Tukanoan Linguistic Regionality: Policy Pressures. In H. E. M. Klein and L. Stark (eds), *South American Indian Languages: Retrospect and Prospect.* Austin: University of Texas Press.

Stern, S. J. (1995) *The Secret History of Gender: Women, Men and Power in Late Colonial Mexico.* Chapel Hill: University of North Carolina Press.

Stoll, D. (1982) *Fishers of Men or Founders of Empire? The Wycliffe Bible Translators in Latin America.* London: Zed Press.

Taussig, M. (1987) *Colonialism, Shamanism and the Wildman: A Study in Terror and Healing.* Chicago: University of Chicago Press.

Todorov, T. (1984) *The Conquest of America: The Question of the Other*, trans. R. Howard. New York: Harper and Row.

Torero, A. (1974) *El Quechua y la historia social andina.* Lima: Universidad Ricardo Palma.

Urban, G. (1991a) *A Discourse-Centered Approach to Culture: Native South American Myths and Rituals.* Austin: University of Texas Press.

Urban, G. (1991b) The Semiotics of State–Indian Linguistic Relationships: Peru, Paraguay, and Brazil. In G. Urban and J. Sherzer (eds), *Nation-States and Indians in Latin America*. Austin: University of Texas Press.

Vaughan, Mary Kay (1997) *Cultural Politics in Revolution: Teachers, Peasants, and Schools in Mexico, 1930–1940*. Tuscon: University of Arizona Press.

Viveiros de Castro (n.d.) The Gift and the Given: Three Nano-Essays on Kinship and Magic. MS.

Wachtel, N. (1977) *The Vision of the Vanquished*. Hassocks: Harvester Press.

**11** Legalities and Illegalities

*Mark Goodale*

This chapter examines the anthropological study of law in Latin America. My goal here is threefold. First, I describe a key insight from anthropology about the way law and its normative cousins are constituted in Latin America by locating these processes within a more general, perhaps polemical, series of arguments about Latin American legality (and illegality). Second, I illustrate these baseline theoretical points through critical soundings in several areas which have drawn the attention of anthropologists of, and in, Latin America. It is simply not possible to present a comprehensive anthropological overview of law in Latin America, even if this were a stated intention; the anthropology of law in Latin America remains much too incipient for this. Yet it is possible to sketch the range of current research and reflection on law in Latin America that draws from insights anchored within the anthropological tradition. This is not the same as identifying a putative legal anthropology *of* Latin America, which does not, in any event, exist in any meaningful sense. But it is worthwhile to use this opportunity to describe the outlines of an emergent set of topics for inquiry and social action, in part so that the reader may judge the usefulness of pursuing the problem of law in Latin America through a combination of ethnography, nonfoundational social theory, and cultural critique. Finally, by taking the measure of current anthropologies of law in Latin America through a necessarily abbreviated, but substantive, discussion of illustrative topics, I will also indicate potential new ethnographic and critical spaces for engagement.

The skein of law in Latin America, as elsewhere, can be understood from various angles of approach. First, one can adopt a jurisprudential framework, in which law is understood as the body of rules enacted by a legitimate sovereign – first the colonial empire, then the nation-state – which has the responsibility for enforcing and protecting such rules. Because Latin American "law" in these terms was heavily influenced by European models – Spanish, obviously, but also French and German – which were themselves significantly indebted to the Roman civil law, it has orthodoxly required the trained attention of official jurisprudents, whose task is not so much to make or interpret the law, as to discover and then codify it. In Latin America, as in other civil law regions, specific laws are not made, but deduced from the supposedly timeless current of transcendent or natural law that structures social relations. Because the anthropological approach to law is so radically different from the jurisprudential, it is all the more important that one recognizes that the jurisprudential has been, since the constitution of "Latin America" in the 16th century, the official and thus dominant epistemic orientation to the normative.

A second important analytical framework for understanding law in Latin America resembles Anglo-American legal realism. In this mode, law cannot be reduced to its logical expressions, nor to the institutions that are charged with revealing it. Rather, the whole range of law's instrumentalities – constitutional courts, provincial notaries public, national legislatures, urban bar associations, rural *tinterillos* (literally "scribes," but better, "unofficial lawyers") – are determined by a set of consequential nonlegal forces: political, economic, cultural, and moral. Yet despite the fact that Latin American legal realism creates important spaces for inquiry beyond the artificially drawn boundaries entailed by the deductive and hegemonic legal "science" of law faculties and constitutional courts, this approach is still constrained by its reliance on a formal definition of law. In other words, a politically or economically determined law is still imagined to be a body of rules that can only legitimately flow from the machinery of the nation-state.

But there is another way in which law in Latin America can be conceptualized and then encountered: the anthropological. By anthropological I do not, and, indeed, cannot, mean simply an approach to normative theory and practice in Latin America developed and pursued by professional anthropologists, whether foreign or "native." Rather, an anthropological framework for studying and criticizing law describes a diverse range of theories and practices that are nevertheless united by a set of common – even if unstated – theoretical assumptions and patterns of sociolegal praxis.

First, anthropologies of law in Latin America convert the formal or state legal ideologies that circumscribe the legal within philosophical or political boundaries, into objects for research and critique. An anthropological approach locates law as part of much wider social and economic processes, which are themselves permanently imbricated within, and constitutive of, the very fabric of Latin America itself. In other words, anthropologies of law confirm a different kind of truth embedded in Malagón Barceló's aphorism that "America was born beneath the juridical sign" (1961:4).

Second, an anthropological orientation does not assume that "law" can only be approached through its instrumentalities, whether state, provincial, institutional, or professional; that is to say, law's content and meanings are not limited to what can be captured within empirically valid cause-and-effect relationships. Instead, anthropologies of law are as concerned with legal consciousness and identity as with dispute resolution; they give as much priority to the traditional social memory that conditions present understandings of rights and wrongs as to the movement by indigenous peoples in Latin America to codify these understandings in national constitutions.

Third, the anthropological approach to law is open source: it is nondisciplinary, noninstitutionalized (but see the Red Latinoamericana Antropología Jurídica, RELAJU, the Latin American Network on Legal Anthropology) and, increasingly, nonelite, to the extent that working class, union, and peasant intellectuals and their collective representatives employ an anthropological framework as part of broader legal and political movements. This is not merely the result of its diametric opposition to hegemonic orientations to law in Latin America, although this marginality does mean an anthropological framework will be available to some simply through exclusion; rather, its theoretical and technical openness is also a consequence of a kind of purposive epistemological flimsiness. Finally, anthropologies of law in Latin America, despite their incipience and diversity, are characterized by a counterhegemony, by their linkage with a range of social justice movements at all meaningful social levels. This is something that anthropologies of law in Latin America perhaps share with the anthropology of Latin America more generally; but those who employ an anthropological approach to the legal overwhelmingly do so as part of broader projects for social and economic transformation, in part because the legal is the key institutional and intellectual mode through which Latin America's historic power imbalances have been justified and reinforced.

This description of an emergent anthropological approach to law in Latin America is also an argument for its value compared with the alternatives. In what remains of this chapter I will give substance to this argument through a discussion of specific topics where this value has been most apparent. But before I do this, I would like to anticipate the discussion's progression through its full circle, as it were, in order to make several claims about what anthropological studies of law in Latin America can tell us about the nature of legality itself in Latin America. First, they show that law in Latin America is essentially discursive. What this means is that the bodies of rules, regulatory practices, and categories of normative meaning – i.e. "law" – that are found throughout Latin America are not primarily self-contained and self-reproducing systems directed toward social control or the maintenance of public order, as a jurisprudential analysis would emphasize; rather, they are better understood as open systems of representation that produce both regimes of truth and categories of social subjectivity which these regimes encapsulate. Second, legal discourse understood in this way is arguably the most consequential system of representation in Latin America; and this has been true since the colonial period, as Latin American historians like Steve Stern (1982) and others have demonstrated. Third, the systems of representation we can describe as "law" mediate the production of other, nonlegal structures of meaning and social practice, such that one must locate the legal in order to fully comprehend what appear to be the distinct economic, political, and religious dimensions of Latin American culture and society. In this sense, law in Latin America is constitutive in a way that economics and politics, for example, are not. Finally, anthropologies of law in Latin America point to the ways in which legal discourse is produced dialectically: the spaces of the legal are in constant motion *with* the spaces of the nonlegal or illegal. I say "in constant motion" because legality and illegality are never finally settled discursively, but rather remain two necessary parts of the same conceptual framework within which "law" itself can serve its purposes. One important implication of this dialectical understanding of law in Latin America is the fact that vigilante associations, favela courts, and other "marginal" sites of legal praxis should not be seen as merely peripheral to law, or a reaction against it. Rather, legality and illegality are fundamentally interdependent within a more basic system of representation and, in many cases, hegemony.

This dialectical understanding of law that I develop here has been reinforced most recently by Deborah Poole in an essay on justice and community in Peru. Here Poole (2004) reconceptualizes the relationship between the state and the "margins" as going beyond the merely spatial to evoke the biopolitical topoi within which identity is constituted in relation to structures of political domination, as much as the more obvious topographic markers that create lines in the body politic: checkpoints, national frontiers, "the tracks" (to invoke bell hooks's indelible metaphor for marginality). Poole uses the roadside ritual through which the state in Peru "locates" peasants by checking names against lists in order to subject a whole series of assumed relationships to critical scrutiny: the relationship between centers and margins; the relationship between the state and justice; and the relationship between what she calls "threat and guarantee." But "between" has a double meaning here, which is why Poole's study of checkpoints informs the anthropological understanding of law in Latin America more generally. She argues that firmly established categories like the "state" or "law" must be seen as mere framing devices rather than actual references to sites where social practice unfolds. As she says, the more important set of anthropological questions concerns that "highly mobile, tangible, and embodied space through which the power of the state is felt as [a] slippage" in which "the legitimacy of the state is brought into contact with the sometimes arbitrary forms of power that underwrite the sanctity of law" (2004:36). For Poole the law's constitutiveness in Latin America is expressed through the delicate interplay between contexts of grave danger and the promise of the state to provide its citizens certain guarantees; as I have argued, this dynamism can be tracked anthropologically through the categorical "clash" between the legal and illegal. But in both cases the law's categories are rendered, in Poole's felicitous phrasing, "illegible and opaque" (2004:37).

All of these central findings from anthropological studies of law in Latin America have admittedly been rendered quite abstractly; this is partly due to the fact that relatively few people have drawn out the important theoretical implications from the small but growing body of Latin American legal anthropology. But there is something else. Because anthropologies of law in Latin America have been, as I have argued, often pursued in the context of profound struggles for social justice and, in some cases, self-determination, it is all the more important that alternative conceptual frameworks for understanding law receive sustained treatment; that is to say, my position here is that a more well-developed anthropological approach to law in Latin America can play a role in movements for social change. As with the theoretical implications described above, this more programmatic contention will become clearer through an analytical survey of the range of current key topics within Latin American law.

## NETWORKS OF LAW

There is a specialization within the anthropology of law more generally that studies "legal pluralism": the existence of multiple legal systems within the same juridical and social spaces (see generally Merry 1988; see also Griffiths 1986; Guevara Gil and Thome 1992). Most of the influential ethnographic descriptions of legal pluralism, as well as theoretical frameworks for understanding these processes, are associated with regions outside of Latin America. This is because "official" legal pluralism was never adopted either during the colonial era, or by the newly independent nation-states. Official legal pluralism, which characterized much of colonial Africa and southeast

Asia – most notably Dutch Indonesia – was a specific approach to "managing" large amounts of colonial territory and large indigenous populations. Typically, two official legal systems were allowed to function simultaneously, with certain spheres being within the jurisdiction of colonial courts – criminal and commercial matters, for example – while other, more "cultural" or "local" areas were delegated jurisdictionally to what came to be understood as "customary law": family affairs, real property, marriage. But apart from the effect de jure legal pluralism had in prolonging colonialism through the official oversight and indirect control of local legality, it also resulted in the consolidation of intralocal and intraregional legal "systems" by forcing multiple and often culturally quite disparate populations to legitimate their traditional legal practices within what was inevitably a limited number of official customary legal institutions. Rather than preserving local legality and fostering a degree of autonomy, official legal pluralism actually led to the transformation, or in some cases, destruction, of real normative diversity in areas that came within its ambit.

In Latin America, by contrast, de jure legal pluralism was never prevalent, because colonial governments – and the nation-state after independence – were never able to create unified, but multiple, legal orders as part of wider strategies for social and political control. De facto legal pluralism was the result, in which a plurality of legal systems, or, in Roberto Da Matta's formulation, "codes of conduct" (1987:323), were unofficially associated with different classes and regions, and identified with urban or rural spaces. This fact partly explains why studies of legal pluralism have never been common within Latin America. After the Conquest, "law" became by definition "state law." Although as a matter of social practice, people continued to use alternative, unofficial legal structures for certain claims, at the same time people were also forced by circumstance to participate in governmental legal processes, even if at times such participation was politically strategic rather than purely "legal." Moreover, states in Latin America had every reason to deny the existence of legal pluralism within their borders; to do otherwise would mean to acknowledge a basic weakness in national sovereignty, which depends, among other things, on internal legal hegemony. But the difficulties with understanding legal pluralism in Latin America become compounded because those who have a stake in alternative legal structures – often rural people living at the margins of national legal consciousness – likewise have every reason to deny the existence of what is for them often the "real" law, a law that serves not only to resolve their conflicts, establish and reaffirm their rights and obligations, etc., but also serves as a potent symbol of community resistance to state power (see Goodale 2002a, 2002b, 2008; Rappaport 1994; Santos 1995).

In spite of these difficulties, an anthropological interest in legal pluralism in Latin America has increased, particularly over the last 15 years. This movement has come primarily from scholars (Goodale 2008; Iturralde 1990; Izko 1993; Pasara 1988; Santos and García Villegas 2001), self-representing Latin American social and political activists (Macas 1994) and indigenous intellectuals (Conklin and Graham 1995; Hale 1997; Stephen 1995; Wright 1988; see also Varese, Delgado and Meyer, this volume), although one can look to the constitutional amendment processes in Colombia (in 1991) and Bolivia (in 1994–99), for example, as evidence that even political elites in some countries were willing to consider the possibility that legal pluralism existed within their borders (Van Cott 2000). And this clearly is a promising avenue for future research and analysis, in particular because the international and transnational legal regimes that are becoming increasingly influential in Latin America – e.g. international human rights, commonly ratified instruments like International Labor Organization (ILO) Convention 169 – contain provisions that recognize and legitimate the fact of multiple and equal normative systems within sovereign nation-states.

The problem, however, is that most existing models for understanding legal pluralism are inadequate for Latin America. Because the study of legal pluralism is indelibly associated with the historical conditions of de jure legal pluralism in colonial Africa and southeast Asia, analyses have tended to impose an artificial and simplistic dichotomy on the actual complexity of legality within particular regions. This is reflected in a long line of debates over "legal levels" or the relationship between "state law" and "customary" or "folk law." Although it is doubtful whether these debates produced anything of enduring analytical value even for the specific cases to which they were directed, there is no question that they can tell us almost nothing about legal pluralism in Latin America. But instead of categorizing law into "levels" or distinct and competing "systems," an anthropological approach to law in Latin America shows that legality is distinct in its totality in relation to other (nonlegal) systems of meaning, yet internally diffuse, nonlinear, and, despite all ideology to the contrary, nonhierarchical. How, for example, would it ever be possible to assert that "state law" – which is itself not a monolithic normative entity – is paramount in a country like Bolivia, where for a large majority of the population symbols of state law are at best only one part of much larger legal repertoires, one source of normative tools in what is a highly dynamic marketplace of legal ideas?

Perhaps the best alternative framework for understanding legal pluralism in Latin America is that used by Boaventura de Sousa Santos (1987, 1995) to describe legality in Pasagarda, a pseudonymous favela in Brazil. His approach to legal pluralism is described as "interlegality." As he explains, this

> is not the legal pluralism of traditional legal anthropology, in which the different legal orders are conceived as separate entities coexisting in the same political spaces, but rather, the conception of different legal spaces superimposed, interpenetrated and mixed in our minds, as much as in our actions, either on occasions of qualitative leaps or sweeping crises in our life trajectories, or in the dull routine of eventless everyday life. We live in a time of porous legality or of legal porosity, multiple networks of legal orders forcing us to constant transitions and trespassings. Our legal life is constituted by an intersection of different legal orders, that is, by *interlegality*... Interlegality is a highly dynamic process, because the different legal spaces are nonsynchronic, and thus result in uneven and unstable combinations of legal codes (codes in a semiotic sense)... Such a conception of legal pluralism and interlegality calls for complex analytical tools. (Santos 1995:473; emphasis in original)

The move to interlegality provides anthropologists and others with a theoretical tool that is nearly complex enough to capture the multiplex, multidimensional reality of legal pluralism in Latin America; in particular, as posed by scholars such as Boaventura de Sousa Santos, interlegality assumes that fine distinctions between legal practice and legal imaginings are false distinctions. Anyone who has spent much time conducting participant-observation in legal forums – whether state courts or the house of a village official who has legal responsibilities – knows that such sites are more than just the locations people must come to in order to have disputes resolved. They are not just legal "spaces," i.e. locations where law is done. These areas are legal "places," sites of negotiation over legal (and nonlegal) meanings and identities, places that are understood by legal actors often primarily through their emotions and memories of rights and obligations. Indeed, by conceptualizing law in such terms, it is often difficult to see where law begins and ends. A Latin American legal pluralism conceptualized in this way is both permanently shifting, and potentially subversive.

## SUBALTERN POLITICS IN A NEW REGISTER: RIGHTS MOBILIZATION AND THE COMING OF RIGHTS NGOs

Over the last 20 years, there has been a profound transformation in the way subaltern populations in Latin America understand the nature of a set of long-term problems, locate themselves socially and morally in relation to these problems, and envision the possibilities for redressing them. At broad levels there are patterns to social problems throughout Latin America: rural people constantly struggle to maintain access to productive land and other basic resources, like irrigable water; hereditary, military, and business elites conspire to preserve stark inequalities in wealth; the military is employed by elites against those who would organize to protest economic and social injustice; a rural to urban continuum exists in which rural areas – with the exception of those which are unusually productive for some reason – are systematically deprived of a proportional share of national resources; in nations with large indigenous or Afro-Latin American populations, endemic racism and a discourse of whiteness reinforce ethnic and class hierarchies; and in large cities, parallel sovereignties have emerged within which coteries of the marginalized and oppressed seek to meet basic human needs at the same time they strive for more – a modicum of dignity.

For much of the 20th century, there was really only one type of framework within which programs for social change in Latin America had any meaning and validity: those derived from anticapitalist social theory, whether Marxist, socialist, anarcho-syndicalist, social democratic, Maoist, Trotskyist, or social millenarianist. Despite the range of expressions, what united these attempts to alter the direction of Latin American economy and society was their fundamental antiliberalism. Motivated, in part, by the violence of the civil, guerrilla and counterinsurgency wars of the 1980s and 1990s, however, subaltern populations across the entire range in Latin America have come to anchor their programs through appeals to the inherently liberal language of human rights (see chapters by Rojas-Perez and Sanford, this volume). At the same time, however, indigenous movements in Mexico, Bolivia and elsewhere have also actively intervened to reshape human rights discourse through concepts of economic and collective rights, which serve as a check on the ontological (and ethical) primacy of the individual as the bearer of rights in liberal philosophy, and challenge the absolute necessity of understanding and then resolving social problems in terms of individual rights and obligations.

In other words, the same discursive spaces that are created by the growth and influence of human rights in social practice – that is, apart from the enactment of international human rights instruments in national legislation – simultaneously reinforce a preexisting normative framework in which rights are the foundation for the accumulation of private property. The implications of this discursive tension have already become apparent in one area: the complex relationship between the rights of indigenous peoples and intellectual property rights (see Greaves 1994; Hayden 2003; see also Hayden, this volume). While indigenous peoples throughout Latin America have adopted a rights framework to prosecute old claims by asserting rights in culture, land, and local knowledge practices, this same framework provides the legitimacy for normalizing such countervailing developments as the rise in transnational biomarkets, the capitalization and then commodification of indigenous knowledge – e.g. the infamous Kayapo–Body Shop experiment (Turner 1995) – and, in what amounts to the dissolution of the orthodox legal distinction between persons and things (Pottage and Mundy 2004), the movement toward reifying (and thus commodifying) the blueprint for human life itself.

Yet despite the unacknowledged dilemma created by the emergence of human rights discourse as a supplemental paradigm for struggle and resistance in Latin America, anthropologists, and their co-subjects and collaborators have used this reframing of social problems to transform more than simply the possibilities for emancipatory social practice. There has also been a corresponding shift in anthropology's relationship to human rights more generally, which was originally stimulated by research and activism in Latin America. The best example of this can be seen through the institutional history of the American Anthropological Association's Committee for Human Rights, which emerged through the activities of a small group of professional anthropologists, indigenous activists, and nongovernmental associations active primarily in indigenous Amazonia. The culmination of these activities was the 1999 Declaration on Anthropology and Human Rights, which, apart from its epistemological significance for the anthropological engagement with human rights, reflected the fact that the AAA had become a human rights NGO active in Latin America, and elsewhere (AAA 1999). This development reflected a major transition within professional anthropology after several decades of anthropological indifference to human rights following the defense of a cultural relativist position vis-à-vis human rights in the 1947 AAA Statement on Human Rights (AAA 1947). This shift by the world's largest association of professional anthropologists paralleled much more modest, but similar, collaborations between anthropologists, human rights activists, and local leaders in places like Mexico, Bolivia, Colombia, and Guatemala (see Sanford, this volume).

Although very few anthropologists have made the emergence of human rights discourse in Latin America a topic for ethnographic and critical inquiry, rather than simply a vehicle for ethical engagement (but see Goldstein 2004; Goodale 2002a, 2008; Postero 2007; Speed 2007) there are now several important new spaces for investigation. First, anthropologists of law in Latin America must study the mid-range effects of the rise of human rights discourse, particularly to see whether or not subaltern populations are experiencing greater exploitation at the same time as they employ what can be a powerful legal framework for the recognition of local grievances. Second, because the rise of human rights discourse in Latin America has been so exponential – facilitated in part through the ongoing intervention of an array of (mostly) western European NGOs – anthropologists have the opportunity to use research and reflection on these shifts in legal consciousness and identity in order to contribute to wider understandings of the globalization of human rights more generally. In this sense, like Sally Merry's (2006) work on "localizations" of human rights in other parts of the world, anthropologists can study the finely grained effects that are the result of the introduction and reworking of the transnational normative framework of "human rights." Finally, anthropologists of law in Latin America who study human rights will continue to develop new epistemological contexts within which research and nonacademic ethical engagement relate to each other in innovative ways.

## LEGAL ETHNOGRAPHY IN UNSTABLE PLACES

If law in Latin America can be usefully understood as a system of representations that mediate the production of a range of other social meanings, then anthropologists should also be able to provide a sense of the contexts in which law functions. In a recent volume that explores the uncertainty, and possibility, associated with ethnographies of "unstable places," Kay Warren (2002) argues that an anthropology of "fragments, instabilities, and incomplete transitions" is an innovative response to the decentering of the nation-state and a corresponding rise in ethnic violence, sociocultural transgression, and the volatility of transnational capital and labor markets. An anthropology of instability requires researchers to resist the tendency to become "complicit in the misrepresentation of normative...politics as stable systems." To do this, anthropologists must continue to scrutinize intellectual conjurings that produce a "world of bounded units," whether they appear as islands of political authority, or as the more circumscribed planes of culture (2002:380–381). The result is an ethnography of interstices: the spaces between periods of political consolidation and (neo)liberal hegemony, the gaps that open up within liberalism's master narratives. And an engaged anthropology reconceptualized in this way is also deeply, though critically, collaborative (Hale, this volume); anthropologists and other social actors work together to create new expressive genres that "capture the contradictory currents of change, changing social fields, and the failure of state institutions and older models of citizenship in the face of difficult transformations and transitions" (Warren 2002:391).

The critical pursuit of instability also demands that anthropologists reconsider the assumption, which anthropological theory – and social theory more generally – has tended to share with liberal ideology (in Latin America and elsewhere), that social identity across the range rests on the intactness of social and political structures. Although this point is not typically framed in precisely this way, the idea is central to anthropological studies of political and social violence in Peru (Degregori 2003), the constitution of collective memory in the wake of profound social disruption (del Pino 2003; Sanford 2003), and in attempts to use anthropology to come to terms with the "fragmentation of experience" that accompanies a near-permanent sense of public helplessness in the face of protracted conflict (Jimeno 2001). Moreover, as Warren confirms for Guatemala, social actors throughout Latin America are compelled to perform culture within a state of permanent and "dramatic political change," and this constant structural dynamism rises to the level of social-ontological transformation, so that the practice of everyday life can no longer be measured by degrees of distance from a kind of social or political steady state, but must be reconceptualized in such a way that "dramatic" change is allowed to occupy a benchmark role in both ethnographic research and sociocultural theory. It should be emphasized that this framework for studying and reflecting on the relationship between social practice and political change is not a version of historical materialism in postnationalist clothing;

rather, it reflects the synthesis of a maturing critique of transnationalism and translocalism with a broader reconsideration of ethnography as the methodology of social transformation *par excellence* (see Goodale 2002a, 2006a, 2006b).

But the argument for an ethnography of instability in Latin America is not simply innovative as applied to engaged research in the political spaces "crossed by colonialism, war, and [the]...new national and transnational arrangements" (Greenhouse 2002:11). An ethnography of instability is also an argument for a radically different framework within which legality in Latin America can be understood. More obvious recent events in Latin America – the Americanization of the longstanding civil war in Colombia, the fight between the Brazilian government and indigenous peoples over resource extraction in the Amazon, the struggle against child plantation labor in the Dominican Republic, the campaign of the EZLN (Zapatista National Liberation Army) to rethink how politics is done, or the Bolivian electorate's rejection of an unholy alliance between national elites and transnational capital – suggest new instabilities associated with failed political and economic transitions. The idea of permanent incompleteness, however, also gives new, even if paradoxical, meaning to the anthropological account of law. Despite the fact that official state and jurisprudential orthodoxy maintain that "law," to be legitimate, must serve as the bedrock that sustains Latin American societies at their most basic levels, especially when all else fails or is in transition, law in contemporary Latin America is as fragmentary as political and economic systems. Because law and legal institutions are fragmented, they are necessarily unstable; in other words, law in Latin America is dynamic (not the timeless codification of natural or divine principles), multiplex (not monolithic, as in the "rule of *the* law"), and contingent (not the predictable result of either political or intellectual processes).

Yet I diverge here from an analysis of instability in Latin America that locates this social fact only in relation to the periods of "large-scale drama" that characterize postconflict societies or those still struggling with the dislocating effects of post- or neo-colonialism. I argue instead that fragmentariness in Latin America reflects a basic fact of legal ontology, and one, moreover, that is most readily apparent to the anthropologist studying the lived experience of law through its many trajectories, most of which are not spectacular, but are rather simple extensions of ordinary social actors' identities and interests. Indeed, to the extent that legal *stability* is created in Latin America, it is often to be found in periods of political and social high drama, as, for example, during the epochs of military rule, when an artificial and (often) brutal legal singularism is imposed on populations. This is not to say, of course, that everyday life in Latin America should not be understood through ethnographies of the extra-ordinary, particularly when the exceptional and spectacular are actual expressions of profound social trauma and disarticulation, or when social actors transform them into what Warren describes as the "symbolism of subordination" (Warren 1989). But if instability is to serve as a replacement framing device for ethnographic analyses of the warp and woof of law's registers in Latin America, it must be instantiated where it is most explanatory, which is at the points where law intersects with social practice, or, even more, where law becomes a basic articulation of it.

Legal ethnography in unstable places in Latin America – which are, to be clear, simply the places were law is done – reveals perhaps something even more unexpected than the fact that instability describes the essential condition of law from Columbia's constitutional court (García Villegas 1993) to the creation of sociolegal categories in Chiapas (Collier 2002). It also suggests that the permanent fissures created by imperfectly integrated legal jurisdictions, the practical impotence of centralized orthodox jurisprudence, and the impact of transnational legal and human rights discourses do not simply lead to a kind of neutral structural dynamism. Rather, these legal interstices also emerge as spaces of intense (if undramatic) contestation and latent social transformation. This last point needs underscoring: although it is true that the fragmentariness of law in Latin America creates ever present conditions for subaltern resistance to large-scale structural injustice, equally important is the fact that legal instability constitutes the means through which what Laura Nader (1981) has called "little injustices" can be meaningfully addressed in thousands of rural hamlets, urban favelas, and neighborhood associations and *sindicatos*, as well as in the offices of provincial police officers. In other words, the anthropology of permanently incomplete legal transitions is also an anthropology of reversal, in which indigenous peoples, campesinos, miners, and the urban poor are able to employ a wider range of legal strategies than their elite counterparts, whose experience of law is often more constrained by geography, social class, and the burdens of privilege. This is not to say, of course, that in times of extraordinary social drama the subaltern do not find themselves subject to the often violent power of a suddenly rigid set of legal instrumentalities. But this possibility, I would argue, only serves to underscore the more general pattern of legal disarticulation that provides historically marginal populations in Latin America with the ability to position themselves strategically, reinforce social identities, and to push beyond the constraints of region and nation to engage with potentially empowering transnational ideas and practices.

## THE CONSTITUTION OF LAW

Recent anthropological studies of law in Latin America contribute to an emergent framework within which the relationship between legality and illegality, order and violence, urban and rural, and even center and periphery, can be more productively understood. Legal identity in Latin America, like identity more generally, is constituted in part through the juxtaposition of formal oppositions. Orthodox legal doctrines reflect this conceptual alignment in the way that social acts are judged and social actors located in relation to standards of right conduct; that is to say, people are normatively either inside *or* outside the law. I should emphasize that this is not an empirical description of actual social practice, of the complex ways in which people move between these two normative poles, so that one can be both inside *and* outside the law, as Olivia Harris and contributors to her edited volume have argued (Harris 1996; see especially Bouysse-Cassagne 1996). But the constitution of legal identities is a social process that unfolds disjunctively: the seal of a notary public is either properly affixed to a contract for the sale of land, and thus the document – and associated transaction – is "legal"; or the stamp is improperly affixed (or omitted or secured at the wrong time in an established sequence) and thus the document (and underlying transaction) is rendered "illegal." A young man is accused by hamlet authorities in Bolivia's Norte de Potosí of disturbing the peace by brawling during a recent fiesta, during which a serious injury results. The young man is either brought, against his will if necessary, to the provincial *juzgado de instrucción*, where his case is heard after a police investigation, in which case he is "inside" the law; or hamlet authorities (especially the corresponding ayllu's *jilanqu*) consider his actions without bringing them to the attention of state officials, and, if he is found to be at fault, he is directed immediately to the hamlet whipping post, where he is vigorously whipped. In the latter the young man's social identity has – even if temporarily – been reestablished outside and against the law. Finally, a suspected thief is caught by locals in one of São Paulo's sprawling favelas. He is either taken to the nearest police precinct, which constitutes the "legal" response and locates the suspect within the law; or the man is dragged to the nearest lamppost and hanged by the neck – an act of normatively *illegal* community rage.

Yet even though law in Latin America is constituted dialectically, through the continuous contrast between the spaces of the legal and the spaces of the illegal, the actual social-normative content created through this process is not structurally determined, historically inevitable, or even fixed in relation to the two basic points within the broader system of representation designated as "law"; acts or norms that are considered "legal" can become "illegal," and vice versa. What is most important about this admittedly polemical framework within which ethnographic studies of law in Latin America can be most innovatively understood is that it reconceptualizes the relationship between legality and illegality without denying the discursive power of these seemingly diametrically opposed categories for ordinary social actors. In other words, the sociolegal theory grounded in current studies of law in Latin America makes the process through which legality and illegality emerge as opposed categories a main topic for ethnographic research and critical analysis. At the same time, it poses these categories as actually bound dialectically within the same normative system of representation.

To say this is not, however, to impose a rigid analytical structure on what is actually a much more complicated set of categorical relationships, which are, as I have already argued above, in constant relative motion, so that the legal and illegal as interconnected normative spaces are never finally established; they are, to connect with the last section, permanently incomplete. But this understanding does require a broader and less ideological view of some very consequential moments of violence and disrupture in Latin America. It also demands a clearer analysis of the way crimes and punishments are not simply predictable responses from actors either inside or outside the law, but are rather expressions of more fundamental networks of economic and social power that depend on the apparent permanence of legal concepts and categories.

A framework for studying and reflecting on law's meanings in Latin America that is reconceptualized in this way also demonstrates how difficult it is to adopt an approach that is overly concentric, in which social acts and actors are located at various absolute distances from "the law" – those ideas and practices that conform to a set of normative ideals. The possibilities and challenges of this analytical realignment can be seen through recent accounts of what, from the orthodox perspective (not reflected in the studies themselves), appear as actors or movements at the margins, meaning located at the blurred boundary that separates the legal from the illegal. Whether the particular case study involves the emergence of armed peasant patrols, like Peru's *rondas campesinas* (Starn 1999), or the surge in *linchamientos/ajusticiamientos* ("lynchings") in Bolivian periurban barrios (Goldstein 2004), or the growing sense of "security as a private matter" among subalterns in Brazil's urban shantytowns (Caldeira 2001), in each instance the "law" opens up to reveal interconnected and diverse types of normative praxis, rather than examples of social action that can be easily located in relation to "law."

A good recent ethnographic account of the way law is constituted dialectically in Latin America is Daniel Goldstein's compelling analysis of lynchings on the outskirts of Cochabamba, Bolivia, in which performative violence enacted in the local (and, through the media, national) public sphere expresses both subaltern resistance and conformity. As Goldstein explains:

> Vigilante lynchings in Cochabamba are more than just attempts at vengeance, efforts to satisfy individual or collective psychological cravings for reprisal...They also must be seen as expressive moments in the lives of people historically silenced, denied avenues to communicate their demands or to lament their conditions to an audience that might be able to offer them official redress. Lynchings in this context are not merely parallel justice systems intended to substitute for the inadequate enforcement of state law; nor can they be seen simply as "mob violence"...Lynchings are also spectacles, intended to catch the eye of an inattentive state and to perform for it visually and unmistakably the consequences of its own inaction. (2004:182)

What emerges from Goldstein's analysis is a complicated portrait of social and normative life among Cochabamba's poor and disenfranchised. On the one hand, community members in the district of Villa Pagador know that lynchings of suspected criminals violate national law, and they also have an acute sense that lynchings are taken by the Bolivian middle classes and elites as evidence of the "inherent viciousness of the people" who employ them to dramatic effect. But on the other hand, as in other parts of Bolivia – urban and rural – where the state and its instrumentalities have all but been evacuated, people in Villa Pagador have been left to create strategies of social control, and constitute modes of practice with real normative status, through means that are both "illegal" and "legal" at the same time. It is true that the most narrowly defined conception of "law," that is, one based on legitimate state institutions capable of enforcing rules, would deny any normative validity to the mobilizations of community violence that Goldstein describes. Yet an orthodox and jurisprudential approach does not bring us any closer to understanding the meanings of lynching, nor their function in what could be understood as a locally emergent ethical theory (an ethical theory that is far removed, it is true, from the liberal political theory that animates current Bolivian policies). Moreover, the community ritual associated with what Goldstein calls "spectacular violence" is highly aestheticized. When a "carnival" of illegality is the method through which the powerless attempt to create order from chaos, it is clear that the anthropologist does not gain from pursuing in isolation the discourse of the "rule of law" or "due process"; more illuminating is to study the system of representation that encompasses both lynchings and elite responses to them.

## CONCLUSION: THE SOCIAL PRACTICE OF LAW IN LATIN AMERICA

Anthropological studies of law in Latin America demonstrate how unproductive it is for the researcher or cultural critic to artificially distinguish between legal theory – or law "in the books" – and legal practice, the unsystematic range of efforts to create order out of the wide gap between official law and the messiness of everyday life. Close ethnographic, ethnohistorical, and critical attention to normativity in Latin America reveals the richness of what is an integrated sociolegal practice, in which social actors create locally meaningful codes of conduct and systems of values that are derived from multiple – and contested – conceptual sources, including transnational legal regimes, national legal codes, "customary" legal principles, and, as important, what can be understood as a perpetually emergent "vernacular jurisprudence." These diverse theoretical strands are woven together *through* the course of individual and collective agency, a social process that is both potentially emancipatory and fraught, at times, with danger. In other words, in order to better understand the social practice of law in Latin America, anthropologists, activists, and others must continue to search for the meanings of "law" where they are to be found: at the intersections of "legality" and "illegality," legal theory and practice, violence and peace.

## REFERENCES

AAA (American Anthropological Association) (1947) Statement on Human Rights (by the Executive Board of the American Anthropological Association). *American Anthropologist* 49:539–543.

AAA (American Anthropological Association) (1999) Declaration on Anthropology and Human Rights. Executive Board, American Anthropological Association, June.

Bouysse-Cassagne, T. (1996) In Praise of Bastards: The Uncertainties of *Mestizo* Identity in the Sixteenth- and Seventeenth-Century Andes. In O. Harris (ed.), *Inside and Outside the Law: Anthropological Studies of Authority and Ambiguity* (pp. 98–124). London: Routledge.

Caldeira, T. (2001) *City of Walls: Crime, Segregation, and Citizenship in São Paulo*. Berkeley: University of California Press.

Collier, J. (2002) Analyzing Witchcraft Beliefs. In J. Starr and M. Goodale (eds), *Practicing Ethnography in Law: New Dialogues, Enduring Methods* (pp. 72–86). New York: Palgrave/St Martin's Press.

Conklin, B. A. and Graham, L. R. (1995) The Shifting Middle Ground: Amazonian Indians and Eco-politics. *American Anthropologist* 97:695–710.

Da Matta, R. (1987) The Quest for Citizenship in a Relational Universe. In J. Wirth, Edson de Oliveira Nunes, and Thomas E. Bogenschild (eds), *State and Society in Brazil: Continuity and Change* (pp. 307–335). Boulder: Westview.

Degregori, C. I. (ed.) (2003) *Jamás tan cerca arremetió lo lejos. Memoria y violencia política en el Perú*. Lima: Instituto de Estudios Peruanos.

del Pino, P. (2003) Uchuraccay. Memoria y representación de la violencia política en los Andes. In P. del Pino and E. Jelin (eds), *Luchas locales, comunidades e identidades*. Madrid: Siglo XXI de España Editores.

García Villegas, M. (1993) *La eficacia simbolica del derecho. Examen de situaciones colombianas*. Bogotá: Ediciones Uniandes.

Goldstein, D. (2004) *The Spectacular City: Violence and Performance in Urban Bolivia*. Durham, NC: Duke University Press.

Goodale, M. (2002a) Legal Ethnography in an Era of Globalization: The Arrival of Western Human Rights Discourse to Rural Bolivia. In J. Starr and M. Goodale (eds), *Practicing Ethnography in Law: New Dialogues, Enduring Methods* (pp. 50–71). New York: Palgrave/St Martin's Press.

Goodale, M. (2002b) The Globalization of Sympathetic Law and Its Consequences. *Law and Social Inquiry* 27:401–415.

Goodale, M. (2006a) Ethical Theory as Social Practice. *American Anthropologist* 108:25–37.

Goodale, M. (2006b) Toward a Critical Anthropology of Human Rights. *Current Anthropology* 47(3):485–511.

Goodale, M. (2008) *Dilemmas of Modernity: Bolivian Encounters with Law and Liberalism.* Stanford: Stanford University Press.

Greaves, T. (ed.) (1994) *Intellectual Property for Indigenous Peoples: A Sourcebook.* Oklahoma City: Society for Applied Anthropology.

Greenhouse, C. (2002) Introduction: Altered States, Altered Lives. In C. Greenhouse, E. Mertz, and K. Warren (eds), *Ethnography in Unstable Places: Everyday Lives in Contexts of Dramatic Political Change* (pp. 1–34). Durham, NC: Duke University Press.

Griffiths, J. (1986) What Is Legal Pluralism? *Journal of Legal Pluralism* 24:1–56.

Guevara Gil, A. and Thome, J. (1992) Notes on Legal Pluralism. *Beyond Law* 5:75–102.

Hale, C. R. (1997) Cultural Politics of Identity in Latin America. *Annual Review of Anthropology* 26:567–590.

Harris, O. (ed.) (1996) *Inside and Outside the Law: Anthropological Studies of Authority and Ambiguity.* London: Routledge.

Hayden, C. (2003) *When Nature Goes Public: The Making and Unmaking of Bioprospecting in Mexico.* Princeton: Princeton University Press.

Iturralde, D. (1990) Movimiento indio, costumbre juridica y usos de la ley. In R. Stavenhagen and D. Iturralde (eds), *Entre la ley y la costumbre. El derecho consuetudinario indígena en América Latina* (pp. 47–63). Mexico City: Instituto Indigenista Interamericano.

Izko, X. (1993) Etnopolitica y costumbre en los Andes bolivianos. In A. Wray (ed.), *Derecho, pueblos indígenas y reforma del estado* (pp. 183–206). Quito: Abya Yala.

Jimeno, M. (2001) Violence and Social Life in Colombia. *Critique of Anthropology* 21:221–246.

Macas, L. (1994) An Interview with Luis Macas. *Multinational Monitor* 15:21–23.

Malagón Barceló, J. (1961) The Role of the *Letrado* in the Colonization of America. *The Americas* 18:1–17.

Merry, S. E. (1988) Legal pluralism. *Law and Society Review* 22:869–896.

Merry, S. E. (2006) *Human Rights and Gender Violence: Translating International Law into Local Justice.* Chicago: University of Chicago Press.

Nader, L. (1981) *Little Injustices: Laura Nader Looks at the Law.* 60 min. videocassette. Boston: Public Broadcasting Associates.

Pasara, L. (1988) *Derecho y sociedad en el Peru.* Lima: Instituto de Estudios Peruanos.

Poole, D. (2004) Between Threat and Guarantee: Justice and Community in the Margins of the Peruvian State. In V. Das and D. Poole (eds), *Anthropology in the Margins of the State* (pp. 35–65). Santa Fe: School of American Research Press; Oxford: James Currey.

Postero, Nancy Grey (2007) *Now We Are Citizens: Indigenous Politics in Postmulticultural Bolivia.* Stanford: Stanford University Press.

Pottage, A. and Mundy, M. (ed.) (2004) *Law, Anthropology, and the Constitution of the Social: Making Persons and Things.* Cambridge: Cambridge University Press.

Rappaport, J. (1994) *Cumbe Reborn: An Andean Ethnography of History.* Chicago: University of Chicago Press.

Sanford, V. (2003) *Violencia y genocidio en Guatemala.* Guatemala City: F & G Editores.

Santos, B. de S. (1987) Law: A Map of Misreading. Toward a Postmodern Conception of Law. *Journal of Law and Society* 14:279–302.

Santos, B. de S. (1995) *Toward a New Common Sense: Law, Science and Politics in the Paradigmatic Transition.* New York: Routledge.

Santos, B. de S. and García Villegas, M. (eds) (2001) *El caleidoscopio de las justicias en Colombia.* Bogotá: Colciencias–Instituto Colombiano de Antropología e Historia.

Speed, S. (2007) *Rights in Rebellion: Indigenous Struggle and Human Rights in Chiapas.* Stanford: Stanford University Press.

Starn, O. (1999) *Nightwatch: The Politics of Protest in the Andes.* Durham, NC: Duke University Press.

Stephen, L. (1995) Women's Rights Are Human Rights: The Merging of Feminine and Feminist Interests among El Salvador's Mothers of the Disappeared (CO-MADRES). *American Ethnologist* 22:807–827.

Stern, S. (1982) *Peru's Indian Peoples and the Challenge of Spanish Conquest: Huamanga to 1640.* Madison: University of Wisconsin Press.

Turner, T. (1995) Neoliberal Ecopolitics and Indigenous Peoples: The Kayapo, the "Rainforest Harvest," and the Body Shop. *Yale School of Forestry and Environmental Studies Bulletin* 98:113–127.

Van Cott, Donna Lee (2000) *The Friendly Liquidation of the Past: The Politics of Diversity in Latin America.* Pittsburgh: University of Pittsburgh Press.

Warren, K. (1989) *The Symbolism of Subordination: Indigenous Identity in a Guatemalan Town.* Austin: University of Texas Press.

Warren, K. (1998) *Indigenous Movements and Their Critics: Pan-Maya Activism in Guatemala.* Princeton: Princeton University Press.

Warren, K. (2002) Toward an Anthropology of Fragments, Instabilities, and Incomplete Transitions. In C. Greenhouse, E. Mertz, and K. Warren (eds), *Ethnography in Unstable Places: Everyday Lives in Contexts of Dramatic Political Change* (pp. 379–392). Durham, NC: Duke University Press.

Wright, R. M. (1988) Anthropological Presuppositions of Indigenous Advocacy. *Annual Review of Anthropology* 17:365–390.

CHAPTER 12 Borders, Sovereignty, and Racialization

*Ana M. Alonso*

Scholars recently have proposed that Latin American Studies be reconceptualized in order to deal more adequately with current, hemisphere-wide processes – massive transnational migration, globalization, and the workings of US hegemony – which cannot be captured by traditional spatial scales. Carlos Rico Ferrat, a Mexican intellectual and diplomat, argues that Mexico is a "Latin North American nation" because its history has been shaped by transnational forces and forms of integration (Thelen 1999). Anthropologist Lynn Stephen suggests that we "work with the concept of 'The Américas' to incorporate areas that have been geographically divided into North America, South America, and the Caribbean" (Stephen 2005). At the same time, scholars of regions such as the American Southwest are adopting a transnational perspective; the Greater Southwest is also Greater Mexico (Brady 2000). A critical pan-Americanism seems to be emerging, offering scholars an opportunity to "scale things differently" (Brady 2000) and to rethink "many of the categories and assumptions that have underlined the theoretical developments, research agendas and even the methodologies" of Latin Americanist anthropology (Stephen 2005).

This chapter is written from a pan-Americanist point of view. Hemisphere-wide processes are not solely a contemporary phenomenon; hence I adopt a historical perspective which emphasizes the *longue durée*. Instead of privileging the center, I foreground the periphery. This allows me to highlight and interrogate similarities between key works in the Anglo-American anthropology of non-Indian Mexican Americans and Mexicans in novel ways. In this chapter, I read William Madsen's 1964 book *The Mexican-Americans of South Texas* (Madsen 1973) in relation to long-term cycles of contested sovereignty, racialization, and nation formation in the US–Mexico borderlands. I read Oscar Lewis's *The Children of Sánchez* (1961) in relation to caricatures of Mexicans whose genealogy lies in the border area, to a long history of US violations of Mexican sovereignty, and to Mexico's mestizo nationalism.

Today the borderlands consists of the 960,000 square miles comprised by the ten border states in the US and Mexico. Borderlands scholarship has been dominated by regional perspectives; the significance of the area to understanding broader processes of US and Mexican nation formation has been largely ignored. Yet the very existence of bounded national space is predicated on that of the borders which define and contain it. The US–Mexico borderlands has been a key site for the construction of American and Mexican nationalism – both products of a contrapuntal relationship linked to struggles over sovereignty. This region, "where the United States and Latin America have interacted with one another most intensely" (Martínez 1996:xiii), has been the most important flashpoint in struggles over sovereignty between Mexico and the US. The border features prominently in the US government's most egregious violations of Mexican sovereignty. During 1835–36, the US supported the cause of Texas independence from Mexico, annexing Texas in 1844. After the Mexican–American War of 1846–48, the US acquired approximately half of Mexico's territory – almost one million square miles. The US intervened in the Mexican Revolution of 1910–20 on more than one occasion, attacking and occupying Veracruz in 1914, and sending the Pershing Punitive Expedition across the border in 1916 in pursuit of the revolutionary Pancho Villa

State sovereignty is commonly defined as entailing authority as well as a monopoly of violence within a territory. However, state authority and control over violence in border areas are not only "multidimensional but highly variable" (Thomson 1994:9; Alonso 1995b), often challenged by bandits, rebels, and vigilantes. From a border perspective, sovereignty is not an attribute but rather, an ongoing and variable project of states and of groups which is more or less realized in practice. In addition, as Hansen and Stepputat argue (2005), the state is not the only "sovereign body." Other territorially based sociopolitical bodies – from Indian nations to corporate communities – also compete for sovereignty both in relation to each other and to the state. Rights to resources, property and territory are key stakes in these struggles which are often legitimated by ethnocentric distinctions between "us" and "them," "here" and "there." Since at least the 19th century, US nationalism has proclaimed the superiority of whites versus Indians, Asians, blacks and Mexicans, while the supporting ideology of Anglo-Saxonism has stressed the merit of pure races over hybrids. This ideology has located Anglos at the center and other groups – internal others – at the margins of the nation. Moreover, it has also been the basis for a hemispheric hierarchy of sovereignty which contradicts the Westphalian ideal. The US has accorded full sovereignty to itself and Canada (the "developed," "civilized" nations) while denying it to "underdeveloped" Latin American nations. The long history of US intervention in the internal affairs of Latin American nations makes this more than obvious.

Hobbes, one of the most influential theorists of the modern state, "sharply divides the spatial dimensions of the world between … a realm of sovereignty and law and … a 'state of nature'" and violence (Robinson 2003:5). Rights to property and resources are accorded to those who submit to the sovereign and are categorized as "civilized," just as they are denied those who will not submit and are categorized as unpropertied "barbarians" living in a "state of nature." Such a vision of the state (and the binary oppositions it posits between law and violence, order and chaos, civilization and barbarism, property and "empty land," has long underpinned borderlands' struggles over sovereignty – among colonial powers, between the settler colonists and Indians, between Anglos and Mexicanos, and between the US and Mexico. By focusing on the making of the borderlands, the anthropological lens can help to break down assumptions of geographic stability and allow us to see the organization and representation of space as products of shifting social relations and power struggles. In this sense, anthropology has a particular contribution to make to "scaling things differently."

## CYCLES OF CONQUEST AND ETHNO-RACIAL FORMATION IN THE BORDERLANDS

The borderlands has never been a stable geographical entity. Instead, it has been an unstable product of multiple struggles for sovereignty initiated by the arrival of the Spanish to Northern New Spain in the 16th century (Martínez 1996:xv). Following Mexican Independence in 1821, the borderlands became *el Norte*, Mexico's North. After the US annexation of Texas in 1844, and its conquest or purchase of half of Mexico's territory in 1848 and 1854, large parts of *el Norte* became the American Southwest. Each of these broad cycles of conquest and colonialism – the Spanish, the Mexican and the Anglo – can in turn be broken down into finer periods.

Borderlands' "cycles of conquest" (Spicer 1981) have also been cycles of ethno-racial formation (Menchaca 2001). Ethno-racial formation is a historical product of structural inequality, not a natural outcome of cultural or phenotypical differences (Alonso 2004). Categories such as "Anglo" and "Mexican" are not foundational; instead they are the product of processes of colonialism buttressed by the ideologies of Anglo superiority such as "Manifest Destiny," an expression originally coined in 1845 by the journalist John O'Sullivan to justify the US annexation of Texas (O'Sullivan 1845a; see also 1845b). Manifest Destiny held that "Anglo-Saxons" should bring democracy and progress to "lesser" peoples by conquering their territory and usurping their property; only then would these lands become productive (Acuña 2000). Anglo-Texans, for example, claimed that Anglo-Saxon enterprise, perseverance, moral worth and democratic ideals had turned Texas from the "boundless wilderness" it had been under Mexican rule into "a country of population and worth" (Kökény 2004). Not only did Anglos introduce a new property regime which did not respect communal lands and resources, and which reduced land to a commodity, but also, they actively broke their own laws in order to dispossess Mexicans and indigenous peoples of their lands (Hernández 2001; Montejano 1987).

Though Anglo-American stereotypes of Mexicans did not arise exclusively in the border region (Weber 1988:161), this area was key to their development and to the colonialism they legitimated. Manifest Destiny justified Anglo colonialism of the borderlands: the ethnocide of Indians, the enslavement of blacks, and the economic dispossession and political marginalization of Mexicanos in what had once been their country (Acuña 2000; Hernández 2001; Montejano 1987; Martínez 1996, 2001; Menchaca 2001). Ironically, Anglo-Americans racialized Mexicans (Weber 1979; Hietela 1997; Gutiérrez 1993; Anderson 1998; Menchaca 2001) in terms very similar to the ones Mexicans had earlier applied to the *indios bárbaros*; now they were the barbarians (Alonso 1995b; Nugent 1993).

The discourse of Manifest Destiny conflated national origin and race. Anglos considered themselves to be "at the top of the great chain of being" and placed Africans, Native Americans and Mexican "mongrels" at the bottom (Hietela 1997:52). Anglos' views of Mexicans drew on the "Black Legend" which alleged that "Spaniards possessed an unusual number of serious character defects such as extreme cruelty, treachery, pride, fanaticism, cowardliness, corruption, decadence, and authoritarianism" as well as "indolence" (Weber 1979:62, 1988:161–167; Gutiérrez 1993). Yet Anglo politicians, writers, officers and soldiers used similar adjectives to stigmatize both Mexicans and Indians. This suggests that such views were also shaped by Western notions of property which were "deeply invested in a colonial geography, a white mythology in which the racialized figure of the savage plays a central role (Blomley 2003:124). "Whether 'savages' or 'greasers,' the lesser breeds appeared lazy, treacherous, dull and backward. They occupied valuable lands they neither appreciated nor developed. They had no concept of good government, no grasp of science and technology, no work ethic, no respect for real religion" (Hietela 1997:53). Because of their relative "weakness" (so the story went), Native Americans and Mexicans would be unable to halt the "juggernaut" of Anglo-American Progress (Hietala 1997). Nor could they stop the march of liberty, according to the 1836 Texas Declaration of Independence. From the perspective of the signatories, "political separation" from Mexico was the Texans' only choice since "the Mexican people have acquiesced in the destruction of their liberty … they are unfit to be free and incapable of self-government" (reproduced in Martínez 1996:16; see Kökény 2004). Ironically, these "unfree" Mexicans had legally abolished slavery, while the freedom-loving Texans wanted independence so that they could overturn Mexico's laws and reinstate slavery.

Many Anglos attributed Mexican "weakness" to the racial "degradation" consequent upon miscegenation between Spaniards and Indians (Weber 1988:160–162; Gutiérrez 1993; Martínez 1996; Vélez-Ibáñez 1996:72–75). For example, in 1846 the editor of the *New York Herald* characterized the Mexican–American War as a struggle of the pure Anglo-Saxon race against the "imbecility and degradation of the Mexican people":

> The idea of amalgamation has always been abhorrent to the Anglo-Saxon race on this continent. Wherever they have spread themselves, they have kept aloof from the inferior races, and the result is … that barbarism has receded before the face of civilization. It is the manifest destiny of the Anglo-Saxon race to people this vast continent. (Cited in Hietala 1997:53)

The clearest statement of "Anglo-Saxonism" was written by Josiah Strong a few decades later, in 1885. In *Our Country*, Strong (1963) argued that due to their "genius for colonizing," and their persistent energy and vitality, Anglo-Saxons were destined to conquer the entire world.

Conquest and its accompanying warfare are frequently construed as a testing ground for masculinity, as a struggle between men in which women are the tokens. In 1848, Sam Houston, the hero of the Texas War of Independence and a staunch proponent of American territorial expansionism, salaciously advised Anglo men to "annex" Mexican beauties (Greenberg 2005:88). Although it was destined to crush Mexican men, the "juggernaut" of American expansion might spare the señoritas. Some Anglos thought that miscegenation between Anglo men and Mexican women was acceptable since their "pure blood" would overcome the defects of a lesser heritage.

Not only were these views widespread in the 19th century but they continued into the 20th (Vélez-Ibáñez 1996), invoked to justify the American invasion of Mexico during the Revolution of 1910–20 and, as the editorial cartoon in figure 12.1 suggests,

**Figure 12.1** John T. McCutcheon, "Civilization Follows the American Flag," *Chicago Daily Tribune*, April 23, 1914.

to encourage the US conquest of Mexico. John T. McCutcheon, one of the most famous American political cartoonists, was stationed in Veracruz during the US occupation in 1914. In the top register of his cartoon, McCutcheon employs many of the stereotypes discussed here in order to portray the borderland states of Mexico prior to American conquest. The states, personified as Mexican men, are represented as indolent, ignorant and debased, as is evinced by the men's slack posture, dirty, tattered clothes, and downcast gazes. These men clearly lack a work ethic or enterprising spirit. Notice that the cruelty, authoritarianism, thievery and violence attributed to Mexican men and in particular, to Mexico's leaders, is symbolized by the gun and whip in the hands of the bandit figure on the far right.

The second register of the cartoon presents quite a contrast. Here the borderland states are under American dominion. The Anglo-Saxon men who personify them look you straight in the eye, unlike their shifty counterparts in the first register. They are upright, enterprising and prosperous citizens, shining examples of American manhood. Only the *bandido* personifying Mexico remains in a degraded state. As this cartoon makes evident, the stigmatization by Anglos of Mexican masculinity was part of the process of racialization linked to US expansionism (Greenberg 2005; Weber 1988).

"Anglo" and "Mexican" were part of a broader set of categorical distinctions which included "black," "Indian," and different types of Asians (Montejano 1987; Gutiérrez 1993; Menchaca 2001). Prior to the US conquest, many of the borderlands Mexicanos had emphasized their Spanish descent. The Treaty of Guadalupe Hidalgo specified that Mexicans who chose to remain on the US side of the border could become American citizens (Menchaca 2001; Saldaña-Portillo 2004). Since only whites could become citizens, Mexicans in states such as Texas were classified as "other white race" for legal purposes (Wilson 2003). In 1930 "the Census Bureau enumerated Mexicans as a separate race, specifically, as persons born in Mexico, or with parents born in Mexico, and who were 'not definitely white, Negro, Indian, Chinese, or Japanese'" (Wilson 2003). In the face of the Mexican government's objections, "the 1940 Census reclassified persons of Mexican descent as 'white' if they were not 'definitively Indian or of other nonwhite race'" (Wilson 2003). However, the conflation of nationality and race in everyday practice put into question Mexican Americans' status as citizens. As late at the 1960s one could find Anglos saying things such as "The Meskin's not a white man but he's a hell of a lot whiter than a nigger" (cited in Madsen 1973:13).

Class dynamics crosscut the distinction between Anglos and Mexicans (Vélez-Ibáñez 1996). In some areas of Arizona (Sheridan 1986), northern New Mexico, (Montgomery 2000) or southern California, for example, Anglos married into the old borderlands elite or developed business and commercial ties with its members (Carrigan and Webb 2003; Vélez-Ibáñez 1996:59–60). Some of Texas's Mexican elite even supported the cause of Texan independence (Weber 1988:145–146). Claiming descent from the original Spanish colonists and emphasizing their purity of blood, these Hispanics became the beneficiaries of the flip side of the Black Legend, that is, the romance of Spanish colonialism and Old Mexico (Montgomery 2000; Carrigan and Webb 2003; Sheridan 1986; Lloyd 1986). Though they were also targets of discrimination, some of these "descendants of the Conquistadors" escaped the worst forms of exploitation and oppression (Montgomery 2000; Carrigan and Webb 2003).

Mexican laborers – dispossessed and marginalized descendants of the pre-1848 population as well as subsequent immigrants – were discriminated against as members of a "mongrel" race. They suffered the ill effects of agrarian dispossession, labor market segmentation, and political disenfranchisement, as well as residential, educational and religious segregation (Acuña 2000; Vélez-Ibáñez 1996; Montejano 1987; Hernández 2001). Segregation operated through informal mechanisms which fostered "social apartness" (Menchaca 2001), evinced in the attitude of one Anglo-Texan who did not want Mexicans in her church: they "don't dress well you know, and they eat garlic. I think it might cheapen our church if they worshipped there" (cited in Madsen 1973:65).

Mexicanos did not accept these changes passively. Many contested Anglo colonialism, drawing on the "weapons of the weak." Some turned to social banditry or outright rebellion, leading to decades of insurgency and counterinsurgency on the border, particularly in California and Texas (Hoefle 2004). Anglos construed resistance as crime; Mexicans, they argued, were "a cruel and treacherous people with a natural proclivity toward criminal behavior" (Carrigan and Webb 2003:419). Rebels were merely "bandits." This made them legitimate targets of law enforcement agencies such as the California or Texas Rangers. During counterinsurgency operations in 1915, Texas Rangers shot or hung as many as 5,000 Mexicanos, many of them American citizens (Vélez-Ibáñez 1996:75). Mexicanos were lynched by Anglo mobs while law enforcement agencies looked the other way (Carrigan and Webb 2003; Martínez 1996:143). Lynching was one of the ways in which Anglo sovereignty and economic control over the borderlands was asserted (Carrigan and Webb 2003).

Negative views of Mexicans – as feminized, lazy peons or hypermasculine, violent bandits – spread beyond the borderlands. The offensive "sleeping Mexican" stereotype has even made its way into contemporary, nationally syndicated cartoons. For example, in a cartoon printed in the *Arizona Daily Star* on February 6, 2006, an Anglo retiree can only take a nap when he puts on a Mexican sombrero and serape.

## EVERYDAY RACISM, CARICATURE, AND BANDITS

Anglos and Mexicans are not homogeneous social groups with mutually exclusive cultures; rather, they are ethno-racial groups which have formed in relation to categorical distinctions. These groups are internally stratified by class, location, generation, gender, and other axes of social difference. There can be considerable sharing of cultural repertoires across these ethno-racial boundaries even though each group holds on to its emblematic customs. In addition, social relations among individuals classed as "Anglo" or "Mexican" do not always conform to the social apartness enjoined by orthodox discourse. In practice, these ethno-racial distinctions are applied in context-specific ways. However, the breaching and blurring of boundaries does not entail their dissolution. Those who have disproportionate access to cultural, social, political and economic capital do not easily give up their privileges. Hence, ethno-racial boundaries are continually reinforced by violence, by institutional means, by spatial apartness, by labor market segmentation, as well as by seemingly innocuous everyday practices. Such forms of everyday racism include "disparagement humor" (Ford and Ferguson 2004), expressed in jokes, mock Spanish (Hill 1993), or caricatures.

A caricature is an "exaggerated or debased likeness" which can be grotesque or ludicrous (*Oxford English Dictionary*) but may also be "cute." Caricatures play an important role in ethno-racial formation. By turning people into "types," caricatures can represent social groups through a few exaggerated, easily reproducible elements. By portraying the stigmatized as grotesque, debased, or simply silly, caricatures normalize and elevate the image of the racializing group.

Weber points out that Mexican men, rather than women, were the main focus of Anglos' negative stereotypes (1988:155–158). Since the middle of the 19th century, the cruel and sinister "bandit" has been a common Anglo image of Mexican men. By "breaking the law," bandits challenge state sovereignty. Bandit images proliferated during the Mexican Revolution and particularly after Pancho Villa's 1916 attack on Columbus, New Mexico. In the editorial cartoon in figure 12.2 (reprinted in Rich and De Los Reyes 1996:137), for example, Uncle Sam is elevated over a grotesque image of Pancho Villa as an infantilized bandit, a naughty Mexican child, who won't take his medicine even if it is "for his own good" (the title of the cartoon). Uncle Sam has no choice but to force the "pacification pill" down the recalcitrant bandit's throat: "Come on! You've got to take it sooner or later and you might as well take it now." "Pacification" here is tantamount to US intervention, invasion or even "annexation" of Mexico, as is implied by the sign on the wall, "Civilization follows the flag." Now clean and well-dressed, Uncle Sam's already "pacified" sons, the Philippines, Panama, Nicaragua and Cuba, look on in amusement. With the exception of the Philippines, these "civilized," Americanized children have fair complexions and Caucasian features. The assumptions behind this cartoon are those of the 1904 Roosevelt Corollary to the Monroe Doctrine which maintained that as the "policeman" of the Western hemisphere, the US had the right to intervene in the affairs of any Latin American country engaged in "chronic wrongdoing." It also illustrates the gendered imagery of US imperialism: Uncle Sam is the epitome of hegemonic masculinity, the paternal statesman who knows how to correct the misbehavior of unruly, dirty boys and maintain order in the body politic.

McCutcheon's caricatures of Mexico and Mexicans are tinged with sadism. Caricatures provide an acceptable way to express and enjoy largely unconscious emotions about the "Other"; these include contempt, disgust, hostility, and hatred. Ford and Ferguson (2004:82) have found that people are more apt to enjoy violent images or behavior when these are cast in a humorous light. Humor gives permission to members of the racializing group to make light of their mockery (Ford and Ferguson 2004:83; Hill 1993). Caricatures of the Mexican bandit changed over time in relation to the salience of insurgency and counterinsurgency in the border area and to the character of US–Mexico relations. Beginning in 1933, Franklin D. Roosevelt instituted the "Good Neighbor Policy" which eschewed armed intervention and stressed

**Figure 12.2**   John T. McCutcheon, "For His Own Good," *Chicago Daily Tribune*, 1916.

cooperation with Mexico and other Latin American countries. Mexico joined the Allies during the Second World War; the Bracero Program, which brought thousands of Mexican laborers to replace Americans fighting overseas, was seen as Mexico's contribution to the war effort. The policy of cooperation led the US State Department to ask Hollywood to create more positive images of Latinos. Disney's *Saludos Amigos* (in 1943) and *The Three Caballeros* (in 1944) were a response to this demand. The Mexican caballero was "Panchito Pistoles," a pistol-toting rooster dressed in *charro* attire, who guides Donald Duck through fun-filled adventures in sunny Mexico such as Donald's crazed pursuit of Acapulco beach babes.

Caricatures such as Panchito Pistoles and the 1950s Speedy Gonzalez are examples of what I call soft or "cute racism," which has a paternalist, and sometimes even affectionate, component. Denial of racism is most plausible when the caricature is "cute." Children are often taught racism through cute caricatures and other forms of visual and verbal play. Though some of these caricatures may not be consciously considered to be racist by the targeted group, others, such as the Frito Bandito, become objects of enduring controversy.

The happy-go-lucky, singing and dancing "Frito Bandito" was used to advertise Frito's corn chips in the 1960s. Frito had a huge handlebar mustache, a big, friendly smile and "cute" proportions (compare him to "Hello Kitty," a near universal example of Japanese kitsch). His supersized sombrero boasted a bullet-hole at the top. His chest was crossed with cartridge belts containing ammunition for the revolvers on either side of his waist.

Frito is an infantilized version of the stereotypical Mexican bandit, one whose masculinity has been cut down to size. Indeed, he is probably a caricature of the Mexican revolutionary Pancho Villa, who was infantilized in the 1916 cartoon by McCutcheon discussed earlier. Infantilization of racialized groups allows the adult members of the racializing group (whose judgment is implied to be "more adult") to laugh at their fears. Infantilization renders the Other "harmless"; since the harmfulness of such images is occluded, they are considered "appropriate for children." Because "cute racism" appears to erase prejudice, it facilitates its covert transmission.

Frito had his own "wanted poster"[1] which stated that he was a thief who was sneaky and hard to catch. "He loves cronchy Fritos corn chips so much he'll stop at nothing to get yours. What's more, he's cunning, clever and sneaky!" The use of *cronchy* here is an example of soft linguistic racism, as is Frito's heavily accented cute trash English (he says "keeds" instead of "kids," "dem" instead of "them"). Though the cuteness takes the edge off, the association of "trash English" with Mexicans for an implicitly Anglo audience still indexes the purported inferiority of Mexicans, lack of education, intelligence and "culture" and the alleged superiority of Anglos and their language. "Bandito," like other "mock Spanish" terms is an instance of what Jane Hill calls "incorporation" whereby qualities of the "Other" are domesticated and appropriated by the dominant group (Hill 1993). Like other symbols of the sunny South – big hats, burros, guitars, margaritas, señoritas with roses between their teeth – Frito gives Anglos permission to be uninhibited, mischievous and fun-loving.

Frito erases a history of Mexicano resistance, sanitizing bloody border insurgency and counterinsurgency. Yet many Anglos do not understand why the Mexican Anti-Defamation Committee found the "cute" Frito Bandito offensive and why it called for a ban on the bandit in 1970. How caricatures are perceived depends, among other things, on whether the viewer is or is not a member of the targeted group (Ford and Ferguson 2004; Hill 1993). Indeed, the Bandito is now an object of nostalgia for

Anglos. Frito T-shirts, boxer shorts, thongs, mugs, coasters, refrigerator magnets, and mousepads are for sale on the web and originals are very collectible.[2]

As in the case of racist caricatures of blacks such as "mammy," or "sambo," Frito, the "sleeping Mexican," and others, such as the Kahlua liqueur bottle señorita, are domesticated "Others," part of the material culture of day-to-day life. Like other forms of disparagement humor, these everyday objects, consumed and used by whites, create "a normative climate of tolerance of discrimination" (Ford and Ferguson 2004:79). These objects are still with us today.

Anyone living in the Southwest of the US is familiar with the wide range of objects which bear the image of the "sleeping Mexican" peon, face covered by his big sombrero, back leaning against a cactus; these include light-switch plates, lamps, Edwin Knowles crockery, leather purses, restaurant neon signs, plant pots and salt and pepper shakers. Anglos often do not see these objects as racist; indeed some claim that they demonstrate their affection for things Mexican. Some Mexican Americans would agree; everyday racism is sometimes not even visible to those who are its targets. But others say they cannot understand why another Mexicano would have "sleeping Mexican" objects in their home: "It's like saying Mexicans are lazy and you are *flojo* too."

## "What you learned about Mexico you probably got from Speedy Gonzalez" (*The Mexican*, 2001): Caricaturing, Racialization, and Scholarship

Scholars do not mechanically reproduce orthodox discourses or caricatured images of the Other simply because they are members of the dominant group. However, their writings are inevitably in dialogue with racializing rhetoric and images that are part of the universe of discourse. Many Anglo scholars have engaged such rhetoric in order to criticize it. They have answered back. However, as Gutiérrez (1993) points out, others have let caricatured images of Mexicanos creep into their work. As late as 1979, one American historian argued that European and American assessments of the Spanish and Mexican Californios as "indolent" were not based on racism, but instead on reality, since they had "developed an especial depth to the *mañana* habit" (Langum 1978:196). More recently, S. P. Huntington (2004) has alleged that Mexican Americans suffer from the "*mañana* syndrome."

Scholarly caricatures are serious rather than humorous, but they are still exaggerated and grotesque representations of the Other. They debase the targeted group while implicitly elevating the image of the dominant group and purging it of negative characteristics. The "macho" is one of the most common caricatures in the Anglo-American anthropology of Mexico and Latin America. Homogenized, flat, and wholly negative depictions of machismo are instances of cultural racism which recall the ubiquitous Anglo caricature of the bandit.

Chicano scholars (Rosaldo 1985:406–409; Romano 1967) consider William Madsen's ethnography *The Mexican-Americans of South Texas* to be heavily impacted by cultural racism. Menchaca (1997) provides an apt summary of his point of view: "Madsen argued that Mexican-American culture was the root cause of their inability to succeed in America. ... Allegedly their cultural core – which was composed of familism, Catholicism, honor, and machismo – led these people to behave dysfunctionally." These core cultural traits purportedly explained the different class positions of Anglos and Mexicans: "Anglo financing and planning carried out by Latin labor transformed this remote outpost of Mexican culture into a prosperous and thriving area" (Madsen 1973:8). This sentence could have come straight out of the Texas Anglo-Saxonism of the 19th century (Kökény 2004).

Apparently, only Mexicans have problematic masculinities. According to Madsen, machismo creates lines of tension outside the family, promoting conflict among men who are sensitive to offense and ready to use physical violence to avenge slurs on their honor. This alleged combination of low self-esteem and exaggerated assertion of masculinity is both a product and a cause of family dysfunction. In their role as fathers, machos are supposedly "authoritarian"; they are harsh, distant and violent toward their sons and this has negative consequences for the sons' personality development (Madsen 1973:54–55). Husbands govern all aspects of their wives' behavior and have a culturally recognized right to beat them for disobedience; wives supposedly enjoy such violence (Madsen 1973:20–23).

The norm for Madsen is an idealized Anglo masculinity organized around enterprise, rationality and profit (recall McCutcheon's cartoon above). Implicitly contrasting Mexican men with this ideal, Madsen reduces them to a caricature which fuses the stereotype of the "bandit" and the "indolent" Mexican. Mirande (1986) points out that such a portrayal of machismo is based on meager evidence. Gutman (1997) calls into question this negative and falsely homogenized view of Mexican masculinity, arguing that there are many different ways of being a man in Mexico.

In my own archival and ethnographic research in rural Chihuahua, I investigated the complexity of Mexican masculinity compared to the caricature of machismo (Alonso 1995b). Wife-beating in Chihuahuan villages as well as in Hispano communities of New Mexico was generally considered a cowardly abuse rather than a masculine right (Alonso 1995a; Deutsch 1987). Mexico's 1871 Criminal Code permitted wife-beating to be prosecuted as a punishable crime and provided for the arrest of violent husbands (Alonso 1995a). In contrast, wife-beating was largely regarded as a private matter in the US until the 1970s, and Congress did not pass the "Violence against Women" Act until 1994 (Prah 2006). Historians Deutsch and Arrom challenge the widespread idea that Mexican women suffered more ill-treatment than American women in the 19th and early 20th centuries (Deutsch 1987; Arrom 1998). Indeed, Hispano and Mexican women had legal and social advantages US Anglo women did not. Arrom points out that the 19th century Mexican legal system gave women more rights to property than they had in England or the US (Arrom 1998). Daughters inherited equally and married women had a right to half of the community property. Deutsch's work on New Mexican Hispano families from 1880 to 1940 shows that decision making was a joint affair and that women enjoyed a high degree of respect and autonomy (Deutsch 1987). Other work has emphasized the complexity and heterogeneity of contemporary Chicano households and family relations (Vélez-Ibáñez 1996; Zavella 1987).

## FROM THE DEGENERACY OF RACE TO THE PATHOLOGY OF CULTURE

Beginning in the 1920s, American intellectuals such as Franz Boas criticized the notion that physical differences among human populations had any sociological significance. He and his students Margaret Mead and Ruth Benedict spearheaded the rise of the concept of "culture," which replaced "race" as a way of explaining human differences. Each culture was thought to be integrated by its own configuration of psychological themes and traits which shaped child socialization and led to the formation of distinct types of "social personality."

Culture and personality typologies replaced racial typologies, substituting cultural essentialism for biological reductionism. Anthropologists who worked for the intelligence services during the Second World War extended the culture and personality approach to "national character studies" in order to help the American military understand the "mind" of the enemy. Such studies naively reproduced stereotypes about national cultures and the "modal personality structure" purportedly identified with them (Bock 2000).

Not much of a leap in logic was required to apply these ideas to the understanding of "ethnic" differences, conceived of as cultural differences between social groups. The assumption was that social inequalities in American society would be overcome as outgroups came to accept the Anglo-Saxon values of the American middle class through a process of cultural assimilation (Cayton and Williams 2001). Social science studies of Mexican Americans during the 1960s and 1970s provided a scientific rationale for cultural racism: "an overwhelming number of them depicted Mexican values as not only opposite to American values but detrimental to achievement by Mexicans in the United States" and hence, "inferior" (Vélez-Ibáñez 1996:84). These studies had a huge impact on educational policy, which tried to divest Mexican Americans of their language and culture (Vélez-Ibáñez 1996:85). Such assimilationist attitudes give the lie to the idea that the concept of culture is necessarily a more progressive way of accounting for human differences than the concept of race.

Comparing and contrasting the lot of European immigrants with American blacks or Mexican Americans, scholars such as W. Lloyd Warner (Warner and Srole 1945) began to think about class as a factor shaping assimilation. Poverty, conceived in cultural rather than structural terms, came to be seen as the obstacle to ethnic/racial assimilation by social scientists as well as policy-makers. Accordingly, during the 1960s and 1970s, the lack of "advancement" of racially oppressed groups was attributed to their "dysfunctional" family structures and patterns of child socialization, which were thought to generate pathological personality traits (US Department of Labor 1965). Like caricaturing, this schematizing approach reduced "personality" to a few exaggerated though recognizable elements.

## Oscar Lewis's Caricature of the Mexican Lumpenproletariat

Anthropologists, such as William Madsen and Oscar Lewis, discovered pathology in other cultures' configurations of "traits" and the typical personalities linked to them. Indeed, there are striking similarities between Madsen's characterization of Tejano culture and Oscar Lewis's depiction of the "culture of poverty" in *The Children of Sánchez*:

> Some of the social and psychological characteristics include…a high incidence of alcoholism, frequent resort to violence in the settling of quarrels, frequent use of physical violence in the training of children, wife beating, early initiation into sex, free unions or consensual marriages … a strong predisposition to authoritarianism, and a great emphasis on family solidarity – an ideal only rarely achieved. Other traits include a strong present time orientation with relatively little ability to defer gratification and plan for the future… a belief in male superiority which reaches its crystallization in machismo or the cult of

masculinity, a corresponding martyr complex among women, and finally, a high tolerance for psychological pathology of all sorts. (Lewis 1961:xxvi; see Rigdon 1988 for a longer list of traits)

Lewis's theory of the culture of poverty has been the object of numerous commentaries and critiques (see Rigdon 1988 for an overview; for recent commentary see Aceves Lozano 1994; Díaz Barriga 1994). According to Lewis, who was influenced by the national culture theories of both Ruth Benedict and Lloyd Warner (Rigdon 1988), groups characterized by the culture of poverty were not only lower class but also largely people of color – blacks, Mexicans, Puerto Ricans and Native Americans (Briggs 1998:91). Culture of poverty theory, as outlined by Lewis and applied by others to Mexican Americans or American blacks, was implicitly grounded in ethnic/racial stereotypes which it helped to perpetuate (Rosaldo 1973; Briggs 1998). As McCarthy and Yancey conclude, in their attempts to portray "the negative consequences of caste victimization, social scientists have ... unwittingly provided scientific evidence for white held stereotypes" (1971:648–649). But how could this be? Most of these social scientists were liberal antiracists. Part of the problem lay in their assumptions about normative and pathological cultural and personality traits.

The pathological is defined, either implicitly or explicitly, as a departure from an ideal norm. Reading between the lines of *The Children of Sánchez*, it seems that Lewis unthinkingly took an idealized image of middle class culture to be the norm (see document 66, Rigdon 1988:228–229). Lewis's image of the white middle class was just as distorted as his view of the poor. Income and class "are far less significant factors than he had assumed in the incidence of domestic violence, child abuse, incest, alcoholism," drug abuse, and free unions or unstable marriages (Rigdon 1988:120; Dunaway et al. 2000).

Since Lewis was a socialist, critics are often surprised by his views, expecting them to be more enlightened. Yet, in addition to Benedict's configurationalism and Lloyd Warner's views on ethnicity and race, Lewis was also influenced by Marxism. I suspect that the reason more commentators have not picked up on this aspect of Lewis's intellectual genealogy is that Lewis, like other left intellectuals who were followed by the FBI in the US, telegraphed his Marxism, relying on key terms and allusions rather than on explicit statements. "Lumpenproletariat" is one of these key terms.

In the "Introduction" to *The Children of Sánchez*, Lewis identifies the culture of poverty with the "lumpenproletariat" rather than the working class (1961:xxv). For Karl Marx (who coined the term): "The lumpenproletariat were those who were propertyless, unemployed and whose methods of earning a living placed them outside the productive process. In addition, Marx described them as having a distinct attitude, morality and mental state: they did not want to work, they were thieving" (Hayes 1988). Marx's notion of a distinctive lumpen morality and mental state provided one of the bases for Lewis's culture of poverty theory, with its emphasis on values, traits and psychological characteristics.

As a self-proclaimed humanist, Lewis eschewed doctrinaire views, calling himself "an eclectic materialist" (Rigdon 1988:2). Though he recognized the importance of economic factors, he was more interested in the cultural traits and psychological dispositions that reproduced poverty (document 66, Rigdon 1988:228). Above all, he wanted to put a human face on poverty through an "ethnographic realism" that would purge anthropology from its technical jargon and draw on the representational techniques of novelists. Lewis considered this to be anthropology's "new historic task" (document 48, Rigdon 1988:219–220). According to Lewis, this would result in "a much more profound and balanced picture of the lower class than was provided us by Friedrich Engels and other nineteenth century researchers" (document 51, Rigdon 1988:221).

Lewis was uncertain as to how to improve the lot of the lumpen: he "waffled on the question of whether radical or reformist solutions" were best (Rigdon 1988:155). He thought a reformist solution was possible in the US. For example, he recommended that the Johnson administration fund "psychiatric therapy for the poor" implemented by "middle class people" who had undergone sensitivity training (Rigdon 1988:154). As he grew to understand that poverty was not merely an outcome of psychology and culture, Lewis moved from psychological to revolutionary solutions.

Whether or not the lumpenproletariat should or should not be considered a revolutionary force was a matter of debate in Marxist and socialist circles. In *The Communist Manifesto* of 1848, Marx described the lumpen as the "'dangerous class,' the social scum, that passively rotten mass thrown off by the lowest layers of the old society." Nevertheless, he conceded that "they could be swept into the movement by a proletarian revolution" (Marx in Tucker 1978:482). By 1852 Marx had changed his mind, since the lumpenproletariat had fought on the side of reaction in the French counterrevolution of 1848 (Marx in Tucker 1978:601). Mao Zedong's views were more optimistic; though he considered the lumpen to be dangerous, he also thought they were "great fighters" who could become a revolutionary force under the right guidance (Mao Zedung 1926).

In *The Children of Sánchez*, Lewis argued that the culture of poverty fostered a "critical attitude to some of the values and institutions of the dominant classes, hatred of the police, mistrust of government." Hence, it had a "counter quality and a potential for being used in political movements aimed at the existing social order" (1961: xxvii). In a letter to C. Wright Mills written in 1960, Lewis stated that "conditions are ripe for great social changes" (document 137, Rigdon 1988:271).

Lewis believed that the lumpen could become a revolutionary force under an authoritarian leader (Rigdon 1988:157), and that they could be liberated from their sad lot by socialism. In 1962 he wrote a letter to anthropologist Eric Wolf stating: "Once the poor begin to identify with larger groups or with larger causes, once they become class conscious or become socialists or Communists, they rapidly begin to lose ... the culture of poverty." Indeed, Lewis went to Cuba in 1969 with the hope of confirming that the Revolution of 1959 had destroyed the class system and hence, the culture of poverty (Rigdon 1988:99–100). He was disappointed to find that things were otherwise (document 146, Rigdon 1988:278–279).

Lewis's ideas about the lumpen were shaped not only by race and class but also by the values of a hegemonic masculinity organized around calculation, expertise, rationality, and self-restraint (Connell 1995). Members of the elite, in different times and places, have typically regarded the subordinated masculinities of the lower classes as dissolute, undisciplined, unruly and violent (Hughes 2004; Greenberg 2005). Lewis was no exception; he portrayed the "Mexican macho" as sexually rapacious, authoritarian, violent, lacking in self-control and unable to defer gratification or plan for the future.

One of the remarks of Jesús Sánchez, the patriarch of the family, suggests that the masculinity of the poor was characterized by more ambiguity, ambivalence and complexity than Lewis's caricature of machismo would lead us to believe:

> Yes, at times we men want to be very strong and very *macho*, but at bottom we aren't. When it is a question of morality or a family thing that touches the very fibers of the heart, it hurts and a man cries when he is alone.... And at times those who believe themselves to be machos are really not so when they are alone with their conscience. They are only braggarts of the moment. (Lewis 1961:5–6)

Unfortunately, Lewis accepted his informants' stories at face value, not considering that they might be braggadocio instead of unembellished truth.

Chicano and Mexican scholars have noted that Anglo anthropologists such as Lewis and Madsen interpreted literally informants' jokes and apocryphal stories about men and masculinity (Rosaldo 1985:409–410, 1987:74–75; Díaz Barriga 1994). Fidel Castro seems to have agreed. In a letter to sociologist Lowry Nelson, dated March 27, 1968, Lewis described Castro's reaction to *The Children of Sánchez*: "For example, he thought that Manuel [Jesús Sánchez's son] was a classic picaresque type and such a good story teller that it would be difficult to know when he was describing events and when he was just making up a good yarn" (document 144, Rigdon 1988:276).

In both New Mexico and Mexico, popular speech genres, including narrative, jokes and *el relajo*, were impacted by the picaresque tradition (Lamadrid 1995; Díaz Barriga 1994). The picaresque narrative was a comic genre which originated in Spain in the 16th century. *El pícaro* (or *el pelado* in Mexico) was an antihero, a womanizer, a rascal and an idler who would rather live by his wits than by work. To what extent were Manuel's stories shaped by such popular narrative traditions? To what extent was Lewis's portrayal of machismo based on a naive or even literal interpretation of such roguish stories? The Sanchez family had a radio. Was the narrative of Jesús Sanchez's daughter, Consuelo, shaped by the conventions of the melodramatic *radio-novela*? How might this have impacted Lewis's notion that poor Mexican women suffered from a "martyr complex"?

Lewis's caricature of Mexican lower class masculinity recalls the negative images of Mexican men in the rhetoric of Manifest Destiny. In *The Children of Sánchez*, Lewis does not link machismo to the degeneracy of racial and cultural mixing. But other anthropologists have done so. For example, in *Conflict, Violence, and Morality in a Mexican Village*, Lola Romanucci-Ross characterized her fieldsite as "mestizo – a mixture of racial and ethnic elements" which had "an internally varied culture based upon the partial, diluted and impoverished remains of both Indian and Spanish civilization" (1973:5–6). A notion of mixture as degeneracy underlies Romanucci-Ross's concern with conflict, morality and machismo. Eva Hunt takes exception to her one-dimensional and "biased" portrayal of machismo, "as a negative attribute, psychologically damaging, sociologically harmful, and culturally degrading" (Hunt 1975:948).

The negative portrayals of non-Indian or "mestizo" Mexicans in Anglo ethnographies ran contrary to Mexican nationalism. Nation-state formation in Mexico had to contend with the imperial designs of the United States, with the colonial legacy of ethno-racial inequality, and with the multiple sovereign bodies that characterized a country that had just been through a decade of social revolution (from 1910 to 1920). In contrast to Guatemala and Peru, two other countries with large indigenous populations which did not undergo successful popular revolutions, Mexico developed a distinct and much more stable form of popular sovereignty.

For the architects of post-Revolutionary nationalism, the sovereign popular subject was to be the *mestizo*, conceived as the ideal blend of the Spanish and Indian. The figure of the mestizo represented the transformation of heterogeneity into homogeneity, the bridge between the past and the future, the common origin point for the nation. The Indian element in the mestizo was to ground the nation's claim to territory, providing a continuity of blood, and rooting the nation's history in that of ancient, precolonial civilizations, whose art and mythology were praised as expressions of national spirit. By contrast, the European element was to guarantee the nation's future through its purportedly greater capacity for enlightened scientific knowledge (Alonso 2004).

This mythohisory of mestizaje emerged as a challenge to North American imperial ambitions, which, as discussed earlier, rested on a notion of Mexicans as a "mongrel race" purportedly incapable of governing themselves. Mestizo nationalism and pan-Americanism envisioned a Mexico and a Latin America which would play a significant role in world history, challenging the supremacy of the United States in the Americas and the superiority of Anglo-Saxon racial "purity" and culture (Alonso 2004). Not surprisingly, Mexican concerns about US annexation of its northern states during the 20th century "were fueled by American discrimination against Mexicans and Mexican-Americans" in the borderlands (Lomnitz 2005). Indeed, "the experience of discrimination in the United States has helped to sustain Mexican nationalism for a century and a half" (Lomnitz 2005).

Mexico's anthropological tradition was, from the beginning, an integral part of nation-state formation (see chapters by Nahmad Sitton and Walsh, this volume; see also Alonso 2004; de la Peña 2005; Krotz 1991; Lomnitz 2001). "Mexican antagonism to neocolonial attitudes on the part of North America" made the relationship between Mexican and US anthropologists a "sensitive" one (Gledhill n.d.).

Given the historical context, it is not surprising that *The Children of Sánchez*, published in Spanish in October 1964, became an object of great controversy in Mexico. In February of 1965, the venerable Mexican Society of Geography and Statistics (MSGS) filed a legal complaint in the Attorney General's Office, accusing Lewis, and the Mexican publisher which had brought out the Spanish translation, of breaking a number of federal laws regarding obscenity and defamation of Mexican institutions and ways of life (Rigdon 1988:289–293; Arriaga 1965). Lewis was also accused of fabricating data and of being a spy.

Manuel Arriaga Rámirez outlined the rationale behind the MSGS's accusation in a speech given on March 16, 1965, subsequently published as a pamphlet (Arriaga 1965). The MSGS had several problems with Lewis's book. First, the resemblance between Lewis's portrayal of Mexican "mestizos" and the rhetoric of Manifest Destiny did not escape the MSGS's members; they accused Lewis of defaming the Mexican nation and dragging its name, dignity and decorum through the mud (Arriaga 1965:22). Arriaga stated that Lewis had portrayed the Mexico of the humble classes as "imbued with misery, pain and sacrifice; with the poor all living in hovels, dedicating themselves to smoking marijuana and using drugs, to practicing fornication even in public market stands, barely covered by a blanket which leaves nothing to the imagination" (1965:24). Lewis had portrayed the Mexican poor in such false and negative terms so that he could "conclude that all of the political authorities in Mexico are a gang of bandits who must be eliminated ... and that this chaos would only come to an end when a US president comes to govern us and we are ruled by North American laws" (Arriaga 1965:24; see Lewis 1961:493–495). This was a direct attack on Mexico's "sovereignty"; Arriaga alleged that it might be linked to a broader conspiracy to destabilize Latin America, making it easy prey for US imperialist ambitions (1965:26). This may well be a reference to the infamous Project Camelot, run by the US Army and the Department of Defense, which recruited scholars to do research on the potential for insurgency and counterinsurgency, including American intervention, in nations in which the US had an interest (Solovey 2001).

Second, Lewis attributed the continuing poverty of the lumpen to the failures of the Mexican Revolution (Arriaga 1965:10; see Lewis 1961:xxviii–xxxi). Third, Lewis alleged that in the face of these failures, social unrest in Mexico was a likely outcome (Arriaga 1965:11; Lewis 1961:xxx–xxxi). Lewis was eventually cleared by the Mexican Attorney General's Office. However, similar charges were to dog his subsequent fieldwork. The publication in 1966 of his Puerto Rican family study *La Vida* "led to charges that the book was a slur on the Puerto Rican people and their culture" (Rigdon 1988:165). Lewis's Cuba project was terminated and his fieldwork materials were confiscated by the Cuban government in 1970; one of his main informants was sent to a labor camp as a political prisoner (Rigdon 1988:167).

The suspicions which dogged Lewis's research in Latin America were not unreasonable in the face of the long history of US intervention in the area. After all, "Latin American studies was created as a geographical discipline in large part to generate information that could be used in advancing US foreign policy and development interests," particularly during the cold war (Stephen 2005; Solovey 2001). With respect to Latin America, time and again the US violated the respect for the internal sovereignty of other states enjoined by the Westphalian vision of international order.

## CODA: A NEW CYCLE OF RACIALIZATION?

Globalization has increased the flow of labor across the US–Mexico border. The North American Free Trade Agreement, implemented in 1994, caused many small, rural producers in Mexico to go under. Since the mid-1990s, entire Mexican towns have been emptied of their able adult men. Globalization has also increased the demand for cheap labor in the United States; without it, business sectors claim, they will be unable to compete. Since "illegal aliens" have no legal rights, businesses can pay them the lowest wages. Like debt peonage or slavery, illegality is a mechanism used to secure a cheap and dependent labor force that can be superexploited and discarded at will (de Genova 2002).

The US government's border policy has been a result of contradictory imperatives. On the one hand, government policies seek to foster capitalist accumulation by maintaining access to cheap (illegal) labor and an open border. On the other hand, politics has come to rely more and more on the state's provision of "security" to its citizens through the defense of territorial sovereignty. "Security is not only the physical protection of a regime and its associated social order, but also a political function ... Without the state to ensure basic security," so the story goes, "there would be no civilization" and no nation (Bislev 2004:283).

Anglo nativists in the borderlands and their sympathizers feel betrayed by the federal government: they think it has left the border unsecured. They believe that the "flood" of "illegals" is imperiling all aspects of security in the border area. Mothers Against Illegal Aliens, a civic group formed in 2006, alleges that illegals are making it "unsafe to raise children in the United States" and undermining "the American family" (McCombs 2006:B1).[3] They allege that illegals carry diseases, such as tuberculosis and leprosy, and "dumb-down public education" (McCombs 2006:B8). Illegals are believed to pollute the environment, endangering the biosecurity of the border (Buchanan and Kim 2005). The shifting ethno-racial demographics of the border states is said to imperil the predominance of the superior values of Anglo-Protestant civilization which are responsible for order and prosperity. Illegals are supposedly "importing poverty," endangering economic security. They are accused of undermining the social fabric with their bad habits, poor morals and criminal behavior, threatening to drag everyone down to their level (Buchanan and Kim 2005). Though these claims may seem far-fetched, they are becoming increasingly mainstream as groups against illegal immigrants proliferate and attract new members. In Arizona alone in the spring of 2006, there were several of these groups: the Minuteman Civil Defense Corps, the American Border Patrol, Arizonans for Border Control, Border Guardians, and Mothers Against Illegal Aliens. The arguments they use resonate with those developed by such influential neoconservative intellectuals and policy-makers as Samuel P. Huntington (2004).

Since the 1990s, but particularly after 9/11, many inhabitants of the borderlands have been calling on the state to "secure our Southern border." National sovereignty is supposed to be at risk since Anglo nativists believe that Mexico is engaged in a demographic and cultural "reconquest" of the American Southwest. The Mexican–American war is being fought again, they claim. Some assert that the Mexican army is deliberately entering US territory in order to menace the nation's sovereignty. Others fear that Hispanics will rebel and form their own "Republic of the North" out of the borderland states (Moore 2002).[4] This fear of reconquest has a long history because Anglo sovereignty over the border area has never been wholly secure (Martínez 1996:xiv).

On nativist websites but also in news weekly articles the "unsecured border" is referred to as "ground zero," a border equivalent of the World Trade Center (Banks 2006). This reflects a sense of the border as a leaky container, with a fence as "full of holes as Swiss cheese"; anything might cross. Current fears even extend to the doings of "illegal cattle" (Banks 2006). Mexican cattle are supposedly crossing the border to "trespass" on American land and eat American grass, degrading pasture land, or worse, "mingling" with American herds. Like human illegal entrants, these "undocumented cattle" are thought to carry disease. Though there are no confirmed reports of foot-and-mouth disease in Mexico, nativists allege that "terrorists" could "inoculate" Mexican cows with the virus, turning them into weapons of bioterror (Banks 2006).

The struggle for Anglo-American sovereignty in the borderlands has entered a new phase. A powerful pro-immigrant movement, supported by more Latinos than Anglos, has emerged in response to nativism. At the same time, the border is being remilitarized. The rhetoric of low intensity warfare in the border area not only recalls that of Manifest Destiny, but also that of the current Iraq war. Popular Anglo stereotypes of Mexicans in today's borderlands echo those of the past, but with a new twist. Since the attack on the World Trade Center in September 2001, the figures of the Mexican "illegal" and bandit/smuggler are being linked metonymically to that of the Arab "terrorist," not only by the US Department of Homeland Security, but also by the increasingly numerous and vocal supporters of the new nativism. Some Anglos accuse Mexicans of smuggling Arabs across the border. Others believe that these smugglers themselves are Mexicans of Arab ancestry. Yet others worry that since Mexicans and Arabs supposedly resemble each other physically, Middle Eastern terrorists could pass as Mexican illegals (Buchanan and Kim 2005). The phrase "Arab machismo" has proliferated to such a point that it is even being used by scholars. For example, in a report for the liberal Center for Global Justice, historian Ross Gandy asserts that "the Spanish conquistadors stamped Arab machismo on Mexican culture" (Gandy 2005).

Beliefs linking Mexicans to Arabs are disseminated through numerous websites such as that of the Minutemen or the United Patriots of America.[5] These vigilante groups are actively recruiting armed volunteers to help secure the border, promoting a masculinity which equates freedom with the personal right to deploy violence. The negative potential of this form of masculinity is occluded by a vision which makes the Other, the Mexican-cum-Arab, the only barbarian.

In the face of these developments, we need to reexamine the celebrations of an oppositional borderlands "hybridity" inspired in the field of Cultural Studies by the writings of the chicana feminist Gloria Anzaldúa (1987). The US–Mexico border needs to be defined, however, not only in relation to the shared cultural repertoires and creative energies celebrated by Anzaldúa, but also with reference to structural inequality and "the massive state apparatuses of the boundary" (Heyman 1994:51). In addition, as Blomley emphasizes, "the establishment of colonial property regimes and the creation of the propertied world of the West inside the frontier have their violences" (2003:126)

The settler colonists of New Spain and Mexico fought indigenous groups for this land; they were conquerors who in their turn were conquered – by the Anglos. But the "mestizos'" role as colonial agents in borderlands history is suppressed by Anzaldúa. She draws on the rhetoric of "mestizaje" in constructing a folklorized, Aztec Indian voice as a source of authenticity for her own voice, erasing the real history of indigenous groups in the borderlands. Moreover, borderlands Mexicanos do not all identify themselves as mestizos. The Namiquipans of Chihuahua or the Hispanos of New Mexico and Colorado, descendants of the original frontier settlers, are strongly identified with their "Spanish" heritage and consider themselves to be *blancos* (Alonso 1995b; Nugent 1993; Vila 2000).

The complexity of identity formation in the border area is not captured by Anzaldúa's celebration of mestizaje and boundary crossing. As Vila (2000) points out, border residents have not just been simple "boundary crossers", they have also been "boundary reinforcers." Racism in the borderlands has never been just an Anglo attitude toward Mexicans. Racism toward Indians on the part of the frontier's settlers antedates the arrival of the Anglos. Moreover, today, racism distinguishes and divides whiter from the browner Mexicanos. This is because interculturality in itself does not promote tolerance – indeed the real complexity of cultural flows is often repudiated by the reinforcement of social boundaries through practices such as segregation which continue to characterize the border area.

"Culture" becomes problematic when it is severed from society, history and concrete human practice. Indeed, it becomes as pernicious as the concept of "race." This goes against the grain of established wisdom in anthropology, which insists that the concept of culture is more progressive than the concept of race. "Race" naturalizes social differences, rendering them immutable, while "culture" promises change. Yet change should not be valued uncritically, nor should "culture" be let off the hook. According to Seymour Hersh (2004), Raphael Patai's *The Arab Mind* of 1973, a classic of anthropological "national character studies," has been used to define American policy in Iraq and practices of torture in Abu Ghraib prison. This book has long been considered an indispensable bible on Arab behavior by the US military (O'Neil-Ortiz 2005).

National character studies were discredited by anthropologists in the 1970s, along with the theories of "culture and personality" on which they are based. Since then, they have been marginal to the discipline of anthropology. However, outside of anthropology, "culturalist interpretations of differential human development are back" (Maxwell 1997:137). Neocons such as Lawrence Harrison (2001) argue that cultural values, cognitive orientations and forms of child socialization account for the success of some nations and ethnic groups and the failure of others, including Latinos and Latin Americans. "The argument is that Anglo-Protestant culture encouraged thrift, education, merit, community, and work, whereas Catholic Iberian values and culture encouraged the opposite – sloth, corruption, backwardness, all the bad things that made Latin America stagnate while Anglo America grew" (Maxwell 1997:137). Sound familiar? Lewis's culture of poverty thesis has been updated and extended to the international level.

Harrison's close collaborator Samuel P. Huntington has recently provided an intellectual justification for resurgent Anglo nativism. In *Who Are We?* Huntington identifies Anglo-Protestant values as the "cultural core" of the American nation and argues that this core is under threat due to the increasing number of "Hispanics" in the US and their foreign, Catholic values. An understanding of border history demonstrates that Huntington's "cultural core" has its genealogy in the 19th century Anglo-Saxonism invoked to ennoble the bloody realities of the myth of Western expansion so central to Anglo-American sovereignty.

In this chapter, I show how the territorial politics of sovereignty at the US–Mexico border totalizes the imagined community of "Americans" and individualizes subjects through a binary logic of classification which situates persons as "citizens" or "illegals," "property owners" or "trespassers," "people like us" versus "criminals," "smugglers," "terrorists" or even "invaders." Stigmatized versus normalized categories of persons are racialized in different ways according to their degree of "brownness" or "whiteness," signified not only by phenotypical markers but also by signs of class and lifestyle. I stress that this politics has colonial roots and shows how subjectification, violence, and property have been interlinked in the conquest of the northern frontier of Mexico and in the militarization of today's border area.

As a "shifter," sovereignty can only be understood when situated in specific ethnographic and historical contexts. This is a task eminently suited to the fine lens of anthropology. Rather than taking sovereignty for granted, anthropologists might draw on ethnographic and historical methods in order to question the link between the state and sovereignty (Hansen and Stepputat 2005).

A border perspective on sovereignty can reframe important issues in current Latin American anthropology such as contemporary struggles for indigenous autonomy. If state sovereignty is an ongoing and multidimensional project, an outcome of social struggles and compromises rather than a given, it can be reconceptualized as partible instead of as absolute. Granting "autonomy" within states to indigenous groups need not be seen as a threat to sociopolitical order, but instead can be viewed as the result of a new social pact in which sovereignty is redefined and redistributed.

## NOTES

1  Unfortunately, Frito Lay would not give us permission to reproduce the wanted poster in this chapter. However, there are images of the wanted poster and other Frito paraphernalia on the web; use "Frito Bandito" to do a search.
2  At www.cafepress.com/bandito, accessed Feb. 18, 2006.
3  See also on the website of the group: www.mothersagainstillegalaliens.org/?page_id=7.
4  See also David Sadler's website, www.david-sadler.org/pages/news/immigrate/aztlan/aztlan.htm.
5  See www.minutemanhq.com/hq/ and www.unitedpatriotsofamerica.com.

## REFERENCES

Aceves Lozano, J. E. (1994) Oscar Lewis y su aporte al enfoque de las historias de vida. *Alteridades* 4(7):27–33.
Acuña, R. (2000) *Occupied America*. New York: Longman.
Alonso, A. M. (1995a) Rationalizing Patriarchy. *Identities* 2(1–2):29–48.
Alonso, A. M. (1995b) *Thread of Blood: Colonialism, Revolution and Gender on Mexico's Northern Frontier*. Tucson: University of Arizona Press.
Alonso, A. M. (2004) Conforming Disconformity: "Mestizaje," Hybridity and the Aesthetics of Mexican Nationalism. *Cultural Anthropology* 19(4):459–490.
Anderson, M. C. (1998) What's to Be Done With 'Em? Images of Mexican Cultural Backwardness, Racial Limitations, and Moral Decrepitude in the United States Press, 1913–1915. *Mexican Studies/Estudios Mexicanos* 14(1):23–70.
Anzaldúa, Gloria (1987) *Borderlands/La Frontera: The New Mestiza*. San Francisco: Aunt Lute Books.
Arriaga, M. (1965) *Dos libros sobre Mexico*. Mexico City: Sociedad Mexicana de Geografía y Estadistica.
Arrom, S. M. (1998) Mexican Women: Historical Perspectives. *DRCLAS News* (Winter). At www.fas.harvard.edu/~drclas/publications/revista/women/arrom.htm, accessed Mar. 8, 2006.
Banks, Leo D. (2006) A Matter of Numbers. *Tucson Weekly*, Jan. 19.
Bislev, S. (2004) Globalization, State Transformation, and Public Security. *International Political Science Review* 25(3):281–296.
Blomley, N. (2003) Law, Property, and the Geography of Violence: The Frontier, the Survey, and the Grid. *Annals of the Association of American Geographers* 93(1):121–141.
Bock, P. K. (2000) Culture and Personality Revisited. *American Behavioral Scientist* 44(1):32–40.
Brady, M. P. (2000) Scaling the West Differently. *Western American Literature* 35(1):97–104.

Briggs, L. (1998) *La Vida*, Moynihan, and Other Libels: Migration, Social Science, and the Making of the Puerto Rican Welfare Queen. *CENTRO Journal* 14(1):75–101.

Buchanan, S. and Kim, T. (2005) The Nativists. *Southern Poverty Law Center Intelligence Report* (Winter). At www.splcenter.org/intel/intelreport/article.jsp?aid=576&printable=1, accessed Mar. 8, 2006.

Carrigan, W. D. and Webb, C. (2003) The Lynching of Persons of Mexican Origin or Descent in the United States, 1848–1928. *Journal of Social History* 37(4):411–438.

Cayton, M. K. and Williams, P. W. (2001) Ethnicity and Race. In M. K. Cayton and P. W. Williams (eds), *Encyclopedia of American Cultural and Intellectual History*. New York: Scribner's Sons.

Connell, R. W. (1995) *Masculinities*. Berkeley: University of California Press.

de Genova, N. (2002) Migrant "Illegality" and Deportability in Everyday Life. *Annual Review of Anthropology* 31:419–447.

de la Peña, G. (2005) Social and Cultural Policies toward Indigenous People: Perspectives from Latin America. *Annual Review of Anthropology* 34:717–739.

Deutsch, S. (1987) *No Separate Refuge: Culture, Class and Gender on an Anglo-Hispanic Frontier*. New York: Oxford.

Díaz Barriga, M. (1994) El relajo de la cultura de la pobreza. *Alteridades* 4(7):21–26.

Dunaway, R. G., Burton, Jr, F. T., Evans, V. S., and David, T. (2000) The Myth of Social Class and Crime Revisited: An Examination of Class and Adult Criminality. *Criminology* 38(2):589–632.

Ford, T. E. and Ferguson, M. A. (2004) Social Consequences of Disparagement Humor: A Prejudiced Norm Theory. *Personality and Social Psychology* 8(1):79–94. At www.granma.cu/ingles/febrero02-4/9embajad-i.html, accessed Mar. 8, 2006.

Gandy, R. (2005) Mobilizing Latin American Women for the Fightback against Globalized Oppression. At www.globaljusticecenter.org/papers2005/gandy_eng.htm, accessed Mar. 10, 2006.

Gledhill, J. (n.d.) Autonomy and Alterity: The Dilemmas of Mexican Anthropology. At www.socialsciences.man.ac.uk/socialanthropology/documents/Gledhill_AutonomyandAlterity.pdf, accessed Feb. 28, 2006.

Greenberg, A. S. (2005) *Manifest Manhood and the Antebellum American Empire*. New York: Cambridge University Press.

Gutiérrez, D. (1993) Significant to Whom? Mexican Americans and the History of the American West. *Western Historical Quarterly* 24(4):519–539.

Gutman, M. G. (1997) The Ethnographic (G)ambit: Women and the Negotiation of Masculinity in Mexico City. *American Ethnologist* 24(4):833–855.

Hansen, T. B. and Stepputat, F. (2005) *Sovereign Bodies: Citizens, Migrants, and States in the Postcolonial World*. Princeton: Princeton University Press.

Harrison, L. E. (2001) Introduction. In L. E. Harrison and S. P. Hutchinson (eds), *Culture Matters: How Values Shape Human Progress*. New York: Basic Books.

Hayes, P. (1988) Utopia and the Lumpenproletariat: Marx's Reasoning in The Eighteenth Brumaire of Louis Bonaparte. *Review of Politics* 50(3):445–465.

Hernández, Sonia (2001) The Legacy of the Treaty of Guadalupe Hidalgo on Tejanos' Land. *Journal of Popular Culture* 35(2):101–109.

Hersh, S. (2004) The Gray Zone. *New Yorker*, May 24.

Heyman, J. M. (1994) The Mexico–United States Border in Anthropology: A Critique and Reformulation. *Journal of Political Ecology* 1:43–65.

Hietela, T. R. (1997) "This Splendid Juggernaut": Westward a Nation and Its People. In R. W. Johannsen et al. (eds), *Manifest Destiny and Empire*. College Station: Texas A & M University Press, University of Texas at Arlington.

Hill, J. (1993) "Hasta La Vista Baby": Anglo Spanish in the Southwest. *Critique of Anthropology* 13:145–176.

Hoefle, S. W. (2004) Bitter Harvest: The Frontier Legacy of US Internal Violence and Belligerent Imperialism. *Critique of Anthropology* 24(3):277–300.

Hughes, A. (2004) Representations and Counter-Representations of Domestic Violence on Clydeside Between the Two World Wars. *Labour History Review* 69(2):169–184.

Hunt, E. (1975) Untitled review. *American Anthropologist* 77(4):946–949.

Huntington, S. P. (2004) *Who Are We? The Challenges to America's National Identity.* New York: Simon and Schuster.

Kökény, A. (2004) The Construction of Anglo-American Identity in the Republic of Texas. *Journal of the Southwest* 46:283–308.

Krotz, E. (1991) A Panoramic View of Recent Mexican Anthropology. *Current Anthropology* 32(2):183–188.

Langum, D. J. (1978) Californios and the Image of Indolence. *Western Historical Quarterly* 9(2):181–196.

Lamadrid, E. R. (1995) The Rogue's Progress: The Picaro from Oral Tradition to Contemporary Chicano Literature. *Melus* 20(2):15–34.

Lewis, O. (1961) *The Children of Sánchez.* New York: Random House.

Lloyd, G. (1986) *The Californios.* Tucson: University of Arizona Press.

Lomnitz, C. (2001) *Deep Mexico, Silent Mexico.* Minneapolis: University of Minnesota Press.

Lomnitz, C. (2005) Mexico's Race Problem. *Boston Review* (Nov.–Dec.). At www.bostonreview.net/BR30.6/lomnitz.html, accessed Feb. 20, 2006.

Madsen, W. (1973[1964]) *The Mexican-Americans of South Texas.* 2nd edn. New York: Holt, Rinehart and Winston.

Mao Zedung (1926) *Analysis of the Classes in Chinese Society.* At www.chairmanmao.org/eng/wen.htm, accessed Feb. 18, 2006.

Martínez, O. (1996) *The US–Mexico Borderlands: Historical and Contemporary Perspectives.* Wilmington: Scholarly Resources.

Martínez, O. (2001) *Mexican Origin People in the United States: A Topical History.* Tucson: University of Arizona Press.

Maxwell, K. (1997) Western Hemisphere. *Foreign Affairs* (May–June).

McCarthy, J. D. and Yancey, W. L. (1971) Uncle Tom and Mr. Charlie: Metaphysical Pathos in the Study of Racism and Personal Disorganization. *American Journal of Sociology* 76(4): 648–672.

McCombs, B. (2006) Group Says Entrants Adversely Affect Kids. *Arizona Daily Star,* Feb. 19, pp. B1, B8.

Menchaca, M. (1997) *History and Anthropology: Conducting Chicano Research.* Occasional Paper 11. JSRI Research and Publications. At www.jsri.msu.edu/RandS/research/ops/oc11.html, accessed Feb. 8, 1996.

Menchaca, M. (2001) *Recovering History, Constructing Race.* Austin: University of Texas Press.

Mirande, A. (1986) Chicano Fathers: Response and Adaptation to Emergent Roles. SCCR Working Paper 13. Stanford Center for Chicano Research, Stanford.

Montejano, D. (1987) *Anglos and Mexicans in the Making of Texas, 1836–1986.* Austin: University of Texas Press.

Moore, A. (2002) Is Mexico Reconquering American Southwest? *WorldNetDaily,* Jan. 4. At www.worldnetdaily.com/news/article.asp?ARTICLE_ID=25920, accessed Mar. 8, 2006.

Montgomery, C. (2000) The Trap of Race and Memory: The Language of Spanish Civility on the Upper Rio Grande. *American Quarterly* 52(3):478–513.

Nugent, D. (1993) *Spent Cartridges of Revolution. An Anthropological History of Namiquipa, Chihuahua.* Chicago: University of Chicago Press.

O'Neil-Ortiz, J. (2005) Raphael Patai, Military Arab Studies, and Leftist Academia. *Penumbral,* Apr. 18. At http://penumbral.org/Archive/Raphaelpatai, accessed Mar. 11, 2006.

O'Sullivan, John L. (1845a) Annexation. *United States Democratic Review* 17:5–10.

O'Sullivan, John L. (1845b) The Great Nation of Futurity. *United States Democratic Review* 6(23):426–430. Cornell University Making of America series, at http://cdl.library.cornell.edu/cgi-bin/moa/moa-cgi?notisid=AGD1642-0006-46, accessed Feb. 5, 2006.

Prah, P. M. (2006) Background on Domestic Violence. *CQ Researcher Online*, Jan. 6.

Rich, P. and De Los Reyes, G. (1996) Mexican Caricature and the Politics of Popular Culture. *Journal of Popular Culture* 30(1):133–145.

Rigdon, S. M. (1988) *The Culture Façade: Art, Science, and Politics in the Work of Oscar Lewis*. Urbana: University of Illinois Press.

Robinson, P. S. (2003) The Contours of Spatial-Temporal Politics "After" the State: From Gated Neighborhood to Anarchist Street-Party. Paper presented to conference on Gated Communities: Building Social Division or Safer Communities? University of Glasgow, Sept. 18–19.

Romano, V. O. (1967) Minorities, History and Cultural Mystique. *El Grito* 1(1):5–11.

Romanucci-Ross, L. (1973) *Conflict, Violence, and Morality in a Mexican Village*. Palo Alto: National Press Books.

Rosaldo, R. (1973) Chicanos: Social and Psychological Perspectives. *American Anthropologist*, NS, 75(4):1003–1004.

Rosaldo, R. (1985) Chicano Studies, 1970–1984. *Cultural Critique* 14:405–427.

Rosaldo, R. (1987) Politics, Patriarchs and Laughter. *Cultural Critique* 6:65–86.

Saldaña-Portillo, M. J. (2004) "Wavering on the Horizon of Social Being": The Treaty of Guadalupe Hidalgo and the Legacy of Its Racial Character in Americo Paredes's "George Washington Gomez." *Radical History Review* 89:135–164.

Sheridan, T. E. (1986) *Los Tucsonenses*. Tucson: University of Arizona Press.

Solovey, M. (2001) Project Camelot and the 1960s Epistemological Revolution: Rethinking the Politics–Patronage–Social Science Nexus. *Social Studies of Science* 31(2):171–206.

Spicer, E. (1981) *Cycles of Conquest*. Tucson: University of Arizona Press.

Stephen, L. (2005) Reconceptualizing Latin American Anthropology: Some Ideas for the Future. Address to the Society for Latin American Anthropology, Annual Meetings of the American Anthropological Association, Nov. 30–Dec. 4.

Strong, J. (1963[1891]) *Our Country*. Rev. edn (1st edn 1885). Cambridge: Belknap Press.

Thelen, D. (1999) Mexico, the Latin North American Nation: A Conversation with Carlos Rico Ferrat. *Journal of American History* 86(2):467–480.

Thomson, J. E. (1994) *Mercenaries, Pirates and Sovereigns*. Princeton: Princeton University Press.

Tucker, R. C. (ed.) (1978) *The Marx-Engels Reader*. 2nd edn. New York: W. W. Norton.

US Department of Labor (1965) The Negro Family: The Case for National Action. Office of Policy Planning and Research, US Department of Labor.

Vélez-Ibáñez, C. G. (1996) *Border Visions*. Tucson: University of Arizona Press.

Vila, Pablo (2000) *Crossing Borders, Reinforcing Borders: Social Categories, Metaphors, and Narrative Identities*. Austin: University of Texas Press.

Warner, W. L. and Srole, L. (1945) *The Social Systems of American Ethnic Groups*. Yankee City Series, vol. 3. New York: Yale University Press.

Weber, D. J. (1979) Here Rests Juan Espinosa: Toward a Clearer Look at the Image of the "Indolent" Californios. *Western Historical Quarterly* 10(10):61–69.

Weber, D. J. (1988) *Myth and the History of the Hispanic Southwest*. Albuquerque: University of New Mexico Press.

Wilson, S. H. (2003) Brown Over "Other White": Mexican Americans' Legal Arguments and Litigation Strategy in School Desegregation Lawsuits. *Law and History Review* 21(1):145–194. At www.historycooperative.org/journals/lhr/21.1/forum_wilson.html, accessed Feb. 8, 2006.

Zavella, P. (1987) *Women's Work and Chicano Families*. Ithaca: Cornell University Press.

# CHAPTER 13 Writing the Aftermath: Anthropology and "Post-Conflict"

## Isaias Rojas Pérez

In this chapter I am concerned with the problem of violence in "post-conflict" Latin American societies. If one truth has emerged from anthropological work on war, it is that violence has continued as a permanent, even defining feature of "post-conflict" societies in Latin America. Since the early 1980s, legal and political theorists of democratic transitions have used the notion of "post-conflict" to render political transformations brought about by the end of military dictatorships and civilian wars, and the subsequent establishment of democratic regimes in Latin America. It assumes the existence of two clearly bounded orders (the predecessor and successor) that are linked through the interregnum of the transition. The transition, in turn, is imagined as the exceptional moment wherein the political body leaves behind the violence and arbitrariness of the past and enters into a newly inaugurated present that is imagined as released and decontaminated from such violence and arbitrariness. Since one of the central problems these transitions face is how to deal with massive state crimes and human rights violations of the past, more recently legal and political theorists have advocated for ad hoc official bodies such as truth and reconciliation commissions (TRCs) as essential mechanisms of such transitions. Based upon the well publicized South African Truth and Reconciliation Commission, these scholars consider reconciliation and forgiveness as efficacious channels to bring about the refoundation of national political orders in the aftermath of massive political violence (Minow 1998).

It is important to emphasize that the idea of truth commission first originated in Latin America. In the late 1970s, a truth commission was appointed in Bolivia to investigate political crimes committed during the military dictatorship of Garcia Meza (Hayner 2001). This commission was disbanded by another military coup d'état before it could release its report. The subsequent experiences were successful in various degrees. In 1983, the civilian regimen of Raul Alfonsin appointed a truth commission (Comisión Nacional de Investigación de Personas Desaparecidas, CONADEP) to investigate the disappearance of more that 10,000 Argentineans during the military dictatorship. In 1991, the civilian regime of Patricio Aylwin appointed a truth commission to investigate the crimes of the military dictatorship of Augusto Pinochet in Chile. Similarly, as a result of a United Nations brokered peace agreement, truth commissions were appointed in El Salvador, in 1992, and Guatemala, in 1996, to investigate war atrocities and gross human rights violations during the wars in those countries. In one of the more recent experiences, a truth and reconciliation commission was appointed following the fall of President Alberto Fujimori by the caretaker administration of Valentin Paniagua. It was subsequently ratified by President Alejandro Toledo in 2001, and charged with the task of investigating atrocities and human rights violations committed during two decades of counterinsurgency campaign in Peru.

These Latin American experiences are very different from the South African one. While in South Africa political elites appealed to human rights, religion and cultural relativism to produce a discourse of forgiveness and reconciliation aimed at national centralization (R. Wilson 2001, 2003), in Latin America the discourses of national reconciliation and human rights have had a more ambiguous relationship and have not overlapped. Rather than forgiveness and reconciliation, discourses of human rights in Latin America have been appropriated and mobilized by nonstate actors. As such, Latin American TRCs have helped to propel a popular struggle against impunity that has fissured ruling elites' discourses of national reconciliation. In Latin America, victims and survivors of state crime have found in human rights the enabling language with which to challenge state-led efforts to bring closure to the past. Certainly, these experiences have had differentiated outcomes, which points to the idea that they are different among themselves as well.

Recent anthropological work on Latin American society, politics and culture in the aftermath of the guerrilla and counterinsurgency wars of the 1970s, 1980s and 1990s provides an opening for exploring such differences. More specifically, it allows us to ask first, whether "post-conflict" is a viable category in the Latin American context; and, second, whether it is possible to make a clear differentiation between "normal" forms of violence typical of the "post-conflict" as opposed to "abnormal" forms of violence typical of war periods. This is not to say that there are not differences between violence in war and violence in peace; however, to frame the analysis exclusively in terms of "before" and "after" scenarios obscures the specific ways in which violence repeats, but also differentiates, itself in "post-conflict" settings. In this sense, I suggest that rather than focusing its sights on the idea of "post-conflict," anthropology might better take up the concept of *repetition* as a key to understanding the complexities of violence in contemporary "post-conflict" Latin America.

Two caveats: First, I use the notion of "post-conflict" as a descriptive category for referring to the historical period that marks the end of civilian wars and dictatorships and the emergence of discourses and practices that Hale (2002) has called the "neoliberal cultural project." Used by ruling elites to deepen inequalities and injustice, these discourses and practices have also brought languages of cultural and minority rights that people have appropriated and used unexpectedly. Second: The notion of Latin America as region encompasses three different (sub)regions that politically, economically – and certainly, academically – can operate as "regions" on their own: The Southern Cone, Central America, and the Andean Region. While not exclusively, I will concentrate here on one country in each of these (sub)regions: Argentina, Guatemala, and Peru respectively. In the first case, there is comparatively more anthropological work on violence in

Argentina than other countries of the Southern Cone. Similarly, Guatemala has concentrated intense anthropological work in comparison with other countries such as El Salvador or Nicaragua. Finally, Peru is one of the two countries in the Andean region affected by violence that is undergoing a situation of "post-conflict."

## VIOLENCE AND TERROR: REPETITION AS DEATH-DEALING MACHINE

Writing on the experience of the Guatemalan Commission for Historical Clarification (Comisión para el Esclarecimiento Histórico, CEH), historian Greg Grandin (2000) says that any history that attempts to come to terms with Latin American political repression has to deal with the problem of repetition, both of the violence itself and of memories of the violence. If writing history assumes that the past is in a certain way completed (Nora 1989), how can this history be written if such a past continues to take place in the present? As Grandin (2000) says: "The past keeps intruding on the present; not, however, in the form of memory – even though we would like to convince ourselves that political violence is a thing of the past – but in reality, in the form of new victims."[1]

Anthropologists have situated their work on violence in post–cold war Latin America within and against this uncanny entanglement of violence as memory and as repeated reality. How has this relationship between repeated violence and remembered violence been rendered? A central thesis that emerges from this body of work is that more than two decades after the beginning of democratic "transitions" in Latin America and the end of the cold war era, violence has anything but ended. On the one hand, and with the important exception of Colombia, the forms of violence typical of the counterinsurgency campaigns and military dictatorships of the 1970s and 1980s have been halted in the region. On the other hand, however, forms of violence associated with this period of national wars against the threat of communism continue to take place. In this sense, anthropological work provides a means to contest the notions of "post-conflict" and "transition" as they circulate in both academic and popular understandings of contemporary Latin America.

### Violence as legacy

The concept of legacy has provided one important category for analyzing the repetition of violence in Latin America. Koonings and Kruijt (1999), for instance, use that notion to explain how, in spite of the emergence of democratic regimes and successes of economic stabilization of the 1990s, violence, terror and fear continue to operate in the present. They argue that transitions to civilian rule and peace agreements in Latin America had little impact on those parts of national military apparatuses that unleash violence against civilian populations. Violence, moreover, has ceased to be the resource only of the powerful and increasingly appears as an option for a multitude of actors in pursuit of all kinds of goals. For Koonings and Kruijt (1999), this arbitrariness of social violence in post-conflict settings is a long-term consequence of the everyday arbitrariness of the regimes of terror of the 1970s and 1980s, and testifies to the incapacity of the state to uphold a legitimate and peaceful internal order in the postwar era. In short, in this view, the inability of the post-conflict Latin

American state to restore its monopoly on violence and to impose a "rational" order has resulted in a de facto democratization of violence. An arbitrary, irrational violence remains firmly in place as a legacy of a past violence that has changed tenor, but not disappeared.

Certainly, there is evidence that supports the notion of legacy and the idea of the "democratization of [arbitrary] violence." In Guatemala, El Salvador and Nicaragua, where levels of violent death are comparable or even higher than during the war period, soaring rates of criminal violence have become the hallmark of a new political economy of violence (Rodgers 2002). In some cases this has involved a shifting landscape of violence, as has occurred for example in Nicaragua, where cities that had been relatively peaceful during the war have now become battlegrounds for common criminals and youth gangs (Galeano 2000). In Guatemala, more than five hundred cases of mob lynching against alleged criminals have taken place since the signing of the Peace Agreement in 1996, all of them in rural areas that had been heavily affected by the government counterinsurgency campaigns of the 1980s (Mendoza 2004). Similar examples can be found in rural areas in postwar Peru and Bolivia (Goldstein 2003).

The notion of legacy, however, falls short in conveying the complexity of the situation in post–cold war Latin America. This notion not only presumes a rational bureaucratic character of the state, but it also is informed by a concept of time in which the present and the past are two blocks of time tidily separated. The past is portrayed as an outdated irrational burden which the rational present has not been able to leave behind completely. The situation, however, as some ethnographic work shows, is far more complex. It is not simply that an anachronistic and arbitrary violence has survived the transition, as the notion of legacy implies. It is that the permanence of old apparatuses of repression is part of the transition itself and the forms of arbitrary social violence present in postwar settings express the very workings of the state in the neoliberal era.

In Guatemala, for instance, Schirmer (1998) shows how the old state apparatus of repression has been reincarnated as "democracy." Drawing from her ethnographic work among Guatemalan military officers who participated in the counterinsurgency campaigns of the 1980s, Schirmer contends that the Guatemalan military crafted a unique "counterinsurgent constitutional state" in which the notion of cogovernance by military and civilians alike is its central framework. In Peru, following a military backed coup d'état in 1992, the new 1993 constitution formalized and sanctioned increasing military power (Rospigliosi 2000). Moreover, a civilian-military regime remained in office for almost ten years, well after the defeat of the Sendero Luminoso (Shining Path) (Poole and Rénique 2003; Degregori 2000; Cotler and Grompone 2000; Kruijt 1999). Both in postwar Guatemala and postwar Peru, the military continue to think of themselves as constructors of the nation-state and, as such, as the final arbiters of the boundaries of lawful opposition. In these countries, the United States national security doctrine and its theory of the "internal enemy" remain in place, and the civilian population continues to be the main target of military surveillance (Schirmer 1998; Kruijt 1999).

These reconfigurations of the military apparatus run alongside neoliberal reforms of the state and economy that have deepened inequalities and imbalances of power throughout the region. Poole and Rénique (2003) suggest that in Peru the state did not need to hide its own forms of violence while introducing neoliberal political and economic reforms. The state of emergency was extended well beyond the defeat of the Shining Path and was justified by repeated pronouncements concerning the "return of terrorism." When this argument was not convincing anymore, the Peruvian state justified a continuing state of emergency by citing the alleged threat posed to Peruvian national sovereignty by Colombian guerrillas (Rojas Pérez 2005). As a result of such uses of fear, as portrayed by Degregori (2000), Peruvian society is trapped in an unending state of emergency. In this sense, overt military violence in post-conflict Peru must be seen as instrumental to the establishment of the neoliberal "market democracy" and "privatized state" (Poole and Rénique 2003). Similarly, in other countries such as Chile, neoliberal reforms were also conducted during authoritarian regimes (Ensalaco 2000).

The violence at work in postwar Latin America is, then, not merely a legacy – in the sense of the long-term consequences of an older form of violence that extends on into the present – but the actual working of contemporary state power. The Latin American post–cold war state needs the repetition of "otherized" violence – in the guise of guerrillas, "terrorists," "drug lords," "cartels" or street gangs – in order to hide the repetition of its own violence grounded on a permanent state of emergency. Thus, rather than thinking about violence as the product of "weak states" that are simply unable to restore their monopoly on violence in post-conflict settings, we might better consider the "new" modes of criminal violence taking place in Latin America as modalities of rule through which the post–cold war Latin American state exercises its power. Rather than merely a problem of legacy, this approach to post-conflict violence underscores how the modern state works by producing "margins" in which the state of emergency is not the exception but the rule (Das and Poole 2004).

Colombia provides perhaps the best example of these workings of the state. It has long been praised as one of South America's oldest and most enduring democracies. However, Colombia is also one of the most violent countries in the region. It boasts one of the highest homicide rates, three times the rate of Brazil and Mexico (Gaviria, 2000), and it is going through a longstanding armed conflict that currently results in nearly 35,000 deaths each year (MacIlwaine and Moser 2003). Pecaut (1999) points out that political violence is closely intertwined with social and criminal violence. This complex of violence has been exacerbated by economic recession and neoliberal reforms (see Arocha and Maya, this volume) and the massive US military and economic assistance implemented since 1999 as "Plan Colombia" (Tickner 2003).

Jimeno (2001) has pointed out that this complex of violence is specific and does not affect everyone equally. In very specific areas, the different types of violent action in Colombia mutually interact in such a way that the distinctions between kinds of violence, violent actors and public and private violence have become blurred. What she sees as decisive, however, is that violence as a disruptive social act connects levels of personality, interaction and social structure not through the immediate occurrence of acts of violence, but rather by producing a common critical sense of social life (see also Jimeno, this volume). This critical sense of social life is a historical construct in which individual and collective habitus come together. Its keystone is the notion of authority. In Jimeno's view, those vast sectors of Colombian society exposed to this complex of violence come to understand authority as being an unpredictable, arbitrary and menacing entity. This way of understanding authority is founded on social experiences of domestic behavior, and that of the agents of institutional authority, and becomes a guide for interactions between people in private as well as public life (Jimeno 2001).

## Fear and terror as historical repetition

While the notion of legacy situates the violence of the 1970s and 1980s as an exceptional moment of violence from which the past extends its influence to the present as undesirable consequence, the notion of "permanent state of emergency" situates contemporary violence in broader contexts of history and power. Many anthropologists have made use of the notion of "culture of fear" – built upon the notion of permanent state of emergency – to go beyond event centered understandings of violence and render the specific ways in which fear and terror have been historically mobilized by states in order to attain compliance from potentially rebellious populations.

Originally, however, the concept of "culture of fear" emerged precisely to render the exceptionality of the Southern Cone military dictatorships' use of terror and fear during the counterinsurgency campaigns of the 1970s and 1980s (Corradi, Weiss Fagen and Garretón 1992). For those scholars who coined the concept, the staggering depth and scope of repression (symbolized by the figure of the *desaparecido*, or "disappeared person") in countries such as Chile and Argentina was unprecedented. None of the military dictatorships in these or other Latin American countries in the past had reached such levels of repression and use of terror. The population was subjected to generalized and centralized violence aimed at creating uncertainty, self-doubt, and insecurity. In such contexts, fear became a form of life, a "culture" that pervaded social relations and ways of situating oneself in the world (Corradi, Weiss Fagen and Garretón 1992).

Lechner (1992) put the argument of "culture of fear" in historical terms by linking it to the formation of the nation-state in Latin America. For him, fear is intimately linked to the political question par excellence – that is, the question of order. However, the question of order prompts an array of diverse responses depending on the culture within which it is posed. In Latin America – Lechner argues – diversity was not perceived as plurality but rather as disorder. As a consequence, nation-building was understood to occur through either the ideological construction of homogeneity or the physical erasure of difference via social and political exclusion, as well as through violence, terror and fear.

Anthropologists also began to work on these broader connections between violence, power and history to produce more complex pictures than Lerner's top-down approach. They introduced a perspective that would necessarily incorporate everyday as well as local experiences of conflict and violence within broader frameworks of history and power.[2] In so doing, anthropologists asserted that the state violence of the 1970s and 1980s was not episodic and exceptional, but chronic and endemic. It was part of a long history of exploitation, oppression, racism, torture and murder in Latin America since colonial times. In elaborating this understanding of the violence that is constitutive of state power, many Latin American anthropologists have drawn from Walter Benjamin's observation: "The tradition of the oppressed teaches us that 'the state of emergency' in which we live is not the exception but the rule" (Benjamin 1969).

Building upon Benjamin's theory of history, Taussig (1984, 1992) has reelaborated the notion of "culture of fear" and introduced the notion of "culture of terror." In his account of the terror and brutality inflicted by white colonizers against Indians in the Amazonian lowlands of the Colombian Putumayo, Taussig contends that it was the fear and fantasies of the whites that led them to inflict murderous torture and brutality against Indians, despite the economic irrationality of destroying scarce labor. The brutality, mutilation, dismembering, and burning of Indians, which many have read as instrumental means to control and extract labor from the Indians, were, in Taussig's reading, productive of a powerful imagery by which qualities of savagery and wildness were attributed to Indians that could be rendered as both productive and dangerous. Taussig also draws on Walter Benjamin's notion of the "dialectical image" to explore how images of Indians and their ambivalent powers circulate within this "space of death" where the violence of the colonizer is rendered as "culture" and, as such, is shared by rulers and ruled alike.

For Taussig, in the contemporary processes of violence in Latin America the state reenacted this "culture of terror". The unremitting assault against the civilian population is carried out through forms that create "spaces of death" in which signifier and signified become unhinged and the structuralist dream of a chainlink of order is disrupted. The surplus meaning unleashed gives rise to uncertainty. The state unleashes forms of violence that operate to blur accustomed realities and boundaries, while denial and silencing are mobilized to deepen uncertainty in social relations. Images of the past are used to construct an imaginary reality that is utilized and appropriated by ruling classes in order to sustain the moral character of reactionary social relationships. The place of the other, savage, or Indian is now populated by images of the burglars, prostitutes, guerrillas, and terrorists, who are to be "cleansed" from the social body (Taussig 1992, 2005). Similarly to the white colonizers, the violence of the state and its rulers is in need of the construction of an other, to whom menace and savagery could be attributed. It is a death-dealing repetition.

Some anthropologists have extended the use of notions such as "culture of fear" and/or "culture of terror" to explain how fear and terror continue to shape social life in post-conflict Latin America, particularly among people directly affected by the violence of the state during that time (Green 1994, 1999; Binford 1996). Their work emphasizes the persistence of fear and terror as ultimate arbiters of social relations among victims of violence in the past. On the one hand, it is fear of the concrete possibility that the violence, torture and killing of the recent past might happen again. In this sense of the term, "culture of fear" comes to be equivalent to the images of recent past violence that haunt the social body and are used for present purposes. On the other hand, "culture of fear" has also been used to refer to the individual and familial experiences of past terror that recur in everyday life in the present. For these anthropologists, the repetition of violence does not merely entail a reconfiguration of the apparatus of violence in post-conflict civilian institutions, but also a mobilization of fear through the disciplining practices that produce compliance in post-conflict settings.

Green (1994, 1999), for instance, claims that fear and terror remain as major mechanisms of sociopolitical control in post-conflict Guatemala in spite of the fact that the scorched earth campaigns, massacres, torture and disappearances came to an end several years before. Drawing on her ethnographic work among Mayan widows in the

Guatemalan highlands, Green contends that it is not only the continuing military surveillance of indigenous communities, but also the conscious elaboration and mobilization of fear and suspicion that draw primarily from recent memories of atrocious violence and death. In this sense, Green argues, fear has penetrated social memory and has accordingly become a chronic condition. It is inseparable from the reality in which people live. It is a "hidden state of emergency" (Green 1994, 1999).

In Peru, the state claimed the official end of the war in 1992, with the capture of the leader of the Shining Path, Abimael Guzman. Rural villages, however, remained militarized under the sway of the Peruvian military for many more years (Theidon 2001; Degregori 1996; Coronel 1996; Ludescher 1999; Starn 1996). For these villages, the return of violence remained a "palpable concern" and their daily life resisted any definition of experience in terms of the dichotomy "conflict" and "post-conflict" (Theidon 2001). This fear of the return of the Shining Path was heightened by military sanctioned projects of pacification, which forced former members of the guerrilla groups to return to the same communities from which they were expelled. These processes of forced reconciliation have deepened mistrust, suspicion and fear among former neighbors, kin and acquaintances who under the sway of the military have to live as "intimate enemies" (Theidon 2004).

In El Salvador, anthropologists have found how once proud guerrilla fighters from the Frente FMLN (Frente Farabundo Marti para la Liberación Nacional) have become poor peasants struggling to eke out an existence by farming small, rocky, hillside fields and how they have come to question their participation in the civil war (Binford 1996). Binford (1996) finds how, additionally, these people have to live face to face with perpetrators of the worst state violence against their neighbors and relatives who have not only been granted amnesty by the government, but have also been enriched through their participation in the counterinsurgency campaign.

Anthropologists have also referred to how the impunity granted to the perpetrators of violence and of state crimes is perceived as the reenactment of regimes of fear and terror in post-conflict settings. Robben points out how the permanence of impunity, in spite of attempts at prosecution in Argentina, continues to bring insecurity and uncertainty to victims of state crime (Robben 1995, 2000). Green (1999) says that impunity makes it clear to everyone in Guatemala who retains power and under what conditions. Zur (1994) speaks of the destructive impact of impunity on social relations and personal identities. Sanford (2003a) speaks of how impunity is a very direct form of violence; it is a law of exception. Impunity appears not only as the condition of possibility for the return of the fear and terror of the past; it is also a repeated violence in the sense that unpunished state crime is the reenactment of the crime itself.

In these ethnographic pictures, fear, uncertainty, and shame are not merely mechanical reflections of the past, but they have also become mechanisms for sociopolitical control and the disciplining of subjects in post conflict settings. The production of uncertainty through denunciations, rumors, innuendo, or gossip, in contexts of impunity is the threshold through which images of past violence are brought back in order to produce compliance in the present. This careful management of the past so as to produce conformity with power holders has become one specific feature through which the state guarantees its control over suspicious populations (Green 1994, 1999).

## From "culture of fear" to "trauma"

Other anthropologists have introduced the notion of trauma to account for how victims reproduce in their everyday life forms of violence inflicted against them in the recent past. As Dickson-Gomez (2002) points out, following Das (2000), the violence of the past enters into the present not only as traumatic memory but also as "poisonous knowledge"; that is to say, as key injured social relationships which make the past encircle the present as atmosphere (Das 2000). The most destructive and long-lasting effects of community violence and war are not seen in individual illness experiences but, rather, in the social relationships of which the individual is only a part (Dickson-Gomez 2002).

Bourgois (2001, 2002) speaks of how in El Salvador revolutionary peasants were traumatized by the same violence they used to resist state violence. Infused into these peasants' everyday life, structural violence, political violence and symbolic violence interact as everyday violence whose destructive power is highly demobilizing and depoliticizing. In this sense, unlike 20 years earlier Bourgois asserts that there is no liberating violence or oppressive violence, just a continuum of violence that is highly destructive of social relationships. Also drawing from her ethnographic work in El Salvador, Dickson-Gomez (2002) argues how, in a social context in which basic social relationships were broken by war, there is a transgenerational transmission of trauma understood not only as a "contagion" of psychological symptoms, but also as the process by which a traumatized worldview of fear, pessimism, and violence is socialized into the next generation.

Suarez-Orozco (1992) says that in post–military dictatorship Argentina, the previously forbidden and denied memories of the dead and disappeared returned in the form of a flood of public images and events. In what was called the "horror show," Argentinean society began to talk compulsively of what had been previously denied and betrayed in the most intimate and basic social relationships (Suarez-Orozco 1992). Drawing from his ethnographic work in Argentina among former protagonists of the "dirty war," Robben (1995, 2000) observes how bitter memories, fear and distrust affect the entire society to the point that there is a "social trauma" related to the past violence of the state.

Similarly, trauma articulated in terms of shame is produced as part of the workings of the same oppressive power structure. Former revolutionaries or victims of state crime blame themselves for having been duped into participating in insurrectionary adventures (Bourgois 2001, 2002; Nelson 1999, 2004); or for being unable to defend their relatives from state violence (Robben 2000; Dickson-Gomez 2002); or for having engaged in lethal violence among themselves (Theidon 2004). State power inflicts upon their former victims what Bourdieu calls "symbolic violence" (Bourgois 2001, 2002).

These ethnographic pictures also speak of the recurrence of fear, terror, and demobilizing violence in post-conflict situations in Latin America. For these anthropologists, violence in times of war is as destructive of everyday life as it is in times of peace (Bourgois 2001, 2002; Green 1994, 1999). However, similarly to the notion of legacy, in these accounts of trauma the violence of the 1970s and 1980s appears as an exceptional and foundational event from which violence extends its destructive effects to the present. In this sense, violence is rendered as something external to the social and cultural order and, as such, as threatening to it. In these accounts, violence and culture are not only clearly divided and opposite, but events of violence are spoken of as momentary departures from cultural norms that would generate harmony over the long term (Margold 1998; Poole 1994). By comparison, the notion of "culture of terror" conveys an understanding of how violence can be productive of the social order itself.

## REPETITION AS POSSIBILITY

Yet other anthropologists have criticized the notion of "culture of terror/fear" as inadequate to describe the forms of violence and conflict that characterize "post-conflict" Latin America. Similar to the notion of "culture of poverty," the central premise of the notion of "culture of terror/fear" is that victims are implicated in sustaining the fear and terror that affect them. As cultural attributes, fear and terror become totalizing conditions that orchestrate all the rhythms of daily life (Margold 1998). Given that terror and fear saturate a social group's vision and distort its capacities to act, rationality is either assumed to be external to the victim's chaotic world, or reduced to a reflex of self-survival. Used in this way, the notion of "culture of fear/terror" does not allow for understanding how it is that agency is assigned and how, for instance, victims display and mobilize cultural resources to respond to the state's atrocities (Margold 1998).

In this section, I consider the work of anthropologists who have been looking at "uses of the past" in which repetition appears as possibility and emergence of the new; i.e. as difference. In short, I present anthropological accounts that can lead us to understand how culture is differently recreated, repeated, and reinhabited in the aftermath of devastating violence.

## Exhumations: political and cultural dissidence

Sanford (2003a) argues that trauma occasioned by terror is embedded in language just as it is embedded in other structures of culture. Silence and forgetting imposed upon indigenous peoples were some of the enduring effects of violence and terror in Guatemala, making it impossible for survivors to contest terror. According to Sanford, shifts in language – which express shifts in power relations – began to take place in the context of the political openings brought about by the peace accords and, particularly, the work of the Guatemalan Commission for Historical Clarification. Sanford shows how survivors of state-led massacres in Guatemalan indigenous communities were particularly interested in the exhumations carried out by the CEH and how, breaking away from fear and silence, they mobilized to request official exhumations in their communities. Couching their mobilization in languages of rights and citizenship, they sought to recover the bodies of their relatives assassinated by the military and to provide them with a "proper burial." Sanford interprets this unprecedented mobilization around exhumations as the moment when, by speaking truth to power, silence and forgetting are broken and indigenous communities are able to retake both the past and public space. Thus, sites of exhumation became collective spaces for local healing and the reconstruction of larger social relations (Sanford 2003a).

The picture Sanford offers shows the emergence of voice and the (re)acquisition of language (language of rights, in this case) that animate such efforts to reinhabit a devastated world. Shifts in language and breaking silence allow for the emergence of voice and new definitions of the self in the aftermath of devastation. However, Sanford does not interrogate how these new definitions of the self are related with the culturally established forms of mourning articulated behind the idea of "proper burial." In other words, how do new definitions of the self engage or reengage with already established cultural forms? We can infer from her formulation that cultural forms are brought back by the emergence of voice and new definitions of the self. Couched in the expression "a proper burial," these forms become crucial for reinhabiting everyday life precisely *because* they were hitherto halted or blocked by the violence of the state.

Robben (2000, 2005) analyzes the topic of exhumations for the Argentinean case, privileging a psychoanalytical perspective to account for the differing reactions expressed by relatives of the *desaparecidos* (the disappeared). These exhumations, which followed the work of the Argentinean Comisión Nacional de Investigación de Personas Desaparecidas (CONADEP), conveyed a devastating truth to Argentine society in that they provided evidence with which to counter not only political denial (Cohen 1996), but also social denial (Robben 2000, 2005; Suarez-Orozco 1992).[3] Initially, Madres de Plaza de Mayo, the leading organization of relatives of the *desaparecidos* in Argentina, favored the forensic procedures. The exhumations provided evidence that the practice of disappearance had actually taken place. They also held out the promise that the perpetrators would be tried and sent to prison. However, as soon as the possibility of justice declined, Madres de Plaza de Mayo split regarding the topic of continuing exhumations. On the one hand, those who favored exhumations considered that they were going to be able to recover the remains of their missing relatives. By providing them a "proper reburial," families sought to simultaneously denounce state violence and vindicate its victims. On the other hand, those who rejected exhumations considered that these procedures were part of a broader scheme of reconciliation put forward by the national government aimed primarily at forgetting rather than vindicating the victims. By rejecting exhumations, the Madres de Plaza de Mayo decided to leave open their wounds and to vindicate their disappeared children through the continuation of their political ideas. These mothers redefined the relationships with their (missing) children through the phrase: "nuestros hijos nos parieron" [our children gave birth to us] (Robben 2000; Burchianti 2004).

In this picture we can also see new definitions of the self taking place in terms of redefinitions of the social relations between mothers and their (missing) children. Robben (2000, 2005) introduces the notion of *impaired mourning* to establish differences between the Madres de Plaza de Mayo who rejected exhumations and those who accepted them. The former considered that reburial would bury the mothers' pain of separation instead of assuring their children's presence through the promulgation of their political ideas. Conversely, the latter went through culturally prescribed norms of proper mourning. Suarez-Orozco (1992) speaks of "interrupted mourning" to refer to the "psychological inability" of the Madres de Plaza de Mayo to bury their *desaparecidos*. This "interrupted mourning," he argues, was turned into a political discourse of resistance.

As presented by Robben and Suarez-Orozco, the "impaired" or "interrupted" mourning of the Madres de Plaza de Mayo hinges on the pathological in that it stands opposed to *proper* mourning. Both authors, however, suggest that cultural transgression allows for the emergence of agency. By not following what are considered "proper forms of mourning," these mothers have opened up a space of essential ambiguity from which they could emerge not only as political dissidents, but also as, say, "cultural dissidents." Burchianti (2004) has emphasized the character of political dissidence of the Madres de Plaza de Mayo, explaining how the redefinition of their social relations with their (missing) children has allowed them to transform a politics of memory into a politics of the present concerned with social injustice and inequality in Argentina today. This political stance has led them to resignify current forms of liberalism as a type of structural violence (Burchianti 2004).

These ethnographic pictures show how repetition in terms of memory is the basis upon which victims of state violence have organized their struggle to contest the project of the refounding of the nation-state in terms of forgetting and closure. Moreover, either by speaking truth to power, such as in Guatemala, or by producing specific forms of political and cultural dissidence, such as in Argentina, these women and men have redefined their broader social relationships. In so doing, they have redefined themselves. Rather than detachment so as to produce "normal" forms of mourning, they have actually showed that mourning is about incorporation or, as Suarez-Orozco (1992) says, about accommodation in the present. In this respect, they also appear clearly as producing formulations of difference in the face of the homogenizing and universalizing projects of nation-(re)building, and their demands of "moving on," under the discourse of national reconciliation. Is the post–cold war Latin American nation state able to live with difference and dissidence?

## Nation-state, nationalism, and multiculturalism

One of the defining features of the military campaigns against insurgency in Latin America was the forced integration of civilian populations into national counterinsurgency projects, particularly in countries with large indigenous populations such as Peru and Guatemala. Hundreds of thousands of men, women and children were grouped in strategic hamlets and forced by the army to organize paramilitary civil defense patrols, charged with local surveillance and "defense" of communities against guerrillas and "terrorists" (for Guatemala see Carmack 1988; Manz 1988; for Peru see Ludescher 1999; Degregori 1996, 1998; Fumerton 2002; Starn 1996, 1998; Coronel 1996; del Pino 1996). The militarization and forced organization of the communities under military auspices destroyed preexisting forms of articulation and organization of everyday life that hitherto had governed social relationships in these communities (Zur 1994; Manz 1988, 2004; Theidon 2004).

The end of the armed conflict raised the question of how populations who had been forcefully integrated into national counterinsurgency projects were negotiating with the state to participate *in* the same state that had previously engaged in genocidal acts of destruction (Nelson 2004) and what the place of memory in these processes was. Anthropologists have noted how, in the post–cold war era, the state in Latin America is allowing forms of collective organization through which entrenched inequalities and discriminations against indigenous peoples would purportedly be overcome (Sieder and Witchell 2001; Sieder 1999; Degregori 1996; Del Pino 1996; Coronel 1996). In Guatemala, for example, the UN brokered peace agreement between the government and the guerrilla forces introduced an important reform by defining the Guatemalan nation-state as multiethnic and pluricultural. This was meant to improve the political representation and socioeconomic participation of Mayan indigenous peoples. Until then, the liberal ideology of the state had effectively marginalized indigenous groups from national identity and from the dominant politico-legal order. The agreement dovetailed with the emergence at the end of the war of an intense indigenous Mayan activism that began to contest existing conceptions of national identity and citizenship in Guatemala (Warren 1998; Nelson 1999, 2004; Sieder and Witchell 2001). Throughout Guatemala, initiatives to rebuild the social fabric destroyed by the war, including the reconstitution of local authorities or conflict resolution procedures, were framed in terms of ethnic specificities that have mobilized international languages of cultural rights. By revitalizing and creating a shared cultural past (Alonso 1988; Anderson 1983), indigenous activists sought to respond to an acute form of ethnic discrimination and the destruction wrought by war, rather than separate or develop a different nationalism (Warren 1998; Nelson 1999, 2004; Sieder and Witchell 2001; Sieder 1999).

In Peru, the national counterinsurgency project was formalized as a new constitution in 1993. As mentioned earlier, this new constitution reformed the Peruvian state according to neoliberal guidelines and sanctioned increasing military power (Poole and Rénique 2003; Rospigliosi 2000; Degregori 2000; Cotler and Grompone 2000). It also incorporated a clause recognizing the "pluricultural" nature of the Peruvian state. However, differently from Guatemala, the mobilization of Quechua peasants of the Andean highlands has not been couched in languages of cultural rights, but rather of military nationalism. These Quechua populations recreated strategic local identities based upon their participation in the war against the Sendero Luminoso in order to place claims on the state. In this way, Quechua peasants have mobilized heroic and masculinized histories of war to articulate political claims that form a continuation of their historical struggle for citizenship and integration into the nation-state (Degregori 1996, 1998; Del Pino 1996, 1998; Coronel 1996; Fumerton 2002; Theidon 2003).

Some anthropologists have criticized these subaltern constructions of identity from a feminist perspective. In Guatemala, Sieder and Witchell (2001) have argued that while ideas of legal pluralism, human rights and indigenous rights have become resources for indigenous people historically marginalized and discriminated against, and the law itself has become a central mechanism to express and formalize multicultural, multi-ethnic relations, these same ideas, languages and discourses have led to an essentialization of an indigenous "Mayan" culture (see French, this volume). Indigenous activists have strategically essentialized their culture as inherently harmonious, atemporal and bounded in order to conform to the languages and discourses established in the Peace Accord and to attain levels of autonomy and self-determination, particularly in the terrain of customary law. The problem with this perspective, Sieder and Witchell (2001) argue, is not only that this essentialization may lead to a further discrimination of indigenous populations, but that under the image of "harmonious culture" patriarchal oppressions against women and children are hidden and perpetuated. What is more, local structures of militarized power that were organized during the war remain in place in many areas where the indigenous movements now claim autonomy and self-determination (Sieder and Witchell 2001; Sieder 1999; Green 1999).

In Peru, Theidon (2003) has similarly asserted that the discourses of masculine popular nationalism among Quechua peasants have obscured women's participation in the war. Because these discourses perpetuate specific forms of gender oppression, the types of democratic politics that take hold in these communities correspond more to a "disjunctive democracy," in which equality and rights are unevenly distributed. The new leadership that has emerged in these highland populations, while more efficacious in their relations with the state, have also reproduced and perpetuated older practices of discrimination and segregation within indigenous populations.

Some anthropologists have suggested a different direction of analysis by focusing on what can be called "state endorsed" subalternism. Hale (2002), for instance, suggests that the "neoliberal cultural project" entails the recuperation of the individual, not through the state as is the case in classic liberal theory, but through nonstate intermediate collectivities which have been endorsed with disciplinary and subject-making powers. The neoliberal state unloads much of its previous responsibilities upon organized local groups, not so much in the perspective of democratization, but of discharging its welfare functions (see also Poole 2006). In this sense, neoliberal political economic policies can coexist perfectly with forms of state endorsed multiculturalism since neoliberalism's cultural project entails a proactive recognition of a minimal package of cultural rights, and a rejection of the rest. The state, however, remains as the ultimate arbiter in defining what a "proper" culture is (Hale 2002).

Collier and Speed (2000) have observed in Chiapas, Mexico, an instance of how the state remains as the ultimate arbiter of what is tolerable. The government uses the language of human rights to overcome indigenous claims for autonomy. While it is permissive with the cultural demands of its indigenous political allies, its attitude is different regarding indigenous organizations and communities who align themselves with other opposition groups. In such cases, where a distinction is made between "good" and "bad" Indians (Hale 2002), the language of human rights is deployed as a means to defend the indigenous individual from customary practices that are deemed offensive or "illiberal" (Poole 2006). Thus, the cultural language of human rights, with its ontological understanding of rights as both individual and universal, is reframed in political terms according to what state power is willing to tolerate in specific contexts of political contestation or subordination.

These pictures show that it is an essential ambiguity moving between threat and guarantee (Poole 2004) that defines the relation between the state and indigenous groups. On the one hand, the state not only allows, endorses, and even promotes subalternism (collective identities) as forms of integration and negotiation or, ultimately, forms of neoliberal governmentality. On the other hand, the state reserves for itself the power of definition of what a "proper" culture is and how it should be exercised. If these forms of "propriety" are exceeded, the state reserves for itself the exercise of forms of violence and repression proper to discipline those "excesses." Rationality is not necessarily a marker of the state, so it can become a guarantor against oppression within subaltern groups, as implied in Sieder and Witchell's and Theidon's critiques. It seems necessary to introduce categories of analysis that go beyond Weberian notions of the rational state.

The situation is even more fraught in Colombia where the 1991 constitution recognized the "multicultural" nature of the nation-state. The indigenous and Afro-Colombian communities were granted political and juridical autonomy and the right to administer their territories within the framework provided by Colombian national legislation. Some indigenous communities started to use these multicultural rights and languages to establish control over highly contested areas (Villaveces 2002), in which the violence of the guerrillas, paramilitary and drug traffickers overlap (see Arocha and Maya, this volume). Thus, the newly acknowledged power of these indigenous communities has to compete with other informal forms of power based primarily upon violence. Some of these forms of power, such as paramilitary groups, are backed by the state itself (Sanford 2003b). The state itself is involved in the production of violence in these areas through its counterinsurgency and antidrug policies. Thus, as Villaveces (2002) says, the formal order of the state represented by indigenous communities coexists in a volatile play of forces with decentered and multifaceted orders represented in the figures of the guerrillas, drug traffickers and state-sponsored paramilitaries.

Ramírez (2001) expresses this situation in terms of a paradox: on the one hand, people see the state as a repressive and even terrorist agent since its presence is actualized in terms of support for paramilitary forces and repression against social demands – for instance those of *cocaleros* (coca leaf growers), who are constituted as delinquents by the state. On the other hand, people also see the state as that which provides public services and possibilities for political participation on a local level. It is a state that constitutes citizens. Some basic questions emerge here: who embodies the state, the indigenous communities or the paramilitary forces? How do we establish clear-cut borders between state and society? How do we understand the complexity of these situations?

Nelson (2004) introduces the idea of the "two faced Indian" and the "two faced state" to capture the fluidity and ambiguity of a relationship called State. Responding to how it is that Guatemalan indigenous communities seek to participate *in* the same state that engaged in acts of genocidal destruction against them, she says that people try to do more than merely survive on the exposed cusp of a marginal place and certainly can reengage the state. However, this reengagement is ambiguous. There are different faces (or subject positions), none of them fixed or unique. In turn, the state has two faces as well: one legitimate, the other criminal, corrupt, and murderous; one rational, the other irrational and magical. In one face the state is the people themselves, in the other face the state is against the people, assessing constantly the risk of people's rebellion. People's interactions with the state are thus configured as a fluid and ambiguous relationship in which there are no clear-cut borders between state and society, rationality and irrationality, threat and guarantee. It is this ambiguity and fluidity that opens up possibilities for difference.

Theidon (2000, 2004) also speaks of the notion of "two-facedness" among Quechua peasants in Peru. However, differently from Nelson's account, Theidon renders the notion as referring to an essentially perverse character. In her interpretation, "two-facedness" expresses features such as hypocrisy, betrayal, and mistrust that erode everyday social relationships. It is the mark of those who have fallen outside of local morality – for instance by joining the Shining Path ranks – and as such have been rendered inhuman. For Theidon, the recovery of "moral community" among Andean, Quechua-speaking survivors of the war requires that relationships between individuals and institutions (e.g. the peasant community and "the state") be straightforward or "one-faced." F. Wilson (1997, 2000) finds a different picture in which understandings of the local in postwar Peru are not restricted to the problem of the recovery of "moral community." She shows how former guerrilla members have become local authorities in their communities during the post-conflict era, occupying an ambiguous position from which they can show both their present efficaciousness in articulating the relation of their communities with the state and their past trajectory as an always present possibility for rebellion and the return of violence.

## LAW, ACCOUNTABILITY, RECONCILIATION

Little ethnographic work has been done regarding how state law addresses the problem of impunity in cases of state crime. Anthropologist Leigh Binford (1996) focuses on the case of the El Mozote massacre carried out by the military against the civilian population in El Salvador, in 1982, to show how impunity is produced by the state itself. The massacre was initially denied by the Salvadorean and US governments. It was only because survivors of the massacre pushed their case that judicial procedures were opened. However, a politically biased judiciary manipulated, and ultimately debunked, its own procedures in order to grant impunity to perpetrators. Based upon the abundant evidence produced by judicial procedures, survivors managed to get their case reopened in the context of the work of the Salvadorean Truth Commission. Finally, these procedures were terminated by an Amnesty Law passed by the government of Alfredo Cristiani. Binford (1996) shows how, in spite of this fact, survivors transformed the site of the massacre into a site for memory.

In Guatemala, there were similar attempts to produce impunity from within the state itself. In spite of death threats and several other difficulties, survivors of state crime managed to have judicial procedures opened in some cases. However, while reaching direct perpetrators such as civil patrollers or low ranking military officers, none of these cases implicated high officials involved in genocidal counterinsurgency campaigns (Sanford 2003b, 2003c). For instance, in a highly publicized trial civilian patrollers were found guilty of participating in a massacre against a civilian population, and sentenced to death, while the military officers who allegedly planned and ordered the massacres were merely summoned as witnesses. Considering this trial, Sanford (2003c) speaks of "the grey zone" of justice – following Primo Levi – to refer to the fact that, although justice and retribution are central for the reconstruction of society in post-conflict settings, national courts distribute legal punishment along the lines of ethnicity, class and gender.

Theidon (2004) shows a different picture in her ethnography on reconciliation in Ayacucho, Peru. She opposes the local process of reconciliation to the one sponsored by the national government. Strikingly, the same Quechua peasants who are seeking integration in the nation-state on the basis of popular nationalistic discourses have reserved for themselves the power of administering (criminal) justice and settling accounts among their members. Through a series of rituals of punishment and redemption inspired by Christian imagery, these communities have reintegrated into their ranks those villagers who, having participated in the guerrilla movement, were considered lethal enemies in the past and have shown repentance in the present. Theidon views these processes of local justice as occurring outside the jurisdiction of the nation-state and considers the forms of reconciliation they achieve as more effective than those sponsored by the state. In this view, the local is configured as a space for the re-creation of inherently moral dispositions and relationships based upon "face to face" knowledge.

Levi's notion of the "grey zone of justice," as developed in Sanford's and others' work, provides a more complex picture of justice and accountability in post-conflict settings. Alongside the moral and ethical problems they encompass, criminal prosecutions of perpetrators of atrocities and state crimes through national courts have a crucial impact in local settings (Sanford 2003a, 2003c; Binford 1996). However, victims of state crime do not seem to comply easily with solutions of reconciliation and closure either at the national level or the local level. Throughout Latin America, victims' experience with law in projects of transitional justice is articulated in terms of specific notions of time and senses of belonging to the nation-state. Truth commissions in Latin America have raised expectations of justice and reparation among victims of state violence who felt that, after several years of delay, their demands had been finally attended to. However, these truth commissions have been experienced more as a discursive event than as a political and legal one capable of bringing change into people's everyday life (Grandin 2005). Sentiments of disappointment and suspicion replace expectations and reinforce people's skepticism regarding their position within the nation-state.

In general, victims are more interested in different kinds of reparation and their notions of justice go beyond (though include) mere punishment of perpetrators. There are specific forms of acknowledgment they seek or expect from legal procedures, such as finding out where the bodies of their missing relatives are in order to give them a proper burial. However, criminal law's traditional focus on perpetrators and its stakes in legality and due process hinder any possibility of these expectations being met in the short term. Accordingly, the experience with law during projects of transitional justice continues to be felt by victims as an experience of sameness, as if nothing will have changed with the advent of democratic transitions. It is as if history and social – and political – relations have been congealed in time. It is as if repetition will return experience to the same historical coordinates. It is a cyclical notion of time that emerges as a counterpoint to projects of nation-building that emphasize amnesia as a means of imposing linear notions of time.

Paradoxically, victims continue to be engaged in judicial procedures seeking legal justice and mobilizing international discourses of human rights brought by truth commissions. It is precisely in these efforts that difference is introduced. In Latin America, a popular struggle against impunity and seeking justice has fissured ruling elites' discourses of national reconciliation and forgiveness. Projects of nation-building that emphasize amnesia have been contested by victims and survivors of state crime, who have found in human rights the enabling language with which to challenge state-led efforts to bring closure to the past. Certainly, these experiences have had differentiated outcomes, which points to the idea that they are different among themselves as well.

## CONCLUSION

Cavell says that there is a repetition necessary to what we call life, or the animate, necessary for example to the human; and a repetition necessary to what we call death, or the inanimate, necessary for example to the mechanical. He says that there are no marks or features or criteria or rhetoric by means of which to tell the difference between them. "From which," Cavell continues, "let me simply claim, it does not follow that the difference is unknowable or undecidable. On the contrary, the difference is the basis of everything there is for human beings to know, or say decide (like deciding to live), and to decide on no basis beyond or beside or beneath ourselves" (1988:158).

As we have seen in this chapter, most of the anthropological work on post-conflict in Latin America is full of images of repetition. Violence keeps returning and framing everyday life, particularly in areas that were affected by war and state violence. However, there are images of mechanical repetition such as the violence of the state. The political violence upon which the project of the liberal nation-state was built looms behind the apparent difference brought about by what anthropologists call "the neoliberal reform" or "the neoliberal project." The new forms of governmentality and subject-making introduced in post–cold war Latin America cannot but repeat forms of violence as part of the new grammar of domination.

There are other forms of repetition, however, that are full of possibilities. These forms of repetition have created spaces of ambiguity in which the possibility for the new emerges. As we have seen in this chapter, anthropologists have also registered the multifarious ways in which victims of violence are recreating their devastated worlds. These forms are not straightforward, clear-cut, or heroic. They are ambiguous, inserted in fluid and ever changing processes, but they are full of possibilities. They are becomings. I consider that Arturo Escobar (2002) invites anthropologists to capture these becomings when he calls for shifting our gaze in anthropological studies on violence. Reflecting from the experience of Colombia, Escobar says that, in studying violence, anthropology needs to release the past, and accordingly the present and the future, from the burden of violence that has been imposed upon it. It is necessary, he says, to untie subaltern memories from their purportedly ineluctable association with violence. For this purpose, Escobar says, it is necessary to shift our gaze and to multiply its positions so as to see from different positions. This shift introduces changes in our gaze's position, in its intensity, even in its luminosity. Anthropologists, he says, need to speak not only from the manifestations of violence, but from those manifestations of life that, in spite of their contact with violence, are never completely determined by it (Escobar 2002).

In this chapter we have seen how many anthropologists have already started this shift of the gaze. Some of them have already found that more than seeing, it is about listening. It is in listening to those spaces of ambiguity, in being caught in them, that anthropology has the opportunity for witnessing the emergence of the new.

## NOTES

1   Grandin refers to the fact that years after the signing of the peace agreement in Guatemala and the return to a civilian rule, state-sponsored crimes continued to take place, as exemplified in the killing of Bishop Juan Gerardi in 1998. Gerardi was bludgeoned to death two days after the release of a report of the Catholic Church on the genocide carried out by the Guatemalan military. The report was even more indicting than the official Comisión para el Esclarecimiento Histórico (Grandin 2000; Manz 2004; Sanford 2003a)

2   This was a later development in Latin American anthropology. Prior to the mid-1980s, the study of state violence and terror remained largely outside the purview of anthropologists

(Margold 1998; Poole 1994; Green 1999). It was in response to the massive violence and terror unleashed by states against civilian populations during the cold war that they shifted their focus to the problem of political violence. This turn to study state violence was made possible both by the declared end of the cold war, which opened up opportunities for field-work in former war zones, and by an epistemological shift introduced by contemporary critical literature on the formation of Western nation-states. This literature, with its critical perspective on how violence and power grounded the formation of the modern nation-states, introduced a set of important questions regarding the ways culture and violence were conceived and theorized in anthropology (Feldman 1991; Poole 1994).

3  It is worth noting that class, ethnic and racial dynamics at work in the Guatemalan and Argentinean cases are very different. In Argentina, most of the victims of the state violence were urban, middle class, white, Spanish speaking professionals or university students. In Guatemala, the vast majority were rural, peasants, non-Spanish speaking indigenous population.

## REFERENCES

Alonso, A. M. (1988) The Effects of Truth: Re-presentations of the Past and the Imagining of Community. *Journal of Historical Sociology* 1:33–57.

Anderson, B. (1983) *Imagined Communities: Reflections on the Origins and Spread of Nationalism.* London: Verso.

Benjamin, W. (1969) Thesis on the Philosophy of History. In Hannah Arendt (ed.), *Illuminations.* London: Pimlico.

Binford, L. (1996) *The El Mozote Massacre: Anthropology and Human Rights.* Tucson: University of Arizona Press.

Bourgois, P. (2001) The Power of Violence in War and Peace. *Ethnography* 2(1):5–34.

Bourgois, P. (2002) The Violence of Moral Binaries. Response to Leigh Binford. *Ethnography* 3(2):221–231.

Burchianti, M. E. (2004) Building Bridges of Memory: The Mothers of the Plaza de Mayo and the Cultural Politics of Maternal Memory. *History and Anthropology* 15(2):133–150.

Carmack, R. M. (ed.) (1988) *Harvest of Violence: The Maya Indians and the Guatemalan Crisis.* Norman: University of Oklahoma Press.

Cavell, S. (1988) *In Quest of the Ordinary: Lines of Skepticism and Romanticism.* Chicago: University of Chicago Press.

Cohen, S. (1996) Government Responses to Human Rights Reports: Claims, Denials, and Counterclaims. *Human Rights Quarterly* 18(3):517–543.

Collier, J. and Speed, S. (2000) Limiting Indigenous Autonomy in Chiapas Mexico. The State Government's Use of Human Rights. *Human Rights Quarterly* 22:877–905.

Coronel, J. (1996) Violencia política y respuestas campesinas en Huanta. In Carlos Ivan Degregori (ed.), *Las rondas campesinas y la derrota de Sendero Luminoso.* Lima: Instituto de Estudios Peruanos.

Corradi, J., Weiss Fagen, P., and Garretón, M. A. (eds) (1992) *Fear at the Edge: State Terror and Resistance in Latin America.* Berkeley: University of California Press.

Cotler, J. and Grompone, R. (2000) El fujimorismo. Ascenso y caída de un régimen autoritario. Lima: Instituto de Estudios Peruanos.

Das, V. (2000) The Act of Witnessing: Violence, Poisonous Knowledge, and Subjectivity. In V. Das et al. (eds), *Violence and Subjectivity.* Berkeley: University of California Press.

Das, V. and Poole, D. (eds) (2004) *Anthropology in the Margins of the State.* Santa Fe: School of American Research Press; Oxford: James Currey.

Degregori, C. I. (ed.) (1996) *Las rondas campesinas y la derrota de Sendero Luminoso.* Lima: Instituto de Estudios Peruanos.

Degregori, C. I. (1998) Harvesting Storms: Peasant Rondas and the Defeat of Sendero Luminoso in Ayacucho. In Steve Stern (ed.), *Shining and Other Paths: War and Society in Peru, 1980–1995*. Durham, NC: Duke University Press.

Degregori, C. I. (2000) *La década de la antipolítica. Auge y huida de Alberto Fujimori y Vladimiro Montesinos*. Lima: Instituto de Estudios Peruanos.

del Pino, P. (1996) Tiempos de guerra y de dioses. Ronderos, evangelicos y senderistas en el Valle del Rio Apurimac. In Carlos Ivan Degregori (ed.), *Las rondas campesinas y la derrota de Sendero Luminoso*. Lima: Instituto de Estudios Peruanos.

del Pino, P. (1998) Family, Culture and "Revolution": Everyday Life with Sendero Luminoso. In Steve Stern (ed.), *Shining and Other Paths: War and Society in Peru, 1980–1995* (pp. 158–191). Durham, NC: Duke University Press.

Dickson-Gomez, J. (2002) The Sound of Barking Dogs: Violence and Terror among Salvadoran Families in the Post-War. *Medical Anthropology* 16(4):415–438.

Ensalaco, M. (2000) *Chile under Pinochet: Recovering the Truth*. Philadelphia: University of Pennsylvania Press.

Escobar, A. (2002) Las violencias a través de otras miradas. *Journal for Latin American Anthropology* 7(1):310–315.

Feldman, A. (1991) *Formations of Violence: The Narrative of the Body and Political Terror in Northern Ireland*. Chicago: University of Chicago Press.

Fumerton, M. (2002) *From Victims to Heroes: Peasant Counter-Rebellion and Civil War in Ayacucho, Peru, 1980–2000*. Thela Latin America Series. Utrecht: Rozenberg.

Galeano, E. (2000[1998]) *Upside Down: A Primer for the Looking-Glass World*, trans. Mark Fried. New York: Picador.

Gaviria, A. (2000) Increasing Returns and the Evolution of Violent Crime: The Case of Colombia. *Journal of Development Economics* 61:1–25.

Goldstein, D. (2003) "In Our Hands": Lynching, Justice and the Law in Bolivia. *American Ethnologist* 30(1):22–43.

Grandin, G. (2000) Chronicles of a Guatemalan Genocide Foretold: Violence, Trauma, and the Limits of Historical Inquiry. *Nepantla: Views from South* 1(2):391–412.

Grandin, G. (2005) The Instruction of Great Catastrophe: Truth Commissions, National History, and State Formation in Argentina, Chile, and Guatemala. *American Historical Review* 110(1):38. At www.historycooperative.org/journals/ahr/110.1/grandin.html, accessed Sept. 27, 2007.

Green, L. (1994) Fear as a Way of Life. *Cultural Anthropology*, 9(2):227–256.

Green, L. (1999) *Fear as a Way of Life: Mayan Widows in Rural Guatemala*. New York: Columbia University Press.

Hale, C. (2002) Does Multiculturalism Menace? Governance, Cultural Rights and the Politics of Identity in Guatemala. *Journal of Latin American Studies* 34:485–524.

Hayner, P. (2001) *Unspeakable Truths: Facing the Challenge of Truth Commissions*. New York: Routledge.

Jimeno, M. (2001) Violence and Social Life in Colombia. *Critique of Anthropology* 21(3): 221–246.

Koonings, K. and Kruijt, D. (1999) Introduction. In K. Koonings and D. Kruijt (eds), *Societies of Fear: The Legacy of Civil War, Violence and Terror in Latin America* (pp. 1–30). London: Zed Books.

Kruijt, D. (1999) Exercises in State Terrorism: The Counter-Insurgency Campaigns in Guatemala and Peru. In K. Koonings and D. Kruijt (eds), *Societies of Fear: The Legacy of Civil War, Violence and Terror in Latin America*. New York: Zed Books.

Lechner, N. (1992) Some People Die of Fear: Fear as a Political Problem. In Juan Corradi, Patricia Weiss Fagen, and Manuel Antonio Garretón (eds), *Fear at the Edge: State Terror and Resistance in Latin America*. Berkeley: University of California Press.

Ludescher, M. (1999) Estado e indígenas en el Perú. Un análisis del marco legal y su aplicación. *Law and Anthropology* 10:122–164.

MacIlwaine, C. and Moser, C. (2003) Poverty, Violence and Livelihood Security in Urban Colombia and Guatemala. *Progress in Development Studies* 3(2):113–130.

Manz, B. (1988) *Refugees of a Hidden War: The Aftermath of Counterinsurgency in Guatemala.* Albany: State University of New York Press.

Manz, B. (2004) *Paradise in Ashes: A Guatemalan Journey of Courage, Terror, and Hope.* Berkeley: University of California Press.

Margold, J. A. (1998) From "Cultures of Fear and Terror" to the Normalization of Violence: An Ethnographic Case. *Critique of Anthropology* 19(1):63–88.

Mendoza, C. (2004) Collective Violence in Post Conflict Guatemala: Understanding Lynch Mobs. Paper presented at the meeting of the Latin American Studies Association, Las Vegas, Oct. 7–9.

Minow, M. (1998) *Between Vengeance and Forgiveness: Facing History after Genocide and Mass Violence.* Boston: Beacon Press.

Nelson, D. (1999) *A Finger in the Wound: Body Politics in Quincentennial Guatemala.* Berkeley: University of California Press.

Nelson, D. (2004) Anthropologist Discovers the Legendary Two-Faced Indian! Margins, the State, and Duplicity in Postwar Guatemala. In V. Das and D. Poole (eds), *Anthropology in the Margins of the State.* Santa Fe: School of American Research Press; Oxford: James Currey.

Nora, P. (1989) Between Memory and History: les lieux de mémoire. *Representations* 26:7–24.

Pecaut, D. (1999) From the Banality of Violence to Real Terror: The Case of Colombia. In K. Koonings and D. Kruijt (eds), *Societies of Fear: The Legacy of Civil War, Violence and Terror in Latin America* (pp. 141–167). London: Zed.

Poole, D. (ed.) (1994) *Unruly Order: Violence, Power, and Cultural Identity in the High Provinces of Southern Peru.* Boulder: Westview.

Poole, D. (2004) Between Threat and Guarantee. In V. Das and D. Poole (eds), *Anthropology in the Margins of the State.* Santa Fe: School of American Research Press; Oxford: James Currey.

Poole, D. (2006) Los usos de la costumbre. Hacia una antropología jurídica del estado neoliberal. *Alteridades* 16(31):9–21.

Poole, D. and Rénique, G. (2003) Terror and Privatized State: A Peruvian Parable. *Radical History Review* 85:150–163.

Ramírez, M. C. (2001) *Entre el estado y la guerrilla. Identidad y ciudadania en el movimiento de los campesinos cocaleros del Putumayo.* Bogotá: Instituto Colombiano de Antropología e Historia.

Robben, Antonious C. G. M. (1995) The Politics of Truth and Emotion among Victims and Perpetrators of Violence. In C. Nordstrom and A. C. G. M. Robben (eds), *Fieldwork under Fire: Contemporary Studies on Violence and Survival.* Berkeley: University of California Press.

Robben, Antonious C. G. M. (2000) The Assault on Basic Trust: Disappearance, Protest, and Reburial in Argentina. In A. C. G. M. Robben and M. M. Suarez-Orozco, *Cultures under Siege: Collective Violence and Trauma.* Cambridge: Cambridge University Press.

Robben, Antonious C. G. M. (2005) *Political Violence and Trauma in Argentina.* Philadelphia: University of Pennsylvania Press.

Rodgers, D. (2002) "We live in a State of Siege": Violence, Crime, and Gangs in Post-Conflict Urban Nicaragua. Working Paper 02-36. Development Studies Institute of the London School of Economics.

Rojas Pérez, I. (2005) La crisis colombiana y Peru. *Colombia Internacional* (Universidad de los Andes, Bogotá) 60.

Rospigliosi, F. (2000) *Montesinos y las fuerzas armadas. Cómo controló durante una década las instituciones militares.* Lima: Instituto de Estudios Peruanos.

Sanford, V. (2003a) *Buried Secrets: Truth and Human Rights in Guatemala.* New York: Palgrave Macmillan.

Sanford, V. (2003b) Learning to Kill by Proxy: Colombian Paramilitaries and the Legacy of Central American Death Squads, Contras and Civil Patrols. *Journal of Social Justice* 30(3):1–19.

Sanford, V. (2003c) The "Grey Zone" of Justice: NGOs and Rule of Law in Postwar Guatemala. *Journal of Human Rights* 2(3):303–405.

Schirmer, J. (1998) *The Guatemalan Military Project: A Violence Called Democracy.* Philadelphia: University of Pennsylvania Press.

Sieder, R. (1999) Rethinking Democratization and Citizenship: Legal Pluralism and Institutional Reform in Guatemala. *Citizenship Studies* 3(1).

Sieder, R. and Witchell, J. (2001) Advancing Indigenous Claims through the Law: Reflections on the Guatemalan Peace Process. In Jane K. Cowan, Marie-Benedicte Dembour, and Richard Wilson (eds), *Culture and Rights: Anthropological Perspectives.* Cambridge: Cambridge University Press.

Starn, O. (1996) Senderos inesperados. Las rondas campesinas de la Sierra Sur Central. In Carlos Ivan Degregori (ed.), *Las rondas campesinas y la derrota de Sendero Luminoso.* Lima: Instituto de Estudios Peruanos.

Starn, O. (1998) Villagers at Arms: War and Counterrevolution in the Central-South Andes. In Steve Stern (ed.), *Shining and Other Paths: War and Society in Peru, 1980–1995.* Durham, NC: Duke University Press.

Suarez-Orozco, M. (1992) A Grammar of Terror: Psychocultural Responses to State Terrorism in Dirty War and Post–Dirty War Argentina. In Carolyn Nordstrom and Jo Ann Martin (eds), *The Paths of Domination, Resistance and Terror.* Berkeley: University of California Press.

Taussig, M. (1984) Culture of Terror – Space of Death: Roger Casement's Putumayo Report and the Explanation of Torture. *Comparative Studies in Society and History* 26:467–497.

Taussig, M. (1992) Terror as Usual. In Michael Taussig, *The Nervous System.* New York: Routledge.

Taussig, M. (2005) *Law in a Lawless Land: Diary of a Limpieza in Colombia.* Chicago: University of Chicago Press.

Theidon, K. (2000) "How We Learn to Kill Our Brothers"? Memory, Morality and Reconciliation in Peru. *Bulletin Institut Français d'Études Andines* 29(3):539–554.

Theidon, K. (2001) Terror's Talk: Fieldwork and War. *Dialectical Anthropology* 26:19–35.

Theidon, K. (2003) Disarming the Subject: Remembering War and Imagining Citizenship in Peru. *Cultural Critique* 54.

Theidon, K. (2004) *Entre Prójimos. El Conflicto Armado Interno y la Política de la Reconciliación en el Perú.* Lima: Instituto de Estudios Peruanos.

Tickner, A. (2003) La "cruzada" mundial contra el terrorismo y las relaciones Colombia-Estados Unidos. In Ann Mason and Luis Orejuela (eds), *La crisis política colombiana. Más que un conflicto armado y un proceso de paz.* Bogotá: Universidad de los Andes.

Villaveces, S. (2002) ¿Por qué erradicamos? Entre bastiones de poder, cultura y narcotráfico. *Journal of Latin American Anthropology* 7(1):226–253.

Warren, K. (1998) *Indigenous Movements and Their Critics: Pan-Maya Activism in Guatemala.* Princeton: Princeton University Press.

Wilson, F. (1997) Recuperation in the Peruvian Andes. *European Journal of Development Research* 9(1):231–245.

Wilson, F. (2000) Representing the State? School and Teacher in Post-Sendero Peru. *Bulletin of Latin American Research* 19:1–16.

Wilson, R. A. (2001) *The Politics of Truth and Reconciliation in South Africa: Legitimizing the Post-Apartheid State.* Cambridge: Cambridge University Press.

Wilson, R. A. (2003) Anthropological Studies of National Reconciliation Processes. *Anthropological Theory* 3(3):367–387.

Zur, J. (1994) The Psychological Impact of Impunity. *Anthropology Today* 10(3).

CHAPTER **14** Alterities: Kinship and Gender

*Olivia Harris*

Given the immense cultural, ethnic and class diversity of Latin American societies, kinship and gender relations in the region are, to say the least, heterogeneous. In this chapter I explore the productive qualities of this heterogeneity, bearing in mind that in an important sense heterogeneity is the ground of kinship and gender at the most general level. The point is worth emphasizing for several reasons. First, the resurgent anthropological interest in kinship has tended to downplay difference and bounded-ness in favour of more open-ended links. Second, an expanded understanding of the range of means by which people create long-term bonds, and the agency involved in making and maintaining them, necessarily brings with it an emphasis on relatedness over unrelatedness, interiority over exteriority, and potentiality over closure (see Carsten 2000). Similarly, approaches to gender have been refashioned in recent decades such that the focus on femininity and masculinity as basic principles of difference or opposition has given way to notions of performance, becoming, and androgyny (Strathern 1988; Butler 1990).

To make a synthesis of anthropological studies of Latin American kinship and gender is clearly impossible. However, as I read around the subject my interest was aroused by a number of issues, some of which preoccupied me in the past, and some of which came out of the vastness and diversity of the regional literature. In the end I have chosen to focus on four themes: the colonial and religious dimensions of inclusion and exclusion across Latin America; the "house" as a means for understanding indigenous social forms; the significance of affinity and alterity in South American kinship; and the ways that difference is expressed through gender. Each of these broad themes points to the idea of otherness by asking how boundedness is construed and how alterity constitutes an aspect of sociality, although they do so, as we shall see, in very different ways.

The history of Iberian colonization and domination casts a long shadow over the self-knowledge of Latin Americans, and equally over the attempts of anthropologists to understand the varieties of social forms. Where these approximate what is familiarly

European or Christian, anthropologists have all too often assumed that American lifeways were derived from European avatars, manifesting a "sameness" that was nonetheless distorted and sometimes disturbing. Conversely, where anthropologists found more obvious heterogeneity, they often supposed that it was a response to the experience of colonial or neocolonial domination. Thus they used to take for granted that the apparent lack of social organization in native eastern Amazonia was due to acculturation and the demoralizing effects of contact with outsiders, or that the system of neighbourhoods (*barrios*) and patron saint feasts in the Mesoamerican and Andean highland communities was colonial in origin. It has therefore proved more complex in Latin America than elsewhere to question the applicability of models of relatedness derived from European cultural practice, given the exceptional depth of colonial history in the region.

How, then, are heterogeneous Latin American persons produced through the workings of kinship, social hierarchy, gender and sexual classifications? What are the processes of inclusion and exclusion that differentiate people and groups? Race certainly remains a powerful operator in Latin America societies today (see Wade, this volume). But how do racial and ethnic binaries operate in the production of persons? Insofar as they identify an excluded other, how does that exclusion work at the level of the person? How do those who are "mixed" identify themselves in this way, and for how many generations? Methodologically similar questions can be asked in contexts that are closer to the classic anthropological understanding of kinship and gender. For example, are women and men thought to be different kinds of beings? In the making of persons is there a bias in favour of the mother's or of the father's contribution, of matrilateral or patrilateral ties? From a different perspective, where affines are symbolized as threatening outsiders, do people produce themselves simultaneously as full human beings and as dangerous and external? The question of alterities, of the constitution of difference in the face of potential sameness, and vice versa, is central to this chapter.

Scholarly debate concerning kinship and social organization is usually confined to particular culture areas – the indigenous worlds of Amazonia, the Andes, Mesoamerica, the circum-Caribbean, the Afro-Americans of the Caribbean and the Atlantic seaboard – and even within these some regions are considered to be more exemplary than others. Then there is the "rest" of Latin America, the demographic majority, its practices and values supposed to derive mainly from Europe. In this chapter I might have attempted a synthesis of the diversities of Latin America, but as a specialist on the Andean region I have found it illuminating to follow some of the debates on different regions, and to let them speak to each other, taking as a given that there has been far more historical contact and interchange than we yet have evidence for. A contrast is apparent between European concepts grounded in legal norms, monotheism and the search for pure, bounded categories, and forms of Latin American personhood that are less absolute, defined more by obligation or work than by birth, or organized around practices that belong not so much to the domain of "kinship" as to that of "religion." Nonetheless, while the contrast between the Euro-Christian and the Native American has continuing salience, equally important are characteristics that override it: the enduring competition for status, and the forms of exclusion and differentiation in personhood that are and were generated by social class, whether the elaborate hierarchies of the great kingdoms and empires, the caste boundaries of colonial society, or the racialized classes of contemporary Latin America.

## CATHOLIC INCLUSIONS AND EXCLUSIONS

The first case I have chosen to focus on is how American, African and European persons became redefined in relation to each other through the prism of colonial hierarchy and Catholic Christianity. A fundamental aspect of the conversion of the New World was the attempted globalization of Spanish and Portuguese kinship and gender norms. A vast literature was generated in the 16th and 17th centuries on questions of heresy and idolatry, but the onslaught on notions of relatedness and sexuality, the project to recategorize personhood and inheritance through civil and canon law, was every bit as profound, and given the greater importance attached to eradicating idolatry, it is striking how much priestly energy was devoted to these issues. The confessionals that were written to guide new American Christians in the finer details of their faith reveal as much or more about how Europeans sought to impose their kinship and gender values and practices. For example, Molina's Confessional of 1569 devoted only 1 percent of its teachings to idolatry, in comparison to 15 percent to sins of the body (Gruzinski 1989:100; see also Barnes 1992).

The aim of the first 12 Franciscan friars, who arrived in Mexico in 1524, was to contribute to the rapid evangelization of the entire world in order to hasten the approaching apocalypse (Leddy Phelan 1956). Unlike Jewish notions of a Chosen People set apart from the rest of humanity, the Christian ideal at its most radical (for example St Paul's "there is neither Jew nor Greek, there is neither slave nor free man, there is neither male nor female, for you are all one in Christ Jesus" in Galatians 3:28) aimed to transcend alterity altogether by the conversion of all peoples into a non-differentiated "community of God." Conversion, in other words, was presumed to put an end to exteriority altogether, and thereby bring history to a close. It is ironical, then, that in Spain of the Reconquista, those populations who refused to join the Christian community were subject to exclusion in the most violent and extreme forms: expulsion or death. Those whose conversion was thought to be strategic rather than sincere were labelled as "impure" in contrast to the "clean blood" of long-established Christian families, and subject to investigation by the Inquisition.

The symbolism of blood was deployed as a means of tracking a non-Christian background over several generations. It undermined the open-ended Christian message of salvation, since those who converted retained the stain for as long as any record or memory of their previous religious affiliation remained. There were attempts to apply the idea of impure blood to the new American converts, but it was used more as an exclusionary device among the colonizers themselves, against those with Muslim and especially Sephardic Jewish forebears (Wachtel 2001; Gose 2002).

Among the American converts, non-Christian practices such as polygamy, and marriage between kin up to the fourth degree, were progressively outlawed. Clerics sought to ascertain which of a man's wives was "legitimate" and to compel him to accept her and only her, by flogging if necessary (for Yucatán see Clendinnen 1987:58). They sought to undermine established relationships between seniors and juniors and between parents and children, and to convert women into nurturing and feminine stereotypes of European motherhood (for northern Mexico see Gutierrez 1991:74–78). In general, preference was given to the patriline, especially in regulating inheritance to high office among ruling elites, and at the same time the legal position of women was systematically downgraded (Silverblatt 1987; Kellogg 1995).

Post-Tridentine values included the dogma that wives obey their husbands at all times; and also the idea that procreative sexual relations within marriage were a debt that must be paid, while all other sexual activity constituted an offense against the Sixth Commandment on adultery (Lavrin 1989). Male homosexuality, the unnameable sin (*el pecado nefando*), was outlawed since it was not only contrary to God's law, but also identified with Islam, and hence politically treasonous as well (Seed 2001:121).

The successful application of these new rules was to be monitored and reinforced through the practice of confession. Foucault (1981) saw the sustained probing through the confessional of the penitent's sexual activities – and also desires and fantasies – as part of a process of individualization, an attempt to create persons who were fundamentally detached from their social context. How successful these efforts were in the New World is obviously questionable, as the work of 20th century anthropology helps to reveal. In practice, most Americans did not confess at all, or misunderstood the purpose of confession to the point of undermining it altogether. And contrary to the Tridentine emphasis on the sinner's free will, the belief that external forces influence behavior – whether other people or cultural traditions more generally – did not disappear (Gruzinski 1989).

The conversion of the Americans to Christianity was not, however, to be furthered by intermarriage with the Europeans. As early as 1498, Queen Isabella issued a decree permitting 30 Spanish women "of good birth" to accompany Columbus's third voyage in order to help colonize the New World and instill Spanish morality. The Emperor himself gave the noble daughter of the Count of Aguilar to Hernán Cortés to marry (Konetzke 1945; Miller 1991:20). In the case of Portugal, well into the 18th century it was not uncommon for girls to be shipped off to Brazil against their will, to ensure the reproduction of a respectable ruling elite (Russell-Wood 1978). Nonetheless, there were also a certain number of strategic marriages between Spanish men and high-ranking, wealthy American women (Burkett 1978), and also between Spanish women and American noblemen and royalty (Carrasco 1997:90–91; Choque 1998).

Stoler's research on colonial rule in South and Southeast Asia in the 19th and 20th centuries, whether Dutch, French or English, demonstrates how rigorously racial distinctions between colonizers and colonized were maintained, through tight control over both European women and the *métis* who were born of unions between European men and local women (Stoler 1997). In 16th century Spain and Portugal, however, the concept of *raza* had different connotations. While continued attempts were made to maintain clear boundaries between colonizers and colonized, in practice these were more typically honored in the breach. Hence the uniqueness of Latin America as a postcolonial population.

The Spanish initially referred to themselves as "Christians" in the New World as they had at home, to distinguish themselves from Moors and Jews. As the Americans converted to Christianity en masse, there was no legal reason to bar them from full membership in the community of Christians of Iberian origin (Herzog 2003). However, the social difference which at first had been expressed in terms of religion, and thence also of "blood," quickly became one of status. American social hierarchies were telescoped and downgraded. While elite families retained more of their status and privileges than has often been assumed (Restall 1997), most Americans (known universally as Indians) became plebeians, while all Spanish in the New World aimed to identify themselves as gentry and therefore as social equals (Seed 1988:21). Despite population loss, especially in central Mexico, the native Americans remained numerically dominant, worked mainly in agriculture and mining, and paid the poll tax (*tributo*) unless they were part of the small surviving elite. The African population worked mainly in the urban centres, often as domestic servants. Since as slaves or ex-slaves they were not descended from free vassals of the King, and were also natives of another place, they could never become full legal persons (Herzog 2003:159). The same was broadly the case also in the Portuguese dominions (Schwartz 1985).

Although there was no legal bar to marriages between Indians and Europeans, social pressures ensured that in practice there were very few. On the other hand, unions were commonplace, and as a result the children they produced were overwhelmingly illegitimate. Hernán Cortés had fathered a child with Malintzin (Malinche), the Nahua woman whose linguistic skills were so central to the enterprise of conquest, but his marriage was to a Spanish noblewoman. Thus the separation in the New World between legal marriage and the multitude of children created outside marriage, and generally between different castes, was symbolically inaugurated in the name of Christian monogamy. For many commentators the informal and unequal relationship between Cortés and Malintzin lies at the heart of Latin American identity to this day, and reflects the profound contradictions in the values that were brought from Europe.

For some two hundred years, to be of mixed parentage (*mestizo* or *mulatto*) by definition meant to be illegitimate in the Spanish colonies (Bouysse-Cassagne 1996). Only in the 18th century did significant numbers of Spanish women for the first time seek to marry mestizos, as some of this category became prosperous with the growth of commercial society. But as the desire for intercaste marriages increased, so did the formal restrictions (Seed 1988:148–149). Even the Church, which had previously supported such marriages when based on free choice, fell into line. In this changing social climate, a more rigorous ban on interracial marriage was proclaimed in the 1778 Royal Pragmatic, although given the legal status of Indians it could only be applied unambiguously to marriage between those of African descent and others. Although the Pragmatic did not fully achieve its stated aims, it signaled an increasing and more explicit consciousness of race and racial origins (Martinez-Alier 1974; Socolow 1989:234–235). Similarly in Brazil, although interracial and interclass marriages were not illegal, social pressure ensured that most marriages were between social, racial and economic equals (Da Silva 1984).

While the Iberians disapproved of marriage between different castes, they accepted as normal and inevitable the extramarital unions between higher status men and lower status women that produced ever more complex mixes of different groups (see Wade, this volume). The Indian ruling elites inevitably saw in such practices a threat to their own social order, not least because mestizos were exempt from paying the Indian tribute. Thus the Peruvian nobleman, Guaman Poma de Ayala, in his great work of 1615, denounced in uncompromising language not only the hypocritical sexual behavior of Spanish officials and priests who raped Indian women or kept them as concubines, but also the sexual freedom of Indian women who flaunted their liaisons with other kinds of men: "The author has seen many whorish indian women with their mestizo and mulatto babies, wearing short skirts, ladies' boots and hats. Even though they are married, they consort with Spanish and black men. And others refuse to marry an indian man" (Guaman Poma 1980:1128).

A central theme of Guaman Poma's work is his resounding condemnation of mestizaje. However, what he means by "mixture" is a status distinction as well as a caste one. He also classifies as mestizo the Andean nobleman who marries a commoner woman, and any child born to them (1980:734; de la Cadena 2005:264). It is questionable how far American women themselves shared his view. Apart from the sexual desire some of them felt for Spanish men, others quickly realized the advantages for themselves and especially for their children of procreating mestizos, rather than feeling a sense of outrage (Bouysse-Cassagne 1996).

The history of gender and marriage during the colonial period reveals the effects of segregation, even though it was not expressed in terms of race. Spanish, creoles and Indians, although all Christians and therefore in an important sense the same, were divided in terms of legal status, and thence of economic and political opportunity. The growing mestizo and mulatto population was illegitimate in all senses of the word, not only conceived outside wedlock, but also consigned to a legal vacuum since in theory it did not exist. Mestizos were partly assimilated within the category of Spaniards but at the same time excluded from most public office, as well as from the world of their indigenous kin. In the less rigidly stratified colonial Brazil, too, slaves were "black" and masters "white" even though both groups were likely to be of mixed Portuguese and Indian ancestry (*mamelucos*), and only gradually did an intermediate category of poor peasants emerge as African slaves replaced Americans (Metcalf 1992).

This long history of illegitimacy has undoubtedly played a part in the negative views of mestizaje held by the elites up to the present day. However, at the same time, there is no doubt that many Iberian men considered, and still do, that they were "improving the race" through conceiving children with women of indigenous or African origin. Even in Mexico, the ideology of a mestizo nation that developed after the Revolution (1911) had clear eugenic undertones, since European stock was still considered to be superior, and a means of improving the indigenous element (see Walsh, this volume). Eugenic projects encouraging immigration from Europe were also popular from the early 20th century. In Brazil with its profoundly mixed population, some even dreamed of a time when they would be "transformed into pure Greeks" (Stepan 1991:135, 148). Gilberto Freyre's famous claim that Brazil was a "racial democracy," and his advocacy of *mestiçagem*, have been substantially undermined by later scholarship (1946; Ianni 1970; see also Wade, this volume).

While an ideology of mestizaje was proclaimed by many Latin American nations over the course of the 20th century, status endogamy and the exclusion of racial others continues. In Guatemala the power and position of the ruling elite has never been seriously challenged, maintained through constant endogamy, and avoiding mixture with "inferior" races. Elite Guatemalan families would not dream of consenting to their children marrying indigenous people, but at the same time, elite men in each generation continue to produce large numbers of illegitimate children with indigenous, mestiza and ladino women (Casaús Arzú 1998:79–82). In Mexico too, the aristocracy maintained its exclusivity even though the Revolution and subsequent policies sought to strip it of its status and influence, and with the rise of a new plutocracy has been able partly to recoup its position (Nutini 2004). In Brazil the Moorish practice of cousin marriage was maintained into the 20th century to preserve elite status and property, against Church pressure and the developing medical science and eugenics, accompanied by an expectation that men would also have *concubinas* and secondary households (Borges 1992; Rebhun 1999).

Wade has recently argued, in terms that evoke anthropological understandings of the equal weighting of patrilateral and matrilateral ties in cognatic kinship, that mestizos are able to retain their sense of two alternative identities (Wade 2005). However, it should be noted that his examples mainly involve people of African descent. In spite of Vasconcelos's invocation of the "cosmic" mestizo race derived from a blend of the different races in the Americas (1925), the ideology of "mixing" between Indians and Europeans in practice is far less transparent. In the case of the Andes, for example, Weismantel has argued forcefully that ideas of race today constitute a powerful binary of exclusion, altering according to context but always contrastive (2001).

While mestizaje does not of course have a constant meaning from the 16th century to the present, it is striking how often greater value is attributed to a single European forebear in different historical contexts, including the present day, and how easily a pale complexion translates into higher social status. Those of "mixed" race who have social aspirations are at pains to deny that they have any indigenous forebears. Conversely, it is common enough for children sired by elite men to grow up poor, not knowing more than the identity of their father, if that. Such processes of identification and repulsion in the constitution of Latin American persons and kin relations are only now beginning to be properly studied (e.g. Stolcke 2004; Smith 1995; Kaur 2005).

This history of mass illegitimacy, and mixing between caste – later race – groups who in theory were separate, is unusual in global terms. There are many studies of mestizaje and hybridity, but few which consider issues of kinship and relatedness. In the case of anthropologists who have studied comparable fields of kinship among Afro-Americans, they have concentrated mainly on family structure. In studying the kinship classifications of populations of European origin it has proved easy to forget all those children conceived out of wedlock (a striking and influential example being Schneider 1980). For these people, the mantra that in Euro-American kinship "blood is thicker than water" (Schneider 1984) rarely applies. It is plausible that current anthropological preoccupations with relatedness are in part the result of the general availability of birth control methods in Europe and America. In other kinds of social environments where birth control has not been available, where a rule of monogamy has been combined with acute status and racial consciousness, and many children are not legitimized, or even recognized by their fathers, ties of blood may be denied not recognized, let alone celebrated.

In indigenous kin-reckoning today, nurture plays as important a role as substance (Weismantel 1995), so that status is not an absolute matter of birth, and race is not a relevant concept, although pale skins are often admired more than darker ones. Insofar as ancestry is valued, it is principally as a means of access to resources, especially land, and not as a marker of social status. Hence the way in which mestizos privilege certain forebears because of their European origins is not something that I have seen documented for indigenous populations, or observed myself. In my experience it is outsiders who are fascinated by the occasional pair of blue eyes in indigenous communities, and take pleasure in speculating who was responsible: a white landowner, a Scottish mining engineer, a Spanish priest…

Nonetheless, warrior groups have often sought to capture enemy women both as a demonstration of their own superior power and as a means of harnessing the power of their enemies. For example Amazonians, and Araucanians in frontier regions of Chile and Argentina, were keen to capture white settler women, who not unusually were unwilling to return when recaptured by local militias, since they fared better living with their captors than in their white communities of origin (Bengoa 1985; Goddard 2000). The interpretation by European sources of such kidnappings tended to be that Native Americans were seeking to "fortify the race," but we must be wary of transposing such typical European values onto populations who did not share European preoccupations with racial difference. As Salomon and Schwartz (1999) have pointed out, there were many strategic and economic reasons why Spanish captives were valuable.

## "THE HOUSE" IN MESOAMERICAN AND ANDEAN SOCIETIES

I suggest that social differences in native American philosophies were not until recently formulated in racial terms, and in this section I explore a model of relatedness that places less emphasis on birth than those emanating from Europe. Having said that, the reproduction of status does of course typically draw on birth as a major source of distinction in American cultures as well as European. In the pre-Christian past, the most extreme strategy by which high-status Americans reproduced themselves as a distinctive category was probably that of the Inkas, whose claim to divine origins was reinforced by the marriage of royal siblings, from whose sons and daughters the heirs of the following generation were selected. More generally, elites across the Americas maintained their separateness through strategic exogamic marriages and patrilineal inheritance.

At the same time, it seems that elites and commoners were bound together through particular kinds of ties, and I draw on discussions of the "house," and "house socie-ties," to explore the constitution of social groups in Mesoamerica and the Andes. Central to the developing literature on the house is the recognition that kinship cat-egories that have conventionally been viewed as incompatible, or at least distinct, can be found in combination or coexistence, in part reflecting status differences between members of a single aggregate which is organized around elite families or lineages (Lévi-Strauss 1983; Carsten and Hugh-Jones 1995; Waterson 1995). The continuing debates over whether Mesoamerican and Andean descent and inheritance should be characterized as patrilineal, bilateral, or bilineal, and whether or when endogamy is a marriage rule, can be sidestepped by following the lead of this literature, as well as Schneider (1984), and privileging indigenous categories, recognizing that the consti-tution of social relations and groups may involve different kinds of practice. For exam-ple, I suggest that in Mesoamerica and the Andes, social units combining commoners with elites were historically defined especially through religious and ancestral cults, and after conversion to Christianity translated into the worship of patron saints.

In 16th century Mesoamerica and the Andes, generic terms were adopted by the Spanish administrators to refer to social units which were also identified in Spanish as *parcialidad* (a division of a larger whole) or *barrio* (neighborhood): for example, *altépetl* and *calpolli* in the Nahua-speaking regions, *chinamit* or *cah* in

Maya-speaking regions, and *ayllu* in the Andes. Populations subject to the Mexica (often known as Aztecs) were obliged to pay tribute on a rotating basis, as allocated to each unit. In the more centralized Inka state, local groupings had been reorganized according to an overarching decimal system, including a division into upper and lower moieties, by means of which tribute labour was allocated. As the Spanish took over this highly efficient system, they generalized the use of ayllu to refer to fiscal units under their respective heads, and reserved the term parcialidad mainly to refer to the moieties.

Part of Spanish policy was to resettle the new subject populations in villages modelled on the Iberian grid plan. In the Andes these villages were in some cases founded on the sites of Inka-period settlements, and because ayllu organization was fundamental to the colonial labour service (*mit'a*), the previous organization under the governance of the local nobility was largely retained. As a result, ayllu structures have remained clear in some places even in the 20th and 21st centuries, with named ayllus occupying the same lands over a period of five hundred years or more (although the precise boundaries are of course subject to change and contestation).

In Mesoamerica, by contrast, a less centralized political field meant that each locality retained more independence, even when tied into tributary relations with the Mexica state of Tenochtitlán (Lockhart 1991; Clendinnen 1991). The Spanish brought devastating population loss to central Mexico, through both disease and war, and the Church played an important role in reorganizing settlements. These *congregaciones* were frequently divided into neighborhoods (*barrios*), each with its own patron saint and confraternity (*cofradía*) organized to celebrate its feast. It was long assumed that these settlement towns, later redesignated as *municipios*, were fundamentally Iberian in conception and identity, marking a profound break with the past. This apparent contrast pervaded mid 20th century scholarship. Leading anthropologists and historians in the Andean region (Luis Valcarcel, José María Arguedas, John V. Murra, R. T. Zuidema, Nathan Wachtel) celebrated the continuities between past and present, while Mesoamerican scholars mainly emphasized discontinuity and loss. The orthodoxy was that cultural practice and social forms in Mesoamerica were the product of the colonial order, and retained very little of their pre-Spanish roots. Drawing on Ricard's account of the "spiritual conquest" which asserted that the early Franciscan friars had initiated a profound transformation of Mexican culture (Ricard 1933), and expanding the work of other North American anthropologists (e.g. Tax 1952), Eric Wolf established an influential model of the "closed corporate peasant community," colonial in origin, into which indigenous populations were typically concentrated (1957; 1959:213–220). Martinez Peláez (1971) similarly declared that the cultures and social practices of Guatemalan Indians were substantially the product of colonial rule.

The assumption of an absolute break inaugurated by the Spanish Conquest went together with a sense of lack, powerfully evidenced in anthropological studies of kinship. Try as they might, few anthropologists found more than occasional lineages, or what they perceived to be fragmentary traces of an earlier patrilineal system (Guiteras Holmes 1951; Pozas and Aguirre Beltrán 1954). In the Andes too, early studies of kinship took a similar course (Stein 1961; Vázquez and Holmberg 1966). The prevailing evolutionist assumptions encouraged the representation of highland Latin America as a region where, even before the Spanish administration, social organization based on large kin groups had given way to the principle of territoriality (Hunt 1976; Nutini 1976). As Wolf wrote for Mesoamerica:

> The diligent ethnologist may still find, among the Otomí-speakers on the fringes of the Valley of Mexico, hamlets based on common descent in the male line and enforced marriage outside the community; or patrilineal kinship units sharing a common name, a common saint, and a measure of social solidarity among the Tzeltal-Tzotzil-speakers of Chiapas, though there too they have lost their former exogamy and common residence which they possessed in the past. But these examples remain the fascinating exceptions to the general rule that, among Middle American Indians as a whole, common territoriality in one community and common participation in communal life have long since robbed such units of any separatist jurisdiction they may at one time have exercised. (1959:220)

Wolf's pessimistic assessment of the irremediable lack of exoticism in indigenous Mesoamerica was derived from the assumption that territoriality as a basis for social relations is transparent and univocal. But he was surely wrong. Colonial and postcolonial barrios had little in common with evolutionary ideas about territoriality as understood through the prism of 19th and 20th century administrative categories.

At the same time that anthropologists were accepting that the ways indigenous peasants understood relatedness could not be assimilated into the dominant Africanist models of exogamous patrilineages exercising "separatist jurisdiction," as Wolf termed it, two edited collections, addressing kinship in Mesoamerica and the Andes respectively, appeared to herald a new research agenda, although bizarrely they seem to have been completed without reference to each other. The Andean volume emphasized bilaterality and the autonomy of individual households (Bolton and Mayer 1977; Lambert 1977); the Mexican collection by contrast, while also calling for a new theorization of bilaterality (Nutini 1976:24), concentrated on larger kin units, and the articulation of kin groups and territory (Nutini, Carrasco and Taggart 1976). However, in practice these books marked more the end of conventional kinship studies in the region, as confidence in established modes of analysis plummeted following the critiques of Needham (1971) and Schneider (1984), and the increasing interest in gender.

Part of this general shift of scholarly interest, and greater conceptual sophistication, was linked to the growth of social and cultural history, permitting the development of a more nuanced and empirically grounded understanding of historical process. In Andean anthropology and history, this led to a reaction against what was seen as an essentialist, ahistorical collapsing of the Inka and colonial past with the present, and a growing concern for historical specificity (Abercrombie 1998; Presta 1995; Poole 1992; Saignes 1995).

The opposite occurred in Mesoamerican anthropology and history, which saw an increased interest in continuities of structural form and symbolic meaning over five hundred years or more. Developing the work of the historian Charles Gibson, who had shown that the Spanish administration relied essentially on preexisting social units in the valley of Mexico, albeit with changes of nomenclature (Gibson 1952; 1964), Hill and Monaghan, in an influential study of Sacapulas in the Quiché highlands of Guatemala, demonstrated that the territorial units known today as *cantones* are the same both as the colonial barrios or parcialidades, and as the precolonial chinamit, and that they retained most of their functions until recently. Carlsen's study of Santiago Atitlán (Guatemala) similarly argues that the congregación of 1547 was not a new creation, but brought together several chinamits and larger groupings of chinamits (Hill and

Monaghan 1987; Carlsen 1997; see also Lockhart 1992). Chance (1996) developed these insights for the Nahua town of Tecali by showing how the Spanish administrative system introduced new constraints, such that some units retained their essential features from pre-Spanish times, while others were fundamentally remodeled.

While I recognize the problems associated with delineating a transhistorical model of social forms in Mesoamerica and the central Andes, part of my argument concerns the flexibility of these forms (calpulli, altépetl, chinamit, cah, ayllu), and also the variation in scale. It is intrinsic to these units to change over time.

Spanish commentators in the early colonial period frequently identified them as "lineages" or kin groups, and erroneously assumed them to be exogamous. They were normally associated with particular land, although in urban centers such as pre-Spanish Tenochtitlán, calpulli were associated with crafts specialisms and had no land (Clendinnen 1991). Historically they were structured through identification with a lord or leader (Carrasco 1976; Hill and Monaghan 1987:32–33; Chance 1996; Platt, Bouysse-Cassagne and Harris 2006). Indeed, the idea that all members of such groups tended to marry out may have arisen because of this identification with ruling lineages, who did indeed practice exogamic marriage, forming alliances with elites from other similar units (Joyce 2001; Arnold 1998). Commoners were probably more oriented to endogamy, conserving land within the group. However, it is clear that common membership did not necessarily depend on common kinship, nor on recognition of an apical ancestor. For example, the Maya chinamit was probably organized around a core family or lineage of high status, but others could equally be members of this "brotherhood" without being kin (Hill and Monaghan 1987:32). Again, Andean ayllus in the early colonial period witnessed massive in- and outmigration, such that in some areas more than half were classified as "outsiders" (forasteros) but could nonetheless be identified as members of the ayllu (Sánchez-Albornoz 1978; Wightman 1990; Powers 1995).

In the characterizations of house societies in other parts of the world, members of a "house" generally conceptualize themselves as a single group through identification with a physical building, often the ceremonial residence of house elders. The pre-Spanish Mesoamerican calpolli, too, meant "great house," and was composed of a number of individual houses. Calpolli were enduring units, drawn together through ritual practice, and also for payment of tribute. Kinship, organized cognatically, was a weak point of identification. The ruler held all rights to land and delegated them to the calpolli as a whole, not to individual kinship groups or households. Relatedness was usually based on residence or other strategic interests, and outsiders could be integrated (Joyce 2001:136–139).

In the central Andes, there is less historical evidence that houses of the elite functioned as an encompassing symbol related to the ayllu in the way that was typical of parts of Southeast Asia, although a few examples from 16th century Charcas suggest that such an association probably existed (Platt, Bouysse-Cassagne and Harris 2006: 66, 663–666). The patriline and the imagery of sperm seem to have been more salient as encompassing expressions of relatedness than the house, in both the Aymara and Quechua languages, although it is hard to determine how much this is due to the colonial influence of the sources (Isbell 1997; Salomon 1997).

In general, it was probably religious cults with their shrines and cult-houses that served as the basis of group affiliation. In the central Andes these cults were dedicated to ancestors of the ruling elite and associated with particular landholdings. They were sufficiently important that even when populations were forced to relocate their settlements by the Inka or the Spanish, the original ancestral shrines remained sites of annual pilgrimage (Howard-Malverde 1990; Del Río 1997). The encomienda certificates that granted the use of Indian Labour to individual Spaniards make it clear that ayllus were identified with a leader, and grouped together under the broader leadership of a noble lineage. The relatedness within such groups was mediated through the shared land that fed them and whose ancestral shrines they provided for.

These criteria cannot of course apply to comparable units today, since the ruling elites have disappeared, reclassifying themselves as mestizo or ladino, and the ancestral cults were a particular target for the priests who sought to eradicate idolatry. A few anthropologists have indicated that the house is a key organizing concept for understanding 20th century kinship practices in Mexico (Monaghan 1996; Sandstrom 2000), and others working in the Andean region have also noted the importance of house imagery (Mayer 1977; Arnold 1992; Gose 1994; Yapita and Arnold 1998). However, beyond individual dwellings, a contemporary practice similar to pre-Christian ancestral cults in the Andes and Mesoamerica is the organization of saints day celebrations. Numerous studies of barrios and municipios in 20th century Mesoamerica, and of ayllus or peasant communities in the central Andes, signal the importance of rotating ritual obligations to the functioning of the unit, and demonstrate how traditional authority structures were linked to the obligation (*cargo*) to celebrate the feasts of the saints. This complex of cargos, cofradías and the saints' day *fiestas* has conventionally been seen as evidence that today's indigenous communities are of colonial origin. However, these southern European Catholic institutions may have been accepted with alacrity because they could be mapped onto established practice.

Carlsen's study of Santiago Atitlán provides evidence of such a process. He notes the imagery of vegetable growth and decay in present-day cofradías such that the elders (*principales*) are identified as the trunk and the ancestors as roots, with clear pre-Christian roots. But the "bundle cult," whose origins lie in the Maya Classic period, in the form it is practiced today is associated with Christian saints (Carlsen 1997). In similar vein Hill and Monaghan suggest that the patron saint of each canton in Sacapulas today is like the founding ancestor in the myth of origin (1987:13), and Monaghan's (1995) study of Mixtec Nuyoo today argues that Nuyootecos realize the "great house" that is their community through cargo service. Arnold (1993) proposes for the Qaqachaka ayllus of highland Bolivia that the patron saints, associated with the founding of the pueblo, are a Christianized form of the mummified ancestors. Finally, Urton has emphasized the central importance of patron saints and their fiestas in the articulation of ayllus of Paqariqtambo (southern Peru), suggesting links with pre-Christian cults (1990:99).

Earlier generations of anthropologists recognized the importance of the fiesta system, but were hampered by the conventional divisions of ethnological knowledge. Thus Tax and Hinshaw, writing of the Maya in the midwestern Guatemalan highlands, note: "Perhaps the institution most important in binding the household to the community is the civil-religious hierarchy, and traditionally a sure criterion of one's acceptance of and by the community has been community service through this institution" (1969:88). This observation is made under an overall heading of "political and religious organization." Whether we see the civil-religious hierarchy as a form of "kinship" is open to question, since members of such groups were not necessarily genealogically related, but it surely constitutes a fundamental ground of relatedness in the region.

These units today (barrios, municipios, peasant communities, ayllus), associated with particular landholdings, are often strongly endogamous, but endogamy never seems to be a rule (Hunt and Nash 1969; Hickman and Stuart 1977; Hill and Monaghan 1987; Sánchez Parga 1990; Ossio 1992). On the contrary, where it is politically or socially disadvantageous, other marriage practices take precedence (e.g. Skar 1998; Spedding 1998). In the central Andes it is striking how rarely ayllus are imagined as groups of kin in spite of the high rates of endogamy recorded in some cases (although Isbell 1978:105 documents an exception in Ayacucho, southern Peru). Land is associated with particular ancestors (and more of them male than female) who worked it and handed it on to their descendants, and these forebears are remembered in rituals. When there is great pressure on resources, exclusionary forms such as those emphasizing patrilineal inheritance may prevail (Abercrombie 1998; Arnold 1998:28). But common ayllu membership requires people to cooperate and to exchange labour in highly formalized ways, to mourn their dead, and to celebrate the patron saint or saints together.

It is through meeting these obligations that people have the right to work the land (Gose 1994; Harris 2000). The emphasis on duties to the collective is extraordinarily strong in both Mesoamerica and the Andes, and full personhood has until recently in important senses been a function of membership of the group. As such, the decline – or outright abolition – of collective duties in recent decades, and the growth of legally constituted individual property rights in land, strike at the very heart of indigenous American understandings of personhood, relatedness and identity.

The commensality at the heart of ritual practice is a powerful statement of the bonds constituted and reproduced through nurturing and the giving of food (Weismantel 1995). Similarly, the "territoriality" of these units, long associated by evolutionary thought with the "political" domain, may be the grounding of a relationship realized through the work of agricultural production and consumption. Seen from this perspective, the question of whether, and to what degree, units such as the calpolli, the altépetl, cah, chinamit or ayllu were or are kinship groups ceases to be salient. Endogamy, where practiced, is a reiteration of solidarity and shared interests within such units, but where circumstances dictate, they can easily absorb outsiders, so long as they fulfill their obligations in the form of labour and ritual and festive contributions; those who did not, or do not, fulfill these obligations are expelled. There is, then, often a pragmatic quality to the attribution of kin ties.

The centrality of religious cult in this understanding of relatedness may also help to explain the importance of godparents in these societies. Compadrazgo is generally assumed to be an institution of Mediterranean origin, but the speed and extent to which it was adopted in Mesoamerica and the Andes suggests that this supremely optional form of kinship also had American roots, corresponding to the fluidity and openness of local cultures of relatedness. Compadrazgo ties can be created in many different ways, and on the basis of many different relationships. They can be between close kin, virtual strangers, or patrons and their clients. In some areas anthropologists have noted that individuals may have as many as ten different godparents, and powerful patrons may have compadres and godchildren running into the hundreds (Laughlin 1969; Nutini 1984; Spedding 1998).

However, it would be distorting to emphasize only fluidity and the potential for inclusion. The same features of these social groups are also a means by which opposition, competition and alterity may be articulated. The fact that incomers might, and may, become part of a particular cult- and land-group does not mean that their differential status would be quickly forgotten. In both the Andean and Mesoamerican regions, for example, the prevailing dual organization in at least some cases originated precisely as a means of differentiating conquerors or in-migrants from the established population. Dual divisions – usually between upper and lower moieties – remain an important way in which boundedness and opposition are expressed within a larger landholding unit.

Within such groups too, for all their potential open recruitment, certain relationships must have embodied differentiation. In the past status distinctions were key markers of alterity. In recent times – at least in the Andean region – it is arguably relations of affinity that most obviously play out antagonism and opposition within any land-group.

## Affinity and Alterity: Amazonia and the Andes

In order to explore this suggestion, I turn to the anthropology of Amazonia. Stable groupings of the kind I have outlined for the Andean region have proved hard to identify in much of indigenous Amazonia, although the dualist systems and moieties which have been described for Gê and Bororo groups of Central Brazil are expressed in many different forms and practices (Maybury-Lewis 1989; Seeger 1989). In the main, ethnographers have emphasized fluidity, the performative and optional quality of relationships and the primacy of dyadic interpersonal relations over group sociality (Rivière 1984).

Studies of isolated indigenous groups by Amazonian ethnographers have concentrated unprecedented effort on understanding the micropolitics of kinship and affinity, part of a broader collective attempt to rethink established anthropological models and concepts, since in Amazonia, as in much of Latin America, they have generally proved to be a handicap.

Drawing on Overing's and Rivière's work, a number of studies have shown how in Amazonia social groups are constantly created and remade, especially through sharing and conviviality (Gow 1991; Overing 1989; McCallum 2001). Those who live together in this way are often identified by ethnographers as "consanguines," since little distinction is made between shared bodily substance and the fact of living together. However, it is by no means clear how far shared bodily substance – of blood or anything else – is a defining quality of relatedness, and other terms have been suggested for this ongoing practice of producing intimacy and relatedness, indeed of procreation itself, for example "familiarization" (Fausto 1997; Taylor 2001) or "consubstantialization" (Rival 1998; Vilaça 2002). In general, relatedness has a range of associations in local usage – vegetative imagery, feeding, or the transmission of names – and cannot be restricted to notions of shared bodily substance implicit in the concept of consanguinity. The house, too, has proved to be an important means of constituting and expressing kinship, even among Gê groups such as the Kayapo whose social organization has been more easily assimilated into conventional anthropological models (Hugh-Jones 1995; Lea 1995; Rivière 1995).

In a similar vein, marriage and affinity have been extensively reinterpreted by Amazonian anthropologists, and are seen more as a function of the constitution of a coresidential group as an endogamous kindred than as alliance between groups (Overing Kaplan 1975). This approach to affinity is in part the consequence of the widespread occurrence of kinship terminology organized in two sections which stand as spouse exchangers to each other: the so-called Dravidian type kinship system, famously elaborated by Dumont with reference to South India (1953), but its applicability increasingly questioned to the point where some now claim that the only "true" two-section kinship is to be found in Amazonia (Taylor 1998; Viveiros de Castro 1998b; also Henley 1996). How far people who use the terminology of a two-section system actually marry the people who stand terminologically in an "affinal" relationship is however open to question, and in many instances it seems that the terminology is adjusted to fit practice rather than vice versa (Killick 2005; Lepri 2005).

People outside the coresidential group have generally been viewed with suspicion and hostility in indigenous Amazonia, but at the same time, alterity and the contrast between inside and outside is of central importance in sociality and cosmic reproduction (Overing Kaplan 1981). The outsider has been increasingly identified by anthropologists working in Amazonia with the potential affine. Given the common two-section marriage system, it is not surprising that native Amazonians often prefer to marry within their settlement, and such affinal relationships are reworked to make them "consanguineal." By contrast, marriage with outsiders and strangers is seen as dangerous and problematic, but it is such people who retain their "affinal" status. Indeed, since actual marriage and the reproduction of children leads to a kind of domestication of affinal otherness, it has become increasingly emphasized that the truest affines are those with whom marriage has *not* taken place. There is thus a common association of the categories enemy, cannibal and affine (Descola 1993; Rivière 1993; Taylor 2001).

However, for all it is dangerous and threatening, alterity is also productive. For example, Viveiros de Castro has described the Araweté "passion for exteriority" which he memorably phrased as the "enemy's point of view" and Amazonian "perspectivism," and has pursued this line of enquiry by proposing that in Amazonia the paradigmatic, default relationship is not filiation but affinity, a potential characterized not by marriage alliance but by predation and hostility (1992, 1998a). Since "consanguineal" relationships (understood as those of mutuality and coresidence) have to be constantly made and remade through daily life, Viveiros de Castro proposes that we can understand Amazonian categories better if affinity, understood as difference, is seen as prior to, and encompassing kinship: "consanguinity is *non-affinity* before anything else" (2001:27).

Broadly speaking, Viveiros de Castro's argument is the antithesis of, and perhaps an inevitable backlash against, those who have emphasized the "aesthetics of conviviality," the "power of love," or broadly the culture of relatedness in Amazonian studies (e.g. Santos Granero 1991; Overing and Passes 2000). In Viveiros de Castro's formulation, enmity is the basis of sociality, and the figure of the affine has come to stand for irreducible alterity.

In sharp contrast to native Amazonian studies, affinity has not attracted much attention among ethnographers of highland Latin America, and where it has, it refers to actually existing marriage relations rather than an axiomatic cosmology of otherness.

However the debates over Amazonian categories of relatedness can perhaps shed light on the importance attributed to affinal figures in the Central Andes. Spouse-takers play an important part in key rituals, and a number of Andean ethnographers have indicated that affinal kin are identified with a greater specificity than are consanguineal relationships. For example, Mayer writes of the "clarity and precision with which Tangorinos [Húanuco, Peru] were able to explain *masha* and *lumtshuy* [i.e. DH (daughter's husband) and BW (brother's wife)] categories to me ... compared with the imprecise and 'what for?' questions that I received when I tried to take [a] genealogy and categorize ... relatives according to *casta* and *ayllu* categories" (1977:79).

Affinal relationships often involve violence (Harvey 1994; Van Vleet 2002). Moreover, affinity involves a lifelong relationship of asymmetry or inequality, in which the male wife-taker must perform services, especially ritual ones, for his father/brothers-in-law, and women for their husband's family. There is historical evidence that these relationships were understood in similar ways in the 16th century (Gose 1994:78; Ossio 1998:286).

The particular role of wife-takers is sometimes associated with predators. They are often expected to serve alcoholic drinks during rituals until the desired state of inebriation, and identification with the pre-Christian ancestors, has been achieved. Moreover they are sometimes explicitly seen to be predatory creatures of the wild, for example serpents, jaguars and bears in a 1603 description of a house-roofing ceremony (Ossio 1998:269), or condors who, according to a well-known 20th century myth, carry their young brides off to their craggy nests on the mountain tops (Harris 1994).

This imagery of the condor is found in a slightly different form in Huaquirca (Apurimac, Peru) where the wife-taker son-in-law is quintessentially an outsider, identified with the mountain deities themselves, of whom condors are a physical manifestation. In Gose's analysis, affinity is always expressed as difference (Gose 1994:78, 201–202). Others have described the imagery of robbery and capture when a girl is taken secretly at night to her future husband's house, or the war imagery in marriage rituals.

The image of the wife-taker as a predatory outsider, resonant with the image of affinity in native Amazonia, seems hard to understand in Andean communities where in reality he is often a close neighbor. The male affine who helps to build your house, harvest your crops, becomes in ritual symbolism the quintessential Other. As children are born and the new household consolidates its productivity, the imagery of predation is complemented by more domesticated association. For example, the bride can be seen as a female condor who brings her animal wealth to the new household, and the bridegroom as the male lead llama (*tilantiru*) who carries produce from the warm valleys back to the highlands (Arnold and Yapita 1998:219). Nonetheless, in some Central Andean rituals the wife-taker remains throughout his life a predatory figure, associated with the mountain deities.

The value attached to male affines is closely linked to how notions of interiority and exteriority are deployed. In interpreting the apparent paradox by which a male affine who is part of the same landholding group can also take on the role of permanent outsider, the understanding of affinity in Amazonia can perhaps prove insightful. In contrast to Andean symbols of affinity, closely associated with the living figures of actual wife-takers, the value of affinity can be detached from any actual social relations, and many anthropologists have shown how native Amazonian groups seek either to keep strangers at bay or to reclassify them as kin. Yet, as Viveiros de Castro has noted, exteriority is at the heart of Amazonian sociality: "alterity is an internal relation. The outside [is]…immanent in the inside" (2001:27). In the light of such formulations, it is plausible to suggest that within the solidary, endogamic landholding groups found all over the Andes, alterity exists as a necessary condition for the reproduction of sociality, not just in the sense of marriage and the production of children, but also in the more generic sense represented by the wild creatures of landscape deities.

It is worth pointing out, nonetheless, that these relationships of exteriority or alterity are in principle reciprocal. If a man treats his sister's or daughter's husband as a predatory outsider, he simultaneously fulfills this role with respect to his own wife's kin. Similarly, native Amazonians who conceive of strangers as potential cannibals as well as potential affines are undoubtedly aware that they are perceived in a similar way by others. How far does this apply also to relations with white people? A Cashinahua Amazonian can transform into a Nawa (outsider, gringo), and this would involve having sex with foreigners as well as eating their food (McCallum 2001:166). But by and large this reciprocity of perspective is missing in relations between people of European origin and the "Indians" they so often despise. This perhaps is at the heart of the difference in the way that alterity is understood by the various populations that inhabit Latin America today.

## WOMEN, MEN, AND DIFFERENCE

These heterogeneous expressions of personhood, relatedness and alterity indicate that gender is not always the main symbolic form in which the power or the difference of the other is expressed. Some ethnographers suggest that consanguinity and affinity are the central means by which persons are conceived as same or different, and that gender is not a significant symbol of difference. Descola (2001) in particular has argued that affinity is the marker of alterity in native Amazonia, and that the primordial contrast is between human and nonhuman, rather than between human women and men, and Course (2005) makes a comparable argument for the Mapuche of southern Chile. For the central Andes some have suggested that the contrast between duality and singularity is more significant than that between female and male (Platt 1986; Harris 2000).

Furthermore, where historians and anthropologists have considered gender relations and gender symbolism of indigenous cultures, they have often highlighted patterns which are in stark contrast to Euro-Christian understandings of gender difference or encompassment. At their most general, such formulations have a utopian quality. Thus Miller for example asserts: "men and women throughout the Americas thought of their lives and work as truly separate and equal (not but equal)" (Miller 1992). Utopianism aside, there is plenty of evidence for this kind of gender parallelism in the precolonial civilizations of both Mesoamerica and the Andes, in which women and men are seen as occupying parallel spheres, and where there seems to be a constant effort to balance and compare, rather than oppose.

For example Inka kinship was probably grounded in parallel inheritance and bilineal descent (Zuidema 1977). This principle, moreover, seems to have extended into all domains of social life, such that female and male competences were separate and balanced (Rostworowski 1983; Silverblatt 1987). In Mesoamerica too, research on precolonial gender relations has emphasized female autonomy and economic power and a parallel structuring of key activities and leadership roles, although men monopolized the highest offices (Kellogg 1986, 1997; Anderson 1997; Burkhart 1997; Joyce 2001). A different, less formalistic approach draws on recent feminist theory to emphasize fluidity, dynamic alternation, androgyny and transsexual combinations, but again avoids emphasising gender difference as such (e.g. Isbell 1997; Sigal 2000).

Gender parallelism has also been described in ethnographies of the Andean region; for example Isbell (1978) found parallel descent in naming practices in Chuschi (Ayacucho, Peru). In similar vein, Arnold's exploration of sperm lines and matrilineal blood lines in Qaqachaka (Bolivia) suggests that neither is subordinate to the other. Sperm kin are more lineal, more concentrated in space, inheriting land, while blood kin spread "horizontally" across the landscape, as do the livestock that are inherited matrilineally (Arnold 1988, 1992).

We have seen that an extraordinary effort was made from the early 16th century to globalize southern European norms of gender and kinship, continuing into the 20th century as new frontiers were colonized. These norms included monogamous nuclear families, pronounced sexual difference, the superior status and authority accorded to men, the suppression of homosexual relations, and the chastity of women, and they attached high value to the nurturing, self-sacrificing mother. However, it is clear from the brief examples I have presented that not all aspects of Mediterranean gender norms and practices were endorsed by the Catholic missionaries, nor were they fully successful in replacing existing understandings of personhood and relatedness.

The question remains how far the practices and values of the non-indigenous majority of Latin Americans reflect their southern European origins, in which gender difference and encompassment of the female by the male is often so pronounced (leaving aside the impact of African and Asian cultures on certain regions and localities). Some anthropologists have found the honor and shame complex of southern European cultural traditions helpful for understanding the dynamics of female chastity and maternal suffering in peasant communities of central Mexico and northwest Argentina (Melhuus 1990; Stølen 1996). And yet the transforming experience of migration is also fundamental to the complex that is Latin American gender relations today: the long historical experience of a shortage of suitable white women, the desire of elite groups to maintain their privileged position in a context of increasingly racialized hierarchies, the solitude of the frontier and the endless half-acknowledged miscegenation between racial groups that officially should maintain their separateness.

There are other factors too, that are important for understanding how certain expressions of gendered identity become stereotypic. One of these is popular culture. A key figure here is the Latin American *macho*, the defiantly autonomous man whose agency derives in part from his capacity for violence, typified by Oscar Lewis's portrayal of Jesús Sánchez (1962; Gutmann 1996:248; see also Fonseca 2003). While this figure is widely seen to be the paradigm of Latin American masculinity, his genesis is probably quite recent, often thought to have arisen out of the expressions of defiant bravado at the threat of intervention by the US, on the part of Mexican revolutionaries at the beginning of the 20th century. As represented in countless Mexican *corridos*, or folk ballads, and extended throughout the region, the *macho* has come to symbolize a quintessentially Latin American identity. It is intriguing, then, to learn that it probably developed through a long historical dialogue between North American and Mexican popular culture, and especially through the lives of solitary cowboys or *vaqueros* (Paredes 2003), rather than originating in a constitutive antagonism to the Anglo-American colossus to the north.

In this example, the macho stereotype consolidated elements drawn from varied sources, and coalesced through its expression in music at a time of danger. An analogous argument is made by Archetti (1999) with regard to another paradigmatic expression of Latin American masculinity: football styles, especially those of Argentina. Archetti shows how this English game gradually became in Argentina a means of competing with and mocking the restrained style of the dominant English in the early years of the 20th century.

The macho stereotype signifies boundedness and opposition not only to the threatening Anglo-American other, but also to the feminine. In many ways he is represented as free from social ties and as reacting with violence to any infringement of his autonomy (Bastos 1998).While one of the principal targets of macho violence is women, subordinate men can also be treated metaphorically as women.

This kind of feminization is central to gender imagery in Latin America (Melhuus and Stølen 1996; Gutmann 2003), although not universal. In contemporary Amazonia, for example, warfare and submission are typically represented through metaphors of pedator and prey, with little emphasis on gender. However, more generally metaphors for diverse forms of domination are gendered. Whether by Aztecs, Inkas, Spanish, national elites, or the US, the defeated and the enslaved are downgraded through representation as the feminine, although these subordinate others respond with their own assertions of masculine pride.

But women have also responded to forms of subordination and symbolic devaluation, especially when it involves violence. It is striking how often women have been drawn to movements of fundamental change which have taken a strong stand against male violence, for example the Shining Path revolutionary movement in Peru (Andreas 1985), the Zapatistas in Chiapas (Hernandez Castillo 2001), and Protestant sects in many regions (Garrard-Burnett and Stoll 1994). Some of the best-known Latin American women's movements began as responses to state violence: the mothers who have walked for years round Buenos Aires' Plaza de Mayo in silent remonstration at the refusal of the Argentinean state to acknowledge that it had killed their children (Franco 1992), the mothers who protested the massacre of Tlatelolco in Mexico City after 1968 (Poniatowska 1972), the Maya women who gathered in the first effective organization during the Guatemalan civil war (CONAVIGUA) to help each other and to protest the deaths of their husbands and sons (Zur 1998), have all become emblematic of Latin American women's movements.

These examples highlight the striking way in which Latin American feminism and demands for citizenship are played out through idealized representations of motherhood and wifely duty far more than in northern Europe, and with less emphasis on liberal individualism (Molyneux 2001:169, 183). In part these movements express the particular effects of lived experience and of political violence, but they also deploy and subvert the stereotypes for maximum rhetorical effect. In so doing, they are also responses to a renewed globalizing movement that developed in the second half of the 20th century, a new onslaught on notions of relatedness and sexuality, another project to recategorize personhood. While the globalizing process of the

16th and 17th centuries came from the Catholic Iberian peninsular, this new diffusion across the globe of gender and kinship values and practices originates from Protestant northern Europe and America. These globalizing values are once again presented as a civilizing force, and are used to negotiate the faultlines of existing kinship and gender relations. How, and how far they will produce a radical transformation of Latin American sociality is yet to be determined.

## REFERENCES

Abercrombie, T. (1998) *Pathways of Memory and Power: Ethnography and History among an Andean People*. Madison: University of Wisconsin Press.

Anderson, A. (1997) Aztec Wives. In S. Schroeder, S. Wood, and R. Haskett (eds), *Indian Women of Early Mexico* (pp. 55–86). Norman: University of Oklahoma Press.

Andreas, C. (1985) *When Women Rebel: The Rise of Popular Feminism in Peru*. Westport: Lawrence Hill.

Archetti, E. (1999) *Masculinities: Football, Polo and the Tango in Argentina*. Oxford: Berg.

Arnold, D. (1988) Matrilineal Kinship in a Patrilineal Setting. Ph.D. dissertation, University of London.

Arnold, D. (1992) La casa de adobes y piedras del Inka. Género, memoria y cosmos en Qaqachaka. In D. Arnold (ed.), *Hacia un orden andino de las cosas. Tres pistas de los Andes meridionales* (pp. 31–108). La Paz: HISBOL and ILCA.

Arnold, D. (1993) Adam and Eve and the Red-Trousered Ant. *Travesía: Journal of Latin American Cultural Studies* 2(1):49–83.

Arnold, D. (1998) Introducción: de "castas" a kastas. Enfoques hacia el parentesco andino. In D. Arnold (ed.), *Gente de carne y hueso. Las tramas de parentesco en los Andes* (pp. 15–66). Biblioteca de Estudios Andinos, no. 2. La Paz: ILCA.

Arnold, D. and Yapita, J. de Dios (1998) *K'ank'isiña*. Trenzarse entre la letra y la música de las canciones de boda en Qaqachaka, Bolivia. In D. Arnold (ed.), *Gente de carne y hueso. Las tramas de parentesco en los Andes* (pp. 525–580). Biblioteca de Estudios Andinos, no. 2. La Paz: ILCA.

Barnes, M. (1992) Catechisms and Confessionarios: Distorting Mirrors of Andean Societies. In R. V. H. Dover, K. E. Seibold, and J. H. McDowell (eds), *Andean Cosmologies through Time: Persistence and Emergence* (pp. 67–94). Bloomington: Indiana University Press.

Bastos, S. (1998) Desbordando patrones. El comportamiento de los hombres. *La Ventana* 7:166–224.

Bengoa, J. (1985) *Historia del pueblo mapuche*. Santiago: Sur.

Bolton, R. and Mayer, E. (eds) (1977) *Andean Kinship and Marriage*. Special Publication, no. 7. Washington, DC: American Anthropological Association.

Borges, D. (1992) *The Family in Bahia, Brazil 1870–1945*. Stanford: Stanford University Press.

Bouysse-Cassagne, T. (1996) In Praise of Bastards: The Uncertainties of *Mestizo* Identity in the Sixteenth and Seventeenth Century Andes. In O. Harris (ed.), *Inside and Outside the Law: Anthropological Studies of Authority and Ambiguity* (pp. 98–121). London: Routledge.

Burkett, E. (1978) Indian Women and White Society: The Case of Sixteenth-Century Peru. In A. Lavrin (ed.), *Latin American Women: Historical Perspectives* (pp. 101–128). Westport: Greenwood Press.

Burkhart, L. (1997) Mexican Women on the Home Front. In S. Schroeder, S. Wood, and R. Haskett (eds), *Indian Women of Early Mexico* (pp. 25–54). Norman: University of Oklahoma Press.

Butler, J. (1990) *Gender Trouble: Feminism and the Subversion of Identity*. London: Routledge.

Carlsen, R. (1997) *The War for the Heart and Soul of a Highland Maya Town*. Austin: University of Texas Press.

Carrasco, P. (1976) Los linajes nobles del México antiguo. In P. Carrasco and J. Broda (eds), *Estratificación social en la Mesoamérica prehispánica*. Mexico City: Instituto Nacional de Antropologica e Historia.

Carrasco, P. (1997) Indian–Spanish Marriages in the First Century of the Colony. In S. Schroeder, S. Wood, and R. Haskett (eds), *Indian Women of Early Mexico*. Norman: University of Oklahoma Press.

Carsten, J. (ed.) (2000) *Cultures of Relatedness: New Approaches to the Study of Kinship*. Cambridge: Cambridge University Press.

Carsten, J. and Hugh-Jones, S. (eds) (1995) *About the House: Lévi-Strauss and Beyond*. Cambridge: Cambridge University Press.

Casaús Arzú, M. E. (1998) *La metamorfosis del racismo en Guatemala. Uk'exwachixiik ri Kaxlan Na'ooj pa Iximuleew*. Guatemala: Cholsamaj.

Chance, J. (1996) The Barrios of Colonial Tecali: Patronage, Kinship and Territorial Relations in a Central Mexican Community. *Ethnology* 35(2):107–139.

Choque Canqui, R. (1998) Parentesco entre los caciques de Pakasa. In D. Arnold (ed.), *Gente de carne y hueso. Las tramas de parentesco en los Andes* (pp. 325–340). Biblioteca de Estudios Andinos, no. 2. La Paz: ILCA.

Clendinnen, I. (1987) *Ambivalent Conquests: Maya and Spaniard in Yucatan 1517–1570*. New York: Cambridge University Press.

Clendinnen, I. (1991) *Aztecs: An Interpretation*. Cambridge: Cambridge University Press.

Course, M. (2005) Mapuche Person, Mapuche People: Individual and Society in Indigenous Southern Chile. Ph.D. dissertation, London School of Economics.

Da Silva, M. B. Nizza (1984) *Sistema de casamento no Brasil colonial*. São Paolo: Editora da Universidade de São Paolo.

de la Cadena, M. (2005) Are Mestizos Hybrids? The Conceptual Politics of Andean Identities. *Journal of Latin American Studies* 37(2):259–284.

Del Río, M. (1997) Relaciones interétnicas y control de recursos entre los Aymaras del macizo de Charcas. Los Soras del Repartimiento de Paria: estrategias de acceso a tierras, siglos XVI–XVII. Ph.D. dissertation, Facultad de Filosofia y Letras, University of Buenos Aires.

Descola, P. (1993) Les Affinités selectives. Alliance, guerre et prédation dans l'ensemble jivaro. *L'Homme* 126–128:171–190.

Descola, P. (2001) The Genres of Gender: Local Models and Global Paradigms in the Comparison of Amazonia and Melanesia. In T. Gregor and D. Tuzin (eds), *Gender in Amazonia and Melanesia: An Exploration of the Comparative Method*. Berkeley: University of California Press.

Dumont, L. (1953) The Dravidian Kinship Terminology as an Expression of Marriage. *Man* 54:34–39.

Fausto, C. (1997) A dialética da predaçao e familiarizaçao entre os Parakanã da Amazônia Oriental. Por uma teoria da guerra amerindia. Ph.D. dissertation, PPGAS, Museo Nacional, Universidade Federal do Rio de Janeiro.

Fonseca, C. (2003) Philanderers, Cuckolds, and Wily Women: Reexamining Gender Relations in a Brazilian Working-Class Neighbourhood. In M. Gutmann (ed.), *Changing Men and Masculinities in Latin America* (pp. 61–83). Durham, NC: Duke University Press.

Foucault, M. (1981) *The History of Sexuality*, vol. 1. London: Pelican Books.

Franco, J. (1992) Gender, Death, and Resistance: Facing the Ethical Vacuum. In Juan E. Corradi, Patricia Weiss Fagen, and Manuel Antonio Carretón (eds), *Fear at the Edge: State Terror and Resistance in Latin America* (pp. 104–118). Berkeley: University of California Press.

Freyre, G. (1946) *The Masters and the Slaves. A Study in the Development of Brazilian Civilization*. New York: Knopf.

Garrard-Burnett, V. and Stoll, D. (eds) (1994) *Rethinking Protestantism in Latin America*. Philadelphia: Temple University Press.

Gibson, C. (1952) *Tlaxcala in the Sixteenth Century*. New Haven: Yale University Press.

Gibson, C. (1964) *The Aztecs under Spanish Rule*. Stanford: Stanford University Press.

Goddard, V. (2000) *The Virile Nation: Gender and Ethnicity in the Re-construction of Argentinian Pasts*. Goldsmiths Anthropology Research Paper. University of London.

Gose, P. (1994) *Deathly Waters and Hungry Mountains. Agrarian Ritual and Class Formation in an Andean Town.* Toronto: University of Toronto Press.

Gose, P. (2002) Priests, Petty Disputes and Purity of Blood: Unauthorized Threats to Old Christian Status in 17th Century Peru. Paper presented at conference on Around the Church, Princeton University, Mar. 1–2.

Gow, P. (1991) *Of Mixed Blood. Kinship and History in Peruvian Amazonia.* Oxford: Oxford University Press.

Gruzinski, S. (1989) Individualization and Acculturation: Confession among the Nahuas of Mexico from the Sixteenth to the Eighteenth Century. In A. Lavrin (ed.), *Sexuality and Marriage in Colonial Latin America* (pp. 96–117). Lincoln: University of Nebraska Press.

Guaman Poma de Ayala, F. (1980[1615]) *Nueva corónica y buen gobierno*, ed. R Adorno and J. V. Murra. Mexico City: Siglo XXI.

Guiteras Holmes, C. (1951) El calpulli de San Pablo Cahlchihuitan. In J. Comas and G. Aguirre Beltrán (eds), *Homejae al Dr Alfonso Caso* (pp. 199–206). Mexico City: Imprenta Nuevo Mundo.

Gutierrez, R. (1991) *When Jesus Came, the Corn Mothers Went Away: Marriage, Sexuality and Power in Northern Mexico, 1500–1846.* Stanford: Stanford University Press.

Gutmann, M. (1996) *The Meanings of Macho: Being a Man in Mexico City.* Berkeley: University of California Press.

Gutmann, M. (2003) Introduction: Discarding Manly Dichotomies in Latin America. In M. Gutmann (ed.), *Changing Men and Masculinities in Latin America* (pp. 1–26). Durham, NC: Duke University Press.

Harris, O. (1994) Condor and Bull: The Ambiguities of Masculinity. In P. Harvey and P. Gow (eds), *Sex and Violence: Issues in Representation and Experience* (pp. 40–65). London: Routledge.

Harris, O. (2000) *To Make the Earth Bear Fruit: Ethnographic Essays on Fertility, Work and Gender in Highland Bolivia.* London: Institute of Latin American Studies Press.

Harvey, P. (1994) Domestic Violence in the Andes. In P. Harvey and P. Gow (eds), *Sex and Violence: Issues in Representation and Experience* (pp. 66–89). London: Routledge.

Henley, P. (1996) *South Indian Models in the Amazonian Lowlands.* Manchester Papers in Social Anthropology, no. 1. University of Manchester.

Hernandez Castillo, R. A. (ed.) (2001) *The Other Word: Women and Violence in Chiapas before and after Acteal.* Copenhagen: International Work Group for Indigenous Affairs (IWGIA).

Herzog, T. (2003) *Defining Nations: Immigrants and Citizens in Early Modern Spain and Spanish America.* New Haven: Yale University Press.

Hickman, J. and Stuart, W. (1977) Descent, Alliance and Moiety in Chucuito, Peru: An Explanatory Sketch of Aymara Social Organization. In R. Bolton and E. Mayer (eds), *Andean Kinship and Marriage* (pp. 43–59). Special Publication, no. 7. Washington, DC: American Anthropological Association.

Hill, R., and Monaghan, J. (1987) *Continuities in Highland Maya Social Organization: Ethnohistory in Sacapulas, Guatemala.* Philadelphia: University of Pennsylvania Press.

Howard-Malverde, R. (1990) *The Speaking of History: "Willapaakushayki" or Quechua Ways of Telling the Past.* Institute of Latin American Studies Research Papers, no. 21. London: University of London.

Hugh-Jones, S. (1995) Inside-Out and Back-to-Front: The Androgynous House in Northwest Amazonia. In J. Carsten and S. Hugh-Jones (eds), *About the House: Lévi-Strauss and Beyond* (pp. 226–252). Cambridge: Cambridge University Press.

Hunt, E. (1976) Kinship and Territorial Fission in the Cuicatec Highlands. In H. Nutini, P. Carrasco and J. Taggart (eds), *Essays on Mexican Kinship.* Pittsburgh: University of Pittsburgh Press.

Hunt, E. and Nash, J. (1969) Local and Territorial Units. In M. Nash (ed.), *Social Anthropology* (pp. 253–282), vol. 6 of *Handbook of Middle American Indians.* Austin: University of Texas Press.

Ianni, O. (1970) Research on Race Relations in Brazil. In M. Morner (ed.), *Race and Class in Latin America* (pp. 256–278). New York: Columbia University Press.

Isbell, B. J. (1978) *To Defend Ourselves: Ecology and Ritual in an Andean Village*. Austin: University of Texas Press.

Isbell, B. J. (1997) De inmaduro a duro. Lo simbólico femenino y los esquemas andinos del género. In D. Arnold (ed.), *Más allá del silencio. Las fronteras del género en los Andes* (pp. 253–301). La Paz: CIASE and ILCA.

Joyce, R. (2001) *Gender and Power in Prehispanic Mesoamerica*. Austin: University of Texas Press.

Kaur, K. (2005) The Power of Surnames: Abjecting Indigenousness in a Guatemalan Ladino Town. Paper presented at International Conference on Mestizajes, Cambridge, UK, Sept.

Kellogg, S. (1986) Kinship and Social Organization in Early Colonial Tenochtitlán: An Essay in Ethnohistorical Analysis and Methodology. In V. R. Bricker and R. Spores (eds), *Ethnohistory* (pp. 103–121), vol. 4 of *Handbook of Middle American Indians*. Austin: University of Texas Press.

Kellogg, S. (1995) *Law and the Transformation of Aztec Culture 1500–1700*. Norman: University of Oklahoma Press.

Kellogg, S. (1997) Tenochca Mexica Women 1500–1700. In S. Schroder, S. Wood, and R. Haskett (eds), *Indian Women of Early Mexico*. Norman: University of Oklahoma Press.

Killick, E. (2005) Living Apart: Separation and Sociality amongst the Ashéninka of Peruvian Amazonia. Ph.D. dissertation, London School of Economics.

Konetzke, R. (1945) La emigración de mujeres españolas en America durante la época colonial. *Revista Internacional de Sociologia* 3:123–150.

Lambert, B. (1977) Bilaterality in the Andes. In R. Bolton and E. Mayer (eds), *Andean Kinship and Marriage* (pp. 1–27). Special Publication, no. 7. Washington, DC: American Anthropological Association.

Laughlin, R. (1969) The Tzotzil. In E. Vogt (ed.), *Ethnology* (pp. 152–194), vol. 1 of *Handbook of Middle American Indians*. Austin: University of Texas Press.

Lavrin, A. (1989) Sexuality in Colonial Mexico: A Church Dilemma. In A. Lavrin (ed.), *Sexuality and Marriage in Colonial Latin America* (pp. 47–95). Lincoln: University of Nebraska Press.

Lea, V. (1995) The Houses of the Mèbengokre (Kayapó) of Central Brazil: A New Door to Their Social Organization. In J. Carsten and S. Hugh-Jones (eds), *About the House: Lévi-Strauss and Beyond* (pp. 206–225). Cambridge: Cambridge University Press.

Leddy Phelan, J. (1956) *The Millennial Kingdom of the Franciscans in the New World*. Berkeley: University of California Press.

Lepri, I. (2005) The Meanings of Kinship among the Ese Ejja of Northern Bolivia. *Journal of the Royal Anthropological Institute* 11(4):703–724.

Lévi-Strauss, C. (1983) *The Way of the Masks*. Seattle: University of Washington Press.

Lewis, O. (1962) *The Children of Sánchez*. London: Penguin Books

Lockhart, J. (1991) *Nahuas and Spaniards: Postconquest Central Mexican History and Philology*. Stanford: Stanford University Press and UCLA Latin American Centre.

Lockhart, J. (1992) *The Nahuas after the Conquest: A Social and Cultural History of the Indians of Central Mexico, 16th–18th Centuries*. Stanford: Stanford University Press.

Martinez-Alier, V. (1974) *Marriage, Colour and Class in Nineteenth-Century Cuba*. Cambridge: Cambridge University Press.

Martínez Peláez, S. (1971) *La Patria del Criollo. Ensayo de interpretación de la realidad colonia guatemalteca*. Guatemala: Ediciones en Marcha.

Maybury-Lewis, D. (1989) Social Theory and Social Practice: Binary Systems in Central Brazil. In D. Maybury-Lewis and U. Almagor (eds), *The Attraction of Opposites: Thought and Society in the Dualistic Mode* (pp. 97–116). Ann Arbor: University of Michigan Press.

Mayer, E. (1977) Beyond the Nuclear Family. In R. Bolton and E. Mayer (eds), *Andean Kinship and Marriage* (pp. 60–80). Special Publication, no. 7. Washington, DC: American Anthropological Association.

McCallum, C. (2001) *Gender and Sociality in Amazonia: How Real People Are Made.* Oxford: Berg.

Melhuus, M. (1990) A Shame to Honour, a Shame to Suffer. *Ethnos* 1(1–2):5–25.

Melhuus, M. and Stølen, K. A. (eds) (1996) *Machos, Mistresses, Madonnas: Contesting the Power of Latin American Gender Imagery.* London: Verso.

Metcalf, A. (1992) *Family and Frontier in Colonial Brazil: Santana de Parnaíba, 1580–1822.* Berkeley: University of California Press.

Miller, F. (1991) *Latin American Women and the Search for Social Justice.* Hanover: University Press of New England.

Miller, J. (1992) A Kinship of Spirit. In A. M. Josephy (ed.), *America in the World: The World of Indian Peoples before the Arrival of Columbus* (pp. 305–337). New York: Knopf.

Molyneux, M. (2001) *Women's Movements in International Perspective: Latin America and Beyond.* London: Palgrave.

Monaghan, J. (1995) *The Covenants with Earth and Rain: Exchange, Sacrifice and Revelation in Mixtec Sociality.* Norman: University of Oklahoma Press.

Monaghan, J. (1996) The Mesoamerican Community as a "Great House." *Ethnology* 35(3):181–194.

Needham, R. (1971) Remarks on the Analysis of Kinship and Marriage. In R. Needham (ed.), *Rethinking Kinship and Marriage.* London: Tavistock.

Nutini, H. (1976) Introduction. In H. Nutini, P. Carrasco, and J. Taggart (eds), *Essays on Mexican Kinship* (pp. 3–27). Pittsburgh: University of Pittsburgh Press.

Nutini, H. (1984) *Ritual Kinship,* vol. 2: *Ideological and Structural Integration of the Compadrazgo System in Rural Tlaxcala.* Princeton: Princeton University Press.

Nutini, H. (2004) *The Mexican Aristocracy: An Expressive Ethnography, 1910–2000.* Austin: University of Texas Press.

Nutini, H., Carrasco, P., and Taggart, J. (eds) (1976) *Essays on Mexican Kinship.* Pittsburgh: University of Pittsburgh Press.

Ossio, J. (1992) *Parentesco, reciprocidad y jerarquia en los andes. Una aproximación a la organización social de la comunidad de Andamarca.* Lima: Pontificia Universidad Católica del Perú.

Ossio, J. (1998) Obligaciones rituales prescritas en el parentesco andino por afinidad. In D. Arnold (ed.), *Gente de carne y hueso. Las tramas de parentesco en los Andes* (pp. 265–289). La Paz: CIASE and ILCA.

Overing Kaplan, J. (1975) *The Piaroa, a People of the Orinoco Basin: A Study of Kinship and Marriage.* Oxford: Clarendon Press.

Overing Kaplan, J. (1981) Amazonian Anthropology (review article). *Journal of Latin American Studies* 13(1):151–165.

Overing, J. (1989) The Aesthetics of Production: The Sense of Community among the Cubeo and Piaroa. *Dialectical Anthropology* 14:159–175.

Overing, J. and Passes, A. (eds) (2000) *The Anthropology of Love and Anger: The Aesthetics of Conviviality in Native Amazonia.* London: Routledge.

Paredes, A. (2003) The United States, Mexico, and Machismo. In M. Guttman, F. V. Matos Rodriguez, L. Stephen, and P. Zavella (eds), *Perspectives on Las Américas: A Reader in Culture, History and Representation.* Oxford: Blackwell.

Platt, T. (1986) Mirrors and Maize: The Concept of *Yanantin* among the Macha of Bolivia. In J. V. Murra, N. Wachtel and J. Revel (eds), *Anthropological History of Andean Polities.* Cambridge: Cambridge University Press.

Platt, T., Bouysse-Cassagne, T., and Harris, O. (2006) *Qaraqara-Charka. Mallku, Inka y Rey en la "Provincia de Charcas," siglos XV–XVII. Historia antropológica de una Confederacióm Aymara.* La Paz: Plural Editores and Instituto Frances de Estudios Andinos.

Poniatowska, E. (1972) *Massacre in Mexico.* New York: Viking.

Poole, D. (1992) Antropología e historia andinas en los EEUU. Buscando un re-encuentro. *Revista Andina* 10(1):209–245.

Powers, K. V. (1995) *Andean Journeys: Migration, Ethnogenesis and the State in Colonial Quito*. Albuquerque: University of New Mexico Press.

Pozas, R. and Aguirre Beltrán, G. (1954) Instituciones indígenas en el México actual. In A. Caso (ed.), *Métodos y resultados de la política indigenista en Mexico* (pp. 171–270). Mexico City: Instituto Ediciones del Instituto Nacional Indigenista.

Presta, A. M. (ed.) (1995) *Espacio, etnías, frontera. Atenuaciones políticas en el sur del Tawantinsuyu*. Sucre: ASUR.

Rebhun, L. A. (1999) *The Heart is an Unknown Country: Love in the Changing Economy of Northeast Brazil*. Stanford: Stanford University Press.

Restall, M. (1997) *The Maya World: Yucatec Culture and Society 1550–1850*. Stanford: Stanford University Press.

Ricard, R. (1933) La "Conquête spirituelle" du Mexique. *Travaux et Mémoires* (Institut d'Ethnologie, Université de Paris à la Sorbonne) 20.

Rival, L. (1998) Androgynous Parents and Guest Children: The Huaorani Couvade. *Journal of the Royal Anthropological Institute* (NS) 4:619–642.

Rivière, P. (1984) *Individual and Society in Guiana: A Comparative Study of Amerindian Social Organization*. Cambridge: Cambridge University Press.

Rivière, P. (1993) The Amerindianization of Descent and Affinity. *L'Homme* 126–128:507–516.

Rivière, P. (1995) Houses, Places and People: Community and Continuity in Guiana. In J. Carsten and S. Hugh-Jones (eds), *About the House: Lévi-Strauss and Beyond* (pp. 189–205). Cambridge: Cambridge University Press.

Rostworowski, M. (1983) *Estructuras andinas del poder. Ideología religiosa y política*. Lima: Instituto de Estudios Peruanos.

Russell-Wood, A. J. R. (1978) Female and Family in the Economy and Society of Colonial Brazil. In A. Lavrin (ed.), *Latin American Women: Historical Perspectives* (pp. 60–100). Westport: Greenwood Press.

Saignes, T. (1995) Indian Migration and Social Change in Seventeenth Century Charcas. In B. Larson and O. Harris (eds), *Ethnicity, Markets and Migration in the Andes: At the Crossroads of History and Anthropology* (pp. 167–195). Durham, NC: Duke University Press.

Salomon, F. (1997) "Conjunto de nacimiento" y "línea de esperma" en el manuscrito quechua de Huarochirí (ca. 1608). In D. Arnold (ed.), *Más allá del silencio. Las fronteras del género en los Andes* (pp. 302–322). La Paz: CIASE and ILCA.

Salomon, F. and Schwartz, S. (1999) New Peoples and New Kinds of People: Adaptation, Readjustment and Ethnogenesis in South American Indigenous Societies. In F. Salomon and S. Schwartz (eds), *Cambridge History of the Native Peoples of the Americas*, vol. 3, part 2 (pp. 443–501). Cambridge: Cambridge University Press.

Sánchez-Albornoz, N. (1978) *Indios y tributos en el Alto Perú*. Lima: Instituto de Estudios Peruanos.

Sánchez Parga, J. (ed.) (1990) *Etnia, poder y diferencia en los Andes septentrionales*. Quito: Abya Yala.

Sandstrom, A. (2000) Toponymic Groups and House Organisation: The Nahuas of Northern Veracruz, Mexico. In R. Joyce and S. Gillespie (eds), *Beyond Kinship: Social and Material Reproduction in House Societies*. Philadelphia: University of Pennsylvania Press.

Santos-Granero, F. (1991) *The Power of Love: The Moral Use of Knowledge among the Amuesha of Central Peru*. London: Athlone.

Schneider, D. (1980) *American Kinship: A Cultural Account*. Chicago: University of Chicago Press.

Schneider, D. (1984) *A Critique of the Study of Kinship*. Ann Arbor: University of Michigan Press.

Schwartz, S. (1985) *Sugar Plantations in the Formation of Brazilian Society: Bahia 1550–1835*. Cambridge: Cambridge University Press.

Seed, P. (1988) *To Love, Honor, and Obey in Colonial Mexico: Conflicts over Marriage Choice, 1574–1821*. Stanford: Stanford University Press.

Seed, P. (2001) *American Pentimento: The Invention of Indians and the Pursuit of Riches*. Minneapolis: University of Minnesota Press.

Seeger, A. (1989) Dualism: Fuzzy Thinking or Fuzzy Sets? In D. Maybury-Lewis and U. Almagor (eds), *The Attraction of Opposites: Thought and Society in the Dualistic Mode* (pp. 191–208). Ann Arbor: University of Michigan Press.

Sigal, P. (2000) *From Moon Goddess to Virgins: The Colonization of Yucatecan Maya Sexual Desire*. Austin: University of Texas Press.

Silverblatt, I. (1987) *Moon, Sun and Witches: Gender Ideologies and Class in Inca and Colonial Peru*. Princeton: Princeton University Press.

Skar, S. Lund (1998) El final de la exogamia. Parentesco andino en terreno abierto. In D. Arnold (ed.), *Gente de carne y hueso. Las tramas del parentesco andino* (pp. 99–114). Biblioteca de Estudios Andinos, no. 2. La Paz: ILCA.

Smith, C. A. (1995) Race-Class-Gender Ideology in Guatemala: Modern and Anti-Modern Forms. *Comparative Studies in Society and History* 34(4):723–749.

Socolow, S. (1989) Acceptable Partners: Marriage Choice in Colonial Argentina. In A. Lavrin (ed.), *Sexuality and Marriage in Colonial Latin America* (pp. 209–251). Lincoln: University of Nebraska Press.

Spedding, A. (1998) Contra-afinidad. Algunos comentarios sobre el compadrazgo andino. In D. Arnold (ed.), *Gente de carne y hueso. Las tramas del parentesco andino* (pp. 115–138). Biblioteca de Estudios Andinos, no. 2. La Paz: ILCA.

Stein, W. (1961) *Hualcan: Life in the Highlands of Peru*. Ithaca: Cornell University Press.

Stepan, N. (1991) *The Hour of Eugenics: Race, Gender and Nation in Latin America*. Ithaca: Cornell University Press.

Stolcke, V. (2004) A New World Engendered: The Making of the Iberian Transatlantic Empires. In T. Meade and M. E. Wiesner-Hanks (eds), *A Companion to Gender History* (pp. 371–389). Oxford: Blackwell.

Stølen, K. A. (1996) *The Decency of Inequality: Gender, Power and Social Change on the Argentine Prairie*. Oslo: Scandinavian University Press.

Stoler, A. (1997) Sexual Affronts and Racial Frontiers: European Identities and the Cultural Politics of Exclusion in Colonial South-East Asia. In F. Cooper and A. Stoler (eds), *Tension of Empire: Colonial Cultures in a Bourgeois World* (pp. 198–237). Berkeley: University of California Press.

Strathern, M. (1988) *The Gender of the Gift*. Berkeley: University of California Press.

Tax, S. (1952) *Heritage of Conquest: The Ethnology of Middle America*. Glencoe: Free Press.

Tax, S. and Hinshaw, R. (1969) The Maya of the Midwestern Highlands. In E. Vogt (ed.), *Ethnology* (pp. 69–100), vol. 1 of *Handbook of Middle American Indians*. Austin: University of Texas Press.

Taylor, A.-C. (1998) Jivaroan Kinship: "Simple" and "Complex" Formulas: A Dravidian Transformation Group. In M. Godelier, T. Trautmann, and F. Tjon Sie Fat (eds), *Transformations of Kinship* (pp. 187–213). Washington, DC: Smithsonian Institution Press.

Taylor, A.-C. (2001) Wives, Pets and Affines. In L. Rival and N. Whitehead (eds), *Beyond the Visible and the Material: The Amerindianization of Society in the Work of Peter Rivière* (pp. 45–56). Oxford: Oxford University Press.

Urton, G. (1990) *The History of a Myth: Pacariqtambo and the Origin of the Inkas*. Austin: University of Texas Press.

Van Vleet, K. (2002) The Intimacies of Power: Rethinking Violence and Affinity in the Bolivian Andes. *American Ethnologist* 29(3):567–601.

Vasconcelos, J. (1925) *La raza cósmica. Misión de la raza iberoamericana*. Paris: Agencia Mundial de Librería.

Vázquez, M. and Holmberg, A. (1966) The Castas: Unilineal Kin Groups in Vicos, Peru. *Ethnology* 5(3):284–303.

Vilaça, A. (2002) Making Kin out of Others in Amazonia. *Journal of the Royal Anthropological Institute* (NS) 8(2):347–365.

Viveiros de Castro, E. (1992) *From the Enemy's Point of View: Humanity and Divinity in an Amazonian Society.* Chicago: University of Chicago Press.

Viveiros de Castro, E. (1998a) Cosmological Deixis and Amerindian Perspectivism. *Journal of the Royal Anthropological Institute* 4(3):469–488.

Viveiros de Castro, E. (1998b) Dravidian and Related Kinship Systems. In M. Godelier, T. Trautmann, and F. Tjon Sie Fat (eds), *Transformations of Kinship* (pp. 332–385). Washington, DC: Smithsonian Institution Press.

Viveiros de Castro, E. (2001) GUT Feelings about Amazonia: Potential Affinity and the Construction of Sociality. In L. Rival and N. Whitehead (eds), *Beyond the Visible and the Material: The Amerindianization of Society in the Work of Peter Rivière* (pp. 19–44). Oxford: Oxford University Press.

Wachtel, N. (2001) *La Loi du souvenir. Labyrinthes marranes.* Paris: Seuil.

Wade, P. (2005) Re-thinking *Mestizaje*: Ideology and Lived Experience. *Journal of Latin American Studies* 37(2):239–258.

Waterson, R. (1995) Houses and Hierarchies in Island South-East Asia. In J. Carsten and S. Hugh-Jones (eds), *About the House. Lévi-Strauss and Beyond* (pp. 46–68). Cambridge: Cambridge University Press.

Weismantel, M. (1995) Making Kin: Kinship Theory and Zumbagua Adoptions. *American Ethnologist* 22(4):685–704.

Weismantel, M. (2001) *Cholas and Pishtacos: Stories of Race and Sex in the Andes.* Chicago: University of Chicago Press.

Wightman, A. (1990) *Indigenous Migration and Social Change: The Forasteros of Cuzco, 1570–1720.* Durham, NC: Duke University Press.

Wolf, E. (1957) Closed Corporate Peasant Communities in Mesoamerica and Central Java. *Southwestern Journal of Anthropology* 13(1):1–18.

Wolf, E. (1959) *Sons of the Shaking Earth: The People of Mexico and Guatemala: Their Land, History and Culture.* Chicago: University of Chicago Press.

Yapita, J. de D. and Arnold, D. (1998) Lo humano y lo no-humano en Qaqachaka. Categorias aymaras de parentesco y afinidad. In D. Arnold (ed.), *Gente de carne y hueso. Las tramas de parentesco en los Andes* (pp. 325–340). Biblioteca de Estudios Andinos, no. 2. La Paz: ILCA.

Zuidema, R. T. (1977) The Inca Kinship System: A New Theoretical View. In R Bolton and E. Mayer (eds), *Andean Kinship and Marriage* (pp. 240–281). Special Publication, no. 7. Washington, DC: American Anthropological Association.

Zur, J. (1998) *Violent memories: Mayan War Widows in Guatemala.* Boulder: Westview.

# CHAPTER 15 *Vinculaciones:* Pharmaceutical Politics and Science

## *Cori Hayden*

In the mid-1970s, Mexican President Luís Echeverría attempted to resuscitate support for his embattled government with some powerful populist and nationalist maneuvers. Chief among these were an effort to bring "health" – and particularly pharmaceutical research and development – back into the hands of the nation and "the people." His measures were bold. Hoping to jump start a long-faltering domestic industry (operating in a context in which 80 percent of the pharmaceutical market was then in the hands of foreign companies), Echeverría stunned transnational drug firms by rescinding patent protection on pharmaceuticals – a move meant to give new Mexican companies a leg-up by allowing them to legally copy or reverse engineer any drug they could. In a highly charged echo of post-Revolutionary expropriations, he effectively nationalized the industry, declaring that all drug companies present on Mexican soil be at least 51 percent Mexican owned (Sherwood 1991:168–169).

At the center of this moment of pharmaceutical nationalism was the matter of medicinal plants (Mexico's "national *herbolaria*") – or perhaps better stated, the project of making medicinal plants *matter*, again, in national research politics. Rejuvenating a research agenda with a long and varied pedigree, Echeverría presided over the inauguration of two particularly notable initiatives and institutions. The Mexican Institute for the Study of Medicinal Plants (Imeplam) was formed to reinvigorate interdisciplinary studies of plants and traditional knowledge, the outcomes of which, it was hoped, would include the identification of active chemical compounds for (domestic) drug production, as well as the formal valorization and incorporation of medicinal plants (and thus "traditional medicine") into the practice of medicine in Mexican hospitals and clinics (Lozoya 1976). Proquivemex was a domestic, state-run company based on barbasco root, a lucrative resource which Echeverría ceremoniously handed (back) not just to the nation, but to the campesinos who gathered the root (Soto Laveaga 2003). The aim was not just to reclaim Mexico's once vaunted place as the world's leading provider of diosgenin (a barbasco derived compound used to synthesize steroid hormones); it was also to stave off unrest in the countryside by transforming poorly remunerated, individual root collectors into "fully fledged participants" in all stages of barbasco production, from collection, to processing, to negotiating with transnational companies. Proquivemex officials hoped that these campesinos would come to see themselves as the collective "owners" of their products and the symbols of a pharmaceutically self-sufficient nation (Soto Laveaga 2003).

As we shall see below, this populist pharmaceutical revolution proved somewhat short-lived. But I remain drawn to the Echeverría years as an orienting device – a beacon, of sorts – in this chapter, for a particular reason. My task here is to map the/a nascent field of the anthropology of science and technology in Latin America, or at least to chart one possible route through such a field. For reasons having to do with my own research interests and experience, this route starts, for me, in Mexico. And, to state the case boldly, there is no more generative site for thinking about the anthropology of science and technology in Mexico than the question of plants and "traditional knowledge," and the ways that both have been rendered knowable and actionable at particular moments. My argument is not that everything comes back or down to plants and their pharmaceutical futures – this is not an exercise in (ethno)botanical reductionism – but rather that we might read *out from* the question of "medicinal plants," and their reanimation in a nationalist-populist project in the 1970s, a cluster of issues that lie at the heart of the social and cultural studies of science and technology in and of Mexico, and that speak powerfully to broader regional and disciplinary discussions. In this chapter, I will focus on three dimensions of Latin American(ist) anthropologies of science and technology to which the matter of plants and pharmaceutical politics directs us.

The first concerns the entwined questions of natural history, colonialism, and the racialized nation, or what scholars of colonial and postcolonial Latin America might think of as the relation between *natural history* and *national history* (see Poole 1997). Second, these 1970s initiatives draw our attention to the question of *vinculación*, or the place of science and technology in 20th century politics of national development and modernization. And third, the reinvigoration of state-funded, plant based research and development projects in 1970s Mexico provides an entrée for placing science, technology, and medicine at the heart of anthropological understandings of sovereignties and citizenship. Indeed, in many parts of Latin America (as elsewhere), current pharmaceutical politics is reconfiguring modes of political and economic rights (and corresponding forms of marginalization) that both require and exceed the nation-state. Echeverría's pharmaceutical nationalism anticipated in some ways contemporary developments in which nations and "communities" are making renewed claims to control over the *raw material* for pharmaceutical research and development (such as plants, microbes, and traditional knowledge) and access to its *outcomes* (most notably, AIDS drugs). These issues, in turn, have a growing presence in anthropological work on indigenous knowledge, public health, economic globalization(s), and modes of state and civil society action.

Together, these three clusters of concerns suggest a productively *discordant* and discontinuous map of the problem space set out for and by anthropological studies of science and technology in Mexico and in Latin America. While they have pharmaceutical politics as their theme in common, I do not intend to smooth these disparate trajectories of inquiry into one seamless field or narrative, but rather to draw on each in order to show the richness and heterogeneity of work in this area. These conversations indeed suggest how work in and of Latin America has contributed to the rapidly growing and still molten field of the anthropology of science more broadly.

## NATURE: (POST)COLONIAL ENCOUNTER AND THE POLITICS OF HYBRIDITY

Let us start with Echeverría's Imeplam, the government institute established in 1975 to foment interdisciplinary research on medicinal plants and "traditional knowledge" as a key to securing the nation's health. Imeplam's mandate was essentially twofold: (1) to catalogue and make an inventory of all of the existing scientific knowledge about Mexico's *flora nacional*; and (2) to develop new therapeutic resources based on coordinated interdisciplinary research on the popular uses, scientific names, chemical properties, and therapeutic and toxicological effects of medicinal plants. While the embattled fate of the second goal has been a source of endless frustration and intense reflection for the researchers once in charge of the institute (see below), the effort to recuperate and thus (re)produce a national ethnobotanical knowledge base *has* proven extraordinarily generative. Since the early 1980s, Mexican ethnobotanists, anthropologists, chemists, physicians, and historians have produced a remarkable collection of inventories *of* inventories, catalogues *of* compendia, and histories of the history of research on Mexico's medicinal flora (see, among many others, Dávila Aranda and Germán Ramírez 1991; Estrada Lugo 1996; Lozoya 1976; Lozoya and Zolla 1983; Rojas Rabiela 1994). Like all literature reviews (the present exercise included), these ethnobotanical, anthropological, and historical accounts *do* things.

### Natural history...

First, these are efforts to reach far back into Mexico's oft-mythologized spaces and moments of colonial encounter, in order to take stock of a scientific knowledge base that is, at every turn, "different from itself" – infused with heterogeneity and syncretisms, and suffused with interestingly diverse political projects. Nature, and knowledge about it, is a complicated thing, as several generations of science studies scholars have repeatedly, and variedly, argued. Woven into these genealogies were the detailed and nuanced 16th century accounts of indigenous uses and classifications of plants, animals, and minerals by the Franciscan missionary Fray Bernardino de Sahagún, the Nahuatl medic Martín de la Cruz, and the Spanish natural historian Francisco Hernández; 18th century Spanish natural histories undertaken in the name of the then new Linnaean classificatory system; Humboldt's rapturous 19th century accounts of American landscapes, natural wealth (particularly, minerals) and civilizations; and countless chronicles in between and beyond. In this way, contemporary Mexican accounts of *la flora nacional* literally write a history of a nation forged out of the encounters and "hybridities" of (post)colonial contact zones. Often arguing against the reification of a static, timeless body of indigenous traditions, many such accounts both institutionalize a particular genealogical procession of authoritative accounts, and highlight the ongoing syncretisms and dynamism that literally lie at the heart of what is now considered "Mexican" folk knowledge. Consider, for example, Xavier Lozoya's argument that foundational 16th century ethnographies of Nahuatl healing practices suggest considerable syncretism between indigenous knowledges and Spanish Galenic theories of humoral flows (Lozoya 1983:261–263), or the frequent acknowledgment that many of the most popular medicinal plants in contemporary usage in Mexico were brought from Europe.

Such arguments about transatlantic flows and transliterations may sound familiar to anthropologists and historians of South America. A growing body of literature on colonialism and independence, particularly in the Andes and Amazonia, has drawn on the history and anthropology of science to place natural history at the heart of our understandings of how nature, nations, and a fundamentally hybrid – that is, transatlantic – scientific modernity itself, have been forged. But while many Mexican ethnobotanical genealogies calibrate their origin point to the moment of colonial contact (see also Mignolo 2000), several key works on the politics of nation and nature in South America turn our attention to the Enlightenment – that is, to the 18th and 19th centuries – as a different kind of origin point.

This period has been of particular importance in such accounts in part because of the coincidence of the 1753 publication of Linnaeus's *Systemae Naturae* (a globalizing system for ordering "all of nature") with a decision by the Spanish Crown to grant British and French scientific commissions access to its formerly closed New World territories (Pratt 1992:25). In the wake of the ensuing flurry of scientific expeditions and chronicles thereof, many parts of the South American continent as well as New Spain became known anew – to British, Spanish, and French reading publics, as well as to American creole elites – through the representational technologies, regimes of vision, and narrative emplotments of natural history and scientific classification (Pratt 1992; Poole 1997). The scientific and political writings of Prussian explorer-scientist Alexander von Humboldt are central to this story, in South America as in Mexico. In Mary Louise Pratt's formative argument, Humboldt's romantic narrations of América's flora, fauna, and civilizations not only represented the interior of the continent; they also (and consequently), fueled nascent independence movements in Peru, Venezuela, Argentina, and elsewhere in the New World (Pratt 1992). But it was not only Humboldt's rapturous accounts that became rhetorical and political resources for creole elites. Deborah Poole argues that modes of visualization that developed with scientific lexicons of classification were put to resignifying effect in Peru in the early decades of the 20th century. Thus (for example) Cusqueño photographers and intellectuals developed a distinctly Peruvian *indigenista* aesthetic that both drew on and challenged European aesthetics of classification and typology (Poole 1997).

These and other related works are read widely outside of Latin Americanist circles and are increasingly gathered (for good or for ill) under the label of "postcolonial science studies" (for a useful discussion of this moniker, see Anderson 2002). The postcoloniality in question here is both a historical placeholder and the mark of a particular approach to thinking about knowledge production itself, in which questions of encounters, mixtures, and submerged practices of authorship loom large (see Mignolo 2000; Rodríguez 2001). To be sure, critical work on the role of scientific knowledge and aesthetics in the "reinvention of América" has paid close attention to the powerful, if not hegemonic, effects of formal natural history and its imperial(izing) imperatives to collect, name, and order the world (Pratt 1992). But these analyses have also placed an analytic premium on natural history's – and its practitioners' – vulnerabilities and permeabilities to New World natures *and* New World interlocutors, both Indian and creole.

The notion of permeability – or what historian Warwick Anderson (2000) evocatively calls, in another context, colonialism's "disordered and unequal reciprocities" – has become crucial to anthropologically informed understandings of the place of science in the making of nature and nation in Latin America. Hugh Raffles notes in his book *In Amazonia: A Natural History* just how important Victorian natural history has been to the constitution of Amazonia as a material/discursive place. In so doing, he also draws our attention to the relationship between British explorer-scientist Henry Bates and his hired informants, who clearly had a great deal to do with selecting species and providing data for Bates's famed collections (Raffles 2002:143). These relationships "throw questions of authorship into sharp relief," leading Raffles to ask, "what happened to Bates' natural science in the moment of encounter with Amazonians and this hyperbolic nature? What mimetics and hybridities ensued from the field politics of intersubjectivity?" (2002:138). For Pratt, the traces of similar kinds of field politics in Humboldt's work prompt some of her key arguments about hidden knowledges and subversions; she wonders how American practices and knowledges "infiltrated" Humboldt's accounts and she inquires, "what hand did Humboldt's American interlocutors have directly and otherwise, in the European reinvention of their continent?" (Pratt 1992:135). We might note that for these authors, the "contact zones" of encounter are not located *in* South America and New Spain, but are constitutive of Europeans' views of modernity and their own subjectivity as well (see Poole 1997; Raffles 2002:149).

But how to describe the nature of these permeabilities and reciprocities? The language chosen to characterize such interconnections matters. Raffles is concerned with, among other things, intersubjectivity in the Amazon and the halls of the Royal Academy in London. Deborah Poole, in her account of the relationship between modern regimes of vision, race, and scientific classification in the Andean postcolonial, works in the idioms of circulation and exchange. Pratt borrows Cuban sociologist Fernando Ortíz's notion of "transculturation" to think about processes of give and take, of mutual inscription and infiltration, in the imperial "contact zones" of the interior of the South American continent.

Transculturation in particular is an analytic that leaves literary critic and postcolonial theorist Walter Mignolo with some worries that are intensely germane to the topic at hand. Mignolo frets that the idea of transculturation is inescapably haunted by its etymological roots, pointing us, despite all intentions to the contrary, to notions of biocultural mixture, and thus to the specter of *mestizaje* (Mignolo 2000:14–16). (This, he notes, despite the fact that Ortíz coined the term to move away from explicitly biologized, Malinowskian notions of acculturation and deculturation: Mignolo 2000:14.) Taking the etymological connection seriously, we might argue that, in fact, we cannot entertain a discussion of histories of knowledge about plants forged in encounter without also entertaining the question of (transatlantic) race politics in Latin American nation-building enterprises.

### ...National history

This, then, is the second point I want to make about the reverberations of ethnobotanical inventorying projects of the kind sparked by Imeplam in Echeverría's Mexico. In Mexico, and arguably (though not only) in Peru as well, late 20th century reconstitutions of a distinctly national *herbolaria* are shot through with the notions of hybridity and mixture that have explicitly underwritten modern nation-building, indigenista, assimilationist projects (see de la Cadena 2000). Former Imeplam anthropologist Carlos Zolla suggested just how effortlessly these domains can be thought together, when he explained to me (in a 1997 interview at his office in the no longer existing National Indigenista Institute in Mexico City) that "with medicinal plants, as with many other things, we are a nation of mixtures." It is a charged analogy, to say the least.

As numerous scholars of race, gender, and nation in Latin America have made so clear, the question of (biocultural) mixture – as problem and as solution – has been absolutely central to the constitution of modern Latin American nationness (among many others, see on Mexico, Knight 1990; Stern 2003; on Peru, de la Cadena 2000; on Colombia, Wade 1995; and, for comparative studies, Graham 1990; Stepan 1991; Appelbaum, Macpherson and Rosemblat 2003). It is perhaps not surprising then that it is in the matter of eugenics and racial science – both of which were intensely well developed in early 20th century Latin America – that anthropology in and of the region has perhaps most explicitly grappled with the question of "science." Nancy Stepan's history of eugenics in late 19th and early 20th century Latin America – a path-breaking work that also occupies a crucial place in broader science studies circles – documents how Mexican, Brazilian, and Argentine national elites, scientists, and writers grappled with and redeployed European scientific theories of race, in an effort to combat European disdain for these new nations and their "unstable racial forms" (Stepan 1991). Against such biologized declarations of exclusion from the orders of progress and civilization, Latin American elites embraced (and thus gave new life to) French, Lamarckian genetics in order to ask "whether racial mixture ... should rather be *encouraged* as a biological process of nation formation" (Stepan 1991:137, emphasis added). Doing much more than placing "science" in its cultural or historical context, Stepan draws on approaches in science and technology studies to show how these scientific practices and projects simultaneously *represented* (or reflected) and *constituted* political and social ideologies, practices, and relations (1991:196–201). She also makes the key point, resonant with the arguments about permeability in the above discussion, that the relationship between European and Latin American sciences was anything *but* a question of mere diffusion from metropole to periphery. Stepan, alongside other scholars such as Alexandra Stern, beautifully demonstrates the dynamic relationship between Latin American science/medicine and heterogeneous and contested forms of European science, from neo-Lamarckian genetics to Italian biotypology (see Stern 2003:197).

Anthropological and historical work on eugenics and mestizaje in Latin America – of which there is a large and growing body of sophisticated literature – has also shown how the deployment of biologized notions of race (entwined with class) in the service of early 20th century Latin American projects of national *re*generation varied in relation to differently inflected national(ist) histories and ideologies. In Argentina, for example, where elites imagined the country as a nation of (European) immigrants, 1920s and 1930s eugenic practices and discourses took shape explicitly in defense of "white civilization" against an encroaching *Latinidad* (see Stepan 1991:139–145); Brazilian eugenics and whitening initiatives were configured through deeply ambivalent understandings of the nation as constituted explicitly by "racial mixture." In Mexico, in strong contrast to Argentina, successive versions of eugenics and racial science were configured through (particular understandings of) the nation's relationship to "Indianness," and a post-Revolutionary resignification of the mestizo, in Vasconcelos's infamous formulation, as the cosmic race (see Walsh, this volume). In the decades following 1917, which marked, more or less, the end of the Revolution, the state threw its weight into modernizing efforts, educational projects, and an official indigenista anthropology based on the argument that while the cultural heritage of indigenous peoples had provided the nation with its distinctive profile, the present and future would belong to a bioculturally assimilated, national mestizo citizen (see Stepan 1991:146–147; Stern 2003; see also Fortes and Adler Lomnitz 1994; Lomnitz 2001:139–140).

In Mexico, plants – and efforts to consolidate knowledge about them – have held more than a metaphorical relationship to such complicated, racialized projects of con-solidating "the nation." As with 20th century indigenismo's constitutive ambivalence toward the place of indigenous peoples in the nation (foundational, but consigned to the realm of the folkloric past), so too is the *flora nacional* an assimilationist narrative. The connections are rhetorical, historical, and institutional. In insistent characteriza-tions of the *herbolaria mexicana* as the "product of five centuries of mixture," as a body of knowledge that is (now) remarkably "uniform" across the republic, and as (therefore) the dominion not of particular communities but of the "population as a whole," many ethnobotanists in Mexico and the chief protagonists and chroniclers of Imeplam's endeavors, including its original director, physician Xavier Lozoya, have both helped represent and constitute this post-Revolutionary story of Mexico pre-cisely as a nation of (biocultural) hybridity (see Lozoya 1983: 261, 268).

To bring this section to a close, we might recall Deborah Poole's argument that late 18th to early 19th century natural sciences of classification – and their particular modes of seeing and of typologizing – helped concretize and sediment an emergent, scientific notion of race (Poole 1997:58–84). It is an argument about the transatlantic origins of a scientific modernity, and of the place of "the Andean postcolonial" therein. But it is also an argument that finds an intriguingly concrete analogue in a particular genre of Mexican ethnobotanical inventories, and their dual horizons: their explicit origin point in the moment of colonial contact, and their implicit conditions of possi-bility, tied inextricably to 20th century projects of national consolidation. Poole might argue that plant science is, in a certain sense, racial science. And if race thinking is a powerful mode of thinking about and defining nations, then *la flora nacional* – that intriguingly hybrid historical product – is, arguably, a kind of *historia patria* (see Cházaro 2001–2002).

## *VINCULACIÓN*: CULTURES OF SCIENCE AND TECHNOLOGY

Following the end of Luís Echeverría's term in 1976, Imeplam underwent numerous downsizings, name changes, and relocations. The institute's ongoing effort to turn medicinal plants into bioactive chemical compounds is now carried out south of Mexico City, at a compact facility housed together with a clinic of the Mexican Institute for Social Security (IMSS), the government's preeminent biomedical research institution and the primary public sector provider of health care. Imeplam now lives on under the name of the Southern Center for Biomedical Research (CIBIS), and its goal has become to mobilize the expertise of an extensive network of Mexican research institutions in pursuit not of pharmaceutical products, but rather herbal medicines, or, "phytomedicines." These are lower technology remedies that do not require the isolation of pure compounds, but rather preserve and use much of the plant in question.

CIBIS has shepherded one such product, the antiparasitical capsule Clauden, all the way through its pipeline, from clinical trials to market-ready packaging. Clauden capsules are filled with ground guayaba leaves, controlled for consistency in the amount of active compound per milligram of "biomass," and rigorously tested through a series of clinical trials. The process that produced Clauden involved no fewer than seven different public institutions in addition to CIBIS, as well as a Mexican company recruited to take on the manufacturing and marketing, and a grower who provided six tons of guayaba leaves for the initial run. But following this massive effort (which was seven years in the making), Clauden now sits on a dusty shelf – not one box has sold, CIBIS's current director told me in 2004 (Jaime Tortoriello, interview, 2004). The "problem" is one that historian Nina Hinke has pointed out in her work on the institute's 19th century predecessor (the National Medical Institute, IMN) as well: there was no substantial or sustainable link between basic research – university and government funded – and private or industrial partners (Hinke, personal communication, 2004). CIBIS, like the IMN a century before, could not find any growers to guarantee a steady, industrial-scale stream of plant material, nor were any domestic companies ready to commit to the ongoing project of manufacturing and marketing these products. CIBIS's director Jaime Tortoriello (Xavier Lozoya's successor) has neither the infrastructure, nor, he feels, a mandate to do the industrial scaling-up himself: "we are a government agency, *not* a company," he emphasized to me in an interview in 2004. And thus it is *basic* research, geared toward public health, to which CIBIS must continue to dedicate itself.

The elusiveness of the "development" aspect of the research and development trajectory of Imeplam, now CIBIS, is a much commented upon source of frustration for many involved in these institutions. While I must confess that I remain both impressed and intrigued by the generativity of their ongoing research efforts, this persistent sense of frustration signals something important – as such, it provokes my second pass through an anthropology of science and technology in and of Latin America. This section is not about *nature* and the entanglements of knowledge thereof, but rather about what many Latin American scholars working on the social studies of technoscience identify as a problem of institutional and national *cultures* of science and technology – in other words, the values, relations, and histories that have defined national and regional technoscience education, policy, and practice, and more broadly, processes of technological development (Bueno and Santos 2003; Vessuri 1987; Casas and Luna 1999; Fortes and Adler Lomnitz 1994; see also Cueto 1997, 1989).

At work in many of these analyses is, as well, a different idiom of relationality and entanglement: not hybridity, mestizaje, or encounter, but rather *vinculación*. Strictly speaking, *vincular* means to connect or link: as in (to choose a nonarbitrary example) to forge links between basic, university based research, the government, and industry. For a well-established and growing community of Latin American scholars working in the social studies of science and technology, *vinculación* – what it looks like, how to promote it, and why it has worked in some instances and failed in others – has become one of the keys to understanding the cultural and social dimensions of science and technology, and their relation to projects of modernization, national development, and the intensified globalization of the markets in which Latin American nations (must) compete (Laura Cházaro, personal communication, 2004).

In this sense, Echeverría's support of Imeplam was not just about reanimating the symbolic and biochemical value of medicinal plants. As many chroniclers of 20th century Mexican politics have noted, the Echeverría years brought with them a technocraticization of the Mexican state, in which science and technology would have a newly important role (Schoijet and Worthington 1993:214; Fortes and Adler Lomnitz 1994:18). Echeverría's support of national science was, without doubt, a "locally" relevant maneuver – an effort to shore up the credibility of the ruling party (Partido Revolucionario Institucional, PRI) in the wake of the 1968 Tlatelolco massacre, repression of dissidents, the demise of the mid-century "Mexican [economic] miracle," teachers' strikes, and growing militancy in many parts of the nation (see Schoijet and Worthington 1993:214; Soto Laveaga 2003). But it was also resolutely in line with broader regional trends promoting "indigenous" (i.e. national) technological capacity-building.

The 1960s and 1970s were decades of great ferment in regional science and technology policy and infrastructure-building, most notably in Castro's Cuba (see Reid-Henry 2005), Argentina, Brazil, and Mexico, with Venezuela also investing comparatively heavily in science and technology (Vessuri 1987). In line with arguments developed by dependency theorists in the UN Economic Commission for Latin America (ECLA), technological self-sufficiency and import substitution became key tenets of national development strategies, and the late 1960s and early 1970s saw the establishment of national science and technology councils (CONICITs) across the region – these were agencies created to promote and fund "local scientific activity" (Vessuri 1987:525). With the explicit development of national science and technology policies in nations ranging from the "big three" (Brazil, Argentina, and Mexico) to smaller nations such as Costa Rica and Ecuador, also came an increasing body of social science work focusing on the efficacy (or not) of these policies. In a fascinating and extensive 1987 review of the social studies of science in Latin America, Venezuela based anthropologist Hebe Vessuri, one of the most influential scholars in this arena, noted that while much of this work was itself technocratic and normative, the "problem" of national science policy also opened up a space for a wave of critical and creative analyses, often by politically engaged scientists themselves, such as Amilcar Herrera and Oscar Varsavsky in Argentina, who were at the forefront of rethinking conventional understandings of underdevelopment, and the relationship between science and politics (Vessuri 1987:530–531).

Vessuri notes the distinctive trajectories that national science policies and critical analyses thereof were to have: the military coup in Argentina in 1976 effectively put an end to this moment of critical engagement with the politics of science in that country, and Vessuri argues that, for a variety of reasons, the scientific community in Argentina was slow to recuperate after the return to democractic rule in 1983. In Brazil, by contrast, the state has maintained a strong commitment to promoting science and technology since the early 1970s. Certainly, as was the case across the region, Brazil's initial explosion of scientific activity began to decrease in the late 1970s, but it gained ground again in the mid-1980s (see below). Vessuri argues that strong political commitments to this arena generated a powerful national scientific community with the capacity to militate for continued support (1987:531), and indeed we might add that Brazil is one of the leading sites of creative work in the social studies of science and technology in Latin America.

Mexico too established its own CONACYT (National Commission on Science and Technology) in the first year of Echeverría's term (1970), making the state a key source of support for academic scientific research and graduate studies. By the end of Echeverría's administration, however, economic crisis there too put an abrupt halt to to CONACYT's "modest momentum" (Schoijet and Worthington 1993:215) in the realm of a national pharmaceutical science. More broadly, Echeverría's successor (Miguel de la Madrid) reinstated pharmaceutical patents, dramatically scaled back state-sponsored efforts to turn medicinal plants into national "health resources" (in the World Health Organization's telling phrase), and implemented a series of neoliberal austerity measures and budget cuts that affected basic science funding across the board. Among the ensuing transformations in Mexican academia was the establishment of the now famous and controversial SNI (the Sistema Nacional de Investigadores – National System of Researchers). The SNI was and remains designed to cushion the blow of declining academic salaries by providing academics with a significant supplement based on (research) productivity. As such, it has become both an indispensable feature of the research landscape and a key target for critics of the ongoing "neoliberalization" of academic research in Mexico (Schoijet and Worthington 1993:215–219).

The political and economic environments of science research and funding have, of course, continued to shift over the last two decades, in Mexico and across the region. So too have the key questions and approaches of Latin American social studies of science and technology. Hebe Vessuri noted in her 1987 review of the field:

> some of the topics that loomed large thirty years ago – for example, the establishment of national systems of science, the ethos of scientific research, or the social identity of the research scientists – are now barely mentioned. Today attention is focused upon the cultural backwardness of particular countries, the cultural and technological heterogeneity of the region, the Science and Technology lag in Latin America vis-à-vis advanced countries, the specific difficulties encountered by industrial firms, the behavior and attitudes of entrepreneurs, and the role of universities in research and development. (1987:520)

In the decade and a half since this assessment was published, an ever growing body of work coming out of Mexico, as well as Brazil, Venezuela, and Argentina, indeed suggests that the sociology and anthropology of innovation itself has become a crucial new direction and preoccupation for science studies scholars in the region (as Vessuri predicted in her review; see Arrellano Hernández 2002). In particular, analysis of the cultural and social values that inform or impede links among academia, government, and industry has become a pronounced analytic priority, particularly in light of rapidly changing demands on research centers and industries (see Bueno and Santos 2003). Along with continued work on earlier foundational concerns such as the "socialization of Mexican scientists" (Fortes and Adler Lomnitz 1994) and the distinct profiles of different national scientific communities, this new direction has also meant using ethnographic analysis to understand the *cultural* configuration of technoscientific processes. Thus, anthropologists of science and technology in Mexico interrogate the subtleties and implicit reference points or premises that underlie collaboration between research centers and businesses (de Gortari 2003:115; see also Casas and Luna 1999);

the construction and mobilization of values such as "trust" in the automobile industry (Bueno 2003); and the contours and effects of networks of knowledge production (*redes*), for example, in the production of hybrid corn (Arrellano Hernández 2002).

A key preoccupation here, as the dilemma of CIBIS and its Clauden capsules so powerfully suggests, is the relationship between basic and applied research. Thus critical studies of science have also explicitly analyzed institutional values – manifest in university policies and measures for career advancement – that strongly favor a notion of pure or basic science and thus that can constrain work in fields that rely on a cross-fertilization with applied and technological work (Adler Lomnitz and Cházaro 1999:129). The problem, Larissa Adler Lomnitz and Laura Cházaro note in their study of the Computer Science and Applied Mathematics department of UNAM (National Autonomous University of Mexico), should be seen as an invitation to university policy-makers and science studies scholars to mobilize an ethnographic sensibility to rethink exactly what constitutes basic and applied research, and how they should be related.

No one has taken up the invitation with more creativity, perhaps, than the Brazilian science studies scholar Ivan da Costa Marques (2004). In his essay on a Brazilian company that reverse engineered Apple computers in the 1980s (much to the distress of Apple), da Costa Marques notes the ways in which notions of basic and applied research themselves were very much at stake. When challenged for not respecting Apple's patents, the Brazilian company (Unitron) argued that in fact it takes a great deal of innovative labor to reverse engineer a Macintosh. This move built on a shift that Brazilian computer professionals and state policy had articulated in how "basic" scientific research itself was to be defined. That is, in the 1970s, basic research in this professional community was redefined as a process that would not necessarily have to treat the semiotic equivalent of "nature" or "basic truths" as its epistemological anchor, but rather could legitimately treat "foreign technology" as its raw material – the stuff to study, work on, take apart, understand, and develop, to national ends (da Costa Marques 2004:21–28). It is a virtuoso analysis, in which it is, indeed, the already-made ("technology") – and not something like "nature" – that serves as the raw material for both a strategic national science, and for the critically engaged social studies thereof.

While da Costa Marques gains a great deal of analytic mileage out of this reversal, it is precisely the question of taking "foreign technology" as a starting point that bothers Xavier Lozoya, formerly of Imeplam. Many of Lozoya's publications have been dedicated to a critique of Mexican "medical culture," in which it is, he argues, all too often "foreign" (medical) cultures, technologies, and approaches that are valorized, to the detriment of autochthonous, national resources and expertise. In his view, Imeplam was a brief hiatus and a significant, if short-lived, opening in a national context in which, for the most part,

> the Mexican state and its health institutions recognize and support the exercise of one particular kind of medicine, that which has been copied from the mix of preventative and therapeutic practices established as valid and efficacious by Western, US medicine. Ignoring the existence of "other medicines," the official model of medical attention in Mexico constantly runs up against serious cultural difficulties which in practice effectively limits its ability to meet its own goals. (Lozoya 2003:17)

Lozoya's complaint indexes a powerful set of discussions about the place of "the traditional" in Latin American modernity – a question that is discussed extensively in work on the anthropology of science, religion, and heterodoxy (see Palmié 2002; Hess 1991). Here, these broad-ranging questions about the cultures of occidental medicine, and a "colonized consciousness" that remains ambivalent about the auto-chthonous (see Lomnitz 2001: 132–140), are wrapped up in the problem of institutional cultures of science funding. Urging, as ever, a look "closer to home" for efficacious therapeutic models, Lozoya has joined many of his colleagues in turning to CONACYT, among other bodies, in search of support for his current research endeavors, based at IMSS in Mexico City. In a lively mock diary account that spans the (again) nonarbitrary period of five centuries of engagement with the study of medicinal plants, Lozoya opens the last of his entries as follows:

> November 10, 1998. I received the notification from CONACYT that our project on the development of medications based on Mexican medicinal plants was not accepted. The rejection is particularly surprising because the request for proposals indicated that… the proposed theme must relate to a field of knowledge that requires support not only for consolidating existing knowledge but for creating links (*vinculación*) between science and the productive sector [industry]. From what we have seen, producing national medicines does not seem to be a priority for those making the decisions about how to use public funds for the sciences. (Lozoya 2001–2002:22–23; my translation)

For Lozoya, there are two bitter pills to swallow here: first, CONACYT's reticence to include research on medicinal plants in the ongoing national project of striving for greater *vinculación*, and, second, the additional fact that European, Asian, and US companies are busily developing products and markets for plant based herbal remedies in precisely the "niche" that Mexico should have cornered long ago (Lozoya 2001–2002:23; 2003).

Indeed it is the material specter of "competition" and competitiveness in conditions described as globalization that looms large over many discussions of *vinculación*. It is relevant that the "problem" in Latin American science and technology studies of "not enough" *vinculación* stands in striking contrast to the problem space explored by numerous science studies scholars working in US and (some) European contexts, in which the analytic topography is often defined in precisely the reverse terms. From the mid-1980s to the present, academic science, particularly in the life sciences, has become ever more linked to what Lozoya would call the productive sector. In the US, as the biotechnology industry was getting started in earnest, Reagan-era government policies encouraged and indeed required enhanced forms of "technology transfer" from universities to the private sector (see Rabinow 1996); meanwhile, the changing topographies of (i.e. reduction in) government support for academic research has contributed to the intensified entanglements of university research, "the public" and the state, and life sciences firms. Whether seen as good, bad, or at the least, undeniably generative of new relationships, such intimacies have provoked pointed analytic and political questions. Thus proliferate analyses of the "triple helix" (the three strands of which are government, university, and private sector research) (Etzkowitz and Leydesdorff 1997) and the "new contract between science and society" (Nowotny, Scott and Gibbons 2001; Latour 1998); of hybridities, fusions and splicing (Haraway 1997); of publicizations and privatizations (Hayden 2003b). These relations resonate, of course, transnationally and are giving new shape to contemporary concerns with *vinculación* in Latin American science and technology studies. We are back, it would seem, to the question of mixture in all of its complexity.

## PHARMACEUTICAL POLITICS: SOVEREIGNTIES AND CITIZENSHIPS

My third and final pass through the question of science and technology focuses on pharmaceutical practice and politics, and how they shape relationships among transnational capital, the state, and forms of citizenship. It is a big cluster of concerns, to be sure, but my argument is that both the general field of biomedicine and the more specific area of pharmaceutical research, development and distribution are powerfully shaping our analytic and political engagements with these questions, which are of great importance to anthropological work in Latin America more broadly. As ever, the Echeverría moment – separated from the present by more than two decades of powerful swings to the neoliberal right across Latin America (and beyond) – both anticipated and crystallized a great deal. For it would seem now that it is in the domain of "the pharmaceutical" in particular that we see, again, assertions of sovereignty that echo Echeverría's explicit moves to nationalize both the pharmaceutical industry and particular natural resources that formed its backbone (Soto Laveaga 2003). Such nationalizations, then as now, have powerful implications for how political and other "rights" are being imagined and negotiated within and across Latin American national borders.

Let me begin this section then by turning to another country – Brazil – where we see the most striking example of how assertions of "the nation" and of national public health have come (back) to a position of viability within what Joao Biehl (2004) calls the international pharmaceutical contract. In the late 1990s, under President Henrique Cardoso, Brazil became well known for its combination of a strong scientific research and development community, powerful activist mobilizations, decentralized, regional public health and epidemiological interventions, and credible threats to break corporate patents on antiretrovirals unless prices were cut. As a result, the Brazilian state has been able to provide free, universal access to AIDS medications and therapies that have been prohibitively expensive for most of the "developing" world – and hence to dramatically reduce its AIDS mortality rate (Biehl 2004). Anthropologist Joao Biehl writes:

> a politicized science fuels this model policy. The strengthening of the country's scientific infrastructure and pharmaceutical industry has been key to the realization of the antiretrovirals law [mandating universal access, 1996] and the sustainability of the distribution policy. When three-quarters of the Brazilian state business has already been privatized, medication production is arguably one of the country's most thriving fields. (2004:115)

It is precisely this kind of strong national scientific base – as the backbone for a national industry – that Echeverría had hoped to stimulate, and that *current* Mexican initiatives to promote a national generic drug industry are again attempting to call into being (Hayden 2007). But there are many reasons not to overstate a resonance between "statist" pharmaceutical politics in Echeverría's Mexico and 1990s events in Cardoso's Brazil (or even in contemporary Mexico). One of them is found in Biehl's important argument that Cardoso's assertions of a national pharmaceutical interest was not enacted in stark opposition to "the market" and transnational industry (the kind of argument we would find in 1970s Mexican pharmaceutical nationalism), but rather was intimately tied to Cardoso's efforts to "internationalize" the Brazilian market (2004:112). For Biehl (drawing explicitly on Cardoso's own formulation), *this* example of "biotechnology for the people" suggests that "economic globalization does not necessarily limit states," but rather can enable new forms of regulation. Indeed in this case it helped provide the conditions of possibility for Brazil's transformation from a struggling welfare state to what Biehl calls an *activist* state (2004:105–107).

Certainly, these are not the only stories to be told about "globalization" and pharmaceutical politics in Latin America. Andrew Lakoff's work has tracked the articulations between the formidable Argentina psychoanalytic community and US and European drug companies seeking to tap into (and hence create) an Argentine market for antidepressants and other psychopharmacological drugs. Here there is a rather uneasy relationship between national science – in this case, one with a strongly Lacanian bent – and recalibrations of modes of diagnosis, treatment, and technocratic rationality required and desired by transnational pharmaceutical industry practices and regulatory regimes (Lakoff 2003, 2004, 2005). If one of the things at stake in this uneasy relationship is the transformation of Argentine clinical patients into research subjects for globalized clinical trials, Laura Briggs's work in Puerto Rico reminds us that such relations have a powerful – and heterogeneous – history in the region. Specifically, she examines how Puerto Rican women have served as experimental subjects quite literally for US imperialism. She argues that the sciences of eugenics and contraception have played a central role in the reproduction of a US empire on the island (L. Briggs 2002).

Despite the quite different articulations of science, state, and economy traversed by these works, they point us to an important triangulation: one in which relations between national research communities (and/or governments), on the one hand, and transnational "pharma," on the other, also help configure relations of citizenship, participation, inclusion and exclusion, or what we could call, in a Foucaultian move appropriate to this material, subjectification. That is, contemporary work on pharmaceutical politics in Latin America (and elsewhere) draws on a robust legacy of critical work on public health, eugenics, and "hygiene" more broadly to argue that "biopolitics" – the management of life – is, of course, politics itself (see Stern 2003). Anthropological work on public health in 20th century Latin America has made clear just how central this regime of knowledge and intervention has been to the allocation of "substantive access to the civil and social rights of citizenship" (C. Briggs with Montini-Briggs 2003:10). Charles Briggs and Clara Montini-Briggs make this observation through their detailed work on Venezuelan public health responses to the 1992–93 cholera epidemic in which indigenous peoples were *excluded* from – and hence made subject to – the social and political rights which Briggs and Montini-Briggs call "sanitary citizenship."

Whereas this notion of sanitary citizenship in Venezuela is, in many ways, constituted by state racism and exclusion, Biehl works with a different inflection of the relation between public health and belonging. Specifically, he suggests that Brazil's AIDS drug distribution policies in particular have helped reformulate notions of rights, belonging, and accountability, such that these are not necessarily provided by or calibrated explicitly to "the state" (2004:125). By highlighting the shift from political citizenship to *biomedical* citizenship as a new form of participation, Biehl's work brings Latin American anthropology into conversation with a growing body of new work focusing on biological citizenship and the contemporary life sciences in US and European contexts.

## BIODIVERSITY AND PHARMA POLITICS: NEW MODES OF INCLUSION AND EXCLUSION

It is not only in the realm of public health or, more specifically, the production and distribution of medications, that pharmaceutical research and development has become central to reformulated notions of belonging, the distribution of entitlements, and exclusions therefrom. For, at the same time that the Brazilian government was initiating its AIDS policies (in the mid-1990s), many nations and indigenous organizations across Latin America and beyond were grappling with another kind of reconfigured "sovereignty" and rights: this time, in the domain of biological resources and "cultural knowledge" used as raw material for drug, agricultural, and biotechnological research and development. Here, as Arturo Escobar's work on the Pacific coast of Colombia makes so clear, knowledge about, claims to, and the management of natural resources serve as modes of (re)configuring participation, identity, and exclusions (see Escobar 1997).

Nowhere is this development more evident than in the recent proliferation of biodiversity prospecting agreements, or benefit-sharing contracts, involving varying combinations of "local" communities, developing country scientists, national research institutes, and foreign biotechnology and pharmaceutical companies. These contracts, which we find in operation in Costa Rica, Mexico, Brazil, Peru, Argentina, Chile, and Ecuador (and in other parts of the "global South"), have arisen following the passage of the 1992 United Nations Convention on Biological Diversity (CBD). Intended in large part to promote sustainable development, the CBD essentially granted nations *sovereignty* over "wild" genetic resources, while also noting that communities and community knowledge must be protected and maintained. In taking these resources out of the "global commons," the Convention set the stage for "source nations" and "source communities" to demand some form of benefits, in the form of, for example, royalty payments, technology transfer, or development funds, in exchange for granting drug and biotechnology companies and researchers access to plants, microbes, and traditional or community knowledge.

This new multilateral promise of "benefit sharing" has raised important questions for the anthropology of science, and beyond. It has, certainly, changed the horizons for a heterogeneous tradition in anthropology, ethnoscience, and ethnobotany that has long sought to document the legitimacy and coherence of "local" or "traditional knowledge," as with Roberto González's recent ethnography of "Zapotec science" (González 2001; see also Posey 1985; Toledo 1995). As such invocations of systematic cultural knowledge are increasingly pegged to the ability of communities to assert control over resources – and to claim "benefits" derived from their commercial exploitation – the implications of such documentation projects shift. This is particularly true of the work of the late Darrell Posey, who was among the most visible researchers to make this move from showing the "sustainability" of (in his case) Kayapó cultivation practices in Brazil, to actively promoting and grappling with new forms of community claims-making (Posey 1985, 1996). A growing body of anthropological work on indigenous intellectual property rights both in national contexts and in international forums such as WIPO (World Intellectual Property Organization) and the UN Working Group on Indigenous Populations explores the possibility of granting indigenous intellectual property. In conversation with indigenous activists and communities across Latin America, this literature also examines the pragmatic costs and benefits of such proposed mechanisms of control over resources, the new associational forms to which they give rise, and the relationship between intellectual property rights and other modes of staking claims such as territorial sovereignty, cultural property, and human rights (see Brown 2003; Coombe 2001, 2003; Greene 2002, 2004; Posey 1996).

Whether framed as intellectual property rights per se, or as other forms of "benefits" to be redistributed, these new promises of "inclusion" in processes of pharmaceutical value production have raised longstanding questions about community dominion and belonging, while giving them slightly new form. Several recent ethnographies of biodiversity prospecting agreements, particularly in Mexico and Peru, concretely address the effects of these promises of redistribution, both for the practice of science in these nations, and for indigenous community rights and entitlements (Hayden 2003a; Greene 2004; see also Brush 1999 on agricultural prospecting in Peru). In a US government-funded bioprospecting project in Mexico, the question of how to designate the benefit-sharing recipients who should "come with" collected medicinal plants brought the now familiar formulation of hybrid knowledges (and the natural/national history question) to the fore in some complicated ways. Participating Mexican researchers invoked the now familiar notion of the hybridity of the *herbolaria nacional* as they argued that because medicinal plants are distributed widely across the republic, benefit-sharing relations should be routed through the national public domain (see also Brush 1999). That is, they collected plants in public spaces, and established benefit-sharing relationships with indigenous community organizations – not because they were the "owners" or "stewards" of plants and knowledge, but because they were engaged in projects that dovetailed with this prospecting program's sustainable development agenda. I have described this move as a "nationalization" of a rather particular stripe (Hayden 2003b).

Shane Greene's work on a separate US-funded project in Peru focuses on a different set of "domaining" practices and negotiations over prospecting's modes of inclusion and exclusion. Greene traces the rather harrowing twists and turns in Aguaruna engagements with bioprospecting, outlining how the constitution of, and relationships among, community organizations were powerfully transformed in anticipation of benefits that would, perhaps, materialize many years down the road (see Greene 2002, 2004). Greene's work shows the fascinating ways in which the efforts of Aguaruna groups to make claims on entitlements wove together a range of idioms for political action and inclusion. These idioms did not always fall neatly in line with the prospecting agents' notions of reward and incentive, but rather drew on rhetorics and movements for autonomy and territorial sovereignty, for human rights, and for cultural and intellectual property (Greene 2002). It is worth highlighting here, as Greene does, that these idioms imply and impel different modes of entitlement, grounds for political action, and assumptions about the definition of community itself.

Highlighted in these examples are several aspects of this new politics of benefit sharing which will bring us back, by way of conclusion, to the question of pharmaceutical politics and their relation to forms of sovereignty and entitlements/exclusions. We might note first, recalling Echeverría's move to give barbasco root "back" to the campesinos who collected it, that the act of articulating "participation" for rural actors through their relations to transnational pharmaceutical companies is not an entirely new phenomenon. What has shifted are the languages and mechanisms through which such processes and relations are configured, and the horizons of such participation itself. Echeverría's move was part of a brief resurrection of the corporatist Mexican state, in which a grid of discourses, institutions, and commitments recognized (and thus helped create) a very particular kind of actor-as-political participant. The political promise of "incorporation" and entitlement through the nationalization of medicinal plants was, at that time, reserved for those who would be organized, and would organize themselves, under the name of "*campesinos*" (peasants). But this configuration of the (incorporable/recognizable) rural political actor shifted in the late 1980s and the early 1990s, with, among other things, growing indigenous rights mobilizations across the "global South" and North America. There are of course many avenues through which to argue, as do many other chapters in this volume, that the category of "indigenous peoples" came to eclipse class based identities such as campesino as a key organizing rubric for rural actors' political agency/subjectivity, both within nations and transnationally (see chapters by Barragán, Seligmann, and Martinez Novo, this volume). In the process, echoing Biehl's arguments above, we might note the ways in which "participation" in these relationships of pharmaceutical sovereignty are redefined, not primarily (as under Echeverría) as conventional forms of political rights that are brokered by the nation-state, but rather as the promise of entitlements conferred through participation in (globalized) processes of value production.

At the same time, however, the continuing salience of the "nation" in assessments of the dominion of medicinal plants, particularly but not exclusively in Mexico, reminds us that the state itself is both recalled and reinvented through these provisional processes of redress. The "old" problem of indigenous versus state sovereignties does not by any means evaporate in contemporary pharmaceutical politics.

## CONCLUSION

Within the diffuse interdisciplinary fields constituted by the anthropology and social studies of science, a move has been afoot over the last ten years or so to move beyond an initial focus on European and US American scientific practices and to think about science and technology in arguably more complex geopolitical and historical frames, in which notions of colonialism, transnational capitalism, distinctive national(ist) histories, indigenous and subaltern studies, and critiques of development loom large. Several place-holding terms have emerged to note both the critique of a "Eurocentric" science studies, and a presumed solution, including multicultural science studies (Harding 1998; Hess 1995) and postcolonial science studies (see Anderson 2002; McNeil 2005). It would have been possible to frame this chapter in those terms, but doing so would have produced an untoward diffusionist effect, in which an analytic move from a European and US American "center" *to* Latin America mimics the very idea it is meant to critique. My fascination with plant and pharmaceutical politics in Mexico and more broadly in the region led me to propose a different point of departure, one that engages with an already robust arena of inquiry within Latin Americanist anthropologies; one that articulates with but is not reducible to a "post-colonial science studies"; and one that grapples not just with science, medicine, and technology narrowly defined, but also with some of the central concerns in broader regional and disciplinary work.

On that last point, what these literatures and approaches (postcolonial and other-wise) *do* have in common is the presupposition (and the capacity to demonstrate) that science and technology are not autonomous domains of practice and knowledge pro-duction, but rather are inextricably entwined with, and are constituted by, particular social, political, and historical relations. Somewhat necessarily, then, I have not only drawn on work that explicitly describes itself as doing "the anthropology of science/technology in Latin America." For better or for ill (and with apologies to any unhap-pily appropriated authors), I have also been somewhat activist in drawing other work into this framework, authors' explicit intentions or framings notwithstanding.

With a particular set of (Mexican) pharmaceutical politics as a point of departure, then, we move through what are in some ways three different versions of Latin American(ist) anthropologies of science, in which issues that emerge in Mexico both resonate with broader regional concerns and highlight a number of historical and political specificities. Thus, late 20th century Mexican government efforts to mobilize medicinal plants as a "resource for the nation" call our attention to complex (post)colonial legacies in Mexico and in South America, in which natural history – as a mode of seeing and classifying – became a resource for postcolonial nationalisms. In Mexico in particular, we can see just how powerfully "plants" come to be entwined with nationalist articulations of a *patria* forged through mixture, hybridity, and mes-tizaje. But the social and political hierarchies inscribed in "nature" are not always the primary object of concern for work in this area. As we see in the work of Latin American science studies scholars, distinctive national "cultures" of development, and the institutional values that may be revealed through ethnographic attention to par-ticular processes of *vinculación* or its "failure," have helped to produce a different domain of inquiry. This aspect of Latin American science studies runs orthogonally, in many ways, to those directions in Anglophone and Francophile anthropology of sci-ence concerned with what we might gloss, overly simplistically, as the problem of "nature" and knowledge thereof. Latin American science studies scholars have put this difference to work with very interesting and generative effects.

Finally, the shifting contours of plant based research and development projects in Mexico (in which the 1970s were one of several key moments) have been inextricable from broader shifts in operative modes of political inclusion and exclusion, within Mexico and across the region. Here, pharmaceutical science and technology provides an entrée into thinking about the (re)assertion of "the" nation-state and the redefinition of political rights and other modes of allocation and distribution of resources, as articulated with international pharmaceutical economies, variously scaled activist and civil society interventions, and intellectual property regimes. If Echeverría's Mexico and the issues raised therein tell us so clearly that the science and technology of the pharmaceutical *is* politics itself, then these works collectively and in their diffuse ways remind us that to study science and technology is to engage with some of the most pressing analytic and political questions facing Latin Americans, and Latin American anthropology, today.

## NOTE

I would like to express my deepest thanks to Deborah Poole for the invitation to be a part of this volume, as well as for her editorial acumen; to Laura Cházaro, the late Nina Hinke, María Josefa Santos, Rebeca de Gortari, Teresa Rojas Rabiela, Carlos López Beltrán, Carmen Bueno, Xavier Lozoya, Casey Walsh, and Jaime Tortoriello for ongoing and formative conversations; to Stefan Helmreich for a generous and careful read; and to Andrew Lakoff, Liz Roberts, and Diane Nelson for their insights on various issues addressed here.

## REFERENCES

Adler Lomnitz, Larissa and Cházaro, Laura (1999) Basic, Applied, and Technological Research: Computer Science and Applied Mathematics at the National Autonomous University of Mexico. *Social Studies of Science* 29(1):113–134.

Anderson, Warwick (2000) The Possession of Kuru: Medical Science and Biocolonial Exchange. *Comparative Studies in Society and History* 42(4):713–744.

Anderson, Warwick (2002) Introduction: Postcolonial Technoscience, *Social Studies of Science* 32(5–6):643–658.

Appelbaum, Nancy P., Macpherson, Anne S., and Rosemblatt, Karin Alejandra (eds) (2003) *Race and Nation in Modern Latin America*. Chapel Hill: University of North Carolina Press.

Arrellano Hernández, Antonio (2002) *La produccíon social de los objetos técnicos agrícolas. Antropología de la hibridación del maíz y de los agricultores de los valles altos de México*. Toluca, Mexico: UAEM.

Biehl, Joao (2004) The Activist State: Global Pharmaceuticals, AIDS, and Citizenship in Brazil. *Social Text* 22(3):105–132.

Briggs, Charles, with Montini-Briggs, Clara (2003) *Stories in the Time of Cholera: Racial Profiling during a Medical Nightmare*. Berkeley: University of California Press.

Briggs, Laura (2002) Reproducing Empire Race, Sex, Science, and US Imperialism in Puerto Rico. Berkeley: University of California Press.

Brown, Michael (2003) *Who Owns Native Culture?* Cambridge, MA: Harvard University Press.

Brush, Stephen B. (1999) Bioprospecting the Public Domain. *Cultural Anthropology* 14(4): 535–555.

Bueno, Carmen (2003) Relaciones de confianza en la cadena de abastecimiento de la industria automotriz. In Carmen Bueno and María Josefa Santos (eds), *Nuevas tecnologías y cultura* (pp. 117–148). Anthropos series. Mexico City: Universidad Iberoamericana.

Bueno, Carmen and Santos, María Josefa (eds) (2003) *Nuevas tecnologías y cultura*. Anthropos series. Mexico City: Universidad Iberoamericana.

Casas, Rosalba and Luna, Matilde (eds) (1999) *Gobierno, academia y empresas en México. Hacia una nueva configuración de relaciones*. Mexico City: Playa y Valdés and Instituto de Investigaciones Sociales, Universidad Autónoma de México.

Cházaro, Laura (2001–2002) La fisioantropometría de la respiración en las alturas, un debate por la patria. *Ciencias* (UNAM, Mexico City) 60–61:37–56. Special issue: *La Imagen de los Indigenas en la Ciencia*.

Coombe, Rosemary (2001) The Recognition of Indigenous Peoples' and Community Knowledge in International Law. *St Thomas Law Review* 14(2):275–285.

Coombe, Rosemary (2003) Fear, Hope, and Longing for the Future of Authorship and a Revitalized Public Domain in Global Regimes of Intellectual Property. *DePaul Law Review* 52(4):1171–1192.

Cueto, Marcos (1997) Science under Adversity: Latin American Medical Research and American Private Philanthropy, 1920–1960. *Minerva* 35:228–246.

Cueto, Marcos (1989) *Excelencia científica en la periferia. Actividades científicas e investigación biomédica en el Perú 1890–1950.* Lima: Tarea.

da Costa Marques, Ivan (2004) Reverse Engineering and Other Respectful Enough Accounts: Creating New Spaces of Possibility for Technological Innovation under Conditions of Global Inequality. MS, Universidade Federal do Rio de Janeiro.

Dávila Aranda, Patricia D. and Germán Ramírez, Maria Teresa (1991) *Herbario Nacional de México.* México, DF: UNAM (Institute of Biology, National Autonomous University of Mexico).

de Gortari, Rebeca (2003) La vinculación academia-empresa desde una perspectiva cultural. In Carmen Bueno and María Josefa Santos (eds), *Nuevas tecnologías y cultura* (pp. 101–117). Anthropos series. Mexico City: Universidad Iberoamericana.

de la Cadena, Marisol (2000) *Indigenous Mestizos: The Politics of Race and Culture in Cuzco, Peru 1919–1991.* Durham, NC: Duke University Press.

Escobar, Arturo (1997) Cultural Politics and Biological Diversity: State, Capital and Social Movements in the Pacific Coast of Colombia. In Orin Starn and Richard Fox (eds), *Culture and Social Protest: Between Resistance and Revolution* (pp. 40–64). New Brunswick: Rutgers University Press. Reprinted in David Lloyd and Lisa Lowe (eds), *The Politics of Culture in the Shadow of Capital* (pp. 201–226). New York: Routledge, 1997.

Estrada Lugo, Erick (ed.) (1996) *Plantas Medicinales de México. Introducción a su estudio.* Chapingo, Mexico: Universidad Autonoma de Chapingo.

Etzkowitz, Henry, and Leydesdorff, Loet (eds) (1997) *Universities and the Global Knowledge Economy: A Triple Helix of University–Industry–Government Relations.* London: Cassell.

Fortes, Jacqueline and Adler Lomnitz, Larissa (1994) *Becoming a Scientist in Mexico: The Challenge of Creating a Scientific Community in an Underdeveloped Country,* trans. Alan P. Hynds. University Park: University of Pennsylvania Press.

González, Roberto (2001) *Zapotec Science: Farming and Food in the Northern Sierra of Oaxaca.* Austin: University of Texas Press.

Graham, Richard (ed.) (1990) *The Idea of Race in Latin America, 1870–1940.* Austin: University of Texas Press.

Greene, Shane (2002) Intellectual Property, Resources or Territory? Reframing the Debate over Indigenous Rights, Traditional Knowledge, and Pharmaceutical Bioprospecting. In Mark Bradley and Patrice Petro (eds), *Truth Claims: Representation and Human Rights* (pp. 229–249). New Brunswick: Rutgers University Press.

Greene, Shane (2004) Indigenous People Incorporated? Culture as Politics, Culture as Property in Pharmaceutical Prospecting. *Current Anthropology* 45 (2):211–237.

Haraway, Donna (1997) *Modest_Witness@Second_Millenium. FemaleMan©_Meets_OncoMouse™: Feminism and Technoscience.* New York and London, Routledge.

Harding, Sandra (1998) *Is Science Multicultural? Postcolonialisms, Feminisms, and Epistemologies.* Indianapolis: Indiana University Press.

Hayden, Cori (2003a) From Market to Market: Bioprospecting's Idioms of Inclusion. *American Ethnologist* 31(3):359–371.

Hayden, Cori (2003b) *When Nature Goes Public: The Making and Unmaking of Bioprospecting in Mexico.* Princeton: Princeton University Press.

Hayden, Cori (2007) A Generic Solution? Pharmaceuticals and the Politics of the Generic in Mexico. *Current Anthropology* 48(4):475–495.

Hess, David (1991) *Spirits and Scientists: Ideology, Spiritism, and Brazilian Culture.* University Park: University of Pennsylvania Press.

Hess, David (1995) *Science and Technology in a Multicultural World: The Cultural Politics of Facts and Artifacts.* New York: Columbia University Press.

Knight, Alan (1990) Racism, Revolution, and Indigenismo: Mexico, 1910–1940. In Richard Graham (ed.), *The Idea of Race in Latin America, 1870–1940* (pp. 71–113). Austin: University of Texas Press.

Lakoff, Andrew (2003) The Lacan Ward: Pharmacology and Subjectivity in Buenos Aires. *Social Analysis* 47:2.

Lakoff, Andrew (2004) The Anxieties of Globalization: Antidepressant Sales and Economic Crisis in Argentina. *Social Studies of Science* 34.

Lakoff, Andrew (2005) The Private Life of Numbers: Audit Firms and the Government of Expertise in Post-Welfare Argentina. In Aihwa Ong and Stephen J. Collier (eds), *Global Assemblages: Technology, Politics and Ethics as Anthropological Problems* (pp. 194–213). Oxford: Blackwell.

Latour, Bruno (1998) From the World of Science to the World of Research? *Science* 280 (Apr. 10):208–209.

Lomnitz, Claudio (2001) *Deep Mexico, Silent Mexico: An Anthropology of Nationalism*. Minneapolis: University of Minnesota Press.

Lozoya, Xavier (1976) El Instituto Mexicano para el Estudio de las Plantas Medicinales, A. C. (Imeplam). In Xavier Lozoya and Carlos Zolla (eds), *Estado actual del conocimiento en plantas medicinales de México* (pp. 243–255). Mexico City: Folios.

Lozoya, Xavier (1983) La herbolaria medicina de México. In Xavier Lozoya and Carlos Zolla (eds), *La medicina invisible. Introducción al estudio de la medicina tradicional de México* (pp. 257–278). Mexico City: Folios.

Lozoya, Xavier (2001–2002) El ojo y la mentira del tiempo. Narraciones de cinco siglos. *Ciencias* (UNAM, Mexico City) 60–61:20–43. Special issue: *La Imagen de los Indigenas en la Ciencia*.

Lozoya, Xavier (2003) *La docta ignorancia. Reflexiones sobre el futuro de la cultura médica de los Mexicanos*. Mexico City: Grupo Editorial Lumen.

Lozoya, Xavier and Zolla, Carlos (eds) (1983) *La medicina invisible. Introducción al estudio de la medicina tradicional de México*. Mexico City: Folios.

McNeil, Maureen (ed.) (2005) *Postcolonial Science and Technology Studies*. Special issue of *Science as Culture* (Summer).

Mignolo, Walter (2000) *Local Histories/Global Designs: Coloniality, Subaltern Knowledges, and Border Thinking*. Princeton: Princeton University Press.

Nowotny, Helga, Scott, Peter, and Gibbons, Michael (2001) *Re-Thinking Science: Knowledge and the Public in an Age of Uncertainty*. Cambridge: Polity.

Palmié, Stephan (2002) *Wizards and Scientists: Explorations in Afro-Cuban Modernity and Tradition*. Durham, NC: Duke University Press.

Poole, Deborah (1997) *Vision, Race, and Modernity: A Visual Economy of the Andean Image World*. Princeton: Princeton University Press.

Posey, Darrell Addison (1985) Indigenous Management of Tropical Forest Ecosystems: The Case of the Kayapó Indians of the Brazilian Amazon. *Agroforestry Systems* 3:139–158.

Posey, Darrell Addison (1996) *Traditional Resource Rights: International Instruments for Protection and Compensation for Indigenous Peoples and Local Communities*. Gland, Switzerland: IUCN, and the World Conservation Union.

Pratt, Mary Louise (1992) *Imperial Eyes: Travel Writing and Transculturation*. London: Routledge.

Rabinow, Paul (1996) *Making PCR: A Story of Biotechnology*. Chicago: University of Chicago Press.

Raffles, Hugh (2002) *In Amazonia: A Natural History*. Princeton: Princeton University Press.

Reid-Henry, Simon M. (2005) The Contested Spaces of Cuban Development: Postsocialism, Postcolonialism and Development. *Geoforum*. Special issue: *The End of Socialism?... Ten Years On*, ed. T. Herschel.

Rodríguez, Ileana (ed.) (2001) *The Latin American Subaltern Studies Reader*. Durham, NC: Duke University Press

Rojas Rabiela, Teresa (1994) Antropología y etnobotánica. In *Symposium Internacional sobre Etnobotánica en Mesoamérica* (pp. 87–97). Chapingo, Mexico: Universidad Autonoma de Chapingo.

Schoijet, Mauricio and Worthington, Richard (1993) Globalization of Science and Repression of Scientists in Mexico. *Science, Technology, and Human Values* 18(2):209–230.

Sherwood, Robert (1991) Pharmaceuticals: US Perspective. In Sidney Weintraub, with Luis Rubio F. and Alan D. Jones (eds), *US–Mexican Industrial Integration: The Road to Free Trade* (pp. 161–179). Boulder: Westview.

Soto Laveaga, Gabriela (2003) Steroid Hormones and Social Relations in Oaxaca. In Casey Walsh, Elizabeth Emma Ferry, Gabriela Soto Laveaga, Paola Sesia, and Sarah Hill, *The Social Relations of Mexican Commodities: Power, Production, and Place* (pp. 81–126). US–Mexico Contemporary Perspectives series, 21. La Jolla: Center for US–Mexican Studies, University of California at San Diego.

Stepan, Nancy Leys (1991) *"The Hour of Eugenics": Race, Gender, and Nation in Latin America.* Ithaca: Cornell University Press.

Stern, Alexandra Minna (2003) From Mestizophilia to Biotypology: Racialization and Science in Mexicio, 1920–1960. In Nancy P. Applebaum, Anne S, Macpherson, and Karin Alejandra Rosemblatt (eds), *Race and Nation in Latin America* (pp. 187–210). Chapel Hill: University of North Carolina Press.

Toledo, Victor M. (1995) New Paradigms for a New Ethnobotany: Reflections on the Case of Mexico. In Richard Evans Schultes and Siri von Reis (eds), *Ethnobotany: Evolution of a Discipline* (pp. 75–92). Portland: Dioscorides Press.

Vasconcelos, José (1966) *La raza cósmica. Misión de la raza iberoamericana.* Madrid: Aguilar.

Vessuri, Hebe M. C. (1987) The Social Study of Science in Latin America. *Social Studies of Science* 17 (3):519–554.

Wade, Peter (1995[1993]) *Blackness and Race Mixture in Colombia.* Baltimore: Johns Hopkins University Press.

Zolla, Carlos (1983) La medicina tradicional mexicana y la noción del recurso para la salud. In Xavier Lozoya and Carlos Zolla (eds), *La medicina invisible. Introducción al estudio de la medicina tradicional de México* (pp. 14–37). Mexico City: Folios.

# 16 Agrarian Reform and Peasant Studies: The Peruvian Case

*Linda J. Seligmann*

Peasant studies and the very category of peasants have diminished dramatically in importance in the discourse of policy-makers and scholars of Latin America alike in the last decade of the 20th, and the early 21st century. The attention to "peasants" corresponded to a particular moment in history. The research and scholarship that grew out of the recognition and debates surrounding the subject of peasants was rich and varied, and challenged existing notions of economic and political systems and how they worked. On the other hand, the concept of peasants was invoked as a political instrument. Its reification and transformation, sometimes into a utopian ideal, blinded many scholars to significant transformations in the ways that rural inhabitants in general were making a living, constructing their identities, and drawing on a wide range of political resources in the process. They were also shifting from one geographic locus to another, across national boundaries and sometimes for long periods of time.

The turn away from peasant studies also occurred in the context of deep violence – political and economic – in Latin America. Profound social upheaval and political violence defined Peru's civil war between the Shining Path guerrilla movement and military and paramilitary forces in the 1980s. It also was the context for the emergence of the Zapatistas in Mexico, the battles of coca growers in Bolivia, the long enduring complex struggles of the FARC and ELN guerrilla movements pitted against drug traffickers and paramilitary wings in Colombia, and of landless workers in Brazil. It is worth noting that a key contributor to the violence associated with these movements, whatever the demands of the various participants, was the state. The second form of violence was an equally brutal but more hidden and insidious economic war, as neoliberal economic policies and commitments to restructuring took hold throughout the continent.

In this chapter, I first address the concept of peasants, what it refers to, and how and when it has been used by anthropologists and policy-makers in Latin America. I discuss salient ideological debates and political platforms that gave rise to the use of the category of "peasants," both as a historical subject and as a political instrument, recognizing that the two are sometimes conflated. I then concentrate on demonstrating how Latin American anthropology, in general, and Peruvian anthropology in particular, have been shaped by debates that have emerged from studies of peasants. Obviously, Peru does not stand in for Latin America and peasant studies have been deeply influenced by events and scholarship in other parts of Latin America, especially Mexico and Cuba. At the same time, there are a number of similarities between the Peruvian case and those in other parts of Latin America, especially in the Andean region. As I develop the themes of this chapter, I discuss the mutual influence between scholarly research and institution-building relevant to these debates in the US and Peru, and the sociocultural and political realities in these respective geographic locations. I argue that a combination of factors, including the peculiar construct of the category "peasant," the failure of both reform and revolution, and the conditions of violence that made field research difficult and made many so-called peasants sometimes wish to seek invisibility, contributed to the demise of peasant studies precisely when the livelihoods of rural and urban dwellers alike were becoming both ever more precarious and indissolubly linked. Many years after the boom in peasant studies, the category itself was subjected to rigorous reappraisal (Kearney 1996), a subject to which we will return at the end of this chapter.

## INDIGENISMO

One major debate that serves as the backdrop for understanding a turn to the creation of the concept of "peasants" as political and economic reality and as an object of anthropological study is the tension that emerged historically between the predominant sentiment in Latin America prior to the Mexican Revolution of 1910 that mestizaje or the mixing of races was essential to the well-being of the nation, on the one hand, and the numerous projects of indigenismo, on the other hand, that emerged in the 1920s and 1930s. Proponents of mestizaje viewed race as a biological phenomenon. Mixing would eventually lead to whitening, underscoring the assumption that non-indigenous blood was fundamentally superior (see Wade, this volume). Indigenistas, inspired by the Mexican Revolution of 1910, thought that race was a social construct born of colonialism and paternalism. They believed that the celebration of Indian culture was integral to the building of a strong and proud nation (see Varese, Delgado and Meyer, this volume). One of the most powerful currents of indigenismo was exemplified by José Vasconcelos's (1997) view that indigenous peoples and their customs, far from being deleterious to the future of nationhood, would instead contribute to a mixed "cosmic race" that would bring together the best of Hispanic and indigenous cultural characteristics. These philosophical currents were not contained within universities. They spilled over into government institutions, such as the Instituto Indigenista Interamericano in Mexico, and into political party platforms.

Influenced by both European socialism and the more idiosyncratic philosophy of José Carlos Mariátegui (1968), the founder of the Peruvian Socialist Party, labor movements in the Andes began to grow, together with a renewed and more positive interest in their own indigenous groups on the part of intellectuals (see Varese, Delgado and Meyer, this volume). As an ideology that drew attention to Andean cultural practices and political economy, indigenismo constituted a radical departure from the usual views that the bourgeoisie held of indigenous peoples. Nevertheless, it is also true that proponents of indigenismo idealized, generalized and further marginalized the Indian population by speaking *for* them. Forms of Andean social organization, like the ayllu, were depicted as utopian socialist units, and native cultural traditions were celebrated as folkloric renditions. The Quechua language was elevated in standing, but any diversion from classical Quechua was considered a loss and a vulgarity, a view that persists among some intellectuals (see Harvey, this volume). A handful of scholars took exception to this romanticized vision of indigenous cultures and more systematically explored and documented them in the context of historical processes.

Indigenismo fostered the optimistic sentiment that the distinctive identities, economic practices and sociopolitical organization of native inhabitants, together with aspirations for nation-building and development, would result in a unique and strong people. At the same time, the assumption, especially among intellectuals and politicians, that while indigenous culture was something to be proud of, it could nevertheless be improved led to efforts to incorporate indigenous peoples into class politics and to integrate them into the Western construct of the nation.

## Cultural Ecology, Community Studies, and Modernization

The Second World War represented a significant philosophical and pragmatic shift (but not without some continuities) from indigenismo, especially among Latin Americanists and policy-makers in the United States. A growing interest in cultural ecology and how environmental conditions interacted with human societies had an impact on the kinds of anthropological studies undertaken during this period. In the late 1940s and 1950s, the *Handbook of South American Indians* was published by the Smithsonian Institution and the Bureau of American Ethnology. It was edited by Julian Steward (1946–59), who had coined the term "cultural ecology." Steward was the primary proponent of defining culture areas as particular forms of social organization that had emerged in dynamic and systemic interaction with the physical environment. He pursued extensive and comparative team research in different world regions in order to argue for environmentally shaped multilinear evolution rather than the progressive, unilinear evolutionary models that had prevailed until then. The *Handbook* was exceptional in its systematic attention to geographic, ethnographic and ethnohistorical data. North American contributors to the *Handbook* began to question the effects of colonialism among indigenous peoples of the Andes, partly in response to the efforts of peoples worldwide to gain independence from colonial powers.

Julian Steward's interest in case studies led to work by his students, among them Bernard Mishkin, George Kubler, and Harry Tschopik, who published detailed case studies of Andean and Mexican peasant communities. They were among the first to begin to inquire into the existence of peasants – as opposed to Indians – and to raise questions about the relationship between cultural traits and class relations within Peru. Kubler also did comparative work, using archival documents to examine racial categories during the colonial period in Mexico.

The end of the Second World War and the beginning of the cold war shifted attention away from the theoretical underpinnings of multilinear cultural evolution, as sketched out by Steward and some of the *Handbook* contributors, toward moderniza-tion theory. In Steward's model, what counted was the "fit" between a society and its environment and how to explain the fit, not whether or not it was at the apex or base of an ideal and progressive model of evolution. In fact, Steward stressed that societies were hardly static, and either environmental conditions or changes in social organiza-tion and technology could lead to a different constellation of subsistence strategies.

In contrast, the assumptions of modernization theory, mixed with strains of indi-genismo, were embedded in the activities of the United States Alliance for Progress and Peace Corps. Many anthropologists working in Latin America in the 1950s and early 1960s got their start in these organizations. They began to display an interest in modernization programs and the "development" of Latin America (see Escobar 1995 on the history of modernization in Latin America and a critique of development theo-ries). The tenets of modernization theory mirror much of early evolutionary theory that assumed progressive stages of economic growth and therefore of social develop-ment (Rostow 1953). While "Western" society – European and North American – remained the ideal that all societies should strive to emulate, many scholars and policy-makers supposed that with proper environmental conditions, societies might acquire the tools to rise in civilized standing and become integrated with the rest of the "developed" world. Undergirded by a model, one that was less Darwinian than Lamarckian, as Nancy Stepan (1991) points out, the stages that societies would pass through were linked to education and technology, and although it was not frequently stated explicitly, race and gender influenced the ease with which societies could be transformed. Indigenous culture was evaluated in these terms and improved educa-tion, hygiene, and infrastructure, in general, were the focus of considerable applied anthropological undertakings in indigenous communities. The view that develop-ment could be engineered successfully was widely embraced, even though the natural resources of Latin America were being funneled to more developed regions of the world. In addition, the terms of trade between Latin America and the United States remained woefully imbalanced, and foreign companies owned or managed many of Latin America's industries. Modernization theorists were convinced that by following the proper recipe for development, assimilation and integration would take the place of discrimination against indigenous populations.

The assumptions of modernization theory were closely linked to the growing eco-nomic power of the United States and anticommunist sentiments. Anthropologists who agreed with the assumptions of modernization theory did their best to describe the living conditions of rural communities in the Andes in great detail, specifying the geography where communities were located, the economic activities of rural inhabit-ants, their social and racial composition and stratification, the political organization of communities, and their cultural and religious beliefs and practices. Their research resulted in a fluorescence of community studies, especially in Mexico and in the Andean region. Among the classical community studies in Peru and Bolivia were those of Richard Adams (1959), Henry Dobyns (1964), Paul Doughty (1968), Allan Holmberg (1966) and William Stein (1961).

In the late 1950s and early 1960s, the first joint projects between Peruvian and North American anthropologists materialized. In the joint Peruvian–US interdiscipli-nary projects, anthropologists tried to combine archaeology with ethnography (the Virú Valley Project), and to experiment with cooperatives and modernization programs. The most notable of these projects was the Vicos Project, sponsored by Peruvians and students of John Murra from Cornell University, which lasted from 1952 to 1963 (Holmberg 1966). One project that did not directly involve North Americans took place in the central Andean highlands, in Huarochirí, in which a team comprised of Peruvians José Matos Mar, Teresa Guillén, Julio Cotler (trained in England), Eduardo Soler, and Francisco Boluarte participated (Matos Mar et al. 1959). If anything, with the exception of the Virú Valley project, these joint undertakings stimulated a serious questioning of the role of North Americans in Peruvian anthropology and many of the assumptions of development and modernization theory at the time. The projects eventually failed in their altruistic efforts to assist "Indians" in throwing off the yoke of exploitation by setting up self-government and cooperatives.

Stein (1961) first wrote about the Vicos Project in a positive light, but then reevaluated it many years later in a far more reflective manner, offering a trenchant critique of it (2003:1–50). Stein noted that the Peru-Cornell team which directed the Vicos project failed to take account of the history in which the Vicosinos were embedded. The Vicosinos, Stein showed, were active agents who had participated in resistance movements, shaping the direction of their own future. Nevertheless, at that time, anthropologists involved in the project viewed Vicos as an entity sealed off from the rest of the world temporally and spatially; and they had great difficulty viewing the Vicosinos as subjects, rather than objects, a perception shared by the very hacendados whose power they wanted to curb. The Vicos Project, with its naive desire to liberate indigenous inhabitants from the control of landed estate owners by substituting Western-style infrastructure and social organization, in particular, inspired many anthropologists to embark on studies of peasants. Interestingly, a number of Peruvians and North Americans who were involved in the Vicos Project joined in designing and implementing the agrarian reform launched by General Juan Velasco Alvarado in 1969. Although the reform was based more on an eastern rather a western European model, it nevertheless incorporated liberal assumptions of peasants as victims without history or a distinctive culture.

Over the years, Latin Americans themselves have continued to struggle with variant images of modernization in the light of nationalist passions, their experience of the geopolitics of dependency, conflicts over the control of resources among national elites, labor, and indigenous populations, and, most recently, the transnational flows of information, aesthetics, technology, and commodities. Anthropologists in the 1950s and early 1960s initially endorsed many of the assumptions of modernization but eventually came to challenge notions of progressive and inevitable stages of development, contributing to a new area of research centered on peasants. Their empirical research and theoretical models led to debates about whether or not peasants existed, and if they did, exactly who they were and the degree of relative autonomy they maintained from both a capitalist economic system and the reach of the state.

Many of the examples discussed in these debates were based on field research in Latin America. The arguments and questions raised had already emerged in a general fashion in the works of Marx, Lenin, Aleksandr Chayanov, Karl Kautsky, Witold Kula, Theodor Shanin, Rosa Luxemburg, and Nikolai Bukharin, among others, but had not been systematically considered in the context of the cultural, economic and political realities of non-European indigenous societies. The concept and reality of peasants became a significant way to explain why theories of modernization were not only inappropriate to the Latin American case but also basically flawed. The position and behavior of so-called peasants led to debates about whether or not the working class, intellectuals, or indigenous peasants would constitute the vanguard of resistance and the bulwark of successful revolutionary movements in Latin America. These differing stances and ideologies would eventually be tested in practice, with sometimes deadly and irreversible consequences for the structure and organization of future resistance movements.

## THE EMERGENCE OF PEASANT STUDIES

The anthropology of what came to be known as "peasant studies" was born in the 1960s. It bloomed in the seventies, and reached its peak of maturity in the late seventies and early eighties, in the context of making sense of land tenure and labor issues, as well as of indigenous practices. By the mid-1960s, peasant and labor movements began to percolate throughout Peru and other parts of Latin America. Policy-makers and national elites sought to squelch the unrest while simultaneously achieving modernization. Anthropologists paid attention to how these movements were structured, their goals and motivations, and to the social organization of peasants, in general. When the anthropology of peasant studies boomed, few questioned exactly *who* peasants were and whether or not they constituted a legitimate historical subject. US anthropologist Eric Wolf's (1966) influential definition of peasants, influenced greatly by his work in Mexico and Peru, was primarily shaped by economic and political criteria. Peasants were anchored to the land, not wholly autonomous from the state and market forces, and relied upon agriculture for subsistence. If they produced a surplus, they might sell it on the market or trade it. Wolf's definition of peasants was undergirded by their position in a class structure and the consequences of that standing on their ability to make political demands on the state, on landed estate owners, and, in general, on incursions on their means of production – land and labor. Consequently, he focused on the economic and political position and plight of peasants. Likewise, English Marxist historian Eric Hobsbawm, who did research in Peru, was among the first to argue that peasants had a political consciousness and that they organized strategically to resist encroachments on their land and exploitation of their labor through banditry and "primitive" rebellion (1959, 1981). He also cautioned that peasant rebellions could not be dissociated from the wider urban social context in which they unfolded (1973).

At the same time that Wolf and Hobsbawm's understandings of peasants had considerable explanatory power, the concept of peasants was also strategically deployed as a political device. Foreign governments, especially the United States, Latin American governments, political parties, those who were called or sometimes called themselves "peasants," and anthropologists themselves invoked the position, needs, and threat posed by peasants as a rationale for implementing particular policies. It thus became difficult to distinguish between the specificity of Wolf's definition in the light of particular economic and political conditions and the instrumentality with which the category of peasants was used and applied to particular populations.

There were more subtle yet significant ways in which "peasant" became a distorted catch-all category. It tended to be associated with indigenous populations who engaged in agriculture. Yet not all peasants were Indians. Far from it. For example, along the Peruvian coast, Chinese Americans and African Americans constituted the primary "peasant" population, working on plantations and sometimes retaining small-holder rights over their own fields (Peloso 1999). Similarly, in Brazil, one of the most powerful "peasant" movements in history (see below) is comprised of poor and non-Indian laborers who have no land at all and often have no experience of ever working as agriculturalists.

A second way in which peasants became identified as a valid albeit somewhat reified intellectual category and historical subject was through the comparisons and generalizations that scholars made between the social and economic organization of lowland and highland societies of the Andes. They argued that lowland dwellers, as "Indians," practiced swidden – extensive, slash and burn – agriculture combined with fishing, and hunting and foraging, and that their kinship structures and socio-political organization contrasted quite sharply with those of peasant highlanders. The latter tended to be more permanently tied to agricultural land, engaged in the market more directly, and practiced bilateral rather than patri- or matrilineal kinship (see, for example, Lyon 1974).

In the course of these debates, as well as organizing peasants and movements on the ground, policy-makers and scholars, many of whom had their start working in the Peace Corps or the Vicos Project, began to consider that agrarian reform might constitute one appropriate model of development in regions where land tenure was inequitable, industrialization weak, and labor relations exploitative. These three prongs – peasants, resistance movements, and experiments with agrarian reform – became building blocks for a major field within anthropology and Latin American studies, broadly constituting peasant studies.

Organizations and institutions sprang up in Latin America that had a direct impact on encouraging studies of peasants. In Peru, for example, more Peruvian universities began offering formal anthropology programs. The International Potato Center was established in 1967; Catholic groups such as the Dominican-based Centro Bartolomé de Las Casas (est. 1974), and the Instituto de Pastoral Andina (est. 1968), and the controversial Summer Institute of Linguistics (SIL), run by Protestant missionaries (est. 1934), became concerned specifically with the survival and place of indigenous groups. (SIL would argue that survival was equivalent to assimilation, the only reasonable option for indigenous populations.) The Peruvian nongovernmental organization DESCO, the Center for Studies and the Promotion of Development (est. 1966), was staffed by technocrats and lawyers who viewed development in the light of whether or not indigenous governance infrastructures could be established and indigenous leaders trained so that they could be adequately represented in a national context. IWGIA, the International Working Group on Indigenous Affairs, based in Copenhagen (est. 1968), and the Mexico-based Instituto Indigenista Interamericano (est. 1940) worked throughout Latin America.

Indigenous groups within Latin America began to question and combat dominant ideologies, and address problems of more immediate pragmatic concern. Syndicates and confederations of indigenous groups, miners, and peasants formed. Publishing houses proved to be perhaps a crucial step toward fostering a native anthropology. In Peru, these presses included the Instituto de Estudios Peruanos and Mosca Azul (est. 1964 and 1972, respectively), and historian Pablo Macera's publication of regional archival documents on haciendas, as well as a number of other historical documents. Mexico had a dramatic effect upon the theoretical approaches of Latin American anthropologists in general. Not only were many Latin Americans trained in Mexico, but Mexican publishing houses, such as Siglo Veintiuno (est. 1966), contributed to the growth of a national anthropology.

From the 1960s to the 1970s, despite the lack of a Peruvian school of anthropology, questions of greater concern to Peruvians began to take center stage. They began to focus more on the effects of internal and external domination, which took the form of dependency theory, and they expressed a simultaneous resurgence of curiosity about the nature of Andean institutions. It was also at this time that the Catholic Church began experimenting with the theology of liberation and sought to analyze what exactly it meant to commit to a preferential option for the poor. Within the United States, as a consequence of the civil rights movement, Vietnam war, and the women's liberation movement, more attention began to be directed to peasant studies, peasant movements, ethnicity, and, at a somewhat later date, women's roles in peasant communities (Harris 1978; Bourque and Warren 1981).

One pioneering and influential work of this time was Eric Wolf's 1969 *Peasant Wars of the Twentieth Century*, which examined peasant resistance movements cross-culturally and demonstrated the capacity of peasants to organize substantial uprisings that challenged national states. As well as writing about indigenous peoples as peasants and their living conditions, anthropologists, some of whom had worked on the Vicos project, such as Richard Patch (1964) in Paramonga, began to examine critically the relationship between landed estate owners (hacendados) and peasants. Simultaneously, US policy-makers became increasingly cognizant of growing unrest among peasants and workers in Latin America in the context of the cold war; and national governments within Latin America sought to control their own resources and economic destiny.

It is fascinating in retrospect that agrarian reform as a novel policy could satisfy such different interests. It appeared, in the abstract, to be a reasonable way to transform the status-conscious hacienda system into more productive agrarian enterprises, satisfy peasant demands for control over their land, and release peasants from exploitative labor relations. Governments, eager to control their own economies and resources, believed that if agrarian reform was successfully implemented, it would result in cheaper foodstuffs for workers in urban areas. Furthermore, encouraged by US Agency for International Development (AID) funds and research undertaken by scholars connected to the Land Tenure Center at the University of Wisconsin-Madison, Latin American governments became convinced that hacendados would transition into entrepreneurial industrialists, encouraging national modernization and thereby avoiding a turn to revolution and communism.

## AGRARIAN REFORM

While debate persisted as to whether or not they constituted a social category or a heuristic construct, so-called "peasants" found themselves very much in the midst of cataclysmic and dramatic transformations of their reality in Peru and elsewhere in Latin America. Their participation in movements demanding rights to their own labor and land, as well as national cries for recuperation of patrimonial resources and a desire to implement alternative models of development, led to a number of experiments with agrarian reform. The experiments were motivated by efforts to assert control over the countryside, restore national order, and gain access to industries and resources that were almost entirely owned by foreign companies.

Throughout Latin America, these experiments with agrarian reform took on different forms and had somewhat different objectives. Bolivia's agrarian reform, closely connected to its labor movement, began as early as 1952. Ecuador's principal agrarian reform took place in 1964, while Peru's most dramatic reform began in 1969. Mexico's most significant agrarian reform took place during the postrevolutionary government of President Lázaro Cárdenas (1934 to 1940). Each of these moments was driven by complex, interacting events and conditions. Agrarian reform projects and the research about them constituted a process more than an event. In different countries, it was marked by particular regimes and a specific legal apparatus intended to lay out the process, but the process itself, as well as the larger context in which it unfolded, inevitably led to changes in the composition of the state and amendments to the legal apparatus. Furthermore, as will become apparent in discussing the future of studies of peasants and agrarian reform, one could argue that new impulses for agrarian reform, often not labeled as such by scholars, have taken place in the 1990s in Mexico (the EZLN, Zapatista National Liberation Army), Ecuador (CONAIE, Confederation of Indigenous Nationalities of Ecuador), Bolivia (the water, coca and natural oil wars), and Brazil (MST, Landless Rural Workers Movement).

In general, the scholars who wrote on agrarian reform either provided overviews and evaluations of agrarian reform on a scale writ large – what it consisted of, how the legal apparatus worked, and how successful it was – or offered case studies of the impact of agrarian reform on a particular region or community. Political scientists wrote some of the best known studies but they tended to emphasize the reform process on the coast rather than the highlands (Cleaves and Scurrah 1980; Lowenthal 1975; McClintock 1981; McClintock and Lowenthal 1983; Duncan, Rutledge and Harding 1977). The questions they asked tended to differ from those raised by anthropologists, such as: How has the composition of the state changed as a result of the reform? Has democracy increased and has the desire for democracy been greater before or after the reform? Is more or less land under the control of peasants after the reform? How has participation by peasants in the market changed since the reform? Did the economic benefits of reform outweigh the cost? Carmen Diana Deere (1985) was one of the few political scientists to address how agrarian reform had affected gender relations among rural women in Latin America.

The publications of anthropologists, in contrast to those of political scientists, provided important documentation comparing and contrasting land tenure and labor systems among Andean peasants, both in the highlands and on the coast, before and after the 1969 reform, thus taking account of and analyzing the historical context in which agrarian reform unfolded in heterogeneous social and environmental conditions (Caballero 1980, 1981; Matos Mar 1980; Matos Mar and Mejía 1980; Montoya 1980; Valderrama 1976). These studies, most of which were not written by North Americans, paid attention to the misfit between the model of reform that was being imposed and the actual organization and labor regimes of rural inhabitants; and the problems created by the tension between control over collective resources, such as irrigation systems, and the heterogeneity of land tenure systems where holdings might be private, held in usufruct, sharecropped, or rented. They also critiqued the role of the state, particularly the centralization of expropriation processes, and the unwillingness of reform officials and many scholars to be attentive to already existing organizations that represented peasants, such as peasant confederations and unions. However, the majority of anthropologists neglected the state as an object of anthropological inquiry and theory.

On a smaller scale, focusing more on the highlands than the coast and relying primarily on case studies, anthropologists looked at how the measures of the agrarian reform, including the introduction of collective cooperatives as the major mechanism of restructuring landholding and labor relations affected political organization, economic differentiation, and tenure systems on a case study basis (see especially Guillet 1979; Hopkins 1985; Seligmann 1995; Skar 1982; Smith 1989). One interesting observation about these studies is that anthropologists whose research concentrated on the coast, as well as political scientists, for the most part relied very little on field research. Furthermore, the documentation provided by the national and local bureaucracies that were in one way or another involved in the reform is not terribly reliable. On the other hand, the case studies, often based on impressive field research, give us an in-depth understanding of how reform was played out at the local level, but it is difficult to determine whether or not these conditions are generalizable.

In addition to the work of anthropologists, historians also embarked at a somewhat later date on eye-opening investigations of the history of land tenure, labor relations, peasant movements and political dynamics. They did research on specific cases, and sometimes wider regions, in which they analyzed local, regional, and national archival data and looked more closely at the composition, behavior and perceptions of state formations (see Burga and Flores-Galindo 1980; Mallon 1983; Nugent 1997; Stern 1987; Thurner 1997). The depth of these research projects breathed life into the sometimes dualistic and reified portrayals of ethnic and power relations in the countryside and made it apparent that inhabitants in countryside and city alike had organizations that represented them, vehicles through which they could communicate and build solidarity and rural–urban alliances, and cultural practices that were central to their identities.

Some of the very best work in the area of peasant studies developed in opposition to approaches that emphasized solely political and economic conditions in the countryside as a subset of universal class structures or, alternatively, that began with the assumption of the primacy and continuity of indigenous culture and structure over time. One significant trajectory focused on the "native structure" of peasant economies and the ways that peasants succeeded in maintaining economic self-sufficiency and autonomy. The earlier work of *Handbook* contributors on cultural ecology and geography helped to shape later work on the role of environmental knowledge, geographical conditions, ecological systems, and historical context in Latin America's peasant economies. The ongoing and failed projects of agrarian reform served as incentives for anthropologists to investigate in greater depth the actual workings of peasant economies. They examined how peasants controlled their resource base, drawing their data not only from contemporary agriculturalists, but also from archival sources and archaeological analyses.

John Murra (1975) coined the concept of verticality to define the unique adaptation of Andean peoples to their environment, arguing that it was the cornerstone of

Andean economic, political and social formations. Murra argued that Andean inhabitants took advantage of the ecological attributes of land according to altitude, which in turn ultimately determined the kinds of economies possible. Rather than needing centralized markets, communities sent members as temporary or permanent settlers to different ecological zones; and they traded products from different zones. On a smaller scale, rather than cultivating contiguous pieces of land, they cultivated multiple strips at different altitudinal locations. His work catalyzed numerous debates and research about variants of the verticality model, and the importance of markets, long distance trade, and reciprocal exchange to peasant economies. Emerging directly out of research on ecological adaptive models such as verticality was subsidiary research on irrigation systems, pastoralism, energy flow systems and ethnobotany, as well as their transformations in the context of colonial mercantile and capitalist economies.

Rather than focusing on environmental, economic and political organization of Andean inhabitants, a number of anthropologists oriented their studies toward discerning what constituted the core and kernel of Andean social organization. Lively debates involved how Andean kinship worked, and the nature of Andean community. As a whole, this research served as a challenge to existing models of agrarian reform being promoted by state officials and by scholars pursuing applied anthropology and development studies. It called attention to heterogeneous kinds of social organization among peasants that had been ignored by reform officials; it emphasized the elaboration of indigenous mechanisms that permitted the optimal use of agricultural land, water, and pasture, and made it clear how historical processes and their consequences had sometimes disrupted native economic and political systems that had worked well in the past, and exacerbated conflict among peasants in the same geographic region. The evidence for systems of production and exchange relying on tenure and labor regimes that diverged sharply from Western-style markets, private land ownership and supply and demand called into question the basic tenets of modernization theory, especially as they were incorporated into agrarian reform policies.

Attention to the specificity of Andean formations also yielded a second but very different approach taken by anthropologists who employed a Lévi-Straussian or structuralist approach (e.g. Zuidema 1964). They rejected the notion of peasants altogether and instead focused on Andean continuities and linguistic, religious, ritual, and kinship structures that could be discerned among native peoples in both the distant past and in contemporary Andean society, stressing the scaffolding of indigenous society rather than its content. Some of the traces of indigenismo can be seen in this approach, which was a very different kind of ethnohistory than the one John Murra had proposed. These structuralist studies contributed to the construction of a somewhat timeless or essentialist identity for Andean people. Indirectly, the studies may have fueled the position held by salvage anthropologists that preserving the past in the present was more important than contemporary struggles among indigenous people for economic and political rights. The dualism vaunted within structuralist analyses of Andean cosmology was itself mirrored in the dueling between a more materialist political economic interpretation and a more platonic, idealist interpretation of ethnohistorical and ethnographic data.

Other anthropologists made use of the category of peasants and the Marxist concept of mode of production to mediate structuralist and materialist approaches. Modes of production theorists began with Eric Wolf's assumption that distinctive material and political social formations could be specified in accordance with how the means of production were controlled. The resulting mode of production – kinship based, tributary, or capitalist – corresponded to distinctive ideologies or superstructures. French anthropologists Maurice Godelier, Claude Meillassoux, Pierre-Philippe Rey, and Emmanuel Terray, however, argued that there was a Western bias to this typology and that mental or cognitive structures were not superstructures but rather were integral to the reproduction of socioeconomic and political formations. They devoted considerable attention to how dimensions of indigenous society other than economic or political organization – religion or kinship, for example – might be the driving force of indigenous economies. In fact, Godelier based his research on modes of production on the Inka case. There were a number of formidable problems with modes of production theory, the most important of which was that different modes of production proliferated, since their articulation and respective "ideologies" varied in accordance with the particular society in question. Despite these shortcomings, an interesting body of work emerged that brought non-Western societies into the center from the margins of political economy.

David Lehmann's (1982) edited volume on ecology and exchange in the Andes brought together some of the most significant research in this area. Tristan Platt and Olivia Harris, although they hailed from the United Kingdom, were heavily influenced by a combination of modes of production theory and French structuralism, as was Jürgen Golte, trained in West Berlin. Golte (1980), for example, argued that Andean rationality depended on the manipulation of time, and that Andean communities were able to adjust wage labor to agricultural production cycles to optimize market conditions because both cycles were unified by the same structure of time. Although he did not consider himself a structuralist in the French tradition, his view that these adjustments were not conscious adjustments made by peasants fell into a kind of mentalist approach.

Gradually, scholars began to reconsider their narrow, community based view of Latin American peasants and broadened their inquiry into the place of Latin American peasants in the context of unequal exchange, world systems theory, the composition and role of the state, urban labor movements, and everyday modes of resistance. Eric Wolf, Eric Hobsbawm (1959), Rodolfo Stavenhagen (1970) and Eric P. Thompson (1963) might be considered the progenitors of these approaches. With the exception of Thompson, all of them did field research in Latin America and they fostered studies of peasant movements throughout Latin America.

In Peru, the military government's decision to implement a radical agrarian reform in 1969 was partly a consequence of the uprisings that had spread throughout the countryside. One of the most important series of uprisings had taken place in La Convención in the mid-1960s in Cuzco, Peru. Hugo Blanco, a native of the Peruvian countryside and peasant leader, had helped to lead the La Convención uprisings. He subsequently provided a blow-by-blow account and analysis of them (Blanco 1972). His work led to more research on peasant and worker uprisings in Peru itself and indicated the crucial importance of circuits of ideas and political, sociocultural and economic linkages that extended far beyond highland villages of the Andes to the jungles and capital cities, and to Europe. Not only did Blanco's account become the basis for additional research undertakings; it was also studied in order to determine strategies for future labor struggles.

The peasant uprisings in La Convención inspired many other land occupations once the reform was well underway. Blanco himself became an international spokesperson for the rights of workers and peasants. These uprisings were not so much about peons diminishing the power of landed estate owners, a phenomenon that had already occurred partly as a consequence of the penetration of capitalism and the growth of agro-industry. Rather, peasants were focused on recuperating the lands that they had lost over the centuries. They were intent on demanding that the reform be implemented broadly and deeply and that it take account of a greater number of different kinds of workers. Many peasants and their leaders had also rejected the government-sponsored reform cooperatives, and were attempting to organize themselves into more inclusive unions, parties and confederations. Some of the most notable of these uprisings in Peru took place in Piura (1972–73), Andahuaylas (1974), and Anta-Urubamba (1979). Some Peruvians saw the growing rural ferment as an opportunity to begin armed revolution in the countryside. The political mobilizations and uprisings nurtured greater political awareness and sophistication among rural inhabitants and workers alike. Diego García-Sayán (1982), one of the original founders of DESCO, wrote a well-documented analysis of the uprisings that took place during this period of ferment.

## The Anthropology of Peasants and Class Struggle

As scholars assessed the impact of agrarian reform and the sociopolitical behavior and worldviews of so-called "peasants," a minor chorus started to question the existence of peasants at all and the casual way in which anthropologists were using the term (Orlove 1977a; Leeds 1977). Were peasants a viable "entity" or were they an artificial construct, as was the peasant community, exemplified most dramatically perhaps by Eric Wolf's (1955) model of the closed corporate community? A cluster of anthropologists argued that class, on the one hand, and market dynamics, on the other, needed to be more systematically considered in revising the model. Anthropologists began to wonder whether internal stratification and dependency were so overwhelming that it was fruitless to consider that peasants could ever maintain a degree of self-sufficiency? Even more pointedly, Alain De Janvry (1981) and, somewhat later, Collins (1988) emphasized the *disarticulation of modes of production*, arguing that the scale of peasant agriculture was such that, even with agrarian reform, it could never constitute an adaptive and viable system but would simply come to subsidize the labor required of so-called peasants in the market economy. Many of the anthropologists pursuing this line of inquiry in the late 1970s and early 1980s were influenced by Marxism and the failure of agrarian reform.

As anthropologists, especially Peruvians, some of whom were trained in Europe, confronted the failure of agrarian reform and the recognition that it was mistaken to view peasants as a monolithic category, they became more persuaded that class analysis provided the key to comprehending the contemporary reality and future of Andean peasants. Their focus varied from narrowly describing specific labor movements and their history (Falcón 1980; Kapsoli 1980, 1987; Sulmont 1974), to more analytical probing of the determinants of peasant economic and political practices. The Cuzco-based journal *Allpanchis Phuturinqa* dedicated an entire special issue to peasant movements (1978), and Rodrigo Sánchez (1978), in a somewhat polemical tone, discounted the vertical ecological control model as an ideology in itself, emphasizing that more attention should be paid to class. Unlike most of the other scholars who were drawing heavily on abstract class analysis to explain the position and roles of Andean peasants, Sánchez (1981) based his work on a detailed case study in Andahuaylas. Rodrigo Montoya, a Peruvian who received his doctorate in Paris, represented perhaps the most interesting divergence of a native Peruvian anthropology from a Western-anchored one. His complex study of the importance of the control of irrigation systems in Puquio – a site where José María Arguedas (1964), one of Peru's earliest ethnographers, had also done significant ethnographic work – drew on ethno-history, ethnography, and Marxism (Montoya, Silveira and Lindoso 1979). Montoya analyzed archival materials to provide historical background on the control of irrigation systems. He narrated the kinds of struggles among and between haciendas and communities in Puquio over water, and then traced how a particular ideology had developed from the unequal control over water among community members that at once splintered the communities and allowed political domination by the hacendados over them.

Peruvian scholars trained in England such as Cotler (1978) and Anibal Quijano (1980) wrote on the consolidation (or not) of national political power and its effects in marginalizing peasants economically and politically. José Matos Mar and colleagues including Fernando Fuenzalida and Julio Cotler (Matos Mar et al. 1975; Matos Mar 1976), Anibal Quijano (1979), and Bourricaud (1970) were among the earliest scholars to begin to theorize about race and ethnicity, together with class and the lack of political power, in explaining the marginalization of peasants. Their work, as a whole, was influenced by the Manchester School. The Manchester School, developed by Max Gluckman in the late 1940s and early 1950s at the University of Manchester, challenged the existing structural-functionalist models of British anthropology by arguing that it was necessary to take account of conflict in society. In particular, they were intrigued by how a wide range of conflicts appeared to be resolved in the colonies and protectorates of the United Kingdom, especially in Africa, where many of them were employed by the British government, without the intervention of the state. They looked systematically and closely at the principles of customary law, their implementation, and their interaction with other legal systems from the West. Ultimately, members of the Manchester School came to view conflict within a functionalist model, describing how conflict itself, through economic, political, or even rhetorical or religious means, could restore a society to homeostatic equilibrium by acting as a kind of safety valve.

Peruvian anthropologists who were influenced by the Manchester School, while they did not necessarily agree with the functionalist view of conflict, looked at the ways that state formations and dominant social hierarchies interacted with local cultural and political practices and processes. The research on peasant and worker movements, and on racial and ethnic conflict, brought about a reevaluation of peasants and agrarian reform in the context of a far more nuanced historical and global context, and encouraged more comparative work on political movements. That politically concerned and activist native anthropologists were making their voices heard and writing passionately about conditions at home was what was most striking and unique about this scholarship.

Some of the "middle ground" excluded by studies of agrarian reform and peasant resistance movements was sketched in by three related areas of scholarship that began to develop in the late 1970s and 1980s. In reviewing this tumultuous and turbulent period of Peru's history, it is possible to see a glimmering of future anthropological research that falls under the rubric of human rights research, the anthropology of international law, and legal anthropology (see Rojas Pérez, this volume). A few studies of lawyers and law, and how the latter was understood as both process and instrument by different sectors of Peruvian society, were published, all by Peruvians. Some of the studies were viewed self-consciously as tools that could be useful to peasants who were seeking to defend their legal rights. Among the prominent contributors to a nascent, indigenous legal anthropology were Guillermo Figallo (1985), Diego García-Sayán (1982), Nerio González (1991), Florencio Díaz (see González and Díaz 1991), and Luís Pásara (1978), most of whom began their research in the context of evaluating the tenets of agrarian reform. This work considered the interaction and logic of customary law, national law, and international law, as well as more practical but crucial concerns, such as citizen access to legal institutions, and how legal personnel interpreted and implemented laws.

A second area of scholarship emerged as a consequence of the failures of agrarian reform and the simultaneous efforts of peasants to gain access to markets and to employment in urban areas. The latter was enhanced by the Velasco regime's explicit endorsement of the legitimacy of squatter settlements in Peru's metropolitan regions. These studies, which spanned urban and economic anthropology, paid attention to the causes and consequences of migration and demographic shifts (Matos Mar 1988), the emergence of new kinds of roles for Andean dwellers as entrepreneurs and brokers (Long and Roberts 1978, 1984), how involvement in commodity markets affected peasant calculations of the value of their labor and agricultural products, as well as their exchange practices (Aramburu 1983; Figueroa 1983; Gonzales de Olarte 1982; Mayer 2002; Orlove 1977b, 1986), and how gender and ethnicity were implicated in urban and rural labor segmentation. The work of Florence Babb (1989), Elsa Chaney and Mary Garcia Castro (1989), Carlos Iván Degregori, Cecilia Blondet and Nicolás Lynch (1986), Jürgen Golte and Norma Adams (1987), and Susan Lobo (1982) systematically began to explore the roles of women as household workers, market vendors, and leaders in urban land seizures. The assumptions underlying this research, deeply influenced by Robert Redfield, suggested that validity remained in conceptualizing the worlds in which peasants moved as "rural" and "urban," but the analyses took account of the unpredictable yet powerful impact of each domain upon the other, and recognized that so-called peasants could be found in city and countryside alike. It would be about a decade later, however, that the entire notion of rurally anchored peasants would be challenged and swept away within the discipline of anthropology. The contributors to the superb edited volume prepared by Brooke Larson and Olivia Harris, with Enrique Tandeter (Larson, Harris and Tandeter 1995) demonstrate well how analyses that took account of historical depth, culture, and political economy together offered a far more nuanced and illuminating view of life in the Andes than prior research that assumed migration occurred between clearly definable urban and rural poles and cultural worlds.

A final area of research, partly as a result of far greater fluidity of movement and interaction among so-called "peasants," began to focus on questions of identity: racial, ethnic, gender, class, and otherwise (see, for example, the work of Robert

Albro (1997), Marisol de la Cadena (2000), Rodrigo Montoya (1998), Ben Orlove (1998), Sarah Radcliffe (1997), Mark Rogers (1998), Mary Weismantel (2001), and Stephen Eisenman (Weismantel and Eisenman 1998)). In addition to notable social differentiation that became apparent during and following the agrarian reform, and the permeability of borders and boundaries, this area of research was greatly influenced, on the one hand, by the far-flung reach of goods and information over distance, and the movements of people, and ironically, on the other hand, by the greater difficulty of doing field research on the ground as many regions of the world where anthropologists worked became more violent and dangerous. Peru was no exception.

## THE DEMISE OF REFORM

Despite the modest success of Peru's 1969 agrarian reform, few anthropologists predicted the violent decades that would follow in its wake. As the Shining Path guerrilla movement made inroads among sympathizers and activists in rural and urban areas, in the highlands and Amazonian lowlands alike, and the Tupac Amaru movement captured the imagination primarily of young university intellectuals, the problems of agrarian productivity, water rights, ecological systems and sustainability, and even alternative modes of peasant organizing and resistance movements, other than civil defense patrols, were set to one side (Starn 1999). Instead, a whole slew of "senderologists" focused on the violence of Sendero, locating its causes in what they viewed as a Quechua mentalité born of racial discrimination, poverty, lack of infrastructure, and relative deprivation (Poole and Rénique 1991).

Only when the dust began to settle did a few scholars remind anthropologists and the general public of the existing political organizing that existed side by side or prior to Sendero among workers and peasants alike in Peru (Poole and Rénique 1992; Stern 1998). Orin Starn (1991) wrote a controversial critique of anthropologists who failed to predict Peru's civil war, claiming that they had not paid attention to the broader historical and sociocultural context in which peasant communities were situated. Unfortunately, the validity of his critique was offset by his own exclusion of the anthropologists and historians whose work did *not* focus on cultural continuities. Interestingly, those in the forefront of analyzing the demise of reform and the rise of violence had been following peasant and worker engagement in labor movements, politics, and education for many years (see, for example, Degregori et al. 1992; Degregori 1996; Manrique 1987, 1988; Poole 1994; Urbano 1991). Their critiques call attention, once again, to some of the ghosts of modernization theory and of indigenismo that tended to ignore structures of inequality, including those fomented by the state itself, as well as the long history of political struggles of rural and urban inhabitants who were not content to be excluded from representation within the nation.

Since the decline of Sendero, very few anthropologists have turned their attention to the countryside and rarely do studies of peasants appear. It is noteworthy that in Enrique Mayer's recent book (2002), a compilation of his own articles and chapters, the majority of which were originally published in Spanish, only a few pieces are based on recent research in the countryside. These pieces are indeed classics but they stand out in a sea of books and articles dedicated to hybridity, performativity, race, identity, transnational migration, neoliberalism, and globalization. Even as anthropologists turn their attention to these phenomena and the best ways to study and theorize about them, the idea of the peasant has transmogrified into the idea of "the Indian" once again. But this "Indian," unlike the Indian of the 1920s, 1930s, 1940s, or 1950s, incorporates what Xavier Albó (2002) calls "plurinationality," and, in addition to hailing from countryside and/or city, is increasingly concerned with political rights that involve the delineation and protection of indigenous and inalienable territory. In turn, the protection of territory is fused with defining indigenous identity. Territory is no longer a question of rural plots of ground for farming or the entity of community, though it may include those elements. Rather, it involves laws that are culturally shaped by and for indigenous peoples and in some instances, may take precedent over other national laws (Collier and Quaratiello 2005; and see Barragán, this volume).

Colombia, Ecuador and Bolivia have moved furthest in defining what is now known as "indigenous law" and, at another level, "international law" (see, for example, Starr and Goodale 2002; Rappaport 1996). Both of these intersect, and sometimes conflict, with national law. Land is involved in these questions but it is the assertion of indigenous rights rather than entitlement of land for subsistence and surplus that takes precedence. It is precisely in those regions where indigenous people have been less incorporated into national political institutions and party dynamics, and where valuable extractive resources of interest to national and international corporations or states are located, that indigenous law and indigenous movements have grown in strength. Peru, for example, where especially since the 1969 agrarian reform, Quechua highland peasants have been engaged in party politics, unions, and peasant confederations, has a weak indigenous movement that is most active in the Amazonian lowlands rather than the Andean highlands. A closely linked research interest for anthropologists has moved from peasants and peasant movements to the political organizing of Indians into confederations across local and national boundaries into other kinds of entities. While some of these entities may be political parties, few of them conform to traditional peasant confederations or union or labor movements. Marc Edelman (2003:10) observes that these "transnational forms" of peasant political organizations differ markedly from those of the past. He notes that many of these organizations "barely knew of one another's existence" a decade ago, but "now routinely exchange information and delegations and mount joint lobbying and protest actions. Their target is not only (though it may include) the state, but rather supranational entities, such as North American Free Trade Agreement (NAFTA), the World Trade Organization (WTO), or large multinational pharmaceutical or agro-industry firms. They have a variety of goals, but two of the most important ones, according to Edelman (2003:11), are to remove agriculture from the trading negotiations and policies of the WTO, and to recognize that food, rather than being a commodity, is a human right. The latter would mean a deep and broad commitment to agrarian reform in that access to food and protection of national agricultural resources would require farmers' access to adequate amounts of land and a commitment to local production of food. Edelman coins this "food sovereignty" (2003:12), in contrast to what the UN's Food and Agriculture Organization (FAO) calls "food security."

## WHY HAVE PEASANT STUDIES VANISHED?

The disappearance of peasant studies has coincided closely with more intense processes of globalization, a high degree of activism among indigenous populations struggling toward greater autonomy, sovereignty and unique constitutional rights, and the rapid decline in agricultural prices that has not ceased over a 20 year period (Edelman 2003). It is in this context that Michael Kearney wrote *Reconceptualizing the Peasantry: Anthropology in Global Perspective* (1996). Kearney argues that the category of peasant had been essentialized and reified for the purpose of distinguishing between laborers who relied heavily upon use value (land) and those who relied heavily upon exchange value (proletarians), both of whom were "lower class." Yet peasants had always been an ambiguous category because they combined use value and exchange value (purchase of tools, sale and purchase of products in the market, etc.) and, in fact, this was one of many reasons why agrarian reform projects were not very successful. They began with inappropriate units of analysis and implementation which derived from opposing peasant economies to Western economies. Kearney argues that these reifications instrumentally contained populations and also succeeded in containing and narrowing anthropological understanding of the populations with whom researchers worked. He also argues that value obtained through consumption (including commodities and ideas) and signification through the donning of evocative signs are highly significant as kinds of cultural capital that can then be transformed or converted and funneled into other kinds of value, as elaborated on by Pierre Bourdieu. Kearney points out that the emphasis on fixed criteria and categories has prevented anthropologists from recognizing that so-called "peasants" traverse the globe, work in cities, engage in artisanry for tourists, and hold down multiple occupations seasonally, donning one identity and then another over short periods of time, and engage in acts of resistance that at one and the same time allow them to reject particular dominant ideologies yet perpetuate the system that demands conformity to those ideologies for purposes of success and upward mobility. He concludes that it has become impossible to think about peasants as a viable category even as class remains a very important dimension with which to comprehend social power.

The fading appeal of peasant studies is curious, however, because many throughout Latin America work the land and the living they make from it subsidizes their labor or that of other household members who work in agro-industry or in nonrural occupations. The reverse is also true. In fact, the efforts to situate peasants in a dualistic modern/urban and traditional/rural dichotomy was always problematic. Peasants *do* exist, but peasant studies have been reborn and need to take a new turn (Edelman 1999). At the same time, peasant studies, in comparison with other areas of research, have been woefully neglected for a number of reasons. Not least has been the disenchantment of anthropologists with the possibility of revolutionary change in which peasants would be major participants. The terrible political violence of the 1980s and 1990s in Peru, in which approximately 69,000 people were killed, according to the recent Truth and Reconciliation Commission in Peru, the difficulties for scholars of doing on-the-ground research in Colombia, and the economic violence throughout Latin America as a consequence of restructuring and neoliberal economic reforms, have shifted the concerns of anthropologists.

A second arguable reason for the neglect of peasant studies is more subtle. More and more women have taken the place of men as primary laborers on community or indigenous lands and most of these women engage in multiple kinds of work. Because they are women, to government entities concerned with agrarian policy they may appear invisible (see Tutino 2002:67–68 for a discussion of the Mexican case). Consequently, it may be that a focus on "development" has shifted attention away from agrarian laborers who may more often be women than men. Carmen Diana Deere and Magdalena León (2001) confirm this in a comparative examination across 12 Latin American countries of the impact of state agrarian reform policies in conditions of neoliberalism, looking at how women have fared, both in terms of control over land and of participation in indigenous movements. Deere and León found that they have not benefited much, not only because of their lack of access to legal titles and participation in formal political organizations, but also because of traditional conditions that prevent them from asserting control over land.

## Processes of Globalization: Neoliberalism, Structural Readjustment, and Nongovernmental Organizations

There has been a growing recognition among anthropologists that, in addition to working toward an understanding of indigenous peoples and the state, and the particularities of their politics, economy, and culture, it is critical to analyze the role and culture of nongovernmental organizations (NGOs). The focus on nongovernmental organizations has gone hand in hand with the deepening and widespread impact of neoliberal economic policies and structural readjustment programs, both of which have been spearheaded by the World Bank and International Monetary Fund. It is important to recognize, then, that a contrast can be drawn between the earlier macro-intervention of Andean nation-states in designing and implementing agrarian reform, as well as other development programs aimed at modernization, and the current intervention (and sometimes substitution for the state) of international nongovernmental organizations in a wide range of development projects. The earlier projects and their underlying philosophical premises encouraged the focus on peasants and peasant economies. The current projects of nongovernmental organizations in Latin America are extraordinarily diverse in their goals. At the same time, weakly democratic governments in Latin America are driven by the pragmatics of a single and relentless capitalist rationale. The consequence is that scant attention is focused on laborers in the countryside; or, when it is, the gaze of the nongovernmental organization worker is quite different from that of the anthropologist.

In tracing the history of peasant studies in the context of globalizing processes, some continuities are apparent. The impetus for particular development trajectories more often than not comes from Europe and the United States. Furthermore, despite the diverse goals of nongovernmental organizations, they share some similarities in that they frequently place emphasis on local, grassroots, and community based fiscal responsibility. In the abstract, this may appear like a good thing. However, in accordance with the premises behind neoliberal governance, it shifts responsibility for such conditions as poverty, racial discrimination, barriers to full citizenship rights, and the lack of educational, social welfare and health facilities away from the government to the individual or local community. It is arguable, in fact, that this very shift to the local may have inadvertently catalyzed the reemergence of indigenous and culture based claims throughout much of Latin America.

While much anthropological research on the consequences of neoliberal economic policies has been in the form of a critique, the same cannot be said of research on nongovernmental organizations in Latin America. More recent studies of NGOs have begun to address how NGOs have come to substitute for government bureaucracies, both nationally and internationally staffed, and how, because of their diffuse organizational structure, they offer potential and actual recipients of their projects little opportunity to hold them accountable. While far more research needs to be done on the work of NGOs among peasants in all their aspects, one tentative generalization I would venture is that NGO workers tend to gather data for purposes of applying particular models of development, even when they are "bottom up" models. Hence, with some few exceptions (e.g. Gledhill 1995), the kind of ethnographic attention to agrarian conditions (cultural, political, and economic) that would provide a nuanced view of peasants within a global context is often missing.

Another reason that peasants are rarely the focus of current anthropological research is because of the complexity of following and understanding linkages that cut across nations and multiple identities. Few anthropologists have been able to address simultaneously questions of political economy and culture except in terms of identity, ethnicity, racial discrimination, and performativity that frequently occlude altogether the meaning of working and maintaining control over land while participating in a particular kind of globalized political economy that has its own history and consequences (see Nash 2001). Anthropologists doing research on the interaction of political economy and culture in terms of identity and performativity run the risk of celebrating hybridity and culture mixing without taking careful account of why and how these transformations are occurring. Jean Rahier puts it very well in a special issue of *Journal of Latin American Anthropology* when he observes: "Scholarly texts about métissage, creolization, hybridization, and its variants have a certain appeal. ... From the perspective of Latin Americanist scholars, this intellectual fashion for celebrating cultural and 'racial' mixings tends to obfuscate the oppressive ideological realities and histories of the societies they study" (2003: 42).

The cautionary note Rahier strikes here and with which I find myself in agreement (see also Hale 1994, 1999) is *not* equivalent to a desire to "freeze" people in place, but rather to demand that a balance be struck between the consequences of the relentless demands of late capitalism and the range of ways that people have been forced to adapt to these demands in order to survive. Mechanisms of adaptation (too often celebrated) have included becoming folkloric icons, modes of exhausting and unstable transnational migration, sustaining complex, heterogeneous, and dispersed social movements, and the elaboration of innovative transnational kinship ties for purposes of expanding communities outside a diminishing agrarian land base and/or indigenous territory. These adaptive mechanisms may "work" but they also entail undesirable sacrifices and a far more precarious livelihood that peoples using these mechanisms often articulate.

A final, but no less significant, reason for the vanishing of peasant studies is that the distance, both socially and physically, between anthropologist and peasant permitted anthropologists to maintain a focus on their subject of interest, whereas today it is far less simple to discern who might or might not be a peasant, and where they may be located at a particular time. Furthermore, tillers of the soil, in jungle, valley, or puna, that is, so-called peasants, may prefer to remain anonymous so that less, rather than more, attention will be paid to the land they occupy. There are reasons for those who are less powerful to slip in and out of particular, recognizable identities or, in a slightly different fashion, to cobble together technologies or models from multiple domains. It is often precisely socioeconomic and political conditions that compel shape-shifting and category blurring. These are astute strategies, but they may go unnoticed by anthropologists as responses to difficult conditions.

## CONCLUSION

Voices within Andean nations are preoccupied with questions directly relevant to land and labor conditions in the countryside. For example, a meeting evaluating the 50 years after Bolivia's agrarian reform gathered together intellectuals, lawyers, and political leaders, many of whom were indigenous (*La Razón* 2003). They discussed why so little attention was being paid to questions of land tenure and agrarian reform, and had different perspectives to offer. Some argued that all cultivable land had already been distributed, hence the problem that Bolivia faced was not so much redistribution of land, but how to deal with population pressure and unemployment as more and more people flocked to the cities or entered the coca economy in the eastern part of Bolivia in the jungle. Others noted that environmental degradation of the existing cultivable base was a growing problem, especially erosion, partly due to demographic pressures, partly to a lack of knowledge. Finally, some observed that there was a need to introduce and refine laws to protect indigenous land rights in the highlands and lowlands. In Brazil, to take another case, the Landless Rural Workers Movement (MST) is one of the largest social movements in the world, with hundreds of thousands of landless peasants mobilizing and risking violent conflicts time and again to occupy unproductive land, or land held by large landowners, in order to force the government to give them rights to it. They have also taken it upon themselves to establish food cooperatives, small agricultural industries, and educational infrastructure. Within these countries, it seems that agrarian reform remains a thorny and critical issue, but now more broadly encompasses other concerns directly linked to making domestic agriculture sustainable, equitable and a dynamic dimension of the national economy.

Even as globalization takes center stage in the discourse of intellectuals, it behooves us to recognize that this process has a long history. Those who till the soil are, and have been, major and complex actors in Latin America, whether we choose to call them peasants or laborers on the land, "Indians," migrants, or community members. They may provide remittances that allow for domestic agriculture to continue or, alternatively, their food production may heavily subsidize industry and their participation in nonagricultural work. The food they produce, the exchange relationships they forge, the entrepreneurial activities they interweave among extended family members, the innovations they arrive at, as well as their treatment of the environment, the political ideas they develop, the social movements they build, and the aesthetic expressions they create are just a few of their cultural, political and economic contributions as participants on the world stage who are increasingly savvy about the challenges they face in forging a livable future. While the former parameters of peasant studies and agrarian reform may be too limiting for this day and age, they provide the guidelines for pursuing and expanding significant research into the interactive dynamics of land, labor, and power within the context of a global setting.

## REFERENCES

Adams, Richard N. (1959) *A Community in the Andes: Problems and Progress in Muquiyauyo*. Seattle: University of Washington Press.

Albó, Xavier (2002) *Pueblos indios en la política*. La Paz, Bolivia: Plural Editores and CIPCA.

Albro, Robert (1997) Virtual Patriliny: Image Mutability and Populist Politics in Quillacollo, Bolivia. *Political and Legal Anthropology Review* 20(1):73–92.

*Allpanchis Phuturinqa* (1978) Special issue: *Movimientos Campesinos*. Cuzco: Centro de Estudios Rurales Andinos "Bartolomé de Las Casas."

Aramburu, Carlos (1983) *Familia y trabajo en el Perú rural*. Lima: Instituto Andino de Estudios en Población y Desarrollo.

Arguedas, José María (1964) *Puquio. Una cultura en proceso de cambio*. Lima: Universidad Nacional Mayor de San Marcos.

Babb, Florence (1989) *Between Field and Cooking Pot: The Political Economy of Marketwomen in Peru*. Austin: University of Texas Press.

Blanco Galdos, Hugo (1972) *Tierra o muerte. Las luchas campesinas en Perú*. Mexico City: Siglo Veintiuno.

Bourque, Susan and Warren, Kay B. (1981) *Women of the Andes: Patriarchy and Social Change in Two Peruvian Towns*. Ann Arbor: University of Michigan Press.

Bourricaud, François (1970) *Power and Society in Contemporary Peru*, trans. Paul Stevenson. New York: Praeger.

Burga, Manuel and Flores-Galindo, Alberto (1980) Feudalismo Andino y movimientos sociales (1865–1965). In *Historia del Perú*, vol. 11 (pp. 11–114). Lima: Juan Mejía Baca.

Caballero, José María (1980) *Agricultura, reforma agraria y pobreza campesina*. Lima: IEP.

Caballero, José María (1981) *Economía agraria de la sierra peruana antes de la reforma agraria de 1969*. Lima: IEP.

Chaney, Elsa and Garcia Castro, Mary (eds) (1989) *Muchachas No More: Household Workers in Latin America and the Caribbean*. Philadelphia: Temple University Press.

Cleaves, Peter S. and Scurrah, Martin J. (1980) *Agriculture, Bureaucracy, and Military Government in Peru*. Ithaca: Cornell University Press.

Collier, George A. and Quaratiello, Elizabeth Lowery (2005) *Basta! Land and the Zapatista Rebellion in Chiapas*. 3rd edn. Oakland: Food First Books.

Collins, Jane (1988) *Unseasonal Migrations: The Effects of Rural Labor Scarcity in Peru*. Princeton: Princeton University Press.

Cotler, Julio (1978) *Clase, estado y nación en el Perú*. Lima: IEP.

De Janvry, Alain (1981) *The Agrarian Question and Reformism in Latin America*. Baltimore: Johns Hopkins University Press.

de la Cadena, Marisol (1998) From Race to Class: Insurgent Intellectuals de Provincia in Peru, 1910–1970. In Steve Stern (ed.), *Shining and Other Paths* (pp. 22–59). Durham, NC: Duke University Press.

de la Cadena, Marisol (2000) *Indigenous Mestizos: The Politics of Race and Culture in Cuzco, Peru*. Durham, NC: Duke University Press.

Deere, Carmen Diana (1985) Rural Women and State Policy: The Latin American Agrarian Reform Experience. *World Development* 13(9):1037–1053.

Deere, Carmen Diana and León, Magdalena (2001) Institutional Reform of Agriculture under Neoliberalism: The Impact of Women's and Indigenous Movements. *Latin American Research Review* 36(2):31–64.

Degregori, Carlos Iván (ed.) (1996) *Las rondas campesinas y la derrota de Sendero Luminoso.* Lima: IEP/Universidad Nacional de San Cristóbal de Huamanga.

Degregori, Carlos Ivan, Blondet, Cecilia, and Lynch, Nicolás (1986) *Conquistadores de un nuevo mundo. De invasores a ciudadanos en San Martín de Porres.* Lima: IEP.

Degregori, Carlos Iván et al. (eds) (1992) *Perú. El problema agrario en debate. SEPIA IV.* Lima: SEPIA.

Dobyns, Henry (1964) *The Social Matrix of Peruvian Indigenous Communities.* Cornell Peru Project Monograph. Ithaca: Cornell University.

Doughty, Paul (1968) *Huaylas: An Andean District in Search of Progress.* Ithaca: Cornell University Press.

Duncan, Kenneth, Rutledge, Ian, with Harding, Colin (eds) (1977) *Land and Labour in Latin America.* New York: Cambridge University Press.

Edelman, Marc (1999) *Peasants against Globalization: Rural Social Movements in Costa Rica.* Stanford: Stanford University Press.

Edelman, Marc (2003) Bringing the Moral Economy Back in … to the Study of Twenty-First-Century Peasant Movements. Comments prepared for an invited session on Moral Economies, State Spaces, and Categorical Violence: Conversations with James Scott. American Anthropological Association Annual Meeting, Chicago, Nov. 19–23.

Escobar, Arturo (1995) *Encountering Development: The Making and Unmaking of the Third World.* Princeton: Princeton University Press.

Falcón, Jorge (1980) *Mariategui. Arquitecto sindical.* Lima: Empresa Editora Amauta.

Figallo Adrianzén, Guillermo (1985) *Política y derecho agrario.* Lima: Editores Empresores.

Figueroa, Adolfo (1983) *La economía campesina de la sierra del Perú.* Lima: Pontificia Universidad Católica del Perú. Trans. as *Capitalist Development and the Peasant Economy in Peru.* Cambridge: Cambridge University Press, 1984.

García-Sayán, Diego (1982) *Tomas de tierras en el Perú.* Lima: Centro de Estudios y Promoción del Desarrollo (DESCO).

Gledhill, John (1995) *Neoliberalism, Transnationalization and Rural Poverty: A Case Study of Michoacán, Mexico.* Boulder: Westview.

Golte, Jürgen (1980) *La racionalidad de la organización andina.* Lima: IEP.

Golte, Jürgen and Adams, Norma (1987) *Los caballos de troya de los invasores. Estrategías campesina en la conquista de la gran Lima.* Lima: IEP.

Gonzales de Olarte, Efraín (1982) *Economías regionales del Perú.* Lima: IEP.

González Linares, Nerio (1991) *Derecho procesal agrario, parte general,* vol. 1. Cusco: Editorial Mercantil.

González Linares, Nerio and Díaz Bedregal, Florencio (eds) (1991) *Temas de derecho agrario contemporáneo.* Cusco: Instituto de Derecho Agrario y Ambiental.

Guillet, David (1979) *Agrarian Reform and Peasant Economy in Southern Peru.* Columbia: University of Missouri Press.

Hale, Charles (1994) Between Che Guevara and the Pachamama: Mestizos, Indians and Identity Politics in the Anti-Quincentenary Campaign. *Critique of Anthropology* 14(1):939.

Hale, Charles (1999) Travel Warning: Elite Appropriations of Hybridity, Mestizaje, Antiracism, Equality, and Other Progressive-sounding Discourses in Highland Guatemala. *Journal of American Folklore* 112(445):297–315.

Harris, Olivia (1978) Complementarity and Conflict: An Andean View of Women and Men. In J. La Fontaine (ed.), *Sex and Age as Principles of Social Differentiation.* London: Academic Press.

Hobsbawm, Eric J. (1959) *Primitive Rebels: Studies in Archaic Forms of Social Movement in the Nineteenth and Twentieth Centuries.* New York: Norton.

Hobsbawm, Eric J. (1973) Peasants and Politics. *Journal of Peasant Studies* 1(1):3–22.

Hobsbawm, Eric J. (1981[1960]) *Bandits.* Rev. edn. New York: Pantheon.

Holmberg, Allan (1966) *Vicos. Método y práctica de antropología aplicada,* introd. Carlos Monge. Lima, Editorial Estudios Andinos.

Hopkins, Diane E. (1985) The Peruvian Agrarian Reform: Dissent from Below. *Human Organization* 44(1):18–32.

Kapsoli, Wilfredo (1980) *Los movimientos populares en el Perú.* Lima: Editorial Juan Mejía Baca.

Kapsoli, Wilfredo (1987) *Los movimientos campesinos en el Perú.* Lima: Atusparia.

Kearney, Michael (1996) *Reconceptualizing the Peasantry: Anthropology in Global Perspective.* Boulder: Westview.

*La Razón* (2003) La tierra se agota en el altiplano y el conflicto se traslada al oriente. July 31. La Paz, Bolivia. Digital edn: www.larazon.com/Sociedad/Julio/soc030731a.html, Sept. 14, 2003.

Larson, Brooke, Harris, Olivia, with Tandeter, Enrique (eds) (1995) *Ethnicity, Markets, and Migration in the Andes: At the Crossroads of History and Anthropology.* Durham, NC: Duke University Press.

Leeds, Anthony (1977) Mythos and Pathos: Some Unpleasantries on Peasantries. In James Dow and Rhoda Halperin (eds), *Peasant Livelihood: Studies in Economic Anthropology and Cultural Ecology* (pp. 215–226). New York: St Martin's Press.

Lehmann, David (ed.) (1982) *Ecology and Exchange in the Andes.* Cambridge: Cambridge University Press.

Lobo, Susan (1982) *A House of My Own: Social Organization in the Squatter Settlements of Lima, Peru.* Tucson: University of Arizona Press.

Long, Norman and Roberts, Bryan (eds) (1978) *Peasant Cooperation and Capitalist Expansion in Central Peru.* Austin: University of Texas Press.

Long, Norman and Roberts, Bryan (eds) (1984) *Miners, Peasants, and Entrepreneurs: Regional Development in the Central Highlands of Peru.* Cambridge: Cambridge University Press.

Lowenthal, Abraham F. (ed.) (1975) *The Peruvian Experiment: Continuity and Change under Military Rule.* Princeton: Princeton University Press.

Lyon, Patricia J. (ed.) (1974) *Native South Americans: Ethnology of the Least Known Continent.* Prospect Heights, IL: Waveland Press. Reissued 1985.

Mallon, Florencia (1983) *The Defense of Community in Peru's Central Highlands: Peasant Struggle and Capitalist Transition, 1860–1940.* Princeton: Princeton University Press.

Manrique, Nelson (1987) *Mercado interno y región. La sierra central 1820–1930.* Lima: DESCO.

Manrique, Nelson (1988) *Yawar Mayu. Sociedades terratenientes serranas, 1870–1910.* Lima: DESCO.

Mariátegui, José Carlos (1968[1928]) *Siete ensayos de interpretación de la realidad Peruana.* Lima: Biblioteca Amauta.

Matos Mar, José (ed.) (1976) *Hacienda, comunidad y campesinado en el Perú.* Lima: IEP.

Matos Mar, José (1980) *La reforma agraria en el Perú.* Lima: IEP.

Matos Mar, José (1988) *Desborde popular y crisis del estado. El nuevo rostro del Perú en la decada de 1980.* Lima: IEP.

Matos Mar, José and Mejía, José Manuel (1980) *Reforma agraria. Logros y contradicciones, 1969–1979.* Lima: IEP.

Matos Mar, José, Guillén de Boluarte, Teresa, Cotler, Julio, Soler, Eduardo, and Boluarte, Francisco (1959) *Las actuales comunidades de indígenas de Huarochiri en 1955.* Lima: Instituto de Etnologia y Arqueología.

Matos Mar, José et al. (1975) *Peru hoy.* 3rd edn. Mexico City: Siglo XXI.

Mayer, Enrique (2002) *The Articulated Peasant: Household Economies in the Andes.* Boulder: Westview.

McClintock, Cynthia (1981) *Peasant Cooperatives and Political Change in Peru.* Princeton: Princeton University Press.

McClintock, Cynthia and Lowenthal, Abraham F. (eds) (1983) *The Peruvian Experiment Reconsidered*. Princeton: Princeton University Press.

Montoya, Rodrigo (1980) *Capitalismo y no capitalismo en el Perú. Un estudio histórico de su articulación en un eje regional*. Lima: Mosca Azul.

Montoya, Rodrigo (1998) *Multiculturalidad y política. Derechos indígenas, ciudadanos y humanos*. Lima: SUR, Casa de Estudios del Socialismo.

Montoya, Rodrigo, Silveira, M. J., and Lindoso, F. J. (1975) *Formaciones económicas y políticas del mundo andino*. Lima: Instituto de Estudios Peruanos.

Montoya, Rodrigo, Silveira, M. J., and Lindoso, F. J. (1979) *Producción parcelaria y universo ideológico. El caso de Puquio*. Lima: Mosca Azul.

Murra, John (1975) *Formaciones económicas y políticas del mundo andino*. Lima: Instituto de Estudios Peruanos.

Nash, June (2001) *Mayan visions: The Quest for Autonomy in an Age of Globalization*. London: Routledge.

Nugent, David (1997) *Modernity at the Edge of Empire: State, Individual, and Nation in the Northern Peruvian Andes, 1885–1935*. Stanford: Stanford University Press.

Orlove, Benjamin (1977a) Against a Definition of Peasantries: Agrarian Production in Andean Peru. In Rhoda Halperin and James Dow (eds), *Peasant Livelihood: Studies in Economic Anthropology and Cultural Ecology* (pp. 22–35). New York: St Martin's Press.

Orlove, Benjamin (1977b) Inequality among Peasants: The Forms and Uses of Reciprocal Exchange in Andean Peru. In Rhoda Halperin and James Dow (eds), *Peasant Livelihood: Studies in Economic Anthropology and Cultural Ecology* (pp. 201–214). New York: St. Martin's Press.

Orlove, Benjamin (1986) Barter and Cash Sale on Lake Titicaca: A Test of Competing Approaches. *Current Anthropology* 27(2):85–106.

Orlove, Benjamin (1998) Down to Earth: Race and Substance in the Andes. *Bulletin of Latin American Research* 17(2):202–222.

Pásara, Luís (1978) *Reforma agraria. Derecho y conflicto*. Lima: IEP.

Patch, Richard W. (1964) *Vicos and the Peace Corps: A Failure in Intercultural Communication*. American Universities Field Staff. Reports Service. West Coast South America Series. N.Y. 11:2.

Peloso, Vincent (1999) *Peasants on Plantations: Subaltern Strategies of Labor and Resistance in the Pisco Valley, Peru*. Durham, NC: Duke University Press.

Poole, Deborah (ed.) (1994) *Unruly Order: Violence, Power, and Cultural Identity in the High Provinces of Southern Peru*. Boulder: Westview.

Poole, Deborah A. and Rénique, Gerardo (1991) The New Chroniclers of Peru: US Scholars and their "Shining Path" of Peasant Rebellion. *Bulletin of Latin American Research* 10(2):133–191.

Poole, Deborah A. and Rénique, Gerardo (1992) *Peru: Time of Fear*. London: Latin American Bureau.

Quijano, Anibal (1979) *Problema agrario y movimientos campesinos*. Lima: Mosca Azul.

Quijano, Anibal (1980) *Dominación y cultura. Lo cholo y el conflicto cultural en el Perú*. Lima: Mosca Azul.

Radcliffe, Sarah (1997) The Geographies of Indigenous Self-representation in Ecuador: Hybridity, Gender and Resistance. *European Review of Latin American and Caribbean Studies* 63:9–27.

Rahier, Jean Muteba (guest ed.) (2003) *Mestizaje, Mulataje, Mestiçagem in Latin American Ideologies of National Identities*. Special issue of *Journal of Latin American Anthropology* 8(1).

Rappaport, Joanne (guest ed.) (1996) *Ethnicity Reconfigured: Indigenous Legislators and the Colombian Constitution of 1991*. Special issue of *Journal of Latin American Anthropology* 1(2).

Rogers, Mark (guest ed.) (1998) *Performance, Dance, Identity and Historical Consciousness in the Andes*. Special issue of *Journal of Latin American Anthropology* 3(2).

Rostow, Walter (1953) *The Process of Economic Growth.* New York: Norton.

Sánchez, Rodrigo (1978) The Model of Verticality in the Andean Economy: A Critical Reconsideration. *Actes du XLII Congrès International des Américanistes* (1976) 4: 213–232.

Sánchez, Rodrigo (1981) *Toma de tierras y conciencia política campesina.* Lima: IEP.

Seligmann, Linda J. (1995) *Between Reform and Revolution: Political Struggles in the Peruvian Andes, 1969–1991.* Stanford: Stanford University Press.

Skar, Harold (1982) *The Warm Valley People: Duality and Land Reform among the Quechua Indians of Highland Peru.* Oslo: Universitetsforlaget.

Smith, Gavin (1989) *Livelihood and Resistance: Peasants and the Politics of Land in Peru.* Berkeley: University of California Press.

Starn, Orin (1991) Missing the Revolution: Anthropologists and the War in Peru. *Cultural Anthropology* 6(1):63–91.

Starn, Orin (1999) *Nightwatch: The Making of a Movement in the Peruvian Andes.* Durham, NC: Duke University Press.

Starr, June and Goodale, Mark (eds) (2002) *Practicing Ethnography in Law: New Dialogues, Enduring Methods.* New York: Palgrave Macmillan.

Stavenhagen, Rodolfo (1970) *Agrarian Problems and Peasant Movements in Latin America.* Garden City: Doubleday.

Stein, William W. (1961) *Hualcán: Life in the Highlands of Peru.* Ithaca: Cornell University Press.

Stein, William W. (2003) *Deconstructing Development Discourse in Peru: A Meta-Ethnography of the Modernity Project at Vicos.* Lanham: University Press of America.

Stepan, Nancy (1991) *"The Hour of Eugenics": Race, Gender and Nation in Latin America.* Ithaca: Cornell University Press.

Stern, Steve (ed.) (1987) *Resistance, Rebellion, and Consciousness in the Andean Peasant World, Eighteenth to Twentieth Centuries.* Madison: University of Wisconsin Press.

Stern, Steve (ed.) (1998) *Shining and Other Paths: War and Society in Peru, 1980–1995.* Durham, NC: Duke University Press.

Steward, Julian (ed.) (1946–59) *Handbook of South American Indians.* 7 vols. Smithsonian Institution, Bureau of American Ethnology Series. Washington, DC: US Government Printing Office.

Sulmont, Denis (1974) *El desarrollo de la clase obrera en el Perú.* Publicaciones Previas, no. 1. Lima: Pontificia Universidad Católica del Perú.

Thompson, Eric P. (1963) *The Making of the English Working Class.* New York: Pantheon Books.

Thurner, Mark (1997) *From Two Republics to One Divided: Contradictions of Postcolonial Nationmaking in Andean Peru.* Durham, NC: Duke University Press.

Tutino, John (2002) Globalizaciones, autonomías y revoluciones. In Leticia Reina and Elisa Servin (eds), *Crisis, reforma y revolución. Mexico: Historias de fin de siglo* (pp. 25–85). Mexico City: Editora Taurus.

Urbano, Henrique (ed.) (1991) *Poder y violencia en los Andes.* Cuzco: Centro "Bartolomé de Las Casas."

Valderrama, Mariano (1976) *Siete años de reforma agraria peruana: 1969–1976.* Lima, Pontificia Universidad Católica de Perú, Fondo Editorial.

Vasconcelos, José (1997[1928]) *The Cosmic Race.* Bilingual edn, trans. and annotated Didier T. Jaén, afterword Joseba Gabilondo. Baltimore: Johns Hopkins University Press.

Weismantel, Mary (2001) *Cholas and Pishtacos: Stories of Race and Sex in the Andes.* Chicago: University of Chicago Press.

Weismantel, Mary and Eisenman, Stephen (1998) Race in the Andes: Global Movements and Popular Ontologies. *Bulletin of Latin American Research* 17(2):121–142.

Wolf, Eric (1955) Types of Latin American Peasantry: A Preliminary Discussion. *American Anthropologist* 57:452–471.

Wolf, Eric (1966) *Peasants*. Englewood Cliffs: Prentice-Hall.

Wolf, Eric (1969) *Peasant Wars of the Twentieth Century*. New York: Harper and Row.

Zuidema, R. T. (1964) *The Ceque System of Cuzco: The Social Organization of the Capital of the Incas*. Leiden: Brill.

CHAPTER **17** | ## Statistics and Anthropology: The Mexican Case

*Casey Walsh*

In a recent survey essay, Victor Toledo (2002) describes the emergence of ecological anthropology as a new "hybrid discipline" built on the foundations laid by cultural ecologists such as Julian Steward and Angel Palerm, and incorporating systems theory and, more recently, a turn to politics. A key innovation of ecological anthropology in Mexico, he argues, has been to question disciplinary boundaries, incorporating the methods and theoretical insights of other social sciences, hard sciences and history in forging a new, interdisciplinary research agenda that offers the possibility of easing the current environmental "crisis" in Latin America by making development sustainable. Other scholars seeking to transcend the fragmentation and excessive specialization of scientific disciplines recall the search for utopia that characterized early modern thinking about the Americas (Krotz 2002), and the harmonious relations postulated by Franciscan thinkers between humans and the rest of the world's living beings. According to the logic of these histories, the constitution of modern disciplinary thinking amounted to a certain fall from grace, a rupture between humans and their environment. In this light, anthropology's "hybrid" effort to understand human society as a complex ecological, social and cultural whole offers traces of an intellectual Eden where scholars study and promote more sustainable human uses of resources and treatment of the environment.

The history of ideas presented in this chapter shows that an interdisciplinary, ecological approach is a feature of Mexican anthropology in general, and is neither a "hybrid" novelty nor a survival of premodern intellectual traditions, but rather an alternate strain within modern statistical thought. Before anthropology, demography, political science, sociology and other social science disciplines took form in the 19th century, statistics was wide-ranging, "general useful knowledge" that included many kinds of narrative, pictorial and enumerative descriptions of social groups and processes. As the scientific disciplines took shape in the late 19th century, the discipline of statistics became much more numerical, while anthropology maintained, to a large degree, the comprehensive, encyclopedic manner of presenting information about people and places. To understand the ecological and interdisciplinary way of thinking central to regional anthropological studies in Mexico, we need to understand the dynamics of this intellectual inheritance. Tracing this history of statistics will, at the same time, help identify the political and conceptual origins of the long and intimate relation between modern Mexican anthropology and the formation of the postrevolutionary state (Warman et al. 1970; see Nahmad Sitton, this volume).

Statistics enables one to abstract, enumerate and represent all kinds of social phenomena, thus making it possible to display, view and evaluate a vast amount of information about the world at once, and to compare and contrast very different kinds of things. By the 18th century statistical knowledge came to be considered by many Europeans as the essential characterization of the nation-state, and governments created statistical offices to define themselves and their power. Colonies and empires received the particular attention of states eager to know the extent and status of the far-removed resources and populations under their rule. It was in the 19th century, however, that the expansion of governments and bureaucracies all over the world gave rise to a "vast avalanche" (Hacking 1982) of statistical knowledge, and a concurrent popularization of statistical concepts such as "population," "type," and "normal."

Historians have begun to explore the histories of the prominent actors and institutions during the constitution and professionalization of Mexican statistics in the 19th and 20th centuries (Urias Horcasitas 2000; Meyer Celis 1999; de la Peña and Wilkie 1994), linking this knowledge to the formation of the nation-state, and the development of capitalist social relations. Two powerful features of statistical forms of knowledge aided the establishment of a Liberal political and economic framework of private property, taxation, and military service. First, as Sergio de la Peña (1994:72–74) argues, statistical language has a technological strength which derives from its utility as an intellectual tool used by state officials and capitalists. Knowing about aspects of social groups, such as their productivity, wealth or age, allowed Mexico's rulers to make the quotidian decisions of government and business: such as whether or not to buy or sell cotton or sugar; whether or not to build a railroad; how many teachers were needed in a city. Furthermore, statistical, numerical language facilitated communications between regional, national and international bourgeoisies otherwise divided by language and culture. As such, it was a language exceptionally well suited to the tasks of managing state and economy. Because of these features, statistics can be considered the "strong language" (Asad 1994) in which the business of capitalism and state formation was conducted. Finally, statistical concepts of population and type are at the heart of the intellectual effort to find and forge a national population in Mexico, defined by an array of interrelated biological, moral and psychological features (Meyer Celis 1999).

This chapter examines statistical representations of Mexico during the late 19th and early 20th centuries, in an effort to trace the origins of the "ecological" way of thinking in Latin American anthropology. This approach to anthropology brings together what are now thought of as separate disciplinary topics: biology, culture, and environment. Statistical representations of the people, resources and social development of Mexico were produced with different goals and aimed at different audiences at different times, and thus differ according to the specific historical contexts of their production, circulation and consumption. Because a comprehensive discussion of these changes in statistical thought and representation in Mexico would be an enormous task, I focus on three works that are emblematic of anthropology's shifting relationship to statistical forms: Antonio García Cubas's 1876 book *The Republic of Mexico in 1876*; an 1893 publication by García Cubas titled *Mexico: Its Trade, Industries and Resources*; and anthropologist Manuel Gamio's 1916 publication *Forjando patria* (Gamio 1960). These statistical "moments" correspond roughly to three well-defined periods in the history of Mexico: from Independence to the Porfiriato (1820–84); the Porfiriato (1884–1910); and the Revolution (1910–40).

While statisticians in the early 19th century treated a wide array of biological, cultural and social factors in a descriptive, narrative way, by the time of the modernizing dictatorship of Porfirio Diaz (1884–1910) statistics had become both more numerical and more narrowly focused on economics. Faced with revolutionary disturbances that Porfirian statistics, with its more limited scope, failed to predict or prevent, Gamio argued for an anthropology that recovered the earlier statistical attention to regional cultural, biological and social diversity, as well as a less enumerative and more narrative style. Widely considered the founder of postrevolutionary Mexican anthropology, Gamio fused race, history, politics, economics and culture into a regional ecological analysis that still defines much of the discipline in Mexico (de la Peña 1988), as elsewhere in Latin America (see Gordillo, this volume).

## MERCANTILE STATISTICS

The term "statistics" referred to a great variety of intellectual activities during the first three quarters of the 19th century in Mexico. Following Alexander von Humboldt, whose 1811 treatise *Political Essay on the Kingdom of New Spain* fundamentally influenced all subsequent statistical work, Mexican statisticians practiced a kind of wide-ranging humanistic science that included topics that would later fall into the domain of professional disciplines such as politics, ethnology, archaeology, geography, medicine, biology or demography. The production of what these thinkers called "general useful knowledge" was dominated by the predominantly liberal intellectuals of the Sociedad Mexicana de Geografía y Estadística (Mexican Society for Geography and Statistics, or SMGE). Founded in 1833, the SMGE was the third such society in the world, and in many instances its members were the same people who ran the state and managed the economy. Liberal reformer and president Benito Juarez was perhaps the most prominent member. This kind of statistics has been labeled "mercantile" statistics because of its role in facilitating the accumulation of merchant capital, and the construction of hemispheric trade networks managed by the wealthy merchants of the northeast United States (Salvatore 1998). The Mexican liberals of the SMGE organized an effort to centralize state power, stimulate economic production, and promote internal and international commerce, all severely affected by the half century of civil war and foreign aggression that followed independence. In a project modeled on the experience of French state formation, the intellectual basis of this larger effort was to be the collection and publication of statistical information on the people, products and resources of the country. The national state's efforts to collect statistical information concerning localities and regions met with indifference and resistance on the part of local and regional powers, largely because statistics were used to levy taxes and conscript soldiers.

In 1853 the Mexican Secretaria de Fomento (Ministry of Development) was created under the tutelage of Miguel Lerdo de Tejada, and between 1861 and 1872 Antonio García Cubas conducted four statistical surveys for Fomento, commissioned in part to determine the effects of the land reform legislation drafted by Lerdo de Tejada. These surveys provided the data for a series of publications, including *The Republic of Mexico in 1876: A Political and Ethnographic Division of the Population, Character, Habits, Customs and Vocations of Its Inhabitants*, produced "with the view of removing the wrong impressions that may have been left on the minds of the readers of those works which, with evil intent or with desire of acquiring notoriety as novelists, have been composed and published by different foreigners in regard to the Mexican nation" (García Cubas 1876:1). In García Cubas's opinion, Mexico needed European colonists to develop a thriving economy and other features of a "civilized" country. He therefore wrote to dispel what he felt were popular misconceptions about the bodies and work habits of Mexicans, misconceptions which would discourage Europeans from immigrating to Mexico. He also carefully described the wealth of natural resources that Mexico offered to colonists, and included vivid images in the book of Mexican landscapes and people. "So many and so propitious gifts as those with which Nature has enriched Mexico," he wrote, "cause it to be one of the choicest countries in the world for colonization; but in order to attain this desirable object, it is requisite to make known those vital elements and fountains of wealth that yet remain unexplored" (1876:1).

While the writings of García Cubas during this period contain great descriptive detail about the material riches of Mexico (1857, 1874a, 1874b, 1877), the human resources are the primary subject of *The Republic of Mexico*. In his representation of the people of Mexico, García Cubas integrated social, biological and cultural elements, identifying three racially, culturally and regionally defined groups of Mexicans: "the white race and more direct descendants of the Spaniards, the mixed race and the Indian race" (1876:13). His first task was to defend the racial purity of the "white" Mexican elite against defamation by European travelers who, he felt, "would have done well in abandoning the routine of classifying the Mexican nation among the redskins. It is supposed that the thirst for speculation has obliged [those writers] to excite curiosity, by presenting the most extravagant types, instead of those that in their equality with Europeans, would attract little or no special attention" (1876:15–16). Together with their biological whiteness, elite Mexicans were defined by their European fashion and culture

The statistically derived concept of "type" is of central importance to the representations in García Cubas's 1876 book. The "types" discussed below are portrayals of populations by representative instances of those populations; they are examples of imagined means. That is to say that, while García Cubas may have used actual people as models for his "types," these people were considered "typical" because they conformed to visualizations of the norms of those populations. At the same time, the populations themselves were configured and delimited using statistical techniques. The preoccupation demonstrated by García Cubas with defining and defending racial and social boundaries depended to some degree on the statistical conceptualization of social groups as pure, ideal-typical abstractions.

Geographical region was of central importance to the ecological relation established by García Cubas between race and culture in his description of Mexican "types."

**Figure 17.1**    Mercantile statistical rendering of Mexican types.
*Source*: Antonio García Cubas, *The Republic of Mexico in 1876: A Political and Ethnographic Division of the Population, Character, Habits, Customs and Vocations of Its Inhabitants* (Mexico City: La Enseñanza, 1876).

The middle image in figure 17.1 is labeled "Washerwoman and servants, guard with bullion from Real del Monte," a mining area near Pachuca, Hidalgo. Here García Cubas shows us that the "lower class" of Mexicans are clean, well dressed, and not too different looking from the elite. The lower frame shows people from Guadalajara, dancing and working. In other figures from the 1876 book we are presented with the "jarocho" types from Veracruz, also defined both by place and material culture, as well as physiology. Curiously, the only people actually labeled "mestizos" in the captions are two women from the Yucatan peninsula. In these images García Cubas refers to the people by their jobs and geographical origins rather than by race, evidence of the importance of class and place to the racial-cultural amalgam that made up the "types" central to the descriptive project of encyclopedic statistics.

Statistical knowledge was also fundamentally historical, and a concept of development lay at the heart of García Cubas's understanding of the relationships between race, environment, society and culture. This is clear in his discussion of the mestizo. He argues:

> The natural inclination of the mixed race to the habits and customs of their white brethren, as well as their estrangement from those of the natives, is the reason that many of them figure in the most important associations of the country, by their learning and their intelligence, including in this large number the worthy members of the middling classes. From this powerful coalition, the force of an energetic development naturally results, which is inimical to the growth of the indigenous race. (1876:16)

In this narrative and in the visual images presented alongside it, the productive capacity of the Mexican nation is linked directly to its mestizo racial status. And the capacity of the mestizo nation to create this economic "development" is linked directly to the whiteness of both the existing Mexican elites, and the potential European and North American immigrants who were the intended audience for García Cubas's book. "Development" and "progress" were both racial and political-economic concepts, and the development and progress of the Mexican nation through European or North American colonization implied the whitening of Mexico through mixing with colonists and the creation of new generations of mestizos (García Cubas 1874b:62–63).

The statistics presented in *The Republic of Mexico in 1876* were directed at an audience of potential European and American colonists, who would have had access to this sort of book through a set of institutions that also emerged in the second half of the 19th century: expositions, public museums, and public libraries (Leach 1994; Muratorio 1994; Rydell 1984; Tenorio-Trillo 1996; Williams 1982). The images shown here come from a copy of the book held by the New York Public Library, a copy that was originally donated to the Philadelphia Centennial Exposition of 1876. In fact, in Mexico statistical data was gathered and books were produced for the explicit purpose of display at exposition exhibits and libraries, and for discussion at the international congresses on statistics, race, archaeology and colonial sociology that were held in conjunction with these expositions (Tenorio-Trillo 1996).

## PORFIRIAN STATISTICS

In 1882, as a result of sustained pressure from Antonio García Cubas and Emiliano Bustos, the government's statistical agency (which dated from 1852) was refounded as the Dirección General de Estadística (General Directorate of Statistics, or DGE) within the Ministerio de Fomento (Ministry of Development). Antonio Peñafiel, who soon after assumed the directorship of the DGE and remained its head throughout the Porfiriato, was a key figure in the establishment of a statistical apparatus during this time. The "encyclopedic" kind of statistics practiced earlier by Alexander von Humboldt (1769–1859), García Cubas and others gave way to a set of specialized, professional academic disciplines institutionalized in universities, museums, and state agencies. The Porfirian era also witnessed the blossoming of bureaucracies which generated a huge amount of statistical information. Mexican statisticians who had previously dedicated themselves to producing "general useful knowledge," now focused their attention on measuring and monitoring the movements of an array of newly constituted social facts of this developing society: production, profit, imports and exports, currency exchange, labor migration, etc. The progress and development of the Mexican nation came to be understood by changes in the numerical indicators of these social facts. This more purely enumerative statistics was a language spoken by managerial capital (Chandler 1977) and by the vast bureaucracies erected by these capitalists and their colleagues in government. Mexican statisticians wrote their publications in this language in hopes of generating confidence among the new foreign investors.

The venues in which these statistical representations circulated and were displayed also changed. The statistical publications of the mercantile era were housed in public libraries, private homes and expositions. When the international expositions began around 1850 they were dedicated to demonstrating the advances of science and the progress of "man," but by the 1880s they had become massive marketplaces exhibiting the prime materials and products of the world. The expositions maintained their didactic nature throughout these changes, and they gradually became a place to educate the consumer desires of the emergent European and North American middle class. In fact, the transformation of expositions into markets was paralleled by the creation of the department store and the modern museum. As William Leach (1994) shows, through the free exchange of directors and curators, the creation of "design" as an art form, and the focus of late 19th century and early 20th century museums on presenting the "industrial arts" of the world, the modern museum and department store developed hand in hand. The statistics produced by the DGE, for example, were displayed at the 1889 and 1900 Paris Expositions alongside a dense array of products and images, and the director of the DGE, Antonio Peñafiel, was in charge of the Mexican pavilion at the expositions.

One institution which exemplified the fusion of exposition, museum and department store, and of different kinds of information, was the Philadelphia Commercial Museum. Created in 1894, it was a permanent exposition, holding exhibits from all over the world, garnered from other expositions. "The collections now on exhibition," the museum's publicists said, "comprise materials of great variety, all arranged in such a manner as to illustrate graphically the habits and customs of other lands, their resources and articles of production, the character of their commerce, their chief items of consumption, and their race characteristics" (*Commercial America* 1904:10). Among the exhibits were the famous "life-groups" which displayed mannequins of human bodies, and an exhibit which arranged the material culture (the "productive arts") of the world's peoples in serial form so as to facilitate comparison of cultures and their location within hierarchical evolutionary progressions. The museum was also quite clearly a market, where businessmen could survey the variety of the world's products and make investment and consumer decisions. For businessmen who needed more specialized information than that provided by the museum displays, the Philadelphia Commercial Museum provided the services of its Foreign Trade Bureau Library, a sort of statistical clearing house fed by the bureaucracies of national and colonial states (Philadelphia Commercial Museum 1910). While the general useful knowledge of earlier statistics was divided into different academic disciplines, kinds of presentation and domains of study, and while statistics became a much narrower and more numerical kind of knowledge, statistical images and publications shared institutional homes with displays of commodities, artifacts and bodies. Moreover, these institutions utilized the statistical technique of displaying very different kinds of things so as to allow comparison. In these institutions, statistical representations of the Mexican economy were positioned in relation to, and made commensurate with, arrays of commodities and racially ordered displays of bodies.

One of the statistical works almost certainly held by the Philadelphia Commercial Museum's library is Antonio García Cubas's *Mexico: Its Trade, Industry and Resources*, published in 1893 to coincide with the Chicago World's Fair. The subject of this book is Mexico's "trade, industries and resources" – rather than "the population, character, habits, customs and vocations of its inhabitants" discussed in García Cubas's 1876 publication. The author does include a bit of narrative information about the people of Mexico that he originally published in 1874 (1874b), but most of the information is presented in the forms of graphs, charts and tables, and deals with subjects such as mining, shipping, education, and cotton textile production. The visual grammar of the statistical chart conveyed a sense of order, modernity and planning that went beyond the actual numerical or linguistic content of the charts themselves (see figure 17.2).

Although the racialized depictions of bodies and cultures of Mexicans are not found in this work, the same statistical concepts which organized those earlier depictions continue. The Mexican nation is still the subject of statistical representation, but features of that population other than bodies and minds are represented. Thus the argument that mestizos constitute an intelligent hardworking race especially good at the productive arts is made in this work by showing numerical representations of national levels of the production of commodities. The European whiteness of Mexico is represented by a different kind of representational image of the statistical concept of progress – charts and graphs of improvements in hygiene, electricity or education. Mexico's status as a civilized nation is depicted graphically through the enumeration of rising levels of commerce with other "civilized" nations such as the US and Great Britain, rather than by images of Mexican ladies dressed in the latest French fashions.

To a large degree this shift in the nature of statistical knowledge can be seen as a displacement of narrative and descriptive information to anthropology and other disciplines, and the displacement of images of bodies to other parts of the institutions dedicated to displaying statistical information. As the domain of statistical knowledge increasingly came to be expressed through numerical representations, and the discipline of statistics focused on the emergent social facts of managerial capitalism, the analysis of bodies and culture was taken on by other disciplines such as anthropology and archaeology. For example, the organizational force behind Porfirian statistics, Antonio Peñafiel, was an accomplished artist and antiquarian with a deep knowledge of prehispanic art and architecture. Among his more notable creative efforts was the design of the neo-Aztec building that housed Mexico's exhibition at the 1889 Paris Exposition (Peñafiel 1889). But although he published various books related to Mexico's prehispanic art, Peñafiel maintained disciplinary boundaries between his statistics and these other interests. Similarly, representations of race and economy were

## FOREIGN TRADE.

### Entries.

| COUNTRIES. | STEAMERS. Ships. | STEAMERS. Tons. | SAILING VESSELS. Ships. | SAILING VESSELS. Tons. | TOTALS. Ships. | TOTALS. Tons. |
|---|---|---|---|---|---|---|
| Germany | 30 | 44, 889 | 24 | 8,353 | 54 | 53,242 |
| Belgium | ... | ......... | ... | ......... | ... | ......... |
| Brazil | ... | ......... | 7 | 2,158 | 7 | 2,158 |
| Columbia | 64 | 98,477 | 15 | 3,849 | 79 | 102,326 |
| Costa Rica | ... | ......... | 3 | 632 | 3 | 632 |
| Chile | 1 | 80 | 1 | 800 | 2 | 880 |
| Denmark | ... | ......... | 3 | 1,042 | 3 | 1,042 |
| Ecuador | ... | ......... | 2 | 959 | 2 | 959 |
| Spain | 71 | 140,525 | 27 | 3,833 | 98 | 144,358 |
| United States | 460 | 469,329 | 183 | 42,459 | 643 | 511,788 |
| France | 26 | 57,557 | 23 | 8,093 | 49 | 65,650 |
| Guatemala | 1 | 890 | 4 | 1,324 | 5 | 2,214 |
| Hayti | ... | ......... | 1 | 376 | 1 | 376 |
| Hawai | ... | ......... | 1 | 1,297 | 1 | 1,297 |
| Holland | ... | ......... | 2 | 507 | 2 | 507 |
| Honduras | ... | ......... | ... | ......... | ... | ......... |
| England | 96 | 154,083 | 157 | 43,801 | 253 | 197,884 |
| Italy | ... | ......... | 1 | 559 | 1 | 559 |
| Nicaragua | ... | ......... | 1 | 28 | 1 | 28 |
| Norway | ... | ......... | ... | ......... | ... | ......... |
| Argentine Rep | ... | ......... | 2 | 591 | 2 | 591 |
| Venezuela | ... | ......... | 15 | 4,025 | 15 | 4,025 |
| Orders | ... | ......... | 6 | 853 | 6 | 853 |
|  | 749 | 965,830 | 478 | 125,539 | 1,227 | 1.091,369 |

### Departure.

| COUNTRIES. | STEAMERS. Ships. | STEAMERS. Tons. | SAILING VESSELS. Ships. | SAILING VESSELS. Tons. | TOTALS. Ships. | TOTALS. Tons. |
|---|---|---|---|---|---|---|
| Germany | 42 | 74,995 | 40 | 14,597 | 82 | 89,592 |
| Belgium | 1 | 1,486 | ... | ......... | 1 | 1,486 |
| Columbia | 55 | 85,898 | ... | ......... | 55 | 85,898 |
| Costa Rica | ... | ......... | 1 | 739 | 1 | 739 |
| Carried forward... | 98 | 162,379 | 41 | 15,336 | 139 | 177,715 |

G.C.,—4

**Figure 17.2**  Porfirian statistical representation of Mexico's place among nations.
*Source*: Antonio García Cubas, *Mexico: Its Trade, Industries and Resources* (Mexico City: Departamento de Fomento, Colonización e Industria, 1893).

displayed within the same expositions and museums, although in separate places. The public was educated about the connections between the statistical displays of economic progress and the evolution of technologies and bodies more by the reified, statistical form in which they were displayed than by spatial contiguity.

The creation of museums and expositions in metropoles such as Chicago, Philadelphia and Paris took a different shape in Mexico's capital city. The interest that surged during the late 18th century among European states to gather and produce statistical information resulted in the creation, by the Bourbon colonial government, of a Natural History Museum in Mexico City in 1790. In 1825, with the establishment of an independent Mexico, this became the National Museum, which had the mandate of "providing the most exact knowledge of our country, in terms of its primitive population, the origin and process of its sciences and arts, the religion and customs of its inhabitants, its natural production and the properties of its soil and climate" (Castro-Leal and Sierra 1988:513). In the later part of the 19th century the statistical activities and collections of the museum were divided along disciplinary lines (anthropology and ethnology; ethnography; zoology; comparative anatomy; botany, etc.), while maintaining an explicitly national focus, with particular emphasis on Mexico's regional diversity. This orientation complemented the international emphasis of the museums and anthropologies emerging in Europe and the United States, and in 1890, for example, an exhibit of artifacts representing the regions of Mexico was collected for display at the Madrid Exposition of 1892. That same year the museum formalized its role as a teaching institution, a role which would be strengthened after 1910 with the creation of the International School of American Anthropology. The museum's role as the principal center of anthropological education in Mexico was solidified by the participation of foreign teachers such as Frederick Starr, Alex Hrdlicka, Sylvanus Morley, Alfred Tozzer and Franz Boas, as well as Mexicans such as Andrés Molina Enríquez and Francisco del Paso y Troncoso.

As the various disciplines that emerged in the second half of the 19th century narrowed and defined their fields of study, the discipline of statistics became increasingly focused on the numerical information useful for managing the economy in Mexico, with the emergent science of anthropology distanced from knowledge of these aspects of government. Nevertheless, the disciplinary split between statistics and other social scientific and humanistic fields did not mean that enumerative statistical analysis was absent from other newly formed disciplines, such as the anthropological race science of Nicolás León, who was employed as a "naturalist" at the National Museum. Nor did it mean, of course, that the fundamentally statistical concepts of progress and civilization at the core of narrative representations of Mexican racial types were absent from the more enumerative treatments of the socioeconomic facts of Porfirian Mexico. While academic professionalization marked the concentration of a certain kind of statistical thinking in the discipline of statistics, anthropology in Mexico emerged in the late 19th century as the direct heir of the "general, useful" knowledge that characterized earlier, "mercantile" statistics. The consolidation of different strains of statistical thought in different disciplinary and institutional settings in Mexico became even clearer during the long process of revolution and state formation that began in Mexico around 1910.

## REVOLUTIONARY STATISTICS

The last "moment" which I will discuss in this brief history of Mexican statistics is represented by Manuel Gamio's *Forjando patria*, published in 1916 at the height of the Mexican revolution (Gamio 1960). The Mexican Revolution was an incredibly complex affair, irreducible to a thumbnail historical sketch. What is important here, however, is that Gamio argued in *Forjando patria* that works of Porfirian statistics such as García Cubas's 1893 *Mexico: Its Trade, Industry and Resources* played a central role in the social upheaval because they were unable to envision things such as the needs and desires of the racially and culturally diverse indigenous and mestizo population in Mexico. Porfirian government failed because it failed to understand, statistically, the population and territory it sought to govern. Gamio intended *Forjando patria* to be a contribution to the effort to build a new state, and called for wide-ranging anthropological knowledge of the sort that characterized the mercantile statistics of the early 19th century. In a reaction against the Porfirian mode of Mexican statistics, Gamio argued for a more encyclopedic, less enumerative kind of knowledge: an anthropological knowledge that explicitly recognized the existence of "the Indian" and "the Mestizo" as social types and actors, and posited their hearts and minds as objects of inquiry and intervention.

For Gamio, there were two reasons why Porfirian statisticians missed the revolution. First, Porfirian statisticians actively chose not to include information about social tensions in their books and images. Because it was their job to generate confidence among foreign investors, those who produced the statistical information were not interested in showing the social tensions and instability of Mexico. The second reason is that neoclassical Porfirian statistical thinking was ideologically incapable of recognizing and representing such tensions. There was a firm belief among statisticians, economists and other neoclassical thinkers during that period that the unrestrained market would provide for the general health and welfare of society. As Susan Buck-Morss (1995) has shown, neoclassical representations fail to capture the kinds of social and historical dynamics that give rise to riot, rebellion and revolution. There were, of course, people producing other, less enumerative kinds of images and narratives about Mexican society. Statisticians such as García Cubas or Antonio Peñafiel produced works on the history and archaeology of Mexico all through the Porfiriato (García Cubas 1884, 1904; Peñafiel 1890). Andrés Molina Enríquez was well aware of the "great national problems" that faced Mexico, and in 1909 described them in a more narrative manner than his contemporaries (Molina Enríquez 1997). Molina Enríquez's ideas on agrarian politics, development and race had quite an influence among the radical liberals of the Porfiriato, and revolutionary intellectuals such as Manuel Gamio (Basave 1992). But in the circuits of international managerial capitalism, the language spoken during the Porfiriato was neoclassical, and numerical.

While Manuel Gamio was steeped in the alternate Porfirian liberalism of Molina Enríquez, from whom he took classes at Mexico's National Museum, he also owed a good deal of his reformism to his mentor Franz Boas. Gamio studied in the anthropology department at Columbia University around the time when Boas was conducting his craniometry research on immigrants. In 1908, Boas presented his findings before Congress as an intervention into a policy debate marked by eugenicist anti-immigrant arguments. This work formed the basis of his 1911 book *The Mind of Primitive Man*, which is widely considered to be the first major and systematic critique of supremacist notions of racial difference in anthropology. Boas and Gamio were both public intellectuals who struggled to bring progressive anthropological knowledge to bear on social problems. In 1910 Boas accompanied Gamio to Mexico City, where, despite the outbreak of revolutionary political turmoil, they founded the International Americanist School, dedicated to archaeological and anthropological research (Godoy 1977). During 1911 and 1912 Boas gave a series of lectures on

Anthropology at the National University of Mexico, which were based largely on *The Mind of Primitive Man*. Boas returned to New York in 1912, but his influence on Gamio is clearly seen in an essay in *Forjando patria* entitled "Prejudice in Archaeology and Ethnology," in which he reproduced Boas's critique of ideas of racial supremacy.

In *Forjando patria*, Gamio described his understanding of what a Mexican statistics of the revolution should be and do.

> The necessities of a people cannot be determined, nor can its improvement be procured without knowing its statistics. Statistics is a systematic integration of the economic, ethnological, biological, etc., etc., characteristics of human individuals and groups. Knowledge of these characteristics leads to knowledge of the necessities of the population, and suggests the measures to alleviate them. (1960:29)

Gamio thought that statistics should be encyclopedic, or in current terms, transdisciplinary. What it should do was understand the revolutionary nature, address the needs, and ensure the progress of the majority of Mexican people, all of which Porfirian statistics had failed to do. "In Mexico," he wrote, "statistics has tended to the quantitative understanding of the population, but almost not at all to the qualitative, which has been the cause of eternal governmental failures" (1960: 29). He argued that "general, useful" anthropological knowledge be brought back into the Porfirian statistical activities of government, and that, in turn, these Porfirian statistics be made more encyclopedic by including anthropological knowledge about race and culture.

The project Gamio directed in Teotihuacan exemplifies the integral character of his anthropology, its regional scope, and its clear developmental goals. By 1917 Gamio had succeeded in installing anthropology within the emergent Mexican state, and headed the Dirección de Antropología until 1924. He included personnel from many branches of the Secretaría de Agricultura y Fomento in carrying out a massive study of the prehistory, history and ethnography of the Teotihuacan Valley, a representative study of the central highlands that he sought to reproduce in nine other regions of Mexico (Gamio 1979:ix–xii, c–cii). These studies were designed to promote the "physical, intellectual, moral and economic development" of the Mexican nation by providing anthropological, statistical information on the "racial characteristics, material and intellectual culture, idioms and dialects, economic situation and physical, biological environment of the present and past regional populations" of Mexico (1979:x). The publication which resulted from the study is a monumental and detailed five-volume description of "the population of the Teotihuacan valley, the environment in which it has developed, its ethnic and social evolution and social initiatives to improve it" (Gamio 1979).

The fusion of "economic, ethnological, biological, etc., etc." (1960:29) elements in Gamio's anthropology would continue to define his thinking through the 1940s, and has remained at the heart of the discipline in Mexico. Gamio located the root of the revolution in the Mexican indigenous population, and the inability of mestizos and Europeans to understand the Indians.

> Contemporary civilization has not been able to infiltrate our indigenous population because of two great causes: first, the natural resistance with which this population opposes culture change; second, because we do not understand the motives of such resistance, we don't know how the Indian thinks, we ignore his true aspirations, we

prejudge him with our criteria, when we should steep ourselves in his to understand him and make him understand us. An indigenous soul must be forged – albeit temporarily. Then we will be able to labor for the progress of the indigenous class. (Gamio 1960)

In this reconstituted anthropological statistics Gamio placed racial ideology back into state knowledge, and thus into the formation of the postrevolutionary state. Gamio's view of race was not identical to that held by Boas, who sought to prove racial categories empty by showing that more variation existed within so-called races than between them. Boas would not have been entirely comfortable with typifications such as "Indian" and "Mestizo," especially when coupled with Gamio's nationalism. Boas would also not have been happy with the interconnectedness of race and culture in Gamio's thinking, nor his argument that racial development in Mexico should be the object of eugenic social science and government migration and colonization policies (Gamio 1924, 1930, 1931, 1932a, 1932b, 1987; Walsh 2004).

Gamio incessantly argued – through the 1940s – for the need for accurate statistics concerning the racial/cultural populations of Mexico. The concept of race, fused with the concept of culture, was central to Gamio's developmentalist anthropology. Beginning in the late 1910s with the Teotihuacan Project, his longstanding goal was to perfect a statistical definition for racial and cultural groups using the census as his principal measure His representations of race in the 1922 Teotihuacan publication, however, were still very much limited to photographic portraits of racial "types" (see figure 17.3; Gamio 1979). He found an especially receptive environment for his developmentalist statistics in the agrarian reform movement that took place under President Lázaro Cárdenas (1934 to 1940). In 1934, for example, he carried out censuses in the states of Hidalgo (El Valle de Mezquital), Guerrero (la Costa Grande), and Morelos (Cuernavaca). Discarding language and physical appearance as too mutable to serve as indicators of race, Gamio (1937, 1987) seized upon the statistical analysis of material culture as the method by which the Mexican state could definitely know the racial composition of the Mexican nation, and identify those groups which needed development (figure 17.4).

Socioeconomic factors were also important to Gamio's racial/cultural statistics. Gamio argued that the Indigenous and Mestizo groups were biologically "deficient" due to centuries of socioeconomic oppression, and that if their material, cultural conditions were improved, the biological progress immanent in those races could be achieved. By this reasoning, state knowledge of the material culture of the population was the prerequisite for achieving this development:

the standard of living of more than 12 million people is deficient or semideficient, from the material point of view, which brings as a consequence the abnormality of its development in all aspects and principally in the biological. ... The manner to resolve such an inconvenient situation consists not only in procuring the economic improval of this great mass, but also in teaching it to elevate its level of material culture. (Gamio 1987:57–59)

Gamio's focus on artifacts follows the reifying logic of 19th century museology, in which differences in material culture were construed as hierarchical evolutionary relationships between human races or nations. Gathering statistics on material culture and race would be central to Gamio's plan for indigenista politics through the early 1940s (Gamio 1942a, 1942b). By 1946, however, the complexity of doing material

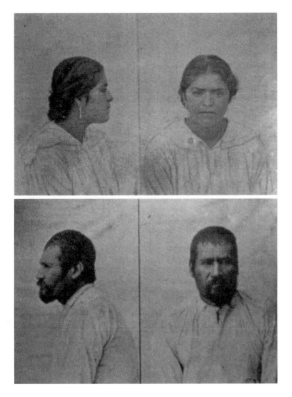

**Figure 17.3**   Revolutionary statistical images of indigenous and mestizo types.
*Source*: Manuel Gamio, *La población del Valle de Teotihuacan* (1922; Mexico City: Secretaria de Agricultura y Fomento, Dirección de Antropología, 1979).

culture surveys of all of Mexico (and the rest of Latin America) persuaded Gamio that language was a much more efficient, albeit inexact, basis for the identification of racial groups and the subsequent enactment of indigenista social programs (Gamio 1946).

Education, in Gamio's view, was a principal vehicle to achieve cultural, economic, social and biological progress. Faced with social disturbances during the revolution that neoclassical statisticians simply failed to see and address, Gamio posited a new arena of statistical research: the subjective, qualitative conditions of the Indian and mestizo populations of Mexico: their "true aspirations"; their "souls." Gamio was not new in positing culture as a terrain for politics, for progressives and radical liberals had been waging a largely unsuccessful educational and moral crusade among the illiterate and (what they considered to be) degenerate masses throughout the Porfiriato (Knight 1991). He is, however, representative of a moment in Mexican statistics that, although present in some form earlier, gained currency in the political culture of state forma-tion after the revolution. Gamio proposed in 1935 that the Secretaría de Educación Pública enact his plan for formal education which recognized, built upon and changed the needs, customs, desires and beliefs of the indigenous groups (Gamio 1987). Gamio also argued that processes of acculturation could be harnessed for educative purposes, and he encouraged the immigration of Europeans and especially the repa-triation of Mexicans from the United States, whose modern culture would act as a

TABULATION OF CHARACTERISTICS
OF THE MATERIAL CULTURE OF THE VILLAGES OF "THE MEZQUITAL
VALLEY," HIDALGO AND "ESCUDERO," GUERRERO

| ORIGIN | | | CULTURE | | | PRODUCTION | | | | RESULT | | | USE | |
|---|---|---|---|---|---|---|---|---|---|---|---|---|---|---|
| Prehispanic | Colonial | Contemporary | Indian | Mixed | Western | Domestic | Regional | National | Foreign | Efficient | Deficient | Damaging | Continuous | Sporadic |

Percent of material objects classified by origin, cultural type, production, result and, use

**"JUAN R. ESCUDERO" COLONY**

| 20.91 | 41.18 | 37.91 | 14.16 | 26.36 | 59.48 | 10.68 | 28.10 | 40.96 | 20.26 | 91.08 | 7.65 | 13.08 | 81.26 | 18.73 |

**VILLAGES OF "EL MEZQUITAL"**

| 43.80 | 43.50 | 12.70 | 37.40 | 25.70 | 36.90 | 17.00 | 40.60 | 28.90 | 13.50 | 80.10 | 14.60 | 5.30 | 93.90 | 6.70 |

**Figure 17.4**  Revolutionary statistical representation of the material culture of rural Mexico. *Source*: Manuel Gamio, *Hacia un México nuevo. Problemas sociales* (1935; Mexico City: Instituto Nacional Indigenista, 1987).

progressive influence on the "inferior" and "deficient" indigenous (precolumbian) and mestizo (colonial) cultures (Gamio 1931, 1987:71–83).

Teaching Mexicans to "raise their level of material culture" was quite explicitly an effort to create new "needs" and "aspirations" – it was an effort to create a mass of consumers. In the 1920s, Gamio's exhortations to support his anthropological efforts to forge consumers and deepen Mexican consumer markets were aimed at US government officials and intellectuals. "As a practical and utilitarian result of this work," he argued to an audience at the Carnegie Institute in 1924, "the Mexican market amounting, to-day, to only three or four million buyers, will be increased to sixteen million, since the indigenous and mestizo inhabitants will then require necessities which can be satisfied only by importation" (1924:126). By 1935 Gamio was making this argument in support of the Cardenista plan to promote national industry. "Needs must be created for them and those which they already have must be modernized," he said; "they must be taught to consume" (Gamio 1987). But for Gamio, all attempts to improve the cultural and physical level of Mexicans; to educate desires, create consumers and stimulate economic development – all these depended on statistical, anthropological knowledge of the subjectivities of rural Mexicans.

Another important innovation made by Gamio was to shift the intended audience of Mexican anthropological statistics from foreign investors and colonists to the population of Mexico, by way of the Mexican state. Although commonsense statistical thinking was fairly well developed by the late 19th century, the neoclassical graphs, charts and tables produced by Porfirian statisticians for state officials and businessmen probably would not have been easily accessible to most Mexicans. The structure and language of Gamio's arguments were chosen to appeal to a national, popular audience well versed in the language of race. Moreover, the pressing issue of Mexican government was controlling rebellion and forging political unity at home, perhaps more than generating foreign investment abroad. Forging the nation, then, was a question of forging a national-racial "soul": delineating the subjective "Indian" conditions of revolution, and then reshaping them through the medium of the Mexican mestizo state.

Gamio's anthropology was a project to generate a national self-consciousness. He contributed his expertise on the topics of culture and nation-building to what Mary-Kay Vaughn (1997) calls the "cultural politics" of Mexico's Secretaría de Educación Pública in the 1920s. During the late 1920s and 1930s he worked on issues of migration, population and development, and participated in efforts to colonize Mexico's northern border with Mexicans repatriated from the United States. In the 1940s he helped found the Instituto Nacional Indigenista (National Indigenous Institute, or INI) and the Instituto Internacional Indigenista (International Indigenous Institute, or III), over which he presided for the next 20 years. In these capacities he was one of the primary forces behind the institutionalization of an encyclopedic kind of statistical knowledge within state anthropology, a national politics of indigenismo and mestizo state formation, and the dissemination of this politics on a popular, cultural level.

## ECOLOGIES OF POWER IN MEXICAN ANTHROPOLOGY

A number of features of Gamio's statistical thinking characterize 20th century Mexican anthropology. The first is the encyclopedic effort to connect many different aspects of human life – economy, politics, culture, biology, etc. – in one discussion. Second, the region has continued to play a central role in the organization of research questions and methods in Mexico. Third, the "integral," regional approach to understanding people and historical process was especially well suited for applied anthropology seeking to promote development in the service of the state. The integral, regional anthropology founded by Gamio flourished in the postrevolutionary era, when the Mexican state promoted such research as the basis for national social-economic development and the formation of a national social and political consciousness.

In the late 1930s and early 1940s, partially in response to the desires of President Cárdenas to promote the development of his home state of Michoacan, collaborative regional studies of the Lake Patzcuaro area were made, under the direction of Daniel Rubin de Borbolla, of Mexico's Instituto Politecnico Nacional, and Ralph Beals of the University of California (Beals and Rubin de Borbolla 1940), and by the Smithsonian's Institute of Social Anthropology (ISA), in collaboration with Mexico's National Anthropology School (ENA) (Foster 1948). In the late 1940s the collaboration between the ISA and the ENA shifted its focus to Tajin, in coastal Veracruz, where ENA student Angel Palerm collaborated with Isabel Kelley (Kelley and Palerm 1950).

Both the Patzcuaro and Tajin regions offered the opportunity to pursue a collaborative, "integral" research agenda including studies of archaeology, history and ethnography, carried out by teams of anthropology students and professors. Julian Steward founded and directed the ISA, and these regional, integral studies contributed to a growing interest among US academics in "Area Studies" such as the People of Puerto Rico Project (Steward et al. 1956) after the Second World War (de la Peña 1988). Contemporary research in the Andes also took on a regional, ecological character under the guidance of the ISA (Tschopik 1947), a tendency reinforced in the concepts of vertical integration developed by John Murra (see Murra 1980).

Gonzalo Aguirre Beltrán further expanded integral, regional, developmental anthropology in Mexico, contributing discussions about intercultural dynamics between mestizos and Indians, and working on a practical level to implement cultural integration in "regions of refuge" (Aguirre Beltrán 1967) through the actions of the INI. "The Mexican school of anthropology," Aguirre explained, "since its initial steps directed research and action toward eminently practical goals, through the employment of interdisciplinary techniques" (1970:127). Like Gamio before him, Aguirre used the region as the social, cultural and geographical unit to organize integral theory, methods and developmental action (Hewitt de Alcantara 1984:47–57). Apart from its home in the INI, integral regional research also found support as part of the protracted effort by the federal government to develop agriculture through the construction of regional irrigation systems in Mexico's river valleys. Gamio himself participated in the planning and colonization of irrigation districts in northern Mexico during the 1930s (Walsh 2004), and Aguirre Beltrán, Alfonso Villa Rojas, Angel Palerm and many others participated in a later generation of regional irrigation schemes (Hewitt de Alcantara 1984:49). From his position at the Universidad Iberoamericana, Palerm directed an ongoing anthropology field school in the region of Texcoco, near Mexico City, where generations of students were taught integral, regional research. These students then went on to found and staff anthropology programs such as those of the Centro de Investigaciones y Estudios Superiores en Antropología Social (CIESAS), the Colegio de Michoacan, and the Universidad Autonoma Metropolitana (UAM) in Mexico City, among others. Guillermo de la Peña, Arturo Warman, and Roberto Varela are some of the more widely known students who propagated the regional approach in emergent institutional settings. And, despite important critiques of Mexican anthropology's developmental relation to the national state, the regional study continues to form the basis of discipline-straddling research aimed at understanding Mexico's national community and identity (Lomnitz-Adler 1992, 1998). As Mexico experiences the effects of globalization, the fracturing of the political pact forged after the revolution, and the emerging environmental crisis, problems of regional diversity and national integration promise to loom large, generating new iterations of regional, integral research.

## REFERENCES

Aguirre Beltrán, Gonzalo (1967) *Regiones de refugio. El desarrollo de la comunidad y el proceso dominical en mestizoamerica.* Mexico City: Instituto Nacional Indigenista.
Aguirre Beltrán, Gonzalo (1970[1958]) *El proceso de aculturación y el cambio sociocultural en Mexico.* Mexico City: Universidad Iberoamericana.

Asad, Talal (1994) Ethnographic Representation, Statistics and Modern Power. *Social Research* 61(1):55–87.

Basave Benitez, Agustín (1992) *México Mestizo. Análisis Del Nacionalismo Mexicano En Torno a La Mestizofilia De Andrés Molina Enríquez.* Mexico City: Fondo de Cultura Económica.

Beals, Ralph and Rubin de Borbolla, Daniel (1940) The Tarasca Project: A Cooperative Enterprise of the National Polytechnic Institute, Mexican Bureau-Indian Affairs, and the University of California. *American Anthropologist* 42(4):708–712.

Buck-Morss, Susan (1995) Envisioning Capital: Political Economy on Display. In Lynne Cooke and Peter Wollen (eds), *Visual Display: Culture beyond Appearances.* Seattle: Bay Press.

Castro-Leal, Marcia and Sierra, Dora (1988) *Las instituciones,* vol. 7 of Carlos García Mora (ed.), *La antropología en México. Panorama histórico.* Mexico City: Instituto Nacional de Antropología e Historia.

Chandler, Alfred Dupont (1977) *The Visible Hand: The Managerial Revolution in American Business.* Cambridge, MA: Belknap Press.

*Commercial America* (1904) *Commercial America* (Philadelphia) 1(1).

de la Peña, Guillermo (1988) *Las cuestiones medulares (Etnología y antropología social),* vol. 4 of Carlos García Mora (ed.), *La antropología en México. Panorama histórico.* Mexico City: Instituto Nacional de Antropología e Historia.

de la Peña, Sergio (1994) Visión global de los orígenes de la estadística. Guía de forasteros y nativos a la historia de la estadística económica nacional. In Sergio de la Peña and James Wilkie, *La estadística económica en México. Los orígenes* (pp. 5–126). Mexico City: Siglo Veintiuno.

de la Peña, Sergio and Wilkie, James (1994) *La estadística económica en México. Los orígenes.* Mexico City: Siglo Veintiuno.

de Mier, Sebastián (1900) *México en la Exposición Internacional de Paris.* Mexico City: Secretaria de Fomento.

Foster, George (1948) *Empire's Children: The People of Tzintzuntzan.* Mexico City: Imprenta Nuevo Mundo.

Gamio, Manuel (1924) *The Present State of Anthropological Research in Mexico and Suggestions Regarding its Future Developments.* Washington, DC: Pan-American Union.

Gamio, Manuel (1930) *Mexican Immigration to the United States: A Study of Human Migration and Adjustment.* Chicago: University of Chicago Press.

Gamio, Manuel (1931) Migration and Planning. *Survey Graphic* 66:174–175.

Gamio, Manuel (1932a) *Comentarios sobre la evolución de los pueblos latino-americanos.* Rome: Comitato Italiano por lo Studio dei Problemi della Popolazione.

Gamio, Manuel (1932b) *Sugestiones para el estudio de las poblaciones primitivas en los paises indo-ibéricos de America.* Rome: Comitato Italiano per lo Studio dei Problemi della Popolazione.

Gamio, Manuel (1937) An Analysis of Social Processes and the Obstacles to Agricultural Progress in Mexico. *Rural Sociology* 2(2):143–147.

Gamio, Manuel (1942a) Calificación de características culturales de los grupos indígenas. *América Indígena* 2(4):17–22.

Gamio, Manuel (1942b) Las características culturales y los censos indígenas. *América Indígena* 2(3):15–19.

Gamio, Manuel (1946) La identificación del indio. *América Indígena* 6(2): 99–104.

Gamio, Manuel (1960[1916]) *Forjando patria. Pro nacionalismo.* Mexico City: Editorial Porrua.

Gamio, Manuel (1979[1922]) *La población del Valle de Teotihuacan.* Mexico City: Secretaria de Agricultura y Fomento, Dirección de Antropología.

Gamio, Manuel (1987[1935]) *Hacia un México nuevo. Problemas sociales.* Mexico City: Instituto Nacional Indigenista.

García Cubas, Antonio (1857) *Noticias geográficas y estadísticas de la republica mexicana.* Mexico City: J. H. Lara.

García Cubas, Antonio (1874a) *Atlas metódico para la enseñanza de la geografía de la república mexicana, formado y dedicado a la Sociedad Mexicana de Geografía y Estadística.* Mexico City: Sandoval y Vázquez.

García Cubas, Antonio (1874b) *Escritos diversos de 1870 a 1874.* Mexico City: Escalante.

García Cubas, Antonio (1876) *The Republic of Mexico in 1876: A Political and Ethnographic Division of the Population, Character, Habits, Customs and Vocations of Its Inhabitants.* Mexico City: La Enseñanza.

García Cubas, Antonio (1877) *Álbum del ferrocarril mexicano. Colección de vistas pintadas del natural por Casimiro Castro.* Mexico City: V. Debray.

García Cubas, Antonio (1884) *Cuadro estadístico.* Mexico City.

García Cubas, Antonio (1893) *Mexico: Its Trade, Industries and Resources.* Mexico City: Departamento de Fomento, Colonización e Industria.

García Cubas, Antonio (1904) *El libro de mis recuerdos.* Mexico City: Antonio García Cubas.

Godoy, Ricardo (1977) Franz Boas and his Plans for an International School of Archaeology and Ethnography in Mexico. *Journal of the History of the Behavioral Sciences* 13:228–242.

Hacking, Ian (1982) Biopower and the Avalanche of Printed Numbers. *Humanities in Society* 5:279–295.

Hewitt de Alcantara, Cynthia (1984) *Anthropological Perspectives on Rural Mexico.* London: Routledge and Kegan Paul.

Kelley, Isabel and Palerm, Angel (1950) *The Tajin Totonac: Part 1, History, Subsistence, Shelter and Technology.* Washington, DC: US Government Printing Office.

Knight, Alan (1991) Intellectuals in the Mexican Revolution. In Roderic Camp, Charles A. Hale, and Josefina Zoraida Vázquez (eds), *Los intelectuales y el poder en México.* Mexico City: El Colegio de México/UCLA Latin American Center Publications.

Krotz, Esteban (2002) La otredad cultural entre utopía y ciencia. Un estudio sobre el origen, el desarrollo y la reorientación de la antropología. Mexico City: Universidad Autonoma Metropolitana/Fondo de Cultura Económica.

Leach, William (1994) *Land of Desire: Merchants, Power, and the Rise of a New American Culture.* New York: Vintage Books.

Lomnitz-Adler (1992) *Exits from the Labyrinth: Culture and Ideology in Mexican National Space.* Berkeley: University of California Press.

Lomnitz-Adler, Claudio (1998) *Modernidad indiana. Nueve ensayos sobre nación y mediación en México.* Mexico City: Planeta.

Meyer Celis, Leticia (1999) *Entre el infierno de una realidad y el cielo de un imaginario. Estadística y comunidad científica en el Mexico de la primera mitad del siglo XIX.* Mexico City: El Colegio de México.

Molina Enríquez, Andrés (1997[1909]) *Los grandes problemas nacionales.* Mexico City: A. Carranza.

Muratorio, Blanca (ed.) (1994) *Imágenes y imagineros.* Quito: FLACSO.

Murra, John (1980[1955]) *The Economic Organization of the Inka State.* Greenwich, CT: JAI Press.

Peñafiel, Antonio (1889) Explication de l'edifice mexicain al l'Exposicion Internacionales de Paris en 1889. Barcelona: Espasa.

Peñafiel, Antonio (1890) *Monumentos del arte mexicano antiguo. Ornamentación, mitología, tributos y monumentos.* Berlin: Ascher.

Philadelphia Commercial Museum (1910) *The Commercial Museum, Philadelphia.* Philadelphia Commercial Museum Press.

Rydell, Robert (1984) *All the World's a Fair: Visions of Empire at American International Expositions, 1876–1916.* Chicago: University of Chicago Press.

Salvatore, Ricardo (1998) The Enterprise of Knowledge: Representational Machines of Informal Empire. In Gilbert M. Joseph, Catherine C. LeGrand, and Ricardo D. Salvatore (eds), *Close Encounters of Empire: Writing the Cultural History of US–Latin American Relations.* Durham, NC: Duke University Press.

Steward, Julian et al. (1956) *The People of Puerto Rico.* Urbana: University of Illinois Press.

Tenorio-Trillo, Mauricio (1996) *Mexico at the World's Fairs: Crafting a Modern Nation.* Berkeley: University of California Press.

Toledo, Victor (2002) Antropología y ecología. Aportes y perspectivas de un planteamiento interdisciplinario. In Guillermo de la Peña and Luís Vázquez León (eds), *La antropología sociocultural en el México del milenio* (pp. 540–556). Mexico City: Instituto Nacional Indigenista/Consejo Nacional para la Cultura y las Artes/Fondo de Cultura Económica.

Tschopik, Harry, Jr (1947) *Highland Communities of Central Peru*. Washington DC: Institute of Social Anthropology.

Urias Horcasitas, Beatriz (2000) *Indígena y criminal. Interpretaciones del derecho y la antropología en Mexico, 1871–1921*. Mexico City: Universidad Iberoamericana.

Vaughn, Mary Kay (1997) *Cultural Politics in Revolution: Teachers, Peasants, and Schools in Mexico, 1930–1940*. Tucson: University of Arizona Press.

Walsh, Casey (2004) Eugenic Acculturation: Manuel Gamio, Migration Studies, and the Anthropology of Development in México, 1910–1940. *Latin American Perspectives* 31(5):118–145.

Warman, Arturo et al. (1970) *De eso que llaman antropología mexicana*. Mexico City: Nuestro Tiempo.

Williams, Rosalind (1982) *Dream Worlds: Mass Consumption in Late Nineteenth-Century France*. Berkeley: University of California Press.

PART **III** Positions

# CHAPTER 18

# Indigenous Anthropologies beyond Barbados

*Stefano Varese, Guillermo Delgado, and Rodolfo L. Meyer*

A Call to Certain Academics

That we no longer know anything, that we are backwardness itself, that we will be
given a new head

That our hearts are no good either, frightened as a swallow, crying like a bull being
pierced by the sword, none of this is good

Certain academics say this, bred on our very land, getting fat, making up stories along
the way

Let them talk, let them go on talking to themselves

What is it our brains are made of? What is it our hearts are made of, dear academics?

The rivers are screaming out so that these academics leave unmoved their deep waters,
the golden dusk, the golden dawn, the silver stones

Our heads, our brains are made of that golden night, those silver stones, so also are our
fingers

What is it then that will always make it the river, dear academics?

Run and get your binoculars, go and look and try to grasp its depth, if you are so able

Five hundred potato flowers are watching so that you not take from earth, the golden
dusk, the silver days

Your eyes can't see them, they are my brains, they are my heart.

Poem by José María Arguedas, translated from the Quechua

The Peruvian poet, writer and anthropologist José María Arguedas wrote "A Call to
Certain Academics" in Quechua just a few years before his death in 1969. A foundational
voice in Peruvian and Latin American anthropology, Arguedas was born "white" *and*
mestizo in 1911 in the Peruvian Andes. The son of a provincial middle class lawyer,
as a young child he was relegated by his unloving stepmother to indigenous servants
and commoners, who raised and nurtured him in Quechua language and culture until
he was eight years old. This short formative period of Arguedas's life transformed him
into an Andean *Runa*, a blue eyed, light skinned indigenous person who could speak

and write equally well in Quechua and Spanish and who soon became one of the most outspoken defenders of the millions of Andean indigenous peoples of Peru. Arguedas began to publish in Quechua and Spanish in his early twenties. At age 30 he published his first novel, *Yawar Fiesta* (1941, and Arguedas 1985). In the following editions of the novel, Arguedas included an essay that he had published in 1950 in the journal *Mar del Sur* (Arguedas 1950). In this essay Arguedas writes as one of the very first indigenous anthropologists about the characters of his novel, the indigenous community, the Andes, the *indios*, the mestizos, the town, and the provincial elite. His descriptive analysis of the social setting of the novel is clearly anthropological, and so is his definition of some of the terms he uses throughout his work: *indio, Indigenista, Indianista*. Arguedas, however, rejects the notion that his fiction writings can be called indigenista: "my novels *Agua* and *Yawar Fiesta* have been called *indigenista* or Indian. And that is not the case. It's a matter of their being novels in which the Andean Peru appears with all its elements, in its disturbing and confused human reality, in which the Indian is only one of many different characters" (Arguedas 1985:xiii).

In 1963 Arguedas earned a doctoral degree in anthropology at the National University of San Marcos, Lima, with a comparative dissertation on the Spanish peasant communities and the indigenous Andean communities (Arguedas 1968). Thereby, he officially entered Peru's anthropological profession and academia, which in the previous few decades had grown dramatically under the patronage of other Andean archaeologists-ethnographers. Some of the early anthropologists, such as Julio C. Tello and Luis E. Valcárcel, were Andean by place of birth and, at least in the case of J. C. Tello, were Quechua speakers and members of indigenous communities. Before them, in the early 20th century, other intellectuals, writers and artists had contributed to the establishment of a school of thought, creativity and political activism that became known throughout Latin America as *indigenismo*. What is different in the case of José María Arguedas is that up till then in modern Peru, very few intellectuals (social scientists or humanists) had been willing to accept their indigenous ancestry in public, much less claim either a generic indigenous identity or a specific one (Quechua, Aymara, Moche, Uru, or any other indigenous affiliation of the dozens of ethnicities existing in the country). Arguedas, a "white mestizo" educated and socialized by Quechua peoples, was the first intellectual and trained anthropologist of modern Peru who was willing to openly abandon his class and ethnic origin and fully assume the despised cultural identity of the impoverished and disenfranchised natives of Peru. This existential position and political decision earned him a high degree of ostracism by the intellectual elite of Peru and arguably some level of marginalization by the literary community of Latin America (Vargas Llosa 1996).

The dialogue that Arguedas had hoped to open between the indigenous Andean and the academic anthropologists and intelligentsia of Peru failed at that time. The colonial and eurocentric formation of Peru's intellectual constituency was unprepared to accept a conversation that implied a thorough process of decolonization, the acknowledgment of different epistemologies, and the possibility of an indigenous anthropology: "What is it then that will always make it the river, dear academics?"

In this chapter, we discuss the artificiality of the indigenista/indigenous divide that has been underscored since the late 1940s by Mexico's governmental policy toward indigenous peoples and followed closely by most of the Latin American states with larger demographic contingents of aboriginal peoples. "Indigenismo," from Mexico to Argentina, has become the dominant discourse (and policy) on indigenous peoples elaborated and imposed by the state, while "Indianismo" is increasingly meaning the Indians speaking for themselves. While indigenismo aspires to be a hegemonic argument that neutralizes alternative visions on issues of multi-ethnicity, Indianismo, in its various and multifaceted expression, is the counterhegemonic and pluralistic response that opens the dialogue of the whole society on the central theme of the "right to diversity."

## THE PAST IN THE FUTURE

Three hundred and fifty years before Arguedas wrote his poem "A Call to Certain Academics," Huaman Puma de Ayala, a Quechua native intellectual and scholar from the central Andean region of Huánuco in Peru, wrote explicitly for King Philip III of Spain the long treaty Nueva Corónica y Buen Gobierno (1615) (Adorno 1988) as the first ever systematic critique of European colonialism in the Americas.[1] Huaman Puma was blatantly opposed to the direct rule of the invading foreigners and argued strongly in favor of land and territorial restitution to the indigenous peoples, as well as the restoration of the original Andean governance and polities. Strongly anticlerical and antibureaucratic, he condemned the rapacity, corruption, and thievery of the Spaniards, while acknowledging the ideal expectations and possible benefits of the imported Christianity. Huaman Puma's acceptance of the foreigners' faith, however, is mediated by his radical symbolic reinterpretation of Christian cosmology. In his drawing "Mapamundi of the Kingdom of the Indies" (1615) (Adorno 1988:89–99) Huaman Puma reorganizes the conventional European symbolic representation of the world in Andean indigenous terms: the center of the world is now Cusco, not Jerusalem; and the six cosmic axes (north, south, orient, occident, zenith, nadir) are now transformed into the four "corners" (Tahuantinsuyu: four suyu) and the two cosmic poles of the indigenous axis mundi – upper/lower (hanan/hurin), which are now part of an indigenous cardinal points system that reconfigures the universe as social, cultural, "natural" home of the indigenous peoples. The indigenous Andean community, or ayllu, is once again recomposed and refounded by Huaman Puma's description and analysis as a cosmic site of multiple dualities related through the principles of complementarity and reciprocity.

Huaman Puma's dictum "Pachacama, maypim canqui?" [Creator of the world, where are you?] refers to both the loss of the knowledge of God by previous indigenous generations, and the chaos or inversion of a world order which has been brought about by the European conquest. The fact "that there is no God and no king. They are in Rome and in Castille" (Adorno 1988:140) marks, for Huaman Puma, a theological and ontological disconnection, as well as a political distance separating Andean indigenous peoples from any form of legitimate authority. It is this distance – symbolized by the far-off European king and the dismembered and buried Inka monarch – that causes Huaman Puma to doubt the possibility of dialogue across barriers between differing civilizations (Adorno 1988:141–142). Toward the end of his "Letter to the King," and after having produced hundreds of pages of writings and drawings of critical indigenous ethnography and colonial sociology, Puma becomes a skeptical anthropologist who mistrusts the prospect of ever achieving cultural communication between the indigenous and the Spanish worlds, separated by fundamental ontological difference. His final conclusion is that European modes of thinking are inadequate to recount and decipher American indigenous experiences before and after Spanish invasion. This indigenous anthropological precursor rejects the fundamental Christian concepts of theology, history and justice, as well as the narratives that support such worldviews, while unmasking the intellectual and philosophical enterprises that were all created to justify and memorialize the colonial domination and oppression of indigenous peoples (Adorno 1988:142–143). Two hundred and fifty years later Europe would witness, with Karl Marx, a similar radical disclosure of the profound reasons for doubting the honesty and trustworthiness of the intellectual undertaking of European elites in regard to the poor and the non-European world.

At this point a preliminary accounting is due regarding what we can call *indigenous anthropologies.* On one hand, José María Arguedas, a white/mestizo Andean person, is reshaped into an indigenous *Runa* (Quechua speaker and anthropologist) who expresses in a tragic manner the radical difference of cultural values coexisting in modern Peru, as well as the extreme difficulty of communication between the two worlds. In these worlds, indigenous and non-indigenous peoples in Peru, divided by racist and ethnic prejudices, are equally oppressed by a delusion of illegitimacy brought about by a false sense of history and cultural misrepresentations; all of which are sanctified by and are immersed in a "scientific" anthropology that can hardly acknowledge epistemic cleavages and separate rationalities. What good does it do to study years of anthropology if your own culture, you mother tongue, your history, your peoples are all concealed by a scientific apparatus that makes your own indigenous reflection an alienated endeavor? On the other hand, Huaman Puma, one of the first American indigenous critics of colonialism, failed at that time in his anthropological enterprise, while still accomplishing a monumental ethnography of Andean society. In his effort to translate and interpret both cultural worlds, Huaman Puma was coerced into using the invaders' language, Spanish, and with it, all of its intellectual and scholarly arsenal. Huaman Puma's ethnography remained hidden in the archives of Europe for 300 years, until a few members of the intellectual elite of Latin America, Europe and the US rediscovered the text, interpreting it not as a complex hermeneutics of the indigenous peoples' world, but rather as a historical document helpful in interpreting the colonial establishment.

Here arises the paradox of indigenous anthropologies in Latin America. Anthropology, as a discipline of modernity, is founded on the rationalist paradigm that was brought to its full development by the European Enlightenment. The modern model of science, however does not help the understanding of an anti-ontological subject/object such as diverse human societies and cultures in time and space, precisely because these subjects/objects do not possess a constant permanence, and in a strict sense they are not "ontologies." In the same manner, the monologist science of modernity does not allow for a conversation with nature, the world, the landscape, and the cosmos. "Science, according to Kant, does not dialogue with nature, it imposes its language upon her" (Costa Lima 2003:30). The fundamental goal of this mode of knowledge/science is to achieve technical domination over nature and the universe. The failure of José María Arguedas and Huaman Puma to achieve a dialogic communication between the indigenous worlds and the colonial/neocolonial world is based on a dichotomy between a relational indigenous approach as opposed to a Western hierarchical rationality. There is a split between a relational intelligence that approaches the cosmos as a web of relations seeking its meaning through acts of partnership, and an opposite Western logos. The Western logos analyzes the cosmos in attempting to understand it, addressing it as an inanimate entity ruled by laws that can be expressed mathematically, manipulated, and subdued to the ruling principles of modern capitalist cosmology: surplus value and the "market laws." As Max Weber wrote in 1915, "The more the cosmos of modern capitalist economy follows its own immanent laws, the more it becomes inaccessible to any thinkable relation with a religious ethics of brotherhood."[2]

## THE DIALECTICS OF LIBERATION: NATIVE AMERICANS AND ANTHROPOLOGISTS

In the Andean countries, starting in the early 20th century, there were many mestizos and indigenistas who attempted to establish a dialogue with indigenous people. These leaders and intellectuals, who acted as spokepersons and representatives of entire voiceless communities, denounced the forms of discrimination and inequality that oppressed indigenous communities. Among these leaders were Uriel García, the Churata brothers (Quechua, Peru), Pascual Coña (Mapuche, Chile), Eduardo Nina and Fausto Reynaga (Aymara, Bolivia), Dolores Cacuango (Quichua, Ecuador), Quintin Lame (Paez, Colombia), Nele Kantule (Kuna, Panama), Antonio Rodríguez Suysuy (Moche, Peru) and many others who brought to the attention of their national communities powerful indigenous discourses on culture diversity, racism and nation-building. Through their actions, these leaders acted as collective and representative voices. They were indeed the spokespersons and legitimate representatives of entire voiceless communities, challenging the wrongdoings of the nation-state and denouncing forms of discrimination and inequality oppressing their communities. However, none of these indigenous intellectuals were ever given serious consideration by anthropologists as valid interlocutors in the debates on ethnicity and nation-state formation. Even postrevolutionary Mexican intellectuals had difficulty acknowledging the presence of indigenous intellectuals and their contributions to Mexican history and culture. In 1940, during his last year as president of Mexico, Lázaro Cárdenas convened the First Inter-American Congress of Indigenous Peoples (Congreso Indigenista Interamericano). The Congress gathered some of the most visible indigenous intellectuals of the continent, with the noticeable and unfortunate exception of Mexico's delegation, which was formed by non-indigenous anthropologists and politicians (Téllez Ortega 1987).

By the end of the 1960s and the early 1970s, Latin America was witnessing the growth of an incipient but strong indigenous peoples' liberation movement that would soon gather reputation on the international scene, prompting a few Latin American anthropologists to call for an action anthropology and urgent ethnology. Some very important meetings of indigenous peoples and anthropologists took place during this period, precisely when indigenous peoples were striving to internationalize themselves as a social movement and assert their political relevance in the various national arenas. Spearheaded by the 1971 Barbados Group of dissident anthropologists, a more equitable dialogue began to take place between anthropologists and indigenous leaders and intellectuals. In this renewed and tense conversation, issues about the decolonization of knowledge and its social practice assumed a position of centrality, while authoritarian

Western social science with its dominant eurocentric perspective was slowly displaced into an area of critical reevaluation (Acosta 1972; Bonfill Batalla 1981; Nahmad Sitton 1977; Rodríguez and Varese 1981a, 1981b; Varese 1977, 1978).

The year 1977 celebrated a dialogue, for the first time, between a dozen "formally trained" Latin American anthropologists and 17 indigenous intellectuals and leaders (Grünberg 1979). The indigenous participants in the Second Meeting of the Group of Barbados (Barbados II) demanded the decolonization of anthropology, to be turned instead into a social science committed to the struggle for the liberation of indigenous peoples. By calling into question the arrogant centrality of "scientific objectivity," native intellectuals and activists dislodged European presumptions of knowledge reproduction and established a new intellectual domain – open to indigenous and non-indigenous peoples – for the encountering and sharing of cultural and political creativity. At the Barbados II meeting the indigenous participants proposed that researchers *accompany* (rather than objectify) the struggles of indigenous peoples. The goal of both indigenous peoples and anthropologists was to galvanize a renewed sense of humanity in the social contract, based on three main points, collected, at the time, by French anthropologist Michel de Certeau in his now prophetic article (Certeau 1976). De Certeau summarized the following points in the already ongoing struggle of indigenous peoples: first, the passage from a *micropolitics* (of self-managing communities) to a *macropolitics* (federations and multilevel organizations); second, the *collective contracts* with the earth and nature in general, in their dual aspect as economic (cooperatives, collectives) and ecological (harmony with nature); and third, *cultural pluralism*, not monoculture but pluricultures, as an essential component of the self-management perspective.

During these formative years of indigenous anthropology, specifically in the Andean and Amazonian areas, but also in Mesoamerica, ethnic self-awareness about political agency and the persistence of native languages were stressed. This fact probably inspired the early formation of native ethnographers interested in organizing their own materials in their own ethnic language for future generations to study. Following the established tradition of the Andean indigenismo, other trends of studies of indigenous peoples and their struggles emerged in Latin America. Based on the Andean indigenismo of José Carlos Mariátegui, Hildebrando Castro Pozo, Luis E. Valcárcel and José María Arguedas among others, the Mexican indigenismo of Manuel Gamio, Moisés Sáenz, Wigberto Jiménez Moreno, Miguel Covarrubias, Alfonso Villa Rojas, Gonzalo Aguirre Beltrán, and the early Brazilian Indianismo of Cándido Mariano da Silva Rondón, and the young Darcy Ribeiro, new emerging indigenous anthropologies began to influence a small sector of the educated Latin American public with their active defense of indigenous cultures. They alleged racial and ethnic discrimination, economic exploitation and political oppression of indigenous peoples. In a sense, these indigenous voices found in the indigenistas the validation of Native worldviews and their opposition to the overwhelming push of the early modernization projects. "Indigenous anthropologies" emerged to directly deny – rightly or mistakenly – the impact of modernization and industrialization on the lives of indigenous peoples. Both were perceived as destructive forces of "civilization" intruding on traditional life and the autonomy of indigenous communities.

The rise of indigenous anthropology in contemporary Latin America can thus be attributed to the confluence of collective indigenous politics, state policy, and the deeply fractured character of most Latin American societies. On one hand, indigenous communities and individuals sought acknowledgment and full admittance into the national community without having to repudiate their history and culture, and on the other hand the white/criollo/mestizo communities were expressing a series of national-cultural goals which contradicted radically the ideal coexistence of cultural diversity. The "Right to Difference," the famous manifesto by French Marxist philosopher Henry Lefevbre, was just becoming known in Latin America about these times (the 1970s), broadening the debate and the struggle for social justice from a strictly class oriented and mostly economic one to a deeper political commitment to a future society where social equality could be constructed on the bases of legitimate cultural differ-ence and diversity (Bonfil Batalla 1991; Varese 1977). What soon became a domain of contention in the Latin American struggle and dialectics of liberation was the radically different weight given by indigenous peoples and white/mestizos to analytic, pro-grammatic, and strategic apparatuses. While the progressive white/mestizos were rely-ing on strict Marxist class analysis to organize and mobilize the people toward social changes, indigenous leaderships and organizations were bringing to the forefront of their struggles a radical critique of European and North American colonialism and imperialism, extending their criticism to include Marxism and the insensibility of Latin American Marxists to issues of cultural sovereignty and ethnopolitical autonomy (Bonfil Batalla 1981; Rodríguez and Varese 1981a, 1981b).

## INDIGENOUS PEOPLES IN THE ANTHROPOLOGIST'S CLASSROOM

Formal academic training became a necessity for some native intellectuals. The work-ing together of non-indigenous and professional anthropologists and so-called "inform-ants" generated among some indigenous peoples the need to perpetuate, for the generations to come, a desire to preserve narratives of cultural origins and resistance, acknowledging the force of linguistic agency, but also the memory of territorial resto-ration. It is worth noting the fact that control over admissions of indigenous students at national universities constituted an unspoken veto. Their absence was through exclu-sion and often by self-denial; at the same time, their presence was simply not wel-comed, and their levels of retention, when they were accepted, were very low.

Yet, in the face of those concrete constraints and the intentional marginalization of rural and urban indigenous peoples, Western anthropologists more than other aca-demic professionals made their practices, methods, and aims known or filtered to the "native informants" (soon to become research partners) through fieldwork and close collaboration on the ground. An ethics of solidarity has largely been present in the anthropological ethos of various anthropologists, in spite of the not infrequently tar-nished involvement and misbehavior of a few, as in the infamous case of the Camelot Project in Chile and the documented participation of some US anthropologists in counterinsurgency research in Vietnam and Latin America. Despite the presence of other practitioners of disciplines such as sociology and economics, or archaeology for that matter, anthropology had a natural appeal and opportunity for access for indig-enous peoples. After all, ethnographizing meant the careful practices of "thick description" that inspired other forms of dialogue and assistance between professionals and "informants."

On the other hand, by the end of the 1940s, archaeologists such as A. Posnansky, J. C. Tello and A. Lipschutz in Bolivia, Peru and Chile, or J. Imbelloni in Argentina and A. Caso in Mexico had already carved a niche to study the archaeological remnants of "Ancient" cultures. Intricate iconographies, stone carved pieces, codices, and monumental urban centers constituted, to the eyes of indigenous peoples, empirical confirmation that something worthy and important belonged to their pasts and immediate lives. The nation-state would appropriate the honorable Indian past to graft it onto the re-creation of its "imagined community," but to the detriment of the actual presence of indigenous peoples. Left-wing political parties focused on the possibility of transforming the "indigenous masses" into revolutionary cadres, and/or potential members of the early industrial unions in urban and mining centers. Not only that, it was also clear that they, as indigenous peoples, were not part of the dialogue in designing or controlling their own cultural resources, as may have been the case for other forms of popular resistance. Indigenous ideologies and practices, such as the ayllu system in the Andean area, were accommodated to the aims of unionism, and Marxist doxa found its equivalent in indigenous social practices of communal life and utopian ideologies such as the "Return of the Inka" (Flores Galindo 1987).

Once this social process of re/membering started in different regions of indigenous Latin America during the 1940s, 1950s and 1960s, it slowly influenced the designing and implementation of various schools of anthropology, especially in the Andean countries and Mexico. Obviously, the very heavy Western weight of the anthropological discipline, with its traditions of both materialist and more metaphysical components, affected those indigenous peoples touched by the presence of national and foreign professionals doing research on indigenous peoples' materials. Issues of social inequality, cultural and racial discrimination, economic exploitation, and political oppression became the focus of indigenous intellectual activists engaged as assistants or "informants" in anthropological studies. Early indigenous intellectual leaders and activists were calling into question the aggressive impact of modernization, trying to understand this renewed confrontation with the nation-state, now allegedly postcolonial in its structure but discriminatory in its practices.

It is interesting to stress that since the 1940s the notorious Summer Institute of Linguistics (SIL) and its evangelical branch, the Wycliffe Bible Translators, were present and very active in most countries of Latin America. Their well-financed project of translating the Bible into indigenous languages was intended to promote the conversion and "salvation" of indigenous peoples' souls, in addition to easing their assimilation into a US version of Western modernity (Aaby and Hvalkof 1981; see also Harvey, this volume). Yet the real effects of this proposal could not be confined to inspiring "salvation" in another world, while suffering in this one. Instead it furthered legitimization of indigenous languages as valid systems of thought, even for theological, and broader political communication. In a twist of irony that did not escape the attention of the SIL evangelical directives, some of the most radical indigenous political leaders of the Amazon region had been trained as preachers by the Institute.

Parallel to this extensive process of carrying neocolonialist evangelical missions into indigenous communities, the 1960s and early 1970s also witnessed the incursion of the ecumenical movement of liberation theology, and the openness brought in by Vatican Council II (1962 to 1966) regarding other forms of conceptualizing the sacred, and alternative and interrelated forms of indigenous religious practices (G. Gutiérrez 1973). These Western Christian religious institutions of all shapes and forms can be considered responsible, intentionally or not, for the formation of "organic intellectuals" amidst the early manifestations of organized indigenous movements. As a result of the influence of liberation theology, which emphasized social rather than individual sin, priests and missionaries affected by the Christian–Marxist dialogue after the Second World War worked on securing leaders rather than converts among indigenous activists (Garaudy 1970). Some of the tools shared by these newly trained indigenous leaders were ethnographic methods, as well as anthropological theory that recentered traditional knowledge.

The political program of the new indigenous movements included demands concerning language, culture and religion, and history and ethnography, all organized along the central issue of decolonization. It was clear that, behind the native languages that have resisted forced "castellanization," and colonial languages in general, another indigenous view of history and indigenous culture was kept at the core of the collective memory and the indigenous project of autonomy and equality. Castellanization, being obliged to learn Spanish, could also be equated to another unidirectional concept in vogue at the time: acculturation. It denoted a hegemonic social practice that fuses together the notions of social change, progress, development, modernization and national integration without implementing the notion and practice of citizenship. Any resistance to acculturation could be interpreted by the national elites as conservative traditionalism or as an irrational attachment to archaic and obsolete cultural practices. This despite the fact that Cuban anthropologist Fernando Ortiz had already published his famous *Contrapunteo del tabaco y del azúcar* of 1940, where he formulates the notion of transculturations as the correct approach to address nonintrusive cultural changes and exchanges (Ortiz 2002). This was understood as a process in which something is always given in return for what one receives, a system of give and take, a term that does not contain the implication of one certain culture toward which the other must tend, but rather an exchange between two or more cultures cooperating to bring about a new reality (Malinowski 2002: 125).

These formative decades of indigenous anthropologies were accompanied by processes of ethnogenesis or the formation of "new," or in some cases reborn, indigenous ethnicities. This was the case, for example, of the Cocama and Cocamilla in the Peruvian Amazon, the Zenues in Córdoba, Venezuela, and some new "tribal" communities in northeastern Brazil. In most of these cases the interaction between anthropologically trained indigenous peoples and their communities gave rise to territorial demands and specific cultural rights based on collective claims of indigeneity re/membering after a process of cultural and historical introspection. In truth, some of these new claims of indigenous legitimacy became linked to a growing trend in agrarian legislation throughout Latin America which acknowledged specific land and territorial rights of indigenous communities.

We can tie the emergence of this activist indigenous anthropology led by a handful of native intellectuals to the parallel development of a series of formal and nonformal close conversations with non-indigenous anthropologists (see chapters by Barragán and Hale, this volume). In a sense, the creation of an indigenous anthropology could be seen as a journey into the soul of Autochthonous Peoples, armed with concrete proposals to ensure that cultural survival on their own autonomous terms could be a viable alternative to absolute mestizaje, which has been the accepted norm, discourse, or expectation, as an inescapable destiny for indigenous peoples. On the one hand, the nation-state's hegemonic message was that cultural resistance was irrelevant, for modernization would erase the remnants of the past. In this discourse, the past meant the presence of indigenous peoples with their languages, cultures, institutions, material assets, and spiritual legacy and an ethics respectful of nature. Still, modernization has been a distorted, uneven, partial, and discriminating social process linked to an unequal course of urban and rural industrialization (factories, mining, plantations, ranching), built, in most cases, on indigenous land and natural resources, and based on indigenous exploited labor. On the other hand, indigenous cultural resistance and alternative autonomy projects have always been the unconditional program present in the historical horizon of indigenous intellectuals, even more so when such resistance could be articulated in native languages and specific cultural values reconfigured by renewed self-analyses achieved in cooperation with non-indigenous anthropologists.

In the Andean countries and Mexico, indigenous anthropology was substantively redefined from the 1960s onward by the rural to urban migration, the shift from subsistence or community based agriculture to agribusiness and international labor markets, and, in the 1970s and 1980s, the increasing presence of indigenous peoples at university centers. Inspired by the written record left since the 16th century, indigenous peoples focused on reconstructing records, ideas and cultural values that have survived in the practices of concrete contemporary indigenous communities. The circulation of texts that were reintroduced and reinterpreted in various areas of the Americas – such as those by Huaman Puma, Santa Cruz Pachacuti, Joseph de Acosta, Cieza de León, and the *Relaciones geográficas de las Indias* for the Andean countries and Mexico; the *Chilam Balam*, the Annals of the Kakchiquels, and the *Popol Vuh*, for Guatemala; and the various codices for Mexico – opened the indigenous peoples' interest to document actual cultural practices that some non-indigenous anthropologists labeled "cultural continuity." By the early 1980s it was becoming evident in Peru, Bolivia, Ecuador, Colombia, Guatemala, and Mexico that indigenous traditional intellectuals as well as university trained indigenous ethnologists could master the interpretation of texts (in Latin alphabet, in hieroglyphic writing, or other forms of inscription found in ceramic, weaving or monumental works) much more efficiently that nonnative scholars. It would be presumptuous and offensive not to acknowledge the fundamental role played by indigenous intellectuals, either "traditional" or formed in urban universities, in the enormous development of modern ethnohistory, anthropology, archaeology, and linguistics of Latin America.

Part of the cultural recuperation of indigenous intellectual sovereignty, as a fundamental objective of indigenous peoples, has been staged by indigenous intellectuals and non-indigenous scholars in an uneven and contested multidisciplinary field where natives have been previously considered useful – but uneducated and ignorant – informants who could only provide raw material and data to be analyzed only by (white) anthropologists. In retrospect, the enormous development of Andean and Mesoamerican anthropology between 1950 and 1980 most likely could not have been achieved without the participation of numerous unnamed indigenous assistants. This hidden history of Latin American anthropology is finally emerging in the first decade of the third millennium in the works of indigenous scholars trained and now teaching in formal university programs where indigenous knowledges are imparted (Bartolomé 2003; R. Choque et al. 1992; Mamani 1988; Turpana 1987).

## HISTORY RECLAIMED

In the early 20th century a whole generation of indigenous intellectuals and activists became very closely linked to the anarchist political movement and early socialism brought to Latin America by Spanish and Italian anarchists and socialist immigrants. José Carlos Mariátegui, a Peruvian mestizo founder of the Socialist Party of Peru (later Communist Party), who had been exiled to Italy for a few years, addressed the question of indigenous land rights from a class analysis perspective. Mariátegui argued that a Peruvian socialist revolution could only be achieved with the full participation of the indigenous peoples as rural proletarian. Víctor Raúl Haya de la Torre, a member of the Peruvian criollo political elite, called attention to the contributions made by indigenous peoples to the Mexican Revolution and Sandinista's resistance to the US invasion of Nicaragua. In Colombia, the Páez leader Quintin Lame mobilized indigenous communities in collaboration with the Communist Party, by teaching them their "true" history and by stimulating their cultural pride. Quintin Lame considered native knowledge to be the single most important weapon in the fight to achieve liberation and autonomy. Before European-born ideas of social revolution ever came to indigenous America, other indigenous intellectuals and leaders had fought colonial oppression and advocated indigenous peoples' liberation from Spain and the creation of "Indian Kingdoms and Republics". For example, Juan Santos Atahuallpa (in 1742, in Peru's Amazon region and Central Andean region), Tupac Amaru II (in 1780–81, Southern Peru), Tupac Katari and his wife Bartolina Sisa (in 1780–81, Bolivia) and dozens of other revolutionary indigenous peoples in the Andes, Amazonia and Mesoamerica had severely destabilized the colonial establishment and awakened the ancient indigenous ideals of justice, freedom, and restored deities (Barabas 2002; Carmagnani 1988; Rappaport 1990; Taylor 1979; Varese 2002).

In the late 1960s and 1970s, a small number of revisionist versions of Andean history, emphasizing indigenous peoples' active participation in their own struggle for liberation, made their way through the traditionally conservative historiography, reaching indigenous intellectuals and opening new ways of indigenous historical thinking which allowed a repositioning of indigenous perspectives on their teachings, discourses and oral histories (Condarco 1965; Ossio 1973; Millones 1964; Murra 1975; Pease 1973; Piel 1973; Schaedel 1952; Varese 2002; Wachtel 1971). The thoughts and actions of these buried intellectuals and leaders were brought back to life by native intellectuals as inspirational, formative and ethical texts (Reinaga 1970). Parallel to these events and prompted by European authors (Mariscotti 1978), indigenous worldviews contained in manuscripts and lesser known texts were being validated as legitimate components of humanistic and social science scholarship. Historical facts, interpretations, and ideas that had been dismissed as not reliable enough by previous ideological and methodological limitations of the historical craft emerged now with force and impatience in indigenous documents and declarations: "Our imperative is to decolonize history," declared the new indigenous leaders (Bonfil Batalla 1981:38).

## THE AYMARA EXAMPLE

The Aymara of Bolivia constitute one of the most relevant cases of an indigenous nation's reappropriation of its own history. In the 1970s in Chuquiawu Marka, also known as City of La Paz, Bolivia, a group of Aymara students led by anthropologist Sylvia Rivera Cusicanqui founded the Taller de Historia Oral Andina (THOA, Workshop of Andean Oral History; see Barragán, this volume). THOA's objective was to rewrite the history of the Aymara peoples not as the history of an "Other," but rather as a history in which Aymara peoples figured as protagonists. THOA authors used both Aymara and Spanish language to render their accounts.[3] Placing Aymara people at the center of history had an important impact on the process of decolonization, the plight for indigenous peoples' rights, the movement toward self-determination, the emancipation of marginal groups, the strengthening of disenfranchised labor organizations, and the emancipation of indigenous women. Silvia Rivera Cusicanqui left THOA in the late 1980s. Her book *Oprimidos pero no vencidos* (1984) speaks about indigenous peoples' struggles from a peasant point of view. Her recent work on the plight of coca farmers and women's struggles in the city are also key texts in understanding the Andean peoples' process of decolonization.

Other key writings from THOA's indigenous scholars include Carlos Mamani Condori's *Los Aymara frente a la historia* (1992) and Maria Eugenia Choque's works promoting the return of peasants from a labor union oriented organization to the previous indigenous form of communal organization, the ayllu (Choque and Mamani Condori 1997, 2003). THOA's work includes the reinscription of once marginal people's voices emerging from the collective memory through a vital oral tradition. Following the strategy of THOA, a number of scholars later co-worked in association with Aymara people, as in the case of Alison Spedding and Abraham Colque for *Nosotros los yunqueños. Nanakax yunkas tuqinkiripxtw* (2003). In another important trend in Bolivia's indigenous intellectual movement and historiography, native Quechua and Aymara historians and social scientists are studying their counterparts in indigenous communities of the Bolivian Amazon.

## ASSERTING DIFFERENT VOICES IN THE ANDES

Conceptions of indigeneity rest upon different assumptions of cultural identity. Some people claim territory and place, others claim a linguistic-cultural affiliation, and still other groups claim practices of self-determination. Yet, there is another practice that has been at work since even before the beginning of the European invasion. Such a practice is not articulated in a manifesto, and nor does it work at the conscious level, for this conduct has more to do with a way of being Andean, a way of relating to one's own place, the cultural landscape, the environment including plants, animals, water, rocks, underworld, celestial sphere, and other peoples around us. This way of being

Andean is an aesthetic sensibility, a pan-Andean identity that rests upon behaviors emanating from indigenous knowledge and its practice. This knowledge is enunciated through and by language in the symbolic order, and by a material culture belonging now to a diverse people that includes indigenous and non-indigenous communities (Grillo Fernández 1998:128). Being Andean inhabits a different attitude to life and the whole environment, which is perceived and conceptualized as a living organism, thus radically differing from Euro-American culture. It is a difference established, maintained and diffused through Andean forms of signification in the material world of textiles, pottery, stonework, and agro-ecological and architectural landscaping; in the ritual world of dance, music, and performance, and, again, by the use and repro- duction of languages in the symbolic world. Among several languages still in use by millions along the Andes, this difference is marked by the Aymara and Quechua lan- guages which work as guarantors of difference and specific identities.

For Andean intellectuals and writers it is a difficult task to attempt translations of these fields of "indigenous anthropologies" since it seems that there are no equiva- lents in European languages. The best "explanation" would be to experience this attitude to life and the environment, and this way of being Andean, in everyday prac- tice. But again, this way of being is not suitable for an intellectual exercise, but is rather a way of being, knowing, relating, feeling, sensing, living. It is a living that does not favor individualities, but rather relations among all individuals and communities; it is a horizontal complementary structure devoid of hierarchies; it is a living that creates a Self/Other positioning in a nurturing way. It is a living that requires the honoring of the intangible, deities, nature, people, ancestors, animals, mountains, plants, water, rain, lightning, life and death. In sum, it is a whole learned cultural approach that is rooted in Andean forms of signification and Andean languages.

Tristan Platt in his essay "Entre Ch'axwa y Muxsa. Para una historia del pensami- ento politico Aymara" (1987) draws attention to the need for a new way of reading objects, myths, mountains, and legends as new cultural sources that will need to be placed in relation to the imagination of distinct ethnic groups in the Andes. This approach grows out of a need to adjust the use of analytic language to the represen- tational work of the collective memory as it is expressed by ritual, custom, legend and personal anecdote. The problem, observes Platt, occurs when the line blurs between the use of a verified document, or an ethnographic source, and a more creative use that would extend the reference of concepts to new fields and social phenomena. This problem emerges particularly when the researcher is thinking along the lines of his- torical processes, and wants to link them with Aymara analytic concepts. However, what is important in Platt's observations is that he sees the need for two approaches to anthropological work in the Andes: one is a documentary or ethnographic approach, and the second is a more creative approach, even if the difficulty lies in establishing criteria that would help judge any choice to be a legitimate Aymara approach. In addressing this difficulty, Platt acknowledges the importance of attempting to develop an Aymara anthropology.

> But this problem is related with another one: that which tries to establish and create an "Aymara anthropology" as an instrument of self-reflection, and at the same time as a tool to break the communicative fence, and to place oneself in contact with other American and global thinking traditions in conditions of a "balanced symmetry" (tinku). (Platt 1987:124, our translation)

This insight in Platt's work provides an objective that can be coupled with the epistemological disposition that we have described as Andean ("lo andino") to form a strategy for constituting a body of work in diverse fields as Aymara works, and in this case, as Aymara anthropologies. Hence, Aymara anthropologies partake of analytical categories inscribed in the Aymara language, its cultural context and oral traditions, and the documentary evidence disseminated throughout the Andean material world.

The Aymara people not only have different conceptions of space and time, but also, and more importantly, they have some specific linguistic markers for personal location and time orientation which are essential in the construction of discourse. In the grammar of the Aymara language there are *personal knowledge* categories and *impersonal knowledge* categories, which mark explicitly the position of the describer in time and space and in relation to the item being described. The language also implies the impossibility of a clear separation between deities–humanity–nature – the impossibility of knowledge that is not embodied – and a distinct notion of *man*, which is not severed from *woman*. All of these linguistic and cultural markers are needed to maintain a difference that speaks about the culture's values and priorities: a different conceptualization of *humans*, but also a very different and singular *relationship of humans to the land, to nature*, and *to beliefs*. All of these differences are in direct contrast to Euro-American notions of time, space and the *subject*.

Similarly, the notions and practice of place in the Andean cultures challenge Euro-American anthropologies. *Ayllu* and *pacha* (earth) are in dialogue and this conversation takes place in Quechua language (*Runasimi*). "The Pacha is the house of the ayllu and the ayllu is all that lives in the Pacha: the stars, the rocks, the plants, rivers, animals, human beings dead and alive, all is Pacha" (Valladolid 1998:57). The ayllu often has been portrayed, in a very reductive way, solely as an organizational social unit. However, the ayllu is also the place where a set of nonhierarchical relations of nurturing takes place involving deities, nature, and humanity. In this place of regeneration a conversation takes place among all members of the community, including animals, plants, rocks, water, and the land; all of which are treated as part of a family, all are relatives. In this family-conversation the deities (*huacas*) and humanity (*runa*) have equal footing, just as humanity and the natural world (*sallqa*) have equal footing, for woman/man is not the center of this world, nor is she/he above all other living organisms (Grillo Fernández 1998:89–123). Consequently: "In the *ayllu* the activity of its members is not modeled from the outside, it is not the product of a planning act that transcends it, but rather it is a result of the conversations" that take place in an atmosphere of profound equivalency among humans, deities and the natural world (Allen 2002; Rengifo 1998:89). This conversation, this dialogue, does not take place in a vacuum, nor does it take place in a form of intellectualism devoid of an engagement with all the constitutive parts of *Pacha*.

Thus, it is evident that a better approach to indigenous knowledge and indigenous anthropology in the Andes would be an integrated approach, where local knowledge is contingent, interrelated and working in tension with all forms of local life – people, animals, rocks and plants – and now also with other people's cultures and ways of life experienced by humans elsewhere, in a globalized context. Local knowledge now is increasingly becoming also a conversation with foreign forms of conceptualization and thinking.

## KNOWLEDGE AS RESISTANCE

Indigenous anthropologies inevitably answer to five centuries of colonial and neocolonial occupation and oppression of "Indian country" in the Americas. Any attempt to separate analytically indigenous intellectual endeavors and counterhegemonic constructions from indigenous peoples' reappropriation of their knowledge, their history, their collective identity, their intellectual sovereignty, and their ethnopolitical autonomy is bound to fail. Since the early 16th century invasion of their lands by European powers, the indigenous peoples have resisted colonial domination by preserving their forms of knowledge.

Dismemberment of civilization, utopia and secrecy marks the thoughts and historical memory of the indigenous peoples and constitutes the ideological and spiritual structure of their centuries-long cultural resistance, as well as of the cyclical manifestations of their ethnic nationalism. Throughout five centuries of colonial domination, indigenous peoples have repeatedly rebelled. The historiography of these rebellions has only recently begun to be written. Alicia Barabas (2002) analyzes 56 indigenous rebellions of messianic character for Mexico between the 16th and 20th centuries; Taylor (1979) studies 142 indigenous rebellions for a period of 131 years in only three regions of Mexico: Mexico Valley, Mixtec Highlands and the Oaxaca Valley. For a rewrite of the history of the indigenous people of the Andean and Mesoamerican regions see also Carmagnani 1988; Castillo Cárdenas 1987; Rappaport 1990; Stern 1987; Varese 1987, 2002; Wankar 1981.

This thick collective memory of opposition and resistance constitutes the foundation of indigenous social thought and its use of anthropology as a tool borrowed from the dominant society. As already pointed out by Bonfill Batalla (1981) more than 20 years ago, the indigenous liberation movement is centered around seven fundamental processes of cultural reclamation/recuperation that imply a profound knowledge of the historical relation between the colonial occupiers and the indigenous societies. *First*, at the forefront of its strategy of liberation the indigenous peoples put the reclaiming of time, the recuperation of their own history. *Second*, the recuperation of place/space/territory/lands and resources. *Third*, the recuperation of voice, language, and the right to use it creatively and politically. *Fourth*, the recuperation of knowledge, both indigenous and exogenous. *Fifth*, the recuperation of the "moral ecology," as a relation of stewardship, partnership and nurturing of "nature" and the world. *Sixth*, axiological recuperation as the reclaiming of the moral, ethical, spiritual primacy over materialism. Finally, the recuperation of the indigenous aesthetics: music, dances, performance, weaving, art, and literature.

Some of these processes of cultural recuperation and affirmations have resulted from a forthright collaborative alliance between indigenous intellectuals and anthropologists. They have included Guillermo Bonfil Batalla's creation, in the early 1980s, of the program of Indigenous Ethnolinguistics (a M.A. graduate program directed at members of indigenous communities located initially in Patzcuaro, Michoacán, later in Tlaxcala, and later in Mexico City). The program has awarded numerous M.A. degrees to indigenous intellectuals and activists, mostly from Mexico, but also from other countries. The intellectual production of the "etnolinguistas indígenas" has been an outstanding contribution to the development, in Mexico and other countries, of a corpus of materials for bilingual education and printed materials in indigenous languages. A certain number of these indigenous linguists have earned doctoral degrees in linguistics and anthropology (see Bartolomé 2003).

In the early 1980s, under the leadership of three Mexican anthropologists, Guillermo Bonfil Batalla, Rodolfo Stavenhagen and Leonel Durán, the Mexican government established a national program of Popular and Indigenous Cultures with the mandate of training members of indigenous communities and "mestizo" social scientists, humanists, and natural scientists in transcultural dialogue and the establishment of joint projects of culturally appropriate ethnic development. Some of the indigenous participants in this program have become active intellectuals, writers, and spokespersons of the indigenous autonomy movement in Mexico (Castellanos 1994, 2002, 2003).

Between 1969 and 1975 Peru witnessed a progressive governmental push to recognize Andean peasants' land rights, as well as the territorial claims of indigenous peoples of the Amazon region. (On Peruvian agrarian reform, see Seligmann, this volume.) The process of defining and titling indigenous territories in the Amazon required both a massive mobilization of the communities themselves and the self-training of leadership cadres knowledgeable and ethnically committed to their own peoples. The process and interaction of social scientists and Amazonian Natives around central issues of territoriality, management and governance generated intellectuals and activists who later organized themselves in national and international ethnopolitical organizations (Brysk 2000; Varese 1994).

There are many other Latin American examples of creative relations between indigenous peoples mobilized by national and international politics, and anthropologists who dedicated themselves to contributing in solidarity to indigenous struggles for autonomy. One of the most notable is the case of the Miskitu, Sumo, Rama and Creoles of Nicaragua before, during and after the Sandinista Revolution. The complex and conflictive struggle of the indigenous people to achieve autonomy within a socialist revolution which was, at least initially, insensitive toward ethnic claims of sovereignty required delicate collaborations between indigenous leaders and anthropologists that most of the time resulted in sophisticated indigenous cadres: indigenous anthropologies formed in the praxis rather than in the classroom. In the specific case of the Atlantic coast of Nicaragua, anthropologists and indigenous leaders worked together toward a political program that tended to minimize class contradictions while emphasizing ethnic-cultural commonalities (Hale 1994).

## History, Ecology, and Indigenous Resistance

Two disciplines seem to have demonstrated more sensibility than anthropology and other social sciences regarding the indigenous peoples' political emergence and their intelligentsia. On one hand, we are thinking of the historians who, by epistemological mandate and necessity of method, position themselves at a prudent distance from events and, as a consequence, perform a factual treatment that neither questions nor radically confronts the cultural – and therefore ethical – premises of the analyst. A great many of the works compiled by Steve J. Stern (1987) for the Andean case are illustrative in this respect, although it could be asked why Stern himself and several of the authors avoid the use of ethnic denominations or the terms "indigenous" or

"Indian," preferring that of generic *campesino/peasant*, when they refer to indigenous societies. With the possible exception of the central Andes, however, historians have, until recently, tended to favor the class based category of *campesino/peasant* over other factors of ethnicity or collective identity at secondary levels.[4]

On the other hand, we see the ecological approaches of a recent generation of biologists and eco-economists, especially in the case of studies on indigenous people in Mexico, who have known how to recount more sensitively the indigenous peoples' struggles to defend and preserve their autonomy, by focusing concretely on the indigenous resistance in the field of ethnic and ecological knowledge transformed into political strategies (Altieri, Anderson and Merrick 1987; Caballero and Mapes 1985; Posey 1984; Toledo 1978, 1980). We believe that the encounter between the bio-ecologists and the various manifestations of the culture of indigenous resistance, in its modest, daily strategies of use and defense of their territories and resources, as well as the direct verification of the overwhelming, ecocidal arrogance of the dominant societies have enabled them to see and understand the subtle and tenacious political quality of native peoples that has often escaped socio-anthropological attention. Finally, environmentalist concerns have become – perhaps only through imitative osmosis – part of the cultural interests of Latin America's middle classes and, as a consequence, it was to be expected that a rediscovery of the "noble savage" turned into "noble environmentalist" should have occurred sooner or later.

The paradox in this story is that, precisely during these last 30 years, anthropology in the metropolis (especially the US) has become involved increasingly in an effort to define ethnicity, and the formation, meaning and deployment of identity categories, especially in regard to the political and economic dimensions of social organization (Williams 1989). So, while anthropologists are trying to untangle a complex network of theoretical and methodological problems derived from the redefinition of the boundaries between the traditional areas of study (domestic units, rural community, indigenous region), and the redefinition of the analytical contexts (world economy and politics in interdependence with the rural campesino community), indigenous peoples in Latin America are once again fully entering the political scene as politically militant ethnic groups. Until recently, scholars working within the hegemonic social sciences of political science and sociology have been unwilling to accommodate the implications of indigenous political activism for their disciplinary practices. Yet anthropology, like all social sciences, is not only a field of study but also a field for social struggle (Bourdieu quoted in Kearney 1990). In their epistemological and methodological definitions, in the choice and definition of the "object" of study, in the paradigmatic construction of the "other," anthropologists, despite their best wishes, frequently remain tied to the hegemonic project – in the Gramscian sense of hegemony as struggle – of the class and ethnicity of which they are a part.

In July of 1990, the representatives of 120 Indian nations met in Quito to celebrate the continental meeting "500 Years of Indian Resistance." The Declaration of Quito begins with these words: "We the American Indians have never abandoned our constant fight against the conditions of oppression, discrimination, and exploitation that were imposed on us because of the European invasion of our ancestral territories." The meeting was held a few weeks after the conclusion of negotiations between the government and the Ecuadorian Indian organizations. These negotiations marked a truce in one of the strongest Latin America indigenous uprisings of the past few years.

According to independent analysts, it was the most important popular mobilization of the country's last decade (*Andean Report*, London, 1990). More than 100,000 indigenous people participated in a demonstration that lasted several weeks and kept the highways to Quito and other cities around the country closed to all access. Territorial recovery and control, self-determination, economic-political autonomy, and Indian self-government were the central demands of the uprising and were taken up again in the continental meeting.

Analyses of the long conclusions and resolutions of the meeting reveal that the political platforms of the organized indigenous peoples of the hemisphere are basically identical to the demands that have driven indigenous struggles during the last five centuries:

- Recovery and recuperation of the territories lost because of the colonial and national occupation.
- Defense and recuperation of the natural resources and the environment destroyed by mercantile exploitation.
- Right to maintain, reestablish and develop the indigenous economies based on community solidarity and principles of reciprocity.
- Respect for the sovereignty of indigenous nationalities, right to self-determination and political autonomy.
- Right to the full use and development of indigenous languages.
- Right to the use and development of one's own culture, forms of spirituality, scientific-intellectual development without oppressive and authoritarian interference of Christian evangelization and colonizing educational systems.

Organized indigenous peoples recognize that the struggle

> has acquired a new quality in recent times. This struggle is less and less isolated and more organized. Now we are fully conscious that our definitive liberation can only be expressed as the full exercise of our self-determination. Our unity is based on this fundamental right...without Indian self-government and without the control of our territories, there can be no autonomy...[In] our general struggle strategy [we seek] the full exercise of self-determination through the Indian peoples' own governments and the control of our territories...[for this] it is necessary to have an integral and in-depth transformation of the state and national society; that is, the creation of a new nation. (Declaration of Quito 1990)

The spiritual basis for the indigenous resistance, insurrection, and autonomous political projects are found in conceptions of humanity and nature that are essentially community oriented.

> We do not feel we are the owners of [nature]: it is our mother, not merchandise; it is an integral part of our lives; it is our past, present and future. We believe, in this sense, that what is human and the environment itself is not only valuable for our communities or for American Indian peoples. We believe that this way of life is an option, an alternative, a light for the peoples of the world, oppressed by a system sustained on domination over men, between peoples, on the domination of nature; a system where individuality comes first, where the rights of the people are empty declarations that are incoherent with that which is practiced...because, for the capitalist system, diversity, commons good, solidarity, autonomy and self-determination only represent obstacles to exercising imposition,

exploitation and domination....In light of these reflections...we wish to look at the history of our peoples...the history that intends to hide the invaders, despising and denying our cultures, treating them as archaic and backward, to justify the invasion, the genocide, the permanent pillaging over 500 years, and denying their historical responsibility. (Declaration of Quito, Resolutions:6)

The achievements of Quito 1990 must be seen as a continuation of the dialogues of the 1971 and 1977 Barbados meetings between Indians and committed anthropologists. The visible "object" of ethnography, the Indians of the Americas, answers back with full agency. The dialogue built in the Barbados meetings reached far. The object of research, at this point, cannot be disciplinary anymore: A new concretely *decolonizing* anthropology – holistic and interdisciplinary – creates the coming together of new forms of problematizing reality, but it is also committed to offer solutions to – rather than simply analyses of – given situations. Indeed the Barbados dialogues and the agency of indigenous peoples have very much been represented by a 21st century anthropology that has relinquished "studying" the Indians of the Americas. Self-reflection has become a necessary way to rethink human prejudice and Western intellectual prerogative. In a sense, indigenous peoples forced anthropologists to historicize, self-reflect and risk the comfort of writing the predicament of culture.

## THE DIALECTICS OF OPPOSITION: INDIGENOUS ANTHROPOLOGIES

The continental indigenous peoples resistance movement is disinterring its gods. It has done it over and over again in the last two decades: in Chiapas, Mexico (Zapatista Maya insurrection), in Bolivia (Cocaleros struggle, "water wars," general uprisings against neoliberalism), in Guatemala (Maya civil war resistance and postwar reconstruction), in Colombia (constitutional reforms, antiwar movement), in Chile (land recuperations), in Venezuela (political organization in support of social reforms). The movement is taking the utopian ideals out from the underground, from the secrecy to which they had been relegated during centuries of oppression. The spiritual sustenance for these political and cultural actions is centered on a moral system that favors the principles and norms of reciprocity above those of individual accumulation, and privileges an ecological concept of the cosmos and nature above the utilitarianism characteristic of European "modernity." This moral ecology grants to the collective and individual right to subsistence an essential, undeniable and nonnegotiable civilizing role. Rooting the indigenous cultures in a normative system that assumes reciprocity and sharing in the social and the ecological spheres as the central axis of the political-cultural platform, and project itself, reveals an idealist and – why not? – a utopian tone.

An alliance between *indigenous anthropologies* and their dissenting, contradictory and dialectical couple, *academic anthropology*, is not only possible but also inevitable. It implies a reappropriation of the political and cultural space by indigenous communities and intellectuals who were forced underground, and by the non-indigenous intellectuals and practitioners disillusioned by military authoritarianism, and experiencing skepticism and despair at given stages of Latin America's recent history. Such a process of cultural creation – and therefore political inventiveness – needs a strong belief in a future scenario in which diversity and the right to be different will be as important as the right to social equality and political justice. Last but not least, as was expected, the development of indigenous agency throughout the Americas makes us aware of the strong potential of the ecological, anthropological and indigenous philosophies and correlations that are leading indigenous peoples toward broader and more effective forms of participation in elected governments.

The December 2005 presidential elections of Evo Morales Ayma, the first Aymara elected to lead as head of the Bolivian state since its inception in 1825, is but a logical consequence of indigenous peoples' rethinking of politics and globalization while seeking self-determination. President Morales Ayma is calling for the total restructuring of the Bolivian state in a nation of indigenous majority. In times of neoliberalism and globalization that strongly recommend the shrinking of the state and the reduction of welfare and safety nets for the poor, the Aymara president calls for a reinvented state that delivers rather than abdicates its responsibility. To the globalizing forces and the inevitability of a highly interconnected world that places hardship on historically exploited peripheral areas, Aymara President Morales Ayma responds that the Indian country's riches of land, water, oil, natural gas, minerals, preserved forests, high levels of biodiversity, cultural diversity and millennial heritage of social organization will be the tools for defeating the never solved poverty of Bolivia and its indigenous peoples. Can we think of a better prospect for academic anthropology than to position itself on the side of these renewed indigenous anthropologies that are betting all their resources to make this world better than the one we found?

## NOTES

Chapter epigraph translated from Quechua to English by Guillermo Delgado-P. with Norma Klahn. The poem was originally titled "Huk Doctorkunaman Qayay" and published in Quechua in the *Suplemento Dominical* of *El Comercio* in Lima, July 17, 1966; reprinted in José María Arguedas, *Temblar/Katatay* (Lima: Editorial Ausonia, 1972), p. 50.

1 For this section on Huaman Puma de Ayala we draw on Rolena Adorno's excellent study (1988).
2 Max Weber, "Zwischenbetrachtung," 1915, republished in *Gesammelte Aufsatze zur Religionssoziologie*, vol. 1 (Tübingen: J. C. B. Mohr, 1988), p. 544, cited in Costa Lima 2003:42, our translation from Spanish.
3 Interestingly, this indigenous Latin American movement of historical recuperation was happening a few years earlier than the Subaltern Studies movement in South Asia (see Guha 1983), which has become the flagship of postcolonial analysis in English speaking academia. Two decades earlier, in 1968, Varese published a study on the campa-ashaninka peoples of eastern Peru (Varese 2002) in which the history of resistance to colonial invasion and domination is written from within the indigenous nation using "emic" or endogenous interpretive categories.
4 The Andean bibliography that bears witness to a greater sensibility of historians to the question of ethnicity and "Indianness" of the historical subject is relatively abundant. Suffice it to cite only a few of the most relevant texts: first, the foundation works of Murra (1975, 1978); Flores Galindo (1986, 1987); Ossio (1973); Pease (1973); and Stern (1987). For the case of the Andean jungle of Peru, see the study by Zarzar (1989) on the pan-Indian rebellion of Juan Santos Atahualpa in the 18th century, as well as the revision on the same insurrection by Stern (1987), and Varese's own work from some years ago (see now Varese 2002). For the case of Mesoamerica there are also important historical works in this line.

To cite only a few: Barabas (2002) has conducted a detailed and fundamental study of religious ethnohistory and anthropology of the Indian resistance movements in Mexico over four and a half centuries of colonial occupation; see also Carmagnani 1988; Farris 1984; Taylor 1972, 1979; Whitecotton 1977, among many others.

## REFERENCES

Aaby, P. and Hvalkof, Søren (1981) *Is God American? An Anthropological Perspective on the Missionary Work of the Summer Institute of Linguistics.* Copenhagen: International Working Group on Indigenous Affairs (IWGIA).

Acosta, L. (1972) Etnología y colonialismo. *Casa de las Américas* (Instituto Cubano del Libro, Havana) 12(71) (Mar.–Apr.):97–101.

Adorno, R. (1988) *Guaman Poma: Writing and Resistance in Colonial Peru.* Austin: University of Texas Press.

Allen, C. (2002[1988]) *The Hold Life Has: Coca and Cultural Identity in an Andean Community.* Washington, DC: Smithsonian Institution Press.

Altieri, M. A., Anderson, M. K., and Merrick, L. C. (1987) Peasant Agriculture and the Conservation of Crop and Wild Resources. *Conservation Biology* 1(1) (May):49–58.

Arguedas, J. M. (1941) *Yawar Fiesta.* Lima: Compañía de Impresiones y Publicidad. In English in Arguedas 1985.

Arguedas, J. M. (1950) La novela y el problema de la expresión literaria en el Perú. *Mar del Sur* 9:66–72. A revised version in English in Arguedas 1985.

Arguedas, J. M. (1968[1963]) *Las comunidades de España y del Perú.* Lima: Universidad Nacional Mayor de San Marcos, Biblioteca de Cultura Superior, Departamento de Publicaciones.

Arguedas, J. M. (1985) *Yawar Fiesta,* trans. Frances Horning Barraclough. Austin: University of Texas Press.

Barabas, A. (2002[1987]) *Utopías indias. Movimientos sociorreligiosos en México.* New edn with chapter added. Mexico City: Plaza y Valdes.

Bartolomé, M. A. (2003) Las palabras de los otros. La antropología escrita por indígenas en Oaxaca. *Cuadernos del Sur* 9(18):23–50.

Bonfil Batalla, G. (ed.) (1981) *Utopía y revolución. El pensamiento político contemporáneo de los indios en América Latina.* Mexico City: Editorial Nueva Imagen.

Bonfil Batalla, G. (1991) *Pensar nuestra cultura. Ensayos.* Mexico City: Alianza Editorial.

Brysk, A. (2000) *From Tribal Village to Global Village.* Stanford, California: Stanford University Press.

Caballero, Javier and Mapes, Cristina (1985) Gathering and Subsistence Patterns among the P'urepecha Indians of Mexico. *Journal of Ethnobiology* 5(1):31–47.

Carmagnani, M. (1988) *El regreso de los dioses.* Mexico City: Fondo de Cultura Económica.

Castellanos Martínez, J. (1994) *Cantares de los vientos primerizos. Wila che be ze lhao.* Mexico City: Editorial Diana.

Castellanos Martínez, J. (2002) *Relación de hazañas del hijo del relámpago. Da kebe nho seke gon ben xhi'ne guzio.* Oaxaca: Instituto Oaxaqueño de las Culturas.

Castellanos Martínez, J. (2003) *Diccionario zapoteco-español/español-zapoteco. Variante Xhon.* Oaxaca: Gobierno del Estado de Oaxaca, Secretaría de Asuntos Indígenas.

Castillo Cárdenas, G. (1987) *Liberation Theology from Below: The Life and Thought of Quintín Lamé.* Maryknoll, NY: Orbis.

Certeau, M. de (1976) Dans le silence d'une action discrète, la longue marche indienne. *La Lettre* (Paris) 188 (Apr.):14–15.

Choque, M. E. and Mamani Condori, C. (1997) *Inkan Amtawipa.* La Paz: THOA/Aruwiyiri.

Choque, M. E. and Mamani Condori, C. (2003) Reconstitución del ayllu y derechos de los pueblos indígenas. El movimiento indio en los Andes de Bolivia. In Esteban Ticona (ed), *Los Andes desde Los Andes* (pp. 147–170). La Paz: Ediciones Yachaywasi.

Choque, R., Soria Choque, V., Mamani, H., Ticona, E., Conde, R. et al. (1992) *Educación indígena. ¿Ciudadanía or colonización?* La Paz: THOA/Aruwiyiri.

CIPCA (Center for Research and Promotion of the Peasantry) (1976) *Los Aymaras dentro la sociedad boliviana.* La Paz: CIPCA.

Clastres, H. (1975) *La Terre sans mal. Le prophétism Tupí-Guaraní.* Paris: Seuil.

Condarco Morales, R. (1965) *Zárate, el temible Willka. Historia de la rebelión indígena de 1899.* La Paz: Burillo.

Costa Lima, L. (2003) La función social de la historia. ¿Cómo pensarla? *Historia y Grafía* 21(11):19–53.

Declaration of Quito (1990) Declaration of Quito. Indigenous Alliance of the Americas on 500 Years of Resistance. *SAIIC Newsletter* (Oakland, CA) 5(3–4):21.

Farriss, Nancy (1984) *Maya Society under Colonial Rule. The Collective Enterprise of Survival.* Princeton NJ: Princeton University Press.

Flores Galindo, A. (1986) *Europa y el país de los Incas. La utopía andina.* Lima: Instituto de Estudios Peruanos.

Flores Galindo, A. (1987) *Buscando un Inca. Identidad y utopía en los Andes.* Lima: Instituto de Apoyo Agrario.

Garaudy, R. (1970) *Marxism and the Twentieth Century.* London: Collins.

Grillo Fernández, E. (1998) Development of Cultural Affirmation in the Andes? In F. Apffel-Marglin (ed.), *The Spirit of Regeneration* (pp. 124–145). London: Zed Books.

Grünberg, G. (1979) *Indianidad y descolonización en América Latina (Documentos de la Segunda Reunión de Barbados).* Mexico City: Nueva Imagen.

Guha, R. (1983) *Elementary Aspects of Peasant Insurgency in Colonial India.* Delhi: Oxford University Press.

Gutiérrez, G. (1973) *A Theology of Liberation.* Maryknoll, NY: Orbis.

Hale, Charles R. (1994) *Resistance and Contradiction: Miskitu Indians and the Nicaraguan State, 1894–1987.* Stanford: Stanford University Press.

Kearney, M. (1990) Borders and Boundaries of State and Self at the End of the Empire. *Journal of Historical Sociology* 4(1):52–74.

Malinowski, Bronislaw (2002[1940]) Introducción. In Fernando Ortiz, *Contrapunteo del tabaco y del azúcar* (pp. 123–133). Madrid: Ediciones Cátedra.

Mamani, M. (1988) Agricultura a los 4000 metros. In Xavier Albó (ed.), *Raíces de América. El mundo Aymara* (pp. 75–131). Madrid: Alianza Editorial.

Mamani Condori, C. (1992) *Los Aymaras frente a la historia. Dos ensayos metodológicos.* Chukiyawu/La Paz: THOA/Aruwiyiri.

Mariscotti, A. M. (1978) *Pachamama Santa Tierra. Contribución al estudio de la religion autóctona en los andes centro-meridionales.* Indiana, supplement 8. Berlin: Iberoamerikanisches Institut.

Millones, Luis (1964) Un movimiento nativista del siglo XVI. El Taki Ongoy. *Revista Peruana de Cultura* 3 (Oct.):134–140.

Murra, J. V. (1975) *Formaciones políticas y económicas en el mundo andino.* Lima: Instituto de Estudios Peruanos.

Murra, J. V. (1978) *La organización económica del estado Inca.* Mexico City: Siglo XXI.

Nahmad Sitton, S. (1977) *Siete ensayos sobre indigenismo.* Mexico City: Instituto Nacional Indigenista.

Ortiz, Fernando (2002[1940]) *Contrapunteo cubano del tabaco y el azúcar.* Madrid: Ediciones Cátedra 2002.

Ossio, J. (ed.) (1973) *Ideología mesiánica en el mundo andino.* Lima: Edición de Ignacio Prado Pastor.

Pease, F. (1973) *El dios creador andino.* Lima: Mosca Azul.

Piel, J. (1973) Rebeliones agrarias y supervivencias coloniales en el Perú del siglo XIX. *Revista del Museo Nacional* (Lima) 39:301–314.

Platt, T. (1987) Entre Ch'axwa y Muxsa. Para una historia del pensamiento politico Aymara. In T. Bouysse-Cassagne et al. (eds), *Tres reflexiones sobre el pensamiento andino* (pp. 61–132). La Paz: Hisbol.

Posey, D. (1984) A Preliminary Report on Diversified Management of Tropical Forest by the Kayapó Indians of the Brazilian Amazon. In G. T. Prance and J. A. Kallumky (eds), *Ethnobotany in the Neotropics*, vol. 1: *Advances in Economic Botany* (pp. 112–126). New York: New York Botanical Gardens.

Rappaport, J. (1990) *The Politics of Memory: Native Historical Interpretation in the Colombian Andes*. Cambridge: Cambridge University Press.

Reinaga, F. (1970) *La revolución india*. La Paz: Burillo.

Rengifo Vásquez, G. (1998) The Ayllu. In F. Apffel-Marglin (ed.), *The Spirit of Regeneration* (pp. 89–123). London: Zed Books.

Rivera Cusicanqui, S. (1984) *Oprimidos pero no vencidos. Luchas del campesinado Aymara y Quichua, 1900–1980*. La Paz: Hisbol/CSUTCB.

Rodríguez, N. and Varese, S. (1981a) *El pensamiento indígena contemporáneo en América Latina*. Cuadernos de Información y Divulgación para Maestros Bilingües. Mexico City: SEP-DGEI.

Rodríguez, N. and Varese, S. (1981b) *Experiencias organizativas indígenas en América Latina*. Cuadernos de Información y Divulgación para Maestros Bilingües Mexico City: SEP-DGEI.

Schaedel, R. P. (1952) La representación de la muerte del Inka Atahuallpa en la fiesta de la Virgen de la Puerta en Otuzco [Perú]. *Escena, Órgano de la ENAE* 4(8):23–25.

Spedding, A. and Colque, A. (2003) *Nosotros los yunqueños. Nanakax yunkas tuqinkiripxtw*. La Paz: Editorial Mamahuaco/PIEB. An excerpt in English at www.bolivianstudies.org 4(2) (July–Aug. 2004).

Stern, S. (ed.) (1987) *Resistance, Rebellion, and Consciousness in the Andean Peasant World, 18th to 20th Century*. Madison: University of Wisconsin Press.

Taylor, W. B. (1972) *Landlords and Peasants in Colonial Oaxaca*. Stanford: Stanford University Press.

Taylor, W. B. (1979) *Drinking, Homicide, and Rebellion in Colonial Mexican Villages*. Stanford: Stanford University Press.

Téllez Ortega, J. (1987) La época de oro. In Carlos García Mora (ed.), *La antropología en México. Panorama histórico*, vol. 2: *Los hechos y los dichos (1880–1986)* (pp. 15–35). Mexico City: Instituto Nacional de Antropología e Historia.

Toledo, Víctor Manuel (1978) El uso múltiple de la selva bajo el conocimiento tradicional. *Biótica* (Mexico City) 3(11):85–101.

Toledo, Víctor Manuel (1980) La ecología del modo campesino de producción. *Antropología y Marxismo* (Mexico City), no. 3:35–55.

Turpana, A. (1987) *Narraciones populares del país Dule*. Mexico City: Factor Ediciones Literarias.

Valladolid Rivera, J. (1998) Andean Peasant Agriculture: Nurturing a Diversity of Life in the Chacra. In F. Apffel-Marglin (ed.), *The Spirit of Regeneration* (pp. 51–88). London: Zed Books.

Varese, S. (1977) Una dialéctica negada. Notas sobre la multietnicidad mexicana. *Revista Mexicana de Ciencias Políticas y Sociales* (UNAM, Mexico City) (Nueva época) 23 (Apr.–June):35–51.

Varese, S. (1978) Defender lo múltiple. Nota al indigenismo. *Nueva Antropología* (Mexico City) 9:33–47.

Varese, S. (1987) La cultura como recurso. El desafío de la educación indígena en el marco de un desarollo nacional autónomo. In Madeleine Zúñiga, Juan Ansión and Luis Cuevas (eds), *Educación en poblaciones indígenas, políticas y estrategias en América Latina*. Santiago: UNESCO/OREALC/Instituto Indigenista Interamericano.

Varese, S. (1994) Los Dioses enterrados. Política de la resistencia indígena. In Jacinto Arias Pérez (ed.), *Arreglo de los pueblos indios*. Bilingual edn (Tzeltal, pp. 403–432; Spanish, pp. 433–463). Tuxtla Gutiérez, Chiapas: Instituto Chiapaneco de Cultura.

Varese, S. (2002) *Salt of the Mountain: Campa Asháninka History and Resistance in the Peruvian Jungle*, trans. Susan Giersbach Rascón. Norman: University of Oklahoma Press. Spanish original, *La sal de los cerros*. Lima: Universidad Peruana de Ciencias y Tecnología, 1968.

Vargas Llosa, M. (1996) *La utopía arcaica. José María Arguedas y las ficciones del indigenismo*. Mexico City: Fondo de Cultura Económica.

Wachtel, N. (1971) *La Vision des vaincus*. Paris: Gallimard.

Wankar (1981) *Tawantinsuyu. Cinco siglos de guerra qheswaymara contra España*. Mexico City: Nueva Imagen.

Whitecotton, J. (1977) *The Zapotecs: Princes, Priests, and Peasants*. Norman: University of Oklahoma Press.

Williams, B. F. (1989) A Class Act: Anthropology and the Race to Nation across Ethnic Terrain. *Annual Review of Anthropology* 18 (Oct.):401–444.

Zarzar, A. (1989) *Apo Capac Huayna, Jesús Sacramentado. Mitto, utopía y milenarismo en el pensamiento de Juan Santos Atahualpa*. Lima: Ediciones Centro Amazónico de Antropología y Aplicación Práctica.

# 19 Afro-Latin American Peoples

*Jaime Arocha and*
*Adriana Maya*

The 12 million captives who were forcefully taken by Europeans from Africa to the Americas are responsible for the first global and massive process of cultural reinvention undertaken by humankind (Inikori 1998). In fact, during just a few decades of the 16th century, Wolof, Mande, Bijago, Bran, Zape and other people from the regions of Mali, Senegal, Gambia and Guinea, living within narrow margins of captivity, created techno-environmental, techno-economic, linguistic, social, political and symbolic prostheses which allowed them not only to survive forced deportation and enslavement in the New World, but to originate ingenious forms of resistance against loss of freedom, and in other cases to produce gold, silver, sugar and cattle surpluses for their captors. Later on, during the 17th century, and until the 1890s, other people from the valleys of the Congo, Niger, Volta and Cross rivers would replicate a cultural revolution whose analysis should have been paramount for the archaeological, ethno-historical and ethnological research that began to flourish during the first half of the 20th century.[1]

Despite the fact that scholarship on Afro-Latin Americans has reached unprecedented levels in the last ten years, specialized anthropological journals such as *Current Anthropology* or *American Anthropologist* still publish very few essays about those people's cultures, history and racial relationships, as compared to the number of articles on indigenous people of the same region. This asymmetry is consistent with the way in which the Spanish and the Portuguese treated people of African descent in their colonies. While, during the early 1500s, the European legal system defined Amerindians as human beings, and tried to protect them under their states' humanitarian institutions, the Black codes classified African captives as "merchandises," allowing torture as a means to control resistance (Friedemann and Arocha 1986:15–18). Official protection of these people was not fully ruled until the last decades of the 18th century (Arocha 1998b:382).

In terms of this unevenness, which is also reflected in the modern field of human rights, it could be said that perhaps Jean Stubbs and Pedro Pérez Sarduy were too optimistic when they chose the title *No Longer Invisible: Afro-Latin Americans Today* for the book they compiled with cases from Brazil, Colombia, Cuba, The Dominican Republic, Puerto Rico, Mexico, Nicaragua, Panama, Costa Rica, Belize, Honduras, Venezuela, Peru, Ecuador and Bolivia. In 1995, the nongovernmental organization Minority Rights Group published that work, acknowledging that Afro-Latin American ethnic identity and its historical visibility were part of the new generation of human rights recognized by the United Nations in 1992 (Minority Rights Group 1995). The volume corroborated what other analyses were saying, particularly since the 1980s: one of the main sources of racial discrimination and exclusion of people of African descent in Latin America and the Caribbean consists of the process by which their lives, contributions and needs are edited out from historical, aesthetic, political, social, health, educational, demographic and cultural narratives and records (Pérez Sarduy and Stubbs 1995:2, 3).

Social scientists bear responsibility for the persistence of these particular forms of discrimination. The case of Brazilian historian Gilberto Freyre is representative of the trend that became preponderant in Latin America during the first half of the 20th century. In 1930, he published *Casa grande e senzala*, reinforcing the myth of origin held by most Latin American nations. In this myth, Iberian institutions, including plantation slavery, are classified as benevolent in comparison to their Northern European counterparts. Their paternalistic nature allowed for mestizaje, which consists of multiple racial and cultural mixtures. Mestizaje, in turn, is said to have given origin to supposedly mobile and open societies, which in turn accounted for the consolidation of the so-called "racial democracy" (see Wade, this volume). This model was applied to explain, on the one hand, the emergence of syncretistic religions, such as the Cuban Santería and Brazilian Candomblé, both of which are said to mingle the Yoruba and Roman Catholic traditions. On the other hand, it was also utilized to elucidate how black people's blood diluted as it mixed with the Indians' and Europeans', therefore accounting for the apparent disappearance of men and women of African descent from the high Andes of Peru, Bolivia, Ecuador and Colombia, as well as from Argentina and Uruguay (Celestino 2004).

During the 1940s, anthropologists like Gonzalo Aguirre Beltrán (1946) in Mexico began to combat invisibility by publishing accounts of the contributions made by African descendants to the Mexican nation, and by describing the mechanisms by which they were denied labor rights, education and health care. A more radical point of view was forwarded by Afro-Brazilian thinker Abdías do Nascimento (1987), who claimed that, insofar as mestizaje emphasized the positive effects of whitening and dilution of Africanness, it constituted a form of genocide against black people. This critical perspective gained acceptance during the 1980s, influencing the present-day wave of affirmative action policies whose most prominent manifestation consists of the quota system for admission of Afro-Brazilian students in that country's universities (de Carvalho 2005).

In keeping with an ethical and political commitment against the pernicious effects of invisibility, in this chapter we explore recent anthropological work on Afro-Latin Americans, giving special emphasis to those populations whose territories connect the Andean mountain ranges of Colombia and Ecuador with the Caribbean Sea and the Pacific Ocean. We will refer to territories within which personal services, extraction of woods and pearls, and mining of gold and silver shaped both the trade and enslavement of African captives (Klein 1986:26–33; Sharp 1976). By contrast with sugar and tobacco plantations, gold mining settlements were rather small and highly dispersed along riversides (Whitten 1974:81–92). After the 1750s they started to receive small numbers of *bozales* (African-born captives), either because plantations in the Caribbean islands or in Brazil needed more forced laborers, or because locally born captives became available in slave markets such as that of Popayán (Klein 1986:36–37). North Atlantic scholars have generally been less interested in these more tenuous or clandestine traces of Africanness, focusing instead on the more explicit continuities between Yoruba, Kongo and Igbo religious expressions and the Santería, Palo de Monte and Abakuá secret societies in Cuba (Fernández and Porras 2003:27–28), Candomblé in Brazil, and voodoo in Haiti or Jamaica (de Carvalho 2004c:80–81; Verger 1993). Despite advances in studies about Latin America and the Caribbean, scholars in the North continue to associate indigenous America with Mexico and Peru, and Afro-America with Cuba and Brazil (e.g. Wolf and Hansen 1972; Winn 1995).

By and large, the reflections that follow refer to Afro-Colombians. However, most of the problems we will identify have or will apply to people of comparable ancestry from Ecuador, Panama and Venezuela. Our thoughts result from ethnohistorical and ethnographic studies about people of African descent who gave origin to diverse communities on the mainland and the islands of the Caribbean, as well as in the Andean river valleys and Pacific lowlands of Ecuador and Colombia. Today many of these people face opposing pressures produced by two seemingly contradictory processes set in motion by neoliberalism: the promotion and celebration of diversity and cultural patrimonies through cultural policies and constitutional reforms; and the weakening or removal of the national legal frameworks that safeguard ancestral ethnic territories and polymorphous systems of production.

As with other groups approached by anthropologists in Latin America, the study of Afro-Latin Americans must begin with a consideration of the national and international political context. Despite its recurrent genocides and ecocides, the modern eurocentric state persists in its utopia of productivity. Hence the present-day neoliberal interests in the wood, mineral, genetic, solar, radioactive and hydraulic resources of the lowlands of the Caribbean and the Pacific. Globalized geopolitical competition therefore explains why those people whose African forebears settled in these regions are either under surveillance by regular Colombian soldiers and policemen, or under fire from left-wing guerrillas or right-wing paramilitary squads, known as United Self-Defense Groups of Colombia (Autodefensas Unidas de Colombia, AUC). Members of the AUC are frequently denounced because of their association with regular Colombian soldiers and policemen (León 2004). Directly or indirectly, these and other armed actors foster or benefit from the private investment through which long-established multicrop sustainable agricultural systems have come to be replaced by monocrop industrialized cultivation of African oil palms, grasses to feed cattle, or plants for illicit use, mostly coca.

The government's commitment to monocropping is part of President Alvaro Uribe's goal to convert Colombia into a biodiesel power by increasing oil palm cultivation from 170,000 to 600,000 hectares by 2010, mostly in areas surrounding the ports of Guapi and Tumaco on the Pacific coast (*Diario del Sur* 2004; INCODER 2004; Presidencia de la República de Colombia 2005). Considering the surfaces to be cleared, in 2005 Congress approved the so-called Forestry Law separating land ownership from the ownership of trees, therefore effectively allowing lumbering corporations to bid for humid tropical forest resources that are (supposedly) protected either by international agreements, or by laws derived from the 1991 Colombian constitution. These laws legally recognize Amerindian and Afro-Colombian communal and collective territories, and lend legitimacy to these groups' calls for sustainable development (Foro Nacional Ambiental 2005).

Other new laws dealing with privatization of water sources and rural development have been denounced by human rights organizations because of their potential to facilitate legal appropriation of those lands now belonging to black and Indian communities that members of illegal groups began to control through extortion and threats (Camacho 2004; Flórez and Millán 2007:194–200; Molano 2004). The same humanitarian organizations object to the lack of concern by the executive branch and its supporters in Congress for the reparations required by ethnic victims of armed conflict. Hence the doubts cast upon the government's commitment to the ongoing peace process with the right-wing AUC according to the framework defined by Law 975 of 2005. After signing agreements to stop their military operations, make public confessions of their crimes and accept imprisonment while waiting for their convictions, several of these war lords either continued to manage their criminal structures from jail, or reoriented their strategies, while those paramilitaries who dissented from the peace process competed further to monopolize strategic regions like the Pacific (Comisión Nacional de Reparación y Reconciliación 2007). The executive argues that between 2005 and 2007 the paramilitaries ceased to exist. However, the first report filed by the Disarmament, Demobilization and Reincorporation team of the National Commission for Rehabilitation and Reconciliation expresses worry about emerging paramilitary groups who are mainly responsible for maintaining the steady flow of Afro-descendants who have been violently displaced from their ancestral domains since 1997. These people look for refuge in urban and metropolitan spaces, such as Cartagena, Medellín, Cali, Bogotá, Esmeraldas (Ecuador) and Jaqué (Panama) (*Cambio* 2001; Flórez and Millán 2007:21–38; Molano 2002).

Operation Genesis undertaken by the Colombian Army between January 24 and February 27, 1997 against a guerrilla front affiliated to the FARC was mostly responsible for the displacement of 15,000 Afro-Colombian peasants from the river valleys of Cacarica, Curvaradó, Jiguamindó, Domingodó, Truandó and Salaquí, tributaries of the lower Atrato river in the Pacific lowlands (Flórez and Millán 2007:204, 205). Community councils representing the communities of Cacarica and Truandó had recently signed land titles legitimizing their collective domain over their ancestral territories. Eight years later, in October 2005, several NGOs succeeded in repatriating some of these refugees. The people who returned to Curvaradó and Jiguamindó found that while they were away, several corporations had not only claimed 10,000 hectares of their collective territory, but planted them with oil palms (Flórez and Millán 2007:209, 214). The government argued that the titles obtained by the investors were legal, and that human rights activists were unjustly demonizing industrialized monocrop cultivation (*El Tiempo* 2005).

## MEMORY, CULTURE, TERRITORY

In 1625, Alonso de Sandoval, a Jesuit priest living in Cartagena, published *De instaurata aethiopum salute*, the first treatise with systematic information approaching ethnohistorical and ethnographic representations of the African captives whose descendants created the territories discussed in this chapter. After the publication of that monumental – and still understudied – text, several centuries would pass before another Jesuit priest, José Rafael Arboleda, and a black medical doctor, Manuel Zapata Olivella, published other nonpejorative studies of African retentions. Arboleda studied in Northwestern University with Melville Herskovits and searched for traces of Africanness in the Caribbean lowlands. Zapata, who was a self-educated novelist, developed a dissident theory of mestizaje based on fieldwork in the same area (Friedemann 1984b:544, 545). Rather than acclaiming racial and cultural mixtures for optimizing whitening, Zapata Olivella (1984) described mestizaje as the means for the propagation and persistence of Africanness among Amerindians and descendants of Europeans. On the first anniversary of his death, which occurred in November 2004, several African American scholars announced that his major work, *Changó, el gran putas*, would finally be translated into English.

Two other prominent Afro-Colombian anthropologists were Rogerio Velásquez and Aquiles Escalante. The former was educated and later taught at the National Ethnological Institute – which would later become the Colombian Institute of Anthropology and History (ICANH). Nonetheless, Velásquez was not permitted to publish his work in that institute's journal, the *Revista Colombiana de Anthropología* (Friedemann 1984b:545–549). His fine ethnographical pieces instead were published in the *Revista Colombiana del Folclor* – a fact which partially explains why his contributions remained dispersed, until 2000, when the ICANH published *Fragmentos de historia, etnografía y narraciones del Pacífico colombiano negro*. He is also well known for his novel *Memorias del odio* about how racism against blacks of the Choco fueled the uprising by intellectual Manuel Saturio Valencia, who was publicly executed in 1907 (Friedemann 1984b:547).

Aquiles Escalante also studied at the National Ethnological Institute and got his M.A. at Northwestern under the direction of Melville Herskovits (Friedemann 1984b:542, 554). Upon returning from the United States, Escalante began to work at the Universidad del Atlántico, where he founded the journal *Divulgaciones Etnológicas*, with emphasis on the Caribbean lowlands. There he published his pioneer fieldwork on Palenque de San Basilio, the village located near Cartagena, belonging to the group of maroon societies that began to flourish in the Caribbean lowlands from the second half of the 16th century. However, his best-known contribution is *El negro en Colombia*, published by the National University of Colombia in 1964, with a classical application of the "encounter model" developed by his North American professor during the 1930s and 1940s.[2]

The dialogues that these five seminal figures established between western, central western and central Africa and the northwest corner of South America nourished the work of Nina S. de Friedemann, perhaps the most influential and controversial figure in the anthropology of Afro-Colombia. After graduating in 1959 from the Colombian Institute of Anthropology, she began an intensive career, sustained until her death on October 29, 1998. Her ethnographic and ethnohistoric explorations took her to a variety of Afro-Colombian communities, beginning with those of the Afro-European Protestants of the Caribbean islands of San Andrés, Providencia and Santa Catalina (Friedemann 1964–65, 1967), and continuing with the artisan gold miners and agriculturalists of the Güelmambí, a river whose waters flow to the southern Pacific coast

(Friedemann 1971, 1984a). Together with photographer Richard Cross and linguist Carlos Patiño, she returned to the Caribbean mainland, to carry out fieldwork in the already mentioned Palenque de San Basilio, a community whose members speak a creole language derived from the Kikongo of central Africa, are organized in moieties and age groups known as *kuagros*, and celebrate the *lumbalú*, a set of funeral rituals akin to those practiced by Bantu people in the Congo river valley (Friedemann 1979; Friedemann and Patiño 1983). Those types of organizations seem to have predominated among African maroons whose settlements had mushroomed since the late 1500s along the low valleys of the Cauca and Magdalena rivers, in the Chota valley of Ecuador, and in the region of Barlovento in Venezuela. They began to decline in the mid-1700s (de Carvalho, Doria and Neves de Oliveira 1995:13–73; Friedemann and Patiño 1983).

In Palenque, Friedemann's attention was drawn to the persistence of African memories among the different dance groups who participate in the Carnival of Barranquilla (Friedemann 1985), a festival declared by UNESCO in 2003 as a cultural patrimony of humankind. During the 1980s, she returned to the Pacific coast to examine effects of multinational gold mining on artisan mining and multicrop cultivation (Friedemann and Arocha 1986:301–378; Friedemann 1989); craft manufacturing among communities which had suffered the effects of the tsunami of 1979 (Friedemann 1989); and the rites and myths around several Afro-American deities, such as the virgin of Atocha in Barbacoas, San Francis or *San Pacho* of Quibdó (behind whom the Yoruba orisha Orula hides), and Anancy the trickster, personified by a spider. Anancy stories were brought by Akan speaking people of Ghana and the Ivory Coast, and continue to be told in those African countries, as well as in many communities of the Caribbean and Pacific coasts (Friedemann and Vanín 1991; Friedemann 1995). Finally, during the 1990s, she published the journal *América Negra* to strengthen knowledge about the connections between Africa and the Americas and to improve South-to-South academic communications.

Throughout her career, Friedemann stressed the importance of studying the history and ethnology of western, central western and central Africa, as a means to better comprehend the societies formed by African captives and their descendants in the Americas. The Martinique poet Édouard Glissant (2002:16) maintains that those were the only humans who, by means of violence, were converted by Europeans into *naked migrants*. Hence the exceptional value of those African memories with which they arrived. Under the conditions of marginality and exclusion that characterized their lives, enslaved people reinterpreted and reconstructed the memories that would constitute their main resources for forging the mental, technological, social and symbolic prostheses necessary to rebuild their lives in the new ecosystems and societies to which they had been forced to adjust (Mintz and Price 1995). Traces of Africanness consist of those reinterpreted African memories, whose force has been hypothesized to correspond to the intensity of resistance against enslavement which captives and their descendants set into motion (Friedemann 1993; Maya 2005; Zapata 1984).

German linguist Ulrich Felischmann (1993) used the concept of *Afrogenesis* to describe how traces of Africanness come to animate Afro-American cultures. In Colombia, proponents of Afrogenesis also tend to hypothesize that after shipment from the ports of western and central Africa, captives neither ceased to reinterpret their memories to create new cultures, nor to resist enslavement (Maya 2005).

In reference to Cuba and Brazil, Andrews (2004:69–71, 73, 74) depicts the workings of *cabildos* and other mutual aid associations of people of African descent. During the 1820s and 1830s, they originated such Afro-American religions as Santería and Candomblé (within the Yoruba tradition), Abakuá (following beliefs held by the Igbo) and Palo Monte (recreating rituals practiced by Kongo, Ngola and Ki-kongo, among other ethnic groups of the Congo river basin belonging to the Bantu linguistic family). The cults multiplied the opportunities for underground gatherings of people of comparable origin. By sharing culture and language, members of these sects not only practiced solidarity, but formed pressure groups capable of controlling stevedores, artisans and other port and urban laborers who helped fuel the chain of rebellions that the book documents for the early 1800s. Resistance against loss of freedom accounts for the specificities of Afro-Latin American movements to claim those territories they consider ancestral, and their autonomy with respect to equivalent movements launched by indigenous people (Arocha 1998b). In reference to population surveys and censuses, Afrogenesis favors questions pertaining to cultural-historical identity over questions based on racial categories (Arocha et al. 2002).[3]

The opposite paradigm corresponds to the concept of *Eurogenesis* (or *Euroindogenesis*), in which black cultures are seen to have been constructed through a mixture of indigenous and European cultural repertoires. While advocates of such hybridizing models show interest in marooning and other forms of resistance against slavery, they may be trapped by stereotypes that depict captives, especially women, as docile subjects (Wade 1997:298–300). For example, advocates of this approach to cultural history emphasize the abolition of slavery in the 1850s as the most important milestone in the production of black culture. Furthermore, for some of them, black ethnicity only began to thrive after the constitutional reform processes of the 1990s, as a spin-off (or imitation) of the territorial claims voiced by indigenous peoples (Restrepo 2002; Cunin 2003:64–65; Hoffman 1999, 2002). Last but not least, with respect to population censuses and surveys, they give preference to racial categories over ethnicity (Urrea, Ramírez and Viáfara 2004).

Brazilian anthropologist and ethnomusicologist José Jorge de Carvalho is an advocate of Afrogenesis who focuses on the insertion or seclusion of people of African descent with respect to both global and local territorial, cultural, social and political scenarios. He coined the concept of *exophilia* (2004c:183) to describe the simultaneous processes of exclusion and inclusion to which people of African descent and their cultures are subjected. Corporations, nongovernmental organizations (NGOs) and cultural industries, including tourism, not only seem to accept, but also to applaud the Africanization of European and North American cultural repertoires. However, at the same time, people belonging to those institutions foster the annihilation of musical, religious and other Afro-American traditions by converting them into fetishes of exoticism and sensuality that circulate and are consumed within globalized spaces. They further contribute to the extinction of Africanness, on the one hand by decontextualizing, misinterpreting and trivializing ancestral and original meanings, which can be secret and sacred, and on the other hand, as has happened with the Afro-Brazilian sacred chants of the *congadas*, by copyrighting those patrimonies as if multinational corporations had created them (de Carvalho 2004a, 2004c). Last but not least, accounting for dark skin color and other corporal traits, the same agencies segregate the creators and keepers of those memories from the lives of their nations.

When Robert Jaulin (1970) first denounced ethnocide as the elimination of a particular people's culture, he insisted that its main feature was the denial of otherness. De Carvalho has built on this concept to argue that cultural annihilation can also come about through the seemingly "positive" celebration of cultural diversity. This paradoxical development also appears in the midst of other contradictory occurrences, including and especially the dismantling of the national legal structures that gave legitimacy to ancestral territories, and the armed conflicts that threaten to spread from Colombia to Ecuador, Panama, Venezuela, Peru and Brazil as a result of the US backed Plan Colombia and Andean Initiative (Bonilla 2004; Restrepo 2004).

## THE CULTURAL POLITICS OF NEOLIBERALISM

Beginning in the mid-1980s, several Latin American countries witnessed the rise of popular political or ethnic movements for territorial, sociocultural, economic and political rights. Activists in Nicaragua, Brazil, Colombia and Ecuador argued that the models under which Latin American nations had consolidated had failed (Barillas et al. 1989; Comisión de Estudios sobre la Violencia en Colombia 1987:105–133; Díaz 1989; Menezes 1989; Heredia 1989; Stavenhagen 1989; Wray 1989). Their strategies were based upon assimilation, and thus the effective exclusion of those who either could not integrate, or those who dared to defend their cultural and political autonomy vis-à-vis the nation-state. These activists seek to redefine nationhood and citizenship by claiming permanent rights to cultural diversity and ancestral communal territorial domains. During the late 1980s, beginning with Nicaragua and Brazil, and following with Colombia in the early 1990s, citizens voted for and approved new constitutions recognizing the multicultural and pluri-ethnic makeup of their societies (de Carvalho 2004b; Helg 2004; van Cott 2000).

In the case of Colombia, soon after July 8, 1991, when the new constitution was approved, the government of César Gaviria named the Special Commission for Black Communities with the purpose of changing transitory article 55 into what would become known as Law 70 of 1993. That law's main achievement was to recognize Afro-Colombians as an ethnic people (Vásquez 1995:13), and hence as subjects of those rights which Convention 169 of the International Labor Organization defined for indigenous and tribal peoples. In May 1991, a few months before the new National Constitution was signed, the Colombian Congress ratified ILO Convention 169, thereby granting it the status of a national law (Sánchez 2001:23). As a result, Afro-Colombian communities gained the means to demand state recognition of, and collective title to, their ancestral territories. The law also requires national and multinational corporations to consult with community leaders before exploring for oil or other minerals, or undertaking any development projects that could affect ancestral territories (Gaviria 2004; Vásquez 1995:17). On paper, Convention 169 also shields collectively held territories from land speculators or violent expropriation (Gaviria 2004; Vásquez 1995:15). In the context of ongoing violence and continuing seizures of land by members of paramilitary organizations, it is especially important that the Colombian government can now be held accountable for violations of those territories (Diócesis de Quibdó 2004).

This charge is particularly meaningful considering that between 1997 and 2004, community councils in the river valleys that flow to the Pacific coast were able to gain collective land titles to more than five million hectares. The success of this experiment also had to do with the recognition of new forms of democratic participation in the 1991 constitution. In a country where armed conflict has extended to most of its regions, it is very significant that such a wide-ranging agrarian reform process was attained by nonviolent legal means (Almario 2004). It is also meaningful that the different presidential administrations under which this process of ethnic tolerance has unfolded have not fully recognized its relevance and paradigmatic nature. Nor have they been able to curb the armed violence that undermines legal reordering of ancestral lands.

The Ecuadorian constitution of 1998 also opted for multiculturalism as the principle defining nationhood, and its articles 83 and 84 recognized Afro-Ecuadorians as ethnic people. Grassroots organizations have taken advantage of that political opening to launch a process of territorial redefinition comparable to the Afro-Colombian one. With respect to this challenge, a positive stimulus consists of the cultural and historical traditions that those people share on each side of the Ecuador–Colombia border. In his classic work on the Afro-Ecuadorian cultures of the Pacific coast, Norman Whitten (1974) notes the relevance of the marimba within secular and religious contexts. The marimba is a wooden xylophone whose ancestry in western and central Africa is not only morphological, but musical: descendants of enslaved people retained the peculiar western and central African procedures and scales necessary to tune the instrument (Miñana 1999). Later on, during the early 1980s, in a joint project with Jaime Arocha, Friedemann traced the intricate social networks through which Afro-Colombian fishermen from Tumaco constantly crossed the maritime boundaries to purchase outboard motors, spare parts and nylon strings for their nets. Indeed, Afro-Tumaqueños have responded to government neglect with threats of secession to Ecuador (Friedemann and Arocha 1986:301–378). Only the growth of armed conflict on the Colombian side has jeopardized those cultural, commercial and social exchanges.

Traditional polymorphous production systems have also disintegrated, however, compromising the Afro-Ecuadorians' well-being (Antón 2003). Looking for a way out of this predicament, the mayor of Esmeraldas activated international contacts to implement a complex development scheme, involving: (1) opening the Institute of Afro American Studies as a means to address the relative invisibility of Afro-Great Colombian studies; (2) the construction of a *marimbódromo* or large musical arena which would house marimba masters, schools and luthiers, and hosting an annual competition of marimba players from both sides of the border; (3) international sponsorship of archaeological projects on the Ecuadorian remains of the Tumaco-La Tolita cultural complex, including a five star hotel where visitors could consume both indigenous archaeological riches and Afro-Colombian and Afro-Ecuadorian culture – in addition to the tropical beaches of the area. In March 2004, three members of the scientific committee of UNESCO's Slave Route Project were invited to Esmeraldas to evaluate the proposal. To their surprise, besides the officials who had summoned them, the three experts met a group of North American potential investors. Therefore, they agreed to write a document protesting commodification of indigenous archaeological treasures and Afro-Ecuadorian ancestral patrimonies (personal communications by Miguel Barnet,[4] August 25, 2004, and Luz María Martínez Montiel,[5] August 23, 2004).

While the Ecuadorian initiative involves a local government, in Colombia the presidency itself took the lead role in delivering the documents required by UNESCO for classifying the linguistic, musical, social and religious repertoires of Palenque de San Basilio as intangible cultural patrimonies of humankind (Presidencia de la República de Colombia 2004) – a process that successfully concluded in late 2005. However, the excluding side of exophilia explicitly contradicts these types of proposals, as it is openly practiced by illegal armed groups. The left does not accept ethnic dissent, while the right promotes ethnic cleansing.

## LARGE-SCALE ENGINEERING PROJECTS, WAR, AND DISPLACEMENT

In addition to the armed conflict, Afro-Colombian territories are also threatened by the competition to monopolize the lowlands of the Colombo-Ecuadorian Pacific coast and the lowlands of the Caribbean. In the Amazon forests and the Orinoco floodplains, loose state controls allow local entrepreneurs supported by illegal armed groups to extract gold, oil, radioactive minerals and tropical biodiversity (de Rementería 2004). Exploitation of such resources ranks high among the priorities of the Free Trade Area of the Americas (ALCA) and the Free Trade Agreement (Tratado de Libre Comercio) (Flórez 2004). Therefore, planners are designing ambitious engineering projects to connect the plains of the Orinoco with the Caribbean lowlands, and the Amazon forests with the Pacific lowlands of Colombia and Ecuador (Acosta 2004; Antón 2004). Two of these projects should be mentioned here: a proposed new channel connecting the Caribbean Sea with the Pacific Ocean through the Truandó river, an affluent of the Atrato; and a line to pump natural gas from the Gulf of Maracaibo in Venezuela to the Bay of Tribugá on the Pacific coast.

As these forms of modernization advance, the war machines compete to monopolize the region. At least during the last 20 years, the Colombian Armed Revolutionary Forces (Fuerzas Armadas Revolucionarias de Colombia, FARC) have been in the middle and low parts of the Atrato river, while the National Liberation Army (Ejército de Liberación Nacional, ELN) was in the San Juan river. However, attacks on civilians occurred so infrequently that people felt that the war had not yet begun in the Chocó. However, when paramilitaries killed a peasant leader from the Baudó in May 1992, people sensed that deep changes were to come. In fact two years later a dissident group of the Popular Liberation Army (Ejército Popular de Liberación, EPL) appeared in the Baudó, taxing people and killing those peasant leaders who did not agree with them. By February 1995, we registered the first groups of internal refugees building what they thought would be temporary shelters in Quibdó. We tried to conduct a survey about the origins of these people and their reasons for leaving home. However, we could not perform this task after receiving several anonymous threats. Around July 1995, another insurgent guerrilla group, the Benkos Biojo, expelled the EPL dissidents. The winners practiced racial Afrocentrism, but they then had to face the Armed Revolutionary Indigenous Forces, a guerrilla group with an Indocentric ideology, which exclusively defended the interests of the indigenous people of the area. These two groups are together blamed for the insertion of paramilitary squads, whose threats and massacres cause further displacement.[6]

Public order also deteriorated in the rest of the Department. Massive displacements of peasants have occurred in the middle and lower Atrato, Truando, and

Bojayá rivers, as well as in the municipality of Juradó. While people argue that the proposed new channel is too costly, and that construction will take a long time to begin, land speculation had an early start, and has to be added to other features of the area which ease the export of cocaine and the importation of weapons. These include abundant waterways and well-hidden natural bays. Disputes over control over these resources explains the high frequency of armed confrontations. One of the most devastating occurred on December 11, 1999, when the town of Juradó was almost totally destroyed, and its inhabitants dispersed, looking for refuge and defense. Some of those who were displaced migrated to Jaqué in Panama, where they filed official claims against Panama after they were refused political asylum and mistreated as illegal invaders (*Cambio* 2001:35).

Another well-documented massacre occurred in the Cacarica river in February 27, 1997. Soon after the Genesis Operation already mentioned, a group of paramilitaries affiliated with the United Self-Defense Groups of Colombia (AUC) accused the peasants of being accomplices of the guerrillas (Flórez and Millán 2007:205). They carried out several public executions and forced others to leave their ancestral collective territories. A month later, we wrote a letter to President Samper protesting the forced exodus, demanding prompt reparation, and citing the fact that the community councils of the area were the first ones to sign collective titles granted by Ernesto Samper's own government (Arocha 1997). A month later, the Presidential Advisor for Displaced People answered the letter, assuring the signatories that the government was interested in defending those who had received their collective titles, and would offer warranties so that peasants could return soon (García 1997).

Between 2000 and 2001, different human rights nongovernmental organizations sponsored the formation of peace communities to guarantee the safe return of displaced persons. However, the government was expected to assume a firmer commitment to the future of these people, considering that the same self-defense organizations were responsible for new massacres and genocides of indigenous and Afro-Colombian people along the Yurumangui, Raposo and Naya rivers. A year later, the same armed groups were threatening to repeat their atrocities in the same communities (Comisión Intereclesial de Justicia y Paz 2004; US State Department 2002). Then, in May 2002, another genocide occurred in the town of Bellavista on the Bojayá river, where guerrillas affiliated to the FARC fired a gas cylinder rocket into a church where 150 people were looking for refuge from guerrillas and paramilitary fighting (Diócesis de Quibdó 2004).

Evidently, throughout these years a pattern has developed, consisting of the emergence of paramilitary groups as soon as members of community councils sign the documents granting them collective domain over the ancestral territories guaranteed by Law 70 of 1993. Let us take the case of the upper Baudo river valley. On May 21, 2001, Andres Pastrana, who at that time was the president of the country, intended to commemorate the 150th anniversary of the official abolition of slavery by delivering in person the collective title which had been issued by the Colombian Institute of Agrarian Reform. The celebration never took place due to activities of the same paramilitary squads (Diócesis de Quibdó 2004). The particular ferocity of these actions against indigenous and Afro-Colombian people moved Eduardo Pizarro (2001), who by then was exiled in the United States, to speculate that perhaps the Ku Klux Klan had served as an inspiration for the extreme forms of ethnic cleansing carried out by Colombian paramilitaries. Paramilitary combatants also systematically threaten to kill those who identify and recover the bodies of dead relatives and friends (Molano,

2002:81–82). For Pacific coast Afro-Colombians, the most important religious rituals are wakes and funerals. Therefore, being forbidden to sing their *alabaos*, or hymns of praise (Whitten 1974:203), to say farewell to their dead is like losing the reason to live (Arocha 1996, 2002).

A final consideration has to do with the perpetuation of war and its spread to other areas of the Andean-Caribbean region. Obeying mandates by successive US governments, Colombian policies against cultivation of coca and poppies include repression of peasant producers by state armed forces, and aerial spraying of chemical herbicides (Molano 2004). These practices have been shown to favor high prices for cocaine and heroin on the streets of New York (*Cambio* 2001:16–23), and hence the continual relocation of crops that are marketed for illicit use. Aerial spraying of coca plantations in the Department of Putumayo (Colombia) resulted in forced displacement of people toward Ecuador and the expansion of coca and poppy cultivation to other areas along the Pacific coast. Needless to say, these processes have had disastrous implications for collective territorial claims by Afro-Colombian community councils, many of whose members have been forcibly displaced. Comparable events have occurred near the border between the Department of Chocó and Panama, whose government – as noted previously – expelled several groups of Afro-Colombians who had been displaced by armed conflict.

Negotiations of Free Trade Agreements exclude subsidies paid by the US government to North American farmers (Molano 2004). Importation of these farmers' products will mean further bankruptcy of small peasant enterprises in the Andean-Caribbean region. This juncture implies two different options, both in favor of war. On the one hand, peasants can simply refrain from growing licit food crops and begin cultivating coca and poppies – the two crops that support illegal armies (de Rementería 2004). On the other hand, unemployment in rural zones will grow, thus optimizing recruitment options for illegal armed groups (Collier 2001).

## Cultural Maneuvers with Essences and Stereotypes

Afro-Latin Americans thus face not only growing armed confrontations, but also the practices implemented by cultural predators. Victims have responded by complex negotiations in their day-to-day existence. We have observed some of the spaces where recent migrants and violently displaced Afro-Colombians struggle to rebuild their lives. Research by the Afro-Colombian Studies Group of the National University of Colombia about recent migrants from the Pacific to Bogotá involve the following projects:

1   Socio-cultural and Demographic Study of Residents of African Descent in Bogotá, sponsored by Bogotá's Secretary of Government and the National University of Colombia;
2   Study of Interethnic Coexistence within the Educational System of Bogotá, funded by the Secretary of Education of Bogotá and the National University of Colombia;
3   Routes, Roots, Paths and Memories of Afro-Colombians in Bogotá, funded by the Research Directorate of the National University of Colombia;

4  Displaced Afro-Colombians in the Municipality of Soacha: Between Repatriation and Urban Insertion, sponsored by the Research Directorate of the National University of Colombia.

These studies show that many of those victims do not remain passive, even after receiving death threats, or after witnessing genocides and public executions. These are traumas comparable to the ones their ancestors experienced during the slave trade because of their capacity to profoundly disrupt the sense of self, as well as their relationships with their ancestral territories, and with their living or dead relatives.

Many of those people who were expelled from their lands had developed systems of production based on multicrop agriculture, artisanal gold mining, fishing, and shellfish collection (Arocha 1999b). In the meantime, women managed their own agriculture by building and maintaining *zoteas* next to their homes on riversides or beaches. *Zoteas* consist of wood platforms on which women place old and discarded kitchen pots, plastic containers or canoes (Arocha 1999a). With help from their children and husbands, they looked for ant hills in the forest and collected the little soil pellets that those insects leave at the entrance. After transporting that fertile soil, they placed it in the different containers and sowed food plants, herbs to season dishes or cure ailments, but especially the trees that would become *ombligos* or navels of newborns. Women plant the seeds of those trees after learning that they are pregnant. Little tree and belly grow at the same time, and the first one is transplanted with the placenta, when the mother gives birth. From thereon, she will teach her son or daughter to recognize that tree with the name of *mi ombligo* ("my bellybutton"), thus making it part of himself or herself.

These people might not have been rich, but they were autonomous. However, once in the city, those competences which integrated them with their forests and rivers seem useless. We have identified two distinct groups of recent migrants. The first consists of impoverished producers who began to arrive during the early 1990s, as modernization gathered force in the Pacific and polymorphous production began to collapse (Arocha 1999b). Generally, the second group is made up of violently displaced migrants, whose numbers became significant after 1995, when armed conflict thrived in the same region. In Bogotá and its surrounds both groups find more radio stations to listen to, more television channels to watch and more printed materials to see and read. Cultural industries construct and distribute stereotypes availing themselves of Afro-Colombian phenotypes, simplified cultural traits and ancestral traditions, among other raw materials. While those Afro-Colombians who settled in Bogotá before the 1990s may actually denounce the racist content of some of those stereotypes, recent migrants tend to accept them as avenues to insert themselves in urban labor markets. These maneuvers depend on culture, understanding it also as a "combative" source of identity consisting of "each society's reservoir of the best that has been known and thought" (Said 1994:xiii). Hence, handling of cultural essences and reinterpreted memories are also part of exercises by which people adjust their day-to-day behavior to the expectations that stereotypes create, and contribute to making those stereotypes even more exotic.

We have worked with two groups of impoverished producers. Most of them are young adult men and women who have left their children behind at their original homes with their mothers. Women work as maids and men as construction workers.

One group of these migrants come from Paimadó, near Quibdó, the capital of the Department of Chocó (Camargo 2002; de la Rosa and Moreno 2002), and another one from Boraudo, a small port village further north (Abello 2004). The former settled in Los Cerezos, a working class section toward the northwest, while the latter live in the Veinte de Julio, a more traditional working class neighborhood near downtown Bogotá. Both subgroups occupy small and crowded multifamily dwellings that face paved streets and where public services are reported as good.

Like others from the same regions (González 2002; Godoy 2002), these women manipulate two stereotypes around food: "Black women are good cooks" and "Black food tastes well and has aphrodisiac properties." Sticking to the first one has helped them to find part-time and full-time jobs as cooks in houses of rich people where having a black servant has become prestigious. The second label is partially responsible for the growing number of restaurants in Bogotá offering a tropical atmosphere and selling food from the Pacific.

Each year, before Christmas, black women living in those two neighborhoods return home, bringing electrical appliances, furniture, clothing and other expensive presents for their relatives and friends. Usually, they also take with them the umbilical cords of those babies who were born in Bogotá during that year, so that in their hometowns and with their mothers, they will be able to perform all the ceremonies around the newborn's umbilicus. In Bogotá, these women refrain from carrying out these rituals because of their semi-secret nature, and because the proper trees with which to establish spiritual kinship ties are not available. Something similar occurs with the dead, whose bodies are sent home so that the proper rituals can be performed.

Aside from forms of racial discrimination they had not suffered before, impoverished producers say they are not doing badly in their new milieu. In fact, they are even giving origin to a new form of territory, which includes the Colombian capital of Bogotá as part of their customary domains. Violently displaced migrants, on the other hand, do not do as well. They arrive in shantytowns such as the Heights of Cazuca in the industrial city of Soacha, which extends south of Bogotá. There one sees tiny, flat-roofed, brick houses built over superficial foundations, next to shacks made of cardboard and plastic sheets. Both of them cling to steep hills almost devoid of vegetation. Each year the heavy rains of October and November may sweep away two or three of these fragile homes. On top of the loose topsoil one sees dozens of black rubber hoses carrying water to black plastic tanks holding the 500 liters which are pumped only every 28 days. The myriad of pipes running along the ground grows as new settlers arrive and agree among themselves to purchase tubes and connectors, while requesting cisterns from the NGO Médecins sans Frontières (MSF). By contrast with this informal or unofficial nongovernmental water supply system, every dwelling place has its respective gauge to measure electricity consumption. To the recently privatized Bogotá Electric Company, it is important to register a new house, to install the corresponding measuring device, and to begin charging for every watt used.

Autonomy gives way to dependence as some people learn how to beg for money, or to apply for humanitarian aid and low-skilled, low-paying jobs such as bricklaying, cooking, cleaning or unloading trucks in the nearby wholesale vegetable market. On average, these Afro-Colombian women and men earn 25 percent less than the minimum daily wage of Col. $13,000 (US$5), and they cannot expect to receive social security or any other legal fringe benefits. Yet they continue to struggle for a better life.

Samuel Pardo, for example, is a 35-year-old man who, in 1991, received threats against his life and had to leave his community on the Atrato river. Accepting that, for many people, "Black men are good soccer players," he opened a soccer school in Soacha and was able to recruit a good number of black and non-black students. Not only because he kept some youngsters off the streets of a neighborhood full of violent gangs, but because of his creativity, several foreign embassies and NGOs have supported his effort, while the private business sector awarded him a prize for his entrepreneurial success. He used the money to expand his school, and later on, holding on to the stereotype that "Blacks are good performers," he began to offer lessons on traditional music from the Chocó. However, some of his students also introduced modern contemporary Afro-American beats such as hip hop, reggae and reggaetón. This mixture of traditional and contemporary musical expressions, with the dancers' exaggerated sensual movements, brought more success to the troop. Some upper class high school students were so impressed by the ensemble's performances that they decided to become its agents and began to raise funds for an upcoming international tour.

Other Afro-Colombians who play with stereotypes and essences are barbers and hair stylists (Vargas 2003), street vendors of tropical fruits (Meza 2002), artisans, *santeros* or priests of Santería, the Afro-Cuban religion, and Roman Catholic priests. The last two religious officers have developed controversial innovations. On the one hand, considering that the sacred cowry shells used in divination ceremonies are not easily available in Bogotá or are too expensive, santeros have replaced them with soda bottle caps, which they bend to imitate the folds of the original shells (Velasco 2003). On the other hand, Catholic priests belonging to the Commission of Afro-Colombian Religious Life are introducing variations to their masses to bring them into line with the challenges of increasing racial discrimination, war and violent displacement (Quintero 2004). One of the essences to which they have appealed is "traditional African clothing." Thus, wide tunics made with colorful fabrics and hats of the same material are replacing traditional Roman Catholic chasubles. Another is percussion music. A marimba ensemble plays rhythms that became popular during the feasts that people from Quibdó celebrate in October to honor Saint Francis or *San Pacho*, their patron saint. Because the original words of these songs are highly erotic, the priests replace them in the mass with those of sacred chants. A dozen youngsters wearing "typical" attires from the Pacific form two rows of dancers who accompany the priests in processions from the entrance of the temple to the altar. Once the celebrant finishes dancing around the altar holding the Bible above his head, he offers his sermon. Dancers then approach him, bringing wine and bread, as well as more unorthodox offerings such as flowers and a wooden canoe paddle, which is an important symbol from the rivers flowing to the Pacific. The priest closes the mass by reciting, "Bless us God of life who is Father, Mother, Son and Holy Spirit." This change in liturgy not only responds to gender consciousness, but to a desire to Africanize Catholicism by introducing gender dualism, as it appears in the "pataquíes" or narratives about the different roads taken by the orishas (Arce and Ferrer 2002:265).

Therefore, in the face of dismantled traditional production systems and war, and in order to compensate for the negative effects of migration and violent displacement, Afro-Colombians seem to be making creative uses of stereotypes and essences.

The question, however, is how they will manage to avoid being trapped by them, and hence barred from having access to other work and social options that require specialized skills and higher education. This problem is worth reflecting on because, during Uribe's government, we have identified a true ethnoboom around Afro-Colombian music, food, hairstyles and body aesthetics. Both the official and the private sectors sponsor this hyperpromotion of black cultural patrimonies, thus extending a veil over the development of policies that violate or impede implementation of the legal instruments provided for in the 1991 constitution to combat racism and intolerance (Arocha 2006).

## ACCOUNTING FOR AFRO-COLOMBIAN PEOPLE

President Andres Pastrana's term lasted from 1998 until 2002. During those years, Law 70 (passed in 1993) began to be applied to regions outside the Pacific coast. People of African descent in the Caribbean lowlands began to file claims for communal ownership, and Afro-Colombians in Bogotá and other major cities set in motion consulting commissions provided for in Law 70. However, experts and policy-makers knew little about the total numbers of Afro-Colombians, their regional distribution and population movements. These data became indispensable for claiming rights molded by the ethnic past, as recognized by the 1991 Colombian National Constitution. Therefore, for the first time, the 1993 national population census asked for a person's ethnic affiliation, origins and social trajectory. While indigenous people knew how to answer those questions either by saying how they called themselves or how other people called them, and how their genesis was portrayed by their myths, Afro-Colombians did not or could not. This situation has several causes: On the one hand, with independence from Spain, the terms that Spaniards invented to name people of African descent disappeared. On the other hand, until the 1990s social scientists had barely studied the Afro-Colombians' past and cultures. As a result, neither experts nor grassroots organizers have access to a recorded corpus of origin stories and myths, such as those on which indigenous organizations routinely draw (Rappaport 2005). Indeed surveyors' inquiries regarding Afro-Colombians' ethnic affiliations were greeted with confusion and surprise. Consequently, results consisted of negligible population figures and percentages, and confusing migration patterns (Arocha et al. 2002:26–33).

Since then, there has been much debate concerning the use of racial versus ethnic categories in the counting of those considered as ethnic "minorities." Between 1998 and 2000, with the financial support of national and international institutions, and both regional and local governments, social scientists from the University of the Valle (Universidad del Valle) and the National University of Colombia began to design and implement statistical studies to learn when and how many people of African descent had immigrated to the cities of Cali and Bogotá, where they lived and worked, and if they had experienced discrimination. While the first team leaned toward Eurogenesis and racial indicators, the second identified with Afrogenesis and questions about ethnic identity. However, differences were not openly confronted until 2001, when experts from University of the Valle analyzed Stage 110 of the National Home Survey, which the National Department of Statistics (DANE) carried out throughout 13 metropolitan areas of the country. The University of the Valle team applauded the

methodology employed by the DANE. Surveyors requested that people being interviewed identify with one of the phenotypes portrayed by a set of four photographs of
"black," "mulatto," "mestizo," and "white" young people very well dressed, perhaps
employed and well educated (Urrea, Ramírez and Viáfara 2004:219). These experts
maintained that the methodology offered the most accurate results so far, and proposed applying it to the upcoming national population census, considering that in
reference to Afro-Colombians "no national feelings of shared ethnic membership are
freely expressed by significant groups of the population" (2004:217).

There are disagreements with that perspective. On the one hand, it leaves ethical
worries unanswered. The International Labor Organization's Agreement 169, which
the Colombian Congress endorsed and thus converted into Colombian national law,
requires that population surveys specify ethnic affiliation, and not racial type, and that
in cases of doubt, other members of the same ethnic community be consulted about
specific choices (Chang et al. 2002). On the other hand, our own study showed that
Afro-Colombians not only shared ethnic affiliations, but public consciousness about
them. Again, the problem had to do with the lack of scholarly research on Afro-
Colombians. In the course of our study we found that people interviewed employed
ethnic denominations about which some scholars had spoken, such as *libres* (free people) and *renacientes* (reborn people), and other terms that were emerging within the
new urban contexts, such as *afro* and *niche*, while at the same time denominations
derived from the person's place of birth were also gaining acceptance, especially as
people from the same town began to change the clusters they formed into communities explicitly sharing origins, history and symbols. An additional criticism has to do
with the limitations of those instruments in accounting for people like the so-called
*culimochos* of the south Pacific. While their phenotypes fluctuate between what people
call "white" and "mestizo," they openly claim affiliation with Afro-American cultures
(Rodríguez 2001). Last but not least, our own survey asked about ethnic affiliations,
and produced accurate results (Arocha et al., 2002:42–45). Careful training of surveyors on matters of Afro-Colombian culture and history must also be covered when
counting people who belong to ethnic minorities.

Notwithstanding the relevance of this discussion, the three studies discussed here
coincided in that people of African descent faced increasing forms of discrimination in
all metropolitan areas of Colombia. Racism at the workplace, lower income due to
skin color, and restricted access to public services, especially education, were not only
rampant, but showed signs of future deterioration. Hence the relevance of the National
Population Census, scheduled for May 2005. The National Department of Statistics
created a special unit to address this matter. It sponsored meetings with representatives of the grass roots, scholars and policy-makers in order to address the question
about counting Afro-Colombian people. Until September 2004, the proposed survey
forms emphasized questions on ethnicity, to be double-checked by means of questions on race. However, these inquiries were eliminated from proposed census forms
after Carlos Caballero, the Department's director, resigned. President Uribe's secretary banned a press conference by Caballero on recent statistics on violence. Numbers
showed that effects of the government's antiterrorist program, known as Democratic
Security, did not measure up to expectations, in spite of restrictions on civil liberties
(IEPRI 2004). Soon after the new director Ernesto Rojas was named, he made public
a new questionnaire which seemed intended more to establish domestic surveillance

than to find out what population changes had occurred as a result of the war. Discussions about how to count Afro-Colombians became irrelevant because all the sections from the previous forms disappeared. Grassroots organizers and scholars denounced yet another strategy to perpetuate the invisibility of Afro-Colombians (Mosquera 2004).

Nonetheless, these people succeeded in their claims, and the National Statistics Department included the question: "according either to your physical features, to your origin or culture, you are [ ... ] Black, Mulato, Zambo, Afro-Colombian, a person of African descent, Palenquero [from Palenque de San Basilio], o Raizal [from San Andrés, Providencia or Santa Catalina]."[7] However, when the surveys began, people found that there were two types of questionnaire to be applied at random, according to the instructions appearing on the handheld digital screens of each surveyor: a short one, asking for name, sex, age, address and foods taken during the last 48 hours; and a long one, which included the questions on racial and ethnic identities. Leaders of Afro-Colombian organizations were recruited to monitor census data gathering. Some of them reported that in spite of training sessions and the TV educational advertisement shown by the main channels from October 2005 (CNTV 2005), most of the interviewers' training on how to inquire about matters of ethnic and racial identity left much to be desired. Indeed, some interviewees still had trouble understanding words like *zambo* and *afrodescendiente*, while others were reluctant to call themselves *negros* or *negras* (personal communications, Rudecindo Castro, January 20, 2006, and Gererdo Martínez, February 1, 2006). These monitors regretted that the words *moreno* and *morena* were excluded, and reported that districts with large Afro-Colombian populations were yielding low numbers of black people. A new stage of the process began in January 2006, to include the rural areas of Afro-Colombia. Nonetheless, the monitors already mentioned remained highly skeptical.

## Dismantled Afro-Colombian Ethno-Education

One of the first clues about the counter-reform which the administration of Alvaro Uribe intended to initiate was the objection that the Minister of Education raised in reference to the ethnic character of Afro-Colombians. In fact, she officially addressed the Center for Social Studies of the National University of Colombia requesting an informed concept on the definition of ethnic minorities, taking into account that black people amounted to 26 percent of the country's population. The Center's answer was based on the thesis developed by the NGO Minorities Rights Group: Ethnic minority is defined by its exclusion from the power structure, and not by demography alone (Malik 2002). The rest of the concept was about the specificities of Afro-Colombian cultures, as well as their African roots.

It seems that the minister did not accept that concept and proceeded to close the Division of Afro-Colombian Education and to postpone indefinitely the publication of the first Ethnographic Atlas of Afro-Colombia, and to make it available through the webpage of the ministry.[8] These two innovations had to do with the implementation of the Afro-Colombian Studies Program which Law 70 of 1993 required for the entire school system. The program had three main purposes: (1) to make Afro-Colombian history and culture visible; (2) to increase levels of ethnic tolerance in most national and local spaces; and (3) to supply the high quality teaching materials necessary to implement the Afro-Colombian Studies Program. Those materials have been almost unavailable as a consequence of scholarly disdain for communities of African descent.

The Atlas had begun to be prepared in 2002. Adriana Maya, project coordinator, formed a team of highly recognized experts on the contributions made by people of African descent to the symbolic, spiritual, aesthetic, environmental, and sports repertoires of Colombia. The Atlas also includes digitalized colonial maps of Africa and the New Granada, as well as plates from the late 18th century Botanical Expedition and the mid 19th century Chorographic Commission. These illustrations were complemented by media and documentary photographs. The project also called for distribution of the Atlas to all schools in the country, and especially to urban schools, where the number of Afro-Colombia students had been increasing due to forced displacement; leading in some cases to rising interethnic tensions.

Our attempt to help to counterbalance official neglect toward the Afro-Colombian Studies Program consists of an intensive course we have been offering to elementary and high school teachers of public schools in Bogotá since 2004. We have named it "Elegguá and the Roads of Tolerance." It focuses on the ethnic origins of Afro-Colombians, on the cultures and societies created here by African captives and their descendants, basing themselves on their memories and on their struggles for freedom, and on studying invisibility and stereotyping as highly persisting forms of racism. Emphasis is also placed on the ethnography of their own schools. We have found that our students/teachers set in motion pedagogical practices capable of eroding invisibility, at the cost of reinforcing stereotyping. This paradox speaks about the challenges involved by the process of overcoming four centuries of indoctrination in favor of "white" superiority. It also means that it is necessary to open more spaces for discussion, bibliographical exchange and follow-up procedures (Arocha et al. 2007). However, structural changes will only come about with the creation of institutes on Afro-Colombian studies by the country's whole university system, a task which perhaps will be easier now with the marketing boom of African Diaspora studies (Lao-Montes 2007:309).

## CAN EXOPHILIA BE CHECKED?

Invisibility, as a form of pernicious discrimination against Afro-Latin Americans, feeds a distorted anthropological perspective on the whole continent. However, it is also a source of low levels of self-knowledge and esteem. In 1999, when our research team surveyed a representative sample of Afro-Colombian homes, it found that more than 80 percent of those interviewed did not know anything about Law 70, the mechanisms of participatory democracy it introduced, or the newly founded Chair on Afro-Colombian Studies (Arocha et al. 2002:68, 69). Five years later, another team affiliated to the same group repeated some of these same questions, along with others about territorial rights, to a small sample of refugees. The former tendencies were confirmed, causing concern in that most of those interviewed came from the middle course of the Atrato river, which is the scene of the widest ranging collective titling project since the approval of Law 70 in 1993 (Sarmiento and Torres 2006).

The breach between the achievements of Afro-Colombians in the legal arena and popular knowledge and appropriation of the new rights is consistent with "exophilia" and the contradictory policies developed to implement the 1991 constitutional reform. It also resonates with developments in other Latin American countries where multiculturalism has been embraced as official "policy" (de Carvalho 2004b; Hale 2005; Sieder 2004). As we have shown, while governmental guidelines and practices are increasingly timid in reference to ethnic inclusion, environmental sustainability and participatory democracy, they are firmly supportive of unchecked infrastructural modernization, economic opening, "free trade," and cultural industries that convert ethnic patrimonies into merchandise for globalized consumption. We cannot deny that those policies have attempted to safeguard Afro-Colombian cultural patrimonies, such as those of the Carnival of Barranquilla and the language and symbolic capital of Palenque de San Basilio. However, at the same time, they have weakened the structural basis for full ethnic inclusion by neglecting (1) the technological, economic and legitimate military instruments to defend and consolidate those Afro-Colombian territories which have taken shape as a result of the collective land titling provided for by Law 70; (2) the educational programs which Colombians in general, and Afro-Colombians in particular, will require if they are to understand fully the implications for their lives of the changes introduced in 1991; and (3) the means to comprehend how Afro-Colombian traditional or polymorphous systems of production have reached environmental sustainability, and how they might serve as viable alternatives to monocropping of oil palms, grasses, coca leaves and opium poppies.

Last but not least, exophilia weakened the potential in the Colombian constitutional reform to impede the propagation of armed conflict. Without the necessary means to strengthen ancestral territories and sustainable management systems, the Colombian government can only give lip service to ethnic inclusion and apply forms of cosmetic multiculturalism. One way to minimize the chances of ethnic annihilation by means of exophilia consists in supporting the creative cultural maneuvers through which Afro-Colombians have remade their lives following the disintegration of their traditional production systems, and their forced displacement from ancestral territories. Another way to combat ethnocide is the continuous pressure that – despite threats and assassinations – Afro-Colombian organizations exert in favor of full implementation of collective land titling processes and the Afro-Colombian studies program. Finally, a third method – which has flourished in relationship to indigenous peoples – is to build international solidarity with Afro-Latin American communities through the work of committed scholars and human rights organizations. We hope that this publication will contribute to strengthening awareness of Afro-Latin American problems, and their centrality to anthropological discussions of ethnicity, rights and political activism.

## NOTES

1   This segment is based on Mintz and Price (1995). However, the definition of culture as a set of prostheses whose design, testing, use, transmission and replacement depend on learning and symbols is ours.

2   The encounter model "posits the existence of two 'cultures,' one African and one European, which are brought into contact in the New World by white colonists and black slaves. [It ... ]

requires that the researcher choose between two neat but questionable 'explanations' of the African side of the equation [ ... ] (1) [ ... ] the existence of a generalized West African cultural 'heritage'; or (2) to argue that the bulk of Africans in that colony came from some particular 'tribe' or cultural group [ ... ] [In his classical book, *The Myth of the Negro Past*, Melville Herskovits conceived West African unity in terms of] overt or explicit social and cultural forms such as 'patrilocality,' 'hoe agriculture,' 'corporate ownership of land,' and so forth" (Mintz and Price 1995:7, 9).

3   In the opening pages, in each chapter, and in the appendix, Andrews (2004) formulates and tries to solve the question of how people of African descent have been counted by government officials or by themselves. One emphasis is on the intricacies of self-ascription to census categories that are not well suited to assess how many persons recognize themselves as "blacks" or mulattoes, after being subjected to whitening since their arrival from west and central Africa.

4   Miguel Barnet is a Cuban novelist and poet who studied under ethnologist Fernando Ortíz, the most important figure of Afro-Cuban studies. Barnet is the director of the Fundación Fernado Ortíz in Havana. In 1966 he published *Biografía de un cimarrón*, a classical work on marooning.

5   Luz María Martínez Montiel is a Mexican anthropologist who studied with Gonzalo Aguirre Beltrán, expanding his contributions with academic programs such as Mexico-Afroamérica, and The Third Root. She also is co-founder of UNESCO's project The Slave Route.

6   Besides sources reviewed, our perceptions on the propagation of armed conflict throughout the Pacific originate from the research project Baudoseños: Interethnic Peaceful Coexistence and Ecological Polyphony, which we developed between 1994 and 1996 with sponsorship from the National University of Colombia, the Corporation for the Development of the Chocó Department, the Colombian Fund for the Development of Science and Technology (Colciencias), the North–South Program of the University of Miami and UNESCO. Co-investigators included historian Orián Jiménez, anthropologists Javier Moreno, Natalia Otero and José Fernando Serrano, and biologist Stella Suárez (Arocha 1998a, 1998b, 1999a, 1999b, 2002).

7   "de acuerdo con sus rasgos físicos, su pueblo o su cultura, usted es ... Negro(a), Mulato(a), Zambo(a), Afrodescendiente, Afrocolombiano(a), Palenquero(a), o Raizal" (CNTV 2005).

8   See www.colombiaaprende.edu.co/html/etnias/1604/article-85713.html, accessed Oct. 5, 2007.

## REFERENCES

Abello, Martha (2004) Boraudó. Una cultura afrochocoana en Bogotá. B.A. thesis, Department of Anthropology, Faculty of Human Sciences, National University of Colombia.

Acosta, Mauricio (2004) Megaproyectos y desplazamiento. Tras las claves del Chocó. In *Chocó. Agua y fuego* (pp. 59–66). Documentos CODHES, 1. Bogotá: Consejería para los Derechos Humanos y el Desplazamiento (CODHES).

Aguirre Beltrán, Gonzalo (1946) *La población negra en México*. Mexico City: Editorial Fuente Cultural.

Almario, Óscar (2004) Dinámica y consecuencias del conflicto armado en el Pacífico. Limpieza étnica y desterritorialización de Afrocolombianos e Indígenas y multiculturalismo de estado e indolencia nacional. In Gustavo Montañez Gómez, Fernando Cubides, Socorro Ramírez, and Normando Suárez (eds), *Dimensiones territoriales de la guerra y la paz en Colombia* (pp. 641–682). Bogotá: Red de Estudios Territoriales, Universidad Nacional de Colombia.

Andrews, George Reid (2004) *Afro-Latin America, 1800–2000*. Oxford: Oxford University Press.

Antón Sánchez, John (2003) Organizaciones de la sociedad civil afroecuatoriana, diagnóstico. In *Diagnóstico de la problemática afroecuatoriana y propuestas de acciones prioritarias*. BID ATN/SF-7759-EC. Quito: Cooperación Técnica.

Antón Sánchez, John (2004) La guerra y sus efectos socioculturales en la región pacífica. Territorio, proyecto de vida y resistencia de los afrodescendientes. In Gustavo Montañez Gómez, Fernando Cubides, Socorro Ramírez and Normando Suárez (eds), *Dimensiones territoriales de la guerra y la paz en Colombia* (pp. 741–757). Bogotá: Red de Estudios Territoriales, Universidad Nacional de Colombia.

Arce, Arisel and Ferrer, Armando (2002) *The World of the Orishas*. Havana: Editorial José Martí.

Arocha, Jaime (1996) Pensamiento afrochocoano en vía de extinción. *Revista Colombiana de Psicología* 5–6:216–223.

Arocha, Jaime (1997) Comunicado para el Presidente de la República en referencia a los desplazados del Bajo Atrato. Photocopy, Santafé de Bogotá.

Arocha, Jaime (1998a) Etnia y guerra. Relación ausente en los estudios sobre las violencias colombianas. In Jaime Arocha, Fernando Cubides, and Myriam Jimeno (eds), *Las violencias. Inclusión creciente* (pp. 205–234). Santafé de Bogotá: Colección CES, Centro de estudios sociales, Facultad de Ciencias Humanas, Universidad Nacional de Colombia.

Arocha, Jaime (1998b) La inclusión de los Afrocolombianos. ¿Meta inalcanzable? In Adriana Maya (ed.), *Los Afrocolombianos* (pp. 333–395), vol. 6 of *Geografía humana de Colombia*. Santafé de Bogotá: Instituto de Cultura Hispánica.

Arocha, Jaime (1999a) *Ombligados de Ananse. Hilos ancestrales y modernos en el Pacífico colombiano*. Santafé de Bogotá: Colección CES, Centro de estudios sociales, Facultad de Ciencias Humanas, Universidad Nacional de Colombia.

Arocha, Jaime (1999b) Redes polifónicas desechas y desplazamiento humano en el Afropacífico colombiano. In Fernando Cubides and Camilo Domínguez (eds), *Desplazados, migraciones y reestructuraciones territoriales* (pp. 127–148). Santafé de Bogotá: Colección CES, Centro de estudios sociales, Facultad de Ciencias Humanas, Universidad Nacional de Colombia.

Arocha, Jaime (2002) Muntu y Ananse amortiguan la diáspora afrocolombiana. *Palimpsestus* 2:92–103.

Arocha, Jaime (2006) Afro-Colombia en los años post-Durban. *Palimpsestus* (Facultad de Ciencias Humanas, Universidad Nacional de Colombia) 5:26–41.

Arocha, Jaime and Friedemann, Nina S. de (eds) (1984) *Un siglo de investigación social. Antropología en Colombia*. Bogotá: Etno.

Arocha, Jaime, Ospina, David, Edidson Moreno, José, Díaz, María Elvira, and María Vargas, Lina (2002) *Mi gente en Bogotá. Estudio socioeconómico y cultural de los afrodescendientes que residen en Bogotá*. Bogotá: Alcaldía Mayor, Secretaría Distrital de Gobierno and Centro de Estudios Sociales, Facultad de Ciencias Humanas, Universidad Nacional de Colombia.

Arocha, Jaime, Guevara, Natalia, Londoño, Sonia, Moreno, Lina del Mar, and Rincón, Liliana (2007) Elegguá y respeto por los afrocolombianas. Una experiencia con docentes de Bogotá en torno a la Cátedra de Estudios Afrocolombianos. *Revista de Estudios Sociales*, Dossier *Raza y Nación II* (Facultad de Ciencias Sociales, Universidad de los Andes, Bogotá) (Aug.): 94–105.

Barillas, E., Herrera, A., López, M., Ortiz, L., and Pérez de Lara, O. (1989) Formación nacional y realidad étnica en Guatemala. *América Indígena* 49(1):101–130.

Bonilla, Adrián (2004) Las dimensiones y las condiciones del la regionalización del conflicto colombiano. In Gustavo Montañez Gómez, Fernando Cubides, Socorro Ramírez, and Normando Suárez (eds), *Dimensiones territoriales de la guerra y la paz en Colombia* (pp. 133–144). Bogotá: Red de Estudios Territoriales, Universidad Nacional de Colombia.

Camacho, Alvaro (2004) La reforma agraria del Uribe izquierdista. *El Espectador*, Sept. 19. At www.elespectador.com/2004/20040919/opinion/nota18.htm, accessed November 9, 2004.

Camargo, Alejandro (2002) *Paimadó: Territory and Culture*. Research Report, Project Routes, Roots, Paths and Memories of Afro-Colombians. Bogotá: Afro-Colombian Studies Group, Center for Social Studies, Faculty of Human Sciences, National University of Colombia.

*Cambio* (2001) Guerra en Chocó. *Cambio*, Aug. 13, p. 35.

Celestino, Olinda (2004) Encuentro de los afrodescendientes e indígenas en las Alturas Andinas. In Jaime Arocha (ed.), *Utopía para los excluidos. El multiculturalismo en África y América Latina* (pp. 131–158). Bogotá: Colección Centro de Estudios Sociales, Facultad de Ciencias Humanas, Universidad Nacional de Colombia.

Chang, Giselle, Guevara, Marcos, Hernández, Omar, and Murillo, Carmen (2002) Cuantificar la diversidad cultural. La experiencia del censo del año 2000. In *IV Congreso Centroamericano de Antropología*. San José: Departamento de Antropología, Universidad de Costa Rica, Museo Nacional de Costa Rica.

CNTV (2005) Las caras lindas de mi gente negra. A TV educational advertisement in CD format. Comisión Nacional de Televisión, Bogotá.

Collier, Paul (2001) Causas económicas de las guerras civiles y sus implicaciones para el diseño de políticas. *El Malpensante* 30:31–53.

Comisión de Estudios sobre la Violencia en Colombia (1987) *Colombia. Violencia y democracia*. Bogotá: Universidad Nacional de Colombia.

Comisión Intereclesial de Justicia y Paz (2004) Sin Olvido 3. La masacre y desplazamiento del Naya. Electronic message distributed on Apr. 13.

Comisión Nacional Especial para las Comunidades Negras (1993) Acta No. 2, Subcomisión de Identidad Cultural. *América Negra* 6:181–195.

Comisión Nacional de Reparación y Reconciliación (2007) Disidentes, rearmados y emergentes, ¿Bandas criminales o tercera generación paramilitar? Informe 1. Área de desmovilización, desarme y reconciliación. At www.cnrr.org.co/new/interior_otros/informe_1_DDR_Cnrr.pdf.

Cunin, Elizabeth (2003) *Identidades a flor de piel*. Bogotá: Instituto Colombiano de Antropología e Historia, Universidad de los Andes, Instituto Francés de Estudios Andinos, Observatorio del Caribe.

de Carvalho, José Jorge (2004a) Las culturas afroamericanas en iberoamérica. Lo negociable y lo no negociable. In *Los Afroandinos de los siglos XVI al XX* (pp. 177–205). Lima: UNESCO.

de Carvalho, José Jorge (2004b) Las tradiciones musicales afroamericanas. De bienes comunitarios a fetiches transnacionales. In Jaime Arocha (ed.), *Utopía para los excluidos. El multiculturalismo en África y América Latina* (pp. 47–78). Colección Centro de Estudios Sociales. Bogotá: Facultad de Ciencias Humanas, Universidad Nacional de Colombia.

de Carvalho, José Jorge (2004c) Los Afroandinos en el siglo XXI. De la diferencia regional a la política de identidades. In *Los Afroandinos de los siglos XVI al XX* (pp. 78–91). Lima: UNESCO.

de Carvalho, José Jorge (2005) *Inclusão étnica e racial no Brasil. A questão cotas no ensino superior*. São Paulo: Attar Editorial.

de Carvalho, José Jorge, Doria, Siglia Zambrotti, and Neves de Oliveira, Adolfo (1995) *O quilombo do rio das ras. Histórias, tradicoes, lutas*. Salvador: Editorial da Universidade Federal da Bahia-Centro de Estudios Afro-Orientais.

de la Rosa, Laura and Moreno, Lina del Mar (2002) *The Paimadoseños in Bogotá*. Research Report, Project Routes, Roots, Paths and Memories of Afro-Colombians in Bogotá. Afro-Colombian Studies Group, Center for Social Studies, Faculty of Human Sciences, National University of Colombia, Bogotá.

de Rementería, Ibán (2004) La guerra en Colombia. Un conflicto por el uso alternativo de los recursos naturales. In Gustavo Montañez Gómez, Fernando Cubides, Socorro Ramírez, and Normando Suárez (eds), *Dimensiones territoriales de la guerra y la paz en Colombia* (pp. 37–44). Bogotá: Red de Estudios Territoriales, Universidad Nacional de Colombia.

de Sandoval, Alonso (1987[1625]) *De instaurata aethiopum salute, un tratado sobre la esclavitud*. Madrid: Alianza Editorial.

*Diario del Sur* (2004) Hoy Álvaro Uribe presidirá consejo comunal en Tumaco. *Diario del Sur*, Oct. 15. At www.diariodelsur.com.co/octubre/16/tumaco.php, accessed Nov. 6, 2004.

Díaz Polanco, Héctor (1989) Etnias y democracia nacional en América Latina. *América Indígena* 49(1): 35–56.

Diócesis de Quibdó (2004) Carta abierta al Presidente Álvaro Uribe Vélez. In *Chocó. Agua y fuego* (pp. 21–28). Documentos CODHES, 1. Bogotá: Consejería para los Derechos Humanos y el Desplazamiento (CODHES).

*El Tiempo* (2005) Reversazo del incoder les Quitó 10mil hectáreas a negritudes, comunidades de Curvaradó y Jiguamiandó las afectadas. *El Tiempo* (Bogotá), Oct. 23.

Fernández Martínez, Mirta and Porras Potts, Valentina (2003) *El Aché está en Cuba*. Havana: Editorial José Martí.

Felischmann, Ulrich (1993) Los Africanos del Nuevo Mundo. *América Negra* 6:11–36.

Flórez, Margarita (2004) *La integración silenciosa*. Bogotá: ALCA-Temas, Plataforma Colombiana de Derechos Humanos, Democracia y Desarrollo.

Flórez López, Jesús Alfonso and Millán Echavaría, Constanza (2007) *Derecho a la alimentación y al territorio en el Pacífico colombiano*. Bogotá: Misereor.

FONADE (1997) Concurso Público Internacional de Méritos No. 001-97. *El Espectador*, Feb. 16, p. 2B.

Foro Nacional Ambiental (2005) *Los bosques naturales en el proyecto de ley forestal*. Policy Paper 9. Bogotá: Fescol, Universidad de los Andes (Facultad de Administración), Fundación Alejandro Ángel Escobar, Fundación naturea, GTZ, Tropenbos Internacional Colombia y Ecofondo.

Freyre, Gilberto (1930) *Casa grande e senzala*. Rio de Janeiro: José Olympo.

Friedemann, Nina S. de (1964–1965) Ceremonial religioso funébrico representativo de un grupo negro de la Isla de San Andrés (Colombia). *Revista Colombiana de Antropología* 13:147–182.

Friedemann, Nina S. de (1967) Miss Nansi, Old Nansi y otras narraciones de folklore de la Isla de San Andrés (Colombia). *Revista Colombiana de Folklore* 4(9):213–234.

Friedemann, Nina S. de (1971) *Minería, descendencia y orfebrería, litoral Pacífico colombiano*. Bogotá: Universidad Nacional de Colombia.

Friedemann, Nina S. de (1979) *Ma Ngombe. Guerreros y ganaderos en Palenque*. Bogotá: Carlos Valencia Editores.

Friedemann, Nina S. de (1984a) Estudios de negros en la antropología colombiana. In Jaime Arocha and Nina S. de Friedemann (eds), *Un siglo de investigación social. Antropología en Colombia* (pp. 507–572). Bogotá: Etno.

Friedemann, Nina S. de (1984b) Troncos among Black Miners in Colombia. In W. Culver and T. Graves (eds), *Miners and Mining in the Americas*. Manchester: University of Manchester Press.

Friedemann, Nina S. de (1985) *Carnaval en Barranquilla*. Bogotá: Editorial La Rosa.

Friedemann, Nina S. de (1989) *Criele criele son. Del Pacífico negro*. Bogotá: Planeta Colombiana Editorial.

Friedemann, Nina S. de (1993) *La saga del negro. Presencia africana en Colombia*. Santafé de Bogotá: Instituto de Genética Humana, Facultad de Medicina, Pontificia Universidad Javeriana.

Friedemann, Nina S. de (1995) *Fiestas*. Santafé de Bogotá: Villegas Editores.

Friedemann, Nina S. de (1997) Diálogos atlánticos. Experiencias de investigación y reflexiones teóricas. *América Negra* 14:169–178.

Friedemann, Nina S. de and Arocha, Jaime (1986) *De sol a sol. Génesis, transformación y presencia de los negros en Colombia*. Bogotá: Planeta Editorial.

Friedemann, Nina S. de and Patiño Rosselli, Carlos (1983) *Lengua y sociedad en el palenque de San Basilio*. Bogotá: Instituto Caro y Cuervo.

Friedemann, Nina S. de and Vanín R., Alfredo (1991) *Chocó, magia y leyenda*. Bogotá: Litografía Arco.

García, César (1997) *Respuesta al pronunciamiento hecho por diferentes personas sobre los desplazados del Bajo Atrato Chocoano*. Santafé de Bogotá: Consejero Presidencial para los Desplazados.

Gaviria, Carlos (2004) Sentencia C-169/01, del 14 de febrero de dos mil uno (2001). In Alexandra Córdoba and Martha Eugenia Villamizar (eds), *Cartilla consecutiva de la jusrisprudencia y marco legal, legislación afrocolombiana* (pp. 569–576). Bogota: Ministerio del Interior y de Justicia, República de Colombia.

Glissant, Édouard (2002) *Introducción a una poética de lo diverso*. Barcelona: Étnicos del Bronce.

Godoy, Mónica (2002) *La cultura alimentaria de los Afrocolombianos y Afrocolombianas en Bogotá*. Research Report, Project Routes, Roots, Paths and Memories of Afro-Colombians in Bogotá. Bogotá: Afro-Colombian Studies Group, Center for Social Studies, Faculty of Human Sciences, National University of Colombia.

González, Reina Raquel (2002) *Aires del Pacífico. Una metáfora de las relación entre lo público y lo privado*. Research Report, Project Routes, Roots, Paths and Memories of Afro-Colombians in Bogotá. Bogotá: Afro-Colombian Studies Group, Center for Social Studies, Faculty of Human Sciences, National University of Colombia.

Hale, Charles R. (2005) Neoliberal Multiculturalism: The Remaking of Cultural Rights and Racial Dominance in Central America. *PoLAR* 28(1) (May):10–28

Helg, Aline (2004) Constituciones y prácticas de las minorías de origen africano. Una comparación entre Colombia y Cuba. In Jaime Arocha (ed.), *Utopía para los excluidos. El multiculturalismo en África y América Latina* (pp. 23–46). Colección Centro de Estudios Sociales. Bogotá: Facultad de Ciencias Humanas, Universidad Nacional de Colombia.

Heredia, Walter (1989) Perú. Estado-comunidades indígenas amazónicas. *América Indígena* 49(1):193–215.

Hoffmann, Odile (1999) Identidades locales, identidades negras. La conformación del campo político en Tumaco. In Michel Agier, Manuela Álvarez, Odile Hoffmann, and Eduardo Restrepo (eds), *Tumaco. Haciendo ciudad* (pp. 245–276). Bogotá: Instituto Colombiano de Antropología e Historia, IRD, Universidad del Valle.

Hoffmann, Odile (2002) Conflictos territoriales y territorialidad negra en caso de las comunidades afrocolombianas. In Claudia Mosquera, Mauricio Pardo, and Odile Hoffmann (eds), *Afrodescendientes en las Américas. Trayectorias sociales e identitarias, 150 años de la abolición de la esclavitud en Colombia* (pp. 352–368). Bogotá: Universidad Nacional de Colombia, Instituto Colombiano de Antropología e Historia, Institut de Recherche pour le Développement, Instituto Latinoamericanos de Servicios Legales Alternativos.

IEPRI (Instituto de Estudios Políticos y Relaciones Internacionales de la Universidad Nacional de Colombia) (2004) Reformar el DANE para recuperar la confiabilidad de las estadísticas en Colombia. *El Espectador*, Sept. 19. At www.elespectador.com/2004/20040919/opinion/nota11.htm, accessed Nov. 6, 2004.

INCODER (Instituto Colombiano de Desarrollo Rural) (2004) 318.162 hectáreas entregó el presidente a familias afrocolombianas. At www.incoder.gov.co/noticias/verNoticia.asp?Id=176, accessed Nov. 6, 2004.

Inikori, Joseph E. (1998) Les Aléas méconnus de la traite transatlantique. Sources, causes et implications historiographiques. In Doudou Diène (ed.), *La Chaîne et le lien. Une vision de la traite négrière* (pp. 130–151). Paris: UNESCO.

Jaulin, Robert (1970) *La Paix blanche*. Paris: Seuil.

Jimeno, Myriam, Sotomayor, Lucía, and Valderrama, Luz M. (1995) *Chocó. Diversidad cultural y medio ambiente*. Santafé de Bogotá: Fondo FEN.

Klein, Herbert S. (1986) *La esclavitud africana en Amércia Latina y el Caribe*. Madrid: Alianza Editorial.

Lao-Montes, Agustín (2007) Decolonial moves: trans-locating African Diaspora spaces. Cultural Studies, vol. 21, nos. 2–3, March: 309–338.

León, Juanita (2004) Las traiciones de Segovia. *El Malpensante* 57:32–47.

Malik, Iftikhar H. (2002) *Religious Minorities in Pakistan*. London: Minorities Rights Group.

Maya, Adriana (1992) Las brujas de Zaragoza. Resistencia y cimarronaje cultural en las minas de Antioquia. *América Negra* 4:85–100.

Maya, Adriana (1994) Propuesta de estudio para una formación afroamericanística. *América Negra* 7:139–158.

Maya, Adriana (1996) Legados espirituales en la Nueva Granada, siglo XVII. *Historia Crítica* 12:29–41.

Maya, Adriana (2005) *Brujería y reconstrucción de identidades entre los africanos y sus descendientes en la Nueva Granada, siglo XVII.* Bogotá: Premios Nacionales a Obra Inédita, Ministerio de Cultura.

Menezes, Claudia (1989) Estado y minorías indígenas en Brasil. *América Indígena* 49(1):153–170.

Meza, Andrés (2002) Mensaje estético o estrategia autosuficiente. Vendedores afrocolombianos en la dinámica del comercio callejero en Bogotá. B.A. thesis, Department of Anthropology, Faculty of Human Sciences, National University of Colombia.

Miñana, Carlos (1999) *Afinación de las Marimbas en la costa pacífica colombiana. Un ejemplo de la memoria interválica africana en Colombia.* Bogotá: Departamento de Antropología, Facultad de Ciencias Humanas, Universidad Nacional de Colombia.

Minority Rights Group (ed.) (1995) *No Longer Invisible: Afro-Latin Americans Today.* London: MRG.

Mintz, Sidney and Price, Richard (1995) *The Birth of African-American Culture: An Anthropological Perspective.* Boston: Beacon Press.

Molano, Alfredo (2002) *Desterrados. Crónicas del desarraigo.* Bogotá: El Áncora Editores.

Molano, Alfredo (2004) Neo reordenamiento territorial. *El Espectador*, Nov. 14, p. 16A.

Mosquera, Claudia (2004) Letter to President Alvaro Uribe about the 2005 Population Census. Afro-Colombian Studies Group, Center for Social Studies, Faculty of Human Sciences, National University of Colombia, Bogotá.

Nascimento, Abdías do (1987) *O genocídio do negro brasileiro. Proceso de um racismo mascarado.* Rio de Janeiro: Paz e Terra.

Pérez Sarduy, Pedro and Stubbs, Jean (1995) Introduction. In Minority Rights Group (ed.), *No Longer Invisible: Afro-Latin Americans Today* (pp. 1–18). London: MRG.

Pizarro, Eduardo (2001) El Ku-Klux-Klan. *El Espectador*, May 12, p. 2.

Presidencia de la República de Colombia (2004) *Palenque de San Basilio. Obra maestra del patrimonio intangible de la humanidad.* Bogotá: Presidencia de la República de Colombia, Ministerio de Cultura, Instituto Colombiano de Antropología e Historia, Consejo Comunitario Kankamaná de Palenque de San Basilio, Corporación Festival de Tambores y Expresiones Culturales de Palenque de San Basilio, and Institución Educativa Técnica Agropecuaria Benkos Bioho.

Presidencia de la República de Colombia (2005) *Pide Uribe a los campesinos nariñenses no desacreditar el cultivo de la palma africana.* Bogotá: Secretaría de Prensa de la Presidencia. At www.presidencia.gov.co/prensa_new/sne/2007/mayo/05/05052007.html.

Quintero, Patricia (2004) La pastoral afrocolombiana en Bogotá. M.A. thesis, Department of Anthropology, National University of Colombia.

Rappaport, Joanne (2005) *Intercultural Utopias: Public Intellectuals, Cultural Experimentation, and Ethnic Pluralism in Colombia.* Durham, NC: Duke University Press.

Restrepo, Eduardo (2002) Políticas de la alteridad. Etnización de "comunidad negra" en el Pacítico Sur Colombiano. *Journal of Latin American Anthropology* 7(2):34–59.

Restrepo, Luis Alberto (2004) Los países vecinos ante en conflicto colombiano. In Gustavo Montañez Gómez, Fernando Cubides, Socorro Ramírez, and Normando Suárez (eds), *Dimensiones territoriales de la guerra y la paz en Colombia* (pp. 125–132). Bogotá: Red de Estudios Territoriales, Universidad Nacional de Colombia.

Rodríguez, Stella (2001) Piel mulata, ritmo libre. Identidad y relaciones de convivencia interétnica en la costa norte de Nariño, Colombia. B.A. thesis, Department of Anthropology, Faculty of Human Sciences, National University of Colombia.

Said, Edward W. (1994) *Culture and Imperialism.* New York: Knopf.

Sánchez, Beatriz Eugenia (2001) El reto del multiculturalismo jurídico. La justicia de la sociedad mayor y la justicia indígena. In Boaventoura de Sousa Santos and Mauricio García Villegas (eds), *El caleidoscopio de las justicias en Colombia*, vol. 2 (pp. 5–140). Bogotá:

Colciencias, el Instituto Colombiano de Antropología e Historia, Siglo XXI Editores and Universidades Nacional, de los Andes y de Coimbra.

Sarmiento, Sandra and Torres, Oscar (2006) Experiencias y expectativas de negociación entre organizaciones afrocolombianas y Estado. El caso de los desterrados en Soacha. B.A. thesis, Department of Anthropology, Faculty of Human Sciences, National University of Colombia, Bogotá.

Schwegler, Armin (1996) *"Chi ma nkongo." Lengua y rito ancestrales en el Palenque de San Basilio (Colombia)*. 2 vols. Frankfurt: Vervuert Verlag.

Sharp, William (1976) *Slavery on the Spanish Frontier: The Colombian Chocó: 1680–1810*. Oklahoma, Oklahoma University Press.

Sieder, Rachel (ed.) (2004) *Multiculturalism in Latin America: Indigenous Rights, Diversity and Democracy*. New York: Palgrave Macmillan

Stavenhagen, Rodolfo (1989) Comunidades étnicas en estados modernos. *América Indígena* 49(1):11–34.

Triana, Adolfo (1987) Bases de una nueva legislación de minorías. In Comisión de Estudios sobre la Violencia en Colombia (ed.), *Colombia. Violencia y democracia* (pp. 276–290). Bogotá: Universidad Nacional de Colombia.

Urrea Giraldo, Fernando, Ramírez, Héctor Fabio, and Viáfara López, Carlos (2004) Perfiles socioeconómicos de la población afrocolombiana en contextos urbano-regionales del país, a comienzos del siglo XXI. In Mauricio Pardo, Claudia Mosquera, and María Clemencia Ramírez (eds), *Panorámica afrocolombiana. Estudios sociales en el Pacífico* (pp. 213–268). Bogotá: Instituto Colombiano de Antropología e Historia and Universidad Nacional de Colombia.

US State Department (2002) *Country Reports on Human Rights – 2001*. Washington, DC: Bureau of Democracy, Human Rights and Labor, digitally distributed by Colombian nongovernmental organization Ideas para la Paz, Mar. 6.

van Cott, Donna (2000) *The Friendly Liquidation of the Pas: The Politics of Diversity in Latin America*. Pittsburgh: University of Pittsburgh Press.

Vargas Álvarez, Lina María (2003) *La poética del peinado afrocolombiano en Bogotá*. Bogotá: Instituto Distrital de Cultura y Turismo.

Vásquez, Miguel A. (ed.) (1995) *Las caras lindas de mi gente negra II, legislación nacional para comunidades negras*. Bogotá: Red de Solidaridad Social–Plan Nacional de Rehabilitación.

Velasco, Mónica (2003) Pa'que baje el santo. La Santería: práctica mágico-religiosa de los afrocolombianos en Bogotá. Bogotá: B.A. thesis, Department of Anthropology, Faculty of Human Sciences, National University of Colombia.

Velásquez, Rogerio (2000[1935–59]) *Fragmentos de historia y narraciones del pacífico colombiano negro*. Bogotá: Instituto Colombiano de Antropología e Historia.

Verger, Pierre Fatoumbi (1993) *Orixás. Deuses yorubas na África e o Novo Mundo*. Sao Paulo: Corrupio.

Wade, Peter (1997) *Gente negra, nación mestiza*. Medellín: Universidad de Antioquia, Instituto Colombiano de Antropología, Siglo del Hombre Editores, and Ediciones Uniandes.

Whitten, Norman E., Jr (1974) *Black Frontiersmen: A South American Case*. New York: John Wiley.

Winn, Peter (1995) *Americas: the Changing Face of Latin America and the Caribbean*. Berkeley: University of California Press.

Wolf, Eric and Hansen, Edward (1972) *The Human Condition in Latin America*. Oxford: Oxford University Press.

Wray, Natalia (1989) La constitución del movimiento étnico-nacional indio del Ecuador. *América Indígena* 49(1):77–100.

Zapata Olivella, Manuel (1984) *Changó, el gran putas*. Bogotá: Remandes.

# CHAPTER 20

# Reconceptualizing Latin America

*Lynn Stephen*

Latin American anthropologists often begin from the standpoint of solidarity and shared citizenship – legal, cultural, and social – with those they conduct research with. This critical perspective has much to offer non-Latin American anthropologists who conduct fieldwork in the Américas. In addition, the intellectual inheritance given to us by anthropologists based in Latin America and the Caribbean has much to offer all anthropologists who work both at home and abroad in terms of getting us to rethink how US empire and global hegemony are part and parcel of the field within which we operate and participate as natives and citizens.[1] In fact, a standpoint of shared citizenship is useful not only as a way to conceive of relationships between anthropologists and those they work with, but also for rethinking the way we approach geography.

This chapter builds on the contributions of our Latin American anthropological colleagues to suggest how we might reconceptualize Latin America as well as how we theorize and carry out anthropological research. Beginning with a decentering of the US in relation to Latin America, I suggest that we work with the concept of "The Américas" to incorporate areas that have been geographically divided into North America, Central America, South America, and the Caribbean. Within the area we can call "The Américas" I put forward some ideas for how to conceptualize flows of people, capital, and culture. On the one hand, my suggestions question the container of the nation-state as our primary focal lens by considering transborder processes, identities, and institutions. On the other hand, I will also suggest ways in which we still have to consider the "nation" in our discussions because of the strong historical presence of nationalism in creating categories that have powerful roles in defining how people are inserted into relations of power. We also have to deal with states which still have a great deal of power to define who does and does not have access to the formal rights associated with citizenship, legal residency, and more. Continuing with a decentering of things US, the remainder of my chapter develops the insights anthropologists based in Latin America and the Caribbean have offered to us historically which can help us to reframe our concepts and methods in a transborder space which puts us on the same social and political playing field as our fellow "Americans."

## THE AMÉRICAS

"Américas" is a term which attempts to put everyone from North, Central, South America and the Caribbean on equal footing and to recognize all historical and cultural contributions to the continent (Stephen et al. 2003:22). One of the pitfalls of this all-encompassing term is that it can tempt us to move into new levels of homogenization and to lose sight of local, regional, and national particulars that come into play in their claimed places of origin as well as in multiple other sites where they are deployed through a variety of means. We can no longer suggest that the cultural and historical entity we call "Latin America and the Caribbean" exists solely below the Rio Grande, and south of Florida. In my own research in Oregon, I work in the town of Woodburn which is now at least 51 percent Latino, primarily immigrants from Mexico who have settled into this town in several different waves since the 1950s. Or if we move to the east coast, there are 551,004 Latinos in Queens, including 69,875 Dominican, 60,298 Colombians, 57,716 Ecuadorians, and 55,418 Mexicans (*Queen's Tribune* 2004). In east Los Angeles 98.6 percent of the population is Latino (primarily from Mexico), as is 65.8 percent of the population of Miami, Florida, primarily from Cuba, Puerto Rico, Nicaragua and Honduras (US Census Bureau 2001).

In many US cities and towns there are significant and sometimes dominant populations of immigrants from a wide range of Latin American and Caribbean countries. These can include different waves of immigration, or those who were simply always there – as in the case of the southwest. The presence of so many immigrants from a wide range of Latin American countries, but in the greatest numbers from Mexico, has diversified the public space of many communities in terms of restaurants, businesses, schools, and cultural institutions, as well as resulting in a wide range of civil society organizations, including hometown federations that can incorporate thousands of members, religious based organizations, and increasingly the representation of Latin American immigrants in the organized labor movement. Immigration from one country to another within Latin America and the Caribbean is important to consider as well. For example, in 1914 one third of Argentina's residents were born abroad – 40 percent of the foreign born were from Italy and about 35 percent from Spain. By 2005, the Center for Latin American Migratory Studies (CEMLA) in Buenos Aires estimated that there were 600,000 Bolivians in Argentina. The 2001 census put the number at 233,000 (Egan 2005). In addition, large numbers of Peruvians and Paraguayans are also living and working in Argentina. Immigrants are laboring in the construction sector as well as textile factories and in agriculture. The presence of different kinds of immigrants from Bolivia, Peru, and Paraguay is changing the face of Buenos Aires and other Argentinean cities in the ways that Mexican immigration has transformed many parts of the United States, both urban and rural, given the large numbers of immigrants and their widespread settlement.

Different waves of migration have recreated "Mexico" in cities and towns such as Santa Ana, California and Woodburn, Oregon. For indigenous migrants who settle in these areas, life often functions as a significant extension of Mexico in these locations in both positive and negative ways. In order to fully contextualize the experiences of transborder individuals and communities, we need to look at the ways that nationalism and national cultures are reconstructed within the boundaries of cities and towns in the

United States by Latin American immigrants themselves. An additional part of this context is also the unique ways that people from different Latin American and Caribbean countries have been constructed by non-Latin Americans as well as Latinos in particular regions of the US and/or within particular types of institutions. Vilma Santiago-Irizarry offers a model for looking at how immigrants from different places can be essentialized and stereotyped in relation to "Latino" culture in bilingual, bicultural psychiatric programs in New York City. She found that "reproduction of a medical ideology that systematized cultural traits and behaviors associated with being Latino into an array of psychologized symptoms resulted in the construction of a stereotypical Latino patient by Latino health practitioners" (Santiago-Irizarry 2001:115). Similar types of research can be carried out in any location in the Américas.

In another example, Gabriela Vargas Centina poses the following set of questions in terms of how to think about immigrant communities and individuals in the Yucatan both today and in regional Yucatecan history. She writes,

> for example, in places like Yucatan, with the new identity politics, now we have "indigenous Koreans" who are native Maya speakers, and "Maya people" who do not speak Maya. And the leader of the Maya movement in Yucatan, Guillermo May, is of Korean descent on both sides, and does not speak Maya. Of course, General May, the famous Maya rebel leader, was born in Korea and grew up in Yucatan as a Maya speaker in the nineteenth century. (Personal communication, October 2005)

This raises a whole host of questions about how to conceptualize not only regional Yucatecán-ness, but indigenous identity and Mayan ethnic identity as well. Juan Castillo Cocom, a Mayan, Yucateco anthropologist at the Universidad Pedagógica Nacional, Yucatán, Mexico takes on these questions in situating himself in relation to analyzing the party politics of Maya identity in Yucatán.

> Sometimes I hear voices. I think I am in that quincunx that anthropologists describe as "the" Maya (cosmos, culture, identity, religion, race, milpa...). Sometimes I think I am talking to the gods, but my friends at 7-Eleven in the plaza of Mérida tell me they are only anthropologists. Sometimes I think I am talking to an anthropologist and it is just myself; but I am an anthropologist. Sometimes I talk to other Maya in the Wal-Mart on Paseo Motejo – and it happens to be myself. Sometimes I do talk to myself, but I do not know who I am! Sometimes I am a Maya and sometimes I am a post-Maya. I am also a Mayanista or mayista and at other times a post-Mayanist.... I am a sociologist, Indígena, anthropologist, Mexican Yucateco, and none of these things. (Castillo Cocom 2005:133)

Juan Castillo Cocom's reflections offer double insight into the ways that identities meet at a point of suture where there is, he says, respect. This passage allows us to see the interior and exterior points of suture for the mosaic of identities Castillo Cocom manages personally both in his daily interactions and in his research on Maya identity in party politics. His perspective echoes the kinds of challenges and awareness faced by those who do their fieldwork where they live.

In my own work on the west coast of the US I have thought long and hard about how to conceptualize the Mexican spaces in Oregon and California (Stephen 2007). One possibility would be to follow Nick De Genova's suggestion that cities with significant populations of immigrants from Latin America be considered as a part of Latin America. He suggests the specific concept of "Mexican Chicago" in relation to the large number of Mexican immigrants there (De Genova 1998: 89–90, 2005). Offered as a corrective to perspectives that see Latin America as "outside the United States," and assimilation as the logical and desirable outcome of migration, De Genova suggests that "rather than an outpost or extension of Mexico, therefore, the 'Mexican'-ness of Mexican Chicago signifies a permanent disruption of the space of the US Nation-state and embodies the possibility of something truly new, a radically different social formation" (2005:190). Others have used the words "transnational" community to characterize this kind of space (Besserer 2002, 2004; Kearney 1990, 1995a, 1995b, 1998, 2000; Rouse 1992, 1995; Levitt 2001; Glick Schiller 1995, 2003). Another characterization, particularly when referring to grassroots organizations, is "binational civil society," suggesting parts of transnational communities that participate in their national country of origin, in their country of settlement as well as creating unique third spaces that can be called "transnational" (Fox 2005a, 2005b).

Politically, we need to be aware of how we package our discussion of transnational communities in light of books such as Samuel P. Huntington's *Who Are We? The Challenges to America's National Identity*, published in 2004. Here Huntington argues that Mexican and other Latin American immigrants are the most immediate and serious challenge to America's traditional identity – defined as "Anglo-Protestant" – because they fail to assimilate. "As their numbers increase, Mexican-Americans feel increasingly comfortable with their own culture and often contemptuous of American culture," he states (2004:254–255). Huntington opens his book with a description of the American flag at half mast while other flags are raised, and then moves directly into a description of a Mexico–US soccer match in Los Angeles in 1998. There images prevail of drunken Mexicans pelting garbage at the American team and at "US" (i.e. Anglo) fans waving American flags. This soccer match is not in Mexico City, Huntington notes, but in Los Angeles. He quotes an upset "US fan" who feels he should be able to raise the American flag without a response from Mexican soccer fans. This is the image of the future that Huntington implies – loss of American culture and even actual territory to Mexico and Mexicans. They will not assimilate, they will take over (2004:5).

Many scholars have pointed out that much of the evidence is to the contrary – that within two or three generations, Mexican immigrants do integrate many aspects of US popular and consumer culture into their lives, as well as coming to speak English (see Alba and Nee 2003). Mexican immigrants pay taxes and social security, are serving in the US military, and hold a wide range of jobs in the US economy. In 2001 there were 109,487 Hispanics – many of Mexican origin – enlisted in the US Armed Forces, 9.49 percent of the total (Krauze 2004:32). More than 36,000 service members are noncitizens, making up about 5 percent of active duty service members. About a third come from Mexico and other Spanish-speaking countries and the rest are from China, Vietnam, Canada, Korea, India and other countries (Ritthichai 2003). There are 1.1 million veterans of Hispanic origin (US Census Bureau 2003).

One positive contribution of work on transnational communities is that it has encouraged scholars to work outside the container of the nation/state and the kinds of binary divisions which have permeated so much of social analysis such as global/

local, national/transnational. Peggy Levitt and Nina Glick Schiller state the following of local, national, transnational and global connections:

> In one sense, all are local in that near and distant connections permeate the daily lives of individuals lived within a locale. But within this locale, a person may participate in personal networks, or receive ideas and information that connect them to others in a nation-state, across the borders of a nation-state, or globally, without ever having migrated. By conceptualizing transnational social fields as transcending the boundaries of nation-states, we also note that individuals within these fields are through their everyday activities and relationships, influenced by multiple sets of laws and institutions. (2004:5)

It is certainly important to consider the "national" in the "trans" part of migrant and immigrant histories and experience – particularly when it comes to the recognition or lack thereof of basic human and labor rights often connected to their positions in relation to the legal frameworks of the nations they are moving between. I want to suggest, however, that we have to look beyond "the national," as De Genova (2005) and other recent theorists do, in order to understand the complete nature of what people are moving or "transing" between. In the cases of the indigenous Mixtec and Zapotec migrants I study, the borders they have crossed and continue to cross are much more than national.

In many communities such the Mixtec community of San Agustín Atenango and the Zapotec community of Teotitlán del Valle (both in Oaxaca, Mexico), where migration to and from other places has become a norm that spans three, four, and now five generations, the borders people cross are ethnic, cultural, colonial, and state borders within Mexico as well as the US–Mexico border. When Mixtecos and Zapotecos come into the United States, they are crossing a new set of regional borders that are often different than those in Mexico, but may also overlap with those of Mexico (for example the racial/ethnic hierarchy of Mexico which lives on in Mexican communities in the US). For these reasons, it makes more sense to speak of "transborder" migration rather than simply "transnational." The transnational becomes a subset of the "transborder" experience. While we might want to avoid using the term "border" to avoid a literal sense of state borders and substitute the word "transboundary" instead, I am reluctant to let go of the "border" because, while migrants and immigrants are moving across boundaries other than those of nation-states, in the case of many immigrants who begin as undocumented the literal "border" remains strongly etched in their psyches and memories of coming to the US (see Stephen 2004; see also Alonso, this volume).

In major cities, such as Los Angeles, and other places where many transborder migrants are concentrated, Saskia Sassen argues that such cities emerge as strategic sites not only for globalized economic processes and the concentration of capital, but also for new types of potential actors. While Sassen concentrates her analysis on global cities such as Los Angeles, New York, Tokyo, Paris, London, Brasilia, Mexico City, and others, some of the characteristics she attributes to global cities – denationalized platforms for global capital and sites for the coming together of increasingly diverse mixes of people to produce a strategic cross-border geography that partly bypasses national states – can also be found to some degree outside of global cities in many parts of the Américas (Sassen 2004:649). Woodburn, Oregon is such a place. By the year 2000, Woodburn was 50 percent Latino and 44.5 percent of the population was of Mexican origin, as discussed above.

In these cross-border geographies, Sassen suggests that it is important to capture the difference between powerlessness and "the condition of being an actor even though one is initially lacking in political power." She uses the term "presence" to name this condition. She suggests that in the context of the strategic space of the global city, people like transborder indigenous Mexican migrants can "acquire a presence in the broader political process that escapes the boundaries of the formal polity. Their presence signals the possibility of a politics" (Sassen 2002:22). The specific context will determine what kind of politics. In Los Angeles, for example, a wide range of nonformal political participation has emerged from Mexican immigrant presence, from federated hometown associations and transborder organizations that negotiate directly with US and Mexican public officials (see Fox and Rivera 2004), to major participation in unions like UNITE-HERE (see Milkman 2005). UNITE-HERE is a union with over 450,000 active members that represents workers in apparel and textile manufacturing, apparel distribution, apparel retail, industrial laundries, hotels, casinos, restaurants, food service and airport concessions. Participation in these forms of nonparty politics has also led to groups such as UNITE-HERE having influence in mayoral races in Los Angeles.

The ever increasing numbers of Mexican immigrants and most recently of indigenous migrants in the western US (and elsewhere) can have similar results in terms of those actors developing a "presence" that can exist as a precursor to more organized political participation. This may also be the case for the 600,000 Bolivians of different kinds in Argentina as well. The notion of "presence" is important in two senses and can be a useful analytical tool in conceptualizing the Américas. First, a significant concentration of people who are connected through preexisting kin, community, and other networks is necessary in order to build critical mass for any kind of consistent organizing from an internal perspective. Secondly, presence is important as projected into the larger community that any organizing effort exists with – in other words, the presence of a particular kind of group of people in a particular community shapes the context within which any social movement takes place. As stated by Sassen in terms of global cities:

> current conditions in global cities are creating not only new saturations of power, but also operational and rhetorical openings for new types of political actors which may have been submerged, invisible or without a voice. A key element of the argument here is that the localization of strategic components of globalization in these cities means that the disadvantaged can engage the new forms of globalized corporate power, and secondly that the growing numbers and diversity of the disadvantaged in these cities under these conditions assumes a distinctive "presence." This entails a distinction between powerlessness and invisibility or impotence. (2002:21)

Even in smaller cities such as Woodburn (population 20,000) and Salem, Oregon (population 142,940), "the localization of strategic components of globalization," such as the integration of commercial agricultural and food processing at a global level localized in food processing plants that work with fruits and vegetables from around the world, cross-border labor contracting, widespread availability of the internet, email, phone cards and cell phones, and consular outreach programs that target immigrant populations outside their home country, have provided conditions for new kinds of political presence and organizing. The strategic components of globalization involving technology which link transborder communities also exist in a contradictory context in which communication by cell phone may be accompanied by lack of access to medical care, crowded housing conditions, and inadequate nutrition on both sides of the border.[2]

## NATIONAL, RACIAL, AND ETHNIC IDENTITY CATEGORIES IN THE AMÉRICAS: A FEW BRIEF POINTS

Within the ongoing diasporas, settlements, and resettlements of peoples within the Américas, national identities or what we might call national moments fade in and out of importance, depending on the context. This is also the case with ethnic and racial identities as well. Borders, boundaries, and senses of belonging are subject to temporalities that shift with specific context – depending on who are literally or symbolically present and what the meaningful lines of "in" and "out" are in the particular situation, event, or symbolic space.

While immigrants are often homogenized in relation to their national identities such as "Mexican," "Colombian," or "Dominican" or "Cuban," using national origin as an identity category can reproduce and mask importance differences and heterogeneity within a national population. Within Mexico, indigenous peoples are incorporated into a colonially inherited system of merged racial/ethnic classification (see Stephen 2002:85–91). While such categories are certainly historically and culturally constructed and not biological, they continue to operate with political and social force in many parts of Mexico as well as among Mexican-origin populations in the US. When indigenous families from San Agustín Atenango and Teotitlán go elsewhere in Mexico, as soon as they identify themselves as from Oaxaca they are immediately classified as "chaparitos" (short ones), "Oaxaquitos" (little people from Oaxaca), "Inditos sucios" (dirty little Indians), and – despite the fact that most are bilingual – told that they can't "speak" because of use of their native Mixteco or Zapoteco (see Fox and Rivera-Salgado 2004:12). These derogatory terms not only follow them to other parts of Mexico, but are frequently employed in the US by the Mexican-origin population there as well. Whether it is in the public schools, in local businesses, or in the surrounding labor camps, the belittling of indigenous peoples that occurs in Mexico is often repeated in Oregon and California. This reality is something that is articulated not only by Mixtec and other indigenous migrants, but by non-indigenous Mexicanos as well.

Within the larger constellation we have traditionally called Latin America and the Caribbean, there are also homogenizing terms that are usually tied to projects of colonialism, nationalism, and national identity creation. The best known of these categories is "mestizo," which has served as a way of erasing indigenous and African heritage from national identities or as a way of diminishing its importance in relation to "white" and "Spanish" origins. Beyond that however, mestizaje and by implication the hybridity associated with that represent complex processes of long-term, unequal dialogues "in social fields of domination, exploitation, and subjectification," as pointed out by Marisol de la Cadena (n.d.) and Ana Alonso (2004). As such, mestizaje has also been the cornerstone of nationalist projects that were explicitly anti-imperialist and anticolonial and which used the idea of racial and cultural mixture to create a new homogeneity in the face of a colonial past and US imperialism (Alonso 2004:462). While we have often remembered to contextualize historically and politically the terms we so often take for granted such as "mestizo" and "indigenous," we don't often pause to reflect about how such terms in the US and other regions have taken hold in the present. What does it mean to identify as "mestizo" or "Indian" in Los Angeles or New York in 2006? How do American Indians in the US read immigrant "Indians" from Latin America? How do Chicanos, Mexican Americans, Anglos, and African Americans in the US read "mestizos"?

We need to do the same for categories handed to us more recently by both government agencies and social movements. In the US, this entails unpacking the relationship between race and the terms Hispanics and Latinos. With regard to the categories of "Latino" and "Hispanic" and "Chicano" and their further elaborations in the 1990 and 2000 censuses, conflation of race and ethnicity has always been at the heart of the matter. Popular cultural understandings of race in the US are built on four colors that roughly correspond to geographic areas: black (Africa), white (Europe), red (Native North America), and yellow (Asia). As Clara Rodríguez (2000), Roger Sanjeck (1994), and others have pointed out, these four color groups continue to have corresponding categories on census forms, despite a slew of critiques that show there is no basis for them. The 1980 and 1990 census forms used the four color scheme in the race question, but the specifics varied. In 1980 and 1990, people were requested to "fill in one" racial category. This was followed by the question: "Is this person of Spanish/Hispanic Origin," followed by primarily national identity designations, "Mexican/Mexican-American/Chicano, Puerto Rican, Cuban, and Other Spanish/Hispanic." In the 1980 and the 1990 census forms, the person filling out the form was asked to specify what "Other" means. In 1990, specific examples were provided, "Print one group, for example, Argentinean, Colombian, Dominican, Nicaraguan, Salvadoran, Spaniard, and so on" (US Census Bureau 1990).

One of the most interesting results that emerged from analysis of the 1980 and 1990 censuses was that more than 40 percent of Hispanics choose the "other race" category – i.e. not self-identifying as "white," "Black" or "Negro" or "Indian" or "Asian or Pacific Islander." In addition, many who chose the "other" box wrote in the "name of their 'home' Latino country or group to 'explain' their race – or 'otherness'" (Rodríguez 2000:7). The referents put in the "other" race box were often cultural or nation-origin terms such as Dominican, Honduran or Boricua (Puerto Rican). Rodríguez suggests that this indicates "the fact that many Latinos viewed the question of race as a question of culture, national origin and socialization, rather than simply biological or genetic ancestry or color" (2000:7). By the year 2000, the percentage of Hispanics who choose the "other race" category was 51 percent (Huizar Murillo and Cerda 2004:280). As pointed out by Jonathan Fox, in choosing to answer the race question with "other," Latinos are thereby creating their own de facto racial category.

The 2000 census contained two other interesting changes. First, the term "Latino" was added to the question wording and response options "Spanish/Hispanic/Latino." The term "Hispanic" was included for the first time in the 1980s census and was disparaged by many as an inaccurate, government created category. The term "Latino" refers to people in the US of Latin American or Caribbean origin and is a term born of social struggles and activism, much like Chicano. As explained by Arlene Dávila:

> By the 1960s and 1970s, however, the terms "Hispano" and "Hispanic" were seen to be contrary to the cultural nationalism that accompanied larger struggles for civil empowerment by both Chicanos and Puerto Ricans and thus a denial of their identity and a rejection of their indigenous and colonized roots. Ironically, it was shortly after these cultural struggles that the US government coined the offical designation of "Hispanic" to designate anyone of Spanish background in the US. This explains why

Latino activists generally regard "Hispanic" as more politically "sanitized" terminology than "Latino/a" even though both terms are equally guilty of erasing differences while encompassing highly heterogeneous populations that can be equally appropriated for a range of politics. (2001:15)

Other scholars have made similar points, including Susana Oboler, who has suggested that the creation of the label "Hispanic" not only conflated differences between Chicanos and Puerto Ricans as they were engaged in nationalist movements that were increasingly militant, but also disproportionately empowered Cuban exiles (1995: 81–84). De Genova and Ramos-Zayas make a similar point (2003:4).

The other significant change in the 2000 census was to put the "Spanish/Hispanic/Latino" question first. Then the form asks what the person's race is, providing 15 printed options, along with "some other race," as well as allowing people to mark one or more races. The 2000 census was also the first time that indigenous Mexicans could make their presence known through two distinct census categories. A campaign mounted by the Front of Binational Indigenous Organizations (FIOB) encouraged indigenous immigrants to register their presence in the census, particularly in California. Here is how this occurred.

One of the racial options, "American Indian or Alaska Native," left a space to indicate a specific "tribe." According to the census bureau, American Indian or Alaska Native refers to

people having origins in any of the original peoples of North and South America (including Central America), and who maintain tribal affiliation or community attachment. It includes people who indicated their race or races by marking this category or writing in their principal enrolled tribe such as Rosebud Sioux, Chipewa, or Navajo. (US Census Bureau 2001:2)

The 2000 census showed a significant growth in the number of people who self-identified as "American Indian" *but also* in the number of people who identified themselves as both Hispanic and American Indian. In other words, self-identified Latin American indigenous migrants could "identify both ethnically as Latinos and racially as American Indians" (Fox 2006:45). In the 2000 census, 407,073 people reported themselves as both "Spanish/Hispanic/Latino" *and* American Indian and Alaskan Native. This was 1.2 percent of the total Hispanic population (US Census Bureau 2001:10, table 10). This significant growth resulted in headlines such as "California Overtakes Oklahoma as State with Most American Indians" in the *San Jose Mercury News*, signaling not only the growth in indigenous migrants primarily from Mexico and Central America, but also the beginning of self-designation on the census (Huizar Murillo and Cerda 2004:279). Most did not write in a "tribe" as this is a US based concept which makes no sense in the Mexican and Central American context where, until the 1980s and 1990s, pan-ethnic identities such as "Mixtec," "Maya," and others were not commonly used (see Kearney 1995a, 2000; Nagengast and Kearney 1989; Warren 1998). Looking historically at the ways in which racial, ethnic, and national-identity categories are created, debated, challenged and assimilated can provide some important common strategies for how to think across the Américas.

## TRANSBORDER THEORIZING: LESSONS FROM LATIN AMERICA AND THE CARIBBEAN

Beyond trying to think about how to characterize the people of the Américas and their movements, social networks, and economic, political, and social lives, we also have to think about the role of transborder theorizing and framing in terms of where we get our concepts to think with. Few people would debate the statement that Latin American Studies was created as a geographical discipline in large part to generate information that could be used in advancing US foreign policy and development interests in Latin America and the Caribbean. Latin America and the Caribbean have been constructed with US-centric priorities and visions. At the same time, however, the founding of innovative research centers and organizations such as the Latin American Faculty of Social Sciences (FLACSO, founded in 1957) in Chile, Argentina, Brazil, Costa Rica, Cuba, the Dominican Republic, Ecuador, El Salvador, Guatemala, and Mexico; the Latin American Council for Social Sciences (CLACSO, founded in 1967) in Argentina; the Brazilian Center for Analysis and Planning (CEBRAP, founded in 1969) in Brazil; The Center for Research and Advanced Studies in Social Anthropology (CIESAS, founded in 1973) in Mexico; the Center for Social Investigations (CIS, founded in 1942) at the University of Puerto Rica, and Casa de las Américas in Cuba (founded in 1959) are examples of important Latin American and Caribbean centers of theorizing on economic, political, cultural, and social life (Stephen et al. 2003:6). While economic theories from some of these centers made their way into US intellectual life, the same cannot be said for anthropology.

As observed recently by Gustavo Lins Ribeiro,

> Although anthropologists have long been weaving transnational networks, most of their own work – including systems of funding, training and publishing – remain bound within the confines of nation-states. This is mostly because anthropologists keep their allegiances to cliques that operate within these boundaries and partially derive their prestige from being members of national circuits of power. Thus, nation-states remain the primary space where the reproduction of the profession is defined in particular ways. (2005:5)

Brazilian, Colombian, Mexican, and other Latin American anthropologists have been at the forefront of helping us not only to reconceptualize Latin American anthropologies, but also to imagine "World Anthropologies at a planetary level in an open-ended way, despite their historical origin in European modernity and modernity's connections with colonialism, capitalism and globalization," to use the words of the World Anthropologies Network Collective (WAN 2003:265–266).[3]

A first step in envisioning world anthropologies, according to Eduardo Restrepo and Arturo Escobar, is "contestation of the subalternization associated with the taken-for-granted 'dominant anthropologies'…This contestation is not only discursive…it is indispensable to reverse the asymmetrical ignorance that goes into the processes of hegemonization/subalternization" (2005:115). Asymmetrical ignorance refers to anthropologists who work at the "center" ignoring what goes on elsewhere or believing that what happens in their intellectual circles is either representative of what is going on in the rest of the world or has universal value (Restrepo and Escobar 2005:115; Mato 2001:128). Specifically the logic of world anthropologies seeks to challenge the current paradigm of national anthropological traditions in which some traditions and paradigms have more power and authority than others. This proposal goes beyond proclaiming simply that European and US models of anthropology are hegemonic. In the reflections of Latin American anthropologists on their own intellectual history, the notion of "nacio-centrism" is prominent, suggesting the ways in which specific intellectual orientations are centered on the concept of "nation" – and on specific nations and specific nationalisms (see Elias 1989; Jimeno 2005:8). Thus, although it is true that anthropologists of "the south" (Krotz 1997) have been peripheralized in the global domination of US and European theory, in many cases the relatively narrow focus of some national anthropologies has served to reinforce marginalization by constraining access to anthropologies from other Latin American countries, as well as by excluding other forms of knowledge production (Jimeno 2005).

Like Jimeno's underlining of the results of nacio-centrism in Colombian anthropologies, the proposal for World Anthropologies seeks to make visible different kinds of knowledge producers (see Restrepo and Escobar 2005 for a lengthy discussion). For example, during the last two decades of the 20th century, indigenous peoples and Afro-Latin American peoples in Latin America began to press successfully for their governments to recognize certain rights premised on social and cultural difference. By the year 2000, Canada and 16 Latin American countries, from Mexico to Argentina, had undergone constitutional reforms that guaranteed fundamental rights to indigenous peoples, and in some cases to Afro-Latins as well (see Arocha and Maya this volume). A wide range of social movements, NGOs and research centers also now focus on indigenous and Afro-Latin rights. Nevertheless, the expertise and knowledge of activist intellectuals associated with these movements has not been sufficiently taken into account in formulating policy, setting research agendas, and in thinking through long-term strategies for further empowerment – nor has this knowledge been influential in the canon of Latin American and Caribbean anthropology – with some notable exceptions of efforts within Latin American countries and academies to work collaboratively with others as knowledge producers.

As stated by the World Anthropologies Network, we should be working to make visible the "different knowledges that central anthropologies (just as normalising 'expert knowledges' everywhere) ignore, disqualify or subordinate" (WAN 2003:266). Thus, as the WAN collective authors point out, testimonio is still not taken as a form of knowledge in its own right or certainly not on a par with novel theories about it. The same could be said for reports written up by *curanderos* or other practitioners of Native medicine, whose writing may be fodder for analysis by medical anthropologists, but is not seen as a legitimate knowledge form in and of itself. Only when hired as official consultants by a deputizing expert agency or individual do alternative knowledge producers become experts in their own right (see also Hayden, this volume). This happened recently when Zapotec and Mixtec healers were brought to California by certified medical experts to advise other medical experts on the importance of Native healing techniques in dealing simultaneously with the emotional and physiological aspects of illness for effective treatment (Khokha 2005). A step in this direction might begin with Ramos's suggestion that anthropological expert reports, advisory statements, and other forms of advocacy work must see the light of day (Ramos 2000). If such reports became legitimate anthropological knowledge then maybe the input from nonanthropological collaborators in such reports would receive more authority as well.

Latin American colleagues have been communicating with us about the peripher-alization of Latin American and Caribbean anthropologies for quite some time. In a special issue of the *Journal of Latin American Anthropology* in 2000, Roberto Cardoso de Oliveria explored the productive tension between scholarly communities located in the "periphery" and those in metropolitan centers. He suggested that Brazilian anthropology has been heavily influenced first by French anthropologists (particularly Lévi-Strauss) and then increasingly by Anglo-American anthropologists. Latin American anthropologists, he writes, have carried out research primarily within their own national territories, are often dependent on foreign countries for advanced professional training, and are plagued by institutional weaknesses, including lack of access to good libraries, and few full-time professorships (Cardoso 2000:20).

Estabon Krotz, in a widely cited article on the silencing of anthropologies of the South, published in 1997, discussed how in Latin America those studying and being studied are citizens of the same country; the importance of the different political, economic, and social contexts that anthropologists of the South work in and its effect on their perspectives; the way that importation of scientific and technical knowledge from the North blocks the production and diffusion of traditional and locally gener-ated knowledge; and the ways in which these first three areas have contributed to erasing the historical antecedents of Latin American anthropology (1997:244–247). Krotz's basic points have come to serve as the pivot points for debate not only among Latin American anthropologists, but also among those constructing the Network for World Anthropology in a context that attempts to equalize the playing field and to de-emphasize the influence of the nation-state as the container delimiting and defin-ing anthropological discourses.[4]

Because the majority of Latin American and Caribbean anthropologists have a long history of conducting their research at home, they have developed a great deal of useful experience in the politics of accountability and of being citizen activists simultaneously with their professional and academic roles as anthropologists (see Jimeno 1999, 2000, 2005). Alcida Rita Ramos aptly noted in 2000 that "in Brazil, as elsewhere in Latin America, to do anthropology is a political act" (2000:173). Teresa Caldeira expanded this discussion in the introduction to her book *City of Walls*, where she describes functioning as a public intellectual in Brazil and what that means and how that subject position is undercut when she publishes first in English with a US press:

> In Brazil, as in other postcolonial countries, intellectuals have a prominent role in public life. They think of themselves first as public intellectuals working to influence public debates, and only second as academics…Moreover most public intellectuals (including anthropologists) conceive of their work as a civic responsibility. This view shapes their relationships with their fellow citizens and with the subjects of their research. When public intellectuals study their own cities, they tend to write as citizens not as detached observers. This means that they talk not only to fellow intellectuals but to the broadest public they can reach. It also means that even when they write in a scientific and authoritative tone, and in spite of all the inherent powers of a social and professional elite, their view of society is more liable to contestation both by other social analysts and by fellow citizens. Theirs is only one position in a public debate.…However, by writing in English I lose the public space for engaging in debates with other citizens of the city. And although I still translate and publish the same works in Portuguese, an undisguisable American accent changes the way I am read in Brazil. (Caldeira 2000:7–8)

Myriam Jimeno has also articulated the tension inherent in the dual position of being a researcher and a fellow citizen with those who are subjects of inquiry. She states of the history of Colombian anthropology since the mid-1940s:

> In countries such as Colombia, anthropological practice is permanently faced with the uneasy choice between adopting dominant anthropological concepts and orientations or modifying them, adapting them, rejecting them, and proposing alternatives. The need to adapt the practice stems from the specific social condition of anthropologists in these countries; that is our dual position as both researchers and fellow citizens of our subjects of study, as a result of which we are continually torn between our duty as scientists and our role as citizen... (Jimeno 2005)

Her point, like Ramos's, is that political neutrality is impossible when one identifies as a citizen in the shared polity of the people one is researching. This shared interest in the political implications and influence of research leads to a set of questions that are quite distinct from the position of someone who considers themselves an "outsider" in relation to their research project and who perceives that they move in and out of the field.

The shared experiences of anthropologists who conduct their studies among those with whom they share citizenship – not just legal, but cultural and political citizenship (Rosaldo 1997) in terms of "political communities and systems of rights that emerge at levels of governance above or below those of independent states or those that cut across international borders" (Bauböch 2003:704) – have much to offer us in terms of rethinking Latin American and Caribbean anthropologies. These experiences come historically from anthropologists based in Latin America and the Caribbean, but also increasingly from those based in the US, Canada, Europe, and other places that have belonged to those traditions that defined the anthropological canon.[5] The lessons learned from decentering the notion of the field and seeing ourselves as always "in the field" can work not only for those who conduct research at home in the context of their daily lives, but also for those who go elsewhere to conduct research (see Uribe 1997; Stephen 2002:13–15). Operating as citizens not only of individual or multiple nations (in a legal and cultural sense), but also as citizens of the planet in our role as anthropologists is one way to open up our thinking. Most of us don't push hard enough in terms of how we position ourselves in the sociopolitical proximity of our subjects in a globalized Américas characterized by an indistinct boundary between the practice of anthropology as a discipline and the social action we take as citizens (Jimeno 2005:5).

As Ramos tells us about Latin American anthropologists, "The combination of academia and activism leads the anthropologist along theoretical and research paths that favor the dynamics of stormy and conflicting social forces, rather than the stability of homeostatic systems" (2000:173). From the 1960s through the late 1980s to the early 1990s, Latin American anthropologists lived directly under the influence of a US cold war policy that supported outright military dictatorships in Argentina, Brazil, and Chile, and supported pseudo-democratic regimes that were controlled by militaries in Central America and some other countries. The simple reality of dirty wars, human rights violations, lack of participatory democracy, and the creation of suspected subversives in many Latin American countries strongly influenced the education, priorities, and individual perspectives of US, Caribbean, and Latin American anthropologists. This period and the present, which some would call postcolonialism and some simply new colonialism or empire, "is characterized by a paradoxical condition marked both by a rejection of the colonial past and by colonialism's continuing and pervasive traces – it is not just applicable to indigenous people; instead, it characterizes Latin American societies as whole systems of stratified relations" – including the anthropologists in them (Alonso 2004:460). The flip side of Latin American postcolonialism during the past several decades is the construction of US empire, in Latin America and elsewhere, and the generation of a US-centric mono-vision that strongly affects the perceptions of people living, working, and educated in the United States.

## POST–9/11 RHETORIC AND US FOREIGN POLICY IN LATIN AMERICA: MORE LESSONS FOR THEORIZING

Perhaps with the kind of post–September 11 society we now live in here in the United States, US anthropologists and others can begin to understand the kinds of priorities and perspectives generated by the other September 11, 1979 in Chile and related situations in other countries at other times. Part of learning from the theoretical and methodological innovations of Latin American and Caribbean anthropologists has to do with recognizing how US foreign policy operates in the Américas and has become integrated with antiterrorism rhetoric.

Here is an example from 2005 of our national discourse equating Latin Americans who disagree with US policy with terrorists. In August of 2005, the popular evangelist Pat Robertson called for the assassination of Venezuelan President Hugo Chavez on his television news broadcast "The 700 Club" which has an audience of more than a million viewers:

> There was a popular coup that overthrew him [Chavez]. And what did the United States State Department do about it? Virtually nothing. And as a result, within about 48 hours that coup was broken; Chavez was back in power, but we had a chance to move in. He has destroyed the Venezuelan economy, and he's going to make that a launching pad for communist infiltration and Muslim extremism all over the continent.
>
> You know, I don't know about this doctrine of assassination, but if he thinks we're trying to assassinate him, I think that we really ought to go ahead and do it. It's a whole lot cheaper than starting a war. And I don't think any oil shipments will stop. But this man is a terrific danger … This is in our sphere of influence, so we can't let this happen. We have the Monroe Doctrine, we have other doctrines that we have announced. And without question, this is a dangerous enemy to our south, controlling a huge pool of oil, that could hurt us very badly. We have the ability to take him out, and I think the time has come that we exercise that ability. We don't need another $200 billion war to get rid of one, you know, strong-arm dictator. It's a whole lot easier to have some of the covert operatives do the job and then get it over with. (Media Matters for America 2005)

These sentiments were echoed later in 2005 when Evo Morales was elected as the first indigenous president of Bolivia. During a 2002 vote in Bolivia, the US embassy warned they would withdraw all aid from the country if Morales was elected, and that sent him surging in the polls (Howden 2005). Washington is also rumored to have privately labeled Morales as a narcoterrorist. Increasingly as Latin American countries have moved against the preferences of the US government in terms of electing presidents, seriously questioning free trade agreements, and wanting to control regional institutions like the Organization of American States, individual countries, leaders, and unnamed groups of immigrants have been cast in a language of exclusion, equating rejection of US neoliberal development plans with an anti-US and therefore proterrorist position.

In addition to moving US policy into our framing of Latin America, we also need to challenge our current national discussion on homeland security by refocusing it on what human security can mean in the Américas – here in the US as well as in other locations. Human security has to do with access to essentials such as food, housing, education, health care, and employment. In many ways the Zapatista movement could be called a movement for human security in its initial basic demands and it has been joined by other social movements throughout the Américas in challenging the underlying philosophy of life and assumptions of neoliberalism (Harvey 1998; Stephen 2002).

## Los Nuevos Desaparecidos: US Foreign Policy in Latin America with Current Realities

US national political discourses that frame Latin America and Latin Americans as potential terrorists in relation to our "homeland security" use already institutionalized language that equates undocumented immigrants with illegality and potentially terrorism. One specific strategy for unraveling this logic is to research patterns of militarization across the Américas, examining the role of the US in this process in the past and present. I have begun that in one project I call Los Nuevos Desaparecidos. During the 1980s and 1990s, groups that identified themselves as families and kin of the disappeared in Latin America came to have a significant political presence. Identified primarily as "mothers" of the disappeared, groups such as the Madres de la Plaza de Mayo from Argentina and CO-MADRES of El Salvador drew worldwide attention to the brutal practices of military dictatorships in the Southern Cone and the pseudo-democracies of Central America that were in fact run by the military. Analyses in the 1990s have provided ample evidence of US knowledge of the kinds of practices that resulted in widespread assassinations, disappearances, and rape as weapons of political intimidation. Since the end of the cold war – marked by most with the fall of the Berlin wall and in our hemisphere with the peace processes in El Salvador and Guatemala – public oversight over the continued role of the US military and foreign policy in the region has decreased, with the exception of Colombia.

In this project I draw our attention to what I am calling "los nuevos desaparecidos, asasinados, y muertos" of the late 20th and early 21st centuries that are occurring on the US–Mexico border – hundreds of women who have been raped, sexually brutalized and murdered in a range of border cities and now on the Mexican–Guatemalan border as well as within Guatemala and the thousands of men, women, and children who die crossing the US border or are simply never found. The militarization of both borders, high rates of immigration from Mexico (of people from a variety of nations), the integration of various kinds of smuggling operations in the 1980s and 1990s at key points on both of Mexico's borders, and the integration of former counterinsurgency specialists from the Salvadoran, Guatemalan, and Mexican militaries with cartels who control the borders are at the heart of the patterns of desaparecidos we are seeing now. While the context of militarization and the patterns of abuses perpetrated against women and men who were labeled as "subversives" during the civil war in El Salvador are distinct from those we encounter on the border regions of Mexico in the 1990s and beyond, there are related elements and patterns that should draw our attention.

US border defense policy since the mid-1990s has converged with the emergence of Mexico as the major drug transshipment point from Central and South America into the US to produce what can aptly be termed as border war zones. The victims in these war zones are "los nuevos desaparecidos, asasinados, y muertos" – the new disappeared, assassinated, and dead. The intense violence and danger which has become ordinary in these border zones is directly related to the presence of drug cartels, high levels of impunity for crimes such as rape, murder, and mutilation, and the high levels of corruption on both sides of the border funded with billions of narco dollars. The high levels of profits, totaling in the billions of dollars every year, make human smuggling extremely lucrative. While United States officials are quick to condemn drug and human traffickers, they seldom pause to consider the role that US border defense policy has had in pushing migrants into such dangerous circumstances.

Military and paramilitary cultures of masculine violence based on the feminization of victims and their sexualization are certainly a factor in the nature of the violence perpetuated against girls and women from Ciudad Juarez and Chihuahua. In addition, such cultures of violence also seem to permeate smugglers and their accomplices who are in the business of moving Mexican men, women, and children across the US–Mexico border. What is missing from many US government analyses of the "border crises" are two elements. One is a consideration of how forcing migrants into isolated sectors of the desert has contributed to the situation. The other is consideration of how not providing a road to legalization continues to push people into coming in as undocumented.

In large part these observations are part of a philosophy that calls for recognizing and adjusting the status of large numbers of people who are already here and contributing economically, socially, culturally, and politically to both the US and Mexico. In addition, we need to radically rethink the current strategies for militarizing and patrolling the border. Much higher levels of cooperation and teamwork are necessary with the justice system and various police and armed forces of Mexico. The primary routes for crossing from Mexico into the US are not controlled by the US border patrol, but by interlinked groups of drug and people smugglers based on both sides of the border who clearly pay protection money to armed forces and the police. Until the very high levels of corruption within the Mexican justice system and armed and police forces are addressed on a binational basis, with similar standards on the US side of the border, the high levels of danger currently associated with crossing will not decrease. As long as a culture of violence and impunity characterizes our border zones then women, men, and children will continue to face deadly peril as they live in border cities and cross into the US.

## CONCLUSIONS

Recasting Latin America and the Caribbean as part of The Américas offers us an opportunity to rethink many of the categories and assumptions that have underlined the theoretical development, research agendas, and even the methodologies that have characterized both Latin Americanist anthropologies and the anthropologies of Latin

America and the Caribbean. While US-centric priorities and views have shaped the work of US based anthropologists conducting research in Latin America and the Caribbean, the nation-centric realities of specific histories and nationalisms have also resulted in certain constraints for anthropologists based in Latin America and the Caribbean. In both contexts, alternative knowledges and epistemologies existing outside of the academy and policy arenas have usually been silenced. We might work within the framework suggested by world anthropologies in which we seek to "transform the uneven conditions of possibility of production/circulation of anthropological thinking at large" (Restrepo and Escobar 2005:119). This new kind of structure also incorporates "the Caribbean," which has often been silenced in area-studies based labels and structures that simultaneously erase Afro-Latin and Afro-Caribbean histories and cultures as well. This proposal implies not only changing historical relationships between anthropologists, but also those between anthropologists and their collaborators, and the kinds of knowledge products that are the result of research. Multilingual, web based, video, radio and audio formats are important in reversing the kind of knowledge circulation that has characterized much of our intellectual history. We can take many of our cues from the kinds of structures, organizing strategies, and information production offered by the rich array of social movements in the Américas, as we work together to widen and deepen the anthropological horizon on our continent and on our planet.

## NOTES

1    Taking into account all of the important work of anthropologists from Latin America and the Caribbean is an impossible task. My coverage of the Caribbean is very scant here and reflects the biases of my own training as a "Latin Americanist." I urge readers to consult with Karla Slocum and Deborah Thomas's excellent review (2003) of Caribbean anthropology that touches on many of the themes here.
2    I thank Patricia Zavella for this point.
3    Arturo Escobar's writing on the "Latin American modernity/coloniality Research Program," drawing together the insights of Latin Americans and Latin Americanists for reconceptualizing modernity, highlights some of the strains of thought that have also contributed to the type of thinking represented by the World Anthropologies Network. He states, "The conceptualization of modernity/coloniality is grounded in a series of operations that distinguish it from established theories of modernity. Succinctly put, these include the following: (1) an emphasis on locating the origins of modernity with the Conquest of America and the control of the Atlantic after 1492, rather than in the most commonly accepted landmarks such as the Enlightenment or the end of the eighteenth century; (2) a persistent attention to colonialism and the making of the capitalist world system as constitutive of modernity; this includes a determination not to overlook the economy and its concomitant forms of exploitation; (3) consequently, the adoption of a world perspective in the explanation of modernity, in lieu of a view of modernity as an intra-European phenomenon; (4) the identification of the domination of others outside the European core as a necessary dimension of modernity, with the concomitant subalternization of the knowledge and cultures of these other groups; (5) a conception of eurocentrism as the knowledge form of modernity/coloniality – a hegemonic representation and mode of knowing that claims universality for itself, and that relies on a confusion between abstract universality and the concrete world hegemony derived from Europe's position as center" (2004:35).
4    Mexican anthropologist Estabon Krotz notes in a later discussion on the state of Mexican anthropology that because of the remarkable developments and growth in the field of

anthropology in Mexico, it is impossible to generalize about the position of all Mexican anthropologists. He states, "on the one hand, the presence of anthropologists in diverse areas of public administration and national political debate remains strong. Yet on the other hand, the weakness of profession-based organisms has made it impossible to join forces or coordinate any internal debate nor direct one towards society at large; in addition, there is an ever-widening divide between anthropologists who work in academic institutions and tend to assume the representation of the entirety of Mexican anthropology, on one side, and, on the other, those who work in state administration and frequently penetrate, in very creative ways, into both the public and private sectors, including the growing sector of Non-Governmental Organizations" (Krotz 2006:19). Thus Krotz suggests that we should be wary of creating nationally based positions for anthropologists from Latin American and Caribbean countries.

5   See for example the work of Zavella 2003; Davis 2004.

# REFERENCES

Alba, Richard and Nee, Victor (2003) *Remaking the American Mainstream: Assimilation and Contemporary Immigration.* Cambridge, MA: Harvard University Press.

Alonso, Ana María (2004) Confronting Disconformity: "Mestizaje," Hybridity, and the Aesthetics of Mexican Nationalism. *Cultural Anthropology* 19(4):459–490.

Bauböck, Rainer (2003) Towards a Political Theory of Migrant Transnationalism. *International Migration Review* 37(3):700–723.

Besserer, José Federico (2002) Contesting Community: Cultural Struggles of a Mixtec Transnational Community. Ph.D. dissertation, Department of Cultural and Social Anthropology, Stanford University.

Besserer, José Federico (2004) *Topografías transnacionales. Hacía una geográfica de la vida transnacional.* Mexico City: Universidad Autónoma Metropolitana, Unidad Ixtapalapa, Divisón de Ciencias Sociales y Humanidades.

Caldeira, Teresa P. R. (2000) *City of Walls: Crime, Segregation, and Citizenship in São Paulo.* Berkeley: University of California Press.

Cardoso de Oliveira, Roberto (2000) Peripheral Anthropologies "versus" Central Anthropologies. *Journal of Latin American Anthropology* 4(2)/5(1):10–32.

Castillo Cocom, Juan (2005) "It Was Simply Their Word": Yucatec Maya PRInces in YucaPAN and the Politics of Respect. *Critique of Anthropology* 25(2):131–155.

Dávila, Arlene (2001) *Latinos, Inc.: The Marketing and Making of a People.* Berkeley: University of California Press.

Davis, Dana-Ain (2004) Manufacturing Mammies: The Burdens of Service Work and Welfare Reform among Battered Black Women. *Anthropologica* 46:273–288.

De Genova, Nicholas (1998) Race, Space, and the Reinvention of Latin America in Mexican Chicago. *Latin American Perspectives* 25(5):87–116.

De Genova, Nicholas (2005) *Working the Boundaries: Race, Space, and "Illegality" in Mexican Chicago.* Durham, NC: Duke University Press.

De Genova, Nicholas and Ramos-Zayas, Ana Y. (2003) Latino Racial Formations in the United States: An Introduction. *Journal of Latin American Anthropology* 8(2):2–17.

de la Cadena, Marisol (n.d.) Mestizos Are Not Hybrids: Genealogies, Dialogues, and Mestizajes in Peru. MS, Department of Anthropology, University of California at Davis.

Egan, Louise (2005) Argentina Economic Hook Coaxes Back Immigrants. Reuters, Oct. 31. At www.msnbc.msn.com/id/9876730/, accessed Nov. 10, 2005.

Elias, Norberto (1989) *El proceso de la civilización.* Mexico City: Siglo XXI.

Escobar, Arturo (2004) "Worlds and Knowledges Otherwise": The Latin American Modernity/Coloniality Research Program. *Cuadernos del CEDLA* 16:31–67. At www.unc.edu/~aparicio/WAN/EscobarWorlds.doc, accessed Feb. 4, 2006.

Fox, Jonathan (2005a) Mapping Mexican Civil Society. Background paper for conference on Mexican Migrant Civic and Political Participation, Woodrow Wilson International Center for Scholars, Washington, DC, Nov. 4–5. At www.wilsoncenter.org/news/docs/Mexican-MigrantCivilSocietyFoxFinal1.pdf, accessed Oct. 3, 2007.

Fox, Jonathan (2005b) Unpacking Transnational Citizenship. *Annual Reviews in Political Science* 8:171–201.

Fox, Jonathan (2006) Reframing Mexican Migration as a Multi-Ethnic Process. *Latino Studies* 4:39–61.

Fox, Jonathan and Rivera Salgado, Gaspar (2004) Building Civil Society among Indigenous Migrants. In Jonathan Fox and Gaspar Rivera-Salgado (eds), *Indigenous Mexican Migrants in the United States* (pp. 1–68). La Jolla: Center for US-Mexican Studies, Center for Comparative Immigration Studies. University of California, San Diego.

Glick Schiller, Nina (1995) Editor's Foreword: The Dialectics of Race and Culture. *Identities* 1(4):iii–iv.

Glick Schiller, Nina (2003) The Centrality of Ethnography in the Study of Transnational Migration: Seeing the Wetland Instead of the Swamp. In Nancy Foner (ed.), *American Arrivals: Anthropology Engages the New Immigration* (pp. 99–128). Santa Fe: School of American Research Press.

Harvey, Neil (1998) *The Chiapas Rebellion: The Struggle for Land and Democracy.* Durham, NC: Duke University Press

Howden, Daniel (2005) Latin America's Newest Socialist Revolution. *New Zealand Herald*, Dec. 20. At www.nzherald.co.nz/location/story.cfm?l_id=11&ObjectID=10360679, accessed Feb. 2, 2006.

Huizar Murillo, Javier and Cerda, Isidro (2004) Indigenous Mexican Migrants in the 2000 US Census: "Hispanic American Indians." In Jonathan Fox and Gaspar Rivera-Salgado (eds), *Indigenous Mexican Migrants in the United States* (pp. 279–303). La Jolla: Center for US-Mexican Studies, Center for Comparative Immigration Studies, University of California at San Diego.

Huntington, Samuel P. (2004) *Who Are We? The Challenges to America's National Identity.* New York: Simon and Schuster.

Jimeno, Myriam (1999) Desde el punto de vista de la periferia. Desarrollo profesional y conciencia social. *Anuário Antropológico* 97:59–72.

Jimeno, Myriam (2000) Le emergencia del investigador ciudadano. Estilos de antropología y crises de modelos en la antropología colombiana. In J. Tocancipá (ed.), *La formación del estado nación y las disciplinas sociales en Colombia* (pp. 157–190). Popayán: Taller Editorial, Universidad de Cauca.

Jimeno, Myriam (2005) Citizens and Anthropologists. Colantropos, Universidad Nacional de Colombia, Bogotá. At www.humanus.unal.edu.co/ces/docs/otros/jimeno_citizens.pdf, accessed Oct. 22, 2005.

Kearney, Michael (1990) Borders and Boundaries of State and Self at the End of Empire. *Journal of Historical Sociology* 4(1):52–74.

Kearney, Michael (1995a) The Effects of Transnational Culture, Economy, and Migration on Mixtec Identity in Oaxacalifornia. In Michael Peter Smith and Joe R. Feagin (eds), *The Bubbling Cauldron: Race, Ethnicity, and the Urban Crisis* (pp. 226–243). Minneapolis: University of Minnesota Press.

Kearney, Michael (1995b) The Local and the Global: The Anthropology of Globalization and Transnationalism. *Annual Review of Anthropology* 24:547–565.

Kearney, Michael (1998) Transnationalism in California and Mexico at the End of Empire. In Thomas W. Wilson and Hastings Connan (eds), *Border Identities: Nation and State at International Frontiers* (pp. 117–141). Cambridge: Cambridge University Press.

Kearney, Michael (2000) Transnational Oaxaca Indigenous Identity: The Case of Mixtecs and Zapotecs. *Identities* 7(2):173–195.

Khokha, Sasha (2005) Oaxacan Immigrants Challenge Health Care System. *The California Report.* KQUED Radio, Nov. 8. At www.californiareport.org/domains/californiareport/archive/R511080850, accessed Oct. 2, 2007.

Krauze, Enrique (2004) Identity Fanaticism: In Defense of Mexican Americans. *New Republic,* June 21, pp. 28–32.

Krotz, Esteban (1997) Anthropologies of the South; Their Rise, Their Silencing, Their Characteristics. *Critique of Anthropology* 13(3):237–251.

Krotz, Esteban (2006) Mexican Anthropology's Ongoing Search For Identity. In Gustavo Lins Ribeiro and Arturo Escobar (eds), *World Anthropologies: Disciplinary Transformations within Systems of Power.* Oxford: Berg.

Levitt, Peggy (2001) *The Transnational Villagers.* Berkeley: University of California Press.

Levitt, Peggy and Glick Schiller, Nina (2004) Conceptualizing Simultaneity: A Transnational Social Field Perspective on Society. *International Migration Review* 38(3):1002–1039.

Lins Ribeiro, Gustavo (2005) A Different Global Scenario in Anthropology. *Anthropology News* 46(7):5–6.

Mato, Daniel (2001) Producción transnacional de representaciones sociales y transformaciones sociales en tiempos de globalización. In Daniel Mato (ed.), *Estudios Latinoamericanos sobre cultura y transformaciones sociales en tiempos de globalización* (pp. 127–159). Buenos Aires: CLACSO.

Media Matters for America (2005) Robertson Called for the Assassination of Venezuela's President. Media Matters for America. Washington, DC. At http://mediamatters.org/items/printable/200508220006, accessed Nov. 10, 2005.

Milkman, Ruth (2005) Latino Immigrant Mobilization and Organized Labor: California's Transformation in the 1990s. Paper presented at conference on Immigrant Political Incorporation. Educational programs, Radcliffe Institute for Advanced Study, Harvard University, Apr. 22–23.

Nagengast, Carole and Kearney, Michael (1989) Mixtec Ethnicity: Social Identity, Political Consciousness and Political Activism. *Latin American Research Review* 25(2):61–91.

Oboler, Suzanne (1995) *Ethnic Labels, Latino Lives.* Minneapolis: University of Minnesota Press.

*Queens Tribune* (2004) The Latinos. In *Patchwork of Cultures,* special issue.

Ramos, Alcida Rita (2000) Anthropologist as Political Actor. *Journal of Latin American Anthropology* 4(2)/5(1):172–190.

Restrepo, Eduardo and Escobar, Arturo (2005) "Other Anthropologies and Anthropology Otherwise": Steps to a World Anthropologies Framework. *Critique of Anthropology* 25(2):99–129.

Ritthichai, Chaleampon (2003) Immigrant Soldiers. *Gotham Gazette,* May. At www.gothamgazette.com/article/immigrants/20030501/11/368, accessed Oct. 17, 2005.

Rodríguez, Clara E. (2000) *Changing Race: Latinos, the Census, and the History of Ethnicity in the United States.* New York: New York University Press.

Rosaldo, Renato (1997) Cultural Citizenship, Inequality, and Multiculturalism. In William V. Flores and Rina Benmayor (eds), *Latino Cultural Citizenship: Claiming Identity, Space, and Rights* (pp. 27–38). Boston: Beacon Press.

Rouse, Roger (1992) Making Sense of Settlement: Class Transformation, Cultural Struggle, and Transnationalism among Mexican Migrants in the United States. In Nine Glick Schiller (ed.), *Towards a Transnational Perspective on Migration* (pp. 25–52). Annals of the New York Academy of Sciences, 645. New York: New York Academy of Sciences.

Rouse, Roger (1995) Thinking through Transnationalism: Notes on the Cultural Politics of Class Relations in Contemporary United States. *Public Culture* 7(2):353–402.

Sanjek, Roger (1994) The Enduring Inequalities of Race. In Stephen Gregory and Roger Sanjek (eds), *Race.* New Brunswick: Rutgers University Press.

Santiago-Irizarry, Vilma (2001) *Medicalizing Anthropology: The Construction of Latino Identity in a Psychiatric Setting.* Ithaca: Cornell University Press.

Sassen, Saskia (2002) The Repositioning of Citizenship: Emergent Subjects and Spaces for Politics. *Berkeley Journal of Sociology* 46:4–25.

Sassen, Saskia (2004) Local Actors in Global Politics. *Current Sociology* 52(4):649–670.

Slocum, Karla and Thomas, Deborah A. (2003) Rethinking Global and Area Studies: Insights from Caribbeanist Anthropology. *American Anthropologist* 105(3):553–565.

Stephen, Lynn (2002) *Zapata Lives! Histories and Cultural Politics in Southern Mexico*. Berkeley: University of California Press.

Stephen, Lynn (2004) The Gaze of Surveillance in the Lives of Immigrant Mexican Workers. *Development* 47(1):97–102.

Stephen, Lynn (2007) *Transborder Lives: Oaxacan Indigenous Migrants in Mexico and the US*. Durham, NC: Duke University Press.

Stephen, Lynn, Zavella, Patricia, Gutmann, Matthew, and Matos Rodríguez, Felix (2003) Introduction. In *Perspectives on Las Américas: A Reader in Culture, History, and Representation* (pp. 1–32). Oxford: Blackwell.

Uribe, Carlos (1997) A Certain Feeling of Homelessness: Remarks on Estebon Krotz's "Anthropologies of the South." *Critique of Anthropology* 17(3):253–261.

US Census Bureau (1990) US Census Form. Facsimiles of Respondent Instructions and Questionnaire. At www.census.gov/prod/1/90dec/cph4/appdxe.pdf, accessed Apr. 8, 2005.

US Census Bureau (2001) Overview of Race and Hispanic Origin. Census 2000 Brief. At www.census.gov/prod/2001pubs/cenbr01-1.pdf, accessed Apr. 7, 2005.

US Census Bureau (2003) US Armed Forces and Veterans. Facts and Features. Apr. 10. At www.census.gov/Press-Release/www/2003/cb03-ff04se.html, accessed Oct. 17, 2005.

WAN (World Anthropologies Network Collective) (2003) A Conversation about a World Anthropologies Network. *Social Anthropology* 11(2):265–269.

Warren, Kay (1998) *Indigenous Movements and Their Critics: Pan-Maya Activism in Guatemala*. Princeton: Princeton University Press.

Zavella, Patricia (2003) Talkin' Sex: Chicanas and Mexicanas Theorize about Silences and Sexual Pleasures. In Gabriela Arredondo, Aída Hurtado, Norma Klahn, Olga Nájera Ramírez, and Patricia Zavella (eds), *Chicana Feminisms: A Critical Reader* (pp. 228–253). Durham, NC: Duke University Press.

# CHAPTER 21

# Places and Academic Disputes: The Argentine Gran Chaco

*Gastón Gordillo*

Early in July 1924, tensions were running high in Napalpí, a state-run indigenous settlement in the Argentinean Chaco. Hundreds of Mocoví and Toba were involved in a millenarian movement that had triggered intense conflicts with settlers and, on July 19, a large police force stormed their main camp, killing between 200 and 300 men, women, and children. This massacre would mark a significant moment in the history of Argentinean anthropology, for various reasons. First, a German-Argentinean ethnographer named Robert Lehmann-Nitsche was doing fieldwork in Napalpí that same month; however, he never wrote a word about these events. The following year, he published an article on "Toba astronomy" based on materials gathered, he mentioned in passing, during "a fifteen-day visit" to Napalpí in July 1924 (1924–25:181). In a disturbing expression of anthropological silencing, the article includes Toba myths about stars but provides no commentary on the massacre or the tense sociopolitical conditions surrounding his fieldwork. Decades later, Napalpí would shape Argentinean anthropology in a different way. In the late 1960s and early 1970s, some of the first attempts to produce more historical accounts of the indigenous groups of the Chaco included analyses of the 1924 massacre.

   In this chapter, I analyze the histories behind these contrasting forms of knowledge production and how they have contributed to the making of Argentinean anthropology. I argue that the history of the discipline in Argentina was profoundly linked to the production of the Gran Chaco as its most important, and politically charged, ethnographic site. Certainly, this was not the only region mapped by national academic centers. Yet the Gran Chaco was arguably the main testing ground where the first systematic expressions of sociocultural anthropology, especially at the universities of Buenos Aires and La Plata, defined their identity and character. For many ethnographers, this region best captured the exoticism they projected onto indigenous cultural practice; for others, it was the place that best exemplified the violence and exploitation that had characterized the experience of indigenous groups in Argentina. This is why, I argue, the Chaco became the battleground of ideological conflicts shaping the local academy. These disputes shed light on some of the political and spatial dynamics of anthropological traditions in Argentina and, more generally, in Latin America; they show that the exoticization of indigenous "others" was challenged from within the discipline from an early stage but also that, in tension with this move, some anthropologists sided with politically reactionary agendas.

My analysis draws on recent approaches to the spatiality of anthropological practice. As authors like Richard Fardon (1990) and Akhil Gupta and James Ferguson (1997) have argued, the history of anthropology has been intrinsically tied to the making of spatially defined patterns of cultural difference. As part of this process, the spatial distance between "the field" and "home" was the precondition for the cultural distance many ethnographers sought to discover in faraway places. In this chapter, I examine how a similar spatial ordering shaped anthropological traditions in a peripheral place such as Argentina, where "the field" and "home" were part of the same national geography. Yet I am also interested in showing how this practice was a multifaceted, contested process of place making.

In the first section, I analyze the factors that set the Chaco apart from Patagonia and the Andean northwest in the Argentinean anthropological imagination. Then, I examine the first wave of anthropological studies conducted in the region by European ethnographers and the rise of diverging anthropological traditions in the 1960s and 1970s, in connection with the political conflicts then transforming Argentina. In the final section, I analyze the new directions taken by Argentinean anthropology in the mid and late 1980s and the geographical and conceptual reconfigurations brought about by these changes.

## THE CHACO AT THE TURN OF THE 20TH CENTURY

The Gran Chaco is a wide, mostly semiarid plain that stretches eastward from the last slopes of the Andes to the Paraná and Paraguay rivers, and north from the Pampas to Chiquitos (southeast Bolivia). For centuries, this region was one of the most important indigenous bastions in South America and the Spanish saw it as the epitome of savagery. The recurrent failure of attempts at conquest fostered myriad images of alterity about this region's indigenous groups but also endeavors to document their practices. As elsewhere in the Americas, Jesuit missionaries produced the earliest ethnographic and historical accounts (Paucke 1944; Dobrizhoffer 1970; Lozano 1989), some of which presented the Chaco as a heathen, perfidious geography under the control of the Devil (Lozano 1989).

In the 19th century, the gradual consolidation of an independent Argentinean nation-state created a more secular discourse about the Chaco. This region emerged as an unknown territory waiting to be explored, mapped, and named, and also as a place of huge economic potential (Arenales 1833). European and Argentinean scientific explorers began making journeys into frontier areas, often combining an interest in botany and zoology with ad hoc attempts at surveying anthropological and linguistic differences (D'Orbigny 1835–47). When the final military assault on the Chaco was launched in the 1880s, scientists and surveyors joined many of the army units sweeping the region (Arnaud 1889; see also Fontana 1977; Seelstrang 1977). Science and violence became part of the same project of conquest, mobilizing a machinery of knowledge production that required not just the military defeat of those populations but also their conversion into objects of study. This was also an attempt to turn older patterns of alterity defined by heathenism and savagery into new forms of difference, now to be read through the lens of concepts such as "race" and "culture."

At the turn of the 20th century, the earlier, largely improvised ethnographic descriptions led to more systematic efforts conducted by academics. Anthropology related studies in Argentina (then closely associated with the natural sciences and paleontology) were based at the Museum of Natural History in Buenos Aires and the Museum of Natural Sciences in La Plata. Francisco Moreno, Florentino Ameghino, Samuel Lafone Quevedo, and Juan Ambrosetti were the dominant figures and the research they conducted and inspired targeted not just the Chaco but also Patagonia and the Andean northwest. The three regions were construed as sources of anthropological knowledge, but this "othering" operated in each of them in different ways. Patagonia was (and continued to be throughout the 20th century) the center of major geopolitical disputes with Chile, and much of the early anthropological work in the region was tied to implicit nationalist agendas. Those concerns were embodied, first, in Ameghino's (quickly discarded) theory that humanity had originated in La Pampa-Patagonia (and therefore in Argentina) and, later on, in studies on the "Araucanization of the Pampas," through which the expansion of Mapuche (Araucanos) groups across the Andes was read as a "Chilean" invasion of sorts that engulfed "Argentinean Indians" (Lazzari and Lenton 2000). The northwest, meanwhile, would attract archaeological work on pre-Inka agricultural societies, and Folklore studies on the blending of indigenous and Hispanic cultural practices.

Within this spatial triad, the Gran Chaco seemed to be culturally and historically more distant from Buenos Aires than the other two. Free of the nationalist narratives that firmly grounded Patagonia within national identities and of the cultural and archaeological sediment left by the relatively "advanced" Andean civilizations of the northwest, the Chaco emerged as the most primitive of the internal frontiers. In short, this was seen as the place whose native population was most radically removed from the modernizing and Europeanized ideal shaping the nation-state. This aura made the region enormously attractive to generations of anthropologists. The Chaco became the territory in Argentina where they sought to fulfill, to borrow from Michel-Ralph Trouillot (1991), the discipline's "savage slot." Yet this was from the outset a slot that mobilized contrasting intellectual projects, some of which would eventually challenge this exoticization.

## THE MAKING AND UNMAKING OF SAVAGERY: THE EARLY DAYS OF CHACO ETHNOGRAPHY

In the 1890s, the first attempt to order the fragmented ethnographic information on the Chaco involved the study of indigenous languages, mostly through already existing sources (e.g. Lafone Quevedo 1898). But scholars began conducting more direct observations soon after. It could be argued that modern Chaco anthropology began at the dawn of the new century with two almost simultaneous, yet strikingly different, events.

In September 1899, the Argentinean government stopped the shipment of 23 Toba men and women ready to be sent from Buenos Aires to Paris to be exhibited at the

1900 World Fair. Robert Lehmann-Nitsche (1872–1938), the scholar who decades later would silence the Napalpí massacre from his accounts, immediately saw the opportunity to study the distant Chaco in Buenos Aires. Regretting that "the European scientific centers were deprived of the opportunity to make direct observations about one of the most interesting and unknown tribes of South America" (1904:264), he decided to take physical measurements on them before they were returned to the Chaco. Holding a doctorate in physical anthropology, Lehmann-Nitsche had arrived in Argentina from Germany two years earlier to join the La Plata Museum. Reifying these Toba men and women as specimens scrutinized by science, he carefully measured each person's body. He registered not just their weight and height but also an overwhelming mass of quantitative information on faces, eyes, noses, ears, feet, legs, hands, arms, and skulls. He also photographed each man's full naked body and each person's face. "There is no doubt," he wrote, "about the purity of the race" (1904:266).

This purportedly scientific obsession with nonwhite bodies was certainly widespread at the time and expressed the racialist paradigms that dominated physical anthropology. As in similar measurements conducted elsewhere among "Negroes," it was apparent that Lehmann-Nitsche was looking for signs of *difference*: i.e. for those markers that would confirm that those bodies were physically distinct from white bodies. The subtext of such a search was that the seemingly obvious cultural difference of the Toba had to have a physical correlate. In his quest for differences and disregard for the relations of power constituting his subjects, Lehmann-Nitsche contributed to setting the tone for future anthropological endeavors that would see the Chaco as the cradle of ontologically different human beings. Almost simultaneously, nonetheless, members of the Swedish aristocracy were setting off to the Chaco on a very different type of anthropological journey.

Led by Baron Erland Nordenskiöld (1877–1932), the Swedish Cordillera-Chaco Expedition of 1901–02 was the first large-scale scientific attempt to study the Chaco and its indigenous population. This expedition gathered information on the geography, zoology, botany, archaeology, and ethnography of a wide region on the Argentinean–Bolivian border, both in the Andes and the Chaco. In contrast to the measurements conducted by Lehmann-Nitsche, Nordenskiöld and his colleagues interacted with indigenous people in their "natural habitat" and made firsthand observations on their social practices. More important, they registered the tense historical conjuncture in which these groups were immersed. The official ethnographer of the expedition was Count Eric von Rosen, who would publish his account about the Chorote over 20 years later (von Rosen 1924). Yet the expedition's most gifted ethnographer turned out to be Nordenskiöld himself, who was initially the group's zoologist. Impressed by his experience in the Chaco, he decided to return for a longer period. In 1908–09, Nordenskiöld organized a new expedition that this time forayed along the Pilcomayo river, in an area beyond the control of the Bolivian and Argentinean armies. In a Malinowskian sense, his fieldwork was still rudimentary. He could barely communicate with his informants, did not spend much time in one single village, and much of his energy was focused on the collection of material artifacts for Swedish museums.

Yet Nordenskiöld was a sensitive and keen observer. His 1910 *Indianlif* (The Life of the Indians, published in Swedish and soon translated into German and French) was a remarkable accomplishment, which captured in a personal prose the experiences of indigenous groups gradually affected by an encroaching capitalist frontier. He described the practices, rituals, forms of social organization, and material culture of several groups, but also their early engagement in wage labor and the conditions of exploitation imposed on them (see 1912:254, 255). Further, his prose is marked by a humanism that avoids an easy exoticization of indigenous practices. Whereas other authors would later on explain indigenous dances in terms of an alleged "fear of evil spirits," he rightly argued that people danced as entertainment (1912:70–71). The spirit of his writing is clear in the closing lines of his chapters on the Chorote and Nivaclé, where he emphasized that they were not "novel heroes" but ordinary people with whom, he hoped, readers could sympathize (1912:131).

The tone and content of Nordenskiöld's writings, however, shifted some years later when he tried to systematize his previous findings based on the diffusionist models popular at the time in continental Europe. The ethnographic richness of his earlier accounts was replaced by a much drier, comparative attempt to chart "lists" of the cultural influences that had constituted Chaco societies. And the previous humanism was replaced by a more conventional distancing. Here, Nordenskiöld reproduced the assumptions of the day about the Chaco as an eminently primitive place, where local groups received their more "advanced" cultural elements (horticulture, weaving, musical instruments) from elsewhere, especially the Andes (1919:267).

Supported and influenced by Nordenskiöld, in 1911–12 another Scandinavian scholar made an inroad into the Chaco: the Finnish ethnographer Rafael Karsten (1879–1956). Holding a doctorate in religious studies, Karsten conducted research roughly in the same region covered by his Swedish predecessors: the Argentinean–Bolivian border. Karsten was the first ethnographer to conduct relatively prolonged, systematic fieldwork in the Chaco and published two major monographs drawing on this experience: *The Toba Indians of the Bolivian Chaco* (of 1923, see Karsten 1970) and *Indian Tribes of the Argentine and Bolivian Chaco* (1932). Even though the latter is clearly his most important work on the Chaco and includes valuable ethnographic data, both books represented a notable break from Nordenskiöld's humanism. Despite having gone to the Chaco influenced by Nordenskiöld, Karsten was harshly critical of him and dismissed him as a "traveler" and "artifact collector" (1932:17, 31, 108, 201). His primary objection was that Nordenskiöld had overlooked the "religious" and "magical" dimensions of indigenous life. The Finnish ethnographer's view of "indigenous religion," however, was particularly rigid and stereotypical. Karsten was among the first to project the image of the "magical thinking savage" onto the Chaco, an image that would haunt Argentinean anthropology for decades. Contrary to Nordenskiöld's interpretations, face tattooing, dancing, and rituals had for Karsten few mundane or aesthetic dimensions and were designed as protection from "evil spirits." This analysis, however, was largely speculative and ethnographically thin. It is worth noting that Karsten admitted, on several occasions, that his informants' explanations were often mundane rather than "magical" or "religious" (e.g. 1970:85; 1932:183).

While these Scandinavian ethnographers aimed their work at a European audience, in Argentina anthropological research on the Chaco was following a different path. First, the discipline was gaining institutional ground. In 1903, an anthropology course (*cátedra*) was established at the Universidad de Buenos Aires (UBA), and the following year Juan Ambrosetti founded the university's Ethnographic Museum, the first research institution in South America solely centered in the study of human cultures. Robert Lehmann-Nitsche positioned himself as the main Chaco specialist in the country and pursued his physical studies further. Not surprisingly given the conditions of his previous work, in 1905 he measured indigenous bodies at a large sugar plantation, La Esperanza (Jujuy), where thousands of men and women from the Chaco worked every year. His quantitative fixation with nonwhite bodies was similar to that of his previous work on the Toba; but this time he wrote a surprising, if brief, critique of the violence unleashed by the military on these groups. He lamented they were "chased without mercy" for, he argued, they were a "cheap and easy to control" labor force that was crucial for the "wealth of the country" (Lehmann-Nitsche 1907:54).

This criticism of state violence led to a paradoxical twist in Lehmann-Nitsche's career, for he would become one of the first scholars in Argentina to argue that anthropology should advise state policy. At a 1910 conference, he proposed that the state put aside reservations following the United States model, where indigenous people could "live their traditions" while providing "cheap labor" (1915:3–5; see Bilbao 2002). This proposal contributed to the debates that in 1912 led to the creation of Napalpí, the state-run settlement where Toba and Mocoví were to be taught "work habits." However, Lehmann-Nitsche's future research would not address these issues again. Now as the head of the Anthropology Section at the La Plata Museum, he did more fieldwork in the Chaco and deepened the distancing begun earlier by building, this time, on the image of indigenous people as myth centered. Once again, his chosen field sites were places where indigenous people were socialized into new codes of discipline: the Ledesma plantation (in 1921) and Napalpí (in 1924). His silencing of the Napalpí massacre symbolizes the type of ahistorical representations he was striving for; but this silence can also be read as a political choice, given his previous support for the establishment of such places. By publishing his results in Spanish and in local journals, Lehmann-Nitsche consolidated the first Argentinean based anthropological construction of the Chaco as an eminently different, mysterious place. Even though this view would have a lasting influence in Argentinean anthropology, reemerging with sheer force in the 1970s, the legacy of Nordenskiöld's humanism would temporarily counter this perspective.

Alfred Métraux (1902–1963), arguably the most important Chaco ethnographer of the first half of the 20th century, played a crucial role in this countermove. Born in Switzerland, Métraux spent part of his childhood in the Argentinean province of Mendoza, where his father settled as a doctor (Bilbao 2002:11–13). Trained at the Sorbonne under Paul Rivet and Marcel Mauss, Métraux spent two years at the University of Gothenburg (Sweden) under Nordenskiöld, where he wrote his dissertation (later defended in Paris) on the material culture of the Tupí-Guaraní. In his thesis, Métraux repeatedly praised Nordenskiöld as "my teacher" (1928:viii, 3). His direct interaction with Nordenskiöld proved profoundly influential, both in his interest in the Chaco and the development of a critical humanism that avoided a simplistic exoticization of indigenous practices. In 1928, under the auspices of Rivet, he was appointed director of the newly created Institute of Ethnology at the Universidad de Tucumán, in northwest Argentina. Suspicious of theory and permanently attracted to ethnographic research, Métraux did fieldwork in myriad settings but focused primarily on the Gran Chaco. He worked among the Guaraní of the Bolivian Chaco (in 1929) and conducted two ethnographic expeditions to the central Chaco, in 1932–33 and 1939, chiefly on the Pilcomayo River.

His 1932–33 expedition was arguably the one that would have a deeper impact on his career. Métraux worked in areas still torn by state violence and was struck by the abuses of the Argentinean military against indigenous people. He was quick to denounce this situation by sending from the field a report to the Société des Americanistes, which published it soon after. The tone of this piece is one of passionate and unequivocal indignation. He denounced the "annihilation" of a "healthy, beautiful race" by "the excrement of civilization": settlers and military officers whose actions were characterized by their "barbarism," "hypocritical evil," and "stupidity" (1933:205). More important, on returning from the field he began denouncing the army's atrocities in the daily *La Nación* and lobbied in Buenos Aires for indigenous rights. As a result, the head of the Honorary Commission of Indian Reservations (Comisión Honoraria de Reducciones de Indios) offered him a post to return to the Pilcomayo and assess the situation (Bilbao 2002:78–79). Yet facing threats by army officers deployed in the area, Métraux decided not to take the job. With little research funding and facing delays in his salary because of the impact of the 1930s Depression, he decided to leave Argentina. In December 1933, he left for Europe and later moved to the United States (Bilbao 2002:80).

While based at the Bishop Museum in Hawaii, Métraux systematized some of his field materials and published his most accomplished ethnographic account of a Chaco group, his "Études d'ethnographie Toba-Pilagá" (1937). This piece confirmed, first, Nordenskiöld's influence on his work. Right from the start, the narrative situated his fieldwork in the midst of the conflicts triggered by the army. And his comprehensive depiction of indigenous life – including shamanism, ritual, political organization, warfare, and festivities – regularly made reference to new historical forces such as the labor migration to sugar plantations or the recent Anglican missionization. His ethnography, at the same time, was superior to Nordenskiöld's: his prose is more analytical and his understanding of indigenous culture subtler. This piece is also significant because Métraux made clear from the outset his critical stance toward Karsten's speculative interpretations. His dismissal of the Finnish ethnographer was swift: "his works are not only light and superficial, but are also full of errors and ridiculous nonsense" (1937:173).

Because his departure from Argentina had been relatively abrupt, Métraux sought to conduct a new expedition to the Chaco to complete his previous findings. In 1939, with a grant from the Guggenheim Foundation, he returned to the Pilcomayo for several months. Even though back in the United States he engaged in other research projects, he continued publishing materials on the Chaco. The most important piece was his "Ethnography of the Chaco" (1946), published in the *Handbook of South American Indians* edited by Julian Steward. This was the most ambitious effort to date to systematize the growing yet scattered information available on this region's indigenous populations. Descriptive in nature and comprehensive in scope, his "Ethnography" was a remarkable achievement that further distanced him from his predecessors. Even though hailing Nordenskiöld, this time he also criticized his speculative diffusionist interpretations (1946:211). Furthermore, he renewed his criticism of the "magical thinking" thesis to explain indigenous cultures, writing, with Karsten in mind: "Chaco Indians do not actually live in the constant fear of spirits that some authors have ascribed to them" (1946:352).

Despite his historical sensitivity and his commitment to the rights of indigenous people, Métraux was in many ways the epitome of the mid-20th century ethnographer, primarily interested in topics such as mythology and shamanism. Issues of social and culture change were not relevant to his analysis, for he firmly believed that such changes would lead to the "disappearance" and "destruction" of indigenous cultures (1946:205). However, his work would leave a mark on Argentinean anthropologists interested in accounting for the historical forces transforming the Chaco.

## INSTITUTIONALIZATION AND THE CHALLENGES OF "SOCIAL CHANGE"

Métraux's work at the Institute of Ethnology in Tucumán influenced a man who would become one of the foremost figures in Argentinean anthropology: Enrique Palavecino (1900–1966), the first Chaco ethnographer born in Argentina. Beginning in 1927, he conducted numerous (if mostly brief) ethnographic trips to the Gran Chaco and played an important role in the institutionalization of the discipline. He directed the Institute at the Universidad de Tucumán, contributed to the creation of the Department of Anthropology at UBA in 1958, and directed the UBA Ethnographic Museum. With Métraux working abroad, Palavecino became for several decades the most prominent Chaco specialist in Argentina. For this reason, his work was more shaped by the political events in the country than that of his European predecessors.

Initially, Palavecino's writings were largely descriptive and tackled some of the same practices (shamanism, body decoration, mythology, subsistence) that had interested the previous generation of ethnographers (see Palavecino 1933, 1935). Yet following Métraux's legacy, Palavecino became increasingly concerned with the critical role that anthropology could play in state policy. In 1934, when he was affiliated with the Museum of Natural History, he participated in a study that anticipated this concern. A businessman had brought a group of Wichí to Buenos Aires to be displayed at an exhibit. The Comisión de Reducciones de Indios intervened to stop the exhibit, but granted researchers at the museum permission to "study" the Wichí prior to their return to the Chaco. The research team was led by José Imbelloni, Palavecino's director at the museum and a rising anthropological figure due to his work on diffusionism in the Americas. Imbelloni took physical measurements and made masks molded on the faces of the Wichí, while Palavecino wrote notes on "language, mythology, and magic" (1935:78). Whereas in 1899 Lehmann-Nitsche had lamented that the Toba he measured were not sent to Paris for further studies, Palavecino was critical of the shipment of the Wichí to Buenos Aires. More importantly, he personally took them back to the Chaco, pursuing an academic practice that was more closely tied to state policies aimed at "protecting" them.

As anthropology was gaining more visibility in state circles, the political constraints on academic practice were also becoming more evident. The rise of Peronism in the mid-1940s, in fact, set Imbelloni's and Palavecino's careers apart. The first two presidencies of Juan Domingo Perón (1946 to 1955) favored those intellectuals deemed close to the official nationalist ideology, which celebrated a "national character" based on the blending of criollos and European immigrants. Palavecino was not well regarded by Peronist functionaries and was removed from the directorship of the

Institute of Ethnology in Tucumán. Imbelloni, who had well-known sympathies for European fascism, became the dominant figure of Argentinean anthropology. Those were the golden days of diffusionist theory in Argentina, championed by Imbelloni and strengthened by the arrival of European scholars after the Second World War, most notably Oswald Menghin. As the measurements conducted on the Wichí illustrate, Imbelloni saw the Chaco as a distant geography that he dissected from Buenos Aires, mostly through studies on physical anthropology, archaeology, and linguistics aimed at sketching the origin of some of the region's cultural features.

The 1955 military coup against Perón undermined the dominance of this intellectual tradition, forced Imbelloni out of the university, and allowed the return of scholars previously censored by Peronism, among them Palavecino (Perazzi 2003:78). When the Department of Anthropology at UBA was created in 1958, Palavecino positioned himself as one of the dominant figures. Under the new ideology of *desarrollismo* ("developmentalism"), epitomized by Arturo Frondizi's presidency (1958 to 1961), Palavecino's earlier interest in state policy led him to write what would become the first anthropological analysis of social change in the Chaco. In a 1959 article, he analyzed the transformations affecting indigenous groups and argued that their alleged "incompatibility" with the national society was not caused by their "racial incapacity" but by the "inadequate treatment" imposed on them (Palavecino 1958–59:389). He also made a call for a "rational state policy" and argued that anthropology had an important role to play, for an "adequate treatment" of these people required "a profound knowledge of native culture" (1958–59:380, 389).

Yet Palavecino had to compete with a rising star in the Department of Anthropology who had a very different agenda: a young, charismatic professor named Marcelo Bórmida (1925–1978). Born in Italy and initially trained in the natural sciences, Bórmida had migrated to Argentina after the Second World War and became a disciple of Imbelloni. For over a decade, he conducted research in archaeology, physical anthropology, and comparative ethnology but by the late 1950s was shifting his interests toward ethnography. With the decline of Imbelloni's star, Bórmida continued at UBA, and deepened, the radical distancing of indigenous people that had been initiated by Lehmann-Nitsche. In this regard, Bórmida's differences with Palavecino had profound ideological connotations. Building on the legacy of politically conservative academic traditions in Argentina, he rejected any anthropology committed to the pragmatics of social change and, in turn, began advocating a hermeneutic of "the archaic mentality."

The influence of Palavecino and Bórmida on new generations of ethnographers, among other factors, would contribute to fracturing Argentinean anthropology for the next two decades. Even though these competing intellectual traditions were forged in offices, classrooms, and libraries in Buenos Aires, they grounded their identity elsewhere: primarily, in the Gran Chaco. The latter emerged as a contested terrain over which a now-institutionalized anthropology molded its contours.

## HISTORY, POWER, AND RESISTANCE: THE DE-EXOTICIZATION OF THE CHACO

The 1960s were years of increasing political polarization in Argentina, marked by the proscription of Peronism, the radicalization of popular organizations (boosted by the 1959 triumph of the Cuban Revolution), and new military coups in 1961 and 1966. Some of the first anthropology graduates (*licenciados*) at UBA began conducting research in the Chaco clearly influenced by this context. Argentinean anthropologists trained in the United States joined this trend. Despite their differences, these scholars were all interested in accounting for the historical forces that had constituted the Chaco at the time of their fieldwork. Their concern for history, in this regard, was deeper than the one we find in Nordenskiöld and Métraux. These two authors had included historical information in their accounts to illustrate the conditions of their ethnographic present; but they were still interested, primarily, in representing indigenous cultures as they had existed prior to their incorporation into the nation-state. In the 1960s, by contrast, ethnographers were keen to analyze the impact of historical forces on the organization and identities of these groups, following a shift also gaining momentum in anthropology in the United States, Great Britain, and France. These interests paralleled the attempt by government agencies to address pressing issues of poverty and inequality, and this confluence between anthropology and state policy was symbolized by the work of Edgardo Cordeu and Esther Hermitte.

In 1963, Edgardo Cordeu, one of the first anthropology graduates at UBA, was hired by the Comisión del Río Bermejo (Bermejo River Commission) to assess the social situation of a Toba village to be affected by an ambitious (but never implemented) canalization project of the Bermejo river. The report submitted by Cordeu (1967) became the first in-depth ethnographic study of culture change in the Chaco. Shortly after, in 1969, the Chaco provincial government hired Esther Hermitte to conduct research on the social conditions of indigenous people in order to evaluate how to "integrate" them into "national society." Hermitte had obtained her Ph.D. in anthropology at the University of Chicago and was based at the Instituto di Tella in Buenos Aires. Leading an interdisciplinary team, in 1970 she and three other anthropologists conducted fieldwork in four indigenous settlements.

A common feature of the reports by Cordeu and by the team led by Hermitte is that they showed that indigenous groups had been deeply transformed by agrarian capitalism and state interventions. Hermitte's team in particular criticized the concept of "integration" for presupposing that these groups were not already part of the regional political economy (1995:97, 181). Both reports, nevertheless, included significant conceptual differences. Cordeu paid considerable attention to the Toba's cultural and religious experience, an interest that would shape his future research. The team led by Hermitte (1995:57, 227–229), in contrast, had a predominantly socio-economic approach and was arguably the first anthropological analysis in the Chaco influenced by Marxism, even if that influence was not made explicit.

The Gran Chaco was being constructed as a place quite different from what earlier generations of ethnographers had imagined. No longer defined by a taken-for-granted distance from the nation's center, the region was now seen as the product of new historical forces. This view did not go unchallenged, as we shall see, but it revealed that a new generation of anthropologists defined their identity as intellectuals committed to social change and to building bridges between regions previously viewed as essentially different. The Chaco began to be de-exoticized in further ways. Some ethnographers conducted fieldwork in indigenous urban settlements, in which people lived as a marginalized labor force. This included Esther Hermitte's 1970 fieldwork in Resistencia (the capital of the province of Chaco) and also the work of Leopoldo

Bartolomé, an Argentinean graduate student at the University of Wisconsin, Madison. Bartolomé conducted fieldwork in Sáenz Peña (province of Chaco) and wrote an article on Toba leadership, where he criticized any attempt at analyzing indigenous leaders without examining these men's close interconnection with state agencies (Bartolomé 1971).

Of the authors mentioned above, Cordeu was the only one who continued building his academic career through long-term research in the Chaco. For a few years, he continued examining the intersections of history and culture and, together with Alejandra Siffredi (another UBA graduate), tackled one of the most significant yet silenced events in recent Chaco history: the 1924 Napalpí massacre. Cordeu and Siffredi were not alone in this endeavor. Elmer Miller, an American anthropologist and former Mennonite missionary who conducted research among the Toba in the 1960s, based much of his 1967 dissertation at the University of Pittsburgh on the massacre, especially as it related to the subsequent rise of Toba Pentecostal churches (see Miller 1979). Cordeu met Miller in Buenos Aires in 1966 and relied heavily on his work. As part of his M.A. research, Leopoldo Bartolomé (1972) also worked on the events in Napalpí and published a historical analysis of millenarian movements in the Chaco. However, Napalpí gained visibility in academic and public circles especially through Cordeu's and Siffredi's 1971 book on that particular topic. That by 1972 several anthropologists had analyzed, within just a few years, the 1924 massacre is significant of the growing historical concerns shaping Chaco ethnography and of the break with the previous academic silencing of state violence.

Yet while these authors were pushing for historical perspectives in anthropology, Marcelo Bórmida was actively forging a school in radical opposition to them. By the mid-1960s, he had consolidated his power as the dominant anthropological figure at UBA. This clout gave him the upper hand in the academic struggle over competing representations of the Chaco. After all, many of the anthropologists advocating historical approaches – Hermitte, Bartolomé, and Miller – worked outside major Argentinean universities and had little influence in the training of new graduates. Cordeu and Siffredi, for their part, had junior positions at UBA and worked under Bórmida. Not surprisingly, Cordeu and Siffredi (1971:164) concluded their book on Napalpí by citing Bórmida at length on the opposition between "mythical" and "rational" thinking. As Argentina's official political landscape was becoming increasingly hostile to research suspected of "leftist leanings," and as Bórmida's influence over anthropology was becoming deeper, the wave of historical studies conducted in the 1960s and early 1970s receded into a silenced background. The days of the mythical savage of the Chaco began.

## THE MYTHICAL SAVAGE: THE RISE AND FALL OF PHENOMENOLOGICAL ETHNOLOGY

In the heated and increasingly violent political environment of the 1970s, Bórmida's rising stardom was the academic expression of the backlash against revolutionary activism then brewing in Argentina. In 1969, Bórmida had conducted his first fieldwork in the Chaco and had published the first sketches of what he would call "phenomenological ethnology." And in the early 1970s he conducted further fieldwork, this time among the Ayoreo of the northern Chaco. Yet the brief democratic spring of 1973 forced Bórmida to leave UBA and create the private research institute that would be the trademark of his school: the Centro Argentino de Etnología Americana (CAEA, Argentinean Center of American Ethnology). In 1973, he began publishing *Scripta Ethnologica*, CAEA's flagship journal. The 1975 intervention of the university and especially the 1976 military coup, which began the most systematic campaign of state terrorism in Argentinean history, enabled Bórmida to return to UBA and strengthen his influence. Under a military dictatorship friendly to "apolitical" forms of ethnographic research, he controlled the Department of Anthropology and most of the anthropology grants from the federal agency for research funding (CONICET). Meanwhile, some of the anthropologists who had pursued socially committed work were sent to jail and tortured. Those who managed to escape physical repression and did not leave the country were based at institutions with relatively low visibility: Hermitte at IDES (Instituto de Desarrollo Económico y Social, a private institute in Buenos Aires) and Bartolomé at the Universidad Nacional de Misiones, in the country's northeast (see Guber and Visacovsky 2000). Continuing with a research shift they had begun prior to the 1976 coup, Cordeu and Siffredi remained at UBA but put aside their previous historical interests and focused much of their work on mythology (Cordeu 1974; Siffredi 1976; Cordeu and Siffredi 1978).

The political context in which phenomenological ethnology arose, with few spaces for ideological or theoretical dissent, contributed to this school's tight hegemony at UBA throughout the mid and late 1970s. Yet the rise of Bórmida's phenomenology was also grounded in its conceptual appeal, for this was the first attempt in Argentina to create a distinctive approach to ethnographic research. Most of the previous anthropological work conducted in the country was either descriptive or followed theoretical concepts produced elsewhere. The exception had been Imbelloni, but his cultural and historical analyses did not include a call for ethnographic research. Bórmida's ultimate goal, in contrast, was to reinvent ethnography. Drawing on Imbelloni's "Americanist" concerns, he also aimed to expand his research beyond Argentina. This partially explains why some followers of phenomenological ethnology conducted fieldwork in the Paraguayan and Bolivian Chaco (Bórmida and Califano) and even the Bolivian and Peruvian Amazon (Califano).

Yet Bórmida's ethnology faced a profound paradox: it was based on a repudiation of theory and, hence, on a self-defeating denial that its phenomenology included theoretical assumptions. Following Husserl, Bórmida argued that the ethnographer's primary task was to leave behind, "bracket," any theoretical preconception that may "distort" ethnographic data (1976:78–79). For Bórmida, concepts such as "kinship," "social relations," or "the economy" were rationalized, Western distortions that pulled the ethnographer away from native cosmologies. He wrote: "The ethnographic culture, formalized and atomized by traditional ethnological concepts and categories, is not a living cultural fact but a corpse to which sociological integrationism gives a fictitious and conventional life" (1976:54). The "corpse" produced by anthropological concepts, in short, had for him nothing in common with the native's cultural apprehension of the world. Drawing on German antipositivism and thinkers such as Benedetto Croce and Lucien Lévy-Bruhl, Bórmida (1976:141) claimed that mythology was the natural cradle of cultural meanings and hence the most important focus of anthropological research.

Bórmida chose the Chaco as the laboratory to pursue this model and, in just a few years, the number of ethnographers working under him multiplied. With an esprit de corps distinctive of groups led by a strong, charismatic figure, researchers such as Mario Califano, José Braunstein, Anatilde Idoyaga Molina, Celia Mashnshnek, Miguel de los Ríos, and Alfredo Tomasini (among others) went to the field following Bórmida's ideas and focused most of their initial work on mythology. Yet these authors' production could not help but be defined by their own assumptions about culture and myth, which made them trip over recurring contradictions. For instance, writing about the Ayoreo, Bórmida wrote that their myths lose "coherence" when they are "forced" into organized ensembles that do not exist in the indigenous mind (1974:42); however, in the same piece, he organized Ayoreo myths into different subgroupings, following criteria that are clearly his own (1974:62). Similarly, Bórmida recurrently referred to the "potency" of mythical beings and material items despite acknowledging that the Ayoreo lack any such concept (1975:74, 127). This use of "rationalist" constructs is particularly apparent in his book on the Ayoreo, coauthored with Mario Califano, which is organized along the same categories Bórmida had dismissed as creating a "corpse": "the economy," "social organization," "political organization," and "religion" (Bórmida and Califano 1978).

These authors' assumptions shaped their research in other, more clearly ideological aspects. In sharp contrast to the socially committed anthropology advocated by Palavecino or Hermitte, Bórmida wrote against any type of involvement with the people under study. For him, avoiding preconceptions implied putting aside "pragmatic" concerns such as "the betterment of a group's living conditions" (1976:44–45). This call for a disengaged anthropology was part of a broader conservative agenda committed to erasing history and power relations from ethnographic accounts. Since the primary goal of phenomenological ethnology was to account for permanent mythical structures "independent of space and time" (Bórmida 1969:47), issues such as state violence, wage labor, or missionization were silenced for the sake of reaching for a mythical consciousness impervious to such forces. Paradoxically, this radically ahistorical approach created the corpse Bórmida was striving to move away from: an alleged culture secluded in rigid narratives kept separate from everyday, historical practice.

This production of a timeless, mythic imaginary about the Chaco was at its peak when in 1978, and quite suddenly, Bórmida passed away. Phenomenological ethnology lost its charismatic founder and Mario Califano emerged as the school's leading figure, both at CAEA and UBA. However, some members of the school were beginning to stretch Bórmida's model beyond its self-proclaimed limits. In a 1978 article on mythology, for instance, Cordeu and Siffredi (1978:160) subtly criticized Bórmida's rejection of ethnological concepts and made a call for a theoretically grounded phenomenology. This break became more explicit in a 1982 piece that Cordeu coauthored with Miguel de los Ríos, in which he openly criticized Bórmida's essentialist and rigid approach to culture (Cordeu and de los Ríos 1982:148–149, nn. 37, 39). Published the same year the dictatorship began to crumble following the defeat in the Malvinas (Falklands) War, this article repositioned Cordeu, together with Siffredi, as the leading reformer of Chaco ethnography. By then, even some of Bórmida's staunchest supporters were expressing doubts. In 1983, José Braunstein published a book on "social organization" and "kinship" in the Chaco that contradicted Bórmida's rejection of such concepts; hence he wrote an apologetic preface trying to explain why his book would not contradict his "esteemed teacher" (1983:13). While remaining loyal to Bórmida's legacy, in the following decade Braunstein nevertheless embarked on research about ethnic boundaries that moved him further away from phenomenology.

By the early 1980s, therefore, the hegemony of phenomenological ethnology was showing cracks and the end of the military dictatorship in December 1983 caused this movement's collapse at UBA. Yet the memory and influence of darker times lingered.

## BÓRMIDA'S GHOST: CHACO SCHOLARSHIP IN THE MID AND LATE 1980S

In 1984, social anthropologists who had been exiled or had been working in private institutes returned to UBA. Accused of gaining their teaching positions under the dictatorship, Califano and Braunstein were forced to leave the university. Anchored in the CAEA, phenomenological ethnology became a marginal, self-enclosed group whose remaining members (especially Califano, Idoyaga Molina, and Mashnshnek) continued doing research abiding by Bórmida's ideas. Yet the momentum in the discipline had clearly moved elsewhere, conceptually and geographically.

The end of the dictatorship marked the return of a social anthropology that, born in the struggles of the 1960s, had sought to break with the "savage slot" assigned to the discipline. Thus, in the mid and late 1980s there was a dramatic increase in research conducted in urban areas and among non-indigenous rural dwellers. Because of the legacy of the dictatorship, many considered that doing research among Chaco indigenous groups was synonymous with doing "right-wing anthropology." Highlighting the weight of spatialized forms of academic production, for some anthropologists a politically progressive discipline had to be grounded *elsewhere*, in less charged places. Yet this distancing showed how strong the essentialization of the region had become in the 1970s, even among those critical of essentialism. By implying that the Chaco should be avoided as a subject of research, this perspective reproduced the idea that historical analyses did not belong there and that the region should be left to the remnants of the old phenomenological guard. Paradoxically, this erased the historical studies conducted in the Chaco in the 1960s and early 1970s, which included central referents for new generations of social anthropologists, such as Leopoldo Bartolomé and Esther Hermitte.

As part of the post-dictatorship reconfiguration of the anthropological academy, Cordeu and Siffredi became the most important figures in Chaco ethnography. It is worth noting that, by then, both were working in the Paraguayan Chaco: Siffredi among the Nivaclé and Cordeu among the Ishir (Chamacoco), reproducing the transnational reach of UBA begun the previous decade. Yet in the 1980s their practice was paradoxical, for it showed the lingering, if indirect, legacy of phenomenological ethnology. Even though Cordeu and Siffredi challenged Bórmida's naive empiricism and produced theoretically sophisticated symbolic analyses, they reproduced his central epistemological tenet: that mythology (as opposed to everyday practice) is the key to understanding indigenous cultures and that mythical narratives can de examined without accounting for the historical forces shaping the informants' subjectivity.

This is particularly apparent in Cordeu. Whereas in the 1960s he had contributed to building an anthropology sensitive to history, in the 1980s he replaced those questions with cultural analyses detached from historical experiences (e.g. Cordeu 1984). It was only in a 1989 article that he examined the "ethnic disarticulation" affecting the Ishir, acknowledging his previous disregard for this topic (1989:546). Siffredi's research followed a slightly different, more eclectic and eventually more historical path. In the early and mid 1980s, her work was still centered on history-free mythological analyses (e.g. Siffredi 1984). However, more in tune with the new historical mood at UBA, by the late 1980s she was drawing on systems theory to study situations of "interethnic friction" (Siffredi 1989). In conjunction with Elmer Miller (whose 1979 book on Toba Pentecostalism reached wide circulation in Argentina), Cordeu and Siffredi influenced new generations of ethnographers interested in symbolic anthropology, social organization, and religious syncretism (see Barúa 1986; Wright 1983, 1988).

Meanwhile, the mid-1980s also marked the return of openly historical perspectives in Chaco scholarship. Former ethnographer-turned-historian Nicolás Iñigo Carrera (1984), who had been part of Hermitte's 1970 team, published an influential book on the role of violence in the proletarianization of indigenous groups, which became the first openly Marxist approach to the analysis of Chaco native people. The renewed interest in history and political economy fostered new studies on seasonal labor migrations, subsistence practices, and the making of ethnic identities. These studies helped bridge the gap between the research conducted in the Chaco and the social anthropology now hegemonic at UBA (see, for instance, Carrasco 1989; Trinchero and Maranta 1987; Mendoza and Gordillo 1989).

In the 1990s, this type of work and a new wave of studies on ethnicity and religious syncretism experienced an enormous expansion. The resulting body of work is so diverse and rich that it deserves an article of its own. Hence, my relatively arbitrary decision to end this analysis in 1989. But a defining feature of the post-dictatorship Chaco ethnography is the weight of the intellectual scars left by the military regime and, in particular, by phenomenological ethnology. The studies produced in the mid and late 1980s were haunted by tacit or explicit efforts to move away from Bórmida: by incorporating cultural theory and/or by accounting for history and power relations. In this regard, no other figure in Argentinean anthropology stirred as much controversy and was as influential as Bórmida, even if that influence can be measured mostly negatively: that is, as attempts to break away from him. For this reason, his legacy goes beyond Chaco ethnography. After all, the mostly urban based social anthropology that consolidated its clout in the 1980s defined Bórmida as its negative alter ego, as the symbol of the type of work that should *not* be done, even if this phantom legacy was rarely acknowledged openly. This is why the influence of ethnographic productions on the Chaco is not limited to scholarship on the region but has shaped Argentinean anthropology as a whole. By the late 1980s, only a small fraction of anthropologists in the country worked in the Gran Chaco. But this spatial diversification had a lot to do with the heated prominence of this region among prior generations.

## CONCLUSION

Several authors have argued that the history of anthropology has been characterized by a recurrent tension between historico-materialist and culturalist approaches (Ortner 1984; Roseberry 1989). The ethnography of the Chaco is no exception, even if this tension includes many gray areas that cannot be reduced to neatly bounded dichotomies. In this chapter, I have tried to illustrate how these multifaceted tensions were played out in the academic production of a particularly charged geography. Yet I have also tried to show that these rival intellectual camps, rather than being the result of two separate blocks clashing with each other, were often part of loosely defined threads that were at points closely intertwined. Both Lehmann-Nitsche and Métraux, for instance, made calls to stop state violence, but their responses to the actual violence affecting their research subjects were strikingly different. Likewise, both Palavecino and Bórmida worked under Imbelloni but then pursued opposite agendas. Palavecino carried forward the legacy of Métraux and Nordenskiöld; Bórmida, breaking with it, developed in turn the cultural distancing fostered by Lehmann-Nitsche and Imbelloni.

These shifting ethnographic representations were, as we have seen, closely related to the political struggles transforming the country. The tight connection between knowledge production, politics, and state policy is certainly not exclusive to Latin America. But to a larger degree than in the so-called liberal democracies of western Europe and North America, anthropologists in Argentina lost their jobs, went into internal or external exile, and in some cases were jailed because of their ideological allegiances. Beginning overtly with the Peronist and anti-Peronist governments of the 1940s and 1950s, ideological discrimination became particularly swift during the 1966–73 and 1976–83 dictatorships. Yet the repression of a critical anthropology advocating change was also parallel to the rise of right-wing counterparts. The case of Argentina confirms that progressiveness is not a natural anthropological trademark and that conservative ideologies can have close correlates in the discipline, especially under authoritarian regimes.

The contestations shaping Argentinean anthropology also illustrate that academic forms of place production are central to disciplinary identities. Ethnographers, by definition, ground their practice in particular geographies. And the selection of field sites is never random but follows assumptions about the type of places that would best suit one's research questions. In Argentina, most of the men and women who played a central role in the history of anthropology grounded their questions, at one point or another, in the Gran Chaco. As the last indigenous bastion in the country, this region evoked intense, contradictory meanings for a discipline charged with the task of understanding and disentangling the nation's internal frontiers. Ethnographers produced and inscribed those meanings on the academic mapping of the region, informing the research of subsequent generations of anthropologists who in turn internalized, reformulated, or challenged those imaginings. It was especially in this geography that some of the most important traditions in Argentinean anthropology were to forge, and fight over, their identity. In doing so, ethnographers produced this region as a distinctive place; and this place, in turn, shaped them as particular types of anthropologists.

## NOTE

I presented an earlier, longer version of this chapter at the Workshop on the History of Argentinean Anthropology held in July 2004 at IDES (Instituto de Desarrollo Económico y Social),

Buenos Aires. I am grateful to Claudia Briones (the paper discussant) and the workshop participants for their comments and suggestions. Deborah Poole, Rosana Guber, and Axel Lazzari read a previous draft and provided me with particularly insightful comments. The opinions expressed throughout the chapter are my sole responsibility.

# REFERENCES

Arenales, José (1833) *Noticias históricas y descriptivas sobre el país del Chaco y el río Bermejo, con observaciones relativas a un plan de navegación y colonización que se propone.* Buenos Aires: Imprenta Hallet.

Arnaud, Leopoldo (1889) *Del Timbó al Tartagal. Impresiones de una viaje a través del Gran Chaco.* Buenos Aires: Imprenta del Río de la Plata.

Bartolomé, Leopoldo (1971) Política y redes sociales en una comunidad urbana de indígenas tobas. Un análisis de liderazgo y "brokerage." *Anuario Indigenista* 31:77–97.

Bartolomé, Leopoldo (1972) Movimientos milenaristas de los aborígenes chaqueños entre 1905 y 1933. *Suplemento Antropológico* 7(1–2):107–120.

Barúa, Guadalupe (1986) Principios de organización en la sociedad mataco. *Suplemento Antropológico* 21(1):73–130.

Bilbao, Santiago (2002) *Alfred Métraux en la Argentina. Infortunios de un antropólogo afortunado.* Caracas: Comala.

Bórmida, Marcelo (1969) Mito y cultura. *Runa: Archivo para las Ciencias del Hombre* 12:9–52.

Bórmida, Marcelo (1974) Érgon y mito. Una hermenéutica de la cultura material de los Ayoreo del Chaco Boreal (II). *Scripta Ethnologica* 2(2):41–107.

Bórmida, Marcelo (1975) Érgon y mito. Una hermenéutica de la cultura material de los Ayoreo del Chaco Boreal (III). *Scripta Ethnologica* 3(1):73–130.

Bórmida, Marcelo (1976) *Etnología y fenomenología.* Buenos Aires: Editorial Cervantes.

Bórmida, Marcelo and Califano, Mario (1978) *Los indios Ayoreo del Chaco Boreal.* Buenos Aires: FECIC.

Braunstein, José (1983) *Algunos rasgos de la organización social de los indígenas del Gran Chaco.* Buenos Aires: Facultad de Filosofía y Letras, UBA.

Carrasco, Morita (1989) Procesos de colonización y relaciones interétnicas en el Chaco formoseño. Articulación social o subalternidad? *Cuadernos de Antropología* 3:90–109.

Cordeu, Edgardo (1967) *Cambio cultural y configuración ocupacional en una comunidad toba, Miraflores, Chaco.* Publicación 123J. Comisión Nacional del Río Bermejo.

Cordeu, Edgardo (1974) La idea de "mito" en las expresiones narrativas de los indios chamacoco o ishir. *Scripta Ethnológica* 2(2):75–117.

Cordeu, Edgardo (1984) Categorías básicas, principios lógicos y redes simbólicas de la cosmovisión de los indios ishir. *Journal of Latin American Lore* 10(2):189–275.

Cordeu, Edgardo (1989) Los chamacoco o ishir del Chaco Boreal. Algunos aspectos de un proceso de desestructuración étnica. *América Indígena* 49(3):545–580.

Cordeu, Edgardo and de los Ríos, Miguel (1982) Un enfoque estructural de las variaciones socioculturales de los cazadores-recolectores del Gran Chaco. *Suplemento Antropológico* 17(1):131–195.

Cordeu, Edgardo and Siffredi, Alejandra (1971) *De la algarroba al algodón. Movimientos milenaristas del Chaco Argentino.* Buenos Aires: Juárez Editor.

Cordeu, Edgardo and Siffredi, Alejandra (1978) La intuición de lo numinoso en dos mitologías del Gran Chaco. Apuntes sobre el mito y la potencia entre los Chamacoco y los Chorote. *Revista del Instituto de Antropología* (Universidad Nacional de Córdoba) 4:159–196.

Dobrizhoffer, Martin (1970[1784]) *An Account of the Abipones, an Equestrian People of Paraguay.* New York: Johnson Reprint.

D'Orbigny, Alcides (1835–47) *Voyage dans l'amérique méridionale.* Paris: Pitois.

Fardon, Richard (ed.) (1990) *Localizing Strategies: Regional Traditions of Ethnographic Writing.* Washington, DC: Smithsonian Institution.

Fontana, Luis Jorge (1977[1881]) *El Gran Chaco.* Buenos Aires: Solar-Hachette.

Guber, Rosana and Visacovsky, Sergio (2000) La antropología social en la Argentina de los años '60 y '70. Nación, marginalidad crítica y el "otro" interno. *Desarrollo Económico* 40(158):289–316.

Gupta, Akhil and Ferguson, James (eds) (1997) *Anthropological Locations: Boundaries and Grounds of a Field Science.* Berkeley: University of California Press.

Hermitte, Esther et al. (1995) *Estudio sobre la situación de los indígenas del Chaco y políticas para su integración a la sociedad nacional,* ed. and introd. Nicolás Iñigo Carrera and Alejandro Isla. Posadas: Editorial de la Universidad Nacional de Misiones.

Iñigo Carrera, Nicolás (1984) *Campañas militares y clase obrera. Chaco, 1870–1930.* Buenos Aires: Centro Editor de América Latina.

Karsten, Rafael (1932) Indian Tribes of the Argentine and Bolivian Chaco. *Commentationes Humanarum Litterarum,* 4. Helsingfords.

Karsten, Rafael (1970[1923]) *The Toba Indians of the Bolivian Gran Chaco.* Oosterhout, Netherlands: Anthropological Publications.

Lafone Quevedo, Samuel (1898) *Arte de la lengua Toba por el padre Pedro Bárcena.* La Plata: Imprenta del Museo de La Plata.

Lazzari, Axel and Lenton, Diana (2000) Etnología y nación. Facetas del concepto de Araucanización. *Avá: Revista de Antropología* 1:125–140.

Lehmann-Nitsche, Robert (1904) Études anthropologiques sur les indiens Takshik du Chaco Argentin. *Revista del Museo de la Plata* 11:263–313.

Lehmann-Nitsche, Robert (1907) Estudios antropológicos sobre los Chiriguanos, Chorotes, Matacos y Tobas (Chaco occidental). *Anales del Museo de La Plata* 1:53–151.

Lehmann-Nitsche, Robert (1915) *El problema indígen. Necesidad de destinar territorios reservados a los indígenas de Patagonia, Tierra del Fuego y Chaco según el proceder de los Estados Unidos de Norteamérica.* Buenos Aires: Imprenta Coni.

Lehmann-Nitsche, Robert (1924–25) La astronomía de los Tobas (segunda parte). *Revista del Museo de la Plata* 28:181–209.

Lozano, Pedro (1989[1733]) *Descripción corográfica del Gran Chaco Gualamba.* San Miguel de Tucumán: Universidad Nacional de Tucumán.

Mendoza, Marcela and Gordillo, Gastón (1989) Las migraciones estacionales de los tobas ñachilamo'lek a la zafra salto-jujeña (1890–1930). *Cuadernos de Antropología* 3:70–89.

Métraux, Alfred (1928) *La Civilisation matérielle des tribus Tupi-Guarani.* Paris: Librairie Orientaliste Paul Geuthner.

Métraux, Alfred (1933) Nouvelles de la mission A. Métraux. *Journal de la Société des Americanistes* 25:203–205.

Métraux, Alfred (1937) Études d'ethnographie Toba-Pilagá (Gran Chaco). *Anthropos* 32: 171–194, 378–402.

Métraux, Alfred (1946) Ethnography of the Chaco. In Julian Steward (ed.), *The Marginal Tribes,* vol. 1 of *Handbook of South American Indians* (pp. 197–370). Washington, DC: Smithsonian Institution.

Miller, Elmer (1979) *Los Tobas argentinos. Armonía y disonancia en una sociedad.* Mexico City: Siglo XXI.

Nordenskiöld, Erland (1912) La Vie des indiens dans le Chaco (Amerique du Sud). *Revue de Geographie* 6(3).

Nordenskiöld, Erland (1919) *An Ethno-Geographical Analysis of the Material Culture of Two Indian Tribes in the Gran Chaco.* Göteborg: Elanders Boktryckeri Aktiebolag.

Ortner, Sherry (1984) Theory in Anthropology since the Sixties. *Comparative Studies in Society and History* 26:126–166.

Palavecino, Enrique (1933) Los indios pilagá del río Pilcomayo. *Anales del Museo Nacional de Historia Natural de Buenos Aires* 37:517–582.

Palavecino, Enrique (1935) Notas sobre la religión de los indios del Chaco. *Revista Geográfica Americana* 2(21):373–380.

Palavecino, Enrique (1958–59) Algunas notas sobre la transculturación del indio chaqueño. *Runa: Archivo para las Ciencias del Hombre* 9:379–389.

Paucke, Florian (1944[17?]) *Hacia allá y para acá. Una estada entre los indios mocovíes, 1749–1767*, trans. and ed. E. Wernicke. Tucumán: Universidad Nacional de Tucumán.

Perazzi, Pablo (2003) *Hermenéutica de la barbarie. Una historia de la antropología en Buenos Aires, 1935–1966*. Buenos Aires: Sociedad Argentina de Antropología.

Roseberry, William (1989) *Anthropologies and Histories: Essays in Culture, History and Political Economy*. New Brunswick: Rutgers University Press.

Seelstrang, Arturo (1977[1877]) *Informe de la comisión exploradora del Chaco*. Buenos Aires: Eudeba.

Siffredi, Alejandra (1976) El papel de la polaridad en la intuición de la potencia. *Scripta Ethnologica* 4(1):147–158.

Siffredi, Alejandra (1984) Los parámetros simbólicos de la cosmovisión nivaklé. *Runa: Archivo para las Ciencias del Hombre* 14:187–219.

Siffredi, Alejandra (1989) Un encuadre articulatorio de las relaciones interétnicas. El caso de la misión multiétnica Santa Teresa (Chaco boreal). *Cuadernos de Antropología* 3:110–126.

Trinchero, Héctor Hugo and Maranta, Aristóbulo (1987) Las crisis reveladoras. Historias y estrategias de identidad entre los mataco-wichí del Chaco Centro-Occidental. *Cuadernos de Historia Regional* 4(10):74–92.

Trouillot, Michel-Ralph (1991) Anthropology and the Savage Slot: The Poetics and Politics of Otherness. In Richard Fox (ed.), *Recapturing Anthropology: Working in the Present* (pp. 17–44). Santa Fe: School of American Research.

von Rosen, Eric (1924) *Ethnographical Research Work during the Swedish Chaco-Cordillera Expedition, 1901–1902*. Stockholm: Fritze.

Wright, Pablo (1983) Presencia protestante entre los aborígenes del chaco argentino. *Scripta Ethnologica* 7:73–84.

Wright, Pablo (1988) Tradición y aculturación en una organización socio-religiosa Toba contemporánea. *Cristianismo y Sociedad* 95:71–87.

# 22 Disengaging Anthropology

CHAPTER

## Alcida Rita Ramos

The last years of the 20th century witnessed a drastic change in Latin American ethnography. From subjects of research to researchers in their own right, indigenous peoples have forced many anthropologists to ponder the ethics and politics of ethnographic research. In an effort to capture the specificities of this sea change as it has unfolded in a particular national context, I focus in this chapter on the ethnography of indigenous peoples as it has been practiced in Brazil. No comparative analysis with other Latin American situations is attempted, although references to them and to cases elsewhere are inevitable. Although there is a family resemblance in the Latin American mode of doing anthropology, there are, beyond the expected similarities, a number of differences in anthropological "accents" which underlie the diversity of historical experiences and theoretical outlooks in the region, as this volume amply demonstrates.

Temporally, the chapter is organized as an exercise in flashback. Divided into two parts, it attempts to reflect not only on the recent turn of events in Brazil, but also on my own perplexity as I have observed this process over the years. The path I have chosen to follow goes from a mode of engagement to one of disengagement regarding both theoretical persuasions and militant commitments. The first part covers a moment when to defend the right of being different meant defending the righteousness of certain anthropological concepts that were created precisely to highlight the value of human diversity. To be politically engaged meant to be critical of what might be called anthropological fads. Hence to defend such ideas as the concept of culture meant to defend indigenous rights in the face of homogenizing trends in both national and international ethnic politics.

Over about five years, my view of the matter changed substantially as I witnessed case upon case of ethnographic frustration on the part of young researchers in less than friendly field situations. It was an opportunity to take stock of the present state of the profession as it has been exercised in Brazil. The analysis of this new moment in ethnographic work has led me to advocate a state of disengagement. But far from an abdication of commitment, this disengagement means a sort of liberation from illusions of grandeur that have blinded ethnographers to the vigor of indigenous will to full agency.

## Engagement

For more than two decades we have witnessed a laudable effort on the part of Anglo-American anthropologists who have insisted on the need for political commitment in ethnographic work by taking native peoples into consideration (Asad 1973; Hymes 1974; Fardon 1990; Fox 1991; Fox and King 2002). They have succeeded in shaking metropolitan centers of anthropological production away from the atomistic torpor that has debilitated the "savage slot," that is, that corner of Western knowledge dedicated to the study of "native" peoples (Trouillot 1991). They have, however, also contributed to the climate of derision that has led some professionals to go overboard and deny altogether the value of studying the local and the distant. "But," asks Herzfeld, "who sets the boundary between importance and mereness?" He continues: "There is a suspiciously close convergence between the refusal to take ethnographic detail seriously and the homogeneity enjoined by nationalist ideologies" (Herzfeld 1997:11).

Common targets of criticism or deconstruction have mostly been the culture concept, otherness, exoticism, and essentialism. Beyond the salutary exercise of periodic checks on the effect of "secondary explanations" (Bunzl 2004:439) that adhere to the discipline along its history (Fabian's 1983 defense of coevalness is one example), the fairness of some positions, especially those leveled at the concept of culture, is open to question. Debates against and in favor of culture have mobilized a number of scholars in the past decade, with, as might be expected, both unexciting and outstanding results. Since most critics of culture stress the concept's negative features without naming names or citing titles, one might be justified in thinking that the object of their objections is the stereotyped image that was created during the final decades of the 20th century of Bronislaw Malinowski's prescriptive formulas for how ethnographic fieldwork should be done and ethnographies written. Critics of this formula have asserted that, by depicting a culture as bounded, ethnographers do its carriers a political disservice. The canonical way of presenting cultures, it is feared, turns anthropology into "a discourse of alterity that magnifies the distance between 'others' and 'ourselves' while *suppressing mutual entanglement* and the perspectival and political fracturing of the cultures of both observers and observed" (Thomas 1991:309, emphasis added). Nevertheless, Thomas concedes that "it is obvious that much anthropological writing is not subsumed within that canon, and that examples of comparative analysis already exist" (1991:316).

The discomfort expressed by authors like Thomas and Fabian with the anthropological bent for othering is justifiable to the extent that the products of ethnography in fact contribute to demeaning non-Western peoples in the eyes of the world power centers. (Chagnon's 1968 portrayal of the Yanomami is a case in point.) However, the denial of significant cultural differences risks inflating even more the already excessive self-righteousness of the West. In their effort to create a field of "native" empowerment, anthropologists concerned with the negative effects of othering risk erasing one of the most valuable assets of the anthropological endeavor – the political and moral importance of cultural diversity.

We must not assume that the anthropological concept of *Other* refers necessarily to a substance, an essence pertaining to the inhabitants of the world fringes. To the contrary, it could and should be taken, *not* as a substantive category, but as an analytical concept that can be found anywhere, from one's neighbors to one's antipodes. "The remote places," says Herzfeld, "are no less relevant than the accessible" (1997:187).

Similarly, sociologists and political scientists in Brazil have berated anthropological studies for their tendency to favor the "popular" and the "quotidian" at the expense of more detached and elevated theorizing (Peirano 1995:13–14). The resulting "state of analytical indigence" is feared like an epidemic disease that threatens to spread over and contaminate the other social sciences. Troubled by opinions of this sort, some anthropologists seem to behold themselves as diminished in the disparaging eyes of their sociology and political science peers whose professional agenda gives priority to impersonal and macro phenomena. Hence, "relevant issues" in "complex" societies are often adopted by anthropologists, not so much due to the perfectly sound conviction that any form of humanity deserves anthropological attention, including its Western manifestations, but rather as "sycophantic adulation," in Herzfeld's exquisite expression (1997:17), of their fellow social scientists, or as a sort of bashful repentance for anthropology's atavistic overattention to the "small and remote" which has kept the profession away from the site where the action is.

In craving for "relevance" and turning their backs to the fringes, anthropologists end up intensifying the taste for exoticism. To study only what is "relevant" – and peoples at the margins of the Western world are almost by definition banned from this exclusive club – is to confirm quite forcefully the inescapable exoticism of the "primitives" that fuels the West's superiority complex. It is not by abandoning basic, local ethnography with native peoples that anthropologists ease the weight of exoticism that has been put upon these peoples' shoulders. Such an attitude can only whet the appetite for the exotic, as the distant Other will continue to be anecdotal and irrelevant to the extent that their inner cultural logic remains unintelligible to the world that has exoticized him in the first place.

Some critics consider that the profession's disregard for broader issues can be traced to the roots of the colonial imagination that hatched anthropology. For this original sin to be expurgated one must retreat from the old ethnographic canon. In other words, anthropological work is politically correct when it inquires into the meanders of Western domination over marginalized or native peoples. In themselves these peoples would not be capable of generating any interest other than in the key of exoticism. It would appear then that they depend on the anthropologist to make them politically visible and relevant by displaying to the world at large their "agonies of oppression" (Herzfeld 1997:23). Otherwise, to study them in and of themselves would amount to doing them a disfavor. Behind this misconception is a centuries old, perhaps impossible to eradicate, incapacity of the West – wherever this is – to relate to cultural differences in any other way than in the mode of inequality: to be different is to be inferior. This notion is so deeply ingrained in Western minds – wherever they are formed – that anthropologists themselves tend to essentialize it. Despite their long and meticulous training designed to counteract this prejudice (in Gadamer's sense of fore-meaning (1975:238)), anthropologists seem unable to break away from its grasp. In their zeal to save the "primitives" from the stigma of inferiority, they end up downplaying cultural specificities as telltale signs of that inferiority. Rather than looking Western arrogance squarely in the face, some metropolitan anthropologists prefer to change the subject and discard the study of cultural specificities as responsible for the production of degrading exoticism. And yet, a good ethnography, be it canonical or not, rather than producing alienating exoticism, has the potential to thwart it by turning inscrutable and glaring differences into intelligibilities or, at least, awakening an appreciation for what we cannot reach. To engage in potentially damaging exoticism is to treat alterity as irreducible to outside understanding. It is to cite empirical details out of context, turning them into fatuous anecdotes or vacuous banalities. A superficial ethnographic account, an inconsequent public talk, a witty, joking or shocking remark to a lay audience are examples of negative exoticism. Ethnic intolerance, paternalism, and cultural submission of indigenous peoples owe a great deal to these written and verbal abuses.

How can the anthropologist try to avoid producing these artifacts of debasing exoticism? Gregory Bateson seems to have searched for an antidote:

> If it were possible adequately to present the whole of a culture, stressing every aspect exactly as it is stressed in the culture itself, no single detail would appear bizarre or strange or arbitrary to the reader, but rather the details would all appear natural and reasonable as they do to the natives who have lived all their lives within the culture. (1958:1)

As unachievable as a Weberian ideal type, this aspiration nevertheless can aptly serve as a remedy against the malignant growth of a Baudrillardian simulacrum. Again the Yanomami case serves us well to illustrate my point. The Yanomami public image has circulated around the world in a reduced, simplified, and highly distorted rendition that has hardly any resemblance to the cultural sophistication with which these people have endowed ethnography. As "fierce people" the Yanomami have been deeply insulted by the mass media: "the rather horrifying Yãnomamö culture makes some sense in terms of animal behavior. Chagnon argues that Yãnomamö structures closely parallel those of many primates [such as] baboon troops" (*Time* 1976). What *Time Magazine* depicted was nowhere near an honest version of the Yanomami, but rather a grotesque simulacrum of an extraordinarily complex reality (Ramos 1987). Reduced and ethically dubious models seem to be a general currency when it comes to the portrayal of flesh and blood Indians (Ramos 1994).

"If it were possible" to meet Bateson's standards, familiarity would supplant exoticism, which in turn would lose much of its virulent simulation. We cannot aspire to do such an exhaustive job as Bateson dreamed of, but we can have thoroughness as our ethnographic horizon. As a matter of fact, to embrace an Other's entire world and still maintain the sense of difference would amount to a sort of contradiction in terms: familiarity with strangeness. The exotic, says Foster, "is always full of surprises; it delights and titillates. To domesticate it exhaustively would neutralize this aspect of its meaning and regretfully integrate it into the humdrum of everyday routines" (1982:21–22). The sense of difference must be maintained if we are to shake off the Metropolis's self-righteousness and halt the perpetuation of the Other's powerlessness. Whenever the Metropolis staggers in the face of confronting otherness, ethnography is redeemed. Whenever the Metropolis is as ethnographically denuded as the fringes have been, the meaning of power undergoes some sort of revision. It is this potential to produce an unsettling effect on established truths that should be the thrust of repatriating anthropology.

This represents an altogether different face of exoticism (Ramos 2003a). It involves the prodigious effort of first trying to understand the logic, the deep sense of the Other, then of finding forms of cultural translation that are deserving of its formidable complexities, to eventually convert the results into instruments for defending the people's right to be different. This means a refusal to adjectivize the subjects of our research, reduce them to a handful of stereotyped features, and make them the object of inane curiosity. A thoughtful ethnography that does not deny its subjects the right of coevalness (Fabian 1983), that is constructed in as complete and sensitive a manner as possible, with ethical commitment, with moral and political respect for alterity, and a critical attitude to banalization, can go a long way to keeping the exotic within the limits of healthy differences. In other words, one can practice ethnography without consuming oneself with guilt.

The other side of exoticism can also be found in the social movements of indigenous peoples who objectify their culture for the purpose of protecting their alterity against the homogenizing pressure of nation-states. The Kayapó of central Brazil (Turner 1991), the peoples of the Brazilian Northeast (Oliveira 1999), the Mayas of Guatemala (Warren 1998), the various indigenous peoples in Colombia (Jackson 1989, 1991, 1995, 1999; Sotomayor 1998), the Dekuana (Yekuana) of Venezuela (Arvelo-Jiménez and Jiménez 2001), or the Argentine Indians (Briones 2003; Gordillo and Hirsch 2003; Hirsch 2003; Rappaport 2005; Warren 1998) are apt illustrations of this rapidly expanding phenomenon. One would do well to learn from non-Western peoples, not only about their cultural specificities as thoroughly as Bateson wished, but also about their strategies, very often regarded by anthropologists themselves as questionable, naive or ineffectual. One should bear in mind that indigenous peoples have a long experience of walking straight on winding trails. What may look like idle wanderings to a Cartesian mind may actually represent the shortest way between two political points, providing us with surprising lessons of creativity (Sahlins 1988, 1992). Underlying processual History there is always a dialectical process that usually unfolds in silence, often going unnoticed, but which has the power to transform the course of events regardless of human awareness. These remarks echo Foster's, written in the early 1980s: "If cultural processes work dialectically, one may expect the proliferation of social meanings posed by the exotic to be controlled, countered and limited by further symbolic machinations" (1982:27). To what extent anthropologists are able and willing to follow up the signs and directions of such design, no doubt identified today as the creativity of the local, is the challenge of the profession in this turn of millennium.

## DISENGAGEMENT

Most of what appears above refers to ideas that moved me up to the turn of the century. Although I am still convinced of the value of ethnographies, and even more so of the political justice in demonstrating the legitimacy of otherness as well as the ethical appropriateness of engagement, I perceive this set of issues in a new light due, in large part, to the recently identified reactions of indigenous peoples to the work of anthropologists. So strong an impression has this new context made on me that I propose a change in paradigm – from engagement to disengagement.

Needless to say, the chapter rests on questions rather than on answers, in part, because we are dealing with an intensely shifting ground. What follows, then, is an attempt to make some sense of a segment of the history in Brazil of interethnic relations in the making, as it were.

## The small and the remote are getting bigger and closer

In the last three decades, if not before, ethnographers working in Latin America, including Brazil, almost unanimously endorsed the proposition of combining research activities among indigenous peoples with advocacy work on their behalf (Ramos 1990, 1999–2000, 2003a). Engagement was the order of the day and ethnography was put at the service of ethnic justice. Such intense commitment to the indigenous cause was bound to affect not only the way research was conducted, but also what was being researched and how. As Albert put it, "the social engagement of the ethnographer can no longer be seen as a personal political or ethical choice, optional and foreign to his scientific project. It clearly becomes an explicit and constituent element of the ethnographic relationship" (1997:57–58).

Research topics came to contemplate not simply the ethnographer's interests but also the need to generate strategic knowledge that might contribute to the defense of indigenous rights. Advocacy became a must among ethnographers in Brazil, with the result that their indigenous subjects were progressively made aware that anthropological research had a strong political appeal.

But while ethnographers who did their major fieldwork in the 1960s, 1970s, and 1980s could choose when to go to the field, what to study and with whom, an imperceptible shift was underway. Anthropologists accustomed to regarding fieldwork as an open and uncontested research base began to realize that they were no longer in control of the field situation. What started as a goodwill disposition on the part of ethnographers to deliver knowledge and political awareness to their research subjects, suddenly changed actors, keys, and motives.

By the 1990s a new generation of ethnographers began to distinctly feel the pressure to conform to local demands, be they in the form of trade goods, machinery, fundraising proposals, or assistance in various activities, as a condition for carrying out their investigation. These constraints on research activities are now part and parcel of doing ethnography. They are usually, but not solely, directed to fledgling ethnographers and take the form of often outlandish demands, given the limited funds normally available to anthropologists, particularly students. Consider, for instance, the paving of a ten kilometer road as the cost of admittance by a specific indigenous group, a situation faced by a Brazilian M.A. student who wished to study the effects of biopiracy that had been inflicted upon that group. Hardened by the experience of being grossly exploited in the name of scientific research, those Indians reacted as though all researchers were out to take advantage of them. In this, as in most cases, this sort of initiatory probation resolves itself with often elaborate negotiations that bind the disheartened researcher to an unforeseen course of action. But most likely the Indians will end up steering the researcher's project to their own ends as a condition for his or her stay in the field. Malinowskian-style fieldwork is definitely a thing of the past, and a wad of tobacco is no longer enough for admission into an ethnographic haven.

As to speaking for the natives, previous experiences with indigenous activism had already put an end to the long habit of taking the anthropologist as their widely acknowledged surrogate. Along the anthropologists' career as political actors (Ramos 1999–2000), they have seen their indigenous subjects take over the task of defenders of their own rights, stipulate conditions or norms for research activities, and affirm their political agency (Caplan 2003).

Now a new time begins in which, having seized the role of political actors, indigenous peoples in Brazil (and elsewhere) are in the process of appropriating the very raison d'être of the ethnographer's work, namely, ethnographies. Anthropologists can now observe the first results of the literacy programs many helped create, and with these, a growing indigenous interest in the production of auto-ethnographies.

Here I am speaking as a Brazilian anthropologist long engaged in indigenous advocacy, particularly on behalf of the Yanomami people. What follows refers to their present situation in Brazil, but what we now witness is not limited to the Yanomami or to indigenous peoples, nor is it an exclusively Brazilian phenomenon (see Varese, Delgado, and Meyer, this volume).

The impact of ethnographic research upon our subjects is much greater than we realize or are prepared to admit. A common experience for many of us who worked with peoples before their exposure to schools was to watch the curiosity, especially on the part of the younger generation, about our constant habit of writing. My field diaries, as certainly those of many colleagues, are at points covered with wavy lines on the margins done by Yanomami as they gazed at my constant chore of inscribing the events of the day. Initially associated with the Protestant missionaries resident in their villages, writing was one of the distinctive features of being *setenabi*, a Sanumá (the Yanomami subgroup among whom I did fieldwork) concept translatable as "the other, White." The connection between writing and power was a relatively easy one to make, as putting marks on a piece of paper could produce spectacular results (see Harvey, this volume). But unlike the missionaries whose immediately perceived interest was in language and preaching (in Sanumá *deusïmo*, from the Portuguese *Deus* (God) + *mo* (verbalizer)), the ethnographers asked a myriad of other questions and actually encouraged habits condemned by the Protestants, such as polygyny and shamanism.

Those were questions that perhaps the people themselves had never asked before, thus setting off a subtle process of auto-curiosity. Thoughts along these lines came to me in the early 1990s when I brought back recollections of my 1974 interviews with an ambitious young man, as I wrote the Portuguese version of *Sanumá Memories* (here I take the liberty of quoting from the US edition):

> I began to think about the issue of self-questioning when later I pondered those encounters with him. What goes into the making of a native philosopher? How is his or her philosophical road paved? The seed of distancing may be sowed by missionaries or any other agents of change, but it is the anthropologist, the spawner of distancing *par excellence*, who often nourishes that seed to germination. In his eagerness to unveil what is implicit, he (as often as she) asks the unaskable, planting doubts about what is taken for granted. In so doing, the ethnographer projects a way of being Western that has neither precedent nor nexus for the people. The very respect for and emulation of the local culture the ethnographer often demonstrates become themselves an impetus for questioning on the part of his or her hosts. (Ramos 1995:319–320)

Considering that learning among indigenous peoples is mostly done by observation and imitation or replication, to attain instruction by intense questioning in ethnographic style seems to have been a striking novelty. Silently, not only have they assimilated this way of learning, but also incorporated some anthropological discourses as devices to make sense of the new order of interethnic relations that are increasingly affecting them (Albert 1993). Observing the ethnographer at work reproducing fragments of local knowledge that were fixed on paper triggered in many a Yanomami in Brazil the desire for literacy. In their case, as in many other situations, I suspect, there has been no reason for alarm that localized ethnographic research might suppress "mutual entanglement," as Thomas seemed to fear.

In 1995, the Pro-Yanomami Commission, the Brazilian nongovernmental organization that had so vigorously campaigned for the demarcation of the Yanomami land (signed by Brazil's president in 1991 after 13 years of intense lobbying), began to work on a literacy program in a limited group of villages. By 2004 there were 38 schools operating in seven regions totaling nearly 1,700 people, 470 students, and 25 Yanomami teachers. Instruction has been mostly done in the local languages, which have become the vehicle for the exchange of written messages that now cover a vast network within the Yanomami Indigenous Land. A number of youths are developing a taste for research. They have taken upon themselves the task of probing into their elders' erudite knowledge of things Yanomami. Also on visits to other indigenous peoples in the country (as part of their school activities), young Yanomami dedicate part of their time researching their hosts.

The still timid empowerment that writing is conferring to the Yanomami has been manifested, for instance, in their use of collective letters to key figures of the Brazilian state demanding respect for their rights, be they in matters of health or land invasions. These letters are publicized via the internet by the Pro-Yanomami Commission and reach a large and varied readership, from government officials to journalists. Writing is at last being harnessed and producing its first effects for the Yanomami in Brazil.

When the Pro-Yanomami Commission was created in 1978, its designers – who included several anthropologists – proposed that its life expectancy would depend on the degree of preparedness of the Yanomami to cope with external pressures (www.proyanomami.org.br). The first step in that direction was to guarantee the official protection of their land rights. Once that was achieved, health and education programs were launched, not only as part of the original purpose of sparing that ethnic group the fate that fills copious volumes on the tragedy of interethnic contact in the Americas, but also to meet a growing and insistent Yanomami demand. Thirteen years after the official land demarcation, the Yanomami in Brazil created, in November 2004, their overarching association designed to promote their languages and culture and steer their interests in as autonomous a manner as possible. As the main supporter of this event, the Pro-Yanomami Commission foresees its own closure in a fairly near future when its original project has been safely accomplished. Once the Yanomami are equipped to directly defend their rights and walk on solid interethnic ground, the Commission will, in Mission Impossible fashion, destroy itself, so to speak. Rather than regarding withdrawal as a defeat, its members consider it a measure of its success.

The Yanomami have reached the 21st century relatively free of the plights that have afflicted the vast majority of the world's native peoples. Land invasions and epidemics have taken a heavy toll, especially along the 20th century (Ramos 1995). But most of the 25 thousand Yanomami (roughly half in Brazil and half in Venezuela) have been spared the enduring material degradation and social humiliation that saturates the history of interethnic contact in the Americas. This situation is highly favorable and conducive to preventive work (land mostly free of settlers, literacy in the native languages, and vaccination campaigns among other advantages). As lived experience cannot be transmitted vicariously, many Yanomami do not fully appreciate the benefit of a vast demarcated territory for their permanent and exclusive usufruct. For them the arduous battle for land rights in the context of opposing national and regional interests is something of an abstraction, as is the notion that land can be the object of private property with considerable market value. These are experience-distant realities that the Yanomami are slowly incorporating, via formal education, and for which their newly created association will serve as a powerful catalyst.

## The ethnographer as supporting actor

Twentieth century anthropology was marked by both severe ethical abuses – such as US undercover activities in Latin America and Southeast Asia (Weaver 1973) – and a substantial concern for ethical conduct toward research subjects (Caplan 2003; Fluehr-Lobban 2003; Víctora et al. 2004). As a consequence ethnographers are haunted by several questions that transcend queries on the morality of the culture concept: how will subjects of research react to ethnographic writings; will negative reactions put a stop to further research; do ethnographers have the moral right to denude other people's lives; how ethical, after all, is the very act of ethnographic research? (Mills 2003:37). As a culmination of the mounting critical awareness on the part of indigenous peoples, there is now the possibility that all these questions may sooner or later become moot the moment these peoples complete the so far budding process of appropriation of ethnographic know-how and set out on a project of auto-ethnographies. If and when that occurs, what will happen to the traditional fieldworker? The resilience of academic habits seems to have shielded anthropologists from exposure to these challenges, especially if we observe the US experience. For years Native Americans like Vine Deloria have taken anthropologists to task on the issue of professional ethics and engagement, with apparently negligible results (Deloria 1988; Mihesuah 1998). Perhaps the hold of the Metropolis has been too strong, suffocating possible activist vocations among academic anthropologists. It would seem that "the natives-speak-back phenomenon" has to take global proportions to be properly heeded by the metropolitan anthropological profession. We are now on the edge of such globalized challenge. In turn, the Latin American, more specifically Brazilian, anthropological condition outside metropolitan centers of production has favored a disposition toward multiple influences, including that derived from the experience of ethnography among indigenous peoples (Velho 1982; Ramos 1990; Ribeiro 2005).

Current examples give us a glimpse of the future roles of today's ethnographers. The Brazilian Uaupés region has witnessed a lively period of literary production by the Tukanoan-speaking Desana and the Arawak-speaking Tariana, who have been granted funds to write a series of books on their own mythology. To bring their project to fruition they requested the assistance of their long-term ethnographer and advocate Dominique Buchillet, who has been in charge of the organization and editing of seven volumes of their Rio Negro Indigenous Narrators series (sponsored by the Federation of Rio Negro Indigenous Organizations, FOIRN, and comprising seven volumes). Her own research on health issues and shamanism, which qualifies her for the task, has given way to the commitment to satisfy that intense indigenous demand for publishing about their own culture. From a leading position as main researcher with projects of her own, she has taken on the role of supporting actress in a feature run by her research subjects.

Similarly, Bruce Albert, who has conducted fieldwork among the Yanomami in Brazil since 1975, had his solo ethnographic research cut short by a demand on the part of his host, Davi Kopenawa, to prepare a book about his life, his culture, and his rich interethnic experience. Albert does the writing, but Kopenawa is the incontestable mentor of the project and author of the narrative. Taking this cooperative type of ethnographic enterprise as highly important and rewarding, Albert has abandoned any idea of returning to the canonical ethnography he practiced for decades.

These cases illustrate what roles the anthropologist can perform in an era when research subjects, in ascertaining their agency and empowerment, keep the ethnographer at arm's length. The intellectual investment of a lifetime begins to bear fruit to those – the research subjects – who made that investment possible in the first place. Like a figurative echo of a cargo cult, this movement aims at apprehending the stuff of ethnography, preferably doing away with the ethnographer, not by the ethnographer's magic, but by a new form of erudition. The dialogical relationship between observer and observed much touted by postmodern authors, albeit in something of a social vacuum, may well materialize as a joint venture where the leading role is no longer with the conventional ethnographer, as in conventional ethnographic writings where almost invariably the senior author is the anthropologist.

The knowledge generated by fieldwork and demonstrated in some political actions, such as the mobilization of public opinion, the organization of support groups, and, perhaps most impressively, fundraising, has convinced our subjects that behind the apparently innocent, idle or irritating curiosity of researchers there is the unsuspected power of ethnographic imaging and othering. Their reactions are not always affable, often causing hurt feelings on the part of ethnographers, but this should not deter us from appreciating the full consequences of our professional activities. Brazilian rules for getting permission to do fieldwork in indigenous areas include the need for the acceptance of the research project by the communities in question. This puts the fate of the researcher's project literally in the hands of the local people. In certain situations sentiments of rejection or of outrageous demands produce such bitterness in the ethnographer as to create a blind spot in her or his consciousness, allowing anger and frustration to replace the need to understand what is actually at stake. Incidents in the field often bring about misunderstandings that have great potential to be productive and should in due time, when the dust has settled, elicit from the anthropologist the urge to reflect upon and analyze new conjunctures of old structures as they unfold under her or his baffled eyes.

Activist anthropologists would do well to shed the fantasy that redeeming goodwill is an automatic safeguard against native refusal to collaborate. In fact, it is not impossible that anthropological benevolence caters to the dominant society rather than to the people being studied, as research subjects clearly perceive and Povinelli shows in the case of Australian Aborigines: "Because anthropologists were people of good-will – people who could demonstrate a real sympathy, knowledge, and passion for Aboriginal society – they could reassure the public that whatever disciplinary protocol they advocated for Aboriginal society was advocated humanely, tolerantly, and on its behalf. It would be just and moral" (Povinelli 2002:122). Many abusive ethnographic portraits of indigenous peoples have been drawn with the good intention of protecting them from offensive judgments about customs regarded as distasteful by the dominant society. These attempts at sanitizing native cultures are as insulting as cases of collective character assassinations and are now the object of angry reactions on the part of the offended people.

The underside of the hurdles that impair research, most often emotionally perceived by wounded ethnographers as unjust treatment in return for their altruistic dedication, constitute a much deeper phenomenon, the intelligibility of which must be sought in the recent history of interethnic relations rather than in the personalized contingency of ethnographic misencounters. After a long trajectory of forced surrender, indigenous peoples in Brazil – and elsewhere – now act upon the urgency to take over the making of ethnographies as symbolic capital. It is as though, from the natives' point of view, ethnography was just too important an enterprise to be left to ethnographers. The symbolically charged quest for the repatriation of the indigenous cultural self, begun with the political act of self-representation, is completed with the appropriation of ethnographic production. This, however, is far from being an easy task. Conveying indigenous logic to non-indigenous audiences without the surrogate anthropologist can be a difficult enterprise, as Huron historian Georges E. Sioui has experienced: "I have often been struck by the great difficulties peoples of Native culture encounter when they try to sensitize outsiders to their traditional values" (1992: xxi). Cultivating the image of the hyperreal Indian (Ramos 1994) is an old habit that will certainly die hard.

In the inverse order of the indigenous commitment to auto-affirmation, the anthropological consciousness in Brazil – and, as we have seen, elsewhere – is gradually retreating from its ethnographic and militant conventions. Tacit questions are in the air still waiting to be explicitly formulated. Will ethnography survive without the conventional ethnographers? Will anthropologists acquiesce to play the role of supporting actors? What might they do in that role: Take on the busy work expected of them by their former research "objects"? Facilitate their access to anthropological theories as tools for refined auto-research? Usher them to the vast world of comparative ethnographies, if, of course, they show any interest at all in theory and comparison, which is by no means an obvious assumption? Simply abdicate their own agency and retreat backstage, converted into a mere convenience for the political purposes of the new actors of self-indigenism? Or rejoice with the new, creative, and so far immeasurable prospects for a new sort of comparative and theoretical work?

The relatively long and established tradition of academic anthropology in Brazil (Ribeiro 1999–2000; Grimson, Ribeiro and Semán 2004; Trajano Filho and Ribeiro 2004) has resulted in a rather ambiguous relationship between ethnographers and their research subjects. If, on the one hand, most ethnographers working with indigenous peoples have adhered to a political commitment that has characterized the study of interethnic relations in the country (Ramos 1999–2000), on the other, the weight of academic authority has not gone unnoticed by their research hosts. For a while, anthropologists were regarded as assets in the various spheres that involved the Indians in issues of human rights. In a slightly caricatural mode, each tribe had its anthropologist who should comply with its demands. Although this pattern survives to this day in a number of interethnic contexts, indigenous leaders are increasingly intent on disentangling themselves from anthropologists as authoritative figures. At most, the latter are permitted to be supporting actors in the field of interethnic politics. For all their good intentions, anthropologists have no longer the paramount role they once had in defending "their people."

Still, of all the possible political partners in the ethnopolitical scenario, Brazilian Indians still prefer to work with anthropologists. Why do they choose to involve anthropologists in their joint ventures? Could it be the respect and appreciation they sense in their ethnographic observers; the fact that ethnographic involvement in research has no strings attached (such as economic or religious entanglements); or the capacity they perceive in ethnographers to propagate their image through power centers? Perhaps a combination of these and other factors have brought about a new relationship in the field. On the bright side of things, if we disregard the differential power that always exists between the academic ethnographer and the people studied, we might conceive of this new association as partnership. What has been commended as complicity – "The basic condition that defines the altered mise-en-scène for which complicity rather than rapport is a more appropriate figure is an awareness of existential doubleness on the part of *both* anthropologist and subject" (Marcus 1999:97) – may no longer be sufficient to describe the novel ethnographic ambiance in countries such as Brazil. While complicity underscores the bond that prolonged interaction may create vis-à-vis those who do not partake of ethnographic intimacy, it is silent about the terms of ethnographic coproduction between the academic researcher and the "native" ethnographer. Complicity is a necessary but not a sufficient condition for the establishment of an ethnographic partnership.

Over and above all the surprises, disillusions, and misgivings that fieldwork has brought about lately, anthropologists, particularly but not exclusively those active in human rights, must be aware of the twofold influence of their ethnographic work. On the one hand, through their example in probing cultural worlds and then in acting in their defense, ethnographers first awakened in their research subjects the urge to act on behalf of their ethnic integrity and political rights. On the other hand, through advocacy work, anthropologists have opened up new lines of investigation, thus contributing to dignify the practical side of the profession for so long lessened as second-rate anthropology under the disparaging epithets of "applied anthropology" or "action anthropology" (Hastrup and Elsass 1990:302, 306, 307; Caplan 2003:14). Both aspects have had profound consequences for the future of ethnography.

From the standpoint of indigenous peoples, there is a clear convergence of interests in their new attitude toward the legacy of anthropologists. Self-defense and self-representation go hand in hand when the Indians, like anybody else, come to realize that knowledge is power and that writing is a mighty instrument for the accumulation of knowledge. Why then leave the wisdom of one's world in foreign hands? And, what is worse, as an incomplete, fragmented, and often distorted picture as ethnographic knowledge, as Bateson envisioned, is bound to be, when in one's own hands that knowledge can reach incomparable degrees of depth, intelligibility, and immediate significance?[1] Might not auto-ethnographies achieve Bateson's vision quest for nonexotic alterity? Together, ethnographic knowledge and political action seem to make up a secular cargo-cult type of package that is on the verge of being retrieved from Westerners and delivered to the native actors who are taking over the interethnic stage. "I wonder," says Stuart Kirsch (2004), whose research and advocacy experience in New Guinea has aroused similar thoughts, "if we are on the cusp of a third era, in which concerns about our participation are being raised by the people with whom we work, who may no longer want us to be involved in projects so closely linked to their own identities and self-determination."

Ironically, in this emergent native trend, ethnographers, the "spawners of distancing *par excellence*" and harbingers of self-inquisitiveness, are greatly, albeit not wholly, responsible for the present boom of cultural awareness and political assertion. Observe, for instance, the widespread transformation of the concept of culture from an academic artifact to an icon of ethnic strengthening and self-determination (Turner 1991; Sahlins 1992, 1993; Ramos 2003b). Witness also the force of the motto "Our knowledge is our trademark" [Nosso saber é nossa marca] that underlines the logotype of the Brazilian Indigenous Institute for Intellectual Property. No wonder traditional ethnographic production is now under suspicion and surveillance, treated as a sort of smuggling or poaching for which consent has seldom been frankly and thoroughly informed.

Why have I chosen the expression auto-ethnographies rather than "native ethnographies" or what we may call "metonymic ethnographies" (like investigating like, such as women studying feminism, blacks studying blacks, homosexuals studying homosexuals, ethnics studying ethnics, etc.)? The main reason for this choice has to do with the former's specific intellectual orientation which differs substantially from the other two. In fact, just about the only thing the three modes have in common is the reduced or even lack of distance between observed and observer. Both "native anthropology" and "metonymic ethnography" follow the canon of metropolitan anthropology with its emphasis on theoretical underpinnings and the pursuit of knowledge for knowledge's sake. Although native anthropologists may resent the state of invisibility to which the Metropolis relegates them (Briggs 1996), they still conform to "the foundational Self/Other divide that organizes classical fieldwork and produces the native anthropologist as a virtual member of the discipline" (Bunzl 2004:436). An integral part of the traditional academic mode, metonymic ethnography has been commended for its appeal for the repatriation of anthropology (Clifford and Marcus 1986). In turn, auto-ethnographies, as far as we can envision a trend, have no perceptible commitment to the academic side of anthropology, and may never have if uncritical emulation of Western intellectual habits continues to be resisted. Basically self-interested in the present phase of ethnic consciousness (again I am speaking about the Brazilian context), auto-ethnographies seem to be geared toward the instrumentality of ethnic assets to be used in contexts of interethnic politics. This view resonates with Mary Louise Pratt's observation: auto-ethnographies "are merged and infiltrated to varying degrees with indigenous idioms to create self-representations intended to *intervene* in metropolitan modes of understanding" (1994:28, emphasis in the original).

It is doubtful that auto-ethnographies will necessarily mirror traditional ethnographies. "Native" appropriation of ethnographic production has a distinctly different rationale, at least as far as we can now detect. Interest in self-representation in the ethnographic mode is political rather than academic, which certainly moulds observation and analysis in a distinct way from the ethnographies academically fashioned. One can expect, for instance, a considerable difference in the choice of research topics, styles, and public. It is even possible that the matter of authorship, important as it has been for Western scholars (*pace* the complications brought about by electronic release), may play a minimal role in the political scenario of auto-ethnographies. It is also reasonable to expect that whatever interest there may develop among indigenous people for the making of ethnographies of the West will have the same primary political, nonacademic quality. There is no reason to assume that the academic orientation of Western-made ethnographies is a precondition for their production. If one of the consequences of ethnographies is that the "know-how" for carrying out research is being delivered to its subjects, it follows that ethnographic research is not an exclusive prerogative of the West.

## Old Malinowski versus New Boas

A new Zeitgeist seems to be rising on the anthropological horizon in Brazil. The stirrings of a "third era," to evoke Kirsch's intuition, appear to be in the air, announcing not only the exit of the anthropologist from center-stage activism, but also the confluence of anthropological praxis and theory. The Malinowskian canon of ethnographic research, responsible as it was for a large portion of anthropology's empirical and theoretical baggage, is no longer feasible or, for that matter, necessary. The "ethnographer's magic, by which he is able to evoke the real spirit of the natives, the true picture of tribal life" (Malinowski 1961:6) is losing its mystery. In looking over the ethnographer's shoulder for so long, the "natives" are now in the process of cracking the secret formula of that magic. One can detect at least two major factors that account for the loss of ethnographic hegemony and for the sense of malaise that has troubled the profession.

On the one hand, the demise of the "research object," that imagined bastion of immanence, has of late caused a great deal of discomfort that was ruthlessly accentuated at the height of the postmodern rebellion. Not a few ethnographers, incomprehensibly oblivious of the historical metamorphosis that transfigured their "informants" into politically smart subjects, were, oddly as it may seem, caught unawares when told that their precious research projects were not and had never been of any interest to their former hosts and so, please, don't come back. Having the ethnographic rug pulled from under their feet, ethnographers seem to have lost their balance and are still stumbling around in bewilderment, stranded fieldworkers in search of the lost field.

This may be more noticeable now in Brazil than elsewhere in Latin America (see, for instance, Barragán, this volume), but it is evident that indigenous ethnography – which, incidentally, has regularly been a minority activity within the anthropological profession in that country – attracts much less attention than other research sites. In fact, some ethnographers have changed fields since their doctoral research. Caught up between two contrasting conjunctures that may well lead to a new and still unpredictable research configuration, most of us are yet to come to grips with a future in which ethnography might be, literally, alien to our training and expectations.

On the other hand, anthropology has become utterly saturated with "ethnographic facts" that for nine decades have been accumulating to overflowing, thus cramming the discipline with an excess of diminishing returns. In nearly a century of professional activity, anthropology attained an extraordinary ethnographic acumen as the result of the continuous and ever growing effort to collect data from all over the world. With this reserve in hand it would seem, to some, that all major points in anthropology's time-honored agenda have already been made, some, in fact, *ad nauseam* and not necessarily by consensus: the universality and primacy of culture, the merits and dangers of relativism, the praise and pride for human diversity. Would the compulsive amassing of data in projects epitomized by Yale's ill-fated and now pretty much forgotten Human Relations

Area Files go on forever toward a sorcerer's apprentice nightmare, if the "natives" did not put a stop to it?[2] Or will it continue in spite of everything to feed the type of anthropological imagination that is bent on forever weaving filigreed turns of mind *à la pensée sauvage* (e.g. Viveiros de Castro 1995)? As US anthropologist Sherry Ortner wrote nearly a decade ago: "Cultural analysis can no longer, for the most part, be an end in itself. The production of portraits of other cultures, no matter how well drawn, is in a sense no longer a major option" (1999:9).

If the Malinowskian mode of ethnographies minimized the intellectual transit between observer and observed, the anthropological script created by Boas left open that possibility. It is perhaps no coincidence that Boas – who helped to train such important anthropologists as Manuel Gamio and Moises Saenz in Mexico – exerted a much greater influence in Latin American anthropology than Malinowski.[3] Recent efforts to restore Boas's influence in contemporary anthropology have pointed toward a new Boasian way of shaping the field. Partly as a response to the barrage of criticism leveled at the concept of culture, Bashkow (2004), Bunzl (2004), Handler (2004), Orta (2004), and Rosenblatt (2004) sift through Boas's thinking to show that the specter of bounded cultures is nothing more than an example of secondary rationalization, "highly charged with emotional value" (Stocking quoted in Bunzl 2004:439), and that the chasm between the knowing subject and the knowable object had no place in his agenda. In fact, "Boas was just as happy if Native Americans generated ethnographic data themselves" (Bunzl 2004:438). In other words, Boas, who came from a Herderian tradition where *Kultur* took on the status of a national essence, significantly enough, conceived for anthropology a sense of culture totally open not only to the work of history, but also to external as well as internal scrutiny. What for so many years lay dormant in the folds of anthropological memory, submerged by successive waves of theoretical novelties, reemerges as ancestral wisdom with the potential to rescue the discipline from a pending impasse.

Thus reloaded, the Boasian matrix could be a suitable instrument to gauge what is now happening in the contested field of ethnography. Far from being a universal panacea for the present anthropological gloomy mood, neo-Boasianism simply offers an opportunity for reflection. It is good to think the current predicaments of the field for it presents "an ongoing condition of the possibility for a meaningful and relevant anthropology" (Orta 2004:485).

Following the lead that Boas, perhaps involuntarily, insinuated, ethnography may very well be on its way to be transferred to its traditional subjects, which in itself is a measure of its success. The habit of observing their observers at work transforming endless questions into knowledge and knowledge into influence has elicited in the "natives" of ethnography the desire to take into their own hands the control of this precious instrument of agency and power. It is to be expected that auto-ethnographies will have a very different flavor from the Western canon in which we have grown up professionally. Observing the observed in the act of observing themselves may be a rewarding conclusion to the long narrative anthropology has composed about Otherness. It follows, then, that both in terms of activism and ethnographic work the ethics of disengagement is in the order of the day.

It goes without saying that disengagement as advocated here is in itself an act of engagement. Indeed, I dare say it is the utmost expression of engagement, for it requires the ethnographer's withdrawal from center stage for it to be occupied by our traditional "others." It is the ultimate recognition that these "others" are at last affirming their full agency as producers of anthropological knowledge. How much more engaged can an anthropologist be in renouncing not only the status of ethnographic authority, but also the decades-long role of nursing the wounds of subjugated indigenous people? How much more mature can anthropology itself be in receiving in its ranks, with open arms, those who for generations have merely been food for its theoretical thought?

## NOTES

1   The question of significance or relevance came home to me during a graduate class when we were discussing Fernando Coronil's *The Magical State*. Invited to the session, Venezuelan anthropologist Nelly Arvelo-Jiménez was amused with the lively debate in which the students and I engaged about the various possibilities of interpreting the Venezuelan context having our Brazilian experience as a comparative yardstick. When asked to comment, our guest declared that all those opinions were very interesting, but, although not wrong, they meant nothing to her. It was a vivid demonstration that what makes sense to an outsider may be virtually meaningless to the insider. Somewhat along these lines Brazilian intellectuals tend to regard Brazilianists' analyses with a grain of skepticism. In the old days of ethnoscience, that was a contentious point, wittily dubbed as God's truth or hocus-pocus (Burling 1964).
2   The Human Relations Area Files were an ambitious project created at Yale in 1949. Its goal was to catalogue every cultural trait ever recorded in ethnographies and other published and unpublished sources.
3   I thank Deborah Poole for pointing this out to me.

## REFERENCES

Albert, Bruce (1993) L'Or cannibale et la chute du ciel. Une critique chamanique de l'économie politique de la nature (Yanomami, Brasil). In *La Remontée de l'Amazone*, theme issue of *L'Homme* 126–128:349–378.

Albert, Bruce (1997) "Ethnographic Situation" and Ethnic Movements: Notes on Post-Malinowskian Fieldwork. *Critique of Anthropology* 17(1):53–65.

Arvelo-Jiménez, Nelly and Jiménez, Simeón (eds) (2001) *Atlas Dekuana*. Caracas: Point Grafique.

Asad, Talal (1973) *Anthropology and the Colonial Encounter*. London: Ithaca Press.

Bashkow, Ira (2004) A Neo-Boasian Conception of Cultural Boundaries. *American Anthropologist* 106(3):443–458.

Bateson, Gregory (1958[1936]) *Naven: A Survey of the Problems Suggested by a Composite Picture of the Culture of a New Guinea Tribe Drawn from Three Points of View*. Stanford: Stanford University Press.

Briggs, Charles (1996) The Politics of Discursive Authority in Research on the "Invention of Tradition." *Cultural Anthropology* 11(4):435–469.

Briones, Claudia (2003) Re-membering the Dis-membered: A Drama about Mapuche and Anthropological Cultural Production in Three Scenes (4th edition). In Gastón Gordillo and Silvia Hirsch (guest eds), *Indigenous Struggles and Contested Identities in Argentina*, theme issue of *Journal of Latin American Anthropology* 8(3):31–58.

Bunzl, Matti (2004) Boas, Foucault, and the "Native Anthropologist": Notes toward a Neo-Boasian Anthropology. *American Anthropologist* 106(3):435–442.

Burling, Robbins (1964) Cognition and Componential Analysis: God's Truth or Hocus-Pocus? *American Anthropologist* 66:20–27.

Caplan, Pat (ed.) (2003) *The Ethics of Anthropology: Debates and Dilemmas*. London: Routledge.

Chagnon, Napoleon (1968) *Yanomamö: The Fierce People*. New York: Holt, Rinehart and Winston.

Clifford, James and Marcus, George (eds) (1986) *Writing Culture: The Poetics and Politics of Ethnography*. Berkeley: University of California Press.

Deloria, Jr, Vine (1988) *Custer Died for Your Sins: An Indian Manifesto*. Norman: University of Oklahoma Press.

Fabian, Johannes (1983) *Time and the Other: How Anthropology Makes Its Object*. New York: Columbia University Press.

Fardon, Richard (ed.) (1990) *Localizing Strategies: Regional Traditions of Ethnographic Writing*. Edinburgh: Scottish Academic Press; Washington, DC: Smithsonian Institution Press.

Fluehr-Lobban, Carolyn (ed.) (2003) *Ethics and the Profession of Anthropology: Dialogue for Ethically Conscious Practice*. 2nd edn. Walnut Creek, CA: Altamira Press.

Foster, Stephen W. (1982) The Exotic as a Symbolic System. *Dialectical Anthropology* 7(1): 21–30.

Fox, Richard G. (ed.) (1991) *Recapturing Anthropology: Working in the Present*. Santa Fe: School of American Research Press.

Fox, Richard G. and King, Barbara J. (eds) (2002) *Anthropology beyond Culture*. Oxford: Berg.

Gadamer, Hans-Georg (1975) *Truth and Method*. New York: Crossroads.

Gordillo, Gastón and Hirsch, Silvia (eds) (2003) Introduction: Indigenous Struggles and Contested Identities in Argentina: Histories of Invisibilization and Reemergence. In Gastón Gordillo and Silvia Hirsch (guest eds), *Indigenous Struggles and Contested Identities in Argentina*, theme issue of *Journal of Latin American Anthropology* 8(3):4–30.

Grimson, Alejandro, Ribeiro, Gustavo Lins, and Semán, Pablo (eds) (2004) *La antropologia brasileña contemporánea. Contribuciones para un diálogo latinoamericano*. Buenos Aires: Prometeo Libros/ABA.

Handler, Richard (2004) Afterword: Mysteries of Culture. *American Anthropologist* 106(3):488–494.

Hastrup, Kirsten and Elsass, Peter (1990) Anthropological Advocacy: A Contradiction in Terms? *Current Anthropology* 31(3):301–311.

Herzfeld, Michael (1997) *Cultural Intimacy: Social Poetics in the Nation-State*. London: Routledge.

Hirsch, Silvia María (2003) Bilingualism Pan-Indianism and Politics in Northern Argentina: The Guaraní's Struggle for Identity and Recognition. In Gastón Gordillo and Silvia Hirsch (guest eds), *Indigenous Struggles and Contested Identities in Argentina*, theme issue of *Journal of Latin American Anthropology* 8(3):84–103.

Hymes, Dell (ed.) (1974) *Reinventing Anthropology*. New York: Vintage Books.

Jackson, Jean (1989) Is There a Way to Talk about Making Culture without Making Enemies? *Dialectical Anthropology* 14:127–143.

Jackson, Jean (1991) Hostile Encounters between Nukak and Tukanoans: Changing Ethnic Identity in the Vaupés, Colombia. *Journal of Ethnic Studies* 19(2):17–39.

Jackson, Jean (1995) Culture, Genuine and Spurious: The Politics of Indianness in the Vaupés, Colombia. *American Ethnologist* 22(1):3–27.

Jackson, Jean (1999) The Politics of Ethnographic Practice in the Colombian Vaupés. *Identities* 6(2–3):281–317.

Kirsch, Stuart (2004) Activist Ethnographies: Politics of the Body, State and Nature in New Guinea. Paper presented at conference on Political Interactions: Research, Advocacy and Representation, Goldsmiths' College, London, Nov.

Malinowski, Bronislaw (1961) *Argonauts of the Western Pacific*. New York: E. P. Dutton.

Marcus, George (1999) The Uses of Complicity in the Changing Mise-en-Scène of Anthropological Fieldwork. In Sherry Ortner (ed.), *The Fate of "Culture": Geertz and Beyond* (pp. 86–109). Berkeley: University of California Press.

Mihesuah, Devon A. (1998) *Natives and Academic: Researching and Writing about American Indians*. Lincoln: University of Nebraska Press (Bison Books).

Mills, David (2003) "Like a Horse in Blinkers"? A Political History of Anthropology's Research Ethics. In Pat Caplan (ed.), *The Ethics of Anthropology: Debates and Dilemmas* (pp. 37–54). London: Routledge.

Oliveira, João Pacheco (ed.) (1999) *A Viagem da Volta. Etnicidade, política e reelaboração cultural no nordeste indígena*. Rio de Janeiro: Contra Capa.

Orta, Andrew (2004) The Promise of Particularism and the Theology of Culture: Limits and Lessons of "Neo-Boasianism." *American Anthropologist* 106(3):473–487.

Ortner, Sherry B. (ed.) (1999) *The Fate of Culture: Geertz and Beyond*. Berkeley: University of California Press.

Peirano, Mariza (1995) *A favor da etnografia*. Rio de Janeiro: Relume Dumará.

Povinelli, Elizabeth (2002) *The Cunning of Recognition: Indigenous Alterities and the Making of Australian Multiculturalism*. Durham, NC: Duke University Press.

Pratt, Mary Louise (1994) Transculturation and Autoethnography: Peru, 1615/1980. In Francis Barker, Peter Hulme, and Margaret Iversen (eds), *Colonial Discourse/Postcolonial Theory* (pp. 24–46). Manchester: Manchester University Press.

Ramos, Alcida R. (1987) Reflecting on the Yanomami: Ethnographic Images and the Pursuit of the Exotic. *Cultural Anthropology* 2(3):284–304. Republished in George Marcus (ed.), *Rereading Cultural Anthropology* (pp. 48–68). Durham, NC: Duke University Press, 1992.

Ramos, Alcida R. (1990) Ethnology Brazilian Style. *Cultural Anthropology* 5(4):452–472.

Ramos, Alcida R. (1994) The Hyperreal Indian. *Critique of Anthropology* 14(2):153–171.

Ramos, Alcida R. (1995) *Sanumá Memories: Yanomami Ethnography in Times of Crisis*. Madison: University of Wisconsin Press.

Ramos, Alcida R. (1999–2000) The Anthropologist as Political Actor. In Gustavo Lins Ribeiro (guest ed.), *Reading Brazilian Anthropologists*, theme issue of *Journal of Latin American Anthropology* 4(2)/5(1):172–189.

Ramos, Alcida R. (2003a) Advocacy Rhymes with Anthropology. *Social Analysis* (Forum series, Australia) 47(1):110–116.

Ramos, Alcida R. (2003b) Pulp Fictions of Indigenism. In Donald Moore, Jake Kosek, and Anand Pandian (eds), *Race, Nature, and the Politics of Difference* (pp. 356–379). Durham, NC: Duke University Press.

Rappaport, Joanne (2005) *Intercultural Utopias: Public Intellectuals, Cultural Experimentation, and Ethnic Pluralism in Colombia (Latin America Otherwise)*. Durham, NC: Duke University Press.

Ribeiro, Gustavo Lins (ed.) (1999–2000) *Reading Brazilian Anthropologists*, theme issue of *Journal of Latin American Anthropology* 4(2)/5(1).

Ribeiro, Gustavo Lins (2005) *Antropologias mundiais. Cosmopolíticas, poder e teoria em antropologia*. Série Antropologia, 379. Brasília: Departamento de Antropologia, Universidade de Brasília.

Rosenblatt, Daniel (2004) An Anthropology Made Safe for Culture: Patterns of Practice and the Politics of Difference in Ruth Benedict. *American Anthropologist* 106(3):459–472.

Sahlins, Marshall (1988) Cosmologies of Capitalism: The Trans-Pacific Sector of the "World System." *Proceedings of the British Academy for 1988*, 1–51.

Sahlins, Marshall (1992) The Economics of Develop-Man in the Pacific. *Res* 21:12–25.

Sahlins, Marshall (1993) Goodbye to Tristes Tropes: Ethnography in the Context of Modern World History. *Journal of Modern History* 65(1):1–25.

Sioui, Georges E. (1992) *For an American Autohistory*, trans. Sheila Fischman. Montreal: McGill-Queen's University Press.

Sotomayor, María Lúcia (ed.) (1998) *Modernidad, identidad y desarrollo. Construcción de sociedad y re-creación cultural en contextos de modernización*. Bogotá: Instituto Colombiano de Antropología/Ministerio de Cultura/Conciencias.

Thomas, Nicholas (1991) Against Ethnography. *Cultural Anthropology* 6(3):306–322.

*Time* (1976) Beastly or Manly? *Time*, May 10, p. 37.

Trajano Filho, Wilson and Ribeiro, Gustavo Lins (eds) (2004) *O campo da antropologia no Brasil*. Rio de Janeiro: Contra Capa/ABA.

Trouillot, Michel-Rolph (1991) Anthropology and the Savage Slot: The Poetics and Politics of Otherness. In Richard G. Fox (ed.), *Recapturing Anthropology: Working in the Present* (pp. 17–44). Santa Fe: School of American Research Press.

Turner, Terence (1991) Representing, Resisting, Rethinking: Historical Transformations of Kayapo Culture and Anthropological Consciousness. In George W. Strocking, Jr (ed.), *Colonial Situations: Essays on the Contextualization of Ethnographic Knowledge* (pp. 285–313). Madison: University of Wisconsin Press.

Velho, Otávio Guilherme (1982) Through Althusserian Spectacles: Recent Social Anthropology in Brazil. *Ethnos* 47(1):133–149.

Víctora, Ceres, et al. (eds) (2004) *Antropologia e ética. O debate atual no Brasil*. Niterói, Rio de Janeiro: Editora da Universidade Federal Fluminense.

Viveiros de Castro (ed.) (1995) *Antropologia do parentesco. Estudos ameríndios*. Rio de Janeiro: Editora UFRJ.

Warren, Kay B. (1998) *Indigenous Movements and Their Critics: Pan-Maya Activism in Guatemala*. Princeton: Princeton University Press.

Weaver, Thomas (ed.) (1973) *To See Ourselves: Anthropology and Modern Social Issues*. Glenview, IL: Scott, Foresman.

# CHAPTER 23

# On the Frontlines: Forensic Anthropology

*Victoria Sanford*

> To forget our past is to risk our future.
> Bishop Juan Gerardi, *Nunca más*

In June of 1994, I began my fieldwork focusing on the exhumation by the Guatemalan Forensic Anthropology Foundation (FAFG) of the clandestine cemetery in Plan de Sánchez. After a six hour bus ride, Kathleen Dill and I reached Rabinal – at the time, a small rural town of about 6,000 inhabitants with some 18,000 more living in surrounding villages (FAFG 1995a:19). It was in the late afternoon on a Thursday and we noticed that all the doors and windows of the houses were shut. We reached Rabinal just as the team was departing for Guatemala City for the weekend to take care of some paperwork. We had missed the FAFG's first week of work at the site. They offered us a ride to the city in the back of the truck. By then, it was nearly four o'clock and we had been in transit (on buses) since six in the morning. We decided to stay for the weekend. There was no public transportation to Plan de Sánchez and it wasn't safe for us to walk to the village alone. So we waited until Monday when the FAFG returned in the early morning to go up the mountain. Though just eight kilometers above Rabinal, it took some 40 minutes for a four-wheel drive vehicle to climb the mountains to reach the small village. It lies so high in the mountains that we left the fog of the morning behind in the valley of Rabinal. We reached the clear morning sky at the top of the mountain. Looking down, we saw a blanket of clouds resting in the valley.

When we reached Plan de Sánchez and began to hike up the hill to the clandestine cemetery, my body was overcome with a cold sweat. My hands were alternately hot and cold, and sweating regardless. I felt lightheaded and my stomach started to cramp. I remembered having seen a video of the first FAFG exhumation in El Quiché. In the video, internationally renowned forensic anthropologist Dr Clyde Snow was holding what looked like a reddish brown walnut in his hand and saying, "This is a piece of brain matter." My feet felt heavy as I continued the short walk up the hill. I began to concentrate on not fainting. I felt like I was going to vomit. "Don't faint. Don't vomit. I won't faint. I won't vomit," I repeated to myself as the conversations around me seemed to drift far away. Then I began to panic. I thought, "I can't faint and I can't vomit. If I do, I will be humiliated in front of the survivors with whom I want to work and I will be incapable of carrying out my research. This is too important." Then, we were at the site.

Much to my relief, there were no visible skeletons because the team never leaves any exposed. They always complete as much as they can before leaving and cover any incompletely excavated skeletons. Recovering from the negative rush of adrenaline, I still felt like I was outside my body. As I stood above a large open pit watching the archaeologists uncover half-excavated skeletons, the lead archaeologist Fernando Moscoso handed me a chopstick and a small paintbrush. He pointed to a section of the grave and said, "If you please, why don't you begin by cleaning out that area over there." I was lost somewhere in what Trinh Minh-ha calls "being in the in-between of all definitions of truth" (1992:13). The "in-between" of I'm not vomiting, I haven't fainted, what a beautiful valley, everything is greener than green, those are real bones, my god two hundred people were massacred here, their relatives are watching. Self-consciously, I felt as if all the people (and especially the peasants) were registering my discomfort until I realized that Fernando was talking to me. Without thinking, I obediently accepted the chopstick and brush. I climbed into the grave, slowly walked over to the section he had indicated and gingerly began to clear away loose dirt. My training in anthropology prepared me to study sociocultural structures, from the community to the nation-state. I had no training in the archaeological skills of site excavation or any of the osteological knowledge necessary to analyze skeletal remains. As I reluctantly began to brush away the earth, I didn't even notice that my friend Kathleen had been sent to work with another archaeologist. Unlike me, Kathleen was well prepared for this type of work because she had extensive knowledge of the human skeleton and skeletal trauma, having had years of working as an x-ray and surgical imaging technician. She also had some training in archaeology. Kathleen was an immediate asset to the team.

As for me, I imagine that as he watched my tentative and clumsy movements, Fernando realized I had no idea what I was doing. He came over to where I was and showed me how to break the dirt and brush more systematically. Soon, I was caught in the intricacies of the excavation and its many puzzles. When I discovered a bone, I had to think about which bone it was, which meant I also had to learn the human skeleton. I had to think about how the skeleton was positioned and how best to uncover it. I had to learn the intricacies of an incredibly tedious process. Fernando supervised my work. He had a lot more confidence in my abilities than I did. When I completed the process of brushing the earth away from the skeleton, Fernando would join me. He would lift and examine each bone. He would show me whatever signs of trauma or damage he found. I would inventory the bones, record any observations of trauma, mark the bags in which the bones were to be stored, and pack them away. As the day ended, I was relieved that I had not had to sit and watch all day. I found patience doing the digging and it was a patience I knew would have eluded me had my role been restricted to that of observer.

The exhumation of a clandestine cemetery is much more than the archaeological excavation of the graves. Each exhumation has four phases. This methodology of the forensic anthropology investigation has been developed by the FAFG through its experience working in Maya communities, often under complicated circumstances, including geographic inaccessibility of isolated communities and lack of adequate facilities for carrying out the work. Indeed, FAFG cofounder and former president Fernando Moscoso wrote his thesis at the Universidad de San Carlos in Guatemala on this process. His 1998 thesis, "La antropología forense en Guatemala," is considered the blueprint for training forensic anthropologists.

The FAFG was founded and began its work in 1992 with the assistance of Dr Clyde Snow and the Argentine Forensic Anthropology Team (Equipo Argentino de Antropología Forense, EAAF). Indeed, founded in 1984, the EAAF was the first forensic anthropology team of its kind in the world and, like the FAFG, it was founded under the leadership of Dr Clyde Snow. Just as the FAFG was founded to investigate massacres by the Guatemalan military regimes of the 1980s, the EAAF was founded to investigate the disappearance of at least 10,000 Argentines during the military regime from 1976 to 1983. Prior to the founding of the Argentine team, investigation into those who disappeared during Argentina's military dictatorship was unscientific and haphazard, which meant that whatever remains were unearthed provided no real forensic evidence for the identification of remains, and certainly no evidence for any court cases.

Forensic anthropology grew out of the post-authoritarian period following the end of the Argentine military regime, when elected President Alfonsin established the National Commission on the Disappearance of Persons (CONADEP), and the Commission, along with the Grandmothers of the Plaza de Mayo (who were grandmothers of the disappeared), requested help from the American Association for the Advancement of Science (AAAS). Thus, a delegation of American forensic scientists and geneticists visited Argentina for the first time in 1984 with a human rights mission. Dr Clyde Snow, a member of the delegation, called for an immediate halt to the non-scientific exhumations that were literally bulldozing through known grave sites of the disappeared. Further, he called on archaeologists, anthropologists and forensic doctors to bring their expertise to the human rights field by developing scientifically replicable methodologies for the exhumation and analysis of skeletal remains. The Argentine Forensic Team was founded shortly thereafter, in 1984, and Dr Snow made numerous visits to Argentina for more than five years to provide training in forensic anthropology for the investigation of human rights violations in Argentina. Eight years later, the Argentine team and Dr Snow jointly assisted in the founding of the FAFG.

In this chapter, I am going to explore the practice of forensic anthropology and its outcomes in Latin America through my own experiences with the FAFG. Forensic anthropology in Guatemala exemplifies the challenges and triumphs of forensic anthropology in Latin America, where survivors of cold war dictatorships continue to struggle to find their lost loved ones, hold proper burials and seek justice in national and regional courts. Thus, forensic anthropology is a scientific research tool as well as a vital component in the search for truth and the struggle to end impunity by legal means in Latin America. Highlighting the Plan de Sánchez case provides an opportunity to witness the effects of the exhumation on the community, as well as see the legal outcomes over time.

## FOUR PHASES OF FORENSIC ANTHROPOLOGY

The methodology of the forensic anthropology investigation has four phases. The first phase includes antemortem interviews, collection of survivor testimony, and archival research. The antemortem interview is conducted with surviving relatives about the height, weight, and physical health history of the victims; this includes any particular life events, such as broken bones, dental work, or abnormalities. This basic information is used to reconstruct the osteological biography of each of the victims, with the goal of using this information in the identification process (Reichs 1998; Joyce and Stover 1991; Human Rights Watch 1991). Later each bone will be compared to each section of the antemortem interview both manually and through the antemortem interview database program. These interviews are conducted by FAFG forensic anthropologists and expert consultants, generally with a translator, since the majority of survivors are monolingual speakers of one of the 21 Maya languages.

Survivor and witness testimony is collected with the objective of locating the mass graves as well as reconstructing the events leading up to the massacre, the massacre itself, and its aftermath. Archival research consisting of review and analysis of all available official, academic, and media documents pertaining to the massacre assists in both forensic research and historical reconstruction.

This first phase is conducted simultaneously with phase two, which is the actual archaeological excavation, because many survivors and witnesses come forth for the first time when the ground is broken to begin the excavation, and others continue to come forward throughout the excavation. Thus, antemortem interviews and the collection of testimony usually continue throughout most of the exhumation.

The archaeological excavation begins with the identification, mapping, and excavation of the massacre site, which is, in forensic terms, the crime scene. It is concluded with the exhumation of the remains and recuperation of all associated artifacts, including personal belongings, clothing, bullet and grenade fragments, etc. This phase utilizes archaeological techniques and each step is documented with technical drawings, photographs, and video because the archaeological context of the clandestine cemetery is completely destroyed by the end of the excavation. These drawings, photographs and video are vital to documenting the crime scene – for example, they provide documentary scientific evidence of the massacre and its specifics, including cause of death, whether victims' hands and/or feet had been bound together, and whether victims were killed before or after being placed in the grave. Antemortem interviews, archival research, testimony collection, and the actual excavations are conducted by FAFG staff, expert consultants, volunteers, and interns. All phases of the exhumation include the participation of expert consultants and trained volunteers invited from national and international universities. To complete the excavation, the FAFG uses an extensive supply of tools ranging from picks, axes, shovels, sifting equipment and other excavation tools, to tape measures and compasses for the elaboration of maps. Additionally, the FAFG uses the necessary camera equipment to document the exhumation. Given the isolated rural locations of many investigations, the FAFG has developed the necessary experience and equipment to establish provisional camps for the duration of this phase. Because of previous investigations in caves and wells, the FAFG also has the training and equipment to scale deep caves.

In the months that I worked with the FAFG in Plan de Sánchez, I assisted in the excavation of more than two dozen skeletons. I learned osteology and forensic archaeology while excavating clandestine graves. And I felt very fortunate because, as Dr Snow told me when he came to visit the site, "You couldn't have a better teacher. Fernando [Moscoso] is one of the best forensic anthropologists in the world."

Dr Snow added, "The thing that most people don't understand is that these guys are the real experts. We may have more advanced technology in our labs in the United States, but these guys have more experience with the bones than anyone else. Look at all the graves here. The bones don't lie and these guys know what they say. They are the real professionals of forensic anthropology."

Indeed, in 1994, FAFG lab analysis was much more laborious than it is today. The first limitation was the small size of the lab and the need to share equipment, which limited the number of skeletons that could be examined at any one time. The second limitation was that the location for storage and lab analysis was determined by the whim of the judge issuing the court order to investigate. In the Plan de Sánchez exhumation, the judge had ordered that we conduct lab analysis within the borders of the department of Baja Verapaz. Thus, we temporarily used the lab equipment and morgue of the hospital in Salamá, the departmental capital, to conduct lab analysis.

The laboratory analysis is the third phase of the exhumation. It consists of scientific examination of each of the bones (206 in total) of each skeleton after it is washed, marked and reconstructed in the lab. This examination determines the cause of death, which refers to the trauma that killed the person (firearm injury, machete or knife wound, strike with blunt instrument, etc.); the manner of death (violent or natural); and the identification of the skeleton (through antemortem interview data, dental records, associated artifacts, and DNA). When it is determined that victims died from firearm projectiles or grenade fragments, lab analysis includes x-rays of affected remains to document fragments still present in bones. Thus, just like a murder investigation in the United States, the contextual, artifactual and ballistic documentation is included in the osteological breakdown which forms a part of the forensic record. Today, the FAFG has its own very large laboratory and, with the new court system, the FAFG's investigations are no longer at the whim of a judge. The FAFG has legal custody of the evidence throughout the investigation. The forensic anthropologists at the lab utilize technologically advanced equipment for slicing and analyzing bones, a microscope for examination of tissue and the calculation of age, as well as other precision instruments and necessary lab furniture.

The most reliable scientific method for the identification of remains is mitochondrial DNA analysis, especially in the Guatemalan cases where the majority of indigenous victims lack medical registers and dental records. Mitochondrial DNA analysis compares the root of a hair or a blood sample of a maternal relative to a DNA bone sample taken from the remains of victims. Unfortunately, there is no mitochondrial DNA laboratory in Guatemala, making it necessary to consult with specialized labs in other countries. The FAFG has had the good fortune of working with Dr Mary-Clair King, who has provided similar collaboration to projects in Argentina, El Salvador, Ethiopia, Rwanda, Bosnia and Croatia. Dr Michelle Harvey, who collaborates with Dr King, has also provided the FAFG with this technical support pro bono.

The fourth and final phase of the exhumation is the processing of the data, interpretation of the evidence, and production of the final forensic report. After completing phases one to three, it is possible to determine the consistencies and contradictions between the written documents, interviews, testimonies, and material evidence from the excavation. The final interpretation is based on the analysis of all facts collected in all phases of the investigation. The information gathered in each phase of the investigation is recorded and processed in database programs. The most effective way to identify victims is to use a database to compare the information collected in antemortem interviews with laboratory analysis of remains. Such a process greatly reduces the possibility of error and increases the speed of identification.

The final report is prepared as forensic evidence for presentation in court. Survivors in the community also receive copies of the report. In Rabinal, the forensic team produced a book and a low literacy monograph about the Rabinal massacres (FAFG 1995a, 1995b). The reports on each exhumation are presented in hard copy and on diskette (which includes digital photos) to the Human Rights Ombudsman, local prosecutors, the Attorney General, relevant nongovernmental organizations, community members and other interested parties. The monograph, *Nada podrá contra la vida* (FAFG 1995b), was circulated in Maya communities throughout the country and became a teaching tool to prepare communities about what to expect in the exhumation process. Later, when I was working in Nebaj, I mentioned to a few close Ixil friends that I had worked in some exhumations. For the rest of the day that was all they wanted to talk about. They asked me for more information. The next time I was in Guatemala City, I picked up some copies of the low literacy monograph. My friends then organized several private meetings in groups of three to four local Ixil leaders. Each time, the monograph was read aloud and the reading was peppered with comments that "the same thing happened here," and questions about how to organize and request an exhumation. Inevitably, the reading of the monograph was followed by a group discussion about La Violencia in different communities and other people who might want exhumations.

## MAKING A CASE

In 1994, two years before the the Guatemalan army and guerrillas had signed the 1996 peace accords, before the Guatemalan army's civil patrols had been demobilized, before the United Nations Mission in Guatemala or any international NGOs had arrived, and before the reform of the judicial system, exhumations were initiated by the Human Rights Ombudsman (PDH), with whom requests for the investigation of human rights violations could be filed by individuals, organizations and/or communities; these requests could also be filed anonymously. For an exhumation to proceed, a complaint had to be filed at the Superior Court. If approved by the Superior Court, it then had to be approved by the Appeals Court, which would then pass it on to the Court of the *Primer Instancia*, the departmental administrative court, which would then issue an order to the local justice of the peace. It was then the task of the justice of the peace to solicit forensic experts to carry out the exhumation. Rabinal's justice of the peace sought out the FAFG because the forensic doctor in Rabinal worked only four hours a day and had no formal training in forensics. The FAFG was appointed as the court's expert. In the new legal system that came into being following the 1996 signing of the peace accords, it is the prosecutor, not the judge or court, that initiates the exhumation. Now, an individual can go directly to the prosecutor to request an investigation. The PDH continues to play an important role, assisting individuals in the filing of their claims with the prosecutor or directly filing claims on behalf of the PDH.

The PDH, the local justice of the peace and representatives from human rights groups regularly visited both sites to accompany and support the survivors and the work of the FAFG. CONAVIGUA (Coordinadora Nacional de Las Viudas de Guatemala, National Coordinating Committee of the Widows of Guatemala) and GAM (Grupo de Apoyo Mútuo, Mutual Support Group) provided food for the forensic team as they worked and also provided the resources for the reburial of remains when they were returned to the communities.[1] Whereas previous exhumations had been initiated by these human rights groups by providing legal support and filing complaints at the request of survivors, the Rabinal exhumations were unique in that they were initiated by local residents with no apparent organizational support.

### Juan Manuel Geronimo's Testimony

I raffled the truth to declare the truth. Before the exhumation, all the people hid everything inside. They concealed their feelings. No one would even talk about what had happened, much less make a public declaration. It just didn't seem possible that a person had the power to declare these types of things at the national level or international level. We decided that we were going to declare the truth of what happened. We were going to do it legally. We decided that we were going to do it together, all the families united. I encouraged everyone to participate. I told them, "Look, please, if they call us, we will all go together. We will all go together and we will go without this fear. I am not afraid. If you support me, you will give me more strength to do this." So, when the Ministerio Público (Public Ministry, Prosecutor) called us, we all went together. When the court called us, we all went together. We said, "We want a Christian burial for our families because they aren't dogs, and we don't want them piled up in those graves like dogs." That's how we did it.

So, we moved forward together. I said, "We won't be afraid. We will do this together. Because if we say that one person is in charge of this work, then we are just giving them a new martyr. But if we are all together, we can do this work. What we are doing is legal and the law isn't going to put all of us in jail." These were the ideas we had and this is how we worked together.

One day, the military commissioners [army-appointed civil patrol leaders] from Chipuerta came here. They had been sent by the chief in Rabinal. They wanted a report. They said, "Who is leading the exhumation here? Who is in charge?" But we just said, "We are all doing this together. We want a proper burial." After they left, we discussed this. Once again, we all agreed that no one would blame anyone else and that no one would say there was a leader. The next thing that happened is that I received a note from the chief of all the PACs [army-controlled civil patrols] in Rabinal. The note said that I was to go to Rabinal to meet with him because he wanted to talk to me. I didn't go.

Several days later, he found me walking down the street in Rabinal. He asked me, "Look, what's going on with this business up there?" I said, "What business?" Then he said, "Look, you, what's going on with this business up there? What's going on with this exhumation?" I said, "Do you mean how will it be done? First, we are going to exhume the remains and then we are going to rebury them. But I don't know when." Then he said, "Who has told you this? Who is behind this?" "No one," I said, "we are doing it by ourselves." "But you are working with an organization, aren't you?" he said. And I said, "No. The only institution is our own strength and commitment. So, if you would like to support us somehow with some money that would be helpful." He didn't know how to respond. He said, "How's that?" And I said, "Well, it would be like an institution helping us. We want to do the exhumation." He just accepted that and walked away confused because I hadn't told him anything.

CONAVIGUA was really helping us. The truth is they explained to us how we could make our declarations, how to complete the forms, and where to take them. We are very poor. We don't have any money for taking buses. So, whenever we had to go to the Ministerío Público or the court, they would reimburse our transportation costs. Thanks to God, they helped us a lot. I hope God repays them for their good deeds. They really struggled to help us. But we did our part. We did all the work ourselves. We made all the trips to file the paperwork. That is why it was important for all of us to go together to do these filings. The widows from CONAVIGUA were in agreement that no one should go alone. They said, "Believe us, if only one person goes by himself, somewhere along the road, in one of those holes, you're going to find him buried." This made a lot of the people scared, but we stuck together. I was never afraid. I don't know why, I just never was.

## THE EXHUMATION IN PLAN DE SÁNCHEZ

There was always a lot of activity at the excavation site. Because exhumations are carried out as an investigatory procedure of the court, municipal police maintain a 24-hour presence to guard the site, observe the excavation, and conserve legal custody of all evidence exhumed. In 1994, Rabinal had only one police officer, so the court requested assignment of several customs police because neither the FAFG nor the community wanted soldiers or paramilitary police at the exhumation site. Four customs police were stationed for three weeks at a time in Plan de Sánchez. They set up a large tent at the base of the hill where they camped – supposedly providing 24-hour security to the area. Each day after the remains were cataloged and boxed by both the forensic team and the police, the boxes were transported to Rabinal where they were stored in the modest office of the justice of the peace.

In tandem with the archaeological procedures, Maya rituals marked different moments of the excavation. Before the ground was broken, the Maya priest (*sacerdote* Maya) conducted a religious ceremony. Maya priests are the keepers of Maya religious tradition (*costumbre*), which the Maya have maintained and reinvented since the arrival of the Spaniards in the 16th century. While many have viewed Maya costumbre as a syncretic blending of Maya belief systems with Catholicism, the cult of Catholic saints is also a blending of Maya religion with Catholicism. Each religion reminds us that belief systems are never static, but always changing. For the Achí, as for other Maya, it is sacrilegious to disturb the remains of the dead because wherever the blood of the dead has spilled in burial, the spirits of the dead hover above. To disturb the bones is to disturb the spirits. However, because it was the desire of the community that the truth of these clandestine graves be known, that their loved ones have proper religious burials, and that there be justice, the Maya priest performed a special ceremony before each grave was opened.

While every culture places significance on its particular burial practices, Maya ritual practices at the graves of ancestors implicate not only the passing of the ancestor but also the identity, rights and responsibilities of the living. Archaeologist Patricia Macanany dates these practices back to before the Conquest and notes that "very few royal tombs were sealed and never revisited; most were periodically reopened for an elaborate ceremony of burning incense. It almost seems as though it was vitally important to maintain open pathways of communication with the ancestors" (Macanany 1995). These rituals at burial sites implicate the enactment of deeply held beliefs about individual and community identity and reckoning in the past as well as the present.

Lighting candles, burning copal incense on the area adorned with red gladiolas and pine needles, the Maya priest would first speak with God to explain why the exhumation should take place and ask permission from God to disturb the bones. Then the priest would call upon the spirits to explain to them that God had given permission for the exhumation to take place. He would plead with the spirits to heed God's call. Instead of using their powers against those who disturb the bones, the priest asked the spirits to use their powers to bless and protect the forensic team and all who worked at the exhumation.

Everyone in Plan de Sánchez worked to support the exhumation. The men organized a schedule so that everyone helped with the manual labor, but also had time to tend their fields. I was struck by the volunteers who came representing popular human rights organizations. These peasant men and women were giving up their time working for their own livelihood to support an exhumation that wasn't even in their own communities. They said they came because they wanted to learn more about the exhumations and because they hoped people would come when they had their exhumations in their own communities. "If we are together, we have greater strength and less fear," explained a massacre survivor from a faraway Chichicastenango village in El Quiché. These volunteers came for ten days at a time. Within the village, each man gave several days a week of his time. All helped to do the heavy digging that was necessary before the delicate brushing work of the excavation could begin. They also carried all the dirt out of the graves to sift it. (This sifting is necessary for finding bullet and grenade fragments.) It was the rainy season, so shelters had to be built over the work sites and gullies had to be dug around the perimeter to prevent the water from flooding the open graves. The work was further complicated by the steepness of the mountainside where many of the graves were located. In all, there were 18 graves, so there was a lot of digging, sifting, and building.

When I first arrived at the site, one of my fears was that I would be overcome by the smell of death. That first day, working in the graves that had been opened and exposed for several days prior, there was no smell, or if there was, I didn't notice it. The flesh had decomposed and the remains were bones still dressed in the clothes that had not yet decomposed. Rather than the trepidation I had expected to feel about being (just being) near the bones, I felt great tenderness because they seemed fragile, vulnerable, and somehow almost noble. These were the final traces that confirmed that a human being, this human being had existed. Sometimes when we opened a new grave or if it was a damp day, a slight smell of life lingered. It wasn't a putrid smell, the earth had long since absorbed the rot of death. The scent that lingered was the light murky smell of birth or a stillborn puppy or that of wine fermenting in oak barrels, not a noxious aroma, but one of movement or transformation in rhythm with the mountains and its pine trees, flowers, rich earth, and luscious green grass.

The scent of burning *leña* (firewood) and the resin used to start cooking fires wafted over the site, blending with all the other smells. As their husbands worked on the exhumation of their first families, the current wives of these men (most themselves previously widowed by massacres) prepared food for the forensic team and anyone else who helped with the work. This meant grinding corn, patting out tortillas, and preparing a large cauldron of beans or soup for what usually amounted to some 35 additional mouths to feed each day. They also prepared *atol* (hot corn drinks) for us twice during the day.

As the forensic team and community members worked on the exhumation, campes-inos from nearby villages walked as many as six hours to reach the site to observe the exhumation. These individuals, like the villagers of Plan de Sánchez, were expressing their support of the exhumation by their mere presence. They were seizing the politi-cal space opened by the exhumation and further extending it. Each day, dozens of people came. Not only was no one in Plan de Sánchez singled out, but the presence of villagers from other communities demonstrated that the people of Plan de Sánchez were not alone. A profound expression of what Michel Foucault called "the power effects of truth" (1980:131).

During the exhumation, local campesinos were always waiting and watching. While the excavation of massacre victims may seem like a gruesome endeavor, it is the pres-ence of these local Maya peasants that enables the forensic team members to do their work. It is not simply the collaboration of local labor that helps. It is also the great respect for the dead and the living, and the spiritual and emotional strength that com-munity members bring to the site, that encourages everyone involved to continue their work each day.

The police were always watching from a distance. They often stood behind a tree and would peek out to watch us. They weren't scared of us or the graves, they were scared of the photographers. A photographer demonstrated to me that all he had to do was take out his camera and the police would scatter running behind trees. When I asked them why they hid, one of the police said, "If my picture is taken here, people might think I support it, that I am taking a side. I could lose my job." At the time, I just thought he meant that military institutions, including the customs police, were against the exhumations.

A few days later, I was excavating a skeleton. It was the skeleton of a woman who was face-down in the grave. She had a shawl wrapped around her upper body. As I opened her shawl, the skeleton of an infant was revealed. The same customs officer came out from behind his tree. He walked right up to the edge of the grave. As he leaned into the grave, he called the other three officers. He said, "Look. Look at this. It is a woman with a baby on her back. They told us these were pure guerrillas. These aren't guerril-las. That's a mother and a baby. That's a crime." As the other police came closer to watch, the villagers joined them. One of the police said, "A woman and her baby. Poor woman. Poor baby. I sure would like to machine gun whoever did that." And all the villagers quietly backed away to the other side of the grave. Still, after witnessing the excavation of this woman with a baby on her back, the officers stopped hiding behind trees and voluntarily began to help with the manual labor in the exhumation.

## "LEAVE THE DEAD IN PEACE"

Each Thursday afternoon, we would return to Guatemala City to do paperwork, visit with friends and family, and rest. Before dawn on Monday, we would be on the road returning to Rabinal. When we reached Plan de Sánchez on the morning of July 25, there were only a few villagers from Plan de Sánchez waiting for us at the grave site and there were no villagers from outside – usually there were several dozen. The mood was somber and everyone was very quiet. The widowers of Plan de Sánchez met with us to explain what had happened.

The day before, on Sunday, the subcommander of the army base in Rabinal had ordered all men from the villages to attend a meeting at the army base. The order was received in the morning. By noon, there were several thousand men waiting in the sun at the base. At two in the afternoon, the subcommander greeted the crowd and began a lecture. He told the peasants not to pursue the exhumations. "The anthropologists, internationals and journalists are all guerrilla," he explained. "You know what happens when you help the guerrilla. Collaborating with the guerrilla will bring back the violence of 1982," he warned. "Now, I am going to give you an order," he said. "Leave the dead in peace" (collective interview, Plan de Sánchez, July 25, 1994).

While the men attending the meeting at the base were too frightened to contradict anything the subcommander said, they were not dissuaded from continuing to work on the exhumation. They had increased local security by coordinating trips to their fields and to Rabinal to ensure that no one ever traveled alone and also to make sure that there were always some men in the village. They recommended to us that we not walk around alone in Rabinal during the daytime, and that at night we not walk around outside at all.

When we suggested that a delegation could go to the capital to denounce the army's threats, the villagers informed us that they had pooled their resources on Sunday afternoon to pay the bus fare for several men to go to the capital to do just that. Thus, the army's threats were denounced to the Human Rights Ombudsman, the court, and the national press. At the end of the week, the army made a public statement in which they claimed that the subcommander was not expressing army policy and that he had been transferred to another base. Word of this statement traveled quickly through Rabinal. By the following week, we were back to several dozen local visitors each day at the site.

Later, Juan Manuel admitted to me that the villagers had held a meeting to discuss what we (the forensic team) should be told about the assembly at the army base. Several people were worried that we might not complete the exhumation if we knew about the army's death threat. Though we never mentioned it to the villagers, we were concerned they might pull out of the exhumation because of the threats. The consensus of this political chess game, however, of both the forensic team and the villagers, was that if the exhumation was not completed, then the army would have more power than it had before the exhumation began. This consensus revealed a highly nuanced understanding of the politics of power relations and also the palpable sensation that on any given day the balance of power could weigh in on the side of either the army or civil society.

This was neither the first, nor the last, threat directed at the team or its work. In March 2002, 11 current and former FAFG forensic anthropologists were under 24-hour protection due to death threats. On February 21, 2002, they received individually typewritten letters: "We will finish you off... you aren't the ones to judge us. If the exhumations don't stop, your families will be burying your bones and those of your children" (personal communication with FAFG president Fredy Pecerrelli, February 24, 2002 and with former FAFG president Fernando Moscoso, February 28, 2002). After a decade of forensic anthropology investigations into massacres and more than 190 exhumations, those threats were intended to intimidate the 11 anthropologists who were scheduled to be called as forensic expert witnesses in forthcoming court cases against current and former high-ranking army officials, and the first case scheduled to be heard was Plan de Sánchez. And as recently as March 2006, FAFG members received death threats.

In terms of the team's response to the 1994 death threat, some members of the forensic team recognized it as a death threat, while others categorized it merely as part of the army's campaign to discredit human rights work. Plan de Sánchez survivors, however, viewed the subcommander's statements not only as a death threat, but also as an order for the civil patrollers to attack us – hence their recommendations about our safety in Rabinal. Though it heightened our consciousness of individual and group security practices, we continued our work routine as always – traveling en masse, never walking alone, never leaving the vehicle unattended, and never arriving or departing at exactly the same time (which was, more often than not, a result of lack of planning rather than the reverse).

Less than two weeks after the army's disclaimer, on August 10, the departmental human rights ombudsman in Salamá and the national PDH received identical death threats: "deija [sic] en pas [sic] a los muertos Hijo de puta" [leave the dead in peace son of a whore]. At the same time, while I was conducting interviews with government officials in Guatemala City, a high-ranking member of the Guatemalan government's Peace Commission (then representing the government and army in peace negotiations) told me that "no member of the forensic team should believe themselves to be immune to violent reprisals." He also emphasized that a US passport should not be assumed to provide protection from such reprisals. When I asked him if this was a threat from the army, he said, "It doesn't matter where I heard this or who told me. And it isn't a threat, it is a warning."

When I later met with the national Human Rights Ombudsman Jorgé Mario García La Guardía and asked him about the death threats the PDH had received, he shrugged his shoulders and showed me a stack of threats he had received. "This is the reality of our work," he said. "If I stopped to contemplate the implications of each of these threats, I would be immobilized." This reminded me of Fernando Moscoso, who once explained how he continued working even when he was tired: "When I am excavating, I am conscious that in a year, or two, or three, the skeleton in the ground might be mine."

By the end of my interview with García La Guardía, it was early evening. He offered me a ride to my next destination because I had mentioned to him that a man had attempted to mug me in Guatemala City several days earlier. When I told the friends I was meeting that the ombudsman had given me a ride and that his security was impressive (the driver and two guards each with automatic weapons), they retorted that I would have been safer walking. "No one rides with the PDH. Those guards and guns are worth nothing if someone drives by and opens machine gun fire."

## "YOU ARE SEEING THE TRUTH"

After all the graves had been exhumed, there were 18 large holes in the earth. The sizes of the graves ranged from eight by ten feet to fifteen by twenty feet. Each was about four to five feet deep. Because it was the rainy season, the holes quickly filled with water. As I looked at the gaping holes in the earth, they seemed to be many things. They looked like miniature versions of the wounds left in the earth by nickel mines or gravel pits. They looked like muddy ponds. The area, which had always been filled with people, was deserted and the holes heightened the empty feeling of absence. My thoughts were broken by the laughter of children who trailed Juan Manuel, Erazmo, Pablo, and José. We sat on a grassy knoll and looked at the empty spaces, the valley below and the mountain range beyond it.

"It looks sad here," said Don Erazmo. "But when we have a proper burial, everyone will live with tranquility." He said this with the knowledge that it was unlikely he would receive the remains of his family members because it appeared that they had been among those who were burned beyond recognition. As he spoke, the children played with each other and climbed on their fathers, seeking embraces.

By the end of the exhumation, I had interviewed all survivors of the massacre still living in Plan de Sánchez. I asked them why they wanted the exhumation. In addition to not wanting their relatives buried "como perros" – like dogs – each person gave me several reasons beyond the proper burial.

The first and most stark reason is the concrete, the real, the hard evidence. You can touch it. It is the bones of the victims we pulled out of the earth. And, as Dr Clyde Snow always says, "The bones don't lie." The army claimed there had been a battle with the guerrillas in Plan de Sánchez. The exhumation clearly showed that the vast majority of victims were women, children, and the elderly. Moreover, the forensic evidence unquestionably demonstrated that the skeletons in the grave were victims of a massacre, not in armed confrontation with guerrillas and not civilians caught in crossfire, as the army had asserted about mass graves throughout the country (FAFG Exhumation File: Plan de Sanchéz Caso 319–93, 5TO (1997)).

Don Pablo asked me, "How could they say these were guerrilleros? How can an infant of six months or a child of five, six, or seven be a guerrillero? How can a pregnant woman carrying her basket to market be a guerrillero?" (Rabinal Testimony no. 7-3, July 18, 1994, my archive). About the exhumation, Don Erazmo told me, "Allí, no hay mentira. Allí, están veyendo la verdad" [There, there is no lie. There, you are seeing the truth].

In 1994, I asked them why an already vulnerable community would put itself at greater risk by supporting and actively collaborating with the exhumation. Don Juan Manuel told me that the community supported the exhumation because they wanted "the truth to come out that the victims were natives of the area. Our children, who knew nothing, who owed debts to no one. They killed women and the elderly who did not even understand what they were accused of by the army. Campesinos, poor people. People who work the fields for the corn we eat."

The community wanted the truth to be known. Don Erazmo said, "We have worked in the exhumation. We have worked for truth." I asked what importance truth could have 12 years after the massacre. This is what I was told:

"We want peace. We want people to know what happened here so that it does not happen here again, or in some other village in Guatemala, or in some other department, or in some other country."

"We strongly support this exhumation and that everything is completely investigated because we do not want this to happen again."

"We do this for our children and our children's children."

"We want no more massacres of the Maya."

"We want justice. We want justice because if there is no justice, the massacres will never end. God willing, we will have peace."

Some said they wanted revenge. All said they wanted justice. There was great hope that someone involved in the massacre would be tried in court and prosecuted.[2] Just as army threats had sent tremors of fear through Plan de Sánchez, and indeed throughout Rabinal, the process of the exhumation restored community beliefs in the right to truth and justice. Rural Maya have a strong community tradition of publicly speaking their objections and seeking redress within the local hierarchy. Moreover, in rural Maya culture, the ancestors help the living move into the future. They continue to play a role in the life of the community. They play an important role in defining place and the significance of place as social space, as living space (conversation with Patricia Macanany, April 12, 2000). In this sense, the exhumations resuscitated local Maya cultural practices and created new space for the practice of citizenship.

It was the combination of the forensic evidence of the exhumations with the visible resuscitation of community beliefs in the right to truth and justice that threatened those implicated in the massacres. Denial that those killed had been unarmed civilians remained plausible only as long as the mass graves were untouched. Exhumations not only provided an accretion of truth within the public space of the community, but also an accretion of forensic evidence for court cases and the beginning of a new national and international understanding of La Violencia. As exhumations have proceeded throughout the country, the collective evidence pointed not only to army massacres of unarmed Maya, but to a carefully planned and strategically enacted genocide (Sanford 2003a, 2003b, 2005a, 2005b). Indeed, a significant finding of the Commission for Historical Clarification (CEH, the Guatemalan truth commission) was that the army had carried out genocidal acts. The FAFG also participated in the investigative process of the CEH, carrying out exhumations commissioned by the CEH (FAFG 2000).

## CONCLUSION

The testimonies of survivors and the forensic analysis of the remains of massacre victims provided evidence for a petition filed by survivors with the Inter-American Commission of Human Rights in 1995 requesting that the Commission pass the case on to the Inter-American Court. Over the years, in Plan de Sánchez, Kathleen Dill and I have often discussed this case with survivors. While allowing for citizen petitions, the Inter-American process is slow. We would reassure one another that something was bound to happen – especially after we knew that the case had been passed on to the Court. Cases can take up to 10 years. "Sooner or later there will be justice" became the refrain for survivors.

On April 29, 2004 the Inter-American Court condemned the Guatemalan government for the July 18, 1982 massacre of 188 Achi-Maya in the village of Plan de Sánchez in the mountains above Rabinal, Baja Verapaz. The Inter-American Court was also convinced that "the bones don't lie" and found the forensic evidence and testimonies to be both credible and compelling. The Court attributed the massacre to Guatemalan army troops. This is the first ruling by the Inter-American Court against the Guatemalan state for any of the 626 massacres carried out by the army in the early 1980s (IAC 2004a; Sanford 2004). The Court later announced that the Guatemalan state is required to pay $7.9 million to the relatives of victims (IAC 2004b).

Beyond the importance of this judgment for the people of Plan de Sánchez, the Court's ruling is particularly significant because the following key points were included in the judgment: (1) there was a genocide in Guatemala; (2) this genocide was part of the framework of the internal armed conflict when the armed forces of the Guatemalan government applied their National Security Doctrine in its counterinsurgency actions; (3) these counterinsurgency actions carried out within the Guatemalan government's National Security Doctrine took place during the regime of General Efrain Rios Montt, who came to power through military coup in March of 1982 (IAC 2004a).

Further, regarding the massacre in Plan de Sánchez, the Court indicated that the armed forces of the Guatemalan government had violated the following rights, each of which is consecrated in the Human Rights Convention of the Organization of American States: the right to personal integrity; the right to judicial protection; the right to judicial guarantees of equality before the law; the right to freedom of conscience; the right to freedom of religion; and, the right to private property (IAC 2004a).

The Plan de Sánchez case was considered by the Inter-American Court at the request of the Inter-American Commission, which had received a petition from relatives of the massacre victims. These survivors requested consideration in the Inter-American Court because of the ongoing impunity and lack of justice in the Guatemalan legal system. There is no doubt that both the forensic evidence and testimonies given by forensic anthropology expert witnesses played a key role in the Court's findings. There are still more than 300 massacre cases supported by forensic evidence pending in the Guatemalan court system, and the FAFG has now completed more than 530 investigations and continues to carry out exhumations throughout the country with the goal of exhuming the 2,000 known clandestine cemeteries (www.fafg.org/).

Since their founding, both the Guatemalan and Argentine forensic teams have gained international prominence as the leaders of forensic anthropology investigations. Throughout Latin America, they apply their expertise in forensic anthropology to the investigation and documentation of human rights violations to produce scientific evidence for court cases and to assist relatives in the recovery of the remains of their lost loved ones. To these ends, they have led forensic investigations in Colombia, Peru, El Salvador, Mexico, and Honduras. Both the Argentine and Guatemalan teams have also carried out forensic anthropology investigations in the Democratic Republic of Congo, Ethiopia, Indonesia, the Ivory Coast, Sierra Leone, Uruguay, Rwanda, the former Yugoslavia, and Sri Lanka, among others (EAAF 2002; FAFG 2005). Significantly, just as the Argentine team replicated itself in Guatemala, the FAFG and EAAF have also continued to replicate themselves by assisting in the establishment of forensic anthropology teams in Colombia, Peru and Mexico. These Latin American forensic anthropology groups founded the Latin American Forensic Anthropology Association (ALAF) and now hold regional meetings to strengthen and professionalize forensic anthropology throughout Latin America (EAAF 2002:126).

## NOTES

This chapter draws on "Strengthening the Peace Process in Guatemala: A Proposal of the Guatemalan Forensic Anthropology Foundation to the Open Society Institute" (Sanford

1998) and on "The Bones Don't Lie," chapter 1 of *Buried Secrets: Truth and Human Rights in Guatemala* (Sanford 2003a). The author thanks Juan Manuel Geronimo and the other survivors of the Plan de Sánchez massacre for their trust and friendship. All interviews are the author's unless otherwise noted. Special thanks to editor Deborah Poole for her patience and support.

1　Other popular human rights organizations, such as CERJ (Consejo de Etnías Runujel Junam, Council of Ethnic Groups Runujel Junam) and FAMDEGUA (Familiares de los Desaparecidos de Guatemala, Families of the Disappeared of Guatemala) have also provided assistance to communities filing legal requests for exhumations and provided resources for food during the exhumations and materials for reburial. The ODHA (Oficina de Derechos Humanos del Arzobispado) has also conducted exhumations.

2　Rabinal Testimony nos 7-3, July 27, 1994; 7-5, July 20, 1994; 7-3, July 18, 1994; 7-2, July 27, 1994; 7-1, July 18, 1994; 7-1, July 27, 1994 (my archive); Plan de Sánchez, collective interview, July 25, 1994.

## REFERENCES

EAAF (Argentine Forensic Anthropology Team) (2002) *Annual Report.* Buenos Aires: EAAF.

FAFG (Fundación de Antropología Forense de Guatemala) (1995a) *Las masacres de Rabinal.* Guatemala City: FAFG.

FAFG (Fundación de Antropología Forense de Guatemala) (1995b) *Nada podrá contra la vida. Investigación sobre tres masacres en Rabinal.* Guatemala City: FAFG.

FAFG (Fundación de Antropología Forense de Guatemala) (1997) Exhumation File: Plan de Sánchez Caso 319–93, 5TO. FAFG, Guatemala City.

FAFG (Fundación de Antropología Forense de Guatemala) (2000) *Informe de la Fundación de Antropología Forense de Guatemala. Cuatro casos paradigmaticos por la Comisión para el Esclarecimiento Historico de Guatemala.* Guatemala City: FAFG.

FAFG (Fundación de Antropología Forense de Guatemala) (2005) Information at www.fafg.org.

Foucault, Michel (1980) *Power/Knowledge: Selected Writings and Other Interviews 1972–1977,* ed. Colin Gordon. New York: Pantheon Books.

Human Rights Watch (1991) *Getting Away with Murder: The Medicolegal System and Human Rights in Guatemala.* New York: Human Rights Watch.

IAC (Inter-American Court) (2004a) Plan de Sánchez Massacre Series C, No. 105 Judgment. At www.cidh.org.

IAC (Inter-American Court) (2004b) Plan de Sánchez Massacre Series C, No. 116 Reparations. At www.cidh.org.

Joyce, Christopher and Stover, Eric (1991) *Witnesses from the Grave: The Stories Bones Tell.* New York: Little, Brown.

Macanany, Patricia (1995) *Living with the Ancestors: Kinship and Kingship in Ancient Maya Society.* Austin: University of Texas Press.

Reichs, Kathleen J. (ed.) (1998) *Forensic Osteology: Advances in the Identification of Human Remains.* Springfield, IL: Charles C. Thomas Press.

Sanford, Victoria (1998) Strengthening the Peace Process in Guatemala: A Proposal of the Guatemalan Forensic Anthropology Foundation to the Open Society Institute. Guatemalan Forensic Anthropology Foundation.

Sanford, Victoria (2003a) *Buried Secrets: Truth and Human Rights in Guatemala.* New York: Palgrave Macmillan.

Sanford, Victoria (2003b) *Violencia y genocidio en Guatemala.* Guatemala City: FyG Editores.

Sanford, Victoria (2004) The Inter-American Court Condemns Guatemalan Government. *Anthropology News,* Oct.

Sanford, Victoria (2005a) The Sanford Guatemalan Genocide Databases. Genocide Studies Program, Yale University. At www.yale.edu/gsp/guatemala/guatemala_maps.html.

Sanford, Victoria (2005b) Violence and Genocide in Guatemala. Genocide Studies Program, Yale University. At www.yale.edu/gsp/guatemala/guatemala_maps.html.

Stover, Eric (1992) *Unquiet Graves: The Search for the Disappeared in Iraqi Kurdistan*. New York: Middle East Watch and Physicians for Human Rights.

Trinh Minh-ha (1992) *Framer Framed*. New York: Routledge.

# CHAPTER 24 Collaborative Anthropologies in Transition

## Charles R. Hale

Anthropology, more than any of the other social sciences, relies centrally on field research, which in turn creates an inherent dependence on collaboration between researcher and subject. Collaboration is a tricky noun. It can signal treachery, as in my dictionary's second definition ("to cooperate treasonably, as with an enemy occupying one's country"), and it also can refer in a straightforward way to a mutually agreed upon relation of collective work. I want to keep the ambiguity in place, at least at the outset, and begin with this general question: What conditions make it possible for anthropologists to convince their research subjects to collaborate with them? There is, of course, no single answer in the present, and less still if we historicize the question. One might even interpret the successive crises that have afflicted anthropology since the 1960s as expressions of collective discomfort with previous generations' accepted and largely unexamined notions of collaboration.

I approach this broader inquiry – into the terms of collaboration – through a more focused lens, which allows me to draw directly on my own experience over the past 25 years. What are the conditions of possibility for white anthropologists from the United States to research and represent contemporary indigenous politics in Latin America? By conditions of possibility I mean the historically given ideological and material relations which permit and facilitate a given set of practices. The best way to begin answering this question is to historicize, asking when current conditions arose, what preceded them, and at least speculatively, how they might fare in the future. Even this bare-bones formulation of the problem brings a third identity category into the picture: dominant culture mestizos (or ladinos), who are both analysts and political actors in relation to indigenous peoples of their societies. My argument, in synthesis, is that the conditions of possibility I have experienced over the past two decades have their roots in a particular cultural-political moment in Latin America, in US universities, and in global political-economic relations in the hemisphere. These conditions, which have encouraged the development of collaborative relations between white US anthropologists and indigenous peoples, in the egalitarian and reciprocal sense of the term, are now beginning to change. This incipient change entails the relative displacement of white US anthropologists, and the increasing centrality of mestizo Latin Americans, amid the persisting assertiveness of indigenous peoples themselves.

Three specific conditions of possibility constituted the emergence of reciprocal relations of collaboration between white anthropologists and indigenous peoples: rising indigenous militancy in national level struggles for collective rights; racial tensions between Indian- and mestizo-led political initiatives; and changes in the sensibilities of US based anthropology toward a special emphasis on close, horizontal relations with "subaltern" research subjects. In the making since the 1960s, these conditions came fully to fruition by the end of the 1980s, when revolutionary and national-popular politics in Latin America had lost their salience and appeal (for contrasting depictions of this shift, see Castañeda 1993 and Grandin 2004). We are witnessing the first glimmers of another shift today, as Latin American states proceed in granting partial recognition of indigenous cultural rights, and neoliberal capitalist development generates ever more entrenched forms of social inequality. Neoliberal multicultural-ism does not eliminate racism and racial hierarchy, but it does produce growing sectors of both Indians and mestizos who face basically similar forms of class based marginalization. At the same time, left-aligned political movements may finally be shaking free of the stubborn racialized legacy whereby mestizos insist on speaking for Indians, insist on knowing how to liberate Indians, insist on denying their complicity with anti-Indian racism. Research relations under these emergent conditions, I suggest, will be more firmly grounded in mestizo–Indian coalition politics, which in turn will pose new challenges for white US anthropologists who seek to carry out research in accordance with collaborative principles.

I develop these propositions by examining three successive phases of anthropological collaboration, and the forces that produced the transition from one to another. These phases are: (1) the immediate postwar period (1945–65), when white US anthropologists worked with mestizo power-holders as their unacknowledged allies; (2) the rise of leftist and revolutionary politics, when mestizo intellectuals took the lead in protest against this academic division of labor (1965–85); (3) the most recent period when indigenous politics has taken on a distinctly national character (1985–present). My concluding reflection, that we are on the eve of a new phase, in part is based on empirical observation, in part extrapolation from these observable trends, and in part, admittedly, a positioned argument for changes that I would like to see happen.

Two caveats are in order. First, this entire chapter focuses on socially constituted categories that do not fully or definitively characterize the subjects they name. All of these categories – white, mestizo, indigenous, Mexican, Maya, etc. – are contingent, contested, and fluid. A second, more substantive caveat follows. My attempt to think broadly about structured relations among these categories of people follows a "racial formation" approach, which directs us to explore the role that race has played in the creation and reproduction of relations of social inequality, as well as in the contestation and transformation of these relations (Winant 2001; Williams 1991; Smith 1995; Gordon 1998). To identify people by the racial categories they occupy (e.g. a white anthropologist) is not to suggest that race is the only relevant facet of our social position, only that this is a crucial, and relatively neglected, facet of the triad that I seek to understand. My approach is *both* to explore these structural relationships, and to allow ethnographic or historical particularity to disrupt them. For example, in the rest of this chapter I work with the category "white anthropologist" without the qualifier "US." In part this is a matter of parsimony; in larger part, however, I do this intentionally, to push the structural-racial analysis as far as it can go, while also allowing ethnographic particularity to push back. I view the category "white anthropologist" as both crucial and inadequate: it directs much-needed attention to the racialized facet of research relations, which might otherwise fade unnoticed into the background; at the same time, it is disrupted by white anthropologists who are Latin American, by US anthropologists who study indigenous issues and who are not white, and by white US anthropologists who defy some feature of this category, even while continuing to occupy it. Such disruptions complicate structural analysis of racial categories, but do not undermine their analytical usefulness; to the contrary, we can best understand both the structural relations and the disruptions by reading them together, in tension with one another.

In sum, advances in the development of horizontal collaborative research relations between white anthropologists and indigenous peoples – advances which I strongly endorse and to which I have attempted to contribute – have been predicated on a conjuncture of sociopolitical conditions that now may be coming to an end. On the one hand, these relations will run an ever greater risk of being complicit with state-driven initiatives of managed multiculturalism, which grant limited rights in the hope of staving off more expansive demands (Hale 2002). On the other hand, with Indian–mestizo coalition politics on the rise, white anthropologists will have to pay greater attention to the particular critiques and needs that these coalitions bring to the fore. While it may be too early fully to discern the contours of this shift, we have much to learn by historicizing the preceding phases, and in so doing, to begin thinking about what comes next.

## White Anthropologists and Their Unacknowledged Mestizo Allies (1945–1965)

Although the general affirmation that anthropology has its roots in colonial power relations is uncontroversial, not so for the question of when (or if, or to what extent) the discipline has broken with this historic legacy. To specify such a break it is not enough to establish when white anthropologists began to sympathize with Indians, to defend their cultures against accusations of inferiority, or even, to defend Indian people against abuse and opprobrium. Rather, one must find practices of anthropological knowledge production directly aligned with efforts to transform the systemic conditions that made and continue to reproduce this racial hierarchy. This more stringent reasoning leads me to suggest that the first key shift in relations between white anthropologists and indigenous Latin Americans came not with the "Boasian revolution" of the early 20th century, but rather, with the rise of left and revolutionary politics in the 1960s. Prior to that historical moment, beginning at least in the 1950s and in some cases going back as far as the 1920s, white anthropologists in the Boasian tradition of cultural relativism attacked the precepts of racial inferiority still common in the social sciences, spoke eloquently and acted energetically against all forms of doctrinal racism, and argued that all cultures, even small, isolated and powerless ones, merit respect, equal treatment, and understanding in their own terms. But in general, those who studied indigenous Latin Americans in this era did not, and perhaps could not, align themselves with forms of political mobilization that would transform the prevailing (neocolonial) racial hierarchy.

A number of factors limited these potential alignments. First, within the emergent postwar Latin American area studies paradigm, anthropology continued to be primarily responsible for what Trouillot famously dubbed the "savage slot": the study of small scale, relatively peripheral or isolated social groups (1991). While some Latin Americanist anthropologists of the era refused this assignation from the beginning (e.g. Adams 1967; Wolf 1957), it was not until the onset of revolutionary upheaval and militancy in the 1960s that they found a collective voice as analysts of national-level political processes. Until that time, they were disinclined to think critically about the kinds of national-level political transformations necessary to address the persisting neocolonial relations that afflicted indigenous peoples. Second, white anthropologists of this era viewed themselves as scholarly advocates of Indians, within a mestizo-dominated political, economic and ideological system that they left unchallenged, and largely unexamined. Third, the social relations of research tended to reinforce this ideological alignment. Specifically, white anthropologists of the postwar generation tended to enter Indian America with the mestizo state, mestizo intellectuals and local mestizo interlocutors as an often unacknowledged source of support and collaboration. Mexico is the paradigmatic case in this regard (Barre 1983). In keeping with indigenista policies of the day, mid-level mestizo professionals and functionaries served as bridges between their own modern social milieu and Indian communities. In keeping with the commonsense endorsement of national mestizo ideology, white anthropologists logically and to some extent necessarily conducted their fieldwork with the help of local mestizo power-holders – school teachers, merchants, provincial professionals, local politicians – both for pragmatic reasons (a comfortable house to stay in, a smooth achievement of research access), and because this positioning was consistent with the Indian-to-mestizo historical change assumed to be inevitable.

A perusal of key works of this era amply confirms the ideological convergence, while substantiation of my assertion regarding the material relations of research would require more detailed scrutiny (e.g. of papers, diaries, notes and the like) beyond the scope of this chapter. John Gillin, a Latin Americanist anthropologist of the early postwar generation, laid out the basic mestizo-centric position with exceptional clarity. Gillin taught at universities of North Carolina and Pittsburgh, served as president of the American Anthropological Association, and worked in both Guatemala and Peru. "We shall endeavor to show," he wrote in a 1949 essay, "that the Latin American culture is, or is on the point of being, a vigorous expression of the aspirations of the mestizo race" (Gillin 1949:164). Charles Wagley and Marvin Harris, two pioneering anthropologists of that generation, shared Gillin's deeply seated belief in the inevitable ascendancy of the mestizo, and by extension, enthusiastically endorsed Mexico's indigenista policies of the day as politically progressive and scientifically grounded (Harris and Wagley 1958). These scholars, like Wolf, Adams and others, had adamantly refused "savage slot" anthropology by studying, from early on, the structural inequalities of Latin American societies from a historical perspective. Yet they still operated largely within a mestizo-centric ideological frame. In some cases, such as anthropologists' close association with Guatemala's Seminario de Integración Social, or Mexico's Instituto Nacional Indigenista, the institutional counterpart to this ideological frame was upfront and explicit; in other cases, the association may have been deceitful and surreptitious, as Sullivan (1989) documents for successive generations of anthropological research in the Yucatan peninsula of Mexico. I am most interested, however, in the ties that were viewed as normal, unremarkable, and unquestioned. This meant that mestizos themselves – as material props for anthropological research – rarely became sustained objects of ethnographic attention, just as national mestizaje ideology was rarely subjected to full critical scrutiny. These were the conditions of possibility for white anthropologists to sympathize with Indians, while conceiving both research and advocacy through a mestizo lens.

A corollary to these largely unacknowledged relations of collaboration was the development of strong intellectual ties and institutional affinities between white anthropologists and mestizo Latin American social scientists. We need to know much more about this facet of the social relations of research: To what extent did white anthropologists depend on local mestizos to get their research on Indians accomplished? How common was it for white anthropologists to recruit their mestizo research assistants or associates as anthropological protégés, and what kinds of policies and politics did the protégés, now informed by the best anthropological training of the time, advocate upon their return? For example, we know that Manual Gamio, Moises Saenz and Gilberto Freyre all studied with Franz Boas; and that more than one from the subsequent generation in Mexico and Guatemala (Alfonso Caso, Antonio Goubaud, de Dios Rosales etc.) studied at the University of Chicago. While more careful comparative work needs to be done, these students seem to exemplify the pattern: they were steadfast in their support for Indian (or Afro-Brazilian) betterment, but thoroughly mestizo-centric in their notions of how betterment would be achieved, and in what idiom it would be expressed.

One final way to characterize the anthropological literature on Indians in Latin America published before 1965 is to note that the scholars in question had little concern for what we now call Indian agency. In some respects, it would be ahistorical to hold them to that standard. The notion of agency itself is a later introduction into mainstream social theory, and Indian people had not yet raised their collective voices in national political arenas, claiming coeval status with mestizos. Whatever Indians were up to during this period, the tendency would have been to downplay possibilities for autonomous cultural-political practice, and to place Indian politics within the logic of mestizo-defined initiative. For example, in a comprehensive review of the anthropology of Latin America published in 1964, Arnold Strickon (1964) places central emphasis on holistic ethnographic description, taxonomy of peoples and their cultures, and acculturation studies, all epitomized by the massive multivolume *Handbook* coordinated by Julian Steward (1963). The emerging trends and topics that Strickon emphasizes include the anthropology of complex societies, social differentiation, urban studies, and the like, exemplified by the multifaceted, team researched Puerto Rico study. Topics related to indigenous politics do not enter, except in a faintly dismissive sentence on the work of Richard Patch, whose work on Bolivia, still in the throes of the 1952 revolution, focuses "*only* on economic, social and political matters" (1964:147, emphasis added). Similarly Stickon's complaint about the extensive anthropological research on Peru is that it has focused mainly on mestizos, "people who, though possibly genetically Indian … are to a greater or lesser degree directly involved in the social, economic, and political life of the Peruvian nation and state"

(1964:145). As of 1964, in sum, Latin American anthropology's proper subjects were rural Indians, the less involvement with the dominant society the better. Even if the notion of political agency had existed at this time, there would have been little need to use it.

While this image of the docile Indian research subject has been noted and critiqued many times before, it is perhaps less evident that these research relations and priorities also depended on relatively docile mestizo collaborators as well. Through participation in the anthropological endeavor, these mestizos achieved an affirmation of their dominance over Indians at the price of subservience to the white anthropologists' civilizational superiority. The first rumblings of the seismic shift in these social relations of research would come not primarily from Indians but from mestizo militants, who framed their attack in the language of anti-imperialist, revolutionary nationalism.

## MESTIZO INTELLECTUALS AS REBELLIOUS SUBJECTS (1965–1985)

The spirit of left-inflected *latinoamericanismo* ran deep in the second half of the 20th century. It inspired armed revolutionary movements in many Latin American countries, and spawned nationalist, social democratic political projects nearly everywhere. It can also be associated with an especially vibrant and original flow of intellectual and artistic production – from dependency theory, to the literary boom of the 1960s and 1970s, to *nueva canción* (new song) – which expressed in diverse idioms the aspiration that Latin America forge a new political path: with greater autonomy from the imperial north, rooted in distinctive regional realities, broadly committed to principles of social justice. A young Argentine doctor left us with an eloquent rendering of this message:

> Although we're too insignificant to be spokesmen for such a noble cause, we believe, and this journey has only served to confirm this belief, that the division of America into unstable and illusory nations is a complete fiction. *We are one single mestizo race* with remarkable ethnographical similarities, from Mexico down to the Magellan Straits. And so, in an attempt to break free from all narrow-minded provincialism, I propose a toast to Peru and to a United America. (Guevara 1995:135, emphasis added)

National ideologies of mestizaje, forged in the course of the 20th century found a welcome place within left-inflected *latinoamericanismo*; indeed, the two were mutually enabling. While Ché's June 1952 toast was precocious (a decade early in relation to my scheme), it succinctly captures this potent convergence, and the soaring political aspirations that soon would follow.

The convergence, in turn, had a deep transformative impact on the anthropology of Indian Latin America. When mestizo intellectuals of the 1960s – steeped in latinoamericanismo and trained in the emerging critical traditions of Marxism, structural economics and Third World nationalism – confronted US anthropology on Indians, they found a target ripe for attack and refutation. Although enjoying the power of their racial, class and geographic provenance, white anthropologists were remarkably vulnerable to critique. Their studies were focused mainly on small-scale rural communities and cultures, rather than broader processes of national politics; their frameworks were generally cast in modernization theory, which posited that societal development would follow a path set forth by powerful countries of the north; they were profoundly shaped by the anticommunist fervor of the 1950s, which left them circumspect, if not viscerally hostile, toward analysis influenced by Marxism. A less noted factor that deepened this vulnerability, building on the argument of the previous section, was their complicity with mestizo dominance. While few could yet fathom Indian research subjects rising up and talking back, their mestizo interlocutors were another matter altogether. White anthropologists depended on mutually enabling relations with local and national-level mestizo intermediaries, yet they became a close-at-hand encapsulation of most everything that one sector of these mestizos was now rebelling against.

This critique of white anthropology had four key elements. The first was anti-imperialism: a basic assumption that white anthropology operated within, and contributed to the advancement of, the imperial designs of the United States in Latin America. While this accusation would be dramatically confirmed in particular cases (e.g. Project Camelot – a social science research project in Peru funded surreptitiously by the US Department of Defense – see critical assessments by Sjoberg 1967 and Horowitz 1974), the general point is probably best understood in line with Talal Asad's well-known critique of anthropology and the colonial encounter (1973). No smoking gun was necessary; ideological convergence and structural inequity were enough. Second, the mestizo critique was also antiracist, but in a peculiarly limited way, focusing almost exclusively on macro patterns of US dominance vis-à-vis Latin American national aspirations. Racism against Indians and Afro-Latins rarely entered the equation as anything more than a corollary of the broader assertion, and the problem of mestizo racism against these peoples had no place at all in this discourse. Third, the critique advanced a frontal attack on the US based anthropological theory of the day, often summarized with the gloss *culturalismo*, and generally juxtaposed to the Marxist inflected emphases on structure, power, political struggle and history. Fourth, and finally, mestizo intellectuals criticized white anthropologists for their lack of political engagement on the side of the oppressed. In keeping with the spirit of the times, they argued for a "decolonized" social science, to produce knowledge aligned with the processes of national liberation underway in their societies (e.g. Stavenhagen 1971). They drew a stark dichotomy, with very little middle ground: were you aligned with W. W. Rostow's "non-Communist manifesto" (1960) or with Eduardo Galeano's *Las venas abiertas de America Latina* (1971)?

The paradigmatic case here is Richard N. Adams, whose extensive work in Guatemala and Central America since the 1950s came under blistering attack in the early 1970s. One ladino intellectual wrote an entire book to denounce his research methods, coining the terms *adamscismo* and *antropología de ocupación*, which would live on in the ladino intellectual political imaginary through the century's end (Flores Alvarado 1973). Adams was in many ways an improbable target for this venom, since his work anticipated many of the criticisms noted earlier, and he led an early effort for stricter ethical standards in anthropological research (for a retrospective analysis of this period, by the author himself, see Adams 1994). But rather than details and complexities of individual cases, the structural relationship is key: ladino intellectuals could not envision and lead their own national-popular political projects from the position of junior partner in alliances with white social scientists from the north. Critique of this unacknowledged alliance was more muted in Mexico, where the revolution had been institutionalized, and the state remained committed to the indigenista policies, which mestizo intellectuals and white anthropologists alike generally shared. In some places – Paraguay, perhaps, or deep in the Amazon – the critique could scarcely be heard. But in general, I contend, the closer the contact with mestizo left intellectuals, the more intensely white anthropologists felt the heat. We were asked to substantively change our approach to anthropological research, or to get out.

In US anthropology departments and their broader university settings at this time, the same basic message already had begun to reverberate. This was an era of widespread questioning of anthropology's complicity with the powerful – from counterinsurgency campaigns in Southeast Asia (e.g. Wolf and Jorgeson 1970) to the culture of poverty in the US inner city (Willis 1969; Valentine 1968). Influential voices in the discipline, including a noteworthy contingent of Latin Americanists, called for anthropology to be "reinvented" (Hymes 1969). By the early 1980s, the critique of ethnographic authority had come to fore, giving white anthropologists even greater reason to question standard ethnographic practices, even though the remedies focused mainly on textual reflexivity (Clifford 1988; Clifford and Marcus 1986). Yet white anthropologists receptive to this reformist impulse and determined to work on issues related to indigenous Latin America faced a dilemma: Did they affirm the emerging critical tradition of mestizo-led "decolonized" social science? Or did they opt to work directly with Indians, and steer clear of the challenge from these mestizo interlocutors? In a few places, for limited periods, history resolved the dilemma as Indians massively participated in mestizo-led movements of social change. But for the most part, white anthropology was forced to choose: to align with the mestizo left, which gave their scholarship a radical thrust, but deferred the problem of mestizo people's anti-Indian racism; or to work directly with Indians, and defer grappling with the critiques and challenges of the mestizo left.

Ché Guevara framed this dilemma in a brilliantly prescient way, in the Peruvian toast cited earlier. His call for a "United America" encapsulated the allure of latino-americanismo, a political project rooted in the region, radically defiant of northern influence and imposition. His invocation of the "mestizo race" as this project's collective protagonist highlighted a colossal blind spot on questions of racial-cultural diversity, which would dog these movements for years to come. For a significant period, however, mestizo leftists cut from the cloth of Guevara's latinoamericanismo became the "native intellectuals" of the region, the authentic voices of an inspiring alternative political project that seemed to legitimately represent the interests of majority sectors in Latin American societies. Whether aligned with guerrilla movements or civil-electoral initiatives, these intellectuals acted and spoke for the entire "mestizo race," that is to say everyone except the Indians who had not yet assimilated, and the white Latin Americans who also refused mestizaje, and became, by definition, *vende patrias* (traitors to the country). Better yet if these mestizo intellectuals had readily identifiable Indian features, since the phenotype–identity conflation common to the region lent support to the assertion that they could speak for everyone. This ventriloquism would only persist as long as Indian intellectuals themselves remained marginal to national politics, and movements for Indian cultural rights and autonomy remained a distant aspiration. Once these movements congealed and Indian intellectuals began to speak out, racism and neocolonialism within the mestizo left became a central focus of their militancy. These Indianist activists and intellectuals needed allies, and given the thrust of their critique, few mestizo intellectuals would rise to the challenge.

The signatories of the 1971 Declaration of Barbados – Guillermo Bonfil, Rodolfo Stavenhagen, Stefano Varese, Darcy Ribeiro and others – are prominent exceptions to this pattern (Declaration of Barbados 1971). They disrupt the general argument presented here, in their critique of *both* anti-Indian racism in their own societies, and apolitical white anthropology from the north. Yet they are exceptions that prove the rule for two reasons. First, while many of the Barbados signatories went on to play key roles in the establishment intellectual communities of their home countries, their radical call to put anthropology to the service of "Indian liberation" did not, in most cases, survive the transition. Second, even these anthropologists faced serious difficulties in establishing horizontal relations with the Indian intellectuals whose movements they championed. In subsequent years, mestizo intellectuals deeply committed to indigenous politics would remain a hardy few; in contrast, for white anthropologists from the north, this solidarity would become a widespread article of faith.

## INDIGENOUS ACTIVIST-INTELLECTUALS SEIZE THE INITIATIVE (1985–2005)

Indianist militancy, as a political project and intellectual position, often emerged from within and in reaction against, mestizo left politics. When Guillermo Bonfil Batalla (1981) compiled an extensive collection of documents from Indian rights movements in 1980, this basic divide between movements still aligned with the left and those who sought cultural-political autonomy predominated. A decade later, a parallel expression of this divide – between Indianist and *"popular"* approaches – split the anti-Quincentenary campaign down the middle (Hale 1994a). Yet by the mid-1990s it was clear to most that the Indianist alternative had won the day. In addition to squaring off with the mestizo left and envisioning cultural-political autonomy for the present, Indianist intellectuals have set out to weave a collective understanding of the past that would dignify their plans for the future: recuperating lost or suppressed histories, chronicling Indian survival and resistance, connecting with intellectual forbears in order to assert continuities from precolonial times to the present (e.g. Cojti Cuxil 1997). Periodic pan-American Indian gatherings, made possible by support from large donors and powerful transnational institutions (from the Catholic Church to the Ford Foundation), helped to advance this collective project (Sanders 1977). The year 1992 – when Rigoberta Menchú received the Nobel Peace Prize and the anti-Quincentenary campaign successfully redefined the historical meaning of 1492 – epitomizes this ascendancy. Indianist intellectuals throughout the continent seized the initiative, insisting on a central voice in all acts of representation of indigenous politics. Anything less would be a perpetuation of the colonial relations that their movements were in struggle to cast aside.

While white anthropology was at times a direct target of this critique, forces internal to the discipline already had anticipated the problem, and conditioned us to welcome the challenge. A major element in this political and theoretical conditioning focused on the need to pluralize our understanding of social inequality, adding race and gender to the central axis of class, and generally paying more attention to how all forms of inequality work through constructions of cultural difference (e.g. West 1990). At least for notions of racial or ethnic hierarchy, this shift fits neatly with a central theme in the indigenous collective assertion. The Pan-American indigenous movement was vehemently and invariably anticolonial: theoretically, white anthropology was included under the rubric of colonial powers, but the primary focus was on the colonizers themselves, their political heirs and ideological allies. Not one Latin American state – left, right or center – escaped the "neocolonial" epithet, and anti-Indian racism, deeply ingrained in mestizo political cultures, became a major focus of critique. Correspondingly, the history of political relations between established mestizo-led leftist projects and rising indigenous movements, across Latin America, followed a remarkably similar pattern: common cause, followed by emerging tensions around issues of hierarchy, strategy, racism and the like, eventually leading to a rupture and the establishment of autonomous organizations, visions and goals. Especially after the rupture, white anthropologists were ideally positioned to enter the breach. By taking the side of the subaltern we could give full expression to our antiracist sensibilities, while at the same time we could enjoy a certain buffer from the most stinging anti-imperialist critique of our mestizo counterparts. In this period, then, white anthropologists and leftist mestizo intellectuals drifted apart, and the former gravitated toward research topics immersed with the task of representing indigenous politics, at times in overtly celebratory terms, at times more critically engaged, but always explicitly aligned.

My own experiences weigh heavily in the preceding description. I began this line of work in the late 1970s as a young college student in Bolivia, when the rupture between Indianist and mestizo left was just beginning to reshape the political terrain. Though with sympathies on both sides, I ended up positioned squarely with the former, and fell in with a group of older (i.e. in their late twenties and thirties) white anthropologists most of whom were working closely with Indian communities in general alignment with these rising Indianist political sensibilities. As a neophyte anthropologist, I developed close relations with an Aymara Indian community based organization in a struggle for empowerment. In contrast, my relationship with the mestizo left intellectual community never quite congealed, strained by a higher level of suspicion and their acute awareness of structural inequalities; I felt I had to work much harder to gain *confianza*, and at the end of three years, had achieved relatively little.

I lived this same tension, even more acutely, in Nicaragua during the 1980s (Hale 1994b). In 1981, revolutionary Nicaragua seemed the ideal place to carry forward commitments with indigenous militancy, while also connecting with a mestizo left project, dramatically brought to fruition in 1979 with the overthrow of the Somoza dictatorship. This did not turn out to be the case. Although positioned inside the revolutionary establishment, my research was marked by deepening dissent from the Sandinistas' mestizo-centric and at times blatantly racist ways. While I did gain Sandinista research clearance for fieldwork in a Miskitu Indian community, the closer the ties I developed with Miskitu research subjects, the more Sandinista suspicions grew. They wanted analysis that would help them manage the Miskitu in transition from armed conflict to negotiated endorsement of autonomy; they got some of this, but cast in an insistent analysis of structural-racial tensions that they preferred to suppress or ignore. I remember coming back to the regional center of Bluefields after a long stint in a Miskitu community, eager to share my anthropological insights, drawing on Miskitu language skills, cultural competency, and abundant fieldwork rapport, only to have my mestizo Sandinista coworkers respond with a wry smile: "those Miskitu sure do love gringos."

A similar triad of relations shaped my experience when I turned to research in Guatemala in the mid-1990s. Guatemalan society was just beginning to recover from the collective trauma of the state-directed counterinsurgency campaign, which defeated the armed leftist movement at the price of an institutionalized terror so brutal and widespread that it remains impossible to fathom (Manz 2004; Schirmer 1998; Sanford 2003; and Sanford, this volume). From the ashes emerged a vibrant Maya cultural rights movement, with one of the largest and most sophisticated cadres of indigenous intellectuals anywhere in the Americas (Warren 1998; Nelson 1999; Bastos and Camus 2003). By the early 1990s, the hallmarks of this Maya movement included its sharp break with the revolutionary left, vehement critique of ladino racism, and insistence on organizational autonomy (a precursor to the demand for political autonomy, which was still too dangerous to mention). Maya intellectuals and activists had their own critiques of white anthropology as well, but they overcame these concerns with relative ease once it became clear that we sided with the Maya, affirmed their critique of ladino racism, and in return for this privileged relationship, were more than willing to help keep the contradictions of the Maya movement from public view. Ladino leftists viewed this alignment with a mix of bemusement, resentment and disdain: at best naive romanticism, at worst a new phase of academic imperialism which fomented racial animus rather than common cause. The intellectual disconnect was equally palpable: white anthropologists came to terms with very little of what ladino scholars wrote (for a rare, early critique along these lines, see Smith 1987), while tracking in minute detail the emerging work of Maya intellectuals; ladino intellectuals still tended to place this white anthropological scholarship in the frame of *antropología de ocupación*.

My proposition, in sum, is that the conditions of possibility for white anthropologists' close identification with indigenous politics included a distancing from the mestizo left, and a relative neglect of the transnational inequities – both racial and political-economic – inherent in our role as privileged interlocutors. A related condition was the continuing tensions between progressive mestizo-ladinos and indigenous movements, grounded in mutual distrust and critique of each other's political and analytical bearings. The signs of change toward a successor phase involve all three partners in the triad: race-progressive mestizos or ladinos, who critique national ideologies of mestizaje and endorse indigenous demands for autonomy; indigenous intellectuals who have affirmed (or reaffirmed) the class dimension of their struggle without ceding their Indianist principles; and white anthropologists who seek dual alignments with both these groups, accepting the tensions, contradictions and awkwardness that results.

These changes have been reinforced by the bitter fruits of a decade of neoliberal multiculturalism, which should be understood both as a form of political-economic restructuring, and equally important, as a mode of governance. On the one hand, Latin American states have taken major steps toward recognition and institutionalization of indigenous collective rights, a shift often described in positive terms as "multicultural constitutionalism," or the "multicultural turn" (e.g. van Cott 2000). These policies have led to unprecedented incorporation of indigenous intellectuals and leaders in high levels of government, to a few experiments of power sharing, and to a series of substantive political changes on the ground that promise to institutionalize multicultural recognition. Yet throughout the region, most dramatically in Ecuador and Bolivia, disenchantment with such efforts of institutionalization has been profound, leading to protest, rupture, and retrenchment in more militant and autonomous forms of political mobilization. On the other hand, the harsh social consequences of neoliberal economic policies have incited dissent throughout the region, and have given rise to an intense search for political and economic alternatives (e.g. Gill 2000). These social consequences have afflicted indigenous peoples and poor mestizos in similar ways, providing new incentives and context for political commonality and struggle. Ecuador and Bolivia, again, offer the most dramatic examples of this emergent Indian-centered class mobilization, but one finds echoes throughout the region, from southern Mexico to Chile and Argentina (e.g. Postero and Zamosc 2005). Not only have collaborative research methods become near imperative in the study of contemporary indigenous politics – a condition in the making since the 1980s – but the collective subject of collaboration appears to be changing as well.

IMPLICATIONS AND QUESTIONS

Relations of research collaboration in anthropology have been shaped by broad historical conditions, within which individual experiences take place and unfold. In the postwar period, for example, I argued that close and often unacknowledged relations of collaboration between white anthropologists and mestizo power-holders left their mark on early scholarship on indigenous peoples; and that the subsequent rise of mestizo dominated latinoamericanismo engendered a break, and conditioned the development of close and affirming relations of collaboration between white anthropologists and Indians. This latter argument is not meant, in any sense, as an act of delegitimation. I place myself squarely with this group of white anthropologists seeking to establish these new research relations, and I defend the analytical and methodological contributions that "we" have made (see also Rappaport 2005; Warren 1998; Field 1998; Graham 2002; Turner 1995). At the same time, I want to reflect on these conditions of possibility, especially their implications for white anthropologists' relations with mestizos, and for efforts of mestizos and Indians to forge closer political ties. This critique points to a process of change, already in motion, which will oblige white anthropologists to renegotiate our relations within the triad.

One further question raised by this line of inquiry involves the parallel between Afro-Latin and indigenous peoples. Some facets of this analysis of the white–mestizo–Indian triad apply directly if "Indian" is replaced by "Afro-Latin." Left inflected latinoamericanismo had the same tendency to subsume Afro-Latins as undifferentiated subjects of national-popular politics; mestizo racism toward Afro-Latins became a politicized bone of contention in roughly parallel ways. A key contrast emerges, however, in the character of white anthropologists' relations with the two peoples. White anthropologists were slower to enter the breach between Afro-Latin and mestizo intellectuals, more hesitant to champion Afro-Latin empowerment. US Black anthropologists, in contrast, have forcefully advanced these analytical-political positions, often while affirming a identification with the African diaspora; in so doing, they have met with especially trenchant critique by mestizo intellectuals, and some white scholars as well (for a paradigmatic exchange, see Hanchard 1994, 2003; Bourdieu and Wacquant 1999). These objections – that the Black scholars are "imperialist" and guilty of importing a US influenced idea of race – have been sharper than parallel critiques of white anthropologists' work in collaboration with indigenous empowerment. Why this contrast? If Native American scholars from the north studied indigenous politics in Latin America would similar patterns emerge?

As mentioned at the outset, the sensibilities and practices of white Latin Americans disrupt the analysis presented here in constructive ways. During the period of ascendancy of revolutionary mestizo nationalism, to identify as white (or *criollo*), as opposed to mestizo or at least as a (racially indeterminate) member of a Latin American nation, was paramount to claiming affinities with US imperialism. Remember that Ché Guevara, coming from the Latin American country with the strongest collective affirmation of European descent, conceived of the continent's revolutionary future as adamantly mestizo. Yet there are many Latin American intellectuals who would probably identify as white or criollo who have played important roles in the critique of US imperialism, the critique of white US anthropology, and in pioneering the politics of solidarity and alliance with indigenous peoples. This duality has led many analysts to turn away from racial categories altogether, and to frame the questions I have posed here in terms of a different triad: indigenous peoples, foreign anthropologists, and non-indigenous national intellectuals. Such an alternative formulation, I contend, obscures more than it clarifies. Scholars have noted for some time that the ideology of mestizaje encompasses precepts of *blanqueamiento* (whitening), which assign systematically high value to the white components of the mix (e.g. Gilliam 1988); recent work on whiteness ideology has reinforced this line of argument (e.g. González Ponciano 2004). This work affirms that the ideological precepts valuing whiteness, and the category of white Latin Americans, are both powerful forces in Latin American cultural politics. While they disrupt the facile association of "white" with the north, and complicate analysis that presents mestizos as the dominant culture in Latin American societies, this does not displace the powerful association of *Latin American* whiteness with privilege, wealth, political clout, modernity, and the like. The wager, then, is that to highlight the category "white (US) anthropologist" also pushes us to clarify the role of Latin American whiteness in the triad, a crucial element of this story that would otherwise tend to be downplayed, euphemized, or simply ignored.

This analysis also suggests that we should keep a special lookout for egalitarian relations between Indians and race-progressive mestizos in the production of knowledge on indigenous agency. This would be an updated expression of the political sensibilities behind the Declaration of Barbados, and the inspiring Latin America based calls for decolonizing anthropology, of more than three decades ago. When I began field research in Guatemala in the mid-1990s, few such spaces existed. There are more now, as ladino acknowledgment of anti-Indian racism reaches a critical mass, and as Mayas begin to differentiate between these ladinos and the rest (Hale 2006). This, in turn, points to a potential coalition politics with far-reaching transformative possibilities, in keeping with emergent regionwide patterns. As this trend strengthens, white anthropologists interested in continued roles in the triad will have to reformulate our position; we will have to hear and respond to a new anti-imperialism, more potent than its Guevaran antecedent because it will be voiced by mestizos who have, to some degree, confronted their own legacy of racial hierarchy, as well as by Indians. Our past efforts to achieve horizontal collaborative relations with indigenous peoples will provide a foundation for dialogue toward these ends, as long as we acknowledge that these efforts, even in the best of cases, never shook completely free from the second dictionary definition, "to cooperate treasonably"; that is, these efforts inevitably suffer from a certain complicity with the very structural conditions that Indian communities find most oppressive.

Finally, within US anthropology departments, the increasing presence of postcolonial and "world" anthropologists, as well as African Americans, Latinos, and Asian Americans, means that US anthropology of indigenous peoples can less and less be equated with white anthropology. Questions come sharply into focus in light of the increasing presence of mestizo Latin Americans, steeped in postcolonial and critical race theory, in US anthropology departments. Does this presence hasten the emergent trend I have identified here, whereby horizontal relations of collaboration between mestizo and indigenous Latin Americans displace white anthropologists, and push forward a reformulation of the triad? (Most writing by these scholars themselves would suggest that the answer is "yes"; for a contrasting view, see Dirlik 1994.) Does postcolonial theory retain its critical edge when its purveyors leave the postcolony for the metropole, to wage the struggle from within?

This brings us back, one last time, to the topic of collaboration. My analysis affirms that among white anthropologists of my generation, the move toward horizontal, collaborative relations with indigenous peoples has been an important innovation. I also suggest that this innovation has been predicated on a certain configuration of cultural politics in the region, which is now beginning to change. These collaborative relations may even have sown the seeds of their own eventual displacement: a resolute commitment to critique of transnational racial hierarchy cannot help but train a bright light on the contradictions in the research relations themselves. Our role as interlocutors of indigenous politics, even when conceived in the most egalitarian of terms, is a little too complicit with neoliberal multiculturalism, and with the persistent power of blanqueamiento ideology, to rest comfortably for long. Successor relations of collaboration, I suspect, will have race-progressive mestizos more centrally present in the triad, with indigenous protagonists at the helm (and in some places, an increased blurring of the boundaries between these two). Since the shift is so incipient, the paradigmatic summary statement may not yet have been uttered. In my image, the speaker is a seasoned indigenous activist-intellectual, steeped in cultural particularities of her own struggle, finely tuned to the persistence of anti-Indian racism, and yet equally comfortable with class based allegiances across the identity divide. When she seizes the moment to make that spontaneous end-of-the-evening toast, which captures the spirit of the coming era, will white anthropology be ready to heed the call?

## REFERENCES

Adams, Richard N. (1967) Nationalization. In M. Nash (ed.), *Social Anthropology* (pp. 469–489), vol. 6 of Robert Wauchope (gen. ed.), *Handbook of Middle American Indians*. Austin: University of Texas Press.

Adams, Richard N. (1994) Guatemalan Ladinization and History. *The Americas* 50(4): 527–543.

Asad, Talal (1973) *Anthropology and the Colonial Encounter*. London: Ithaca Press.

Barre, Marie-Chantal (1983) *Ideologías indigenistas y movimientos indios*. Mexico City: Siglo Veintiuno.

Bastos, Santiago and Camus, Manuela (2003) *Entre el mecapal y el cielo*. Guatemala: FLACSO.

Bonfil Batalla, Guillermo (1981) *Utopía y revolución*. Mexico City: Nueva Imagen.

Bourdieu, Pierre and Wacquant, Loïc (1999) On the Cunning of Imperialist Reason. *Theory, Culture, and Society* 16(1):41–58.

Castañeda, Jorge (1993) *Utopia Unarmed: The Latin American Left after the Cold War*. New York: Knopf.

Clifford, James (1988) *The Predicament of Culture: Twentieth-Century Ethnography, Literature, and Art*. Cambridge, MA: Harvard University Press.

Clifford, James and Marcus, George E. (1986) *Writing Culture: The Poetics and Politics of Ethnography*. Berkeley: University of California Press.

Cojti Cuxil, Demetrio (1997) *Ri Maya' Moloj pa Iximulew. El movimiento Maya*. Guatemala City: Editorial Cholsamaj.

Declaration of Barbados (1971) Declaration of Barbados. In W. Dostal (ed.), *The Situation of the Indian in South America*. Geneva: WCIP.

Dirlik, Arif (1994) The Postcolonial Aura: Third World Criticism in the Age of Global Capitalism. *Critical Inquiry* 20(2):328–356.

Field, Les (1998) *The Grimace of Macho Ratón: Artisans, Identity and Nation in Late-Twentieth-Century Western Nicaragua*. Durham, NC: Duke University Press.

Flores Alvarado, Humberto (1973) *El adamscismo y la sociedad guatemalteca*. Guatemala: Editorial Piedra Santa.

Galeano, Eduardo (1971) *Las venas abiertas de America Latina*. Montevideo: Universidad de la Republica, Departamento de Publicaciones.

Gill, Lesley (2000) *Teetering on the Rim: Global Restructuring, Daily Life, and the Armed Retreat of the Bolivian State*. New York: Columbia University Press.

Gilliam, Angela (1988) Telltale Language: Race, Class and Inequality in Two Latin American Towns. In J. Cole (ed.), *Anthropology for the Nineties* (pp. 522–531). New York: Free Press.

Gillin, John (1949) Mestizo America. In R. Linton (ed.), *Most of the World* (pp. 156–211). New York: Columbia University Press.

González Ponciano, Jorge Ramón (2004) La visible invisibilidad de la blancura y el ladino. In C. R. Hale, J. Gould, and D. Euraque (eds), *Memorias del mestizaje. Cultura politica en Centroamerica de 1920 al presente* (pp. 111–132). Guatemala: CIRMA.

Gordon, Edmund T. (1998) *Disparate Diasporas: Identity and Politics in an African-Nicaraguan Community*. Austin: University of Texas Press.

Graham, Laura R. (2002) How Should an Indian Speak? Amazonian Indians and the Symbolic Politics of Language in the Global Public Sphere. In J. E. Jackson and K. B. Warren (eds), *Indigenous Movements, Self-Representation and the State in Latin America* (pp. 181–228). Austin: University of Texas Press.

Grandin, Greg (2004) *The Last Colonial Massacre: Latin America in the Cold War*. Chicago: University of Chicago Press.

Guevara, Che (1995) *The Motorcycle Diaries: A Journey around South America*. London: Verso.

Hale, Charles R. (1994a) Between Che Guevara and the Pachamama: Mestizos, Indians and Identity Politics in the Anti-Quincentenary Campaign. *Critique of Anthropology* 14(1): 9–39.

Hale, Charles R. (1994b) *Resistance and Contradiction: Miskitu Indians and the Nicaraguan State, 1894–1987*. Stanford: Stanford University Press.

Hale, Charles R. (2002) Does Multiculturalism Menace? Governance, Cultural Rights and the Politics of Identity in Guatemala. *Journal of Latin American Studies* 34:485–524.

Hale, Charles R. (2006) *Más que un indio… Racial Ambivalence and Neoliberal Multiculturalism in Guatemala*. Santa Fe: School of American Research Press.

Hanchard, Michael George (1994) *Orpheus and Power: The Movimento Negro of Rio de Janeiro and São Paulo, Brazil, 1945–1988.* Princeton: Princeton University Press.

Hanchard, Michael (2003) Acts of Misrecognition: Transnational Black Politics, Anti-Imperialism, and the Ethnocentrism of Pierre Bourdieu and Loïc Wacquant. *Theory, Culture, and Society* 2:5–29.

Harris, Marvin and Wagley, Charles (1958) *Minorities in the New World: Six Case Studies.* New York: Columbia University Press.

Horowitz, Irving Louis (1974) *The Rise and Fall of Project Camelot: Studies in the Relationship between Social Science and Practical Politics.* Cambridge, MA: MIT Press.

Hymes, Dell (1969) *Reinventing Anthropology.* New York: Vintage.

Manz, Beatriz (2004) *Paradise in Ashes: A Guatemalan Journey of Courage, Terror, and Hope.* Berkeley: University of California Press.

Nelson, Diane (1999) *A Finger in the Wound: Body Politics in Quincentennial Guatemala.* Berkeley: University of California Press.

Postero, Nancy and Zamosc, Leon (2005) *The Struggle for Indigenous Rights in Latin America.* Brighton: Sussex Academic Press.

Rappaport, Joanne (2005) *Intercultural Utopias: Public Intellectuals, Cultural Experimentation, and Ethnic Pluralism in Colombia.* Durham, NJ: Duke University Press.

Rostow, Walt Whitman (1960) *The Stages of Economic Growth: A Non-Communist Manifesto.* Cambridge: Cambridge University Press.

Sanders, Douglas (1977) *The Formation of the World Council of Indigenous Peoples.* Copenhagen: IWGIA.

Sanford, Victoria (2003) *Buried Secrets.* New York: Palgrave.

Schirmer, Jennifer (1998) *The Guatemalan Military Project: A Violence called Democracy.* Philadelphia: University of Pennsylvania Press.

Sjoberg, Gideon (1967) Project Camelot: Selected Reactions and Personal Reflections. In G. Sjoberg (ed.), *Ethics, Politics, and Social Research* (pp. 141–161). Cambridge: Schenkman.

Smith, Carol A. (1987) Ideologies of Social History. *Critique of Anthropology* 7(2):51–60.

Smith, Carol A. (1995) Race-Class-Gender Ideology in Guatemala: Modern and Anti-Modern Forms. *Comparative Study of Society and History* 37(4):723–749.

Stavenhagen, Rodolfo (1971) Decolonizing Applied Social Sciences. *Human Organization* 30(4):333–357.

Steward, J. H. (ed.) (1963) *Handbook of South American Indians.* New York: Cooper Square.

Strickon, Arnold (1964) Anthropology in Latin America. In C. Wagley (ed.), *Social Science Research on Latin America* (pp. 125s–167). New York: Columbia University Press.

Sullivan, Paul (1989) *Unfinished Conversations: Mayas and Foreigners between Two Wars.* New York: Knopf.

Trouillot, Michel-Rolph (1991) Anthropology and the Savage Slot: The Poetics and Politics of Otherness. In R. Fox (ed.), *Recapturing Anthropology: Working in the Present* (pp. 17–44). Santa Fe: School of American Research Press.

Turner, Terence (1995) An Indigenous People's Struggle for Socially Equitable and Ecologically Sustainable Production: The Kayapo Revolt against Extractivism. *Journal of Latin American Anthropology* 1(1):98–121.

Valentine, Charles (1968) *Culture and Poverty: Critique and Counter-Proposals.* Chicago: University of Chicago Press.

van Cott, Donna Lee (2000) *The Friendly Liquidation of the Past: The Politics of Diversity in Latin America.* Pittsburgh: University of Pittsburgh Press.

Warren, Kay B. (1998) *Indigenous Movements and their Critics: Pan-Mayan Activism in Guatemala.* Princeton: Princeton University Press.

West, Cornell (1990) The New Cultural Politics of Difference. In R. Ferguson et al. (eds), *Out There: Marginalization and Contemporary Cultures.* Cambridge, MA: MIT Press.

Williams, Brackette F. (1991) *Stains on My Name, War in My Veins: Guyana and the Politics of Cultural Struggle.* Durham, NC: Duke University Press.

Willis, W. S. (1969) Skeletons in the Closet. In D. Hymes (ed.), *Reinventing Anthropology* (pp. 121–152). New York: Vintage.

Winant, Howard (2001) *The World is a Ghetto: Race and Democracy since World War II.* New York: Basic Books.

Wolf, Eric R. (1957) *Sons of the Shaking Earth.* Chicago: University of Chicago Press.

Wolf, Eric R. and Jorgeson, Joseph (1970) Anthropology on the Warpath. *New York Review of Books*, Nov. 19, pp. 26–30.

# Index